GLOBALIZING FEMINISMS, 1789–1945

Edinb·   ·versit

This definitive Reader presents a coherent, comprehensive, comparative, and much-needed collective history of women's activism throughout the world.

Including key pieces on the history of feminism from an international group of scholars, the book charts feminists' attempts to restore a balance of power between the sexes against a backdrop of huge cultural, social and political transitions across the world. The collection covers the period from the beginning of the French Revolution in 1789 – a turning point that gave rise to practical efforts to embody principles of rights, liberty, and equality on behalf of women as well as men – up until the end of World War II. The chapters reach out well beyond Europe and the Americas to examine the history of feminisms in Japan, India, China, the Middle East, and Australasia.

This diverse body of material is drawn together through a comprehensive general introduction, and individual section introductions. The chapters are also supported by a global timeline of events, and there is a bibliography of further reading. Brought together for the first time in this volume, these groundbreaking essays show how new light can be shed on historical problems by viewing them through the perspective of women's history, and how this can provide a new understanding of our collective past.

Contributors include Ann Taylor Allen, Padma Anagol, Marilyn J. Boxer, Jacqueline R. de Vries, Ellen Carol DuBois, Louise Edwards, Ellen L. Fleischmann, Patricia Grimshaw, Inger Hammar, Nancy A. Hewitt, Sandra Stanley Holton, Francesca Miller, Barbara Molony, Karen Offen, Florence Rochefort, Leila J. Rupp, Rochelle Goldberg Ruthchild, Anne Summers, Angela Woollacott and Susan Zimmermann.

Karen Offen is a historian and independent scholar, affiliated as a Senior Scholar with the Michelle R. Clayman Institute for Gender Research, Stanford University. Her previous publications include *European Feminisms, 1700–1950: A Political History* (2000).

REWRITING HISTORIES
Edited by Jack R. Censer

GLOBALIZING FEMINISMS, 1789–1945

Edited by Karen Offen

Routledge
Taylor & Francis Group

LONDON AND NEW YORK

First published 2010
by Routledge
2 Park Square, Milton Park, Abingdon, Oxon OX14 4RN

Simultaneously published in the USA and Canada
by Routledge
270 Madison Ave, New York, NY 10016

*Routledge is an imprint of the Taylor & Francis Group,
an informa business*

© 2010 Karen Offen for selection and editorial matter;
individual chapters, the contributors

Typeset in Times New Roman by
Book Now Ltd, London

Printed and bound in Great Britain by
CPI Antony Rowe, Chippenham, Wiltshire

British Library Cataloguing in Publication Data
A catalogue record for this book is available from the British Library

Library of Congress Cataloging in Publication Data
A catalog record for this book has been requested

ISBN10: 0–415–77867–0 (hbk)
ISBN10: 0–415–77868–9 (pbk)

ISBN13: 978–0–415–77867–1 (hbk)
ISBN13: 978–0–415–77868–8 (pbk)

CONTENTS

CONTENTS

CONTENTS

NOTES ON CONTRIBUTORS

Ann Taylor Allen received the PhD in History from Columbia University and is now a Professor of History at the University of Louisville, Kentucky, where she was honored with the university's Career Achievement Award for Research and Creative Activity in 2007. She has also taught in Germany in Bielefeld and Berlin. She has held grants from the German Academic Exchange Service, the Fulbright Foundation, and the National Endowment for the Humanities, and has won article prizes from the Conference Group on Central European History (1989) and the German Studies Association (2002). Her works on European women's and gender history include *Feminism and Motherhood in Germany, 1800–1914* (1991); *Feminism and Motherhood in Western Europe, 1890–1970: The Maternal Dilemma* (2005); and *Women in Twentieth-Century Europe* (2008).

Padma Anagol is the author of *The Emergence of Feminism in India, 1850–1920* (2006). She studied at the University of Mysore and Jawaharlal Nehru University in India, and earned her PhD in 1994 from the School of Oriental and African Studies, University of London. She is currently Lecturer in History at the University of Cardiff, Wales (UK), where she teaches on the history of India from a gender perspective. In 2008 she assumed the editorship of the journal *Cultural and Social History*. Anagol grew up in a bi-lingual extended family in a western Indian region called Maharashtra, whose history is resplendent with tales of heroic queens and highly influential female saints. The Jain community (to which she belongs) has maintained a genealogical tradition and her family has its own stock of tales about powerful women who seemed to exercise their rights astutely and circumvent patriarchal embargos. These stories generated her scholarly interest when she became a history student. She discovered that in order to uncover women's agency she had to "unlearn" some of the received wisdom from the academy and to pay attention to the concept of "experience" that her mother's own deeds had so eloquently revealed. She also determined to use the imperial archive more imaginatively and to work in Indian language sources. She began her first expedition into uncovering the feminist consciousness of women in Maharashtra. Her current project continues with the question of women's agency but moving in a different direction. It concerns a key Indian woman-patriot of the late nineteenth century who produced what is probably the first anti-imperialist tract by a woman but interlaced it with hate for other religious communities such as Indian Muslims and the British. Anagol seeks to understand how the categories of family, nation, economy and womanhood are interlinked in this woman's work.

Marilyn J. Boxer is Professor Emerita of History at San Francisco State University. She is author of *When Women Ask the Questions: Creating Women's Studies in America* (1998,

ix

2001), co-author with Jean H. Quataert of *Connecting Spheres: European Women in a Globalizing World, 1500 to the Present*, 2nd edn (2000), and co-editor with Quataert of *Socialist Women: European Socialist Feminism in the Late Nineteenth and Early Twentieth Centuries* (1978). Her article in this volume, "Rethinking the Socialist Construction and International Career of the Concept 'Bourgeois Feminism'," published in *The American Historical Review* (2007), brings together strands of her work that began in 1970, when she heard in a women's liberation student group in San Bernardino, California, that the only route to equality for women lay through socialism. Beginning doctoral studies that year, she set out to examine the historical record of relations between European feminisms and socialist movements during the period of the Second International. Her 1971 seminar paper on "Marxian Socialism and the Woman Question" led ultimately, after several decades of research and publication in women's history, socialist history, and labor history, to the article included here. Along the way, she also chaired the nation's first women's studies program, at San Diego State University, before becoming dean of the College of Arts and Letters there, and later serving as vice-president for academic affairs at San Francisco State University. These positions provided useful perspective on the academic and activist politics surrounding the history and historiography examined in this article.

Jacqueline R. de Vries is Associate Professor and Chair of History at Augsburg College in Minneapolis, Minnesota. Her interest in the historical relationship between feminism and religion emerged while growing up in the conservative (Dutch) Christian Reformed Church during the second-wave feminist movement of the 1970s. Her dissertation research on British suffragists in World War I led to the discovery that earlier generations of feminists also struggled to reconcile their faith and feminism. Since this essay, de Vries has published numerous essays on gender and religion, as well as a book, *Living Faith*, which chronicles the diverse stories of Presbyterians on the American frontier. Her edited book with Sue Morgan *Women, Gender and Religious Cultures in Modern Britain, 1800–1940* will be published by Routledge in 2010.

Ellen Carol DuBois, Professor of History at the University of California, Los Angeles, is one of the pioneers of modern US women's history, focusing on political history. Her work reinterprets the women's path to full citizenship in terms of women's political agency, internal conflicts and shifts within suffragism itself, and explores suffragism's connections to general themes and developments in political history. In addition to her monographs, *Feminism and Suffrage: The Emergence of an Independent Women's Movement in America, 1848–1869* (1978) and *Harriot Stanton Blatch and the Winning of Woman Suffrage* (1997), she has published many articles, some of which are collected in *Woman Suffrage and Women's Rights* (1998). In addition, Ellen has pioneered two important initiatives in US women's history teaching texts. With Vicki Ruiz, she assembled three editions of the innovative anthology, *Unequal Sisters: A Multicultural Reader in US Womens History* (1990, 1994, and 1999), which challenged and reorganized the field's canonical research around themes of multiculturalism and diversity. And, with Lynn Dumenil, she authored *Through Womens Eyes: An American History* (2005), the first narrative history of US women written in over twenty years. Currently she is developing these concerns through an ambitious history of women's rights globally, outside of Europe and North America, between 1920 and 1970.

Louise Edwards is Professor in the School of Modern Languages and Cultures, University of Hong Kong. She was formerly Professor of China Studies at the University of Technology Sydney (UTS) and Director of the UTS China Research Centre. Born in Aotearoa New Zealand, Louise's interest in the history of global feminism was prompted by that country's celebration of its position as the "first self governing nation" to legislate for women's suffrage in 1893. Her most recent book is *Gender, Politics and Democracy: Women's Suffrage in China* (2008). Other publications on gender include *Men and Women in Qing China* (2001), and three edited volumes with Mina Roces: *Women in Asia: Tradition, Modernity and Globalization* (2000); *Women's Suffrage in Asia* (2004); and *The Politics of Dress in Asia and the Americas* (2007). She is a fellow of the Australian Academy of the Humanities and the Australian Social Sciences Academy.

Ellen L. Fleischmann is Associate Professor of History at the University of Dayton in Dayton, Ohio, and the author of *The Nation and Its "New" Women: The Palestinian Women's Movement, 1920–1948* (2003). She received her PhD in Middle East history from Georgetown University, Washington, DC in 1996. Currently she is working on a history of interactions between American Protestant missionaries and Middle Eastern and American women in the Mashriq, tentatively entitled "'Under an American Roof:' The Encounter Among Women of Greater Syria and American Protestant Missionaries, *c.* 1830–1945." Dr Fleischmann lived and worked in the Israeli-occupied West Bank town of Ramallah from 1986 to 1988, and later did her dissertation research while living there and in East Jerusalem, 1992–1994. She has published numerous journal articles and book chapters, mostly on various aspects of the history of women and gender in the late nineteenth and early twentieth centuries in the Middle East.

Patricia Grimshaw holds the position of Professorial Fellow in the School of Historical Studies at the University of Melbourne, where she received her PhD and taught for many years US and Australian history and Gender Studies. In her research she has sustained a particular interest in settler and indigenous women's political rights in Britain's ex-colonies since her first book, *Women's Suffrage in New Zealand* (1972; rev. edn 1987). Her many publications include *Paths of Duty: American Missionary Wives in Nineteenth Century Hawai'i* (1989), the co-authored *Creating a Nation* (1994), which revolutionized the narrative of Australian national history from a gender perspective, and *Equal Subjects, Unequal Rights: Indigenous Peoples in Britain's Settler Colonies, 1830–1910* (2003). She served as the second president of the International Federation for Research in Women's History (1995–2000) and co-edited the IFRWH conference volume *Women's Rights and Human Rights: International Historical Perspectives* (2001).

Inger Hammar (1942–2007) received her PhD in History at the University of Lund, Sweden in 1999 with a dissertation on "Emancipation och Religion. Den svenska kvinnorörelsens pionjähr i debatt om kvinnans kallelse ca 1860–1900" [Emancipation and Religion: Pioneers of the Swedish Feminist Movement and the Debate over a Woman's Calling, *c.*1860–1900]. Before she turned to historical research, she had taught at the high school level in history, religion and Swedish for almost 30 years. Between 1982 and 1994 she taught at Spyken senior high school in Lund. She particularly enjoyed her research on women's history and women's emancipation, producing several articles, including the article republished in this collection and another in English, "Protestantism and Women's Liberation in 19th Century Sweden," in *Gender, Race and Religions: Nordic Missions 1860–1940*, ed. Inger Marie Okkenhaug, Uppsala: *Studia Missionalia Svecana XCI*, (2003). Her most important work after the dissertation was (in Swedish) *För freden och rösträtten: Kvinnorna och den svensk-norska unionens sista dagar* [For Peace and the

Right to Vote: Women and the Last Days of the Swedish-Norwegian Union], published in 2004 by Nordic Academic Press. Inger Hammar died of breast cancer in early 2007.

Nancy A. Hewitt is Professor II of History and Women's and Gender Studies at Rutgers University, the State University of New Jersey. She has published two monographs: *Women's Activism and Social Change: Rochester, New York, 1822–1872* (1984); and *Southern Discomfort: Women's Activism in Tampa, Florida, 1880s–1920s* (2001). Her edited volumes include *Visible Women: New Essays on American Activism* (with Suzanne Lebsock, 1993) and *A Companion to American Women's History* (2002). She is currently completing work on another edited volume, *No Permanent Waves: Recasting Histories of US Feminism,* from Rutgers University Press (2010). Long concerned with challenging standard narratives of woman's rights and feminism in the United States by incorporating issues of race and class, exploring the religious impetus for equal rights, and recognizing transnational connections, Hewitt has published numerous articles on women's history and women's activism. In this spirit, she is now working on a biography of nineteenth-century abolitionist-feminist Amy Post, whose commitment to racial and class equality and religious radicalism underpinned her advocacy of women's rights. Hewitt is currently (2009–2010) the Pitt Professor of American History at Cambridge University, England.

Sandra Stanley Holton splits her time between England and Australia. She has published two books on the women's suffrage movement in Britain: *Feminism and Democracy. Women's Suffrage and Reform Politics in Britain, 1900–1918* (1986) and *Suffrage Days. Stories from the Women's Suffrage Movement* (1996), as well as a number of articles in journals and edited collections. Her research on the role of the Bright circle in the women's suffrage movement led to her subsequent research on women Quakers, which has appeared in her *Quaker Women: Personal Life, Memory and Radicalism in the Lives of Women's Friends* (2007), and to a series of published articles. At present she is writing a biography of Alice Clark, the Quaker industrialist, suffragist and early historian of women's work. Her other research interests include feminist historiography, and the social history of medicine and of religion. She is a member of the Institute of Historical Research, University of London.

Francesca Miller is the author of the prize-winning book *Latin American Women and the Search for Social Justice* (1992) and co-author of *Women, Culture and Politics in Latin America* (1990). Miller is an independent scholar and writer, affiliated with the Department of History, University of California, Davis. She has served as consultant to the White House press corps and to First Lady Hillary Rodham Clinton. In 2006, Miller spoke on "One Hundred Years of Feminism and Internationalism" at a plenary session of the International Conference of the Latin American Studies Association in San Juan, Puerto Rico. In addition, her chapter, "Latin American Women and the Search for Social, Political and Economic Transformation" appeared in *Capital, Power and Inequality in Latin America and the Caribbean* (2008). She has contributed a dozen articles to the *Oxford Encyclopedia of Women in World History* (2008). Other recent scholarly publications include "Anarquistas, Graças a Deus! 'Italy' in South America," in *Revisioning Italy: National Identity and Global Culture* (1997); "Feminisms and Transnationalism," *Gender & History* 10:3 (1998); "The History of Female Education in the Americas," *El Siglo de Mujeres/Women's Century 1900–2000*, ISIS International (Rome), January 2000; and "Eleanor Roosevelt and Latin America," in *The Eleanor Roosevelt Encyclopedia* (2001). In October 2001, Miller received a research grant from the Institute for Historical Study to support a study of legendary Irish sea warrior Grace O'Malley (1530–1603), "an exploration of gender, survival and history." She is currently engaged in writing a trilogy that explores issues without borders through the lens of contemporary realist fiction in Costa Rica, Brazil and Cuba.

Barbara Molony, Professor of Japanese history at Santa Clara University in California, received her PhD from Harvard University. Co-editor (with Kathleen Uno) of *Gendering Modern Japanese History* (2005) and (with Emiko Ochiai) of *Asia's New Mothers* (2008), she has published numerous articles on women's rights, citizenship, suffrage, and the construction of gender in law, discourse, dress, and culture in modern Japan. She is currently writing (with Kathleen Molony) a biography of pioneering Japanese suffragist, Ichikawa Fusae. She has also been active in the Berkshire Conference of Women Historians, serving as program co-chair for the triennial Berks Conference on the History of Women, and in the Western Association of Women Historians, as program chair and host for the 2009 conference. She is president of the Pacific Coast Branch of the American Historical Association.

Karen Offen is a historian and independent scholar (PhD, Stanford University), affiliated as a Senior Scholar with the Clayman Institute for Gender Research at Stanford University. She is a co-founder and past secretary-treasurer of the International Federation for Research in Women's History, past president of the Western Association of Women Historians, and currently serves on the Board of Directors for the International Museum of Women (San Francisco), as well as on many journal editorial advisory committees. She has received numerous fellowships, awards, and prizes, including a Guggenheim Fellowship. Her most recent book is *European Feminisms, 1700–1950: A Political History* (2000), but she is also known for her contributions to the co-edited documentary collections *Victorian Women* (1981) and *Women, the Family, and Freedom* (1983), which launched her interest in comparative histories of women and of feminisms, and to *Writing Women's History: International Perspectives* (1991). She has published many articles in leading scholarly journals and edited collections in English and other languages, and has lectured on her findings internationally. Her current project is to complete a long overdue book on the "woman question" debate in modern France.

Florence Rochefort, in collaboration with Laurence Klejman at the University of Paris VII, completed a landmark multi-volume joint doctoral dissertation on the history of feminism in France under the early Third Republic, a shorter version of which was published in 1989 as *L'Égalité en marche: le féminisme sous la IIIe République* (1989). She continues her research on the history of women's rights, women's emancipation, and gender issues in republican France and has published many articles on that subject. In 2001 Florence became a salaried researcher with the Centre National de la Recherche Scientifique (CNRS) in Paris, attached to the Group "Societies, Religions, and Secularisation." She directs the program "Gender, Religions, and Secularisations [Laïcités]," where she is revisiting the history of French feminism up to the present with a focus on religion and secularization, and, conversely, re-examining the history of secularization in France through the lens of gender. This research is linked to a multidisciplinary, cross-national examination of questions concerning the intersections of gender, religions and politics and their contemporary significance. Her work on this subject is reflected in a recent edited collection, *Le pouvoir du genre, laicites et religions 1905–2005*, ed. Florence Rochefort (2007). She also serves on the editorial committee of the French scholarly journal *Clio: Histoire, Femmes et Sociétés* and has recently published a book on French women's history for general audiences, *Hier, les femmes* (2007).

Leila J. Rupp is Professor of Feminist Studies and Associate Dean of the Division of Social Sciences at the University of California, Santa Barbara. She is co-author with Verta Taylor of *Drag Queens at the 801 Cabaret* (2003) and *Survival in the Doldrums: The American Women's Rights Movement, 1945 to the 1960s* (1987) and has authored *A Desired Past: A Short History of Same-Sex Sexuality in America* (1999); *Worlds of Women: The Making of an International Women's Movement* (1997); and *Mobilizing Women for War: German and American Propaganda, 1939–1945* (1978). She is also co-editor of the 7th and 8th editions of *Feminist Frontiers*. She edited the *Journal of Women's History* from 1996 to 2004 and is currently finishing a new book called "Sapphistries: A Global History of Love Between Women."

Rochelle Goldberg Ruthchild is a Research Associate at the Davis Center for Russian and Eurasian Studies, Harvard University and Professor Emerita of Graduate Studies at The Union Institute and University. She was the first graduate student to receive a PhD in Women's History at the University of Rochester for her 1976 dissertation, "The Russian Women's Movement, 1859–1917." Her book, *Equality and Revolution: Women's Rights in the Russian Empire, 1905–1917*, will appear in 2010 from the University of Pittsburgh Press. Active in the feminist 'second wave', she is also a member of the production group for the documentary film "Left on Pearl: Women Take Over 888 Memorial Drive, Cambridge," about the feminist action which led to the creation of the longest continuously operating community women's center in the United States.

Anne Summers is Honorary Research Fellow at Birkbeck College, University of London. She was a Wellcome Research Fellow at the Wellcome Unit for the History of Medicine, University of Oxford, from 1986 to 1989, and a Curator of Modern Historical Manuscripts at the British Library from 1989 to 2004. Between 1999 and 2005 she was Honorary Professor of History at Middlesex University. An editor of *History Workshop Journal* since 1975, her publications include *Angels and Citizens: British Women as Military Nurses 1854–1914* (1988 and 2000) and *Female Lives, Moral States: Women, Religion and Public Life in Britain, c. 1800–1930* (2000). Her research on British women reformers made her aware of the extent to which Anglophone literature underplays their internationalism, and led her to design a project on the international dimension of Josephine Butler's campaigns: she headed this project from 2004 to 2007 with funding from the Leverhulme Trust at the Women's Library, London Metropolitan University. Some results of this work have appeared in a special issue of *Women's History Review* (April 2008) and more are forthcoming. Currently Summers is pursuing research on relations between Christian and Jewish women in England, 1840–1940, with support from the British Academy.

Angela Woollacott is Manning Clark Professor of History at the Australian National University in Canberra. She was formerly on the history faculty at Macquarie University in Sydney. Her books include: *On Her Their Lives Depend: Munitions Workers in the Great War* (1994); *To Try Her Fortune in London: Australian Women, Colonialism and Modernity* (2001); and *Gender and Empire* (2006). She is currently completing a book manuscript on three iconic "Australian" women performers of the early twentieth century whose careers fused modernity and racial ambiguity; and embarking on a project funded by the Australian Research Council on gender and culture in settler colonialism from the 1830s to the 1860s, placing Australia in imperial context. Her research on Australian feminists' involvement in British Commonwealth and Pan-Pacific feminisms in the early twentieth century grew out of curiosity about connections between feminism and colonialism, and a desire to show the significance of racial issues and transnational frames for Australian history.

Susan Zimmermann is Professor of History at the Central European University (CEU) in Budapest, Hungary, and an adjunct lecturer at the University of Vienna. She has published two monographs in German: *Splendid Poverty. Poor Relief, Child Provision, and Social Reform in Budapest. The "Social Laboratory" of the Habsburg Monarchy as Compared to Vienna 1873–1914* (1997); and *The Better Half? Women's Movements and Women's Aspirations in Hungary under the Habsburg Monarchy 1848–1918* (1999). Her edited volumes include *Social Policy in the Periphery: Trajectories of Development and Change in Latin America, Africa, Asia, and Eastern Europe* (2001, together with Johannes Jäger and Gerhard Melinz) and *Internationalisms: Transformation of Global Inequality in the 19th and 20th Centuries* (2008, together with Karin Fischer). At CEU she was instrumental in establishing the PhD degree program in Comparative Gender Studies and was responsible for the participation of the Department of Gender Studies in the University of Maryland-led project "Educating for the Future: Building Coalitions and Crossing Boarders in Women's Studies Graduate Education/The Graduate Women's Studies Consortium." Her current research explores the complex history of how international(ist) aspirations and politics were engaged with reinforcing, transforming or challenging global inequality. In this context she has written on the history of antislavery in international politics; the politics (between World War I and World War II) of the International Labour Organisation over labour in "non-metropolitan territories" and of international women's organizations in relation to women's labour in non-Western countries; on socialist women's and men's internationalism in the early twentieth century; and on asymmetric transnational politics of institutionalizing gender studies in higher education.

SERIES EDITOR'S PREFACE

Rewriting history, or revisionism, has always followed closely in the wake of history writing. In their efforts to re-evaluate the past, professional as well as amateur scholars have followed many approaches, most commonly as empiricists, uncovering new information to challenge earlier accounts. Historians have also revised previous versions by adopting new perspectives, usually fortified by new research, which overturn received views.

Even though rewriting is constantly taking place, historians' attitudes towards using new interpretations have been anything but settled. For most, the validity of revisionism lies in providing a stronger, more convincing account that better captures the objective truth of the matter. Although such historians might agree that we never finally arrive at the "truth," they believe it exists and over time may be better approximated. At the other extreme stand scholars who believe that each generation or even each cultural group or subgroup necessarily regards the past differently, each creating for itself a more usable history. Although these latter scholars do not reject the possibility of demonstrating empirically that some contentions are better than others, they focus upon generating new views based upon different life experiences. Different truths exist for different groups. Surely such an understanding, by emphasizing subjectivity, further encourages rewriting history. Between these two groups are those historians who wish to borrow from both sides. This third group, while accepting that every cluster of individuals sees matters differently, still wishes somewhat contradictorily to fashion a broader history that incorporates both of these particular visions. Revisionists who stress empiricism fall into the first of the three camps, while others spread out across the board.

Today the rewriting of history seems to have accelerated to a blinding speed as a consequence of the evolution of revisionism. A variety of approaches has emerged. A major factor in this process has been the enormous increase in the number of researchers. This explosion has reinforced and enabled the retesting of many assertions. Significant ideological shifts have also played a major part in the growth of revisionism. First, the crisis of Marxism, culminating in the events in Eastern Europe in 1989, has given rise to doubts about explicitly Marxist accounts. Such doubts have spilled over into the entire field of social history which has been a dominant subfield of the discipline for several decades.

Focusing on society and its class divisions implied that these are the most important elements in historical analysis. Because Marxism was built on the same claim, the whole basis of social history has been questioned, despite the very many studies that directly had little to do with Marxism. Disillusionment with social history simultaneously opened the door to cultural and linguistic approaches largely developed in anthropology and literature. Multiculturalism and feminism further generated revisionism. By claiming that scholars had, wittingly or not, operated from a white European/American male point of view, newer researchers argued that other approaches had been neglected or misunderstood. Not surprisingly, these last historians are the most likely to envision each subgroup rewriting its own usable history, while other scholars incline towards revisionism as part of the search for some stable truth.

Rewriting Histories will make these new approaches available to the student population. Often new scholarly debates take place in the scattered issues of journals which are sometimes difficult to find. Furthermore, in these first interactions, historians tend to address one another, leaving out the evidence that would make their arguments more accessible to the uninitiated. This series of books will collect in one place a strong group of the major articles in selected fields, adding notes and introductions conducive to improved understanding. Editors will select articles containing substantial historical data, so that students – at least those who approach the subject as an objective phenomenon – can advance not only their comprehension of debated points but also their grasp of substantive aspects of the subject.

Not that long ago, there was no broad history of feminism chronicled by the scholarly community. Insofar as the largely male profession considered feminism, it appeared only in the study of women's suffrage. Yet this has been reversed so dramatically that this series, Rewriting Histories, has, in fact, two volumes on the subject. Nonetheless, one difference between these two books highlights how rapidly and recently this field has emerged. The first, *Global Feminisms since 1945* edited by Bonnie G. Smith and issued just a few years ago, included work by historians but also relied on studies by non-historians. Karen Offen's volume, published a handful of years later, presents scholarly articles. Indeed, historians have finally fully engaged with a topic that long deserved their attention.

Offen provides a striking synthesis through the arguments in the comparative essays that constitute this volume. Although she insists that feminism does have a "bottom line," i.e. challenging masculine domination," the articles selected reveal the historic diversity of strategies, arguments, and tactics, some "relational" and others "individualist," that characterized feminist activism globally before 1945. In this way, one gains an historical appreciation for the complexities of feminism, rather than a present-minded view. Furthermore, her selections advance a novel interpretation in the study of feminism by finding that in certain circumstances, it was religion and religious figures, phenomena and actors not usually connected to feminism that provided the necessary culture for advancing women's rights. Likewise, she makes an important case for the role of international organizations. The book concludes by turning the microscope in the other direction and applying feminist insights to discuss history. This excellent volume holds many surprises worth gleaning.

ACKNOWLEDGEMENTS

I would like to extend my heartfelt thanks to the following individuals, without whom this book would never have seen the light of day: to Jack Censer, for asking me to do it and for his uncommon patience and persistence; to Victoria Peters and Eve Setch, for keeping after me all those years; to Emily Kindleysides, for shepherding the project through with grace and efficiency; to Maureen Allen, undoubtedly the best (and most agreeable) copy editor I have ever worked with. It has been a pleasure and a privilege to work with Routledge and Book Now Ltd., whose staff members have seen to it that this book is as perfect as possible (and, yes, they did, finally, find a way to include the endnotes). And, not least, thanks to the superb scholars and colleagues who agreed to have their articles included and who, without exception, have been cooperative and prompt in responding to all my queries and suggestions. I hope they will be as pleased with *Globalizing Feminisms, 1789–1945* as I am.

Karen Offen
Lenk-in-Simmental, Switzerland
September 2009

The permission of the authors and the following publishers to reprint articles is gratefully acknowledged:

Chapter 1   "Was Mary Wollstonecraft a Feminist? A Comparative Re-reading of *A Vindication of the Rights of Woman*, 1792–1992" by Karen Offen. Reproduced from *Quilting a New Canon: Stitching Women's Words*, ed. Uma Parameswaran. Toronto: Sister Vision, 1996, pp. 3–24. © Karen Offen.

Chapter 2   "Re-Rooting American Women's Activism: Global Perspectives on 1848," by Nancy A. Hewitt. Reproduced from *Österreichische Zeitschrift für Geschichtswissenschaften*, 9:4 (1998), 457–470.

Chapter 3   "Liberty, Equality, Morality: The Attempt to Sustain an International Campaign against the Double Sexual Standard, 1875–1906," by Anne Summers. Reproduced with permission from *Sextant*, nos 23–24 (2007), 133–153.

Chapter 4   "'To Educate Women into Rebellion': Elizabeth Cady Stanton and the Creation of a Transatlantic Network of Radical Suffragists," by Sandra Stanley Holton. Reproduced from *The American Historical Review*, 99:4 (1994), 1112–1136.

Chapter 5   "Women's Rights, Feminism, and Suffragism in Japan, 1870–1925," by Barbara Molony. Reproduced from *Pacific Historical Review*, 69:4 (2000), 639–661. Reproduced with permission of University of California Press.

Chapter 6   "Feminism and Protestantism in nineteenth-century France: First Encounters, 1830–1900," by Florence Rochefort. Translated by Karen Offen from "Féminisme et protestantisme au XIXe siècle: Premières rencontres 1830–1900," *Bulletin de la Société de l'Histoire du Protestantisme Français*, 146 (2000), 69-89. Reproduced with permission of la Société de l'Histoire du Protestantisme Français.

Chapter 7   "From Fredrika Bremer to Ellen Key: Calling, Gender and the Emancipation Debate in Sweden, *c.* 1830–1900," by Inger Hammar. Reproduced from *Gender and Vocation*, ed. Pirjo Markkola. Helsinki: Finnish Literature Society, 2000, pp. 27–67. Reproduced with permission of K. G. Hammar and Pirjo Markkola, and the Finnish Literature Society.

Chapter 8   "Indian Christian Women and Indigenous Feminism, *c.* 1850–*c.*1920," by Padma Anagol. Reproduced from *Gender and Imperialism*, ed. Claire Midgley. Manchester: Manchester University Press, 1998, pp. 79–103.

Chapter 9   "Settler Anxieties, Indigenous Peoples, and Women's Suffrage in the Colonies of Australia, New Zealand, and Hawai'i, 1888–1902," by Patricia Grimshaw. Reproduced from *Pacific Historical Review*, 69:4 (2000), 553–572. Reproduced with permission of University of California Press.

Chapter 10   "Challenging Traditions: Denominational Feminisms in Britain, 1910–1920," by Jacqueline R. de Vries. Reproduced from *Borderlines: Genders and Identities in War and Peace, 1870–1930*, ed. Billie Melman. London: Routledge, 1998, pp. 265–283. Reproduced with permission of Routledge, an imprint of the Taylor & Francis Group, an informa business.

Chapter 11   "Constructing Internationalism: The Case of Transnational Women's Organizations, 1888–1945," by Leila J. Rupp. Reproduced from *The American Historical Review*, 99:5 (1994), 1571–1600. © American Historical Association 1994. All rights reserved. Reproduced with permission of University of Chicago Press.

Chapter 12   "The Challenge of Multinational Empire for the International Women's Movement: The Habsburg Monarchy and the Development of Feminist Inter / National Politics," by Susan Zimmermann. Reproduced from *Journal of Women's History*, 17:2 (2005), 87–117. © 2005 *Journal of Women's History*. Reprinted with permission of The Johns Hopkins University Press. As corrected by the author.

Chapter 13   "The Other 'Awakening': The Emergence of Women's Movements in the Modern Middle East, 1900–1940," by Ellen L. Fleischmann. Reproduced, with some author-approved cuts, from *A Social History of Women and Gender in the Modern Middle East*, ed. Margaret L. Meriwether and Judith E. Tucker. Boulder, CO: Westview, 1999, pp. 89–139. Reproduced with permission of the Perseus Books Group.

Chapter 14   "Latin American Feminism and the Transnational Arena," by Francesca Miller. Reproduced from *Women, Culture, and Politics in Latin America*, ed. Seminar on Feminism and Culture in Latin America. Berkeley, CA: University of California Press, 1990, pp. 10–26. Reproduced with permission of University of California Press.

Chapter 15   "Internationalizing Married Women's Nationality: The Hague Campaign of 1930," by Ellen Carol DuBois. Contributed to this volume by Ellen Carol DuBois. © Ellen Carol DuBois.

Chapter 16   "Inventing Commonwealth and Pan-Pacific Feminisms: Australian Women's Internationalist Activism in the 1920s–30s," by Angela Woollacott. Reproduced from *Gender & History*, 10:3 (1998), 425–448. © Blackwell Publishers Ltd, 1998. Reproduced with permission of Blackwell Publishing Ltd.

Chapter 17   "Feminism, Social Science, and the Meanings of Modernity: The Debate on the Origin of the Family in Europe and the United States, 1860–1914," by Ann Taylor Allen. Reproduced from *The American Historical Review*, 104:4 (1999), 1085–1113. © American Historical Association 1999. All rights reserved. Reproduced with permission of University of Chicago Press.

Chapter 18   "Women's Suffrage and Revolution in the Russian Empire, 1905–1917," by Rochelle Goldberg Ruthchild. Reproduced from *Aspasia*, 1 (2007), 1–35. © 2007, Berghahn Books. All rights reserved. Used by permission of the publisher.

Chapter 19   "Women's Suffrage in China: Challenging Scholarly Conventions," by Louise Edwards. Reproduced from *Pacific Historical Review*, 69:4 (2002), 617–638. Reproduced with permission of University of California Press.

Chapter 20   "Rethinking the Socialist Construction and International Career of the Concept 'Bourgeois Feminism'," by Marilyn J. Boxer. Reproduced from *The American Historical Review*, 112:1 (2007), 131–158. © American Historical Association 2007. All rights reserved. Reproduced with permission of University of Chicago Press.

While every effort has been made to trace and acknowledge ownership of copyright material used in this volume, the publishers will be glad to make suitable arrangements with any copyright holders whom it has not been possible to contact.

SIGNPOSTS – A CHRONOLOGY OF GLOBAL FEMINISMS

This chronology does not include data on most *national* or most *regional* women's organizations and congresses; for Europe, see the chronology in Karen Offen, *European Feminisms* (2000). The last part of the chronology (since 1960) highlights significant United Nations conferences and conventions. My thanks to the authors in this collection and other colleagues who helped fill in precise dates, notably Esther Sue Wamsley, Asunción Lavrin, Guiomar Duenas-Vargas, Fiona Paisley, Grace Leslie, Mary McCune, Tiffany K. Wayne, Nurit B. Gillath, "super-sleuth" Karen Rosneck, and Aparna Basu.

> *1789–1793 Women in Paris demonstrate, begin to form clubs, publish manifestos, and organize campaigns for citizenship during the French Revolution. Movement spreads to provincial cities before being put down. Women from the Low Countries also participate.*

1791   Olympe de Gouges publishes her *Declaration des Droits de la Femme et Citoyenne*

1792   Mary Wollstonecraft publishes her *Vindication of the Rights of Woman* in London and leaves for Paris

1804   The Napoleonic, or French Civil Code severely restricts the status of women, especially in marriage; this code provides a model exported throughout Europe and well beyond

1800–
1848   Campaigns mount in England and the United States to end black slavery; many women participate, only to recognize that they are little more than slaves in their own countries. Continental governments pass laws against freedom of the press and association which dampen all efforts at organization and dissenting speech.

1840   World Anti-Slavery Congress in London (12–23 June); women are excluded from participation and positions as delegates

> *1848 Women's rights demands in Paris, Vienna, Budapest, Berlin, and many other European cities during the revolutions that begin in France in February 1848. In mid-July, American women and men convene in Seneca Falls, New York, to draft a "Declaration of Sentiments," demanding women's rights and the vote. A series of conventions in other eastern cities follows.*

*In Persia, a woman, Qurrat al-'Ayn, became a leader and prophet in the Babi
movement, questioned many Islamic practices, and was unveiled before her
followers in 1848; a rebellious woman, she was finally sentenced to death.*

1868   Marie Pouchelin Goegg founds the *Association Internationale des Femmes* in
Geneva, Switzerland

1875   Inaugural Meeting of the British and Continental Federation (later the
International Abolitionist Federation, Liverpool (19 March)

1876   Centennial Exposition in Philadelphia (10 May–10 October). First Women's
Pavilion at an international exposition. Fourth Congress of the American
Association for the Advancement of Women.

1877   First International Congress of the British and Continental Federation (later IAF),
Geneva (17–22 September)

1878   First International Congress on Women's Rights, Paris (25 July–9 August)

1888   International Council of Women (ICW) founded in Washington, DC, by the
National American Woman Suffrage Association (NAWSA) (25 March–1 April)

1889   Two international feminist congresses held in Paris during centennial of French
Revolution: *Droit des femmes* (25–29 June) and *Oeuvres et Institutions* (12–18 July)
Founding of the *Union universelle des femmes*, in Paris by Marya Chéliga-Loevy

1892   *Congrès général des sociétés féministes*, Paris (13–18 May)

1893   World's Congress of Representative Women (15–21 May), convened by ICW,
Chicago during World's Columbian Exposition.
Second "Women's Building" established

1896   International feminist congresses held in Paris (8–12 April) and Berlin (19–26
September)

1897   International feminist congress in Brussels (4–7 August)

1898   Dutch National Exhibition of Women's Labor, The Hague (9 July–21 September)

1899   ICW Quinquennial Congress in London (26 June–4 July)

1900   Two feminist congresses convened in Paris during the International Exposition:
Oeuvres et Institutions (18–23 June) and *Condition et des Droits des femmes* (5–8
September)
Another Women's Building initiative – privately funded

1902   First International Woman Suffrage Association (IWSA) Conference,
Washington, DC (12–18 February)

1904   Second IWSA Conference, Berlin (3–4 June)
ICW Third Quinquennial Meeting, Berlin (8–10 June)

1906   Third IWSA Conference, Copenhagen (7–11 August)

1907   First International Socialist Women's Conference, Stuttgart (17 August; in conjunction with the Seventh International Socialist Congress, 18–24 August)

1908   Fourth IWSA Conference, Amsterdam (15–20 June)
First All-Russian Women's Congress, St Petersburg (10–16 December)

1909   IWSA, Fifth Conference and First Quinquennial, London (26 April–1 May)
ICW, Fourth Quinquennial Meeting, Toronto, Canada (24–30 June)

1910   First *Congreso Femenino Internacional*, Buenos Aires (18–23 May)
Second International Socialist Women's Conference, Copenhagen (26–27 August)

1911   IWSA Sixth Congress, Stockholm (12–17 June)

1912   International Congress of Women, Brussels (28–30 April)

1913   Tenth International Congress of Women (*Oeuvres et institutions féminines, Droits des femmes*), Paris (2–10 June)
International Abolitionist Federation, Eleventh Congress, Paris (9–12 June)
IWSA Seventh Congress, Budapest (15–21 June)

1914   ICW Fifth Quinquennial Meeting, Rome (16–23 May)

August 1914–November 1918: World War I
Disruption of feminist organizing internationally
Revolution in Russia early 1917; Bolsheviks seize power October 1917

1915   International Congress of Women for Permanent Peace, The Hague (28 April–1 May)
International Conference of Women Workers to Promote Permanent Peace, San Francisco, USA (4–7 July)

1916   Two feminist congresses convened in the Yucatan, Mexico: *Primer Congreso Feminista de Yucatán*, Mérida (13–16 January) and *Segondo Congreso Feminista Local*, Mérida (23 November–2 December)

1917   All-Russian Congress of Women, Moscow (7 April)

1918   First All-Russian Congress of Working Women and Peasants, Moscow (16–21 November)

1919   Joint Delegation (ICW and IWSA) of inter-allied feminist internationalists to the Paris/Versailles Peace Congress convenes to influence the peace talks on women's behalf (February–April)
Second International Congress of Women, Zurich (12–19 May) – Founding of Women's International League for Peace and Freedom (WILPF)
Founding of the League of Nations and the International Labour Organisation
First International Congress of Working Women, Washington, DC (28 October–6 November), preceding and during First ILO Conference (29 October–29 November)

1920   Eighth IWSA Congress, Geneva (6–12 June)
ICW Quinquennial, Kristiania (Oslo), Norway (8–18 September)
First International Conference of Communist Women, Moscow (30 July–3 August)

1921   Third Congress of the Comintern (Communist International), Moscow (22 June–12 July) establishes the International Women's Secretariat and develops "Theses on Propaganda Work among Women"
Third International Congress of Women (WILPF), Vienna (10–17 July)
Second International Congress of Working Women, Geneva (17–25 October)

1922   Pan-American Women's Conference, Baltimore (20–29 April)
International Council of Women of the Darker Races (ICWDR) founded in USA
WILPF Extraordinary Congress, The Hague (7–10 December)

1923   World Congress of Jewish Women, Vienna (6–11 May)
Ninth IWSA Congress, Rome (12–19 May)
First Pan-American Feminist Congress, Mexico City (20–30 May)

First *Petite Entente des Femmes*, Bucharest (1–6 November)
Third (and last) International Congress of Working Women, Vienna (14–18 August)

1924   WILPF Congress, Washington, DC (1–7 May)
ICW Conference on the Prevention of the Causes of War, Wembley, London (2–8 May) in conjunction with the British Empire Exhibition
Second *Petite Entente des Femmes*, Belgrade (1–4 November)
Second Pan-American Women's Congress, Lima, Peru (21 December–6 January 10)

1925   All-America Women's Conference, Washington, DC (29 April–2 May)
ICW Sixth Quinquennial Meeting, Washington DC (4–14 May)
British Commonwealth League conference on "the citizen rights of women within the British Empire," Caxton Hall, London (9–10 July)
Congreso internacional de Mujeres de la Raza, Mexico City (5–15 July)
Third *Petite Entente des Femmes*, Athens (6–13 December)

1926   IWSA Tenth Congress, Paris (30 May–6 June); changes name to International Alliance of Women for Suffrage and Equal Citizenship (IAWSEC)
Congreso Inter-Americano de Mujeres, Panama (18–25 June)
Fifth WILPF Congress, Dublin (8–15 July)

1927   First All-India Women's Conference on Educational Reform (AIWC), Poona (5–8 January)
Fourth *Petite Entente des Femmes*, Prague (1–3 June)

1928   Sixth International Conference of American States, Havana; Women's Plenary Session, 7 February; Inter-American Commission of Women authorized 7 March. Equal Rights Treaty presented.
Second All-India Women's Conference on Educational Reform, Delhi (7–10 February)
First Pan-Pacific Women's Conference, Honolulu (9–19 August)

1929   Third All-Indian Women's Conference (AIWC), Patna (3–7 January)
États Généraux du Féminisme, Paris (14–16 February; also 22–23 March 1930 and 30–31 May 1931)
First International Conference of Rural Women, London (30 April–3 May)
Second World Congress of Jewish Women, Hamburg (4–6 June)
British Commonwealth League Conference (5–6 June)
Eleventh IAWSEC Congress, Berlin (17–22 June); founding of Open Door International
Fifth *Petite Entente des Femmes*, Warsaw (25–28 June)
Sixth WILPF Congress, Prague (24–28 August)
First Arab Women's Congress, Jerusalem (26 October)

1930   First official conference, Inter-American Commission of Women, Havana (17–24 February); Resolution on the Nationality of Women adopted
IAWSEC organizes joint demonstration with ICW on Nationality of Married Women, The Hague, during the League of Nations Codification Conference (14 March)
Second Pan-Pacific Women's Conference, Honolulu (9–22 September); founding of Pan-Pacific Women's Association
Eastern Women's Conferences: Beirut (late April) and Damascus (3–7 July)

ICW, Eighth Quinquennial Meeting, Vienna (26 May–7 June)
Fourth *Congreso International Femenino*, Bogota, Columbia (17–26 December)

1931   All Asia Women's Conference, under auspices of AIWC, Lahore (19–26 January)
ILO endorses Convention on Equal Pay for Equal Work
Liaison Committee of Women's International Organizations established at the League of Nations

1932   Women's massive international petition for peace presented to the League of Nations Disarmament Conference in Geneva (6 February)
First Mediterranean Women's Conference (*Congrès des Femmes méditerranéennes*), Constantine, Algeria (29–30 March)
Seventh WILPF Congress, Grenoble (15–19 May)
General Eastern Women's Conferences in Damascus (14 October) and Baghdad (24 October)
Congrès muselman Général des Femmes d'Orient, Tehran (27 November–6 December)

1933   International Congress of Women, Chicago (16–22 July)
Founding of Associated Countrywomen of the World/*Association Mondiale des femmes rurales* (ACWW/AMFR), Stockholm (26–30 June)

1934   World Congress [*Rassemblement*] of Women against War and Fascism, Paris (4–6 August)
Third Pan-Pacific Women's Conference, Honolulu (8–22 August)
Eighth WILPF Congress, Zurich (3–8 September)

1935   Twelfth IAWSEC Congress, Istanbul (16–25 April)

1936   ICW meets at Dubrovnik (28 September–9 October)

1937   *Congrès international des activités féminines*, Paris (26–30 June)
Fourth Pan-Pacific Women's Conference, Vancouver, BC, Canada (12–24 July)
Ninth WILPF Congress, Luhacovice, Czechoslovakia (27–31 July)

1938   *Congrès international des femmes pour la défense de la paix, de la liberté, de la démocratie*, Marseille (13–15 May)
ICW Quinquennial, Edinburgh (11–21 July)
Eastern Women's Conference for the Defense of Palestine, Cairo (15–18 October)

1939   Thirteenth IAWSEC Congress, Copenhagen (8–14 July)

1939-1945: World War II
Disrupts women's international organizing and meeting

1944   Arab Women's Conference, Cairo (12–16 December) – Founding of the General Arab Feminist Union (AFU), with headquarters in Cairo

1945   Founding of United Nations, San Francisco (April)
International Congress of Women, Paris (26 November–1 December) – Founding of the Women's International Democratic Federation (WIDF) with headquarters in the DDR, but closely associated with the USSR and the Third Communist International

1946   Fourteenth IAWSEC Congress, Interlaken, Switzerland (10–17 August)
Founding of the UN Commission on the Status of Women (CSW), initially as a subcommittee of the Commission on Human Rights (CHR)

1947   *Primer Congreso Interamericano de Mujeres*, Guatemala City (21–27 August)
ICW, First Post-War Conference, Philadelphia (5–12 September)

1948   UN General Assembly adopts the Universal Declaration of Human Rights (December)
Second WIDF Women's International Congress, Budapest (1–6 December)

1949   Second Arab Women's Conference, Beirut (March)
Fifth Pan-Pacific Women's Conference, Honolulu (20 July–3 August)
UN General Assembly adopts Convention for the Suppression of the Traffic in Persons and of the Exploitation of the Prostitution of Others (2 December)

1951   ILO Convention on Equal Remuneration for Men and Women Workers (29 June)

1952   ILO Convention on Maternity Protection (28 June)
International Planned Parenthood Federation (IPPF) founded by women from Norway, the USA and India
United Nations General Assembly approves the Convention on the Political Rights of Women (20 December)

1953   World Congress of Women (WIDF) in Copenhagen (5–10 June) – WIDF raises the women's rights banner

1954   UNESCO publishes Duverger's comparative survey *The Political Role of Women*

1955   Pan-Pacific Women's Conference, Quezon City, Philippines (24 January–6 February)
International Council of Social Democratic Women founded, London (July)
World Congress of Mothers (WIDF), Lausanne (7–10 July)

1958   Fourth World Congress of WIDF, Vienna (1–5 June)
First Asian–African Women's Conference, Colombo, Ceylon (15–24 February)

1961   First Afro-Asian Women's Conference, Cairo (14–23 January)

1963   Fifth World Congress of WIDF, Moscow (24–29 June)

1967   UN General Assembly approves a Declaration on the Elimination of Discrimination against Women (7 November)

1969   Sixth World Congress of WIDF, Helsinki (14–17 June)

1975   United Nations – Launch of International Women's Year (1975) and Decade (1976–1985)
United Nations – World Conference of the International Women's Year, Mexico City (19 June–2 July)

1979   United Nations General Assembly adopts the Convention to End Discrimination Against Women (CEDAW) (3 September)

1980   United Nations – Second World Conference of the United Nations Decade for Women, Copenhagen (14–30 July)

1985   United Nations – Third World Conference on Women, Nairobi, Kenya (15–26 July)

1995   United Nations – Fourth World Conference on Women, Beijing (4–15 September)

EDITOR'S INTRODUCTION

My objective in editing this collection is to provide a comprehensive, thought-provoking, and teachable collection of pathbreaking articles on the comparative history of feminisms around the world prior to 1945. The volume showcases important second- and third-generation findings, emphases, or reinterpretations that rewrite history in significant ways. These articles place the thought and action of feminists at the center of historical analysis and deepen our knowledge through comparison and contrast. *Globalizing Feminisms, 1789–1945* provides a companion volume to Routledge's *Global Feminisms since 1945*, edited by Bonnie G. Smith.

The history of feminisms is, in fact, women's political history. Women's pursuit of citizenship in emerging nations provides the unifying theme for the volume. Although women's suffrage campaigns figure prominently in this collection, it bears repeating that for feminist women, obtaining the vote – and thus decision-making power – within their countries was never the ultimate objective; in democratizing societies, feminists viewed suffrage as the most efficient *means* for women to realize a multitude of other dramatic, even revolutionary changes in prevailing laws, institutions, ideas, and practices – and promoting equal opportunity in education, law, the workplace, and social services. To them, the vote provided a tool for reframing the connections between, and showing the connections among, fields as varied as economics, sexuality, war, and peace. For feminists of either sex (and it bears emphasizing that male feminists existed throughout this period in most countries, though the majority were undoubtedly women), theory and practice were intimately intertwined. Their common goal was to restore a balance of power between the sexes – a balance lacking in male-dominated societies. In fact, they represented a very small cluster of activists operating in hostile environments. Thus, to tell their stories, discourse analysis is not enough; we need to analyze their actions as well, and place both their arguments and campaigns carefully within their immediate historical context – in nearly every case studied here, the rise of sovereign nation-states – that most powerful form of "imagined community."

It would be a mistake to characterize all feminist developments in this period as the "first wave," as is so often done by today's commentators – commentators who have only a dim view of this history. Indeed, it may be more fruitful to think (as I did in my earlier book, *European Feminisms 1700–1945: A Political History*) in terms of multiple "eruptions," even explosions, of feminist initiative. When one engages with the construction of international and transnational feminist networks in these years, in particular, many "waves" and "eruptions" – indeed, many "feminisms" – can be identified.[1] What is more, feminist efforts in various countries or regions can no longer be assumed to exist and develop in isolation; these essays correct earlier accounts which have a strictly national and insular approach.

The bibliography on the histories of feminisms prior to 1945 is ballooning. The articles I have selected for this volume feature the work of historians who (a) analyze and compare developments in more than one national context, or in one national context across time; (b) raise questions about transnational feminist organizing across national boundaries, as, for example, in multinational empires, within the international women's movement itself, and about how these feminist advocates relate to other transnational movements such as socialism and pacifism; and (c) challenge and transform our understandings of a variety of historical issues that have formerly been addressed strictly from male-centered, purely national perspectives. Historians of feminisms, by critiquing their own prior assumptions and illuminating developments that have long been hidden or obscured, question the very structure of male-centered historical "memory," at the local, regional, national, international, transnational, and global levels. They dare to ask how we know what we know, who decided what we should know, and how looking at the same situation from a perspective that places women and gender relations at the center of analysis provides an entirely new understanding of our human condition and its collective past.

I have given preference to articles that are jargon-free and fun to read, whose authors embed their theoretical insights in evidence, context, and narrative. Most feature several feminists and/or organizations and offer a *comparative* perspective; none of these selections feature the work of only one feminist thinker or activist working in an exclusively national framework; in the few cases where a single person's activity is highlighted initially, a comparative dimension is developed. Studies of feminisms before 1945 strongly suggest that even when common patterns emerge, one size does not fit all. In their very variety, these articles can help readers to understand not only the complexities of writing histories of feminisms, but also what can change and what remains the same in relations between the sexes worldwide. What goes around often comes around again, in a somewhat altered form, as male hegemony continues to reassert itself – and as women "forget" their past campaigns and victories. The history of feminisms in this crucial period of history is full of surprises and deserves to be far better known than is currently the case. History suggests that the feminist project of challenging male hegemony can never be fully appreciated or realized without looking backward as well as forward, and across national boundaries. It is inevitably, even today, a work in progress.

Initially, I considered including materials as far back as the fifteenth century, when debates about women's relation to men, notions of equality of the sexes, and the rhetoric of women's rights began to emerge in western Europe, framed by a political vocabulary of slavery and freedom, sovereignty and subordination, and rights and duties. But considerations of length force a practical limitation to the 1789–1945 period. In other words, the chronological scope of this volume extends from the early years of the French Revolution in 1789 – an upheaval that gave birth, and wings, to *practical efforts* to embody as well as invoke principles of rights, liberty, and equality on behalf of women as well as men. As authoritarian monarchs in the nineteenth century faced pressures to allow more representative governments and "citizens" replaced "subjects," these ideals spread throughout the world, forcing more opportunities for public meeting and political expression, as well as efforts to democratize societal decision-making. In this period we see the first attempts to *organize* women and men on behalf of female emancipation within the context of national and, subsequently transnational, citizenship.

The collection's endpoint is approximately 1945, with the end of World War II, the fall of the fascist dictatorships, the horror of the Holocaust, the framing of a new world economic order at Bretton Woods, the dropping of the atomic bomb on Japan, the establishment of the United Nations, and the beginnings of the Cold War between the West and the USSR, decolonization of European empires abroad, and the real take-off of economic globalization. So much changes that 1945–1950 really marks the end of an era, not least for feminist efforts in their earlier incarnations. But this endpoint also marks the consolidation of a particular sort of historical writing, one marked by the victories of political factions who insisted that class trumped gender, and even race, and sought to rewrite the past in a way that denigrated or even obliterated the histories of feminisms. Indeed, reclaiming the history of feminisms has required the current generation of scholars to challenge the very politics of historical (and other forms of) knowledge.

Each of the volume's four parts is prefaced with a brief introduction that situates the chosen articles. With one exception, all of these articles have been published since 1993; one selection has never been published in English, and another was written expressly for this volume. The authors include many (though, alas, not all) of the key authors in the field. I have also included a global time-line, signaling important developments in the history of feminisms worldwide. In particular, this time-line includes founding dates and major conferences of international and transnational feminist organizations from the 1860s to 1950. A bibliography of suggested further readings is located at the end of the volume.

During the last thirty years, scholars in a number of settings have raised the question "what is feminism?" We have debated whether this label, which originated in France and was first claimed by an advocate of women's rights in 1882, can be applied to earlier debates and campaigns in Europe or to developments outside Europe. Based on comparative investigation, my own answer to these questions is a qualified "yes," but a "yes" predicated on a historically informed definition of "feminism" and "feminist" that accommodates much diversity in strategies and tactics, but which, in the final analysis rests on a single "bottom line," a common denominator – which boils down to challenging masculine domination.[2] In other words, "feminism" is not only about advancing the situation or status of individual women; it encompasses theories and practices that address the collective position of all women, privileged or poor, whatever their color, race, ethnicity, or religion, whether from a relational or an individualist perspective, or some mixture of the two. Nor, strictly speaking, is feminism identical with women's organization or women's activism, or with the women's movement more broadly; not all "women's movements" can be considered "feminist." Feminism is specifically concerned with women's emancipation – the struggle for equality and rights, especially the rights of citizenship, or for women's legal, educational, economic, and sociopolitical equality (engaged both by women and by men). Feminism is ultimately about ending women's subordination, which in most earlier contexts squarely confronts existing male-designed institutions, ideas and practices, as well as well-defended patriarchal family structures.

In western Europe scholars have identified proponents of sexual equality beginning with the writings of Christine de Pizan at the French court (1405), and recurring through the sixteenth, seventeenth, and eighteenth centuries. Of particular significance and utility was (as I have mentioned above) the development of a vocabulary (or discourse) of liberty and freedom in opposition to slavery; of equality in sociopolitical regimes marked by once rigid hierarchies rooted in religious beliefs and, subsequently, in appeals to "Nature."[3] Scottish Enlightenment historians, who wrote the first histories of women, missionaries and travelers, and visionaries such as Charles Fourier in his *Theory of Four Movements*

(1808; in French) popularized the notion that the position of women was the primary index of civilization in societies.[4] During the first half of the nineteenth century, as western European progressives campaigned for the abolition of slavery, these ideas and terms also became hugely significant and effective in framing the "woman question." The question posed was whether men's "liberty" was predicated on the "slavery" of women as wives, particularly in the institution of marriage (religious or secular). The accompanying discourse of "rights and duties, or responsibilities" will be highlighted in its relationship to this question. I hope readers will appreciate just how radical the notion of *legal reforms* in the position of women, especially as wives, and including the opportunity to divorce, actually was.

Some scholars have proposed a "paradox" in feminist discourse in the face of an ostensibly hegemonic "abstract" individual, promulgated during the French Revolution.[5] In fact, evidence from the period suggests that feminists even at the outset of these revolutionary years contested any such abstraction, grounding their campaigns not only in the Rights of "Man" but also in materially grounded "equality-in-difference" approaches to sexual equality and women's freedom. Most did not understand this approach as either paradoxical or contradictory. They understood the "rights of women" as *embodied* female (not abstract) individuals, i.e. seeking entitlement as citizens *in terms of* sexual difference and built their campaigns on this basis. Instead of posing the question (as an entire generation of late twentieth-century scholars and feminists did) in dichotomous (either/or) terms, e.g. "equality versus difference," earlier feminists preferred inclusive (both/and) arguments such as "equality-in-difference," and many of them invoked "maternalism" as being a specific instance of a "relational" approach, which had then, and still has, very radical implications. Much evidence suggests, in fact, that most feminists before 1945, wherever they may have lived around the globe, have (more often than not) used what I have called "relational" rather than (or in combination with) "individualist" arguments to ground their case for ending masculine domination, though it is also true that in particular contexts and specific instances (especially in English-speaking countries, where the vocabulary of individual liberty and independence had become part of most people's intellectual landscape or "mentality") some did raise the flag of unbridled personal autonomy. This conundrum deserves to be revisited. Some authors, like Ellen Fleischmann on the Middle East, have raised questions about the very applicability of terminology such as "feminisms" and "women's movements," at least as concerns the early phases of women's organizing in those societies; Fleischmann takes great care to explain her terms, including "movement" and "awakening."[6] If indeed, the bottom line for "feminism" is "challenging male domination," then how might we understand women's activism in contexts that dare not speak feminism's name, yet in which women, as they organize (especially in contexts of nation-building) become deeply involved in debating the "woman question," identifying discriminatory situations and seeking redress?

The historians represented in this volume succeed in conveying the complexity of political scenarios in which feminists, women and men alike, worked hard and over long periods of time to achieve their goals. These investigations should help offset the temptation of some colleagues and their students to indulge in retrospective scolding of earlier feminists for holding beliefs (in "progress," "civilization," or eugenics, for example) or making choices that we ourselves, "enlightened" with the benefit of hindsight, might not invariably approve, much less endorse. These essays should help readers understand – to the extent possible – where these historical actors were coming from and how – and why – they arrived at their choices, arguments, vocabulary, plans of action and execution, and maneuvering in situations that were rarely of their own choosing. These essays also point to the "radicality" – in male-dominated societies – of all feminist activity, and suggest that retrospective labeling of some feminists as "conservative" or "traditional" (so dear to the first generation of historians of feminism) is simply misleading or beside the point, more a product of internal polemics than of the facts of the situation.

The contributions in this volume also underscore the "modernity" of feminist thought and action, in whatever culture one finds it. Like other reformers and revolutionaries, feminists (both women and men) are necessarily pro-active, not content to "suffer and be still." They want to change their societies to make them better for women and children, but also ultimately more satisfactory for men. To quote Mary Wollstonecraft (1792): "[women] may be convenient slaves, but slavery will have its constant effect, degrading the master and the abject dependent."[7] She argues for "rights" for women based on *reason*, of which both sexes are capable. This is a new – repeat *new* – insight from the late eighteenth century on, and, as the essays in the collection demonstrate, it has had worldwide ramifications. To acquire the authority that goes with citizenship, to assert the importance of women's potential contributions to civil society and to political life, feminists necessarily become "modern" by "reasoning," by becoming pro-active, by talking back to power. They develop widely varied strategies and tactics, depending on the particular obstacles they face in their respective cultures. This quest for citizenship for women begins with their increasing activity in "public space," the expanding civil society that is developing beyond the household – breaching the *arbitrary boundaries* between "public" and "private" prescribed (usually by antifeminist men) in law and custom or in religious tradition). In fact, these boundaries were far more intangible and permeable than is generally recognized, and the "public/private" distinction should be squarely identified as a repeatedly invoked counter-revolutionary construction, a hoped-for bulwark against change in the dominion of men.[8]

The selected essays highlight the intersections of feminisms and nationalisms, and efforts at gender reorganization that have accompanied nation-building efforts, profoundly shaping the context in which feminist claims could be framed and pursued.[9] They explore the first ventures of women into international organizing, with due respect to religious as well as secular contexts. They showcase new scholarly perspectives on feminists in other imperial contexts besides the British, the latter being relatively well-covered elsewhere.[10] Conflicts over race and class within and outside of feminist campaigns have been raised in earlier scholarship, and this volume will accord them due importance, though it will not dwell on them.[11]

Not surprisingly, feminist efforts have disturbed many people, who, clinging to older ways of doing things, become extremely uncomfortable, even threatened by changes and efforts to eradicate sexual hierarchies and to reconfigure family structures and belief systems. Thus feminist efforts, while succeeding to a considerable degree, have also energized backlash efforts of vast proportions, not the least important of which takes the form of religious fundamentalism when it does not erupt in domestic violence. Some of the articles in this collection make this point abundantly clear.

Feminist claims emerge or "erupt" in situations where cultural comparisons are underway, where other ways of doing things or of organizing the sociopolitical structure can be observed, changes are thought possible, and remedying injustices – whether legal, economic, or political – have become thinkable.[12] Such observations are based on information brought back by travelers and missionaries about other cultures, practices, and institutions and circulated primarily through print accounts. In fact, print culture plays a huge role in the transmission of feminist ideas, not only within a given society but far beyond. An important element in the history of feminisms before 1945 is that information networks and useful concepts and arguments in print traveled freely, often despite efforts to censor them.[13] Japanese feminists, for example, drew on local sources but also invoked the arguments of Jean-Jacques Rousseau and John Stuart Mill. Russian feminists took away significant feminist elements from their visits to France. Women in India, China, and Japan encountered Christian missionaries who had come to their parts of the world to proselytize – and who took a particular interest in the situation of indigenous women. Feminists around the Pacific Rim and around the Mediterranean compared notes with one other at conferences. Progressive women took part in international women's congresses, and also in topical conferences, on science, on education, on the traffic in women, for example. While discussing issues ranging from girls' education to prison reform, prostitution, "white slavery," and peacemaking in the face of militarism and war, they got to know one another, and began to exchange ideas and strategies for ameliorating the situation of women – and men – worldwide.

Finally, this volume underscores a profoundly important premise and finding of feminist scholarship, irrespective of which area of our world it investigates – namely that issues concerning appropriate relations between men and women, and the shaping of gender roles in a given societal contexts lie at the heart of *all* sociopolitical organization. We now know better than to maintain that feminism is peculiarly "Western," by which generally we mean the Atlantic Rim countries – but it is correct to recognize that *sustained* feminist demands and campaigns did first erupt in the Western world, and to appreciate why this was so. Thanks to the earlier development there of literacy, public education, and a mass print culture, travel, and improved communications, undergirded by the unprecedented growth of a globalizing market economy, feminist ideas germinated and traveled widely. As these conditions developed in other societies outside the West, one quickly finds traces of feminist thinking and activism, of questioning the sexual status quo, especially as notions of human rights and the language of equality and justice kick in. Thanks to increased attention to excavating, retrieving, and archiving sources such as correspondence and the women's press that "men's history" so long deemed insignificant, the development of feminism's history becomes increasingly possible. We will never learn all we would like to know, but the quantum leap in our knowledge even during the last thirty-plus years allows us to think about feminisms as indicative of a truly global sociopolitical movement. This collection is intended to assist not only in stimulating further inquiry but also to "de-block" memory. For in fact, the knowledge of feminism's history during its period of globalizing is a precious legacy to younger generations – especially to today's young people who presume to take women's emancipation entirely for granted and resist the label "feminist" until they encounter obstacles that block their paths to self-realization. "Amazing!" they will say, as many of us once said, "Why didn't I learn about that in school?" This question is one we should all be asking, and insisting on answers.

Notes

1 See *Perspectives on Feminist Political Thought in European History: From the Middle Ages to the Present*, ed. Tjitske Akkerman and Siep Stuurman (London: Routledge, 1998).

2 I refer readers to my articles, "Defining Feminism" (*Signs: Journal of Women in Culture and Society*, 14, no. 1 [1988]: 119–157) and "Origins" (*Feminist Issues*, 8, no. 2 [1988]: 45–51) and to the opening chapter of *European Feminisms* (Stanford, CA: Stanford University Press, 2000). These issues come up again in the comparative case study presented in Chapter 1.

3 See, among many other important essays on feminist developments in early modern Europe, Hilda L. Smith, "Intellectual Bases for Feminist Analyses: The Seventeenth and Eighteenth Centuries," in *Women and Reason*, ed. Elizabeth D. Harvey and Kathleen Okruhlik (Ann Arbor, MI: University of Michigan Press, 1992), pp. 19–38; Siep Stuurman, "L'Égalité des sexes qui ne se conteste plus en France: Feminism in the Seventeenth Century," in *Perspectives on Feminist Political Thought in European History*, ed. Tjitske Akkerman and Siep Stuurman (London: Routledge, 1998), pp. 67–84; Carole Pateman, "The Rights of Man and Early Feminism," *Schweizerisches Jahrbuch für Politische Wissenschaft/Annuaire Suisse de Science Politique*, (1994): 19–31; Sarah Hanley, "Social Sites of Political Practice in France: Lawsuits, Civil Rights, and the Separation of Power in Domestic and State Government, 1500–1800," *American Historical Review*, 102, no.1 (Feb. 1997): 27–52; and "The Family, the State, and the Law in Seventeenth- and Eighteenth-Century France: The Political Ideology of Male Right versus an Early Theory of Natural Rights," *Journal of Modern History*, 78, no.2 (June 2006): 289–332; also Karen Offen, "How (and Why) the Analogy of Marriage with Slavery Provided the Springboard for Women's Rights Demands in France, 1640–1848," and other pertinent essays in *Women's Rights and Transatlantic Antislavery in the Era of Emancipation*, ed. Kathryn Kish Sklar and James Brewer Stewart (New Haven: Yale University Press, 2007).

4 See Jane Rendall, *The Origins of Modern Feminism: Women in Britain, France, and the United States 1780–1860* (Basingstoke: Macmillan, 1985), Chapter 1, and her subsequent sequence of articles on the male scholars who wrote histories of women during the Scottish Enlightenment, especially "The Progress of 'Civilization': Women, Gender, and Enlightened Perspectives on Civil Society in Eighteenth-Century Britain," in *Civil Society and Gender Justice: Historical and Comparative Perspectives*, ed. Karen Hagemann, Sonya Michel, and Gunilla Budde (New York: Berghahn, 2008), pp. 59–78. The notion that women's status was the true index of civilization began with them, and not with the French social theorist Charles Fourier in 1808, as many secondary references, including well-reputed dictionaries and encyclopedias in English and French have long claimed.

5 Joan Wallach Scott, *Only Paradoxes to Offer: French Feminists and the Rights of Man* (Cambridge, MA: Harvard University Press, 1996).

6 See the original version of Fleischmann's essay, pp. 90–95, where she engages with Third World feminist critiques of Western feminism with respect to intersections of women's issues with class, race, colonialism, and nationalism. In fact my historical definition of feminism, although admittedly based principally in European and American materials, remains capacious enough to accommodate a very wide range of non-European approaches to ending women's subordination grounded in unique political, cultural, and social conditions. What is not addressed here is the way in which European terms became politically "loaded," as for example, when most German and many Scandinavian women's emancipation advocates declined to adopt the French terminologies, preferring to speak of the Frauenbewegung or "women's movement," while in other settings, such as Greece, feminism and feminist were transliterated into the local language. The politics of linguistic transfer are at once important and understudied. For instances of debate over using the terms in other settings, see Micheline Dumont, "The Origins of the Women's Movement in Quebec," in *Challenging Times: The Women's Movement in Canada and the United States*, ed. Constance Backhouse and David H. Flaherty (Montreal: McGill-Queens University Press, 1992) and Margaret Ward, "Nationalism, Pacifism, Internationalism: Louie Bennett, Hanna Sheehy-Skeffington, and the Problem of 'Defining Feminism'," in *Gender and Sexuality in Modern Ireland*, ed. Anthony Bradley and Maryann Gialannella Valiulis (Amherst, MA: University of Massachusetts Press, 1997), pp. 60–84. For a thoughtful Anglo-Canadian perspective on what feminism represents, see Marlene LeGates, *Making Waves: A History of Feminism in Western Society* (Toronto: Copp Clark, 1996); reissued as *In Their Time: A History of Feminism in Western Society* (New York: Routledge, 2001). See her Chapter 1 "Feminism and Patriarchy: An Introduction."

7 See this volume, Chapter 1, "Was Mary Wollstonecraft a Feminist?"

8 See *Civil Society, Public Space, and Gender Justice*, ed. Hagemann, Michel, and Budde (note 4 above), and my essay therein, "Feminists Campaign in 'Public Space:' Civil Society, Gender Justice, and the History of European Feminisms," pp. 97–116.

9 See, for European developments, the landmark essays concerning women's organizing efforts in many European countries by leading specialists in *Women's Emancipation Movements in Nineteenth-Century Europe*, ed. Sylvia Paletschek and Bianka Pietrow-Ennker (Stanford, CA: Stanford University Press, 2004), and, for twentieth century developments, *Le Siècle des*

féminismes, edited by a multi-national (Belgian, Swiss, French) Francophone team headed by the Brussels-based historian Eliane Gubin (Paris: Atelier, 2004); *Feminismus und Demokratie: Europaische Frauenbewegungen der 1920er Jahre* [Feminism and Democracy in Europe in the 1920s], ed. Ute Gerhard (Königstein: Ulrike Helmer, 2001); and the special issue "Women's Movements and Feminisms," *Aspasia: International Handbook of Central, Eastern, and Southeastern European Women's and Gender History*, vol. 1 (2007), ed. Francisca DeHaan, Maria Bucur, and Krassimira Daskalova. The first significant collection on feminisms and internationalisms in English appeared as a special issue of *Gender & History* 10, no.3 (Nov. 1998), ed. Mrinalini Sinha, Donna J. Guy, and Angela Woollacott.

10 See *Women's Suffrage in the British Empire: Citizenship, Nation, and Race*, ed. Ian Fletcher, Ian Christopher, Laura E. Nym Mayhall, and Philippa Levine (Routledge, 2000), which admirably covers issues in the suffrage campaigns throughout the empire on which "the sun never sets." Philippa Levine's edited collection, *Gender and Empire* (2004) is part of the Oxford History of the British Empire; its contributors are not primarily discussing the significance of feminisms. Also see Clare Midgley, ed., *Gender and Imperialism*. (Manchester: Manchester University Press, 1998).

11 As, for example, in Michelle Rief, "Thinking Locally, Acting Globally: The International Agenda of African American Clubwomen, 1880–1940," *The Journal of African American History*, 89, no.3 (Summer 2004): 203–222.

12 See Karen Offen, "'Eruptions and Flows': Thoughts on Writing a Comparative History of European Feminisms, 1700–1950," in *Comparative Women's History: New Approaches*, ed. Anne Cova (Boulder, CO/New York: Social Science Monographs/Columbia University Press, 2006), pp. 39–65.

13 Two important studies of early- to mid-nineteenth-century feminist networks are Margaret H. McFadden, *Golden Cables of Sympathy: The Transatlantic Sources of Nineteenth-Century Feminism* (Lexington, KY: University Press of Kentucky, 1999), and Bonnie S. Anderson, *Joyous Greetings! The First International Women's Movement, 1830–1860* (New York: Oxford University Press, 2000).

Part I

OPENING OUT NATIONAL HISTORIES OF FEMINISMS

Introductory remarks

In the early stages of feminism, the most fervent complaints and debates developed around two issues: the education of girls, and the male-dominated institution of marriage. With the coming of the French Revolution, the focus turned to issues of citizenship. Who would be citizens? What was at stake for revolutionaries who defended an "abstract," all-encompassing "universal" man (*l'homme*), yet who in practice insisted that citizens be male heads of households? How dare men block the way to citizenship for women in a newly secularized state? How did citizenship demands evolve in the context of developing nation-states? How did feminists express their demands in various national contexts? How did they find like-minded colleagues? What were their experiences in attempting to organize for change?

Ultimately, feminist critiques of male practices sharpened, as some began to address issues of women's economic disempowerment in the context of marriage and the workplace and others challenged government-regulated prostitution and the "traffic" in women, which they then called "white slavery." The five essays in this section demonstrate the revolution in our knowledge base that proceeds from revisionist and comparative histories of feminisms that extend from Europe and North America to the Far East. They also argue against misreadings of earlier feminists that failed to assess their contributions within the context of possibilities open to them in their own time.

Karen Offen's question, "Was Mary Wollstonecraft a feminist?" may at first surprise readers. By comparing and contrasting the best-known writings of Wollstonecraft, long considered the "first feminist" by British and American scholars, with those of her French contemporaries during the early years of the French Revolution, including Olympe de Gouges, author of the *Declaration of the Rights of Woman*, Offen underscores the extremely radical character of Continental approaches to women's emancipation in the early 1790s, and Wollstonecraft's relative moderation. She highlights the peculiarity of Wollstonecraft's engagement with the French ex-archbishop Talleyrand that marks her "dedication" of the *Vindication of the Rights of Woman*. But she also underscores its significance for demonstrating the prescriptive character of the so-called doctrine of "separate spheres," which Talleyrand deliberately invoked by asserting that the notion of "public utility" trumps the application to women of the abstract rights of "man." Offen also highlights the importance of moral reform in the work of Wollstonecraft, especially her proposal to "desexualize" women, and re-examines her arguments in light of earlier efforts to define feminism historically and comparatively.

Turning to the North American scene, **Nancy Hewitt** challenges the standard narrative of the Seneca Falls Convention in 1848 as the founding moment of US individualist feminism and the fight for the vote. She displaces the centrality of the Americans, not least Elizabeth Cady Stanton, focusing instead on the Quaker abolitionist Lucretia Mott. Hewitt then resituates this episode comparatively with respect to the turbulent context of the 1848 revolutions in Europe, and a far more expansive and radical agenda of righting inequities based not only on sex but also race and class. This agenda encompassed demands coming from a variety of quarters, including the Seneca, the Mexican–American war, and US aspirations to control new territories and other peoples. Hewitt's eye-opening analysis at once bridges the new attention to religion (a topic further explored in the essays in Part II) and the consolidation and upsurge of nation-states as the pivotal arenas in which demands for women's rights – and other rights – played out during the long nineteenth century. Hewitt's work also places the efforts of these American women squarely within what she perceives as an imperial tradition.

Anne Summers's meticulous archival investigation of the continental European networks of the multi-lingual Englishwoman Josephine Butler illuminates the cultural and political differences among Francophone (French and Francophone Swiss), Germanophone (Germany and Germanophone Switzerland), Dutch (Flemish-speaking Belgium and the Netherlands), and Anglophone participants in the British, Continental and General Federation for the Abolition of Government Regulation of Prostitution, which ultimately became the International Abolitionist Federation (IAF). This mixed-sex, multi-national alliance, headquartered in Francophone Switzerland, dedicated its efforts to combating the spread of the "French model" of state-regulated prostitution to other countries. Its members also campaigned against the spreading traffic in women (and "children," which generally referred to under-age girls seeking work far from home) that accompanied the building of railroad networks and increased steamship travel and landed unsuspecting young women in brothels from which they could not escape. Butler's network is unique in its success, when so many other early attempts to form international networks to promote peace and other causes (even the First International Association of Working Men) could not develop much staying power before the 1890s. Butler's bravery and inspirational style, first honed in her campaigns against the Contagious Diseases Acts in England, attracted many progressive reformers from around Europe and even beyond. The IAF succeeded in bringing the politics – and economics – of sexuality to a prominent place on the list of feminist reforms, along with developing a critique of the "double standard" of sexual morality. But, as Summers' investigation reveals, its participants held very different ideas about "social purity" issues and about what subjects concerning women's bodies and sexuality were proper to discuss, in public or at home. Still, this initiative launched a new generation of feminist reformers who did not shy away from the subjects of sex, venereal diseases, and the power relations embedded within sexual intercourse.

Re-engaging with Elizabeth Cady Stanton in the 1880s, **Sandra Stanley Holton** alerts readers to the small yet rich network of transatlantic Anglophone suffragists fostered in the 1880s and 1890s by her lengthy visits to England to rejoin her daughter Harriot Stanton Blatch (who had married an Englishman) and her old friends (often Quakers) from the 1840 World Anti-Slavery Convention. Holton thereby contributes to the emerging history of the radicals' perspectives on suffrage – and, in particular, of their campaigns to challenge and change the English marriage laws, especially "coverture" (the legal nullity of English wives in marriage law), campaigns that had been overshadowed in the standard suffrage history narratives written by the liberal suffrage advocates. In fact, the liberal suffragists, who advocated the far less threatening alternative of woman suffrage only for single, property-owning women, did not welcome the forceful and uncompromising stands on principle that informed the Women's Franchise League's campaigns to endow English wives with property rights as well as rights over their own bodies, and to demand full and unrestricted suffrage, reinforced by claims that emphasized women's labor "both paid and unpaid." Holton thus reveals the strong ties that bound this radical subcurrent associated with Stanton and her daughter to the earlier Garrisonian radical strand of abolitionist (anti-slavery) activity. Holton's revisionist scholarship serves both to expand and rebalance our knowledge and appreciation of the breadth of the American and British suffrage movements, as well as the personal ties that bound them together.

Barbara Molony provides an astute comparative analysis of changes in women's rights arguments in Japan from the Meiji period, when women were barred from political meetings and participation in Japan's emerging civil society, through the constitutional period up to imperial Japan's defeat in 1945. In so doing she highlights an extensive campaign of feminist struggle that lay long buried under the assertions of American occupiers in 1945 that *they* had bequeathed rights to Japanese women. By challenging such accounts, Molony underscores the fact that Japanese feminist discourse had significant indigenous roots as well as imported Western ones (notably through Japanese readings of Jean-Jacques Rousseau and John Stuart Mill). And she also insists on the way notions of "rights" and the "state" evolved from the late nineteenth to the early twentieth century, as the Japanese state became less of a work-in-progress and more of an established entity. With the founding in 1919 of the "New Woman Association" (NWA), Molony situates the Japanese debates in comparison to the West but underscores their originality, particularly with respect to Japanese women's demands for state protection against venereal disease through required premarital testing of men, and the right of women to divorce husbands, as well as the enabling vote and the right to run for political office. She also demonstrates that Japanese feminists' invocation of motherhood (or maternalist) arguments and feminine values could justify very radical demands on behalf of mothers and women workers.

1

WAS MARY WOLLSTONECRAFT A FEMINIST?

A comparative re-reading of *A Vindication of the Rights of Woman*, 1792–1992

Karen Offen

Was Mary Wollstonecraft a feminist? What kind of question is that? How absurd! Hasn't she been claimed as the "first" feminist – a "radical feminist" – "the best known feminist of the eighteenth century" – the "mother of English feminism" and a "feminist foremother"?[1] Why else would feminist scholars honor the bicentennial of her most renowned publication, *A Vindication of the Rights of Woman*, originally published in 1792?[2] Why else would feminist political theorists propose adding the *Vindication* to their list of canonical texts?

The quarrel I have deliberately set up in my title is not as silly as it might first sound. It is ultimately grounded in a project to write a comprehensive history of feminism and in a dispute over the interpretative application of a historically-inscribed terminology: what do we mean when we claim someone, especially someone long dead, as a feminist? Is there justification for applying to Wollstonecraft's *Vindication* these terms, "feminist" and "feminism," which postdate her publication by a full century? For, in fact, both the terms "feminism" and "feminist" entered our English-language vocabulary from the French, only around the 1900; thus they are new words and applicable to Mary Wollstonecraft only anachronistically.[3]

Some years ago I put considerable energy into an analysis of various and conflicting understandings of feminism. I tried to extricate the discussion from the hegemony of twentieth-century polemics and feminist historiography, and attempted to derive from historical evidence spread over time and varied cultural settings a simple yet broad definition that could serve both historical interpretation and current political needs.[4] In light of some objections raised by critics, I judged that there might be further insight to be gained about the problems of definition and anachronism by re-examining contextually the ideas of this eighteenth-century English "founding mother," Mary Wollstonecraft, whose life and works are now superbly documented and easily accessible.[5]

It is important to insist, however, that England was not the only eighteenth-century venue for debate on the woman question. In France especially, but also in the German-, Spanish-, and Italian-speaking world, there existed an extensive, provocative, and widely-circulated body of writing on the politics of gender, which addressed many of the same issues that troubled Mary Wollstonecraft. Jean-Jacques Rousseau has monopolized our attention to this debate in contemporary scholarship, but in fact, there were many other participants, and by no means all of them were men. I think in particular of Josefa Amar y Borbon, arguing in Spain for women's education, and Charlotta Nordenflycht in Sweden, defending women against Rousseau, as well as Madame de Coicy, Etta Palm, and Olympe de Gouges writing in late eighteenth-century France.[6]

It is my contention that we can better evaluate the significance of the *Vindication* for the history of feminism by reading it not only through the lens of contemporary Anglo-American political theory and/or neo-marxist approaches to history and philosophy (as many recent interpreters and commentators have done, and from which we have acquired new insights),[7] but with respect to what we now know to be an older and more comprehensive European context. Therefore, following a brief introduction to Mary Wollstonecraft's life and writings, I propose to re-examine the *Vindication of the Rights of Woman* (often referred to as her "Second Vindication") within this broader context, identifying its most salient themes and situating it particularly with reference to other discussants of the "rights of women" in neighboring France just prior to and during the turbulent epoch of the Revolution.

The *Vindication of the Rights of Woman* was composed by a single, mostly self-educated, inquisitive, thoughtful, and independent-minded woman in her early thirties, from a large albeit fragmented, somewhat economically-distressed lower middle-class English family. She had gained some experience of the world through working for inadequate pay as a ladies' companion, governess, and schoolmistress, as well as through resolving the problems of her several siblings. By 1792 she bore a freshly-minted reputation as a self-supporting writer in the London literary world, and held a number of firm ideas about how contemporary British society could be improved. Mary Wollstonecraft was a Dissenter, a professed Deist, a believer in a rational, all-seeing God, in the immortality of the soul, and in reasonable religion, ideas that were not without specific consequences for her project. Her political ideas (as Barker-Benfield has recently pointed out) were greatly influenced by the Commonwealth tradition of seventeenth-century England.[8]

Wollstonecraft's immediate intellectual context was not, however, exclusively English. It was nuanced by exposure to French culture and reformist ideas, mainly acquired (it would appear) through extensive reading and a general fascination with French culture. Although Mary Wollstonecraft had not been to France prior to 1792 and could not speak the language before that time, she was keenly aware of things French: references to French history, customs, phrases and terms pop up repeatedly in the *Vindication* (e.g., Chap. 4, pp. 113, 117, 136, 138). She was acquainted with at least some of the writings of Rousseau, Mme de Genlis, Mme de Staël and her father, the celebrated French prime minister, Jacques Necker. Moreover, Wollstonecraft and the other members of her circle were all deeply interested in the revolutionary experiment taking place just across the Channel, and in its sociopolitical implications for Britain; already in 1789 the French had proclaimed "the rights of man" and abolished all privileges based on birth/rank. They had thereby created all men "equal" and "free," a goal that the men in Wollstonecraft's political circle shared. In 1790 Wollstonecraft had published her *Vindication of the Rights of Man*, a response to the sharply hostile analysis made of the revolution by her countryman, the arch-defender of "tradition" and "custom," Edmund Burke. Her reply was published several months before the great tract on the rights of man by Thomas Paine, her contemporary and colleague in London Dissent circles. She would subsequently publish an account of the history of the first year of the French Revolution.

Wollstonecraft composed her *Vindication of the Rights of Woman* in six weeks, late in the year 1791. During this year the revolutionaries in France had secularized the Catholic

Church, the king and queen had sought to flee France and had been arrested. About the time Wollstonecraft began to write, the National Assembly had completed its draft of a new Constitution, which the king finally signed in late September. By the date of publication of the *Vindication* early in 1792, the all-male electorate had already elected a new Legislative Assembly to proceed with the work of the revolution, including the tasks of reforming education and restructuring marriage as a secular institution. But it was nearly a year later, in December 1792, when Mary Wollstonecraft ventured to France herself to witness at first hand the extraordinary and increasingly disquieting sociopolitical experiment. By that time, a French translation of the *Vindication* had been published in Paris.[9] Ominously, however, acts of political violence had increased; extremism, both in word and deed, appeared ever more difficult to contain. France had been declared a Republic, and as Wollstonecraft arrived in Paris, the royal family was in prison and the king was about to be tried and executed.

But let us return to 1791, prior to Mary Wollstonecraft's Paris journey, and focus on the content and context of the *Vindication of the Rights of Woman*.

The *Vindication* is a sprawling, verbose, and unsystematic book-length work, 450 pages long in its original edition, comprised of thirteen substantive chapters. It is prefaced with a dedication to the former French bishop and current revolutionary legislator, M. Talleyrand-Périgord, followed by a brief "advertisement" to readers concerning the ostensible limits of the work, and a six-page introduction.

The dedication to the defrocked clergyman Talleyrand sets the context for the *Vindication* and is far more pertinent to the book's content than Anglo-centered readings have suggested. For in the 1791 French constitutional discussions, the place of women in the new regime, the specific issue of women's citizenship, and the correlative issue of what education they should be given was discussed at length in the clubs and in the press.

Indeed, the French constitution-makers of 1791 effectively wrote women out of the new order of citizenship, the "public," consigning them to a domestic, or "private" sphere. Such notions of public and private, derived explicitly from Roman law, figured prominently in the revolutionary discussion in 1791 and 1792. In September Talleyrand submitted a report on national education, in the name of the Constitutional Committee, to the National Assembly: in his lengthy *Rapport sur l'instruction publique. . .*,[10] he argued that both sexes should be educated, and set out a plan for district, departmental, and vocational schools. In the concluding pages of his otherwise very progressive-sounding memoir, however, Talleyrand elaborated a plan of differentiated instruction for women, which he viewed as consequent on their political status, just determined by the new Constitution. In deliberate contrast to Condorcet's earlier appeals to justice and equality for women on the basis of their common reason,[11] Talleyrand argued a brief for societal expediency. Referring to the *Declaration of the Rights of Man* itself, which stated (Art. 1) that civil distinctions could be made only on grounds of public utility, he invoked the utilitarian notion of the greatest happiness for the greatest number, which demanded (in his opinion) that women be excluded from political life and relegated to the household. He curtly dismissed all appeal to abstract principles, and tellingly invoked men's fear of rivalry from women in support of his case.

Surprisingly, Wollstonecraft did not quote from Talleyrand's report in the *Vindication*. If she had, however, at least some of her readers might have been indignant at his argument:

> It is impossible here to separate questions relative to women's education from
> an examination of their political rights. When raising them, one must thoroughly

7

understand their destination. If we acknowledge that they have the same rights as men, they must be given the same means to make use of them. If we think that their share should be uniquely domestic happiness and the duties of *la vie intérieure*, they should be formed early on to fill this destiny.

And Talleyrand elaborated this point to make his meaning unmistakably clear:

> It seems incontestable to us that the common happiness, especially that of women, requires that they do not aspire to exercise rights and political functions. One must seek their best interest in the will of nature. Is it not obvious that their delicate constitutions, their peaceful inclinations, the many duties of maternity, constantly distance them from *habitudes fortes*, difficult responsibilities, and recall them to gentle occupations, to the cares of the interior? And how can one not see that the very principle that conserves societies, which has placed harmony in the division of powers, has been expressed as though revealed by nature when it thus distributed to the two sexes functions that are so evidently distinct? . . . Instead of making them disdain the portion of happiness that society reserves for them in exchange for the important services it demands from them, let us teach them the real measure of their duties and rights. That they will find, not insubstantial hopes, but real advantages under the empire of liberty; that the less they participate in making the law, the more they will receive from it protection and strength; and that especially when they renounce all political rights, they will acquire the certainty of seeing their civil rights substantiated and even expanded.[12]

In light of this highly politicized French context, it is simply amazing to find that Wollstonecraft's *Vindication* opens with a gracious tribute to Talleyrand and not with a direct confrontation of his refusal of political rights to women. What seems more surprising is that the body of the tract hardly discusses *rights* as such, at least not in a way that much resembles the far more concrete framing of the issue of rights in the aftermath of the American revolution against England, i.e., with respect to equality before the law, ownership of property and political participation, freedom of speech and assembly, etc. Even readers of the 1790s might have remarked that the *Vindication* was by no means as directly "political" a work as either Condorcet's *Plea for the Citizenship of Women* (1790), or Olympe de Gouges' *Declaration of the Rights of Woman and Citizen* (1791). Indeed, the concept of "rights," even in a more abstract form, scarcely appears in the first 250 pages of the main text. When Wollstonecraft does discuss "rights" she links them (as does Talleyrand) firmly to "duties" (e.g., Dedication 1, and 233), but even then her allusions to "rights" remain nebulous, occupying a philosophical high ground.

What could explain this initially oblique quality of Wollstonecraft's response to Talleyrand? Was the Dedication simply tacked on to an already elaborated text? Was it perhaps an act of deference to the growing counter-revolutionary conservatism of English public opinion? Or, was the context so clear to her readers at the time that they needed no explicit prompt? The prompt, when it finally appeared on pp. 3–4, however, was both bold and anguished.

> . . . when men contend for their freedom, and to be allowed to judge for themselves respecting their own happiness, be it not inconsistent and unjust to

subjugate women, even though you firmly believe that you are acting in the manner best calculated to promote their happiness? Who made man the exclusive judge, if woman partake with him the gift of reason?

Comparing Talleyrand to a tyrant, "eager to crush reason," she insisted:

> Do you not act a similar part, when you *force* all women, by denying them civil and political rights, to remain immured in their families groping in the dark? . . . They may be convenient slaves, but slavery will have its constant effect, degrading the master and the abject dependent.

Talleyrand, renouncing abstract principle in favor of a utilitarian approach to the ordering of human society, had firmly divided men from women, prescribing for them wholly *separate spheres* and wholly *distinct tasks*, with educational preparation to suit. But in Mary Wollstonecraft's ordering of human relations, she insists on retaining priority for the category "human being," with men and women as complementary sub-categories. In consequence she speaks a great deal in the *Vindication* about the "individual" and about the development of individual character and judgment.

Her understanding of "rights" is pinned squarely on this prior category of "human being" and appeals to concepts of "reason" and "virtue" that are common to all beings – a single standard of *human values*, as it were, based in nature and attempts to understand nature through rationality. When Wollstonecraft does invoke "rights" toward the end of her work, she speaks in the very general terms of natural rights (understood to be prior to sociopolitically established rights): for example, "the inherent rights of mankind" (261); "the rights which women in common with men ought to contend for" (286); "let woman share the rights and she will emulate the virtues of man" (287), and again (287), "rights and duties are inseparable," "the rights of reason." This is far loftier and more philosophical language than that of the *Bill of Rights* or the *Declaration of the Rights of Man and of Citizens*. It is loftier still than the language she deployed in her *Vindication of the Rights of Man*, where she did critique as hollow the much-vaunted English concepts of rights to liberty and property. Consideration of these latter issues, as concerned women, she announced she would deliberately postpone until her second, never written, volume.

There is another key phrase in Talleyrand's text, in fact, that provides a point of entry to the major argument that Wollstonecraft makes throughout the *Vindication*: *"If we acknowledge that they have the same rights as men, they must be given the same means to make use of them."* It is on this brief phrase that Wollstonecraft's entire book turns. From beginning to end, the *Vindication of the Rights of Woman* is less an assertion of *rights* than an elaboration of *means*: the social construction of the sexes through their respective upbringing. It is about education, training, shaping, with respect to what we now call gender; it argues, in sum, for "a revolution in female manners" (84, 266, etc.). It offers a critique of how women are and a plan for what they might become. The bulk of the *Vindication* is about giving women comparable *means* to make use of and act on their natural *rights*, i.e., rights they already possess as rational creatures.

Wollstonecraft's emphasis is thus placed on developing in women more *character*, *judgment*, and *knowledge*, on *improving reason* and *promoting virtue*. Overall, the book does not read as a political treatise in the customary sense of "political," but far more as a treatise on moral education. As such, it provides yet another chapter in the extended debate

9

over women's education that had been raging in Europe since the sixteenth century, gathered yet more force in the eighteenth.[13] Viewed another way, however, it is profoundly political, in the sense that we now understand the social construction of gender as a profoundly political problem. And yet, Wollstonecraft's overt political message is muted as quickly as it is raised: the bulk of the *Vindication* addresses the development of character in women and critiques women who, for various reasons, do not deliberately pursue enlightenment and personal growth in their own long-term self interest. Only sporadically does she insert an indictment of the male-dominated society that allows women to be thus distracted and thereby deformed.

Mary Wollstonecraft suggests early in the *Vindication* that developing these qualities in women might be misunderstood as making women more like men, but she argues that such a (Rousseauean) allegation misses the point. She insists (52) that "the most perfect education . . . is such an exercise of the understanding as is best calculated to strengthen the body and form the heart. Or, in other words, to enable the individual to attain such habits of virtue as will render it independent. In fact, it is a farce to call any being virtuous whose virtues do not result from the exercise of its own reason." Elsewhere she writes (58) "The grand end of their exertions should be to unfold their own faculties and to acquire the dignity of conscious virtue." Still further (92) she queries: "how can a rational being be ennobled by anything that is not obtained by its own exertions?" Only midway through the text does she propose an economically-based "true definition of independence" when she argues that women can develop enough strength to enable them to earn their own subsistence and be independent of men (138). And only 100 pages later does she elaborate briefly on the vocations women might pursue (219, 221–24). These arguments for economic independence, however, constitute brief interludes in an argument that is otherwise far more abstract.

Wollstonecraft's analysis exemplifies Enlightenment philosophical individualism at its peak. But what are its sociopolitical implications? Against what foil were these arguments directed? What were women currently doing that Wollstonecraft found so objectionable?

The problematical issue of sensuality lies at the core of Wollstonecraft's thinking about reason and rights. In the eighteenth century, this took the form of a debate over the issue of women's power and influence, particularly as it manifested itself in the world of aristocracy and wealth. At the heart of this issue lay a politics of the most difficult sort: the deliberate construction (and control) of women by men as objects of desire, women's own often flamboyant cultivation of their beauty and/or sexual attractiveness, and their promotion of luxury, ornament, and fantasy to get what they wanted in a male-dominated world that systematically subordinated them. To Wollstonecraft, this was at once a historical and philosophical problem, and one in which the French nation figured as peculiarly problematic. As she put it early in her Dedication to Talleyrand, " . . . Modesty, the fairest garb of virtue! has been more grossly insulted in France than even in England, till their women have treated as *prudish* that attention to decency which brutes instinctively observe" (Dedication 2). This was a problem that she had already raised in her *Vindication of the Rights of Man* and she returned to it with greater energy in the second *Vindication*.

Space does not permit me to explore this vast European debate about women's power and influence at length; suffice to say that it had arisen in conjunction with a critique of courtly society, aristocratic manners, "learned women" (*bel esprits*), luxury, and encroaching commercialism, and that it eventually spilled over into the New World as well. In France, however, the problem seemed to loom larger precisely because French women of the upper ranks were so highly visible; they were never successfully sequestered, as was the case in many other cultures bordering the Mediterranean. One finds, for example, a number of women who as regents or royal mistresses had been exceedingly influential, though technically illegitimate political players in the monarchies of the *ancien régime*. Moreover in the seventeenth and eighteenth centuries women played a major role in the development of French literary, culture and manners.[14] And of course, at the time Wollstonecraft wrote, the French queen, Marie-Antoinette, was under sharp attack by certain revolutionaries as the very epitome of politically irresponsible seductiveness and sensuality, the very embodiment of all that was wrong with the old regime.[15]

Central to Wollstonecraft's thinking about the conditions for success of the new philosophical and revolutionary ideals, therefore, is the desensualization, or desexification of women in male eyes. She expressed concern about works on education by men "who, consider[ing] females rather as women than human creatures, have been more anxious to make them alluring mistresses than affectionate wives and rational mothers" (31–32). As the *Vindication* unfolds, Wollstonecraft (here mirroring Rousseau) seems virtually obsessed with the problem of women's illicit sexual power (53, 77, 97–98, 249). At one point, responding to Rousseau's concern that "the more [women] resemble our sex the less power will they have over us," Mary Wollstonecraft exclaims: "I do not wish them to have power over men; but over themselves" (107).

To illustrate what she was arguing against, Wollstonecraft repeatedly invoked what she called Mahometan practices, which were much discussed at the time. Her contempt for the enclosure of women in the highly-sexualized setting of the seraglio, or harem, and by extension all things Islamic or Oriental, is repeatedly expressed in the *Vindication* (32, 35, 50, 62, 77, 79, 82, 118, 258, 278).[16]

But Wollstonecraft was no less critical of her own culture: she was no benevolent judge of the flaws of others of her own sex (104–107), and she was greatly disturbed by the current emphasis in public discussion on "love" and "sensibility," and on the novels that promoted it. In these days before her affair with Gilbert Imlay and her marriage to William Godwin, she viewed this emphasis on emotion as transitory, ephemeral and ultimately unhealthy (see p. 63, and Chap. 8).

For Wollstonecraft, the "price" to be paid for attaining virtue – and therefore political liberty – was "modesty," by which she meant that women should deliberately curb the use of sexual attraction to achieve their ends (see esp. Chap. 8). The false regard women had for "reputation" or *appearances* should be rechanneled to the cultivation of chaste practices. In order to accomplish the enthronement of reason and virtue, Mary Wollstonecraft argues against the degradation of women that made them subservient, as she put it (60) "to love or lust." *Restraint on passion and on its cultural celebration was central to her project.* This emphasis has been much criticized by some modern Wollstonecraft scholars, who see it as undermining an essential facet of late twentieth century women's liberation.[17] Without excusing her emphasis, I would reiterate that it remains vital for us, in appreciating Wollstonecraft's actual achievement within the context of its time, to comprehend the reasons for her insistence on modesty and chastity. It was not a matter of eradicating women's sexual power and influence, but of constraining and channeling it toward politically appropriate ends. It was not "passionlessness" but channeled passion she advocated.[18]

Within the broader category of "human beings," Mary Wollstonecraft clearly acknowledged and respected sexual difference, if only with respect to societal roles and a sexual division of labor. Her much-discussed "horse-laugh" claim, wishing "to see the distinction of sex confounded in society" (100) represents a radical break, a utopian parenthesis, in a text that is otherwise permeated with acknowledgement of the irrevocability of sexual distinctions.[19] "Women" and "Woman" are categories she distinguishes and cares about, and she believes that females do have particular responsibilities, or duties, as a sex. She repeatedly acknowledges (32, 62, 75, 138) the superior physical strength of males, and not unlike Talleyrand himself she insists on the importance of women's roles as companions to men and as mothers. She is deliberately "relational," that is to say, she thinks of women-in-relation-to-others in her practical, sociopolitical thinking, even as she is "individualist" in her philosophical approach. In consequence of these two factors, however, and in direct contrast to Talleyrand (who in this instance seems to echo Rousseau) Mary Wollstonecraft positions women in these capacities, and indeed family life itself (as others in her time were also doing), as central to all societal progress.[20] In her view, however, the "domestic" is necessarily part and parcel of the "public," not subordinate to it. So much for the attempts of Rousseau, Talleyrand, and revolutionary republicans to prescribe wholly separate – and hierarchical – spheres. Even if women have duties to fulfil, she argues, these duties are all *human* duties, "and the principles that regulate the discharge of them . . . must be the same" (92). Men's and women's duties are asserted to be of equal importance; Wollstonecraft's notion here is one of "equality in difference."

Wollstonecraft's world view is resolutely heterosexual; she envisions women as the *friends* of men, especially in marriage (63, 284–85), and friendship as a superior bond between the sexes. Wollstonecraft's arguments on this point must also be placed within a centuries' old discussion within humanism over whether there could be friendship between the sexes, or whether it could only exist between "equals," i.e., among men.[21] Revealingly, she cites Rousseau's relationship to "that fool" Thérèse Levasseur as an example of a relationship that did not work (259–60). Elsewhere, in her letters, Wollstonecraft once remarked that she was "half in love" with Rousseau. She had obviously been thinking about how much better off Jean-Jacques would have been with a woman like herself; she certainly strove for friendship with the men in her own life (Henry Fuseli, Gilbert Imlay, and William Godwin) with such a companionate vision in mind.

Wollstonecraft argues for the cultivation and development, in girls, of physical strength as well as mental and moral strength (74–78, 254–55). She issues an encompassing critique of the way upper-class girls are physically as well as mentally constrained in their childhood and youth in order to fashion them for the marriage market in polite society (Chap. 3). From dressing-up to doll-play, Wollstonecraft objects, item by item, to the practices of this constraint. She protests against the narcissism cultivated in girls, and to the falsity and ephemerality of the power women – and in this chapter she points not only to the French but to London "ladies of fashion" (276) – obtain through wile and beauty. This, too, was a chapter in the ongoing critique of women's upbringing and education that dated far back in European history.[22]

But Wollstonecraft did not stop there. She went on to vest the responsibility for progress itself on the alternative model of the knowledgeable, virtuous, and dignified mother-educator, a new ideal type for emulation by eighteenth-century women and by extension, a model for female citizenship. This claim is laid out at the beginning (2–3) of her "Dedication":

> Contending for the rights of woman, my main argument is built on this simple principle, that if she be not prepared by education to become the companion of man, she will stop the progress of knowledge and virtue; for truth must be common to all, or it will be inefficacious with respect to its influence on general practice. And how can woman be expected to cooperate unless she

know why she ought to be virtuous? unless freedom strengthen her reason till she comprehend her duty, and see in what manner it is connected with her real good? If children are to be educated to understand the true principle of patriotism, their mother must be a patriot; and the love of mankind, from which an orderly train of virtues spring, can only be produced by considering the moral and civil interest of mankind; but the education and situation of woman, at present, shuts her out from such investigation.

Thus, the scenario Wollstonecraft develops for the deployment of women's talents and judgment in the role of mother and educator can be seen as a rerouting of women's power and influence into socially and politically productive channels. Like Talleyrand's exclusion, it offers a utilitarian proposal but one that sets on its ear the logic of a domestic/public hierarchy. It is in this sense that we should understand her version of those much misunderstood eighteenth-century arguments for patriotic mothers who can educate their children for citizenship, which informs much of nineteenth-century reform in the particular guise of the "republican mother."[23]

It has to be said, however, that by comparison to political texts published by French women between 1789 and 1791, the *Vindication* does not read as a particularly radical document. While Wollstonecraft's *Vindication* treats women's rights as abstract and comparable to those of men, suggesting half apologetically, in one short sentence, that women ought to have representatives (220), the French texts make specific claims for women's political representation as women. They, too, are infused with the discussion over women's sensuality – which is not denied but rechanneled – and they, too, feature arguments for reforming women's education. What is more, many of them are replete with arguments that draw explicit parallels between the slavery of women and the slavery of blacks. I will not elaborate here the comparison to Condorcet, the most eloquent of the women's advocates during the pre- and early revolutionary period, except to point out that his claims on women's behalf were framed in terms of the arbitrary exclusion of "one half the human race" from a role in framing France's new laws (a claim Wollstonecraft also makes). His well-known arguments for women's rights and citizenship are in many respects similar to those of Wollstonecraft, and she may have drawn inspiration from them. But of this we have no concrete proof.

An extended comparison with the range of revolutionary women's texts has not, so far as I know, been attempted in any other work on Wollstonecraft.[24] Yet these documents are of great interest and remarkable originality. Consider, for example, the "Petition by Women of the Third Estate to the King," dated 1 January 1789. Its authors asked: 1) that women's voices be heard; 2) that the King take up their cause; the authors exhibited no great hopes in the Estates General and were skeptical of the election process itself. And 3) they detailed the women's problems: faulty education, a terrible economic position (especially men usurping women's trades), and grave disadvantages in the marriage market.[25]

Another appeal from 1789, "The *Cahier* of Grievances and Demands of Women," signed by the anonymous Madame B***B*** from Normandy, insisted that women property holders of the Third Estate (as well as women fief-holders and women religious of the first and second estates) also be given the opportunity to register their grievances. Going further, she called for the *representation of women by women* in the Estates General.[26]

In a third text from 1789, "The Request of Ladies to the National Assembly," the anonymous authors remark:

It is altogether astonishing that . . . having cut down a very large part of the forest of prejudices, you would leave standing the oldest and most general of all abuses, the one which excludes the most beautiful and most loveable half of the inhabitants of this vast kingdom from positions, dignities, honors, and especially from the right to sit amongst you . . . . You have broken the scepter of despotism, you have pronounced the beautiful axiom . . . *the French are a free people*. Yet still you allow thirteen million slaves shamefully to wear the irons of thirteen million despots!

This document goes on to condemn "masculine aristocracy," proposing a decree that would not only abolish all the privileges of the male sex, but would also disqualify the masculine "gender" (*genre masculin*), even grammatically, from being considered the more noble gender, and would abolish the male prerogative of wearing trousers![27] Whether this document is authentic or apocryphal (as some have alleged), it manifests a stunningly radical political consciousness.

Etta Palm d'Aelders, a Dutchwoman in her late 40s who had lived for years in France and was active in the *Amis de la Vérité*, spoke to the National Assembly in July 1791, objecting to a provision that would underscore the legal authority of husbands over wives:

It is your duty, it is your honor, it is in your interest to destroy to their very roots these gothic laws that abandon the weakest but most worthy half of humanity to a humiliating existence, an eternal slavery . . . . The hour has struck; justice, the sister of liberty, calls all individuals to equal rights without distinction of sex; the laws of a free people must be equal for all beings, just like the air and the sunshine . . . . The powers of the husband and the wife should be equal and individual . . . .[28]

Last but by no means least we come to the *Declaration of the Rights of Woman* of 1791, a document virtually contemporary with Wollstonecraft's *Vindication* and responding to the same constitutional *impasse* for women. The author, the prolific writer and playwright, Olympe de Gouges, then in her mid-40s, provocatively challenges men who would subordinate women: "Men, are you capable of being just? It is a woman who asks you this question . . . . Tell me! Who has given you the sovereign authority to oppress my sex?"

Taking up where Madame B***B*** left off, Gouges called for a national assembly of women – mothers, daughters, sisters – and for the adoption of a *Declaration of the Rights of Woman*. Paraphrasing the earlier *Declaration of the Rights of Man*, she redefined the sovereign "nation" as *the union of woman and man*. She called for equal participation and equal treatment under the law for both sexes, equal admission to public office, equal punishment for equal crimes, and equal and inalienable property rights for both sexes. Free speech for women would include their rights to speak in public and to name the fathers of their babies. But Gouges was particularly exercised on the subjects of national education, women's vices and the restoration of morals, and conjugal contracts. Her text ends with an astonishingly modern "Model for a social contract between a man and a woman."[29]

All these texts were in circulation in Paris prior to or immediately following Talleyrand's eviction of women from public life and the drafting of Mary Wollstonecraft's *Vindication*.

There seems to be no evidence to suggest – or to counter the suggestion – that Mary Wollstonecraft might have been familiar with any of these women's texts or with their authors. Nor is there any mention of either in her subsequent Paris letters or in her account of the first year of the revolution. This leaves one with many questions but few answers. It is my sense, however, that she probably did not know of them (though she was most likely familiar with the writings of Condorcet). Had she been acquainted with the women's texts, she might have responded to Talleyrand in a firmer and more elaborated manner, acknowledging these sisterly efforts, with which she surely would have had sympathy, and she might even have been inspired to write the second part of the *Vindication* first. She might also have found (had she been able to overlook their backgrounds) some kindred souls in Paris, and, following the fall of the pro-English Girondins from power, avoided the fateful liaison with Imlay, which ironically, kept her pregnant and in hiding outside Paris during the last half of 1793, the height of the Terror but also the peak of women's political activism in revolutionary Paris.

It is time now to return to the question with which we began: can we call Mary Wollstonecraft a feminist? And this raises the questions: What is feminism? Who is a feminist?

Many varied yet specific issues have arisen in the course of feminism's history in differing times and places, and an even wider variety of strategies and tactics for addressing them have developed. Some would claim today that one's classification as a feminist might rest on having a politically-correct position on these particulars. Mary Wollstonecraft emphasized modesty, education, and civic motherhood; she even objected to abortion. Her emphasis on education might be faulted in retrospect for slighting the necessary confrontation with the political and legal institutions that ensured male dominance.

It is my argument, however, that these particular issues, strategies, and tactics should not be confused with, or mistaken for defining characteristics of the broader phenomenon of feminism. I think here specifically of the demands in recent European and American history for women's suffrage or ending legalized prostitution, but other markers are and can also be mistaken for the whole, e.g., rape, abortion, protective labor legislation, sexual orientation, or other arbitrary and culturally-specific forms of reproductive control such as cliterodectomy.

The general definition of feminism I distilled from comparative historical study reads as follows:

> The concept of feminism (viewed historically and comparatively) encompasses both a system of ideas and a movement for sociopolitical change based on a critical analysis of male privilege and women's subordination within any given society. It addresses imbalances of power between the sexes that disadvantage women.

One might better say that "it challenges and seeks to remedy imbalances in power between the sexes." These phrases serve, in any case, to place feminism as a group sexual politics; it is not merely about the frustrated aspirations of individual persons who happen to be female. I then laid out some subsidiary considerations with regard to the concept of "gender," and the play between "issues concerning personal autonomy or freedom" and "basic issues of societal organization" and issues of mutual responsibility. And I added that feminism "aims to destroy masculinist hierarchy but not sexual dualism as such" and "Thus, to be a feminist is necessarily to be at odds with male domination in culture and society, in whatever geographical location or situation in historic time."[30]

Such a historically-derived definition of feminism is both general and broad, applicable to very diverse settings. It is concerned primarily with *process*. This concern with a common process informs my elaboration of a series of behavioral criteria for identifying feminists, "irrespective of geographical location or situation in historic time," i.e., independent of specific issues or approaches. Feminists can be identified as any persons, female or male, whose ideas and actions (insofar as they can be documented) show them to meet three criteria:

1. they recognize the validity of women's own interpretations of their lived experience and needs and acknowledge the values women claim publicly as their own (as distinct from an aesthetic ideal of womanhood invented by men) in assessing their status in society relative to men;
2. they exhibit consciousness of, discomfort at, or even anger over institutionalized injustice (or inequity) toward women as a group by men as a group in a given society; and
3. they advocate the elimination of that injustice by challenging, through efforts to alter prevailing ideas and/or social institutions and practices, the coercive power, force, or authority that upholds male prerogatives in that particular culture.

Certainly, Mary Wollstonecraft's mission is encompassed within the larger definition. Let us see how her contributions, as developed in the *Vindication*, might match up with my three criteria:

1. Mary Wollstonecraft insists on and draws extensively on her own experience and her observations of experiences of other women as evidence in developing her critique. Although she objects to some forms of women's behavior, she contests "masculinist" prescriptions for what women as a group should become, both those of Talleyrand and Rousseau. No question here; her work qualifies.
2. In Wollstonecraft's analysis the issue of female education – or rather lack thereof assessed as deprivation – provides the issue that marks out women as the objects (victims) of institutionalized injustice. Like many other eighteenth-century critics she repeatedly draws analogies between the situation of slaves and women. A critique of institutionalized marriage (the famous unwritten volume II) might have served her purpose more emphatically, but it was not vital to her assessment of institutionalized injustice. Again, she clearly qualifies.
3. Wollstonecraft advocates elimination of institutionalized injustice in several ways. On the level of ideas, she attempts to alter prevailing notions by deploying natural rights arguments based on "reason" to challenge the conventional wisdom underlying women's collective deprivation. She attacks prevailing institutions and practices by challenging the reign of sensuality and positing an alternative model of womanhood and motherhood based on its containment and rechanneling. And though she does not develop the case against male dominance and control mechanisms as much as we might have liked to find, she clearly challenges what she has come to see as systemic domination by "vindicating" women's rights – collectively – as women.

Surely, then, even retrospectively, we can bestow on Mary Wollstonecraft the broad label of "feminist." In comparison with her counterpart, the Christian educator Hannah More (who did acknowledge male rule), she is incontestably more progressive.[31] But we must also situate her feminism by insisting on the contextual comparison to her French counterparts, who because of the revolutionary political setting in which they found themselves, were expressing themselves in a far more vehemently politicized language. In France, the very government of the nation, its laws and its cultural practices had been called into question; in particular, new definitions of citizenship were being established and gender was clearly a central problem in revolutionary politics. In England, one could not go so far. What one might term a cultural and political "backlash" was already in formation in 1791. This may explain why the body of Wollstonecraft's critique turned back on reforming women's behavior, on arguing for friendship between the sexes, on notions of taste, dignified domesticity and responsible motherhood, rather than on indicting men's injustice, or insisting on sharing political power. This may also explain why her protests, which are at times truly eloquent, are more often than not embedded in lengthy apologies, excuses, and qualifications.

Mary Wollstonecraft was a feminist, but a particular kind of feminist, one shaped emphatically by – and limited by – the context of her life and times. She makes abstract, individualist philosophical claims, but she articulates them in a relational sociopolitical framework. By re-reading – and appreciating – her *Vindication* contextually and comparatively, we can celebrate her courage and conviction, two hundred years later, even as we acknowledge the situational difficulties she confronted in drafting this historic *Vindication* on behalf of her countrywomen. In my own case as a historian, aware of the substantial and dramatic advances we have made in women's education, but also in acquiring political, legal, and economic rights since the eighteenth century, such a re-reading of the *Vindication* inspires humility as we struggle with the most difficult challenge of excavating, exposing, and eradicating even deeper and more intricately embedded layers of male authority and control, not only in national and international politics, but within language itself and the systems of knowledge that have been structured by human consciousness and speech.

2

RE-ROOTING AMERICAN WOMEN'S ACTIVISM

Global perspectives on 1848

Nancy A. Hewitt

For many American women's historians trained in the 1960s and 1970s, interest in the field was inspired by their engagement with women's liberation. They were compelled by their politics to recover the roots of modern feminism. Many radical feminists initially found foremothers in the likes of Louise Michel, Emma Goldman, Crystal Eastman, and other turn-of-the-century socialist and anarchist women. Though women's historians of this generation were driven by competing visions of feminism and thus embraced different foremothers, many sought to understand the present through a geneaological excavation of the past. This was particularly true for those studying women's political activism, who moved from contemporary debates about sex equity back through suffrage (socialism too quickly fell by the wayside in the United States) and then Seneca Falls. This article explores the implications of reaching Seneca Falls through this reverse chronological trajectory, and then suggests how we might rethink the history of women's activism by re-embedding Seneca Falls in the world of 1848.

What a world it was – revolutions erupted across Europe; Irish peasants and later defeated German revolutionaries migrated to the U.S. en masse; the Treaty of Guadalupe Hidalgo ended the Mexican-American War, adding new territories and peoples to the United States; *The Communist Manifesto* was published; the Seneca Nation embraced a written constitution for the first time; John Humphrey Noyes established a utopian community at Oneida, New York; New York State granted property rights to married women; slavery was abolished in the French West Indies; U.S. slaves fled North to find freedom; the first Chinese immigrants to North America arrived in San Francisco; the Gold Rush began; the Free Soil Party and spiritualism were founded and both attracted thousands of devotees. This remarkable array of events shaped the meaning of Seneca Falls and the trajectories of women's activism in the mid-nineteenth century U.S.

Yet rarely is the 1848 woman's rights convention conceived as part of these revolutionary developments. Instead, it is most often defined as foremother to the federal suffrage amendment passed in the U.S. in 1920. Disentangling Seneca Falls from suffrage is no easy task. These two events were identified as the touchstones of American women's history long before the field was created. Until quite recently, Betsy Ross stitching the American flag and the Salem Witch Trials were the only other widely-known "women's" events in American History. In 1959, Eleanor Flexner's *Century of Struggle* reinvigorated the narrative that carried women's activism from Seneca Falls to suffrage, but the original story line was crafted by pioneer feminists themselves. In their six-volume *History of Woman Suffrage*, published between 1881 and 1922, editors Susan B. Anthony, Elizabeth Cady Stanton, and Matilda Joslyn Gage claimed Seneca Falls as the birthplace of the women's movement and the Nineteenth Amendment mandating women's suffrage as that movement's greatest achievement.[1]

In recent years, scholars studying African American, immigrant, and working-class women have challenged certain aspects of the story.[2] Focusing on the post-Civil War suffrage campaign rather than its antebellum antecedents, historians have detailed the racist, nativist, and elitist tendencies of many white women activists and highlighted the exclusion of poor, black, and immigrant women from the political organizations and agendas of more well-to-do white suffragists. These challenges have tarnished the image of several pioneer figures and added a few women of color and working women to the pantheon of feminist foremothers, but the dominant story of women's political activism as the struggle for enfranchisement has been left largely intact.[3]

By focusing the analysis synchronically – that is, on events occurring concurrently with the emergence of woman's rights in 1848 – we leave aside the question of how women moved from Seneca Falls to suffrage. We can then ask, instead, how women of various racial, ethnic, and economic backgrounds and of diverse religious, regional, and ideological perspectives defined women's rights in the 1840s. How were these views shaped by the Mexican-American War, mass immigration, European revolutions, debates over slavery, race, and Native American rights? And to what extent did the agenda crafted at Seneca Falls and later woman's rights conventions speak to the concerns expressed by female radicals in Europe and by other communities of women in the United States? The answers offered here are speculative, the intention being merely to open up the landscape of 1848, to relocate Seneca Falls within a more panoramic frame, and to suggest how this might help us write new histories of American women's activism by reclaiming alternative narratives of woman's rights.

First, the legend of the Seneca Falls Woman's Rights Convention – a legend well-entrenched in historical texts and popular memory – must be challenged. The classic version of the story was penned by Elizabeth Cady Stanton in her 1898 autobiography, and has been carried forward by historians from Eleanor Flexner to Ellen DuBois and Anne Firor Scott.[4] In 1840, Stanton found herself, twenty-six years old and newly married, "seated behind a curtain at the World's Anti-Slavery Convention in London in company with the forty-two year-old Lucretia Mott [a well-known Quaker abolitionist]. The unwillingness of the convention to seat women delegates led the two to an animated discussion about the discrimination they were experiencing" and to the decision to call a woman's rights convention on their return to the States.

"Eight years and several children later, Stanton, restless and yearning for intellectual stimulation in the isolated town of Seneca Falls, New York, met Mott again." Joined by three friends of Mott, "they drew up a Declaration of Sentiments, carefully modeled on the Declaration of Independence, listing women's grievances. They then sent out a call inviting interested men and women to discuss the subject of women's rights" at the local Wesleyan Chapel. Much to the surprise of the organizers, some three hundred women and men showed up. The result of the Seneca Falls Convention "was a surge of interest in the 'woman question' and the launching of a vigorous debate that was destined to increase in scope and volume through the next seventy-two years," culminating in the achievement of women suffrage.

Most current accounts of this event accept Stanton's narrative and focus on her leadership and the demand for political equality. The history is thus written as one woman's struggle to craft a public role for herself and to inspire a political movement in support of suffrage. The main actors are nearly all native-born white women, assisted by a few good men – such as Lucretia Mott's husband James, who chaired the Seneca Falls Convention, and abolitionist leader Frederick Douglass, the lone African American participant, who argued vigorously for women's right to vote.

Many other versions of this story could be told, however, highlighting other organizers, other participants and other agendas. Judith Wellman, for instance, has traced three distinct political networks – Free Soilers, legal reformers, and Quaker abolitionists – that converged at the 1848 convention. Nancy Isenberg has just completed a book that places Seneca Falls in the context of contemporary struggles over church politics, property rights, and moral reform. More than a decade ago, I too tried to recast the history of woman's rights, by placing radical Quakers at center stage.[5] Led by Lucretia Mott, these feminist Friends dominated the Seneca Falls organizing committee (Stanton was the sole non-Quaker) and provided somewhere between a quarter and a third of the 100 individuals who signed the convention's "Declaration of Sentiments." A more complete challenge must also examine the links between women activists in the U.S. and their counterparts in Europe as well as between the agendas of Anglo-American women's rights advocates and the concerns of African American, Native American, Mexican/American, immigrant, and working-class women.

A new history of woman's rights might begin by replacing Elizabeth Cady Stanton with Lucretia Mott as the central figure at the Seneca Falls Convention. Mott was, after all, the magnet that attracted such a large Quaker contingent to the meeting. Unfortunately for feminist scholars, she did not produce her own histories and autobiographies; and in Stanton's various memoirs, Mott appears only as an inspiring guide, not as an active coworker. At the time, however, Mott's leadership was widely recognized.[6] The preface to the published report of the 1852 National Woman's Rights Convention, held at Syracuse, New York, argued for the significance of the "Declaration of Sentiments," signed by participants at the Seneca Falls and Rochester conventions of 1848: "at the head of the list," it noted, "stood the name of Lucretia Mott."[7] Mott had spoken at abolitionist meetings in Rochester in late June 1848, and Amy Post, that city's leading antislavery and woman's rights advocate, highlighted the Quaker spokeswoman in her account of the Seneca Falls and Rochester conventions. In correspondence with relatives on Long Island, she referred to Mott as "my model of a perfect woman," while she mentioned Stanton only in passing.[8]

The path that Mott and Post took to Seneca Falls was traversed by many women who shared the faith and politics of these radical Quakers; it is a path that links woman's rights to decidedly different historical connections and contexts than those claimed by Stanton. Unlike Stanton, Mott had not spent the years from 1840 to 1848 in domestic isolation. An avid abolitionist, she was active since the mid-1830s in one of the country's most dynamic interracial organizations, the Philadelphia Female Anti-Slavery Society. Like her Quaker coworkers, she was immersed in efforts to end slavery, advance the rights of free blacks and Indians, protest the U.S. war with Mexico, and secure property law reform. Mott travelled to western New York in the summer of 1848 to attend the Genesee Yearly Meeting of Hicksite Friends, assist Quaker abolitionists in the area, and visit Seneca Indian leaders on the Cattaraugus reservation near Buffalo.[9] At the same time, Amy Post and her Quaker coworkers in the area organized a half-dozen antislavery fairs and conventions, broke with the Society of Friends over their stance on women and abolition, founded a new interracial and sex-integrated religious/reform organization called the Friends of Human Progress, formed a Working Women's Protective Union, and followed the efforts of their radical counterparts in France, Germany, and Hungary.

Events in Europe were widely covered that summer in the antislavery as well as the mainstream press.[10] Several American women who later embraced woman's rights had forged bonds with their abolitionist sisters in England during the 1830s and 1840s. Now they reached out to like-minded women in France, Germany and other parts of Europe, creating a set of international alliances among pioneer feminists.[11] Evidence of these connections appears in the reports of the early woman's rights conventions. In the Syracuse proceedings noted above, a letter appeared from French revolutionaries Pauline Roland and Jeanne Deroin, sent to the "Convention of American Women" from their Parisian prison cell in June 1851. In it, they applauded the courage of the American women and reminded them that the chains of the throne and the scaffold, the church and the patriarch, the slave, the worker and the woman must all be broken simultaneously if "the kingdom of Equality and Justice shall be realized on Earth."[12]

Deroin was a seamstress, a committed Saint Simonian socialist, and a revolutionary. In June 1848, she demanded that her male counterparts recognize women's political and social rights. She claimed the right to vote, ran for the legislative assembly, organized workers, and wrote for *La Voix des Femmes*, an early French feminist newspaper.[13] The events that enveloped Deroin were closely followed by abolitionists and woman's rights advocates in the U.S. The abolition of slavery in the French West Indies, for instance, was applauded by Lucretia Mott, who urged her American compatriots to "take courage" from such advances abroad. "We cannot separate our own freedom from that of the slave"; they are "inseparably connected . . . in France," she noted, and are "beginning to be so in other countries."[14] In Rochester, emancipation in the French West Indies was marked by a city-wide celebration on August 1st, just one day before woman's rights advocates gathered at the city's Unitarian church to complete the deliberations begun at Seneca Falls.[15]

After a July visit to the Seneca (Indian) Nation, Mott claimed that Native Americans, too, were learning "from the political agitations abroad . . . imitating the movements of France and all Europe and seeking a larger liberty. . . . "[16] This concept of a "larger liberty" was central to important segments of revolutionary movements in France and Germany and of radical abolition and woman's rights movements in England and the U.S. These segments were comprised largely of women and men who emerged from utopian socialist societies and radical separatist congregations – followers of Charles Fourier, French Saint Simonians, German religious dissidents, and Quakers who rejected the Society of Friends' restrictions on worldly activity and complete sexual and racial equality.[17] These were revolutionaries who believed that to truly transform society meant rooting out oppression in all its forms – in the family, the church, the community, the economy, the polity – simultaneously. To them, emancipation of any group – slaves, for instance – was inextricably intertwined with emancipation for all groups – workers, women, prisoners, and other subjugated peoples. Ultimately, a cooperative commonwealth based on shared labor and shared resources must replace older forms of rule – monarchies, autocracies, even bourgeois democracies. These radical activists advocated individual rights, but only in so far as they complemented rather than competed with communitarian ideals.

Thus revolutionaries like Deroin and woman's rights advocates like Mott and Post supported voting rights for those currently excluded from the body politic, viewing suffrage as a necessary but not a sufficient means for achieving change. The question was complicated in the U.S. by Quaker women's and men's refusal to participate in a government that tolerated violence against slaves and employed military might in the conquest of Mexico. Members of the Friends of Human Progress, a radical Quaker association founded in summer 1848, argued that women should have the same right to refuse to vote as men, but suffrage was not high on their political agenda. Instead, for them, the woman's rights movement provided one more building block in a multifaceted campaign to achieve racial, economic, and gender justice in America.[18]

Radical Quaker analyses of European revolutionaries turned on the inclusivity of their vision. They applauded Jeanne Deroin and Pauline Roland in this regard, but their enthusiasm for Hungarian freedom fighter Louis Kossuth waned during his visit to the U.S. in the early 1850s, when he failed to speak out against slavery.[19] For Mott, Post, and like-minded coworkers, rights for women remained tied to rights for slaves, free blacks, landless laborers, industrial workers, Native Americans, and Mexicans. When radical Quakers organized the second U.S. woman's rights convention in Rochester two weeks after the Seneca Falls meeting, a woman presided, two local seamstresses were invited to discuss women's economic oppression, and two black abolitionist leaders fresh from the Emancipation Day celebration – Frederick Douglass and William C. Nell – were listed as featured speakers. The convention participants called for equal property rights, pay, access to education and occupations, authority in the church and home, and voting rights, for all women regardless of "complexion," that is race. A month later, a gathering of the Friends of Human Progress added to this list land reform, Native American rights, and the abolition of capital punishment.[20]

Two weeks after the Rochester convention, Frederick Douglass carried the woman's rights message into a new arena – the National Convention of Colored Freemen, held in Cleveland, Ohio. He introduced a resolution providing for the full and equal participation of women and men.[21] William Nell, who three years earlier had successfully advocated women's rights in the militant New England Freedom Association (a group that aided fugitive slaves), spoke on behalf of the resolution. By the mid-1850s, nearly every major free black organization in the North granted voting rights to women and a few included women among their officers.

Though the record among predominantly white antislavery organizations was more uneven, those societies that counted a large number of Quakers and some number of free blacks in their membership – such as the Philadelphia Female Anti-Slavery Society and the Western New York Anti-Slavery Society – were in the vanguard. They consistently sought and recognized the support of their African American colleagues; and, as a result, a small circle of black women and men regularly joined woman's rights conventions as speakers, delegates, and officers. These activists also joined forces to abolish segregated schooling. Frederick Douglass and Amy Post took the initiative in Rochester, New York; Betsy Mix Cowles, a radical Quaker woman's rights advocate, led the fight in Ohio; the Philadelphia Female Anti-Slavery Society made the stand in Pennsylvania; and other Quaker coworkers made the case in Massachusetts.[22]

Free blacks recognized the potential power of these interracial alliances for achieving their primary goals – access to education and jobs, abolition, and aid to fugitive slaves. During 1848, free black women in several cities also demonstrated their own brand of women's rights, one inextricably entwined with racial justice. Charlotte Forten, a member of an affluent free black family of Philadelphia, pursued her work for education, fugitive slaves, abolition, and women's rights quietly and with the support of Lucretia Mott and the Philadelphia Female Anti-Slavery Society. Her counterparts across the North – many from less wealthy backgrounds – organized fundraising fairs, challenged school segregation, and refused to consume slave-produced goods. Some embraced more dramatic strategies. In Cincinnati, for instance, in the summer of 1848, freedwomen used washboards and shovels to fend off slavecatchers harassing blacks in the city.[23] Other free women armed themselves with even more deadly weapons to protect fugitive slaves.

In the South, more drastic measures were required if black women were going to participate in these larger freedom struggles. One particularly daring escape was planned in fall 1848 by Ellen Craft, a slave woman from Macon, Georgia. Married to William Craft, a free black cabinetmaker, the light-skinned Ellen dressed herself as a young gentleman, swathed her jaw in bandages to make it appear she was ill, and boarded a train and then a steamer to Philadelphia, with William posing as her/his manservant. They arrived safely in port on Christmas morning, and became noted abolitionist speakers in the U.S. and England.[24] Ellen literally embodied the meaning of women's rights for slaves – the right to control over one's person and one's family. These were property rights, but of a different sort than those envisioned by most white women.

Like many fugitive slaves and many abolitionists, the Crafts found in England a safe haven and a receptive audience. But they missed immersion in African American society. Though we are just beginning to understand women's roles in the internal workings of antebellum free black communities, fragmentary evidence suggests that here, too, individual rights were lauded only as long as they advanced communal interests. Elsa Barkley Brown, studying Richmond, Virginia, has demonstrated that in the immediate post-Civil War period voting was viewed as a community event, whoever cast the ballot.[25] It seems likely that similar views prevailed in northern black communities before the Civil War.

We do know that free black women and men founded churches and mutual aid societies, established political organizations, ran successful businesses, and demanded access to education, jobs, and voting. As a consequence, they were often castigated for asserting citizenship rights that most whites – North and South – still sought to deny them. Woman's rights advocates were likewise defamed, chastised, even arrested for claiming equal status with white men. In Cincinnati, Ohio, in 1853, a woman who wanted to cast a ballot in a local election dressed herself in male attire. When her true sex was discovered, she was arrested and sentenced to twenty days in jail for impersonating a man and thereby a citizen.[26]

As early as 1848, the rejection of feminine fashion and the embrace of more liberated, and more masculine, dress had become one sign of revolutionary commitment for women radicals in Europe and the U.S. Believing that clothes made the man while corsets confined the woman, a number of radical women sought to free themselves and their sisters from restrictive clothing. Replacing bone stays, cinch waists, and long skirts with turkish trousers, loose blouses and knee-length jackets, dress reformers assumed that ease of movement would aid in women's public as well as private labors. In her bid for freedom, Ellen Craft readily exchanged women's skirts for men's pants. In the case of slaves, however, and others who regularly performed extensive manual labor – Native American farmers, Mexican artisans, and Irish factory workers – women already wore less restrictive clothing than their white middle-class counterparts. Yet the freer clothing donned by these women was not usually linked to emancipation. Rather, the failure of poor and working women or any woman from another culture to wear middle-class white American fashions was viewed by those with wealth and power as a reflection of loose morals and a cry for patriarchal control.

Between 1846 and 1848, the issues of women's dress and men's control intersected with the path of western conquest as the Mexican-American War brought vast new territories under U.S. authority. The cause of widespread protest by abolitionist women and men, the war opened vast new lands in northern Mexico/the southwestern U.S. to Anglo-American planters, traders and settlers. Led by radical abolitionists who abhorred war and the spread of slavery, massive demonstrations protesting "manifest destiny" and war with Mexico were staged in cities across the Northeast. Though some antiwar meetings were invaded by angry mobs and threats of "brute force," radical women abolitionists, supported by their counterparts in England, continued to speak out. Lucretia Mott addressed one such meeting in June 1846, presided over by her Quaker coworker Sarah Pugh. Petitions and protests from women abolitionists and woman's rights advocates circulated in Ohio, New York, and Pennsylvania throughout the war. Some drew parallels with the outrages perpetrated by masters against female slaves and noted the dangers that military men posed to Mexican women.[27]

Of course, not all Anglo-American women had developed such clear political perspectives on the war or the women who were its victims. In 1846, for instance, Mrs. Susan Magoffin, the first U.S.-born white woman to travel in the "New" Mexico territory, carried eastern ideals of true womanhood with her. She noted with shock that Mexican women wore loose blouses, flowing skirts and no corsets. She appreciated the personal warmth and hospitality provided her, but was astonished by her hostesses' freedom of movement and what she interpreted as their loose sexual mores. Yet she also noted the extensive legal rights accorded Mexican women.[28]

Under Spanish law and, after 1821, Mexican law, women retained rights to property after marriage; they could inherit, loan, convey, or pawn property whether single or married; they shared custody of children; and they could sue in court without a male relative's approval.[29] These rights were almost uniformly denied under Anglo-American law. In the areas that came under U.S. control, women's rights had been expanded further during the 1830s and 1840s by residents' distance from the district courts of Mexico. They may also have been influenced by their proximity to Pueblo villages, in which women had traditionally held rights to property and a public voice though such rights had been severely curtailed after the Spanish conquest. In Mexican communities, extended kin groups, communal farming patterns, and collective decision-making as well as more egalitarian legal codes defined notions of women's rights and responsibilities.

Northern Mexico was no feminist utopia, however, as the number and range of court cases against abusive husbands, adultery, assault, property disputes, and debts make clear. Nonetheless, conditions worsened with the signing of the Treaty of Guadalupe Hidalgo. As the region came under U.S. control, government officials, Protestant missionaries, and white settlers used portrayals of local women as sexually promiscuous and culturally inferior to justify the imposition of Anglo-American authority. At the very same time, then, as participants at the Seneca Falls Convention were demanding rights to property, inheritance, and custody, "New" Mexican women were losing precisely those rights as they came under U.S. jurisdiction. Mexican women were not only losing rights, but also claims to respectability by virtue of their dark skin and now "foreign" ways. All but the most affluent were compared, as were their Native American counterparts in the Southwest and California, to southern slaves. Indeed, any group of women in the U.S. considered non-white might be defined as morally and socially inferior.

In the northeastern U.S. non-white women had long been affected by the influx of Euro-Americans. Prior to and for more than a century after contact with Europeans, the Seneca – like other Iroquois groups and like the Pueblo – passed names and property through the mother's line, husbands moved into their wives' households upon marriage, and women controlled agricultural production. Seneca women also held positions of religious and political authority, though chiefs and sachems were almost always men. Over the course of two centuries of trade, warfare, disease, missionary efforts, and governmental pressure, however, the Seneca had lost most of their tribal lands, moved to reservations, and converted to patrilineal descent and men's control of agriculture. In July 1848, they also adopted a new "republican" form of government and a written constitution. Women, who once held veto power over a range of decisions – from the appointment of chiefs to the signing of treaties – were divested of some of their authority, but retained the right to vote. And though Seneca men and women would now elect judges and legislators by majority vote, 3/4 of all voters and 3/4 of all mothers had to ratify legislative decisions.[30]

Several Quaker woman's rights advocates were in correspondence with Seneca resident on the Cattaraugus reservation, and Quaker missionary women described in detail the specific voting privileges accorded women, and mothers, there.[31] Lucretia Mott visited the reservation just before travelling to Seneca Falls; and just after the "Declaration of Sentiments" was published, the Seneca women produced a remarkably similar document. For the next seventy years, white suffragists would point, with some ambivalence, to the Iroquois as emblems of politically empowered women, recognizing the ways that communal ownership of property, matrilineal descent, and shared political and religious authority established foundations for female equality.[32] Yet Iroquois women themselves, like their Mexican and Pueblo counterparts, would slowly lose both rights and respectability as they were forced to embrace Anglo-American laws and customs. And in the post-Civil War period, most woman's rights advocates, having accepted the individual right of suffrage as their primary goal, no longer embraced the communitarian vision of equality and justice that allowed their antebellum foremothers to see the Seneca as a model rather than a problem.

There are other threads to follow as we contextualize woman's rights and women's activism in the 1840s: exiled revolutionaries (whose radical politics led to the support of woman's and workers' rights in the German-language press); Irish immigrants (812 of whom arrived in New York harbor while the Seneca Falls Convention was in session); the Gold Rush and western migration (which pulled apart but also extended the radical Quaker network with new circles of activity forming in Michigan, Indiana, and California). Yet the examples above are sufficient to suggest the potential richness of a synchronic analysis.

In rethinking Seneca Falls, it is important to remember that the movement Elizabeth Cady Stanton championed – a movement based on liberal conceptions of self-ownership, individual rights and suffrage – was born there. But it was not alone, nor was it yet triumphant. Rather, the vision held by the largest and most active contingent of feminist foremothers was rooted in communitarian values and organic conceptions of both oppression and liberation. Linked to agendas promoted by utopian socialists and religious radicals in Europe's revolutionary circles, the ideas advanced by feminist Friends also echoed – if sometimes unintentionally – the experiences of women in those African American, Mexican, and Native American communities founded on extended kinship networks, communal labor and collective rights. Self-consciously engaged in campaigns against slavery, war, and western conquest, and for religious freedom, economic justice and political equality, radical Quakers connected the woman's rights agenda to a broader program of social transformation and more diverse networks of activists. Even with all the limitations and shortcomings of such utopian endeavors and knowing that a more liberal, rights-based vision would ultimately dominate, the legacy of woman's rights radicals is worth reclaiming. For it provides an alternative foundation for modern feminism, one that incorporates race and class issues, critiques of colonialism, socialist foremothers, and an internationalist perspective.

3

LIBERTY, EQUALITY, MORALITY

The attempt to sustain an international campaign against the double sexual standard, 1875–1906

Anne Summers

The organisation which is the subject of this article was founded by Josephine Butler (1828–1906) in 1875 and was known under a number of official names: the British, Continental and General Federation for the Abolition of Government Regulation of Prostitution/for the Abolition of State Regulation of Vice; the Association of Social and Moral Hygiene; the International Abolitionist Federation/Fédération Abolitionniste Internationale, a title adopted in the late nineteenth century, and still used by the contemporary organisation. For convenience I shall refer to it as the 'Federation' and shall summarise its aims under the heading 'Abolitionism'.[1] As an organisation of male and female members, the Federation is not always included in listings of feminist associations of the nineteenth century. Nevertheless it is arguable that the European women's movement of the period 1870–1920 cannot be properly understood without reference to Butler's international campaigns. Hitherto, however, her career has been extensively researched in its British and Anglophone contexts only, with the important exception of the work of Annemieke van Drenth and Francisca de Haan.[2]

The concept of internationalism is a relatively recent one, in which, as we know, all sorts of hopes, some more illusory than others, have been invested.[3] While acknowledging the power of those hopes, and the good will that inspired so many organisations, it may be helpful, both historiographically and practically, to 'deconstruct' the internationalisms of the past, or at least to subject them to critical scrutiny. This is certainly required where women's internationalisms are concerned. The issue is strikingly illustrated by the work of Dr Aya Takahashi on the importation of the western profession of nursing into Japan before World War I. She describes conferences of the International Council of Nurses which maintained an ideal – or a façade? – of parity between delegates, but which Japanese nurses could attend only with government permission, and only if accompanied at all times by male chaperones. She raises the question as to what equality of esteem, and what kind of interchange, could exist between women at such different levels of social emancipation.[4] While the contrast between Japanese and western nurses may be an extreme example, there were also, of course, sharp disparities in the degree of female emancipation in different European countries in the nineteenth century. We should, therefore, not expect a movement of European women in this period to find or agree on a simple or straightforward mode of international co-operation, and such was not the case in the Federation.

The constitution of the Federation declared the state regulation of prostitution to be 'une erreur hygiénique, une injustice morale et une crime juridique' [a hygienic error, a moral injustice and a juridical crime] and declared itself to be 'indépendante de tout parti politique, de toute école philosophique, et de toute confession réligieuse' [independent of any political party, philosophical school, or religious confession]. The regulation system, which operated in most European countries, gave women a licence to earn their living through prostitution on condition of being placed on a police register and submitting to regular, and invasive, checks for signs of venereal disease. This was also the system for licensing brothels. Prostitute and non-prostitute women could be arrested and forced to undergo medical inspection without right of judicial appeal. It was virtually impossible for a woman to remove her name from the police register. This regime originated largely in a military concern to preserve the health of soldiers, was fully elaborated in France during the Napoleonic period, and was exported with the French armies of occupation up to 1815. In most European countries, the system survived the defeat of the French armies. It was not adopted in Britain until the passing of the Contagious Diseases Acts of 1864, 1866 and 1869, and then on a small scale, their application being limited to a few naval ports and garrison towns.[5]

The first concerted campaign against the system seems to have originated in England. Both a male National Association for the Repeal of the Contagious Diseases Acts and a Ladies' National Association for the Repeal of the Contagious Diseases Acts, headed by Josephine Butler, had been launched by the end of 1869. There was much co-operation between the two organisations, including mixed public gatherings and the lobbying of Parliament through those members of the National Association who were M.P.s. In April 1871, less than 18 months after the launch, Butler was writing in bullish mood that Gladstone, the Prime Minister, was on the point of repealing the Acts, and this would show the world what 'nous femmes' [we women] could achieve and how men needed 'de l'avis et de l'aide des femmes dans toutes les questions d'économie domestique et dans la législation qui touche a la vie privée de chaque individu' [the advice and assistance of women in all questions of domestic economy and legislation that touched the private life of every individual]. Following this confidently-anticipated success, the campaign should be taken abroad.[6]

By 1875 it was a different story. Far from being able to export a British success to Europe, the national campaign was both disappointed by the lack of progress at home and alarmed by evidence that Continental medical men were increasingly determined to bring pressure to bear on their British colleagues to conform to this system and to implement it throughout Britain and its empire.[7] Butler's response was to form an organisation to change opinion on the Continent. Following a period of Continental travel, investigation and correspondence she and her British colleagues launched the Federation at Liverpool, her home city, in 1875, and after more travel and networking, held its first international congress in Geneva in 1877. Her contacts were established largely among Protestant communities, through the medium of friends, especially Quakers, and also through her family's liberal connections in Europe. Her sister Harriet Meuricoffre, married into a Swiss-Italian family, was from the first a key member of the organisation.

This article focusses on the strains and contradictions involved in maintaining an international organisation. But before discussing the negatives, it is first necessary to give an idea of the positive influence of the Federation – but for which, there would be little point in spending so much time on its history. Through the Federation, Butler's impact on her contemporaries was felt both in the early years of the international movement – the late 1870s to the early 1880s – and in the 1890s, as a second generation of women came to political maturity. This second-generation effect is something which receives little attention in Anglophone literature. The British Contagious Diseases Acts were suspended in 1883 and repealed in 1886, and Butler's subsequent activities are usually narrated in the context of the campaign against regulation of prostitution in India, then the most substantial component of the British Empire. However, by addressing the European dimensions of her campaigns, it is possible to demonstrate the continuation of Butler's interest in, and influence over, European women's movements in the late 1880s and 1890s.[8]

The present study covers five European countries: Belgium and the Netherlands, Germany, France, and Switzerland.[9] The last became the administrative centre of the Federation, and according to one account, it was here that Butler first heard of the evils of regulation, her informant being the radical feminist Marie Goegg.[10] The encounter with Butler in turn directly inspired women such as Marie Humbert-Droz, wife of the Federation's first Secretary, Aimé Humbert; she founded les Amies de la Jeune Fille, an organisation similar to the Young Women's Christian Association which spread through Europe to provide assistance and advice to young women travelling in search of work; Betsy Cellérier, who founded the fundraising and propaganda organisation l'Association du Sou; and Emma Hess of Zurich, who met Butler at the Lausanne congress of 1887 and played an important role in the development of German-speaking organisations affiliated to those set up in French-speaking Switzerland.[11] In the 1890s Butler's example was of immense importance to a more self-consciously feminist Swiss cohort which included Helene von Mülinen, Emma Pieczynska-Reichenbach, Camille Vidart and Emma Boos-Jegher.[12]

In the Netherlands Butler personally inspired Marianne Klerck van Hogendorp and her sisters to draw up a petition against trafficking, signed by 15,000 women, which was presented to the Dutch Parliament in 1885; at the end of the century the sisters were among the founders of the Dutch National Council of Women. In both the Netherlands and Belgium, male and female abolitionists seem to have organised separately: the Dutch feminist Martina Kramers wrote in 1901 that this impulse to autonomous action had been of great value in the formation of the women's movement.[13] It is perhaps significant that the first female doctor in Belgium, Isala van Diest, took up her first post in a refuge for former prostitutes in 1882. She had qualified in 1879 at Bern and then gone to work in London where she encountered the first generation of British medical feminists. More research is certainly needed on the influence of abolitionism on the first generation of women doctors.[14]

In Germany in 1880, Gertrud Guillaume-Schack founded the Deutscher Kulturbund on lines directly inspired by Butler. Her public meetings on abolitionist issues, together with her connection with the prohibited Social Democratic Party, brought her under the ban of the authorities, and she left Germany for Britain in 1885. August Bebel's famous work *Die Frau und der Sozialismus* showed great sympathy for the anti-regulationist position; the knowledge displayed there of the British movement against the Contagious Diseases Acts and of Guillaume-Schack's own campaign, show the extent of the latter's influence. After her exile, more conservative men and women then took up the cause of the protection of women and girls in Germany.[15] These included Pastor Ludwig Weber, whose Sittlichkeitsverein was established in 1885; Dr Adolf Stöcker, who presided over the Allgemeine Konferenz der deutschen Sittlichkeitsvereine from 1888; and Hanna Bieber-Böhm, who founded the Jugendschutzverein in 1889. However, in the following decade, Butler's torch was grasped by younger and more liberal women such as Anna Pappritz, Katharina Scheven and Minna Cauer. The fierce division of opinion between them and the more conservative German abolitionists is a topic addressed later in this paper. It is worthy of remark that despite the divisiveness of the issue in the German women's movement, that wonderful printed source, the *Handbuch der Frauenbewegung* edited by Helene Lange and Gertrud Bäumer between 1901 and 1906, contains more references to Josephine Butler than to any other Englishwoman or indeed to any other non-German woman.[16]

In France, the movement reflected some of the divisions in society, with a Comité Parisien pour le relèvement de la moralité publique founded largely by Protestant supporters in 1875, and an Association pour l'abolition de la prostitution réglementée established by such liberal figures as Yves Guyot, Victor Schoelcher and the feminist theorist Maria Deraismes (as well as Josephine's Protestant ally and amanuensis, Emilie de Morsier) in 1879. At the international congress of the Rights of Women in summer 1878, these strands merged, as speaker after speaker alluded to Butler's work, especially Deraismes, one of the conveners: '. . . il a fallu qu'une femme d'un grand coeur et d'un vaillant esprit, Madame Butler, prit l'initiative . . . Auparavant, cette colossale infamie se classait parmi les usages reçus.' [It took a valiant and courageous woman to take the initiative. . .. formerly everyone took this colossal infamy entirely for granted].[17] They did so again, more than a decade later, at the international congress of Oeuvres et Institutions Féminines (from which the liberals and radicals absented themselves) held in Paris in 1889.[18] In the late 1890s the young Ghénia de Sainte-Croix (1855–1939) 'découvrit le féminisme grâce à une correspondance avec Josephine Butler qui l'encouragea .. à lutter contre la prostitution' [discovered feminism thanks to her correspondence with Josephine Butler who encouraged her to join the fight against prostitution]. As Madame Avril de Sainte-Croix, she later headed the Conseil National des Femmes Françaises.[19]

And, of course, Butler's influence, direct and indirect, on British feminism after the repeal of the CD Acts is so great as to be almost immeasurable: from the women of her own generation who went from the Ladies' National Association to found the Women's Liberal Federation, to their daughters (figuratively and sometimes literally speaking) who entered the ranks of the socialist and trade union movements. Christabel Pankhurst famously demanded 'Votes for Women and Chastity for Men': the suffragettes' focus on men as the source of venereal infection of women and children did not explicitly acknowledge Butler and the Federation, but this massive reversal of the view of the 'impure' woman as the guilty party in the transmission of disease, which had prevailed at the beginning of Butler's 'crusade,' could not have materialised without them.[20]

Now we turn to the negatives. One might conclude from the fact that the majority of Butler's foreign contacts were Protestant, that a major 'fault line' in the Federation would lie in a division between Protestants and Catholics, and another in the traditional gulf between Britain and 'the Continent' (comprising not just the Channel, but the political legacies of the Napoleonic wars and occupations). But there were other centrifugal forces at work. A glimpse of the problem is provided by the letters of a young German woman named Charlotte Pape. In 1875 she was living in London, an early and ardent (and, indeed, lifelong) supporter of Butler's new Federation. Pape wrote that she had sent to a cousin in Brunswick a letter describing the Federation in such cautious terms 'that no girl of 18 need have blushed at a single word' and had received the following reply, which she translated for her English friends:

> After having read, with great repugnance, all through your letter, I asked my wife, hinting at its contents, to read it also. She declined positively even to look at it. I tell you this to show you what are the feelings of a German woman in regard to such communications, for you, my dear, have become quite English. . . . We were more

than a 100,000 <u>men,</u> and all <u>fathers</u> of <u>families</u> who have made earnest protests to our parliament, two years ago, in this same cause. But what have we to do with English conditions? Or how, after such an energetic protest, should we hope to succeed in alliance with the English movement? – You need not be offended with me, but I had rather not agitate against such a law together with ladies. . . .[21]

This early expression of social and national difference overrode a confessional as well as a familial kinship, since this was one Protestant writing to another. The issue of the public association of men and women remained controversial through much of the history of the Federation, and it was often (but not always) a signal of other areas of difference. It is true, of course, that the British movement for the repeal of the CD Acts had its male and female wings, but by 1875 Britain had a culture of mixed-sex campaigning which was unknown in some parts of Europe. If Pape's correspondence gave Butler early warning where Germany was concerned, her preparations for the Federation's first international congress at Geneva alerted her to the problems she might meet in Switzerland.

Butler learned in 1877 that some of her Swiss male colleagues wished women to be excluded from certain sessions. Worse, some of her Swiss female colleagues not only wished to concede the point, but were asking that English M.P.s in their national delegation lend their support to this exclusion. Butler wrote to Marie Humbert that any voluntary absence from controversial meetings would of course be respected, but that a ruling on exclusion was out of the question. 'Our gentlemen here (in Britain) would look upon such a public act as an abandonment of principle. It is precisely this peremptory exclusion of women by statesmen and others from all participation in council and in debate on such vital questions which has led to the present terrible wrong to Society . . .'.[22]

Nevertheless, local sensibilities had to be considered, and Butler was often forced to compromise. There were always several sexually segregated public meetings on the official programme of each international congress. While planning the congress to be held in Brussels in 1897, Butler commented that Belgium was 'more advanced' than Switzerland, as its conferences were always mixed.[23] This lack of equality in organisational terms meant that women within the movement were operating on different assumptions and in different conditions; and no single factor can be adduced to explain this social disparity. Why should Protestant Germany be different from Protestant England? Was it correct to consider French-speaking Protestant Belgians 'more advanced' than (largely) French-speaking Protestant Swiss?

It is possible that we should be looking at linguistic rather than confessional frontiers on the map of European women's emancipation. Bilingual Switzerland, which was the seat of the Federation's secretariat, presents an interesting case study. The first international congress of the movement was held in Geneva in 1877, and more congresses, and conferences (which were smaller international gatherings), were held in Switzerland than in any other single country.[24] Given that it was the international language of the day, it is not in itself remarkable that the Federation's executive and administrative business and publications were conducted in French. However, it is striking to note the predominance of French-speaking Swiss in the first decade of the Federation's existence. The immediate result of the 1877 congress was, as we have seen, the formation in Switzerland of two important women's organisations, the Amies de la Jeune Fille and the Association du Sou, whose membership frequently overlapped.

That the German-speaking Swiss women came more slowly into the movement may have owed something to the lack of tact of their francophone sisters. Reflecting on the conference proceedings at Basel in 1884, Marie Humbert, the founder of the Amies de la

Jeune Fille, admitted 'que nous n'avions pas assez compris qu'en annonçant des réunions publiques dans une ville allemande, il ne convenait guère de parler surtout une langue étrangère' [that we did not sufficiently understand that in announcing public meetings in a German city, it was hardly appropriate to speak in a foreign language] and regretted 'le désappointement que nous avons causé à nos soeurs de Bâle' [the disappointment we caused for our sisters in Basel].[25] But a few years later, Butler was hopeful that this linguistic cleavage could be turned to advantage. Several German-speaking Swiss women had attended the international conferences as interested observers, and had then gone on to join the 'daughter organisations' of the Federation.[26] Butler wrote that she was 'deeply interested in the opening of a door to Germany through Zurich, for Germany is certainly a great stronghold of masculine prejudice . . .'.[27] This optimism was short-lived, and she and her francophone colleagues were by the 1890s regretting that 'these good friends at Bern & Zurich . . . speak of themselves as "Nous autres Allemands".' (She might, perhaps, have thought of writing 'wir andere deutscher').[28] Although for several years the Association du Sou did embrace women from all the Swiss cantons, centrifugal tendencies were always evident. Nearly all the German-speaking women formally severed their links with the Association du Sou in 1901, stating that they no longer wished to contribute financially to the work of the Federation, and would concentrate on independent, local initiatives in prevention and rescue work.[29]

The dissension between German-speaking and other members of the Federation came to be something of a leitmotif of the Federation's history. Its expression took many forms, one of the most remarkable being a booklet published in Hamburg in 1907 purportedly as a memorial to Butler which, unusually within this genre, exploited the occasion to air many long-standing grievances.

For the author, Marie Fischer-Lette,[30] these included the political and the more personal. She resented the Federation's refusal to recognise Alsace-Lorraine as German. She claimed that Butler failed to make more than one visit to Germany, referring only to her journeys to Frankfurt am Main, Cologne and Elberfeld in 1876, incorrectly stating that Butler had been absent from the Federation's international meeting in Colmar in 1895, and unreasonably reproached her for having, in her extremely frail old age, missed the Dresden meeting of 1904. She also complained that Butler did not give sufficient credit to the German Protestant community for its pioneering and energetic philanthropic initiatives on behalf of women and the poor; and accused her of being prejudiced against Germany, and as considering it to be still under a dictatorial Napoleonic regime.[31]

Given what had happened to Butler's friend Gertrud Guillaume-Schack, and given what she knew of Prussian police regulation of voluntary associations, this is a fair description of her views, though perhaps not to be counted as prejudice. There was the further objection that the statutes of the German organisation required members to be Christian, and excluded socialists outright.[32] By the mid-1880s, Butler was fully aware that Adolf Stöcker was intensely anti-semitic;[33] and the Pastor Ludwig Weber who took a leading role in the Sittlichkeitsbewegung after 1885 became, in the 1890s, an outspoken supporter of Stöcker.[34]

Later, she was much exercised by an article published by another German pastor, one Herr Waubka, and wrote to Anna Pappritz:

He assumes "that we ought not to work with any but orthodox Christians" and he "could have no sympathy with the Hindus who he saw sitting on our platform in Exeter Hall" . . . few things have been to me more pathetic than to see those dark faces in our meetings and to hear their pleadings for the poor Hindu widows and girls who have been badly treated by our English government.[35]

By the 1890s Butler was increasingly exasperated by what she saw as the German-speaking membership's unwillingness to share her commitment to the liberal basis of abolitionist principles. As mentioned above, she already thought 'masculine prejudice' in Germany was a cultural obstacle to co-operation, but, as her very frank letters to Dutch and Swiss colleagues show, she began to believe (or to write as if she believed) that German-speakers were incapable of understanding liberal abolitionism. The people of Bern were accused of an extraordinary 'timidité qui leur empêche de vouloir même écouter des opinions qui ne sont pas tout à fait les siens!' [timidity that prevents them from wanting even to hear opinions which are not the same as their own][36]; a German delegation was 'conceited';[37] a German manifesto was 'rather childish'.[38]

The battle for the soul of the abolitionist campaign embraced some of the most fundamental tenets – and dilemmas – of the politics of liberalism and modernity at the turn of the nineteenth century. Opposition to the phenomenon of commercialised sex might attract individuals and groups with very different motivations and philosophical positions, even within one country, let alone within an organisation whose ambitions were global. During this period of rapid industrialisation and urbanisation in Europe, there were widespread concerns over the apparent increase in the number of prostitute women.[39] The spectacle of extensive migration from the countryside led to fears of a breakdown of the traditional social order, of a decline in church attendance and religious belief, and of the disintegration of the family. Many of Butler's European allies saw both prostitution and the industrial employment of working women in this context. They were principally concerned with the need to re-christianise society and to challenge the secular state.[40] Butler's first supporters in the Netherlands and France, for example, tended to come from those circles in the Réveil movement who had welcomed Elizabeth Fry.[41]

Butler, the daughter and wife of ardent Christians, was in sympathy with these aspirations, but she was also aware of the social and economic conditions which restricted freedom of moral and religious choice, and she was particularly concerned about the lack of decent employment opportunities for women. This issue appears to have sparked off its first extensive debate at the international congress held at the Hague in 1883. The Rev. Hendrik Pierson, superintendent of a rescue home for former prostitutes in the Netherlands, and later President of the Federation, insisted that human nature rather than material misery was the cause of immoral behaviour. The Dutch socialist F. Domela Niewenhuis and the Belgian liberal Alexis Splingard strenuously disagreed, and Butler took their side.[42] She was not a socialist, but she resisted any attempt to divorce abolitionism from the 'social question'. Indeed, the Federation's constitution itself explicitly committed it to the 'scientific' study of prostitution, a permanent enquiry into its moral, economic and other causes and consequences.

Butler's own position on the state regulation of prostitution was rigorously and consistently liberal. Although she considered sex outside wedlock as sinful, she did not think that the state had a right to enforce moral conformity in private matters. Her campaign was one to protect individuals from the encroachment of state power as well as patriarchal oppression. Her Christianity convinced her that each individual had an immortal soul of equal worth with every other. Her feminism led her to the perception that while both sexes participated in the commercial transaction, only one was legally penalised. As a Christian feminist, she insisted that solidarity between women was necessary to override distinctions between 'pure' and 'impure' women which were not Christian, but designed to perpetuate the patriarchal imbalance of power in society.

Butler's domestic and political biography, and the network of alliances she built up, could not have been replicated by any European figure. Her staunchly liberal father was active in the movements to abolish slavery in the British West Indies (hence Josephine's familiarity with the term 'abolitionism') and in the campaign to reform the electoral franchise. Mazzini was a personal correspondent of the family, and the Swiss-Italian family into which Butler's sister married had close links to Garibaldi. Her colleagues in the abolitionist movement included other English men and women with links to the Risorgimento, such as Emily Ashurst Venturi and Jessie White Mario. However, her liberal family was also a deeply religious one; and this was a very great point of difference from some of the liberal and republican circles in France and Italy where Butler looked for support. Butler's own religious faith, meanwhile, could not easily be categorised. Protestant it most certainly was, and fiercely individualistic; it was also mystical and often as distrustful of ecclesiastical establishments as of secular authorities. Her liberal and radical allies included Unitarians, Swedenborgians, socialists and freethinkers, as well as Quakers, Evangelicals and the Salvation Army; and this, of course, was a very great point of difference from some Evangelical Protestant circles in Germany, Switzerland and the Netherlands.

The different elements of the abolitionist campaign – liberalism, feminism and salvationist Protestantism – which Butler united in her own person could not be present to the same extent among all the adherents of the cause. Abolitionists embraced radically different critiques of the state, with much of the religious membership objecting to its secularity while their secularist and liberal colleagues emphasised the dangers of dictatorial and oppressive regimes. The two critiques rarely coincided, and Butler was saddened to find that so many of her co-religionists did not object in principle to state intervention in the personal life of the individual.[43] But although she experienced differences of opinion with Dutch and Belgian adherents, she came to see her German colleagues as the main source of disagreement within the Federation. They above all, she felt, did not share her instinctive distrust of the police and the magistracy, and they seemed positively to welcome state intervention in matters which she considered essentially personal and private.

Even without taking into account different interpretations of political liberalism and differential levels of sexual equality, the goals of the Federation posed enormous philosophical and practical problems for its members. Its constitution defined the state regulation of prostitution as a hygienic error, a social injustice, a moral monstrosity and a juridical crime. But to arrive at an agreed set of definitions of the terms justice, morality and legality was no simple matter, particularly given the Federation's ambitions to include members of any creed or none. Did all moral norms ultimately derive from God? Or was it perfectly possible to have a moral code without a religion? How should one distinguish between morality and legality? Could one demand that state laws conform to a moral code derived from a particular religion? Was it, indeed, possible to challenge the power of the state at all while simultaneously requiring the state to repeal or pass legislation?

Then there was the question of the categorisation of the individual: what was the extent of her or his moral responsibility for her or his actions? How far was it reasonable to speak of individuals being coerced by circumstances beyond their control, such as poverty, lack of education, childhood abuse? Was it possible that the love and forgiveness extended to an individual might be harmful to the collective welfare of society? All these questions were debated at congresses of the Federation and within its sections, and the different answers they elicited often had radically different implications in the realm of practice.

Between 1896 and 1899 matters were coming to a head, and the international meetings of the Federation became increasingly stormy. The German Sittlichkeit movement stated its disagreement with Butler's principles in a number of publications, whose prime author and mover was Hanna Bieber-Böhm, founder of the Jugendschutzverein. These position papers stated that the individual did not have the right freely to dispose of her or his own body, in the first place because it was God's creation, in the second because illicit sexual intercourse damaged society, both morally and physically. The state should be able to penalise adultery, fornication, the transmission of venereal disease, and homosexuality. Forcible medical inspection and treatment was envisaged. In a nod to the doctrine of a single standard of morality for both sexes, German campaigners advocated strengthening police powers against offenders of either sex.[44]

Against this, liberal abolitionists argued that prostitution between consenting adult partners, however immoral it might seem to some, should not come under the censure of the criminal law; they believed that any legislation along these lines could only produce a regime of permanent domestic espionage. They also warned that any punitive measures, in the given state of relations between the sexes, would certainly bear down more heavily on female than on male offenders, and that a single standard of morality would not be achieved through a punitive policy.[45] The liberals in their turn were accused of advocating free love, which most (but not the representative of some Parisian socialists and liberals or – more surprisingly – the Executive Committee member, Auguste de Morsier) vehemently denied.[46] The attempt to find common ground was not wholly unsuccessful: the question of the protection of minors overrode the liberal-interventionist divide, as did the issues of procuring and trafficking. A revision of the Federation's constitution in 1901 which emphasised the autonomy of national sections did something to calm the atmosphere (though in the same year, as we have seen, an important split took place in Switzerland within the women's organisation, l'Association du Sou).[47]

Of course, these questions did not only divide national section from national section, but women from women. It must be reiterated that there were serious differences within as well as between national sections. Not all German-speaking members of the Federation were united behind this strenuous drive for an authoritarian form of abolitionism. In 1899 one of the strongest-worded statements against Hannah Bieber- Böhm's position came from the Swiss feminist (and devout Christian) Helene von Mülinen.[48] In Germany in the same year there were two important secessions from women's organisations. Butler's sympathisers, among whom Anna von Pappritz played a leading role, set up sections of the Federation which were independent of the general German union of Sittlichkeit societies; and the Verband Fortschrittlicher Frauenvereine, under the leadership of Minna Cauer, was founded in a split from the Bund Deutscher Frauenvereine.[49] The issue of support for the Federation appears to have been of central importance in the latter secession.[50]

And, as is well known, not all British women supported Butler's liberal line. The National Vigilance Association, which was set up in 1886 after the repeal of the Contagious Diseases Acts, soon dismayed her by the anti-female and anti-working class bias of its approach to sexual morality. Even worse, from the late 1880s women 'purity campaigners' such as Lady Henry Somerset were to be found supporting the installation of a form of 'police des moeurs' to protect the health of the British soldier in India.[51]

Thus, abolitionism, although a woman's cause, could not mean the same thing to every woman. Some of the 'daughter organisations' of the Federation concentrated on prevention work, and on practical support for women and girls who wished to give up prostitution; they did not work in tandem with men, and might perhaps be seen as remote from the concerns of 'equal rights feminism', and in retreat from the difficult and contentious task of challenging state and patriarchal authority. But for many women, even in the late 1880s, these activities represented a first experience of organisational work outside a narrow sphere of family, church and parish. Activists had to overcome their inhibitions in order to address large assemblies, and they had to be innovators, holding women-only events on a previously unheard-of scale.[52] And it is very important to remember that they were all bringing contentious and taboo subjects into the public domain. Hanna Bieber-Böhm and her colleagues, for example, may have been conservative in Federation terms, but they were still denounced in Germany as 'dämonische Weiber' [demonic women] and accused of 'Schamlosigkeit' [shamelessness].[53]

It is difficult to generalise on the implications for women of involvement in this movement, and it would be interesting to know whether – and in which member states – the Federation impelled women into feminism or acted as a brake on the development of a more radical movement. It certainly seems that in many countries abolitionism offered a route into a radical critique of patriarchy to a large constituency of women who might be thought the least likely to respond to it.

These women did not come from families with liberal or humanist intellectual traditions; they did not come from the numerically small but, in terms of activism, elite religious sects such as the Quakers and Unitarians. They were, mostly, conventionally devout Protestant women. It is true that sometimes, as in France and Belgium, they lived as members of minority communities, as did their Jewish colleagues in the Federation. Often, however, they were the wives and daughters of clergy who represented their national social and religious establishments.

Like many of their British counterparts, these Protestant women had a stronger sense of their obligations than of their rights. They were susceptible to calls to philanthropic work on behalf of those less fortunate and less Christian than themselves – the phenomenon which van Drenth and de Haan call 'the rise of caring power'.[54] The Federation took many of them into this domain, but it also took many of them beyond it, to a critique of society and of the imbalance of power between the sexes. It took them further than any previous feminist movement towards solidarity with women who were, in every meaning of the word, dispossessed; and it took them to the outer limits of frankness (for their times) in confronting the hypocrisies of their own class, and the intimate and bodily implications of patriarchy. It launched a younger generation of women into political feminism and, in many cases, the labour movement.

Finally, we must remember that although the discourse of the 'Dames de la Fédération' was so unlike our own, in one sense at least they were the true pioneers and innovators of the modern women's movement: because for them, the personal became, truly, deeply and shockingly, the political.

4

"TO EDUCATE WOMEN INTO REBELLION"

Elizabeth Cady Stanton and the creation of a transatlantic network of radical suffragists

Sandra Stanley Holton

In the 1880s and early 1890s, Elizabeth Cady Stanton made three extended visits from the United States to Britain and Europe. During this decade, she spent in all some five years living in England, where her daughter, Harriot Stanton Blatch, had married. In this time, she renewed and extended friendships first made during a wedding tour in 1840, and she and her daughter became central figures in a transatlantic friendship network. This was a network that in Britain drew substantially on a kinship circle of women connected with the Brights, a radical reforming Quaker family among whom was the statesman, John Bright. Women of the Bright circle had helped in the formation of every major society and campaign on which the organized women's movement in Britain had been built in the late 1860s.[1]

The Bright circle also provided an important locus of radical suffragism in Britain. At the time of Elizabeth Cady Stanton's return to Britain in the 1880s, however, a moderate current of suffrage opinion dominated the movement there, one whose viewpoint until recently has also informed prevailing understandings of British suffragism during the nineteenth century.[2] Because the more moderate leadership also provided the early chronicles of the movement, these contain little evidence of either this friendship network or the alternative radical perspective on suffrage that it represented.[3] The memoirs of American suffragists, together with the correspondence between members of this network, more of which has recently come to light, provide, in contrast, suggestive evidence on both its extent and nature.[4]

An examination of such evidence together with a reconstruction of this network serves to advance our understanding of radical suffragism in a number of ways. To begin with, it brings into focus clearly for the first time an alternative suffrage leadership among Radical-Liberal circles in Britain in the latter part of the nineteenth century and so broadens our picture of the varieties within suffragism, as well as some of the intellectual and social roots, hitherto neglected, of those varieties.[5] In particular, it points to a continuing transatlantic legacy from the abolition movement in terms of a Garrisonian conception of the reformer's role. It suggests, also, Elizabeth Cady Stanton's part in keeping alive that legacy among British suffragists. In emphasizing the need "to educate women into rebellion," she sought to foster an uncompromising and confrontational approach to the emancipation of her sex. She consistently advised her British colleagues against pragmatic

36

retreats determined by what was thought achievable in terms of franchise reform. Instead, she advised a broadened formulation of the demand for the vote, one more consistent with the conception of the citizenship of women she shared with radical suffragists in Britain.

Central to this conception was the ending of coverture, the doctrine that subsumed the legal personality of wives under that of their husbands. In recent years, Carole Pateman has argued that marriage in modern Western societies forms part of a sexual contract fundamental to the subordination of women in civil society. Although the analysis of marriage offered by the nineteenth-century women's movement lacked the coherence and power of modern accounts, radical suffragism did share many of its concerns. The robbing of women upon marriage of both their property and their rights over their own bodies made impossible the autonomous self-development of the individual, which for Radical-Liberal suffragists was an essential part of true citizenship. The position of the married woman provided for them, therefore, the fullest measure of women's subordination, and the end of coverture was given an importance equal to enfranchisement in their efforts to secure the citizenship of women. Hence the inclusion of married women in the demand for the vote became almost an article of faith for Radical-Liberal suffragists in Britain.[6] It was this that set them at odds with the national suffrage leadership. There, a more moderate stance was adopted, one that sought to concentrate only on breaking down the sexual exclusiveness of the franchise laws as the first essential step to citizenship and that saw the ending of coverture as subordinate to that goal. From such a perspective, single women would form the vanguard for their sex, while married women might be excluded from the demand if their exclusion increased the likelihood of gaining the franchise for some women. From this perspective, too, the Radical-Liberal approach endangered the cause, for it challenged the prevailing sexual order in ways that more moderate suffragists thought impolitic.[7]

Elizabeth Cady Stanton's first and most forceful intervention in the British movement concerned this question, and her intervention was subsequently linked to the formation of a new suffrage society in 1889, the Women's Franchise League. A focus on her friendship network, then, draws attention also to a previously neglected body. The league gave expression to the radical suffragism that had been promoted by Elizabeth Cady Stanton and Harriot Stanton Blatch over the preceding few years and provided a clear continuation of the Garrisonian legacy within the British movement. More specifically, the league was determined to maintain the inclusion of married women in the suffrage demand, and the story of the league's formation clarifies the nature of the tensions and splits that occurred in the British movement in 1888–1889. These splits were understandably glossed over in early histories of the movement, which were to some extent also campaign literature, in which the disclosure of old controversies would not have been helpful.[8] But the effect of such neglect has been to marginalize, when it does not conceal, a continuous radical current that left a significant legacy for the twentieth-century movement in both Britain and the United States.

From the 1890s on, the Women's Franchise League promoted a fresh conception of women's claims to citizenship based on their labor, both paid and unpaid. Harriot Stanton Blatch helped develop this approach and subsequently took it back to the United States. The methods and orientation of the Women's Franchise League also prefigured new directions taken by the British movement in the early twentieth century, notably in the links it attempted to build with the labor and socialist movements.[9] Further, the league provided Emmeline Pankhurst with her apprenticeship as a suffrage leader. Aspects of the league's history suggest, then, certain continuities between nineteenth-century radical suffragism and the militancy of the twentieth-century movement, at least in its initial forms, continuities that the current conceptualizations of suffrage history do not acknowledge.

Ellen Carol DuBois has recently described the women's movement as "a self-consciously transnational popular political movement." She has also questioned existing characterizations of nineteenth-century suffrage movements as generally "conservative," pointing to the valuable links that were forged in Britain, the United States, and elsewhere between the middle-class women's movement and socialist and labor movements.[10] An examination of the activities of the Women's Franchise League, and the transatlantic current of radical suffragism on which it drew, offers further confirmation for such arguments. But, more than this, it helps clarify the social-political basis for such links in a long-established and vigorous radical current within the middle-class women's movement. It suggests also an ideological basis for such a relation in a fresh formulation of the claim for citizenship that emphasized a communion of middle-class and working-class women in their shared labor, both productive and reproductive. Finally, it demonstrates the complex exchange of ideas and approaches that occurred among radical suffragists in Britain and the United States.

Elizabeth Cady Stanton's connections to the groups out of which was to grow the radical wing of the British women's movement went back to 1840. The World Anti-Slavery Convention met that year in London, and one of the American delegates was Henry Stanton, whom she had just married. After the convention, the couple took a tour of Britain and came to know some of the most prominent reform families of the day, especially among the Quakers, who were often their hosts.[11] It was in this way that Elizabeth Cady Stanton formed some of the friendships she revived when she returned to Britain for a series of visits in the 1880s. Contact between reformers in Britain and the United States had increased in the intervening years, encouraging a further exchange of radical ideas between the two continents. It was in these circles that William Lloyd Garrison and Frederick Douglass gradually began to find adherents among British abolitionists, for example. Very often, these friendships carried over into subsequent generations, with the children of Garrison visiting and playing host to the children and grandchildren of friends made by their parents while in Britain many decades earlier.[12]

The Priestmans of Newcastle were one of the Quaker families with whom the Stantons stayed while touring Britain, a family active at this time in both the temperance and abolition movements. Their eldest daughter, Elizabeth Priestman, had recently married a young Quaker radical from Rochdale, John Bright, whose part in the campaign against church rates had already brought him to the fore in local politics. Even though Elizabeth Priestman died from consumption shortly thereafter, the links between the two families survived, most notably through the care of her baby daughter, Helen Priestman Bright. The aunts in the Priestman and Bright families shared the young child's care, as her father joined the Anti–Corn Law campaign then under way, a campaign on which he based his subsequent political career as "tribune of the people." The Anti–Corn Law campaign also provided many middle-class women, including John Bright's sisters and sisters-in-law, with their first experience of politics.[13]

John Bright himself was never a reliable supporter of women's rights, and on occasion he openly declared his opposition to women's suffrage. But his first marriage helped form a Quaker sisterhood that played an important role in the women's movement in Britain.[14] This circle of female kin included his sisters Priscilla Bright McLaren and Margaret Bright Lucas, sister-in-law Ursula Mellor Bright (married to Jacob, younger brother of John), and Margaret Tanner, Mary Priestman, and Anna Maria Priestman (all sisters of Elizabeth Priestman), together with their daughters, stepdaughters, daughters-in-law, and nieces, among whom were Helen Priestman Bright Clark, Agnes McLaren, Eva McLaren, Laura McLaren, Lilias Ashworth Hallett, Anne Cross, and Kate Thomasson.[15] As in the United States, Quaker women such as these played a noteworthy role in Britain in both the Garrisonian wing of the abolition movement and the formation of an organized women's movement during the 1860s. The Bright circle became an influential presence in a radical current within the women's movement in Britain, one that adopted a Garrisonian approach to campaigning.

DuBois has suggested that the Garrisonian conception of the task of reformers as "the agitation of public sentiment" was one of the abolition movement's main contributions to the cause of women's suffrage. She has also argued that Elizabeth Cady Stanton was the suffrage leader who transferred to the women's movement the consistently uncompromising stance of the Garrisonians with regard to ultimate ends. The question of the means by which such ends were to be achieved, in contrast, was work that should be left to politicians. For the reformer, there could be no retreat from principle or reduction of ultimate goals.[16] And this was certainly also the essence of the advice Stanton gave to British colleagues on a number of occasions.

Elizabeth Cady Stanton's diary for her first return to Britain in 1882–1883 indicates a progression from the home of one member of the Bright kinship circle to another. The interests of these women, as of Radical-Liberal suffragists more generally, encompassed women's education, married women's property rights, entry to the medical profession, repeal of the Contagious Diseases Acts, the women's temperance movement, and, of course, women's suffrage. One or more of them had been involved in the founding of each of the first major suffrage societies in Manchester, London, Edinburgh, and Bristol. They were linked by kinship with numerous male politicians and reformers. At one point, for example, Priscilla Bright McLaren was declared "the best represented woman in the Kingdom," having six of her closest male kin in the House of Commons.[17]

Elizabeth Cady Stanton's first return was also the occasion of the marriage of Harriot Stanton to an Englishman, and one of her aims, evidently, was to find mentors for her daughter within the women's movement in Britain. She wrote to Anna Maria Priestman, telling of her daughter and declaring, "I hope much of her in the future as wifehood and motherhood rightly considered are a means of development." Toward the end of this stay in England, Stanton wrote again to the Priestman sisters, this time with a more direct request: "I want you all to know the daughter I leave behind me, and help her to earnest work, in all the great reforms for the development of humanity."[18]

Life in Basingstoke, the provincial market town outside London where Harriot Stanton Blatch now had her home, was clearly a strain for both mother and daughter. Elizabeth Cady Stanton told Anna Maria Priestman that they found it "a very benighted conservative town . . . in fact we find ourselves quite alone in all our radical ideas, on many points." Only among the most advanced circles in Britain did they find a recognition of their own sense of national identity as American radical republicans. And these British circles, in turn, had long looked to their relationship with American revolutionaries and reformers to confirm their own identity as radicals. But many of the institutions and conventions that for British reformers were simply an accustomed part of the political context in which they had to work proved trying for their American friends. On her first visit to the House of Commons, for example, Elizabeth Cady Stanton recorded that women were restricted to a "high perch" in the topmost gallery behind a wire grille. In consequence, she remembered, she and her feather-bedecked companions had appeared to her son, in the freedom of other observation galleries, like exotic caged birds.[19]

At times, different national manners and conventions put the British and American suffragists somewhat at odds. Elizabeth Cady Stanton's forceful anti-clericalism and radical theology could occasion unease among her hosts, since British radicals, even among these Quaker women, were used to greater respect for the authority of the church. When Stanton began work on her last great project, the *Woman's Bible*, several of her friends among the Bright circle responded cautiously at first, although a number of its members subsequently became part of the international committee through which she sought to establish the legitimacy of her task.[20]

The monarchy presented perhaps the most alien aspect of British society. Elizabeth Cady Stanton noted wryly, for example: "The Queen is referred to tenderly in most of the speeches although she has never done anything to merit the approbation of the advocates of suffrage for women." She and Harriot Stanton Blatch refused to contribute to a fund for the queen's Golden Jubilee in 1887, expressing their disapproval of a rich woman who would take the pennies of the poor to build yet more monstrous memorials to her dead husband. Such sentiments would undoubtedly have been shared by many of her friends among the Radical-Liberal suffragists, at least some of whom had republican sympathies. Even the more cautious members of this circle, such as Priscilla Bright McLaren, apologized for the backwardness of her British colleagues and the conservatism of British public opinion and national institutions. "I do not think it is possible for you, with your wide unprejudiced views, thoroughly to comprehend our position here . . . we should be running our heads against a wall were we to go in all at once for all the rights you advocate." It was for this reason, she argued, that British suffragists had to proceed more slowly. "You must forgive me, dear, noble, clear-minded friend, if I cannot knock down at once all our Old World fences. We must creep under them, or climb over them as best we can."[21]

Other British suffragists, however, exhibited no such ambivalence toward their own national heritage. Indeed, figures such as Millicent Garrett Fawcett, with whom Elizabeth Cady Stanton also enjoyed friendly relations, occasionally displayed a sense of superiority deriving at least in part from her national identity as a Briton. She consistently exhibited an unbending, not to say parochial, adherence to British constitutional forms as models of moderation and stability from which she evidently believed the rest of the world could learn much. She took the opportunity for smug national self-congratulation, for example, when asked to contribute to Theodore Stanton's 1884 collection of essays on the women's movement in Europe, emphasizing "practical good sense and moderation" as the distinguishing feature of the British women's movement. She also expressed on occasion her resistance to links between the suffrage movements in Britain and America, refusing to accept the office of president of the International Congress of Women in 1888 with the remark, it was "quite impossible that English women and American women should have anything in common, the conditions of their lives and the purposes of their respective societies being so different."[22]

In some British suffrage circles, then, her American identity might lend Elizabeth Cady Stanton additional credibility, while in others it was, no doubt, something to be excused. Social styles evidently were very different, too. Elizabeth Cady Stanton felt it necessary, after a visit to the Priestman sisters, to apologize in case she and her daughter "overflowed too freely when with you." She explained, "our visit to you was like water to the weary traveller crossing a vast desert," after life in Basingstoke, where "there is not one with whom we can commune with freedom and pleasure, none with whom we can have the least interchange of thought." Elizabeth Cady Stanton commented gratefully, "It is rare one finds three women on the shady side of sixty so bright, so liberal, so ready for new thought on all subjects."[23]

Her initial return to Britain led her to send "many urgent letters" to her close friend and colleague in America, Susan B. Anthony, calling on her, too, to lend her force to the British movement. Stanton's return to Britain in 1882 had occurred at a critical time for the suffrage demand there. A campaign was under way for a further Reform Bill, primarily aimed at extending the franchise to male agricultural workers but also providing an occasion to press once again women's claim to the vote. Susan B. Anthony heard the call and joined Stanton in London in February 1883, where both addressed a major meeting of the National Society for Women's Suffrage. Priscilla Bright McLaren traveled from Scotland especially for the event, and afterward Susan B. Anthony recorded: "Everybody is delighted . . . Even the timid ones expressed satisfaction. Mrs Stanton gave them the rankest of radical sentiments, but all so cushioned they didn't hurt."[24]

The central suffrage leadership remained cautious nonetheless, and the disunity this provoked among her British colleagues provided another trial for Elizabeth Cady Stanton during this visit. At the heart of the discord was the question of whether or not to include married women in the demand for the vote. The issue was of far greater consequence in Britain than America, for two reasons. First, in America, adult male suffrage had been achieved, at least in principle, after abolition. But the franchise in Britain remained property-based, a factor that rendered the British context of suffrage campaigning very different. Second, the doctrine of coverture remained more firmly entrenched in Britain than in the United States, where its erosion in state legislatures had begun in the 1830s.[25] The property basis of the franchise in Britain thus placed single women and married women each in a distinct relation to the existing franchise laws.

Jane Rendall has recently analyzed the several differing liberal conceptions of citizenship on which British suffragists drew in arguing their case. In many ways, this range of views was a strength, and Rendall's analysis indicates the inadequacy of any characterization of suffragism simply in terms of classic liberal individualism. But these different conceptions formed a bitter and longstanding source of conflict among suffragists in Britain. Those whose conception of citizenship was grounded on older radical notions of "independence" based on property holding and tax paying preferred a formulation that would secure the franchise for those unmarried and widowed women who might meet the criteria of independence. The doctrine of coverture, of course, deprived married women of such independence. Upon marriage, a woman lost not only her property in goods, but, equally significant, her property in her own body. Radical-Liberal suffragists appealed to a conception of citizenship derived largely from the work of John Stuart Mill, which emphasized the right to moral autonomy and self-development of every individual as the proper basis for a political system.[26] As a consequence, the married woman represented for Radical-Liberal suffragists the fullest expression of the subordination of their sex. There could be no achievement of real citizenship for women that failed to redress the wrongs of the married woman. The one depended on the other.

The question of whether or not to exclude married women from the demand had divided British suffragists since the formation of the earliest suffrage committees in the mid-1860s, and it continued to divide them until the last years of the nineteenth century.[27] The dominance of the Radical-Liberals in the earliest provincial suffrage societies, and the influence of John Stuart Mill himself, had ensured the defeat of initial attempts to exclude married women from the demand in the first years of campaigning in the late 1860s. A compromise equal-rights formulation of the demand was accepted that neither specifically included nor excluded married women, although the common-law doctrine of coverture meant that married women were effectively, albeit tacitly, excluded by such wording. Couching their demand simply in terms of formal sexual equality, suffragists aimed to appease conservative opinion without offering any sanction to the doctrine of coverture. Given the nature of this compromise, Radical-Liberal suffragists also placed considerable importance on a parallel campaign for married women's property rights as a principal aspect of coverture.

This issue became even more crucial from the mid-1870s on when Lydia Becker, reluctantly and under pressure from Conservative parliamentary suffragists, whose party was in power, agreed to the explicit exclusion of married women from the demand.[28] Anna Maria Priestman endorsed a view of the matter general among Radical-Liberal suffragists: "Why people should be so unmerciful to such an oppressed group I cannot think."[29] The policy of the umbrella organization that united the various suffrage bodies, the National Society for Women's Suffrage (NSWS), went back and forth on this issue over the next few years, as the Radical-Liberal position was alternatively reasserted and attacked. For this reason, changing the legal status of married women took on an added urgency for Radical-Liberal suffragists. From 1875 on, Ursula Bright, together with Elizabeth Wolstenholme Elmy, stepped up the campaign for reform of the Married Women's Property Act.[30] They did so in clear opposition to the views of Lydia Becker, who now urged not only the exclusion of married women from the franchise demand but also a suspension of such efforts to end coverture.[31] Support for such defiance was forthcoming from many among the Bright circle, as well as among provincial Radical-Liberal suffragist opinion more generally, especially in the regions of Manchester, Liverpool, and Bristol, and among those also committed to the repeal of the Contagious Diseases Acts.

Some in these circles also had close links with the free-thought and republican movements of this period and the Owenite legacy on which these movements to some extent drew. Their radicalism occasionally extended to a preference for free unions over marriage—Elizabeth Wolstenholme and Ben Elmy, for example, were only persuaded to a legal marriage in the interests of the women's movement in 1874, when she was some six months pregnant. There is also evidence that Emmeline Goulden offered Richard Pankhurst a similar free union before they married a few years later. Others, such as Alice Cliff Scatcherd, showed their contempt for prevailing conceptions of marriage by refusing to wear a ring or to attend any wedding service in the established church because of the vow of obedience it extracted from women. Priscilla Bright McLaren did bring herself to attend the Anglican wedding of a niece, although she left it loudly protesting, "Well, Annie went in a free woman and has come out a slave!" and afterward poured out her feelings of indignation to the clergyman.[32]

The efforts of Elizabeth Wolstenholme Elmy and Ursula Bright met with success at last in the passage of the Married Women's Property Act of 1882, but ironically this advance only sowed the seeds for further discord. Even though the measure extended the capacity of married women to hold property, it had been so amended in the House of Commons that it left in place the doctrine of coverture. It remained uncertain, therefore, whether married women would or would not qualify to vote under an equal rights measure, for the legal standing of married women remained ambiguously different from that of single women. This situation provoked renewed controversy over the question in the summer of 1883, and it was at this point that Elizabeth Cady Stanton made her first direct intervention in the British movement. At a major London suffrage rally, shortly after the success of Stanton's joint appearance with Susan B. Anthony, one of the leading suffragist members of Parliament denied all intention of seeking to enfranchise women under coverture. Ursula Bright and her supporters had arranged for a call to include married women to come from among the platform party and asked Elizabeth Cady Stanton to join them in this act of defiance. But such opposition was overruled from the chair. The manner in which married women were dismissed from the claim gave rise to "strong protests," for such proceedings had "carried the matter too far even for the most timid." The supporters of Ursula Bright arranged a meeting of the dissidents and called on Stanton to confer with them. The meeting resulted in "a great ferment," for she advised them to continue to demand the vote for all women, married and single.[33]

Elizabeth Cady Stanton not only advised the dissidents but also sought to strengthen the resolve of those among her friends whom she believed were wavering on the issue. Her diary records:

> I have written a letter to Mrs McLaren and Mrs Lucas, which I ask them to read to the Brights and Thomassons, on the wisdom of broadening their platform. I impress on them the fact that to get the suffrage for spinsters is all very well, but their work is to elevate the position of women at all points, and that in calling to every form of injustice and laying bare every inequality they take the shortest way to educate women into rebellion and self-assertion, and men into considera- tion of women's rights and wrongs. That the married women of this movement in England consent to the assumption that they are through marriage, practically represented and protected, supported and sheltered from all the adverse winds of life, is the strongest evidence of their own need for emancipation.

She wrote to prevent her friends from taking the path of political pragmatism and abandon- ing principles she believed fundamental to women's emancipation. Priscilla Bright McLaren responded: "I abhor the idea of degrading marriage as much as my sister Ursula Bright by any positive prohibition of a right because of marriage." But she also firmly expressed the view that "the women of our country are not prepared for some of the things you advise us to put upon our flag . . . The real practical reformer must be willing to climb step by step."[34]

Ursula Bright, for her part, evidently took heart from Elizabeth Cady Stanton's advice, adopting an even more intransigent position on the issue. No longer was it sufficient, in her view, to resist the explicit exclusion of married women from the suffrage demand. From then on, she also argued for their *explicit inclusion*. This position appeared extreme even to many Radical-Liberal suffragists, who sought to uphold an equal rights formula- tion that simply ignored the differing civil status of single and married women. Ursula Bright was never, it seems, a very easy colleague to work with. The women of the Bright circle, who might express an amused tolerance for her idiosyncracies among themselves, felt that she was sometimes disruptively high-handed and provocative. Certainly, she appears to have been most effective when a big fish in a small pond, as was the case with the Married Women's Property Committee and subsequently with the Women's Franchise League. This is not to deny her achievements, especially in helping to secure significant advances in the position of married women. But it does suggest that her conception of the reformer's role was more akin to that of Elizabeth Cady Stanton than was the case, for example, with Priscilla Bright McLaren.[35]

Elizabeth Cady Stanton's association with Ursula Bright in this controversy appears also to have affected the reception of another proposal she and Susan B. Anthony first put before British suffragists in 1883. After the travels of each around Europe in the previous year or so, they believed the time was right for the formation of an international suffrage organization to facilitate the sharing of ideas and experience. Lydia Becker and those around her, however, remained skeptical. Helen Blackburn, Lydia Becker's close colleague as secretary of the National Society for Women's Suffrage, wrote to Anna Maria Priestman that while it was in itself "an excellent idea," caution was advisable, for it had been taken up by "some injudicious people." It is clear from other correspondence among British suffragists that Ursula Bright was considered to be among the injudicious; moreover, there were fears she planned to use this new initiative to take over the leadership of the British movement.[36]

The Bright circle, not surprisingly, proved the most receptive to the plan, and Priscilla Bright McLaren, Margaret Bright Lucas, and Ursula Bright took up the challenge during their farewell meetings with the American suffragists in November 1883. They agreed to establish an international organization based in the United States, with corresponding committees in other countries. Out of this came an international conference of suffragists in Washington in 1888, arranged to coincide with the fortieth anniversary of the Seneca Falls convention, which had marked the formal beginnings of a women's rights movement in America. It is noteworthy that the more moderate leadership of the suffrage movement in Britain consistently failed to accord such international initiatives the same significance as their Radical-Liberal counterparts in these years. Possibly, the international context was more important to the radicals precisely because of their marginal standing in their own country; it served as a valued endorsement of their distinct identity as the radical section of their particular national movement.[37]

By the time of Elizabeth Cady Stanton's next visit, from 1886 to early 1888, the tensions and conflicts among British suffragists had intensified even further. The failure to secure the inclusion of women in the 1884 Reform Act left the movement demoralized, and this demoralization was increased by the general political turmoil in Britain in these years. In 1886, for instance, the Liberal Party split over Prime Minister Gladstone's policy of home rule for Ireland.

Among the Bright circle, Ursula and Jacob Bright remained staunch Gladstonians committed to Irish home rule, as did the Clarks and the members of Parliament who were sons of Priscilla Bright McLaren, Charles and Walter. Priscilla Bright McLaren herself, though sympathetic to the grievances of Ireland, did not believe that home rule would provide any peaceful or long-lasting solution and so associated for a time more closely with women Liberal Unionist organizations, as did her niece, Lilias Ashworth Hallett.

These years were also ones of moral panic, a panic that in turn served to promote a "social purity" response to moral reform in the passage of repressive legislation and in oppressive policing practices. It was a panic prompted initially by the sensationalist exposé of child prostitution by W. T. Stead, a crusading journalist. This campaign had brought forth the National Vigilance Association, in which some of the moderate suffragist leadership figured prominently, while Radical suffragists resisted the repressive policies it advocated.[38] Such tensions were exacerbated by the involvement of the Radical Sir Charles Dilke and the Irish Nationalist leader Charles Parnell as corespondents in two notorious divorce cases in this period.

Elizabeth Cady Stanton's diary makes clear her sympathy for Irish protesters in their struggles with the authorities and also with the disgraced politicians Dilke and Parnell. Ursula Bright and her closest colleagues, including the Pankhursts and Harriot Stanton

Blatch, were also supportive of Dilke and Parnell during divorce hearings. Similarly, Elizabeth Cady Stanton expressed a certain skepticism about the motives of social purity advocates such as Stead.

But if this was a period of turmoil, it was also a time when radicals began to feel more optimistic about achieving substantial social change in Britain. Stanton recorded signs during this visit that women were increasingly ready to fight "even here in slow old England." She was impressed with the younger generation coming into the movement and warned, "[O]f one thing men may be assured . . . the next generation will not argue the question of women's rights with the infinite patience we have displayed this half century." Priscilla Bright McLaren shared these hopes: "We see everywhere women rising to a much higher moral and intellectual stature than twenty years ago."[39]

Even so, the national leadership of the British movement continued to resist the pressure from its radical wing for a more assertive stance. And, once again, Stanton found herself at odds with this leadership over plans for the international conference, which was to meet in Washington the next year. She recorded "a very unpleasant interview" with Lydia Becker and others among the more moderate suffragists over their continuing refusal to cooperate in the venture. She turned to Priscilla Bright McLaren and Anna Maria Priestman, who helped her organize a British delegation.[40] This proved to be an oddly assorted group that included the Radical-Liberal suffragist Alice Scatcherd, the social purity campaigner Mrs. Ormiston Chant, and Mrs. Ashton (May) Dilke.

The inclusion of May Dilke was the cause of yet further controversy, for she had become implicated in some of the scandal surrounding her brother-in-law, Charles Dilke, when he had been cited as corespondent in her sister's divorce case. The unorthodox sexual history of several members of May Dilke's family, as well as suggestions about her own irregular life since being widowed, became the subject of speculation and gossip. Helen Taylor, Mill's stepdaughter and another leading figure in Radical politics, used the presence of May Dilke as grounds to withdraw from participation in the international conference, in connection with which she had been scheduled to address a Senate Committee on Women's Suffrage. Both Elizabeth Cady Stanton and Priscilla Bright McLaren pressed Helen Taylor to adopt a more generous view of the matter, with no success. Stanton showed her solidarity by traveling back to the United States for the conference in the company of May Dilke.[41]

In the year that followed, the tensions within the British movement could no longer be held in check by the national leadership. At the end of 1888, a section that included a number of the Bright circle successfully moved to alter the rules of the National Society for Women's Suffrage. This alteration allowed for the affiliation of other women's organizations that included women's suffrage among their objects. In the view of those who opposed this change, it opened the way for the suffrage movement to be taken over by the women's auxiliaries of the Liberal Party.[42] Certainly, some of the main proponents of change were leading Liberal suffragists, including Priscilla Bright McLaren's son Walter and his wife, Eva McLaren, while many of the leading opponents were Liberal Unionists, such as Millicent Garrett Fawcett and Lilias Ashworth Hallett. These last two joined with Lydia Becker in establishing an alternative society that maintained the old rules of the NSWS.[43]

Lydia Becker's account of this split suggests that the exclusion of married women from the suffrage demand had also been an issue dividing the two groups, and she designated her opponents the "left-wing" and "extreme section" of the movement. It shortly became evident, however, that the leadership of the "new rules" society was itself divided over the issue. Its solution was to support bills that explicitly excluded married women as well as those formulated in terms of equal rights. But it refused to support measures that explicitly included married women. When a group of Radical-Liberal suffragists, including Richard Pankhurst, failed to commit the "new rules" society to oppose any suffrage measure that explicitly excluded married women, these dissidents decided at last on the formation of their own suffrage organization.[44] Elizabeth Wolstenholme Elmy, as often in the past, took the lead in this new initiative, with the help of Alice Scatcherd and Harriet McIlquham.[45]

Harriot Stanton Blatch linked the formation of the Women's Franchise League to her mother's intervention in the British movement some six years before when she had argued for the inclusion of married women in the suffrage demand. Undoubtedly, the formation of this new suffrage organization had arisen out of continuing disputes over this question among British suffragists. It is clear, too, that the league drew on the friendship network formed by her mother's friends and colleagues for its early support. Harriot Stanton Blatch herself took a leading role in the new society, while her mother and Isabella Beecher Hooker both became corresponding members during the year after its formation.[46]

Although the league's leadership drew on a second generation of suffragists, it still presented itself as a continuation of the Garrisonian approach to reform. William Lloyd Garrison, Jr., was among the main speakers at its inaugural meeting. He struck a note that harked back directly to his father's role in the abolition movement, in an insistence that reformers had a very different role from politicians: they must hold to the principle that underlay their cause and not allow themselves to be diverted by any considerations of " policy." He also presented the purpose of the new league as one that held to "moral force" in order "to declare the whole gospel of suffrage without let or hindrance." A similar attitude if more anecdotal tone is evident in Harriot Stanton Blatch's contribution to these proceedings: "The first thing I want to do is to make a little personal declaration, that is, that for the first time in a suffrage meeting in England I feel at home." She recalled her mother's experiences of addressing meetings in Britain, which were always preceded by such warnings as, " 'Now, Mrs Stanton, please do not speak on the Bible question, and please do not touch on the matter of divorce, and, above all things, do not touch on the question of Married Women's Suffrage.' Well, my mother said that at last she felt, with her crown of white hair, like the Jungfrau, rising cold and frigid into the sky, never allowed to melt and show her real heart." A different approach was evidently intended by this breakaway organization.[47]

The history of the league over the next few years suggests that the Garrisonian legacy to the British suffrage movement found its fullest expression here. Political pragmatism was consistently eschewed in favor of principle, especially in the matter of including married women in the suffrage demand. Attention was constantly drawn to the complex of institutions that limited British freedoms, including that longstanding radical bugbear, aristocratic privilege. Hence abolition of the House of Lords also became part of the league's platform. In the work of the league, we also find a commitment to expanding the campaign for suffrage beyond the ranks of middle-class reform and to engaging popular radical support. Elizabeth Cady Stanton continued to encourage such challenges to the approach of the moderate leadership of the British movement. She insisted, for example, on the value of anything that gained the public's attention, whether that attention be good or bad, and emphasized the importance of press coverage for the suffrage demand.[48]

The platform of the Women's Franchise League was an expansive one from the beginning and radical by the standards of the existing suffrage societies. The exclusion of married women from the suffrage demand was, as we have seen, the main spur to its formation, and Elizabeth Wolstenholme Elmy drafted a more extensive suffrage measure for the league to promote. The Women's Disabilities Removal Bill, brought before the House of Commons in 1889 and 1890, included a clause that "no woman shall be subject to legal incapacity in voting . . . by reason of coverture." But the league also sought to address the inequality of women before the law more generally, for its members shared the view of Alice Scatcherd when she told the inaugural meeting, "I, for one, am perfectly tired of joining societies which fight only for a little bit, a little shred, a little fragment of freedom."[49]

By the time of Elizabeth Cady Stanton's last visit to Britain in 1890, she was firmly aligned with the most intransigent of the Radical-Liberal suffragists around the Women's Franchise League. Lydia Becker had recently died, and Ursula Bright had moved into the league's leadership. In Elizabeth Cady Stanton's assessment, Bright now unquestionably stood "at the helm of the woman suffrage movement on this side of the ocean." But the league itself was experiencing some internal division at least in part as a consequence of Ursula Bright's presence, a division that soon led to the expulsion of Elizabeth Wolstenholme Elmy. Elmy feared that the Brights had been brought into the league by the Pankhursts to ease the way for the disgraced Radical Charles Dilke to gain control of it as part of a plan to rebuild his career on a combination of women's and labor issues. Elmy wished, instead, to keep the new organization clear of any divided loyalties that might result from such affiliations.[50]

After the first annual meeting, however, Elizabeth Wolstenholme Elmy was replaced as secretary and resigned from the league.[51] The following year, Harriot Stanton Blatch became the league's joint honorary secretary with Ursula Bright. The records that remain of the league's activities under its new leadership suggest that it continued to conceive of itself principally as the voice of radical suffragism, committed to a more advanced platform than the more moderate societies, deliberately linking itself to the international women's movement, especially to the movement in the United States, and pursuing new sources of support for the suffrage demand in the emerging labor and socialist movements. This last it did mainly by providing speakers on women's suffrage for radical clubs, progressive clubs, and branches of the Women's Cooperative Guild.[52] But from this time on, it also exhibited the Liberal Party loyalties of its leadership, and the Women's Liberal Federation now became a focus for many of its activities.[53]

There are no membership records extant, and the few details provided of league finances in the only surviving minute book suggest that Alice Scatcherd and, to a lesser extent, Ursula Bright were its financial mainstays.[54] A generous reading of its records would be that it attracted a membership of a few hundred. The central executive committee does not appear to have kept in very close touch with local branches established in London and the region of Leeds. Indeed, the work of the league in the Leeds area seems to have run virtually autonomously under the direction of Alice Scatcherd, while individual members of the executive committee on several occasions undertook activities in the name of the league for which they only subsequently sought its endorsement.[55] But such indicators cannot provide a proper measure of the success or significance of the league.

An uncompromising and confrontational activism was what gave the league both its identity and its rationale. It saw itself as the conscience of Radical-Liberal suffragism, constantly keeping its perspective before audiences within both the women's movement and popular radical circles, though without seeking to become a mass movement in itself. This was the character of the league as presented, for example, by Ursula Bright when describing its work to an international audience at the World Congress of Representative Women organized during the Chicago World Fair of 1893. She emphasized the Women's Franchise League's special commitment "in plain language to ask for votes for married women" with the declaration that "the legal position of the wife in England is a scandal to civilization." Ursula Bright also laid claim to "a much broader and bolder" approach than "the ordinary suffrage societies." The platform she outlined was indeed an extensive one: equal political rights and duties; equal educational opportunities; equal wages for equal work; equal access to paid, honorary, or elected public office; equality under family law; equality in the rights and liabilities of contract.[56]

Undoubtedly, though, the league's work also evidenced an unwavering loyalty to Gladstone and to a Liberal Party that had repeatedly thwarted the suffrage demand. In this same address, Ursula Bright offered a somewhat lame explanation for this situation, pointing to the league's altruistic dedication to the cause of Irish home rule and seeking to direct her audience's attention to the "timid counsels" that would exclude married women from the claim, counsels she blamed on the "narrow prejudices of Tories or second-hand Liberals." Bright was attempting to address indirectly those critics of the league who would dismiss it simply as a women's auxiliary of the Gladstonian Liberals. While she demonstrated effectively that her suffrage organization was committed to a broader conception of women's citizenship, she failed convincingly to answer the charges of the league's subordination to Liberal Party faction fighting. Perhaps the better to establish the radical credentials of the league, she also noted in her conclusion: "The leaders of the working men are almost to a man on our side."[57]

This link with the labor movement was central to the approach to suffrage campaigning for a number of the league's leaders. By this time, the league was also looking for support, for example, from the campaign for the eight-hour day, and much of its work was directed toward organizing working-class support for the suffrage demand. At its inaugural meeting, Alice Scatcherd had argued: "There are only two great questions presently before the public. These are the labour question and the women's question. And when we come to consider these questions really they are united; for it is largely on the economic condition of woman that her freedom in the future will depend." She was giving expression to a new perspective on women's rights that proved especially influential in the work of the league, one based on a fresh conception of women's citizenship.[58]

This new perspective began to emerge in radical suffragist argument in the early 1880s, and it based claims to citizenship on the labor of women, operating also on a broad understanding of labor that included every kind of women's work, in reproduction and sexual labor as well as the workplace, in unpaid as well as paid labor.[59] Harriot Stanton Blatch described this perspective as an "economic" approach to the issue, an approach that was to give special attention to the need of working women for the vote. It appealed especially strongly to Radical-Liberal suffragists and clearly informed much of the work of the Women's Franchise League.[60] This new "economic" perspective within the women's movement sometimes also linked women's rights to a critique of social relations under capitalism and emphasized the need to unite industrial women workers with middle-class women in the campaign for the vote. Here, Fabians such as Harriot Stanton Blatch were an important influence. Explaining her women's rights commitment to Beatrice and Sidney Webb, for example, Blatch argued: "Women are the source of the race. Its supreme moulders. To do that work efficiently, they must be politically and economically independent beyond all call. Free they cannot be under capitalism: the capitalistic system and feminism are at war."[61]

Perhaps the most notorious episode in the league's history occurred in 1892, when some of its members intervened at a public meeting in support of a new suffrage bill coming before Parliament. The league maintained, incorrectly, that this measure effectively served to exclude married women. Not content with attacking the provisions of the bill, some league members, led by the socialist Herbert Burrows, stormed the stage. The incident caused considerable unease among some members of the league, even though Burrows and his supporters claimed that it was they, in fact, who had been the initial victims of violence at the hands of Ben Elmy, husband of Elizabeth Wolstenholme Elmy. Some resignations followed, and Burrows was asked to provide the league's executive with his own account in writing, something that was apparently never forthcoming.[62]

The bill in question, though less than an equal rights measure, deliberately avoided any explicit reference to coverture or to married women. It would have given the parliamentary vote to all female local government electors; some married women were already voting under such franchises. It was, then, a further compromise with conservative opinion. But it was one that many Radical-Liberal suffragists such as Elizabeth Wolstenholme Elmy were ready to accept precisely because it reinforced the breach in coverture already established with regard to the local government franchise. The league's rejection of it provides further evidence of its ultra-radical stance on this issue. Harriot Stanton Blatch, for one, believed that the league's opposition to such a compromise was unreasonable and resigned from its executive committee in consequence.[63]

The league's most important legacy for the twentieth-century movement, somewhat ironically, was the part it played in securing a critical amendment to the Local Government Act of 1894. This law admitted married women with the appropriate qualifications to local government franchises on the same basis as single women. At long last, the question of coverture in relation to the suffrage demand was effectively dead.[64] Married women's equal eligibility with single women for the vote had finally been clearly established. Although the old guard of the suffrage leadership continued to dispute the question for a little while longer, the way was clear for an unequivocal demand for equal rights for all women in the parliamentary franchise and for a reunification of the suffrage movement within the National Union of Women's Suffrage Societies, which followed in 1897. The Women's Franchise League had helped achieve, therefore, a situation in which its own existence was no longer necessary—perhaps the most significant achievement for which any such radical reform organization might hope.[65]

Looking back, Harriot Stanton Blatch saw the origins of militancy in both Britain and the United States in the work of the Women's Franchise League during the 1890s.[66] Such a claim appears startling in terms of standard accounts of the British suffrage movement in the nineteenth century, accounts that generally emphasize its moderation, even conservatism. It is startling also in terms of current understandings of suffrage militancy, which is still discussed in terms of the extreme violence of militant demonstrations in the 1912–1914 period.[67] Space does not permit a detailed discussion of this claim. It is worth noting, however, that already in the 1890s some Radical-Liberal suffragists were promoting new tactics, most notably tax resistance, that later became a feature of early militancy.[68] The origins and nature of militancy remain in need of more detailed analysis. Yet it seems likely, in view of the evidence presented above, that some significant continuities did exist between nineteenth-century radical suffragism and twentieth-century militancy, and that our present conceptualization of militancy is inadequate inasmuch as it neglects such continuities.[69]

Elizabeth Cady Stanton herself foresaw that radical suffragism might well take a different course, as those educated in the Garrisonian and Quaker traditions of reform were increasingly replaced by new generations on whom they were an ever-weakening influence. In 1889, she warned that her generation had been "bred in the pacific school of the old Abolitionists, dominated by the non-resistance ideas of Garrison, and where the presence of so many Quakers spread about an atmosphere of brotherly love. But we are passing away, and the new American woman is coming to the front. *Cave Canis.*" The year before, at the first international gathering of suffragists in Washington in 1888, she had issued an even more explicit warning: "It requires no prophet to foretell the revolution ahead when women strike hands with Nihilists, Socialists, Communists, and Anarchists, in defence of the most enlarged liberties of the people."[70] In this way, Elizabeth Cady Stanton had "prophesied and in anticipation, welcomed the militant suffrage movement."[71] She did not live to see twentieth-century militancy begin to hit its stride in both Britain and the United States. But when an Australian suffragist, Muriel Matters, chained herself to the grille in the Ladies Gallery of the House of Commons, and that grille at last came down, it is surely not too fanciful to hear the ghost of her American predecessor chuckling overhead.

WOMEN'S RIGHTS, FEMINISM, AND SUFFRAGISM IN JAPAN, 1870–1925

Barbara Molony

Woman suffragism in Japan, often associated with the liberal politics of the 1920s, was grounded in women's rights discussions of the late nineteenth century.[1] "Rights" were a central issue in a wide variety of Japanese intellectual and political discourses, including feminist discourses, in the late nineteenth and early twentieth centuries.[2] To many contemporary observers, notions of rights were part of the tidal wave of Western ideas engulfing Japan after the Meiji Restoration (1868). The salience of rights in Japanese thought, however, suggests that nineteenth-century concepts of rights drew from indigenous as well as imported ideas. To the indigenous value of self-cultivation through education and ethical development was added the imported notion that the cultivated person was an individual who was entitled to a respected role in civil society or the public arena and, in turn, to inclusion in the emerging modern state. Suffragism, while not yet central to women's rights discourses, would draw, a quarter-century later, on the nineteenth-century quest for inclusion in the state and civil society. What were understood as "rights" expanded by the 1920s, however, paralleling the changes in understanding of the "state" in which those rights would be exercised.

By the 1920s the state had come to appear as an established bureaucratic and political system, under an abstraction (the emperor) theorized as defined by and defining the collective spirit of the *kokumin* (variously defined as "people," "nation," "citizens"). Interwar feminists, who contested the state's limitation of suffrage and other civil rights to men, saw little irony in simultaneously demanding state protection as part of women's rights. That is, in addition to struggling for the right to participate in the state, feminists sought the state's protection *from* certain aspects of public and private society that they viewed as oppressive. These included, but were not restricted to, demands for protection from institutionalized patriarchy, from sexually transmitted diseases, and from miserable economic and labor conditions that led to the suffering and deaths of women and their children. Both forms of rights discussions in the 1920s—resistance against participatory exclusion and denial of suffrage, as well as acceptance of the state's power to protect—took for granted an existing state structure. Meiji-era (1868–1912) discussions of rights had assumed both a more fluid political situation and a less precise definition of rights.

Meiji-era rights discourse

In Japan as in many other societies, "rights" had multiple meanings.[3] Rights discourse was lively and diverse, blending notions of Tokugawa-era (1600–1868) anti-authoritarianism[4]

with frequently conflated "Western" rights discourses. The Meiji-era neologisms for "rights" (*kenri*), "women's rights" (*joken*), "male-female equality" (*danjo byōdō*), and "male-female equal rights" (*danjo dōken*) were, at times, used interchangeably, though their meanings were actually distinct.[5] The terms were also drafted into the service of resistance to or support of other newly created state institutions or categories. State, nation, nationality, ethnicity, and gender were all in the process of mutual construction around the same time, and, in some cases, rights discourse was used selectively to resist the emerging structure of one or another of these categories. Conversely, rights discourse could also be employed to help reify any of these categories or institutions. Women's suffrage was not yet assumed to be central to women's rights, as it would be in the interwar period.

Rights discussions in the late nineteenth century, whether by advocates for men or women, developed in the context of rejecting past (Tokugawa) relations of power and of engagement with foreign ideas. That power (in the form of a state, social norms, laws, customs, and so on) would exist was not questioned; it was one's relationship to power that was under discussion. As feminist theorist Wendy Brown notes, feminisms have often been about "a longing to share in power rather than be protected from its excesses."[6]

Although the earliest discussions of rights in the 1870s and 1880s often did not tie rights explicitly to male gender, Japanese discussants frequently employed the ideas of Jean-Jacques Rousseau, whose vision of a social contract was founded on the rights of men in fraternity.[7] Those men and (the smaller group of) women who clamored for rights in the 1870s demanded political participation or inclusion. By 1890 a tiny minority of men had been awarded the right of inclusion in the state and civil society, but women were pointedly excluded from all political participation, including ascent to the hereditary throne.[8] By the turn of the twentieth century, the requirement of male gender for political participation was taken for granted by many; the state itself was being constructed as a fraternity under a patriarchal emperor.[9] When political rights, in particular suffrage rights, were extended in 1890 to some of the men who had earlier demanded rights of fraternal inclusion, many of those activists followed up on their demands by joining parties and entering the government in some capacity.[10]

Nineteenth-century Japanese advocates for women were of varying minds about both the definition of "women's rights" and the means to achieve them. Some argued for a communitarian inclusiveness reminiscent of Rousseauian ideas espoused in the 1870s. Others, inspired by John Stuart Mill, stressed improved education as a way for women to gain the subjectivity that would make them eligible for rights.[11] Still others believed social and political inclusion must follow the elimination of patriarchal sexual privileges, such as those implied by polygamy, prostitution, and patrilineality.[12]

It was the second approach to rights—through education—that dominated early discussions; suffrage itself would have to await the development of women's sense of themselves as public persons.[13] In the Meiji era, discussions of women's rights were closely related to discussions of women's education, particularly beyond the elementary level. Cultivating a good, moral, ethical, responsible character was a goal of Confucian education as well as of the recently introduced Western-style learning. In turn-of-the-century rights discourse, the centrality of education, with its deep connections to notions of respect and ethical leadership (which themselves imply both agency and a relationship to regimes of power), suggests that rights were closely connected to a yearning for women's subjectivity. Talk of rights takes persons' subjectivity for granted; talk of education as self-cultivation advances the cause of women's subjectivity. For Meiji-era policy-makers and many advocates of women's rights, the immediate goal of women's education was not to prepare them for suffrage but to mold ethical wives and mothers who led by example in the family and in civil society. Such women would be active not in electoral politics but in public activities, such as poor relief or more controversial reforms like those calling for regulation of sexuality.[14] Many advocates for women's rights—though not government policy-makers—saw women's growing roles in the family and civil society as an important step in developing their personhood as a basis for rights.

For other feminists, though, some rights of political participation were necessary. Writer Shimizu Tomoko, for instance, connected the rights of citizens (*kokumin*) with social and moral issues.[15] Women needed to be citizens—to have the right of participation—because they should educate their children as citizens and support their husbands in the exercise of their citizenship. Thus, Shimizu posited in 1890 that women's political rights arose from their relationship with those who had (some) rights. She did not go so far as to demand the right of suffrage for all men and women based on their individual personhood. Rights were relational, not individual, for Shimizu. Women's advocacy groups in the 1880s and 1890s also restructured the political to be more like the social or moral.[16] Advocacy for improving women's conditions connected demands for revision of the Law on Political Associations and Assembly of 1890 (which banned women from political participation, including speaking and public assembly) with concerns about morality, the home, economic conditions, and other issues that emerged as women moved increasingly into public realms of advocacy (civil society). And women's education was essential to this ability to penetrate civil society by creating women's personhood. For late Meiji-era feminists, the state was still an entity in formation. Many believed that women's involvement with the state through their quest for rights was bound to alter that emerging entity.

Taishō-era (1912–1926) feminisms

By the interwar era, feminists and others came to view the state as a fixed entity. Although feminists in the late 1890s had believed that both women and men could take part in state formation as long as they had the personhood that accompanied education, later feminists came to view the state as an established institution capable both of protecting rights against societal or civil oppression and of denying rights to groups or individuals who then would either resist the state or struggle for inclusion in it.[17] The evolution of rights discourse to focus on the struggle for women's inclusion led, by the 1920s, to the demand for women's suffrage.

The dual notion that the state was an entity that consisted of individuals with the right of membership and that it should protect classes of individuals against societal exploitation was reified in the founding of the New Woman Association (Shin Fujin Kyōkai; hereafter NWA) in 1919. To achieve the rights of protection and inclusion, women had first to identify as a class, noted Hiratsuka Raichō, one of the group's three founding mothers (the other two were Ichikawa Fusae and Oku Mumeo). Invited to speak to the All-Kansai Federation of Women's Organizations in late November 1919, Hiratsuka delivered a talk entitled "Toward the Unification of Women."[18] As possessors of rights, Hiratsuka stated, women would be part of the state that would determine "the future." Women were no longer in need of proving their wisdom and talent, as they had been in the late nineteenth century. Rights should be theirs—if only women would communicate and unite to achieve those rights. Her vision of rights included different but complementary roles and identities for men and women. In addition, Hiratsuka articulated two types of feminist rights in her comments—women's rights (*joken*) and mothers' rights (*boken*). She did not raise the issue of voting rights.

Shortly after this speech, Ichikawa joined Hiratsuka to draft the New Woman Association's two central demands, which were eventually presented to the Diet (national parliament). The first demanded revision of the Public Peace Police Law (Chian keisatsuhō) of 1900, which had reiterated the restrictions of the 1890 Law on Political Associations and Assembly. Protest against Article 5 of the Police Law—which prohibited women's membership in political parties as well as attendance at political meetings and rallies—was not new. Socialist women had initiated parliamentary lobbying against it between 1905 and 1909.[19] The post-World War I feminist fight against the Police Law of 1900 was also inspired by the increasing success of women's rights movements outside Japan.[20]

The second major program of the NWA also had foreign parallels. Inspired by recent developments in domestic legislation in Europe and the United States, Hiratsuka proposed that the NWA seek passage of legislation to protect women from marrying men with sexually transmitted diseases and to assist wives who had been infected by their carrier husbands.[21] Legal inequalities, she noted, created hardships for the women so victimized. The Revised Civil Code of 1898 stipulated that a Japanese wife was subject to divorce and two years imprisonment for committing adultery, but a wife was unable to file for divorce should she discover—and venereal disease was a strong indication—that her husband engaged in extramarital sexual relations.[22] The NWA's proposed reform of the divorce laws to permit women to reject syphilitic husbands or fiancés directly challenged the patriarchal family system that gave few rights to members other than the patriarch.[23]

Hiratsuka, Ichikawa, and Oku met with other activists at Hiratsuka's home on January 6, 1920, and prepared two petitions to present to the Diet.[24] The first, which called for revision of the Public Peace Police Law, unambiguously demanded for women the rights, enjoyed by men, of citizenship and inclusion in the state. The second, which would require men's premarital testing for syphilis and permit wives to divorce and collect compensation for related medical expenses and other damages, called for women's protection by the state against potentially deadly excesses inherent in the family system.

The NWA responded to opposition to these petitions in terms of women's familial roles, but in doing so, the organization moved feminist discourse increasingly toward a demand for full civil rights based on suffrage. To those who insisted that women's political rights would destroy the Japanese family by changing the wife's role, Ichikawa argued that revision of the Police Law would, in fact, help women become better wives and wiser mothers; a politically aware mother was better informed and, therefore, able to rear better children. Ichikawa's conflation of wifehood and motherhood sounded natural to her listeners because the discourses on wifehood and motherhood were becoming increasingly blended in the popular mind by the clichéd phrase "good wife, wise mother."[25] Supporters of "motherhood" ranged from conservatives to feminists; the latter stressed that, by valuing motherhood, society would value women. But "wifehood" in its official (state) interpretation was not liberatory. Wives were, at worst, under patriarchal control and, at best, responsible for family-supporting productivity.[26] For wise mothers, who carried out an important role in molding the future, political rights could arguably be necessary; for wives, however, who had no property to protect and who had productive responsibilities to the state and family, political rights might have been harder to justify.

Against criticism that the second NWA demand would undermine the husband's dominance in the family, the organization answered that a husband's venereal disease was even more debilitating to the family and especially its children.[27] This approach also shifted the discourse from wifehood to motherhood, again using the malleability of the discourse on "good wife, wise mother." Meiji-era feminists had identified women's rights with respect for women's full personhood. Women gained subjectivity as respected and educated wives in a society free of patriarchy, polygamy, and prostitution. Meiji women's rights discourses boldly attacked extramarital male sexuality. By the Taishō era, male sexuality was identified with patriarchy, which was supported by law and by the state. To change male sexual privilege, then, Taishō feminists had to cast their arguments in terms of other state-sponsored discourses, particularly "good wife, wise motherism." The petition justified exempting brides from syphillis screening by noting that men's sexual habits were dissolute and self-indulgent. Among women, only prostitutes were so morally lax.[28]

Because sexuality had been politicized by the legal construction of patriarchy, the NWA members found that they had to give priority to efforts to revise the Police Law. It was this emphasis on enhancing the rights of women to participate in politics, even in a limited manner, that led logically to the demand for full individual civic rights. No political activity—and the attempt to change policy on sexuality was now defined as political—could be carried out without first revising Article 5 of the 1900 Police Law. Yet advocating change in the law could itself be construed as a violation of that law. The NWA thus took tentative steps into political action, submitting to the Diet a petition to revise the law. The petition never made it out of committee to the full floor of the Diet before it was adjourned on February 26, 1920.

The NWA resubmitted the petition to a later parliamentary session. In July 1920, Representative Tabuchi Toyokichi called for a revision of Article 5, arguing in terms of protection of women as weak:[29]

> There has recently been much talk concerning freedom of speech, but because this freedom is not respected in this country, there is, even in the Diet, little respect for freedom of speech. . . . I have, therefore, decided . . . to bring this problem to your attention . . . and to obtain your approval for changes in Japan's Police Law. . . . Specifically, [I support] elimination of the word "women" from Article Five of the Public Peace Police Law. Gentlemen, one of the currents of our postwar world is socialism; a second current is feminism, reaching Japan. . . . I wonder if these momentous global changes will penetrate the Japanese Diet? . . . Although I do not advocate giving women complete suffrage at this time, . . . women are also human beings who have a right to free speech. . . . I believe we must exercise the basic premise of "democracy" which fosters concepts of equality and support for the weak. . . . I urge you not to derive pleasure from oppressing the weak, but to work for the thirty million [women] subjects of Japan.[30]

Shortly after Tabuchi's speech, the Diet was adjourned, so there was again no opportunity for a vote.

At a later Diet session, on February 26, 1921, a nearly unanimous House of Representatives recommended revising Article 5 to permit women to attend political meetings and rallies; the prohibition of their joining political parties was not yet lifted, however. Opposition to the bill, even in this compromised form, was greater in the aristocratic House of Peers. The most vocal opponent was Baron Fujimura Yoshirō, president of the newspaper *Taishō nichi nichi shinbun* and a powerful leader in the House of Peers. "The participation of women in political movements is extremely boring," he remarked condescendingly.

55

[I]t goes against natural laws in a physiological as well as psychological sense. It is not women's function to be active in political movements alongside men. The woman's place is in the home. Her role is a social and educational one. . . . Furthermore, women's going out into society and becoming active in political movements will result in a number of extremely bad consequences. . . . Take the example of Queen Elizabeth's reign. . . . What I am saying is supported by our particular traditions, customs, and history. Finally, giving women the right to participate in political movements subverts the family system that is the basis of our social system. I think that the behavior of these new women—these groups of peculiar women trying to become politically active—is extremely shameful. [The issue before us] concerns Japan's national polity. . . . I believe we should oppose [revision of the Police Law].[31]

Fujimura's colleagues heeded his warnings and defeated the amendment in the closing minutes of the Diet session. Without the support of the House of Peers, the bill failed.

While the Diet debated these bills, the women of the NWA turned to other projects that were less likely to be identified as "political." The NWA could, then, rightfully claim not to be purely a political association, something women were prohibited from joining. Ichikawa Fusae, the feminist most closely identified with suffragism by the mid-1920s, downplayed the idea that the NWA was interested only in "obtaining political rights for women."[32] Although Hiratsuka Raichō had stated earlier that women's status and lives could not be improved without removing legal impediments to women's rights—that is, women had to gain equality in the eyes of the law through political rights—most advocates of women's rights presented civil and political rights as means to an end, rather than as ends in themselves. The end they called for was the improvement of women's lives through better health, elimination of poverty, better work conditions, protection of motherhood, and other feminist goals. Indeed, in the early 1920s, the struggle for political rights as an end, rather than as a means, was viewed by nonfeminists as selfish, though feminist social reform was not. Hiratsuka stressed in the first issue of the NWA's journal *Josei dōmei* that suffrage was not an end in itself but a means to inject new feminine values into a masculine political system.[33] In the process of working on reforms in the areas of health or labor, either in opposition to or in collaboration with elements of the state, women were, in fact, acting as if they were members of the state. But without specific and articulated rights, their "citizenship" was always inferior to men's. This did not go unnoticed by the leadership of the NWA, who decided to risk denunciation and expand their demand for more complete inclusion in the state, including suffrage. The December 1920 and January 1921 issues of *Josei dōmei* carried, along with the organization's earlier petitions for revising the Police Law and regulating men's access to marriage, a new demand for revising the House of Representatives Election Law; in 1921 this law restricted the right to vote to males twenty-five or older who paid a minimum direct tax of three yen per year and who had been listed in the election directory for one full year.[34] The form this revision would take was, of course, unclear, but the NWA's new position on suffrage, articulated in *Josei dōmei*, made equal suffrage rights a significant component of women's rights discourse.

Redefining women's political rights as requiring nothing short of suffrage—although the right of participation had first to be secured—engendered a more sophisticated understanding of the diverse strands of women's rights. While some argued that mothers' special contributions to and understanding of society entitled them to political rights, others called for political rights for all women, regardless of whether they were mothers. At the same time, no feminist thought in the interwar period rejected the notion that the state owed women protection—all women, whether as workers, as mothers, or as wives. Demands for equality and for gender-based protections were understood to be different, but rarely were they viewed as antithetical. Some feminists stressed one type of rights activism over another, but suffrage was seen as incompatible with protection of women only for a brief period of time and only in some socialist-feminist thinking.

Among NWA leaders, Ichikawa began to emphasize different aspects of women's rights from those stressed by Hiratsuka during the early 1920s. According to Ichikawa, Hiratsuka's ideology was based on the "principle of mothers' rights" (*bokenshugi*), a concept that she contrasted with her own "principle of women's rights" (*jokenshugi*). Although she did not reject state support of mothers, Ichikawa came to believe that women's political empowerment could be achieved only through recognition of male-female equality.[35] Men's political rights had little to do with their education; the same was true for women's *lack* of political rights. In a 1920 article, Ichikawa articulated her beliefs in terms of the "principle of women's rights" ideology.

> Aren't we [women] treated completely as feeble-minded children? Why is it all right to know about science and literature and not all right to be familiar with politics and current events? Why is it acceptable to read and write but not to speak and listen? A man, no matter what his occupation or educational background, has political rights, but a woman, no matter how qualified, does not have the same rights. . . . If we do not understand the politics of the country we live in, we will not be able to understand conditions in our present society.[36]

Women had not earned equality by gaining subjectivity through education, Ichikawa argued. What women *did*—that is, cultivating themselves through education or fulfilling maternal roles—was still not enough to achieve rights. Only absolute rights based on equality would succeed. And absolute rights required that women find a place of equal membership in an already established state and society.

In April 1924, Ichikawa published an article entitled "Absolute Equality between Men and Women?" in *Josei Kaizō* (Women's Reconstruction), in which she discussed the differences in the United States between feminists demanding complete legal equality with men and those advocating special and distinctive treatment for women, especially workplace protections.[37] She suggested that a similar debate was emerging among Japanese women: "Absolute equality between men and women? Which is right or wrong? I have outlined the problem here and have decided to wait for the comments of other intellectuals."[38]

One intellectual from whom Ichikawa may have wished to hear was socialist feminist Yamakawa Kikue. In April 1921 Yamakawa and others organized Japan's first socialist women's association, the Red Wave Society (Sekirankai). The Red Wave Society's manifesto, written by Yamakawa in 1921, condemned capitalism for turning women into "slaves at home and oppress[ing] us as wage slaves outside the home. It turns many of our sisters into prostitutes."[39] She decried capitalism for engendering (in both senses of the word) imperialism, which deprived women of their male loved ones, thereby defining the problems of capitalism in terms of women's losses rather than men's.[40] But like socialist women elsewhere, Yamakawa would find her feminism marginalized by socialist men and in contention with the positions of nonsocialist feminists.

Like her bourgeois sisters, Yamakawa foregrounded protection of women as a function of the state. But unlike the NWA, she did not take the existing Japanese state for granted.

Rather, she envisioned a state without capitalism. Yamakawa's article, "The New Woman's Association and the Red Wave Society," appeared in the July 1921 issue of *Taiyō* .[41] Criticizing the NWA, she wrote:

> there is absolutely no way in a capitalist society to alleviate the misery of female workers. We believe it is a sin to waste the strength of women workers in a . . . time-consuming Diet movement—that is, in any movement which digresses from the only road to salvation for women, the destruction of capitalism. However, bourgeois gentlewomen, because they cannot trust or imagine a society beyond capitalism, concentrate their energies on alleviating the misery of women workers in a superficial and ineffective way.[42]

By the middle of the 1920s, however, socialist women began to give conditional support to suffragism as an ameliorative measure on the way to changing the state.[43]

Organizing for suffrage

The months after Yamakawa's article appeared saw considerable political activity by women in Japan. Much of this activity arose from the amendment of Article 5, Clause 2, of the Public Peace Police Law.[44] Taking advantage of their newly won right to attend openly political meetings (they still could not join political parties, outlawed in Clause 1), women began to organize new groups through which they could make additional demands. Some worked for women's political rights, while others pushed for an end to licensed prostitution and other goals. Some groups of women, like those involved in housewives' campaigns to rationalize home life, might not have described themselves as women's rights activists, though their leaders often did embrace the demand for women's political rights. Their greater public involvement coincided with and was encouraged by other women's increased public visibility. Women's groups of all sorts blossomed in the early 1920s: consumer groups of varied political persuasions, socialist feminist groups, bourgeois descendants of the NWA, the venerable Women's Reform Society (the Japanese branch of the Woman's Christian Temperance Union [WCTU], founded in 1886), and so on. Feminist reformism permeated Taishō liberal culture, but in mid-1923 it was not coordinated to focus on political rights for women as a class. Activists had to be moved to see the importance of joint activity to achieve political equality.

What moved women was the great earthquake that hit the Tokyo region on September 1, 1923. In the aftermath of the quake, the Women's Reform Society's Kubushiro Ochimi and other women turned to relief work to supply thousands of Tokyo residents with food, clothing, and shelter. Women from Christian churches and other groups in the Tokyo area started distributing milk to children and developed a sense of solidarity through shared compassion and concern. Some were housewives with little or no experience in organized cooperative activities. Others were members of alumnae groups and women's auxiliary organizations. Socialists like Yamakawa worked side-by-side with middle-class Christians and housewives.[45] On September 28, 1923, approximately a hundred leaders from forty-three different organizations agreed to formalize their spontaneous cooperative efforts and joined forces in an organization named the Tokyo Federation of Women's Organizations (Tokyo Rengō Fujinkai).[46]

The earthquake's destruction had created a situation that demanded compassionate cooperation. After the Tokyo Federation finished emergency distribution of food and clothing to the poor and finding shelter for the homeless, many members continued to meet.[47] Sometime in late 1923 or early 1924, the organization divided into five sections: society, employment, labor, education, and government.[48] Within these sections, women discussed a variety of issues, including motherhood protection, licensed prostitution, the problems of working women, and political rights for women. It is significant that they sought to promote women's issues that had already been at the heart of the pre-earthquake feminist movements.

The Tokyo Federation's government section focused on issues of political rights, discussing means of gaining full membership in the state. In November 1924, government section director Kubushiro Ochimi called a meeting of women interested in working for women's political rights.[49] This meeting (on December 13, 1924) spawned the League for the Realization of Women's Suffrage (Fujin Sanseiken Kakutoku Kisei Dōmei), the principal women's suffrage organization in the interwar years. As its name indicated, the league would concentrate on obtaining political rights for women. Political rights, declared the manifesto proclaiming the founding of the organization, were essential to improving the status of Japanese women:

1. It is our responsibility to destroy customs that have existed in this country for the past twenty-six hundred years and to construct a new Japan that promotes the natural rights of men and women;
2. As women have been attending public schools with men for half a century since the beginning of the Meiji period and our opportunities in higher education have continued to expand, it is unjust to exclude women from universal suffrage;
3. Political rights are necessary for the protection of nearly four million working women in this country;
4. Women who work in the household must be recognized before the law to realize their full human potential;
5. Without political rights we cannot achieve public recognition at either the national or local level of government;
6. It is both necessary and possible to bring together women of different religions and occupations in a movement for women's suffrage.[50]

This list is a remarkably clear and succinct statement of the meaning of rights among middle-class feminists in the Taishō era. Article 1 unequivocally contrasted "natural rights of men and women" with venerable "customs" that must be destroyed. That is, Japanese society had buried the rights of individual men and women under unnatural customs. In contrast to the Meiji-era optimism about the ability of education to elevate the status of women, Article 2 of the 1924 manifesto rued the continuing denial of even educated women's rights, although it implied—as did Meiji-era feminism—that there could be a connection between education and rights. Article 3 tied together rights and protection for women, an important Taishō-era concern. Article 4 called for recognizing all women's full humanity, and Article 5 connected rights and recognition in the public sphere, both issues raised in the Meiji era. Article 6, which focused on implementation rather than on fundamental principles, recognized the need for a movement. Thus, this manifesto reiterated some of the Meiji-era discourse of rights in terms of respectability, but also explicitly called on the state to include women. Article 1 suggested, moreover, that merely including women as men were included might be insufficient, since both men and women had natural rights that had been inadequately promoted.

To achieve the goals of the manifesto, the league petitioned the Diet for civic rights. The suffragists' expectations were high; three weeks earlier, in late February 1925, the House of Representatives had passed the promised universal manhood suffrage bill, which eliminated the remaining economic qualifications for male suffrage. Although many liberals welcomed the expansion of the electorate, the league criticized the new legislation because "giving the vote only to men and excluding women is not universal suffrage."[51] Despite the Diet's recent limitation of suffrage rights by gender and its passage of a Peace Preservation Law designed to curb leftist political expression, feminists looked forward to Diet discussions of women's suffrage and welcomed the opportunity to resume lobbying.[52] The league succeeded in convincing a small group of representatives, most of them in their thirties, to introduce several items for discussion:

1. An amendment to the Public Peace Police Law of 1900 (Article 5, Clause 1) giving women the right to join political parties and associations;
2. A petition to encourage women's higher education;
3. A petition for women's suffrage in national elections;
4. A petition to make changes in the City Code (1888) and the Town and Village Code (1888), allowing women to vote and become candidates for office on the local level.[53]

When these four items came up for discussion on March 10—a date designated by suffragists as "women's Diet day" (*gikai fujin dee*) because four of the twenty-five items scheduled for discussion concerned women's rights[54]—some 200 women filled the visitors' section in the balcony overlooking the Diet chambers. Their optimism contrasted with the mocking tone of press reportage that day. Describing those they called "veterans of women's suffrage," the *Tokyo asahi shinbun* newspaper reported that "They talk big in their shrill voices."[55] The following day, the *Asahi* printed a caricature of four Diet members with ribbons in their hair signifying sympathy toward women. Diet speeches in opposition to the proposed petitions and amendment were also bitter. Nevertheless, in the end, the proposals were all approved by the House of Representatives. Three of the items voted on were only petitions and thus did not become law, and the Police Law amendment was killed in the House of Peers, but it is noteworthy that these proposals for expanding women's rights fared as well as they did.[56] The partial success of March 10 gave suffragist women hope that they might achieve civic rights. Suffragists shortened the name of their group to Women's Suffrage League (Fusen Kakutoku Dōmei; henceforth WSL) and made a public appeal for *fusen*. This appeal was symbolically important. *Fusen*, when written with different characters, meant either "universal suffrage" or "women's suffrage." *Fusen* had been on the lips of activists for years but had been virtually synonymous with "male suffrage"; the WSL made a tactical decision to buy into the acceptable discourse on male rights by taking advantage of the homonym.[57] They emphatically stated that *fusen* (meaning universal suffrage) was incomplete without *fusen* (meaning women's suffrage).

As with the decision to change their group's name, middle-class suffragists issued the following declaration defining the scope of their future activities (note the plea to socialist women to reject the primacy of class over gender):

> The foundation for the construction of a new Japan has been laid and, as expected, the [male] suffrage bill was passed by the fiftieth Diet session.

Figure 5.1   Two sets of characters that are both pronounced fusen. The set on the left means "women's suffrage," while the one on the right means "universal suffrage."

> However, along with men who are under twenty-five or who "receive public or private assistance," we women who comprise half this country's population have been left without political rights. . . . Therefore, women should put aside their emotional, religious, and ideological differences and cooperate as women. . . . We should concentrate our efforts on achieving the singular goal of political rights. We should work closely with the political parties but maintain a position of absolute neutrality [in partisan matters].[58]

By 1925, then, the ideology of women's right of full political participation through suffrage had evolved from its Meiji-era origins in women's quest for subjectivity through self-cultivation. Japanese suffragists rallied a diverse collection of women's rights activists in the late 1920s in support of suffrage. Lobbying and holding mass meetings, suffragists struggled for inclusion in the state, recognizing the power of the state to grant or withhold membership. Suffragism continued to be a central feature, fueling the rhetoric and actions of groups dedicated to suffrage as a *sine qua non* of rights as well as being supported by groups with other primary agendas.[59] These latter groups took for granted the desirability of rights, despite their differences concerning the meanings of rights other than the vote, which virtually all supported in varying degrees. Rights within the existing state system might be just a stopgap until a revolutionary state could be created—as socialist women advocated in their feminist demands in the leftist labor movement in the late Taishō era[60]—or they might be framed in terms of inclusion in the existing civil society.[61] In both cases, rights were articulated within existing regimes of power. By 1931 the House of Representatives had proposed and twice approved a limited extension of the franchise. Suffragists opposed the bill, holding out for complete equality. In any event, the House of Peers rejected even the watered-down proposal, and the rise of militarism after 1931 squelched demands based on individual rights as potentially subversive.

Feminists increasingly turned to expressing rights as protections in the 1930s. Inclusion in the state and/or civil society, many feminists came to believe, could be achieved in multiple ways, including consumer movements, "election purification" (anti-corruption) movements, protection of laborers, welfare assistance to single mothers and their children, and other successful public-sphere activities producing gendered social-welfare reforms. Although suffrage was put on the back burner, rights remained a central feature of these various activities. When women finally voted for the first time on April 10, 1946, they achieved full membership in the state, but, as their Meiji foremothers might have suggested, the state would have to be in transition to permit their inclusion.

The state was, indeed, undergoing transformation in the postwar era. That transformation built on the efforts of many disenfranchised groups of the prewar era, including women suffragists, to gain respect and full citizenship. These efforts were familiar to women all over Japan in the postwar years. When the American Occupation forces claimed to have introduced the concept of rights to Japanese women, the latter claimed otherwise. Traveling to remote villages and towns, American military women spoke to groups of women, urging them to exercise the rights benevolently bestowed on them by the Americans. At one such speech, an elderly women rose to her feet and indignantly demanded how the Americans could ignore the efforts of Ichikawa Fusae and her colleagues to gain the vote for women.[62] The Occupation's attempted erasure of history, through condescension or ignorance, has, fortunately, been superseded by numerous studies in Japan and elsewhere that highlight the important role of Japanese feminists in earning political rights.

Part II

RETHINKING FEMINIST ACTION IN RELIGIOUS AND DENOMINATIONAL CONTEXTS

Introductory remarks

For several decades historians of feminisms focused primarily on feminisms in secular (and often anticlerical) and socialist settings, under the assumption that feminism could not exist, much less accomplish any gains for women, within the framework of male-dominated organized religions. The latest wave of scholarship disputes and complicates such an assumption. Even Mary Wollstonecraft, the late eighteenth-century English feminist, has been revisited (in a recent study by Barbara Taylor) with an eye to the depth and significance of her non-conformist Christian religious beliefs. By focusing on the religious roots of secular feminist activity as well as the growth of socially progressive female voluntary associations within – or on the fringes of – organized religion, our contributors provide an entirely new and illuminating perspective on nineteenth-century and early twentieth-century feminist activity.

In evaluating a range of potential contributions and selecting those that follow, I have kept an eye on the central question – do these activists and their activities challenge masculine domination or not, and if so, in what ways? What can we learn from their strategies and tactics? their retreats and advances? from the complexity of the situations in which they operated? Certain key Christian beliefs, common to Catholics and Protestants, such as the doctrine of the equality of all souls irrespective of sex or status, provided some Western feminists with a springboard for organizing against many perceived injustices, but especially on behalf of members of their own sex, most notably in antislavery agitation (which is well documented), missionary activity on behalf of girls and women, and later campaigns against domestic violence fueled by alcohol, sexual slavery, labor exploitation, and the traffic in women and children. Conversion to Christianity allowed some women in India and other Asian societies opportunities to challenge their subordinate status. Although some Christian contexts continued to limit and thwart feminist questioning of male-dominated authority structures and antifeminist Church doctrines, groups such as the World Woman's Christian Temperance Union (WWCTU) success-fully nurtured feminist activism in a number of Asian societies, including China and Japan, even as inquisitive feminists began to engage in the most radical sort of Biblical criticism. St. Joan's International Alliance, established in the later 1920s, brought together a transnational network of progressive Catholic feminists. Women engaged in the Theosophical Society became active advocates of women's emancipation in India as well as in England. Some Protestant Christian women sought to vote in their congrega-tions and to become pastors. In Germany, Jewish women also began to organize to gain a voice within their religion, and in the later 1920s began holding separate congresses to discuss their concerns.

Muslim women in several Middle Eastern societies, including Egypt and Iran, organized to claim a share in their national projects, while women in Turkey found themselves sud-denly enfranchised and unveiled by the Atatürk government. Muslim, Coptic Christian, and Jewish women in Syria and Lebanon during the French mandates, and Egypt during the British occupation, organized to oppose the intrusion of imperial power in the Middle East. In so doing, they fought to find a balance between an often neo-traditionalist male-domi-nated cultural nationalism embedded in religious beliefs and customary observances (par-ticularly in defense of the "conventional" patriarchal, often polygamous family) and an overt effort to agitate for women's rights while not succumbing to the powerful yet danger-ous attraction of Western secular emancipationist currents. In most cases it took a long time before denominationally committed feminists could begin to work together across confes-sional boundaries, much less across the lines that separated Western and Eastern religions.

Florence Rochefort probes the remarkable affinity between feminism and Protestant Christianity in nineteenth-century France following the traumatic revolutionary years. Nominally a Catholic nation, it was France's Protestant women, both Calvinist and Lutheran, especially a few remarkable non-conforming women located on the fringes of their respective churches such as Eugénie Niboyet and Jenny P. d'Héricourt, who engaged with early radical emancipatory movements such as the Saint-Simonians and Icarians and spearheaded women's rights campaigns in the 1848 revolution. Later in the century a net-work of well-off women engaged in progressive Protestant-dominated philanthropic efforts, directed especially at assisting poor women. The more radical of these women, in particular Emilie de Morsier and Isabelle Bogelot (who both had developed connections with American feminists), seeking to address the root causes of poor women's problems rather than simply palliating them, spearheaded the organized movement for women's emancipation by organizing major congresses in 1889 and 1900, and founding the Conseil National des Femmes Françaises (CNFF) in 1901.

Inger Hammar's contribution examines the shift in Swedish feminist efforts, begin-ning with feminist critics like Fredrika Bremer who challenged the Church of Sweden (Lutheran, or Augsburg Confession), the Old Testament, and especially the antifeminist prescriptions of Saint Paul – all the while arguing that equality of the sexes was grounded in Christianity and freedom of the individual. Such dissenting efforts provoked a critique of the sexual double standard and ultimately Ellen Key's revolt against the imperative of "chastity" for women only (as well as against the paid employment of mothers). Key's incitement of women to a liberated sexuality moved outside the carefully constructed Christian feminist framework; her influence spread throughout Europe and even to Asia. Hammar's findings show how feminisms in one particular national setting could evolve over time, but also insist on the importance of the conflicts and rifts that propelled the development of new and opposing feminist factions.

Padma Anagol's examination of indigenous feminism in India revises earlier scholarship by insisting on the agency of Indian (Brahmin, Muslim, and Parsi) women in the area around Bombay (now Mumbai) who converted to Christianity following the arrival of missionary groups from England and the United States. Anagol examines the conversions of Pandita Ramabai, Soonderbai Powar, and Krupabai Satthianadhan – based in a knowledgeable critique of Hinduism and its positional statements on the inferiority of women in comparison with a Christianity in which Christ was envisioned as neither male nor female. These women subsequently established schools for girls and developed a selective critique that allowed them to maintain a distance from European Christianity as well as to affirm their "Indianness."

Patricia Grimshaw takes the discussion of feminism and religion in a different direction by providing a comparative perspective on campaigns for women's political rights in New Zealand, Australia, and the US dependency of Hawai'i. Each of these locations had only recently been settled by whites who had to find working arrangements with already well-entrenched darker indigenous peoples. The World Women's Christian Temperance Union (WWCTU) played a significant part in advancing campaigns for women's suffrage in each location. New Zealand and the Australian colonies were the first to enfranchise women, though in the Australian case the vote came only to white women. Only in Hawai'i did the women's suffrage initiative fail completely. In all three locations the politics of gender were inseparable from those of race and imperial ambitions; efforts of white males to maintain their dominance became prominent in each location, yet in each case the outcome for women's vote differed.

Jacqueline R. de Vries compares "denominational feminist" activities by women and men within the Anglican and Roman Catholic churches in Britain in the early twentieth century, arguing that when feminist efforts in religious contexts are taken into account, the period after World War I (1914–1918) looks much less quiet than earlier historians had asserted. Both the Church League for Women's Suffrage (CLWS, Anglican, founded 1909) and the Catholic Women's Suffrage Society (CWSS, Roman Catholic, founded 1910) advocated women's suffrage, but devised very different strategies, due to their differing locations in British society. With a resurgence of religious feeling in British society following the war, these women found new possibilities for public action. Following the enfranchisement in 1918 of women over 30, Anglican feminists took steps in the 1920s to challenge the male-dominated hierarchy and doctrines of the Church of England, even campaigning for women in the priesthood. Their more beleaguered Roman Catholic counterparts also became more assertive, but did not take on the exclusively male hierarchy. In 1923 the latter's organization became the St. Joan's Social and Political Alliance, which subsequently expanded into a progressive international Catholic feminist network.

6

FEMINISM AND PROTESTANTISM IN NINETEENTH-CENTURY FRANCE

First encounters, 1830–1900

Florence Rochefort

From the Cartesian theologian/philosopher Poullain de la Barre's *Treatise on the Equality of the Sexes* in the seventeenth century to the *Jeunes Femmes* movement in the twentieth century, the contributions of Protestant women and men to the dynamics of women's emancipation in France are remarkable enough to allow the conclusion that privileged ties exist between feminism and reformed religion.[1] This fact, agreed on by specialists on Protestantism and feminism alike, has not yet led to a systematic interrogation of the French case.[2] The current rapprochement of the fields of women's history, social history, and sociology of religions encourages us to take up the challenge. But the exercise is by no means a simple one.

For one thing, the religious or free-thinking affiliations of individuals within the feminist movements are rarely made explicit. For another, religious affiliation is not inevitably the most determinant criterion either for defining individuals or for defining feminist strategies. There is not, so to speak, a Protestant feminism that labels itself thus, contrary to the Catholic current which calls itself "Christian feminism." The tight complicity, at the center of the movement for secularization (*laïcité*), of Protestantism, republicanism, and feminism produces a real syncretism among political, social, and moral options. Paradoxically, the adoption by today's Protestantism of the values of sexual equality, by insisting that openness to these values is intrinsic to Protestantism, tends to erase traces of the sociohistorical process which led to that adoption.[3] Thus, it seems fruitful to envisage the question in terms of encounters, influences, and mutual borrowing, rather than seeking right away to characterize a Protestant feminism. I have sought to bring to light several of these encounters by revisiting the routes taken by certain French feminists who have either emerged from Protestantism or who remained involved with it. The links between their religious convictions and their feminism, the passage of singular individual encounters, and then the collective encounter represented by the adhesion [to feminism] of Protestant women's philanthropy in 1900, have all attracted my attention.

Protestantism in France, understood not only in its confessional aspect but also as a culture and ethical phenomenon, has in fact participated in a process of womanly individuation that characterizes Western societies in general.[4] However, for the clarity of this discussion, we are interested in a more limited definition of feminism, not as a global sociological phenomenon, but as a specific current of French thought which, since the end of the Middle Ages, has been nourished in every epoch by various stimuli to respond to misogyny and to inequities of women's status. The concept of the equality of the sexes could already be found at the center of Christine de Pizan's thinking when she wrote *La Cité des Dames* in 1405.[5] It should be understood in the sense of an equivalence in value that allows women to claim serious respect as well as a serious education. This egalitarian current was strengthened in the course of the seventeenth century through the doctrines of natural law and, subsequently, during the French Revolution it burst forth as a collective expression in the field of politics. Its claims were formulated in terms of equality before the law, and thereafter emphasized the right of women to public instruction as well as to civil and political rights.[6] Facing a Catholic traditionalism that for many decades rejected both individualism and the principles of 1789, nineteenth-century feminism and Protestantism both participated in a sort of post-revolutionary modernity, of which a common denominator was a process of societal secularization. For Protestants, women and men alike, who engaged in the sphere of social action, as for the feminists, the inadequate instruction proposed for women, the refined, sociable role that was reserved for them by the upper classes, the exploitation of lower-class women in the labor force, and finally (in the second half of the nineteenth century) the denunciation of prostitution and the double moral standard, provided them with common meeting ground, common themes of criticism, and, not least, opportunities to meet.

On the other hand, neither Protestantism in its larger guise nor the republican "universalism" which it supported, could easily integrate the notion of equality of rights between the sexes. If Protestantism seemed initially more permeable by an egalitarian dynamic than Catholicism, it also generated a certain fundamentalism which radically opposed the emancipation of women. To encourage girls' education was one thing, to acknowledge consciousness of legal inequalities between the sexes – to see this relationship not as a product of either a divine or natural order, but as an injustice that must be remedied – was another matter. To break with the normative Christian doctrine on the relations between the sexes presupposed a questioning of the very principle of authority, a principle perceived as essential to the preservation of the God-given order. What is more, the endorsement of sexual equality, even of the most moderate sort, seemed highly suspect, even subversive to some; it evoked the pretended fury of the *tricoteuses* or the perceived immorality of "public women," both images that seemed profoundly offensive to the morality of upstanding Christians.[7] Thus, those who supported the ideal of sexual equality were only a minority, on the margins of their milieu, and sometimes they had completely broken with their original confessions (whether Calvinist/reformed or, more rarely Lutheran) in a context where dissidence was not rare, or the theological options were sometimes very opposed, and where one's approach to religion could become highly personal.[8] Eugénie Mouchon Niboyet and Jenny P. d'Héricourt, two nineteenth-century pioneer feminists of Protestant origin, provide contrasting examples of how feminist and religious options might intersect.

Eugénie Niboyet and Jenny P. d'Héricourt: singular encounters between feminism and Protestantism

For the women of 1830, Saint-Simonism offered an unprecedented opportunity to act in the framework of a novel and innovative religious movement. Eugénie Mouchon Niboyet (1796–1883), the granddaughter of a Genevan pastor, grew up in a liberal upper middle-class milieu in Lyon. She moved to Paris to enter the ranks of the Saint-Simonians.[9] There she discovered an exalting socialist and feminist doctrine and took charge of a popular education mission in two Paris *quartiers*. When the head of the movement, Prosper Enfantin, decided arbitrarily to evict women from the Saint-Simonian hierarchy, Eugénie was indignant: "It is by the mouth of a woman that the Saint-Simonian "word" should be, I believe, delivered and preached to the workers. To deny us this opportunity is to deny us Life. To provide individual propagandizing is no doubt important, but this does not suffice for my activity. I like to act on the masses because it is there that I feel all my power. I am an apostle! I have received much and I have much to give – and I beg you, leave me in my element!"[10] Thus we get not only a measure of her sense of betrayal but also of the importance of the priestly milieu of the Saint-Simonians. After her break with Enfantin, Eugénie never stopped her sacred ministry, which she prolonged through journalism, associational life, and political activity in the service of humanity and the cause of women, even as she earned her own living. She founded various publications with the intention of educating women, moralizing society and giving women of letters the possibility of self-expression in print.[11] Having renounced founding a new religion, she renewed her ties with the Protestants and affirmed her fidelity to the "law of Christ." The *Société de la morale chrétienne* exhibited a degree of openness and offered her a milieu that satisfied her continuing need for a social and religious apostolate. But it was as a prison reformer and not as a feminist that she found an echo.[12] Her thoughts about women, even when she particularly valorized the role of mothers in the family, never excited the same interest. The Protestant milieu became open to the woman question during debates over their education, but it was still completely impregnated by the imperious idea of womanly duty. It was not yet thinkable for them that women could aspire to the exercise of their rights in the name of ideals of happiness and individual liberty: they had only the right to duty. Even the idea of natural rights for women was repugnant to the nineteenth-century Protestant "ethos" which was based on the notion of "renouncement." The Protestant philanthropists applied their personal resources only to their engagement in this "ethic of devotion."[13]

Nevertheless, encouraged by the example of the English philanthropist Elisabeth Fry, who visited Paris in 1838, Eugénie Niboyet succeeded in mobilizing the women of the *Société de la morale chrétienne* on behalf of the women imprisoned in the Saint-Lazare prison.[14] Subsequently, the context of the Revolution of 1848 offered her another opportunity to express her feminist convictions, though in an entirely different way. Her positions became more radical, even favoring political equality for women. She created the first feminist daily newspaper *La Voix des femmes* as well as a women's club that earned her only hurtful caricatures and condemnations. In the terrible years that followed the failure of the Second Republic, she partially renounced her radicalism and fell back on demands that were more compatible with her engagement with the *Société de la morale chrétienne*: promoting education and valuation of women's role in the family. Her Christian faith continued to nurture her feminism: "As long as a woman is not in possession of herself, as long as she has no free will, she will remain beneath the mission that God has assigned her in the family," she affirmed.[15] Her egalitarian convictions also influenced her theological interpretations. In her last book, *Le Vrai livre des femmes* (1863), she boldly affirmed that God had created woman at least equal to, if not superior to man, because she came from Adam's rib [side] and not from the earth, and that she was the final work of God.[16] Such a feminist reading was not the prerogative of Protestants; Jeanne Deroin, another 1848 feminist with roots in Saint-Simonism, exhibited the same audacity. Romantic Christianity and the religiosity of utopian socialism had encouraged an entire generation. Conversely, in the heart of Catholicism, tolerance of such radical ideas was far more difficult to come by and led militant women to a radical rupture which Protestants did not find necessary.

The case of Eugénie Niboyet reveals one type of encounter between feminism and Protestantism whose plot can be delineated. Even when she distanced herself from Saint-Simonism, which offered an unparalleled syncretism between feminist, political, and religious utopias, it profoundly marked her. The diffusion of her feminist preoccupations in the revivalist Protestant milieu would not have been possible without the framework of philanthropic action influenced by the English mode. Finally, the Christian inspiration and religious dimension of her feminism caused her to moderate her demands but also led her to an audacious critical reading of the Bible.

Jenny P. d'Héricourt (1809–1875; the initial P. stood for her birth name, Poinsard) was also a feminist with origins in a Protestant milieu who belonged to the generation of 1848. Her interest in moral questions, her political formation in the circle of Étienne Cabet and her feminist engagement in 1848 show similarities with the itinerary of Eugénie Niboyet. Yet her own path was marked by a far more radical rupture with Christian doctrine. A *collaboratrice* at *La Voix des femmes* and co-founder of the *Société pour l'émancipation des femmes* in 1848, Jenny P. d'Héricourt came into her own during the Second Empire, in a spirit of reaction to the authoritarian regime of Napoleon III and the accompanying Catholic offensive. With her articles in the *Revue philosophique et religieuse* and in her work *La Femme affranchie* (1860), she intended to prove that woman had precisely the same rights as man.

Jenny's demonstration rested on a critique of men's writings of that time about women and on a denunciation of positivist and medical discourses that were ferociously anti-egalitarian.[17] The influence of rationalism provoked her rupture with utopian socialism as well as with Christianity. She recognized the theoretical contribution of the Saint-Simonians and even the intellectual debt that women owed them. It was with a truly Protestant solidarity that she felt in communion with the Saint-Simonians (who had been deprived of the possibility to live their faith) without, however, wanting to join them. She reproached Enfantin for not envisaging women's emancipation otherwise than through "free love" and the male-female couple and she argued, on the contrary, for a liberation through work and purity of morals that was focused far more on the woman as individual. Dissociating the cause of women from that of the proletariat, she gave the woman question a greater autonomy – a fundamental condition for the development of a movement that was specifically dedicated to emancipating women. Thus it was that she proposed to found a publication which would not "fly the flag of any social sect and which would eliminate political and religious questions as such."[18] This conceptualization is not without connection with her personal project to reject "the teachings of a dogma that is both worn out and retrograde." Her Lutheran father and her Calvinist mother, "a zealous Protestant who adhered to extremely strict morals," belonged to an "enlightened" milieu, but once Jenny became an adult, she did not find in Christianity either "the satisfaction of [her] religious needs" or the response to her egalitarian ideal.[19] In an article that she consecrated to Christianity and the woman question, she compared the ideas of Abbé Michon and of the revivalist pastor Adolphe Monod, concluding that Christianity "could not contribute, without being illogical and without self-destructing, to the liberty of woman."[20]

Penetrated by the anticlericalism of her time, Jenny P. d'Hericourt opposed revolutionary values to divine authority and the subordination of beings and more especially to the "divine right of the other sex" over woman. Distancing herself both from atheism and materialism, she aspired to "a more encompassing dogma that could accept both conscience and Reason," and she drew closer to the laic and spiritualist religion of Charles Fauvety, whom she called her "oldest friend." Not without humor, she evoked her "sacerdotal vocation" to preach truth, reason, and justice, despite her woman's garb.[21] Women ministers, whom she encountered in the course of her travels in the United States and to which she made admiring references in her articles in the periodical *Le Droit des femmes* (founded in Paris in April 1869 by Maria Deraismes and Léon Richer), fired her imagination. Marginalized and isolated toward the end of her life, Jenny P. d'Hericourt died in poverty and it was only thanks to Charles Fauvety that she was not totally cut off from Protestantism. In the obituary article Fauvety wrote about her, he made the point that a pastor who was "liberal among the most liberal"[22] spoke at her memorial service, after her spiritualist convictions had been acknowledged.

By deciding "to eliminate God from questions of Rights and Duties,"[23] Jenny P. d'Héricourt opened the way to a purely secularized reflection on the specific oppression of women. The republican philosopher Maria Deraismes (1828–1894) devoted herself to this mode of thinking, with a more Cartesian rigor than her predecessor, even as the first militant groups formed to organize for women's rights, primarily in Paris. Among the leading Protestants who joined these groups besides d'Héricourt (then living in Chicago) were Charles Fauvety, the Reclus brothers, and Caroline de Barrau. But it would be no more exact to speak of them as "Protestant feminists" than it would in the case of Eugénie Niboyet. Yet, as representatives of feminist and anticlerical radicalization coming from the dissident Protestant fringe, they appear as a constituent element of the laic republican current that favored sexual equality, in close proximity to the feminism of Maria Deraismes. Their religious dissidence permitted them to fully integrate the egalitarian dimension of feminism without restricting it either to the family or to philanthropic practice. Though still very much a minority, they were in any case less isolated in Protestantism than was Niboyet, and they formed the first necessary link to a larger coming-to-consciousness in a philanthropic Protestant milieu that was evolving rapidly.

The birth of social and philanthropic feminism

The years from 1870 to 1900 witnessed the multiplication of women's philanthropic initiatives. Serving as ambulance assistants and as caregivers for the wounded during the Franco-Prussian War of 1870 and the Paris Commune in 1871 proved to be determinant for those who later led the philanthropic and feminist associations. Many Protestants acquired during these events a caring experience of a new type, both solidarist and patriotic, which renewed the perception of social work they had inherited from the *Reveil* (the French Protestant revival). The journey of Élise de Pressensé (1826–1901) is, in this respect, quite typical. Already in 1865, in a letter to the young historian Gabriel Monod (1844–1912), she expressed a profound discomfort with purely charitable endeavors, which she recognized "as indispensible in our time of transition in which letting people die of hunger and cold out of respect for their dignity would be a poor result of our democratic sensibility." She made it clear that "I don't screw up my face while giving, like the gentlemen depicted by André Léo [Ed: in her novels], but nevertheless I feel sort of disgusted with myself – do you understand me?"[24] According to Monod, the religious crisis Élise was going through "was intimately linked to an intense, primordial need for social action, for devotion to suffering humanity."[25] Élise de Pressensé finally found an answer to her questioning through helping the wounded during the war of 1870 and the Paris Commune. The charity workroom (*ouvroir*) she founded in 1871, at first destined to support widows of the Communards, can be viewed as an extension of her wartime service.[26]

Julie Siegfried (1848–1922) likewise underscored the revelatory role for women played by the war: "Their rudimentary instruction, we must admit, the habit they had acquired of being silent in their families when discussions of a political or religious type broke out, the charity which was in that time the sole philanthropic preoccupation of well-off women, none of that prepared them to play a preponderant role during the war."[27] The rupture caused by the war was, for some, definitive. The charity workshop of Élise de Pressensé offered an innovative example of a workshop that encouraged women in distress to attain financial autonomy through paid work. Julie Siegfried, a delegate from this workshop to the first *Congrès des oeuvres et institutions féminines* of 1889, spoke "to those persons who understand how it is more charitable to assist people by offering work than by offering alms."

The more confessionally oriented charities also altered their practices. Henriette de Witt-Guizot (1829–1908), the daughter of the historian and former prime minister François Guizot, founded a shelter-workplace destined for women who had been freed from Saint-Lazare prison. The reforming spirit during the early Third Republic (1870s) and the influence of social Christianity encouraged her break with the more classical form of charity. A number of philanthropies focused henceforth on specific problems encountered by women and contributed to the evolution of French philanthropy toward social action.[28] This philanthropic vitality lent itself to an opening to the woman question but did not necessarily lead to a feminist positioning. Neither Élise de Pressensé nor Henriette de Witt-Guizot ever adventured onto the terrain of women's rights, but Marguerite de Witt-Schlumberger (1853–1924), Henriette's daughter, and Julie Siegfried, both of whom were engaged in philanthropy, became leaders of the women's suffrage movement. A generational factor may be at work here, but it does not by itself explain this formidable change. Nor is the passage from alms to the practice of mutual assistance sufficient to explain it. It was the contact with abolitionism – the campaign against government-sanctioned prostitution (the so-called "white slavery") and the traffic in women – that became determinant.

The impact of the movement founded in Geneva by the British crusader Josephine Butler in 1875 to challenge government-sanctioned prostitution was very considerable. Even though it did not obtain satisfactory results on French legislation in the short term, it nevertheless contributed to the development of a wholly new consciousness about the inequality of the sexes, especially in Protestant circles.[29] Émilie de Morsier (1843–1896), born in Switzerland and installed in France just before 1870, became very enthusiastic about Butler's abolitionist crusade and stimulated a new feminist current in France. Her liberal convictions drew her to the deputy Yves Guyot, with whom she organized the French branch of the abolitionist movement.[30] According to them, the registration [*encartement*] of prostitutes by the morals police blocked every possibility for these mostly young women to escape from their situation; the very fact that any woman could be arrested in the street on charges of soliciting constituted a very grave threat to their liberty, to morality, and to the rights of man.

Abolitionism provided the ideal terrain for the rendezvous of Protestant philanthropy and feminism. Indeed, the argumentation of Josephine Butler herself drew on a moral, religious, and egalitarian register. Militants from diverse backgrounds joined Butler's crusade. They learned to collaborate in political and philanthropic actions. In fact, the founding of a vigorous relationship with government agencies was not their sole mode of action. As of 1877, the *Union des amies de la jeune fille* proposed to protect girls against the white slave trade and prostitution by creating places for them to stay (*foyers d'accueil*) and placement bureaus to help them find safe employment.[31] The pastor Tommy Fallot (1844–1904), founder of social Christianity, was one of the first to understand – through abolitionism – the urgency of according to women the possibility of supporting themselves and obtaining civil rights. He inscribed this last point on his program when he founded the *Ligue pour le rélevèment de la moralité publique* and joined the *Ligue du droit des femmes* of Léon Richer. The positions of Swiss Protestant feminists such as Charles Secrétan comforted the partisans of social Christianity along the road to embracing the equality of the sexes. When in the 1890s Fallot's League began to privilege, almost exclusively, the struggle against pornography over abolition, the women militants who had been the most dedicated to the struggle for women's rights turned to other groups.[32]

At the side of Émilie de Morsier, Caroline de Barrau de Muratel (1828–1888) and Isabelle Bogelot (1838–1923) also played a provocative role in the philanthropic world and enabled the birth of a feminist philanthropic current. All three were atypical in this milieu, participating in the principal feminist associations and in their congresses. Both Morsier and Barrau came from Protestant families but each had developed a relationship with religion that was entirely personal – and dissident. Caroline de Barrau can be situated among the ultra liberals, "at a distance from the Churches," as Tommy Fallot put it, while Émilie de Morsier even became interested in exploring Buddism and esoteric religion.[33] Their marginality with respect to the Protestants in fact favored their contacts with liberal Catholics. Orphaned at a very young age, Isabelle Bogelot had been raised in a Catholic boarding school, then joined the family of the free-thinking Maria Deraismes, whose footsteps she followed. Bogelot appears to have become a fellow traveler with the Protestants (to use the expression of Jean Bauberot), given the company she kept, her philanthropic activity, her sober and exemplary conduct.[34] The *Oeuvre des libérées de Saint-Lazare* (a philanthropy dedicated to assisting women who were not incarcerated as prostitutes on their release from the Saint-Lazare prison), of which Bogelot was secretary, then director, offered her the occasion to participate in international feminist activities; she consolidated the first link between the American feminists and the French, by attending the 1888 founding conference of the International Council of Women, held in Washington, DC.

Each of these women is remembered as exhibiting an unusual devotion. The pastor Charles Wagner underscored the "great originality" and the "audacious kindness" of Émilie de Morsier who joined "the highest idealism to an energetic need for action." As for Caroline de Barrau, Tommy Fallot insisted she was a "secular saint" who pushed self-deprivation to the most extreme limit. The *Larousse Encyclopedia* (1896 edition) presented Isabelle Bogelot as animated by "an irrepressible need to serve."[35] Barrau shared the abolitionist and liberal convictions of her friend Émilie de Morsier, and both of them joined the *Association pour la défense des droits individuels* (Association for the Defense of Individual Rights). Already enthusiastic about the vital role of the woman educator in the 1850s, Barrau published several articles in the feminist *Almanac* of Jeanne Deroin. She edited two brochures and joined the first feminist group at the end of the Second Empire.[36] We do not know what stimulated her and her friends to join the *Oeuvre des libérées de Saint-Lazare*, which was founded in 1870 by Pauline de Grandpré, the niece of the Catholic prison chaplain, Abbé Michel. But once chosen as the *directrice* in 1882, Caroline de Barrau secularized the group and gave it a new thrust forward.[37] The corollary of this laicization was a revision in attitudes towards the liberated women prisoners and a still more critical attitude toward confessionally based charities. Émilie de Morsier took her cue from the British abolitionist Josephine Butler, whom she quoted to defend her point of view: "I don't like either Catholic or Protestant shelters as they are at present. I don't understand why these poor creatures – orphaned girls, single mothers, women pushed by misery to their last resources – should be judged as though they were guiltier than the rest of society. To invite them especially to declare themselves 'penitent' or 'repentant' is neither just nor reasonable."[38] Nevertheless, de Morsier remained a believer and found narrow anticlericalism insupportable: "On the ruins of religious clericalism, we are seeing sprout and grow a possibly even more dangerous scientific clericalism, which under the pretext of freeing us from prejudice, illusions, and ignorance, also offers us its own infallible catechism. This new clergy, it is true, doesn't burn heretics; it contents itself by declaring that every person who believes in an extraterrestial future or in the existence of divine laws is mentally unstable and even a pathological case."[39] Thus one can understand how the secular spirit of the English reformer could be a stimulus for her. For both Émilie de Morsier and Josephine Butler, a religious motivation provided the essential personal impetus – but a social reading of the condition of woman substituted for moral and religious criteria and insistence on a single moral standard for both sexes opposed a strict Christian moralism. Laicization did not signify a break with Christianity as an ideal and a belief, nor even a privatization of religious morality, because it is explicitly invoked as inspiration and a model. Morsier affirmed wanting to place the divine figure of Christ at the center of the problems raised by civil society and conceived of charity as a value. Her approach to Christian dogma was nevertheless both spiritualist and feminist. She advocated a symbolic reading of Biblical texts and the right of women to teach the religion as pastors and priests. This critical stance propelled Morsier, as it had earlier propelled Eugénie Niboyet and Jenny P. d'Héricourt, onto a terrain that was at once religious and social. Her religious convictions inspired her social vision, but "the social" itself was deconfessionalized and morality took on a universal dimension. The birth of social feminism is tightly linked to this mutation. The refusal to treat women prisoners or prostitutes as inherently guilty had everything to do with refusing to acknowledge Eve's guilt as well as the refusal of Dr. Cesaré Lombroso's notorious theories about the prostitute as "born criminal".[40]

Privileging a social reading of prostitution also favored exchanges with militant feminists who were focused more exclusively on women's access to civil and political equality. A similar concern with replacing the discourse on "woman" with a sociological perspective that insisted on the hardships of real life for "women" in the plural brought together these lay philanthropists and feminists. Their differences depended less on their acknowledgement of inequalities than on the way in which they should be addressed and combatted. In the prefatory remarks to the periodical *Revue de morale progressive* that Émilie de Morsier helped to found in 1887, the distinction between these two currents is very clear and the characteristics of a "social" feminism are laid out. The inequality of the sexes is clearly enunciated: "almost all the injustices that women complain of come from the fact that every question concerning the relations of the sexes has been, to date, resolved in the interest of men." But feminist action seemed limited to a very narrow field of action: "the very useful periodicals that concern themselves especially with women nevertheless restrict themselves to a strictly limited perspective, such as civil rights or political rights." This periodical intended to fill a gap, by consecrating itself to a study of the "social consequences" of these relations.[41] Its action would be primarily moral: "The law does not necessarily encompass the totality of justice: morality is the totality of justice." With regard to a feminism which attached itself to the sphere of law and emphasized working with parliamentary representatives – in this sense it can be called "political" – this socially oriented feminism thought it could resolve these inequalities through philanthropy and moral action. Thus, philanthropic and abolitionist action was viewed as an agent of moral transformation through its social impact, rather than by means of religious proselytizing.

Social feminism thus participated in the construction of an egalitarian laic morality, best symbolized – in the eyes of Émilie de Morsier – by the abolition of government-regulated prostitution.[42]

During the Universal Exposition of 1889 in Paris, social feminism established itself as a more direct competitor of political feminism by organizing its own congress. The organizers of the *Congrès International du droit des femmes*, Maria Deraismes and Léon Richer, found themselves at odds with the organizers of the *Congrès des oeuvres et institutions féminines*, notably its prime mover Émilie de Morsier, on two major points: (1) their refusal of government support and control (*tutelle*) and in particular the patronage of former prime minister (and advocate of protective legislation) Jules Simon, and (2) their opposition, as liberals, to the protectionist (and discriminatory) law that sought to ban night work for women, recently passed by the Chamber of Deputies. For her part, Émilie de Morsier, even though she acknowledged the importance of women's civil rights, had for her principal objective recognition of the social role of secular philanthropy and of all the religious confessions. She had been inspired by the Americans who organized the 1888 congress in Washington (where the International Council of Women had been founded) by bringing together associations that ranged from what the French called *féminines* to *féministes*.[43] At a moment in which the republican leadership was thinking of leaning on the philanthropic sector to resolve the social question, and where the first parliamentary projects for married women's civil rights were being discussed, de Morsier's attempt to step forth as potential partner became a critical move.[44]

Agreeing with the protectionist policies, this philanthropic congress contributed to sketching out a form of social citizenship that opened the way to the acquisition of social rights for women without having to necessarily concern itself with civil and political citizenship. The coming together of secularists, Jews, Catholics, and Protestants in France and from other countries was impressive. The Catholic delegates, however, did not receive permission from the archbishop to attend the congress, which he judged too Anglo-Protestant; he only allowed them to file written reports. In contrast, the links between secularists and "confessionals" in the Protestant camp grew tighter, despite the latters' hesitation about the idea of women's rights coupled with their concerns to obtain greater public visibility for their actions. At the end of the congress, Sarah Monod (1836–1912), co-director of the deaconesses of Reuilly and a supporter of the abolitionist campaign decided to bring together the philanthropic and Christian good works (*oeuvres*).[45] She thus founded the so-called *Conférence de Versailles* (Conference at Versailles) which brought together, at annual meetings from 1891 on, the most important names in Protestant women's philanthropy – including Julie Siegfried and Mme Henri Mallet. In an ecumenical spirit, Émilie de Morsier introduced Sunday prayer as a sign of coming together, after having enthusiastically attended a congress on religions in Chicago. The dialogue between traditionalist philanthropic women and feminist philanthropists quickly bore fruit. Their interests converged principally on matters such as laic morality, denunciation of the double moral standard, the education of girls, and the economic situation of women. Their analyses of the causes may have differed, but their proposed solutions converged: to educate girls according to the modern methods of coeducation; to insist on financial autonomy for working (employed) women; to get rid of government regulation of prostitution; and to moralize society. Between 1889 and 1900, the radicalization of French women's philanthropy is absolutely remarkable – and is documented in the pages of their publication *La Femme*. The success of the feminist movement, whose moderate wing was becoming increasingly important, the growing interest in the "woman question" and the development of Solidarist doctrines (among Republican men), and finally Dreyfusism, all played their parts. Following the deaths of Émilie de Morsier and Caroline de Barrau, others – Isabelle Bogelot, Maria Martin, and Ghénia de Sainte-Croix (known after her marriage in May 1900 as Madame Avril de Sainte-Croix) – carried out the work of explanation and diffusion of feminism in philanthropic circles. By the time of the second *Congrès des oeuvres et institutions féminines* in 1900, adhesion to the program of juridical reform had been agreed on, without neglecting the moral and social aspects; only the question of political rights was deliberately avoided.[46] The differences between secularists and "confessionals," like those between social feminism and political feminism, were in part blurred. Still, the philanthropic women made a point of distinguishing themselves by their moderation and willingly stigmatized the "exaggerations" and "extravagances" of more radical feminists. The Americans, who were in a hurry to establish a French branch of the International Council of Women, counted on the Protestant women to take the initiative. Thus, the foundation of the *Conseil national des femmes françaises* (CNFF; National Council of French Women) in 1901 rested on a subtle alliance between social and political feminists. In all events, the choice of Sarah Monod as its first president and the numerical importance of the philanthropic women gave the CNFF a moderate character and a Protestant tinge that everyone was quite aware of.

With the founding of the CNFF, the encounter between feminism and Protestantism found its first manifestation by giving the philanthropic and social feminists an unprecedented means of expression. The women who headed its various sections (morality, legislative, economic, education, suffrage, sciences/arts/letters, and peace) became real experts on the condition of women and addressed themselves directly to the government to present their reforms. Once the section on suffrage was created in 1906, the CNFF program for legal reform became identical to that of the greater part of the feminist movement. If the envisioned field for action had become significantly larger, the egalitarian approach was always nourished by experience in the social sphere. The references to morality, maternal and feminine qualities – that is to say, women's differences from men – as grounds for women's inclusion and emancipation became even more dominant. For some, the suffrage battle even became an absolute priority. Marguerite de Witt-Schlumberger consecrated herself to this goal in the bosom of the *Union française pour le suffrage des femmes* (UFSF, founded in 1909) and explained her commitment thus: "the men don't give us either the laws or the support necessary to make our social work effective; we are spending our strength and our money without getting adequate results. We will only obtain the reforms we are seeking when we have the vote, and they will be forced to take account of our ideas."[47] The CNFF, the fruit of those who insisted on the passage from philanthropy to social action, thus facilitated the next transition from social action to political action. Julie Siegfried, who succeeded Sarah Monod as president, understood that her own itinerary could serve as an example when she declared: "Let them first come work with us, and philanthropy will lead them to social action, and social action to the vote. The National Council of French Women is a normal school (teacher-training school) one must pass through to teach those women who are not feminists to become feminists."[48] The rallying of the *haute bourgeoisie protestante* (upper-class Protestants) and the confessional philanthropic circles offered feminism a new opportunity, constituting a more specific current that was strongly marked by Protestantism. Faced with the Third Republic's obstinate resistance to women's political rights as well as to a Catholic feminism which opposed even civil equality, the Protestant feminists became increasingly radical. They even implanted an oppositional current at the heart of the Protestant congregations by calling for the adoption of the principle of sexual equality in the Presbyterian councils and pressing for access of women to the pastorate. Their feminism remained marked, however, by a moral strictness that was more inflexible than that of Émilie de Morsier, who was very attached to the notion of liberty. It was as much their exacerbated sense of duty and denial, along with their ideal of moral purity and the family, as the progress of nationalist and familialist currents in the heart of Protestantism that rendered them entirely deaf to new problems of womanly identity, and specifically to the idea of "free maternity." Rights and duties were finally reconciled but in a narrow and constraining conception of liberty and sexuality. Thus this Protestant feminist current, at the very moment where it seemed to delineate itself became characterized, like Protestantism itself, by a tension between liberty and intransigence.[49] Taking account of these new questionings would mark yet a further step in the history of feminism and Protestantism in France where, once again, the passage of contributions by several pioneers, like those of Bertie Albrecht (1893–1943), and Anglo-American influence would allow development of a more collective consciousness like that of the *Jeunes Femmes* movement.[50]

The memory of these encounters between feminism and Protestantism in France has scarcely been transmitted. Today it merits revitalization through contact with women's history. Our time of social and humanitarian crisis lends itself to the rediscovery of the ingeniousness of those who not only participated in the invention of social action but also in the acquisition of equal rights for women. Their coming to feminist consciousness can be understood as part of a process of rupture. This sometimes papers over personal crises which have not always left traces. The discovery of inequality by these women was greatly facilitated early on by the necessity of self-support through the exercise of a profession. This was certainly true for Eugénie Niboyet and Jenny P. d'Héricourt. It might have been the fruit of a *crise de conscience* like that experienced by Élise de Pressensé. The historian Anne-Marie Käppeli has underscored the importance of loss and mourning as a factor that precipitated the trajectories of Josephine Butler and Émilie de Morsier. Whatever the causes, the determining factor seems to have been a formidable need to act, to be useful, and to consecrate one's life to a cause that fell outside the strict limits of traditional Christian charity.

This need for engagement animated a number of women who had been suffocating in those domestic spaces in which habit and convention had confined them; they were treated as civil and political minors who had few outlets in the public realm. The concurrent vitality of the women's Catholic orders is also a tell-tale sign.[51] But despite their social effectiveness, the women in these orders were silenced by the apostolic requirements of the Catholic reconquest which made any opening to ideas of women's emancipation extremely difficult.[52] In contrast, the secular character of Protestantism in France, its permeability to Anglo-American influences and its investment in the social sphere allowed women who engaged in good works to participate outside the strictly religious domain and to initiate themselves in the world of reformist ideas.[53] Their way of reconciling their various commitments is far more novel than the caricature that was subsequently circulated about the "lady bountiful" (*dame patronesse*), or the "bourgeois feminist." These women breathed a new egalitarian dimension into French Protestantism, even as they themselves were influenced by the examples from other Protestant countries. Protestantism thus exhibited its capacity to capture and nourish a certain type of modernity by its moral approach to the social question. The limits of its moral intransigence were counterbalanced by its capacity to renew itself and to absorb egalitarian impulses into its own mode of functioning.

77

7

FROM FREDRIKA BREMER TO ELLEN KEY

Calling, gender and the emancipation debate in Sweden, *c.* 1830–1900

Inger Hammar

Fredrika Bremer (1801–1865) was the first woman in Sweden to challenge publicly the religious framework that since the Reformation had determined the extent of women's calling. She made her debut at the age of twenty-seven with an anonymous work about family life in the Swedish upper classes. With books such as The Neighbours (*Grannarne*), The Home: or Family Cares and Family Joys (*Hemmet*), and Homes of the New World: Impressions of America I–II (*Hemmen i den nya verlden*), she became one of the period's most successful authors. Her work was translated into twelve languages and during her own lifetime reached a wide audience both in Europe and the United States, yet her books are now almost completely forgotten. Instead, successive generations have remembered her as the outstanding figure of Swedish feminism.

The conviction that Christianity bore within it the source of all emancipation impelled Fredrika Bremer to use theological arguments when she joined the debate on the liberation of women. In a secularized understanding of reality, spiritual reality is seen as an abstract construction in the minds of those who hold religious beliefs. A person whose approach to existence is grounded in the absence of a godly dimension is unlikely to see life in terms of living out a calling. Here a human being is understood as a biological being who alone creates the framework that determines the course of his or her life. Bremer's understanding of the world was of an entirely different nature. For her, Christianity was the guarantee of the emancipation of women: it was the patriarchal interpretation of the Biblical account of Creation that had suppressed its liberating message down the ages, denying expression to the freedom that was the cornerstone of Christianity. While remaining loyal to her Lutheran heritage, her Christian world view had a liberal bent. With her demand for a new view of women's vocations, she was to find herself in opposition to the Lutheran state's orthodox gender ideology.

This article will argue that by exposing the religious framework, we can reach the beliefs that were the basis of the pioneering generation's engagement. The analysis centres on the importance of the debate over intellectual education and the neutralization of misogynist norms as a necessary precondition for the emancipation of women.

The religious framework

Ever since the Reformation, the established Lutheran churches of all the Nordic countries had had an unassailable position as the representatives of the states' ideological views.[1]

The religious structure was deeply resistant to ideas that conflicted with the Scriptural authority that was the basis for its tenets. Naturally enough, a reform movement that threatened to destroy the Biblically inspired gender ideology of nineteenth-century Sweden met with fierce opposition from the leading members of the community who saw such reform as a crime against the God-given order of the Creation.[2]

Martin Luther's notion of society can only be understood once it is realized that it was an expression of an agrarian world picture; his departure point was a static peasant community, and in his ideal of the state, the terms *ecclesia* (church), *politia* (state), and *oeconomia* (household) were fundamental principles.[3] From cradle to grave, the individual was incorporated into a patriarchal structure where the household was both the essence and the heart of the state. Both married and single women were expected to live out their days in a home sphere that under ideal conditions provided them with both work and livelihood. The immense social changes in nineteenth-century Sweden undermined the household economy, and in the industrial society that emerged, individuals were left to fend for themselves. From the gender perspective, this meant that many women had difficulties in supporting themselves, which made for ideological and financial confusion amongst the leading members of society. A reform movement intent on broadening the range of activities open to women began to take shape.

It was against this background that the early feminists entered into the social debate.[4] To understand the objections to the emancipatory reforms that were raised by society in general, it is necessary to delve deeper into the period when the Lutheran Church still held sway as the guarantee of the state's ideological view. At its core lay Luther's views on calling.

With his particular construction of gender, Luther had destroyed the limited autonomy enjoyed by women in the religious orders of the medieval Church.[5] In his theology, the Church's thinking on celibacy conflicted with the correct interpretation of human calling. It was thus in polemic against the Roman Catholic Church's exclusive view of celibacy that Luther first formulated his teaching on calling.[6] The idea that a certain way of life should be associated with a truly Christian life was dismissed by Luther, and instead of seeing cloistered life as a higher calling, he was to anchor the ideal of vocation in everyday life.[7] It was here that each and every person, regardless of gender or social standing, would endeavour to serve God and his fellow man.

An underlying supposition in Luther's theology is that God wages his war against evil through two forms of dominion: the spiritual and the worldly. With spiritual dominion God works through the Word, and the goal is man's spiritual well-being. In worldly dominion God works through the Sword, the powers that be, and the outer ordering of society; here the goal is man's earthly well-being. Luther's theology was theocratic – as was the medieval theology that informed his beliefs – and for him both spiritual and worldly dominion was subordinate to God's Creation; the deeds of human beings belong in the worldly sphere, while God exercises spiritual and worldly dominion over one and the same person.[8] The worldly rulers represent God on earth, and the Christian therefore owes obedience to his rulers because they are placed there to see to justice done and to maintain the common weal. Through care for his inferiors and obedience to his superiors, a man lives out his calling. Work belongs to the basic condition for human existence and should be seen by the Christian as inherently good because it benefits his fellow human being and contributes to the creation of a just society.[9] Vocation was not limited to special professions – as was often later the case – such as priest, doctor, or nurse; it also embraced the biological ordering of father and mother, son and daughter. To be a father or mother, husband or wife, was thus a vocation.

For Luther, marriage was essential for the structure of society, and he saw parenthood as a high calling. Life in the home, relationships between parents and children; a life of work, relationships between employer and employee: all these were callings.[10] Woman's active calling he assigned to *oeconomia*.[11] There she should live out her calling, under the man's sovereignty, as spouse, mother, daughter, sister, or servant. In *ecclesia* and *politia* she should exercise her influence through the man.

In societies with an outspoken religious understanding of reality, theology rests upon one or more sources that are given a godlike authority. Within Christianity it is the Bible that embodies this authority. Certain Biblical passages give expression to a misogynist gender ordering, while in others one finds the equality of men and women.[12] In the first verses of Genesis the issue of the equality of the sexes is addressed: "So God created man in his own image, in the image of God created he him; male and female created he them."[13] In the attempt to interpret this passage, the fact that humanity had two genders was to become a dilemma for theologians. Were both woman and man created in God's image?[14] The equation was further complicated by the second chapter of Genesis, which gives a broader and somewhat different version of the Creation. Here God, moved by man's loneliness, decides to create "an help meet for him."[15] The creation of woman becomes a secondary event, in which the existence of the man's body was the condition for her coming into being, for according to this passage the woman was created "of the rib" that in turn was taken "from man."[16] The Bible's explicitness about woman's origins in God's surgical procedure, where the man's body was the raw material, paved the way for the idea that woman was man's appendage. Her God-given duty – to be a helpmeet for the man – also fuelled the notion of woman as a dependent being whom the man to all intents and purposes had at his disposal.

However, it was above all the Creation myth's account of woman as man's temptation and fall that gave legitimacy to her subordination. It was Eve who had led Adam astray, making him disobedient to God and spoiling God's original intent with humankind. Retribution was not far behind. For the man it was his fate to work in "the sweat of thy face," while the woman faced the punishment of "in sorrow" giving birth to her children, to be subordinate to her husband, and to let him be her master.[17] The construction of woman as disobedient and sinful naturally affected the Christian view of humankind. For the women who fought for emancipation while retaining a Christian world view, it was to be of greatest significance how they understood their own tradition's interpretation of humankind as God's image, or *imago Dei*.[18]

For Luther, those passages of the Bible that speak of God's punishment of humankind after the Fall served as a principle in the interpretation of the mutual relationship between man and woman. The ancestress of all women, Eve, had in listening to the serpent defied God's commandment. The chaos she caused in Creation doomed her to subordination for ever more.[19] Her meagre intellect was her downfall: "Yet she did not suspect that the Devil could be there, and there lay her weakness and short-sightedness. Eve was not as wise as Adam."[20] Her intellectual feebleness was for Luther the reason that the man was assigned ultimate responsibility, even over the household. Women, said Luther, certainly could speak "as mistresses" when talking of household concerns, but it was very different when they expressed themselves on matters of state. He wrote that it was not so much that they lacked the words, but rather that their speech was "overwhelmingly childish, muddle-headed, and confused," and he went on to lay down that "woman is created for house-keeping, the man for affairs of state, worldly rule, war, and legal matters, to administer and conduct them."[21]

Women's only opportunity to operate openly in a public context was to take on the role of spokesperson, and to appear as the bearer of a holy message. In both the Biblical and the Christian traditions, there are examples of women responding to just such a call.[22] It was essential, however, that the woman did not use her role as a spokesperson to win honour for herself. Her honour was instead indissolubly bound up with her role in the private sphere, while man – through his actions in the public sphere – was expected to win the honour that was enjoined of him by his role as *pater familias*. The role as spokesperson was reserved for only a few, however, and in the main, woman was expected to exert her influence through her calling as spouse, mother, and housewife. The principle of human equality before God may have been indisputable in Lutheran ideology, but as a result of the belief in the idea of the three estates, each person was allocated a determined position from which to function in society, and which no one could question.

Luther's emphasis on motherhood became a stumbling block for those spokesmen of the religious discourse who, from the middle of the nineteenth century, had to address the delicate issue of how an unmarried woman's vocation should be defined. For Luther, femininity was constituted in motherhood; the origins of woman's God-given calling lay in childbirth. Luther had in fact not ascribed to woman any other calling than the one for which her body was constituted – the bearing of children.[23] However, motherhood was dependent on marriage, and during the nineteenth century this was not an avenue open to all because of the period's demographic imbalance, with an excess of women and lack of men.

When during the nineteenth century calls to broaden the range of women's activities were heard, a conflict developed that can be traced back to the Lutheran idea that vocation gave powerful expression to a complementary view of humankind.[24] For Luther, man and woman had been assigned roles at the Creation, and it was man, not woman, who should appear in the role of *persona publica*. Upsetting this order was seen by the orthodox as a revolt against the division of roles between man and woman that had been laid down by God at the Creation.

Women's roles transformed

In nineteenth-century bourgeois society, the "public man" was a highly respected person. The role of *persona publica* gave men the freedom to move without hindrance in the public sphere. The woman's sphere, on the other hand, was ringed about with restrictions. Admittedly some women could maintain their property independently or work for a living – if the practice of their profession required it – in the public sphere. As authors, individual women could under certain conditions engage publicly in debate. Yet women lacked fundamental political rights, and for the majority it was still the case that the suspicion of sexual impropriety fell on them if they entered public life.[25] The 'public woman' could be interpreted as tantamount to a prostitute or fallen woman. Public life as a concept was thus deeply gendered in nineteenth-century Swedish society, and there was a firm belief that morality and virtue would be harmed if women gained entry.

Society in this period was particularly subject to the economic strains caused by social distress. One early attempt to solve the problems that arose from the industrialization process was to bring together individuals to find a way that made it possible, within the framework of vocation, to help the needy. Since those on the orthodox side of the fence feared an undermining of public morality if even respectable women entered public life, the issue was not uncontroversial. They even feared that women would prioritize philanthropy at the expense of their roles as spouse, mother, and housewife. Naturally, they also came to reflect on whether female philanthropy bordered on the role of *persona publica*.[26] As it was, the need for volunteers in the struggle against social misery came gradually to legitimize women's emergence into "philanthropic public life."[27]

It should come as no surprise that it was in the liberal camp that the leading advocates of emancipatory reform were to be found, since it was here that the belief that the freedom Christianity proclaimed down the ages should apply to both men and women was strongest. Amongst the orthodox of Sweden's established Church, however, the women's demand for emancipation – in the meaning of freedom and liberation – was seen as extremely controversial because the term was already central to Christian doctrine. In Christian dogma, freedom had been won once and for all time by Christ's sacrifice. To claim that a liberation specific to women was necessary thus appeared to question this dogma.

A contributory cause for the resistance was the fact that the demand for women's liberation had originally been raised by the authors and philosophers of the Enlightenment, who had linked it to the ideas of humankind's equal worth then current.[28] The Enlightenment philosophers' sceptical view of the metaphysical dimensions of existence had impelled Christian interpretation into rationalist courses during the later eighteenth and early nineteenth century. During the nineteenth century, the Swedish Church distanced itself from ideas that originated in the Enlightenment's notion of natural rights because they challenged the Christian understanding of freedom.[29] For those women who demanded freedom for their sex, it was necessary to use other arguments than those that had emanated from the leading ideas of the Enlightenment.

On their side in the fight for liberation, the feminists had the liberalism that from the middle of the nineteenth century permeated all levels and areas of society. At the core of liberal thought was the status of the individual personality, and it was apparent to its adherents that it was a contradiction not to grant women status as individuals. Out of liberalism's notion of the independent nature of every human being grew a discussion about women's status in society.[30]

Liberalism had a tremendous influence on the religious thought of the period.[31] As early as 1841, the liberal newspaper magnate Lars Johan Hierta published a translated compilation of the German David Friedrich Strauss' controversial book, *Das Leben Jesu kritisch bearbeitet*, a work that sought to give a mythological explanation for Bible stories.[32] When it was first published, there was consternation in theological circles. *Das Leben Jesu* was seen as the most dangerous attack on Christianity and the Church to date, and in Sweden it became the target of immediate challenges under the Press Law.[33] Behind this law lay without doubt the leaders of the Church of Sweden, who saw Hierta's liberal line in the newspaper *Aftonbladet* as a threat to pure doctrine. The altercation over Strauss' book soon subsided, but in the long run it was to be of great significance in the religious debates in Sweden that were to follow.

In their struggle against scripturally literal views of the Bible, the spokesmen of religious liberalism thus encountered a great deal of resistance. The Saviour of the religious liberals was depicted above all as the Son of Man, and in their Christology the emphasis was placed on the human rather than on the godly nature of Christ. The orthodox reacted violently, and every attempt to interpret the Bible as a manifestation of its historical context was denounced as an attempt to undermine the Bible's standing. The circle of women who, while retaining their Christian world view, publicly argued for the emancipation of women could therefore draw small comfort from those who maintained that the Bible should be interpreted literally. Too many passages lent support to the idea that woman should take a role subordinate to man.

Fredrika Bremer – foremost in the Swedish women's movement

It was Fredrika Bremer who through her political writings gave women a voice in society, and it was without a doubt her engagement that was to carry the emancipation debate to a much wider audience.[34] Early in life she distanced herself from the idea that she should take on motherhood. She was certain that this biological vocation was not to be hers.

Fredrika Bremer herself depicted her childhood as a gloomy one. According to a memoir edited by an elder sister, the young Fredrika was seen by the rest of the family as the odd one out.[35] Desperate to gain attention and appreciation, she constantly behaved in such a manner as to draw down on herself the displeasure of her elders and peers. She was a child whose passionate thirst for knowledge gave offence to adults; when preparing for her confirmation, the priest found her repeated questions irritating in the extreme, not least because he held the view that it was everyone's duty to "believe blindly all that one cannot understand, and otherwise to try to live according to Christ's holy teaching."[36] He believed her questioning to be the expression of an obstinate child's need for self-assertion, and his hostile attitude caused the young girl confusion and bitterness. Long after, Bremer underlined the suffering that the intolerance of her surroundings towards her "questing, questioning" mind had caused her in her youth.[37] Her father's capricious moods and her mother's eccentric ideas about child-rearing – that children should be kept ignorant of the world's evils, should learn only what she allowed, and should eat as little as possible – poisoned their children's existence. Discipline was hard, and any departure from convention resulted in punishment. Their social life was limited, and only during the summers – when the family stayed in the country – were the Bremer children able to enjoy a degree of freedom playing in the forests and fields. Bremer herself recorded that she contemplated suicide from an early age, and that for the whole of her youth she found life empty and meaningless.[38]

There is strong evidence that it was following her father's death, and her release from his patriarchal control, that Bremer threw herself into writing and gained a zest for life. The speed of her rise to popularity was spectacular, and almost overnight she became a literary celebrity both at home and abroad. Success spurred her on, and she found her writing so satisfying that she decided to dedicate her life to her pen.[39] Despite receiving several offers of marriage, she remained convinced that her vocation was not one of spouse, mother, and housewife; she was to be an author, and she had every intention of standing out as a "freethinker."[40]

In theological terms, Fredrika Bremer was fundamentally a rationalist.[41] In her view it was possible for humankind to achieve a religious outlook by means of understanding. In her search as an adult for a valid argument for a Christian understanding of life, she received guidance from the theologian Per Johan Böklin. In an intensive correspondence they explored the burning issues of the day, and together studied both classical and new theology. For Bremer, freedom of thought was the precondition of personal belief, and her Christian understanding showed an increasingly liberal stamp. "Christ is the first originator of true liberalism," she declared in 1839, and several years later she felt sufficiently bold to set her theological reflections down in print.[42]

In her publication *Morgon-väckter* Bremer threw herself enthusiastically into the theological debate, and commented in detail on a Swedish compilation of Strauss' thesis, an act that was to draw criticism from those who in Strauss saw an enemy of Christianity.[43] According to her critics, she did not sufficiently dissociate herself from Strauss, and she found herself accused of standing "on the same ground and basis as the one whom she has chosen as opponent."[44]

The fact that men held sway within the theological canon obscured the feminist reflections on theological issues that had been taken up by Bremer in *Morgon-väckter*. In general her work was seen as an anomaly that only served to bring confusion in the debate. The positive comments that *Morgon-väckter* attracted centred on her enthusiasm for the cause rather than her theological stringency.[45] The time was not yet ripe for the entry of a female interpretation into the theological debate. It would seem likely that her sudden launch into the theological debate stemmed from her eagerness to undermine the Church of Sweden's literalist view of the Bible. By following an interpretation of the Bible that was less literal, one could step around individual passages that spoke of female subordination, which brought with it opportunity to question the construction of gender that formed the basis for views on vocation.[46]

Fredrika Bremer believed that society had circumscribed women's calling by giving priority to the wifely and maternal roles, leaving them with a severely limited range of action which in the end was to the detriment of both women and society: "There are any number of books written to shape woman into good wife and mother, but hardly any to shape her into a good human being and citizen in all walks of life, and independent of marriage," she complained on one occasion.[47] For her such a view belonged to the past, and she lived in the hope that a new way of thinking about women's calling was at hand. Instead of "living for the family, only for the delightful, the restricted, and so on," a woman should be able to live "as a human being, as a citizen of God's kingdom, and as citizen of an earthly society," she argued.[48]

Her attitudes were the result of the period's liberal trends, while at the same time she was firmly anchored in a Christian world view. This conjunction was unproblematic for her because she recognized that the origins of the liberal ideal of human freedom were to be found in Christianity. In a letter to Hierta, the leading liberal of the day in Sweden, she wrote that "those teachings on freedom and universal citizenship that are now at work amongst the people are derived from the teaching first heard in Christianity of humankind's equality before God."[49] A few years before, in a letter to a good friend she had declared that Christianity was "a fairly strong proclamation from on high of woman's equality in right and worth with man, and without which our sex would still languish in its heathen infancy."[50]

The demand for equality for both women and men was for Bremer derived from a Christian world view. Without its liberating message, humankind would still be "in its heathen infancy." She believed that the liberalism of her day was the direct consequence of the comprehension of something that had been hidden from earlier generations; that the freedom of the individual had existed from the moment of Creation. Through continuous evolution, mankind had been granted an ever greater consciousness that freedom and citizenship were due to all. In Bremer's eyes, this meant that the roles that society traditionally accorded to women were now doomed. In future, women's "human and social value" must be stressed far more.[51] As for women themselves, they should view life "from the Christian citizenness' viewpoint." By drawing on the "individual powers" that women possessed, society would be imbued with "the feeling for the holiness, the sense of beauty, the maternal, the caring."[52] As a first step, Bremer recommended philanthropy for the unmarried women of a society. She refused to accept an interpretation of vocation that focused on the wifely and maternal role to such an extent that it became an obstacle to single women; if women would only give themselves to their calling as "the handmaids of the Lord," then "the majority of women in the world, who now scare the timid, will show themselves blessed, and as clay in God the Father's hands to further his kingdom," she wrote.[53]

The unmarried woman's vocation was to tend to the most deprived: "The children, the fallen and imprisoned, the old and unhappy."[54] It was amongst society's failures that the bourgeois class' over-abundant women should find work.[55] The associations that were founded in the middle of the 1850s to organize prison and hostel visits, however, met great resistance according to Bremer, and she also had to admit that there was only a handful who were prepared to take on philanthropic work. Despite this, she saw it as having a certain future. Her lifetime ambition now became to raise and strengthen the consciousness of her "own sex of their calling and work in society."[56]

Gradually Bremer was to arrive at a more radical form of emancipation. By the middle of the nineteenth century she believed it was high time for fresh thought on the sexes' God-given equality, and for women to emerge as social beings. The dilemma was that the Lutheran context did not allow women to appear in the role of *persona publica*. At this point Bremer was at the peak of her writing powers. Her books were known all over the world, and she was immensely popular. During a visit to the United States in 1848–51 she was fêted by the public as a celebrity, and her letterbook from this journey met with great attention, if not all of it positive.[57] Her radical message was fuelled by her stay in the United States, and to drive home the importance of women's admittance to public life she was now willing to sacrifice the fame she had achieved as an author: "I am writing a book that will probably make me more enemies than friends," she wrote in 1855 to a friend. The book in question was "a serious and at times sharp protest" against the narrow-minded and unjust manner in which women in the Nordic countries were treated.[58] She now chose to appear in the role of spokeswoman for feminism, a task bestowed on her by a higher power; all she had to do was obey if she wanted to be true to her calling. "I feel that it is a work which my father in heaven has given me to do," she confided to an English friend as the book reached the public.[59]

When it was published in 1856; *Hertha* was greeted by violent objections.[60] The most severe criticism came from those who upheld Luther's gender construction, and indeed one of Bremer's adversaries snorted that the novel gave expression to social and religious blasphemy.[61] The principal offence against probity was the moment when the novel's heroine is so indecent as to dress a cut on a young man's knee; the author clearly contributed to the undermining of public decency. Bremer never regretted her decision to publish her controversial novel, however, and towards the end of her life she revelled in her courage in having freed herself from "centuries-old swaddling bands" by publishing this book, even though it risked sacrificing her popularity as a writer.[62] She never gave up her attempt to encourage a new view of women, nor the conviction that Christ had sanctioned "women's emancipation" which gave her such a sense of purpose: "I go sometimes whole days with a peaceful joy in my soul over our Saviour's communion with woman in the Gospel, and hers with him."[63]

Bremer's opinion of the forces who opposed the emancipation of women, and held subordination to be a Biblical guiding principle, was critical in the extreme. After a journey to the Middle East late in life, she expressed her dismay at the decadence that she saw as the result of polygamy and the harem. She believed all the societies that allowed polygamy and the harem to be in disarray because of their humiliating view of women.[64] As a result of the manner in which the patriarchal system renounced the New Testament's message of equality to give priority to the Old Testament's message of subordination, then age-old repression of women had been fuelled by the Church.[65] Even if the situation for Western women was different from that of the enslaved women of the Middle East, she recognized that it was still far from satisfactory.

To realize a good society, morality had to be improved. When it came to sexuality, Bremer acknowledged that it was God-given, and thus inevitable, but in order that it did not become the ruination of humankind, it should be ennobled with spirituality. Thus it was essential that man accord the same importance to purity that woman had down the ages. For as long as woman had been seen as the sexual being of the two, every society had wallowed in decadence and degeneration. Bremer bemoaned the fact that the idea of subordination had gained a toehold in the New Testament through Paul, and she had no time for the "Pauline, but not Christian, phrase, 'Let your women keep silence in the churches'."[66]

Throughout her life Bremer was true to her Lutheran upbringing, and yet despite this, she was to arrive at a bitter judgement on Luther himself and more particularly the theology that he had propagated.[67] She was to find no solace in the sectarian movements of the day because of their intolerance and literal reading of the Bible. She was forced to conclude that her own age stood far from the Reformation's liberating view of the Bible: "For the majority of Bible readers the Word is perhaps far more a bond than a release for their spirit. The other Luther, the true interpreter of the Bible, the liberator – when will he come?" she wrote wearily on one occasion to a friend and confidant.[68] In old age, she was still to draw strength and power from Luther's hymn *Ein feste Burg ist unser Gott*.[69] The thing she treasured most in Luther was his demand for freedom in interpreting individual Biblical passages.[70]

Reflecting on the omnipotence of the Lutheran church, she criticized it for creating religious "indifference and thoughtlessness" in its congregations.[71] She herself prized the idea of a united humanity, and was certain that the cry "Mankind! Mankind in its original truth, created in God's image" rang out down the ages.[72] Towards the end of her life, Fredrika Bremer declared once more her absolute faith in the creation of woman, like man, in God's image, and of the rightfulness of women's call for liberation: "It is only the good emancipation that can force aside the bad or stupid."[73]

Fredrika Bremer's heirs

Even during her lifetime, Fredrika Bremer had acquired followers who saw in her "the first and noblest spokeswoman and liberator of Swedish women."[74] One of those who reacted actively to the critique that the press directed against Bremer's *Hertha* was a young woman named Rosalie Roos (1823–1898). After her return from a four-year visit to the United States where she had worked as a teacher and governess, she set about defending Bremer in a series of anonymous articles that countered the attacks to which *Hertha* had been subject in the press. Roos formulated her exasperation with "the persecution system" that struck at anyone who protested against the prevailing view of women.[75] In five unsigned articles in the newspaper *Aftonbladet* between 28 March and 2 April 1857, Roos gave expression of her indignation over the "low attacks that Mlle. Bremer has been subject to by the press." There is every indication that the articles that Roos (who in 1857 married Knut Olivecrona) wrote for *Aftonbladet* had been well thought through. As early as November 1856, in a letter to a close friend, she had deplored Bremer's fate. It vexed Roos to see her misunderstood and even derided "simply because she is a woman, and as such has dared to take on more than her sewing, and has occupied herself with other things than gossiping about her neighbours."

At this point the Swedish Parliament was considering whether women should be able to attain majority, and Roos deplored, not without irony, the conservatism all too evident in those in power. She accused the Swedes of being behind the times because they refused to "grant to woman those rights that other civilized nations have long since granted her." Roos had no time for the leaders of society who believed that "women should not concern themselves with anything but running the home," and who moreover disparaged women in "intellectual matters." Above all else she longed to "lift and ennoble" her fellow women, and she cherished the dream of seeing in her lifetime an Institute for Girls. She was indifferent to the shallow social life of the day, and there were few circles in Stockholm that she considered worthwhile moving in. One woman who met her standards was Sophie Leijonhufvud (1823–1895). Of her, Roos wrote in 1857: "Sophie is very intelligent and truly musical, and pleasant and unaffected besides, so that acquaintance with her has given me real pleasure."[76]

Rosalie Roos' acquaintance with Sophie Leijonhufvud was to be significant for feminism in Sweden. For a period they both had admittance to Fredrika Bremer's salon,[77] and in 1859 they together founded Sweden's first periodical with a distinctively feminist programme. In 1861 Bremer wrote that the periodical, *Tidskrift för hemmet*, was a good portent; in her view, women's awakening and entrance into public debate were steps on the road towards a truly good society.[78]

For twenty-five years *Tidskrift för hemmet* was to serve as a mouthpiece for the still disparate women's rights movement in Sweden. Sophie Leijonhufvud (who married Axel Adlersparre in 1868) was responsible for the periodical's editorial policy throughout its existence. The originality of the authorial voice she developed has been recognized as groundbreaking in the history of the Swedish press.[79] Even during the early days, the editors stated that it was Christianity that set the conditions for true liberation, and in this respect these pioneers were clearly Fredrika Bremer's loyal heirs. At an early stage Bremer herself praised the editors' ambition to use the periodical to point to "all that comes from and leads to Christianity's life-centre."[80] Nor did the periodical bear much good will towards those who pleaded for women's liberation using arguments other than those that originated in a Christian world view. A truly emancipated woman in the editors' eyes was not "what one calls an emancipated woman with a scornful smile or shrug of the shoulders," but rather one who put to good use "the talents with which she is endowed."[81]

It was thus to the Bible that the editors turned to trace the source of the freedom they sought. In this they did not differ from the Christian context against which they rebelled in other respects. They fully recognized the limited support they might expect from this quarter; indeed, on one occasion they openly voiced their disappointment that the Church had warped the Christian message beyond recognition. In its understanding of women, the Church was "far from Christian." Above all they rejected the idea "that woman is and will remain a lower being than man, and therefore should take the same subordinate position towards him that the congregation takes towards Christ." Nor could they accept the concept that childbirth was the necessary condition for woman's "spiritual salvation," nor that "Sarah as she was shown in the Old Testament story" was the best role model for a married woman.[82]

Despite the fierce criticism that *Tidskrift för hemmet* was to direct against the Church's leadership on many occasions, like Fredrika Bremer the editors were to remain loyal to their Lutheranism. Rosalie Roos had since her youth been a faithful adherent of the Church of Sweden. "I thank God that I was born in a country where a state religion prevails and where the young are brought up accordingly," she wrote to a good friend during her stay in the United States. The reason for this outburst was that, in her eyes, the multiplicity of religious movements in America created a confusion and indolence that prepared the way for irreligion rather than for religious freedom.[83] According to Sophie Adlersparre, the Swedish church would stand and fall with its Lutheran tradition: "It has only such a future while the theology retains its Protestant character," she noted in her diary on one occasion.[84]

In other words, the feminist pioneers in Sweden did not confront Lutheranism; instead, they wished to gain emancipation with the help of Luther and liberal theology. For them it was a question of redefining and reinterpreting the idea of women's vocation so that they achieved influence over public life, and not of throwing Lutheran ideas overboard. Towards the Church of Sweden's stance on matters of dogma – in direct contradiction of Luther's understanding of each Christian's freedom before the Bible, according to both editors – the periodical was however extremely critical.

The fight for an education

In Luther's opinion, women were the equal of men in theology and eschatology, and he himself recommended that girls should spend part of the day in study. The Church's teaching role began with a child's christening, and the purpose of all its efforts was to transmit the skills that meant that children would grow into adults who could function as sound members of the Church. In line with the Lutheran tradition, the Church of Sweden had for centuries passed on the basics of knowledge to the whole population without differentiating between the sexes. When the question of higher education for women came to the fore in the second half of the nineteenth century, however, a complicated problem arose.

The subject was for *Tidskrift för hemmet* a crucial one.[85] The editors were well aware that the demand for further education for women would meet with resistance, but they could hardly agree with those who argued that women could dispense with further education. As those responsible for the coming generation, women were entitled to an intellectual education.[86] Generally speaking, the periodical's editors opposed the education of the day, seeing it as far too shallow and gender differentiated.[87] Whilst boys were encouraged to adopt manly fortitude, girls were schooled in submissiveness; the periodical noted grimly that women ran the risk of becoming characterless and weak-minded. The ambitions of the available girls' schools stretched only to teaching their pupils a certain amount of music, drawing, modern languages, and dancing. The total effect of inadequate study, mistaken teaching methods, and absence of mental effort and reflection, was the shallowness that was demonstrable in the women of the day. To make matters worse, the financial drain of keeping daughters in school meant that parents were willing to accept a rate of study that was altogether too fast, and the girls' schooldays were marked by an intensive parroting of lessons that rarely resulted in a deep knowledge.

The editors believed the situation would not be remedied with anything less than a complete state assumption of responsibility for girls' schooling, even if it would not resemble the boys' in all respects. They felt in particular for society's lowest classes, where vanity dictated that one should take after the higher classes and give daughters a shallow education; if necessity and distress later struck, the result was that such young women ran the risk of entering upon a life of immorality, argued the editors. An intellectual education had to go hand in hand with a moral education. At least when it came to women's religious education, all the leading groups of society were united, noted the editors wryly. Here there was no resistance to overcome because everyone was agreed that religious education was indispensable for women. The periodical agreed, while distancing itself from those who for conventional reasons maintained a Christian façade or yielded to religious pride.

According to the editors it was an absolute necessity for women to be given the right to develop their intellectual gifts and fill a place in society. Given the contempt with which people viewed unmarried women, it was important that all were offered the same opportunities to support themselves. In arguing for women's right to new vocations, the editors' favoured Biblical reference was the parable of the Talents. They also stressed individual passages that gave credence to the value of work, above all "the Holy word, 'You will work in the sweat of your brow'." Work could take many forms, but no one should be tempted to think that he or she was free from the duty to work. "The holy Scripture says, 'If any would not work, neither should he eat'," noted the periodical. Young girls were advised to trust in God wholeheartedly for their happiness, but when it came to their support, they should rely upon their own work.[88]

The editors agreed that woman's mission in life was generally speaking that of wife and mother. This did not mean, however, that all women were fitted for this role. Marriage meant if nothing else responsibility and duty, and for the woman it was essential that she see herself as an independent person, and not throw herself into marriage for lack of other means of support. On the contrary, it was of the greatest importance that the woman choose her future husband with care. The editors were conscious that some women overlooked the character of their intended in their eagerness to marry and have their material needs met. Such women did not find favour with the periodical's editors. Instead, they held up examples of women who – in cases where the man was unworthy of a woman's love and respect – chose to remain unmarried. They repeatedly argued that to give women the chance to choose whether they wanted to marry or not, society must increase the range of vocations open to women. Indeed, no one should need to marry because they were financially embarrassed, thereby exposing themselves to the degrading fate of binding themselves to men who did not measure up to standards of decency.[89]

It probably was no coincidence that *Tidskrift för hemmet* so urgently pointed to the superficial education of women in its plea for increased schooling. It seems clear that the leading lights of the Church of Sweden entertained the same misgivings about an education that had no greater ambitions than to prepare young women for social life. By emphasizing that the case for education was dependent on women's wishes to put their God-given gifts into the service of society, the periodical's editors rebuffed the arguments against women's emancipation that stemmed from the more orthodox Christians. They were at pains to show that the periodical was by no means out to undermine the role of wife, mother, or housewife.

The problem of morality was markedly present in every discussion about women's intellectual liberation. When in 1865–66 the Swedish Parliament tabled a report that was intended to give women access to university education, all the orthodox delegates protested at the proposal. For theological reasons, they could not permit women to enter higher education, and they were apprehensive that their presence in the public sphere would only be detrimental to morality.[90] Similar assertions were denied in *Tidskrift för hemmet* by Sophie Leijonhufvud; study could scarcely undermine a woman's modesty or lower her worth, she argued, because in comparison with the ballroom, the lecture room offered far fewer opportunities for immoral conduct. She was certain that giving women the opportunity to pursue their education alongside men posed no danger to true femininity.[91] The orthodox wing of the Church of Sweden judged the situation very differently. So did Rosalie Olivecrona.

From the middle of the 1860s, Rosalie Olivecrona felt uneasy about the current reforming zeal. Ten years before she had attacked the opponents of emancipation, angrily writing: "I dread being in public, I am afraid of the epithet 'blue-stocking' and the system of persecution which in our fatherland assaults every woman who dares to step outside the limited circle in which the lords of Creation in their mercy let her move, work – or vegetate."[92] Now she beat a circumspect retreat Any further extension of women's freedom in her eyes risked undermining women's calling. For Rosalie Olivecrona the key factor was that the education that was intended to train state civil servants should in the future remain reserved for men. Instead of encroaching on men's public life, women should strive to emulate Fredrika Bremer and turn their efforts to helping the poor and rehabilitating criminals.[93]

The difference of opinion between Sophie Leijonhufvud and Rosalie Olivecrona was germane because the different Estates of Parliament were debating a proposal to extend the educational possibilities for women. For Rosalie Olivecrona, who thought that the proposal went too far, it was important that any legislation should clearly set out the boundaries for women's vocations so that they could not be tempted to abandon their God-given role. For Sophie Leijonhufvud, who was enthusiastic about the proposed reform, the freedom to choose both education and vocation was a compelling demand. Given her view of the Creation, it was unacceptable for women to be subordinated by legislation created by men. That said, although she demanded freedom for women to choose their vocations themselves, she was equally convinced that women should only choose such vocations as were compatible with their female nature. Eventually the differences of opinion between the two friends became insuperable, and Rosalie Olivecrona handed in her resignation from the periodical.

From 1868 Sophie Leijonhufvud was the sole editor of *Tidskrift för hemmet*.[94] Gradually she adopted a religious stand that was openly liberal. Without going so far as to defy the Bible, she reserved the right to choose and interpret the Biblical passages that she herself considered central, giving herself free reign in the periodical to prioritize those passages that lent support to the emancipation of women.

The emancipation project threatened

The importance for *Tidskrift för hemmet* of the Christian view of life as the cradle of women's liberation was not without its limits, however. In particular, its contributors disputed the traditional Lutheran interpretation of the liberation that was embodied in Christianity.[95] At the beginning of the 1870s, Sophie Adlersparre and her circle launched an assault on those who held that it was particularly in its spiritual and eschatological aspect that Christianity contained an emancipatory message. Christ had freed the previously so "tightly shackled woman" not only that her "spiritual and heavenly share of inheritance" would be accorded to her. On this account she had even "been reinstated in her original rights on earth as a freeborn human," they claimed.[96] Since Christianity primarily aimed to change the temperament of its adherents, renewal should stretch right across "the social and civil arena." The one was the natural result of the other. In this interpretation, Christianity's concept of liberation broke the boundaries that had hitherto been staked out between male and female vocations. Nor were Christian views on life the target when the periodical protested against the subordination of women; instead their attention was focused on the prevailing gender construction, which they argued conflicted with Christianity's view of humankind. In the last few decades of the nineteenth century, the early pioneers led a stinging attack on the advocates of an 'Eastern' view of women. The legacy of Fredrika Bremer could scarcely be clearer.

According to *Tidskrift för hemmet*, the authors of the Old Testament had been influenced by the Eastern view of women. The Israelites were strongly influenced by a Middle Eastern culture that made women into the medium of man's passions. Polygamy, at least as it appeared in the Old Testament, was to be understood as a necessary consequence of the view of women that was to be found represented in society. This, however, was antiquated and was to be completely ignored in the New Testament, argued the periodical. Thus the fact that Israelite society allowed polygamy at the time when the Old Testament was written down was a result of a local gender construction in the periodical's eyes, and the tendency of the Church tradition to charge woman with "by reason of her sex being the representative of sin" was found deeply offensive. The latter supposedly derived from an Eastern idea that was unworthy of a culture steeped in the Christian tradition. In a polygamous society it was impossible for an individual woman to realize her influence as wife and mother, said the periodical. It was only when the family "through the Reformation was lifted from its earlier despised and dependent position" that women were given a chance to influence society. The Reformation had altered the conditions for women's liberation, but the editor was forced to admit that its emancipatory spirit had been lost somewhere along the way; she still had high hopes that the order of things would be restored, of course. That it had yet to happen could be attributed to "the old prejudice" that women were subordinate to men, a prejudice that "the ancient Eastern, Greek and Roman societies passed on to the medieval, and it in its turn to the present."[97]

According to Sophie Adlersparre and her circle, the Biblical testimony that should be used to define the nature of a true Christian was such as emphasized "that which alone is necessary – atonement and salvation in Christ."[98]

There was an abiding hope that by giving precedence to the New Testament, the early pioneers would finally succeed in razing the patriarchal tradition's wrongful line on subordination. Yet while it was certainly difficult to find proof that Christ had given support to subordination, Paul had at some length, and it was his explicit statements on women's subordination that the Church of Sweden used as its justification for reviving the idea in the second half of the nineteenth century. To the consternation of the leading feminists, the emancipation project found itself threatened by the established Church's determination to strengthen a Pauline interpretation of the mutual relations between man and woman. Sophie Adlersparre took up the problem in the periodical by posing the rhetorical question of whether "the Pauline message" placed obstacles in her path as a woman appearing in a public debate. Should not she, like generations before her, heed the message that women should "keep silence" in public? She concluded that this was not the case: "The woman redeemed and restored by Christ must safeguard if not herself, then the holiness that she bears within herself," she maintained.[99]

Above all, it was the fact that for several decades the Church of Sweden insisted on the reintroduction and use of the marriage formula "Paul the Apostle's admonition in the fifth chapter verses 22, 23, and 25 of the Letter to the Ephesians" that drew the greatest protest from the feminist leaders: "Wives, submit yourselves unto your own husbands, as unto the Lord. For the husband is the head of the wife, even as Christ is the head of the church. Husbands, love your wives, even as Christ also loved the church, and gave himself for it."[100]

Sophie Adlersparre and her circle found it highly questionable to use this passage as the basis for relations between the parties to a marriage. Unfortunately, as they were well aware, as soon as marriage was mentioned their opponents were only too happy to remind them of "Paul and Peters' repetition of these humiliating words." Despite this they were not prepared to acknowledge their primacy: "Certainly the explanation for this will be found in the Eastern, ancient low esteem of woman, which however should not be transplanted into the Western spirit as recently as in our times."[101] Instead they held there were good reasons to let themselves be led by Christ himself in this matter. As for the Pauline line on subordination, the leading feminists had little time for it; it posed a threat to the emancipation project.

In the process of the replacement of metaphysical assumptions about reality by an ideological system that centred on the internal life of the individual, a new threat to the early pioneers' emancipation project emerged – secularization. At *Tidskrift för hemmet*, they were extremely conscious of the danger of teachings that were sceptical towards metaphysically anchored value and norm systems, or indeed dismissed them entirely. The periodical warned its readers against influences of this kind: "Thus one sees the advance of positivism, pantheism, materialism, and scepticism – like incorporeal, imperceptible poisonous vapour – into circles where they are yet unknown. Their effect grows because they fall on fertile ground."[102] Particularly treacherous was positivism, with its misguided ideal of women. Auguste Comte – "the zealous denier of the faith in immortality" – who announced that those who followed his teachings would not have reason to lack "Christianity's dreamt hopes" was a thorn in the periodical's flesh.[103] To make women exclusively the object of the men's adoration, as Comte did, and to prescribe for them a life of passivity and after death a place beside the men appeared to Sophie Adlersparre to be deeply cynical. Comte, who in his last year founded a new religion where he himself intended to function as the high priest of humanity, and which had as its main aim the worship of great men, was by this time viewed with distaste by the early pioneers. The periodical issued also a warning against "the cancer of pessimism" that, by way of Schopenhauer and von Hartman, was continuing to gain a footing in society. Their teachings were dangerous since they were the diametric opposites of Christianity's fundamental understanding of the meaning of life and the hereafter. It also had negative consequences for society's morals, because the pessimists' exhausted world view made them liable to see everything in shades of black.[104] These new beliefs threatened the very heart of the emancipation project.

The struggle for moral reform

Tidskrift för hemmet had already published articles in its early years that witnessed to the fact that the editors were conscious of the social problems that were caused by sexuality.[105] However, it is clear that in this early phase the pioneers avoided openly touching on issues that were seen as controversial where morality was concerned.[106] Gradually, however, they came to protest with increasing vehemence against immoral tendencies, and eventually the liberation project bore the full stamp of an ideological war against the double morals of society.[107] In 1884 the Fredrika Bremer Association (*Fredrika-Bremer-förbundet*) was founded, in which Sophie Adlersparre and her circle gained a platform from which they could operate in a more organized manner. From 1886 the mouthpiece of feminism was called *Dagny*.

To understand the zeal – if not to call it fanaticism – with which the pioneering generation came to embrace the demand for moral reform in the last decades of the century, one must bear in mind the theological reflection that formed the basis of emancipation ideology. For the advocates of feminism, it was principally a matter of destroying the theological construction of woman as "man's fall and temptation," and replacing it with a new construct in which woman – according to God's original intent at Creation and in the right sense – became "the man's help and solace." Woman in the first instance should not be positioned as a gender; the gender role was a threat to the emancipation project. Yet that part of the gender role that embraced wifeliness and motherhood was not seen as a threat to the same extent because as a wife, mother, and housewife, the woman won the honour that according to God's order at Creation was due to her sex. The woman who entered into marriage was also duty bound to accept her gender role in a sexual sense, because it was the condition for achieving the honour that became hers the day she fulfilled her role as mother. That apart, woman's gender role was only to her detriment. The pioneering feminists could therefore not accept a role that positioned women as gendered beings trapped in a sexual, non-reproductive condition. They also turned to evolutionary theory. In any civilized society, sexuality would be reserved for marriage where it would exist in the service of reproduction. The playing out of evolution thus brought with it the benefit that the epoch in human history where instinct had been allowed to dominate became increasingly remote from the present.

With time a new threat that emerged, this time emanating from a wholly different approach to sexuality. According to this new idea that went on to win approval from those who advocated "The new Sweden" – often despite strong opposition from the Christian collective – women should no longer be freed from sexuality. To attain true emancipation, she should instead be liberated to sexuality. Thus it was that leaders of the women's movement came to be viewed as puritanical and reactionary; it was the result of their struggle against what they saw as the false liberation of the sexual emancipation ideologists. The leaders of the women's movement believed themselves to be the representatives of freedom and progress – and "the true emancipation."[108]

When the author August Strindberg published his work *Giftas*, the Fredrika Bremer Association could only condemn it. In his controversial work, Strindberg directed a biting attack against marriage, here shown mainly as a means of support for work-shy women.[109] It also included an attack on the emancipation project of the day, which according to Strindberg contributed to the undermining of motherhood. The book naturally met with the outrage of the pioneer feminists. Even though Strindberg insisted that he too was fighting for the emancipation of women, his emancipation ideology conflicted fundamentally with the ideology that they advocated. For them, the whole of Strindberg's personal philosophy was dominated by a decadence in which "enslavement to blind powers of nature" was the cardinal principle; as for Strindberg's supposed praise of motherhood, they remained unconvinced. While it was true that he prized motherhood highly, he saw it "exclusively from a natural perspective," and "the human mother's calling" was not rated by the author above that of an animal's.[110] The newly established women's movement viewed Strindberg's ideas on human sexuality as conflicting with nature, and his statement that "man and woman should be sexually educated and mature at the age of fifteen" was seen as fundamentally wrong.[111]

It was bad enough that there were men who advocated a sexual norm that would return women to an ancient gender role. There was even greater sense of disappointment when women themselves followed such false prophets. An example was when one of Sweden's largest women's associations published in its journal *Framåt* in 1886 an outline of a novel in which a dying woman complains that she did not respond positively to her sexuality earlier in life. The shocking thing here was that it was a female author "by the presentation to her public of an account that is an expression of a female Strindbergianism of the most disgraceful kind," who aired the thought that women required an outlet for their sexuality that was free-standing from reproduction, wrote Sophie Adlersparre in *Dagny*. Women who in like manner called for freer sexual norms were, according to Adlersparre, inevitably the blind and unconscious tools of an enemy to the women's rights movement.[112]

The newly founded Fredrika Bremer Association raced to censure those sisters who, in paying heed to sexuality, saw a way forward to emancipation.[113] One particularly unfortunate situation for the pioneer generation was to develop when one of its most loyal members, the writer Ellen Key, went over to the enemy.

Ellen Key – apostate

Over the years, Sophie Adlersparre had increased the crowd of her collaborators by drawing in prominent writers and public debaters interested in the problems of modern society. One of them was Ellen Key (1849–1926), whom Adlersparre saw as a great hope for the future. With works such as *Barnets århundrade* and *Lifslinjer*, Key, one of the outstanding figures of Swedish feminism, won international renown as an author. She came even to serve as a source of inspiration for those trying to achieve universal peace. From her early youth she was an eager adherent of the emancipation of women. Her capital with the pioneer generation was great until the time at the end of the century when she began to distance herself from the liberal interpretation of Christianity that she had earlier followed, and formed a set of atheistic beliefs.

Ellen Key's contributions to the periodical during the 1870s witness to the fact that during this period she was wholeheartedly linked with the emancipation ideology of the early pioneers.[114] Gradually, however, she clearly became doubtful, a situation not helped by Sophie Adlersparre, who took the periodical so very much to heart that in Key's eyes she became an unreasonable, if not to say despotic, editor.[115] As time wore on, the atmosphere between them became increasingly tense. When in the 1880s Key produced a controversial article on the women's rights movement, it was the final straw. Sophie Adlersparre decided that in this article Key proved herself "altogether too good-natured, letting herself be lured by the German socialist boss' little ruse, using the women's rights movement as a front and pretext to introduce social democracy's teachings for the benefit of the public." The fact that Key had herself been influenced by August Bebel, who, according to Sophie Adlersparre, joined with Strindberg, Nordau, and Brandes in representing the philistine and degrading currents of the day, was seen as extremely compromising.[116] That she appeared in her article to be ambivalent about the idea of the afterlife, and gave greater priority to ennobling life on earth, made things worse. By denying one of the Christian world view's most central tenets – life after death – Ellen Key deserted the emancipation ideology that she had cherished from an early age.

After Sophie Adlersparre's death in 1895, Key moved even further away from the liberal interpretation of Christianity of her youth. Like Fredrika Bremer before her, she saw in women a guarantee for the good society, but her emphasis on the specific nature of women came in time to rest on evolutionary ideas. Under the influence of Herbert Spencer's theories, she became convinced that it was disastrous for women and men to experiment with biologically determined gender patterns. Increasingly, she withdrew from her emancipation ideology, and she had abandoned its fundamentals by the middle of the 1890s. She replaced a Christian world view with personal belief, and she announced that she wished to see the gender roles of ancient times revived.[117] In two works of 1895, she directed an attack against the feminists that was to threaten the success of their idea of emancipation.[118]

Gradually Ellen Key and the feminists descended into open war. The ostensible reason was a party that was arranged in the honour of the seventieth birthday of the Norwegian author Henrik Ibsen in 1898. Representatives from the Fredrika Bremer Association were present, and Ellen Key had been asked to give the evening's key speech. It was to prove decisive. Her speech, "Torpedo under the Ark," took in her personal interpretation of Ibsen's ideas about women's liberation. Such was the reaction to the speech that a public letter of protest was circulated; in particular, her audience was upset because she had spoken of "the salvation of the personality" in a way that could be interpreted as undermining morality, and she had gone on to extol the time when the "new religion" would replace the one whose sun was now setting. Amongst the signatories to the letter of protest one finds many feminist sympathizers.

By 1900, the women's rights movement was on the brink of partition, and the emancipation ideology that had first emerged with Fredrika Bremer and her immediate successors was coming into question. The difference was that instead of coming from the orthodox theological side, it was the increasingly secularized currents that threw the old emancipation ideology into doubt, with their non-theological approach to emancipation from the perspective of a closed, internal world of the individual. The history of Swedish feminism was about to enter a new phase.

Conclusion

With hindsight we can see that the early pioneers' ideals – taking Christian understandings of freedom and liberation from gender roles as its basis – were doomed to pass. Seen from the social context of the day, however, their emancipation strategy is something that posterity has consistently failed to observe. Why? Perhaps the fact that the contemporary religious framework has been rarely taken into account in an interpretation of relations between the sexes is significant here. Since it has been long assumed that the emancipation of women and secularization went hand in hand, research into the history of Swedish women has spent little time in tracing the strongly Christian tone of the feminist movement.[119] Previous accounts of the Swedish emancipation process have primarily focused on the economy as the crucial factor, while at the same time the Swedish clergy have been indiscriminately labelled as negative towards feminism.[120] The Church, represented by its clergy, has in particular in the Swedish research tradition come to be seen as a hand brake, with the consequence that it is principally religion's role as a restraint on the emancipation process that has been emphasized.[121] In doing so, historians have overlooked the contradictions inherent in the fact that from the middle of the nineteenth century, the women who first initiated and then drove forward the emancipation debate were ideologically anchored in a context that has been labelled as hostile to emancipation.

I have termed such research "religion blind" in the same way that feminist research has termed earlier work "gender blind."[122] Our knowledge of the course of history can only be increased by paying heed to theological argument and debate. Things that are today seen as confusing, obscure, or paradoxical become not only intelligible but also consistent if one interprets them in the light of the world view that influenced and controlled the historical figures in question, with the proviso that one is concerned with a period where the historical context included a theological discourse that formed a more or less self-evident element in the contemporary world view. This was still the case in the nineteenth century, when Swedish society was permeated by a Lutheran view of society, even if it was to begin to unravel in the last decades of the century.

Translation: Charlotte Merton, lightly revised by Karen Offen.

8

INDIAN CHRISTIAN WOMEN
AND INDIGENOUS FEMINISM,
c.1850–c.1920

Padma Anagol

The gender and women's history of India has expanded considerably in recent years, adding to our knowledge of various aspects of women's lives.[1] These have included the marginalisation of women in the economy and popular culture; the impact of colonial law and administrative policies on the role and status of women; the reconstitution of patriarchies via the recasting of the concept of 'womanhood';[2] the cultural politics of gender and the significance of masculinity for the imperial enterprise;[3] and more recently, the historical visibility of women.[4] While these studies represent significant contributions to the field, this chapter shifts the focus to tackle directly the twin issues of consciousness and assertion among Indian women in the colonial era.

Over the years, the position of women in Indian society has been looked at either as part of broader studies in the social and cultural history of India[5] or, more directly, in the attempt to trace the changing role of women in the colonial period.[6] Improvements in the status of women came about from the nineteenth century onwards, such scholars argue, not as the product of a process of conscious assertion on the part of Indian women, but through programmes of social reform devised and carried out by Indian men and the colonial state. In many ways the picture which emerges of Indian women as passive recipients in these processes, has been predetermined by the approaches which scholars have adopted. In the Western impact/Indian response paradigm which informs their work there is little room for women as conscious agents. Instead, women are reduced to mere beneficiaries of the 'awakening' experienced by their menfolk as a result of contact with Western influences. Similar problems arise with studies informed by post-structuralism where the focus is on colonialist and nationalist discourse rather than the female subject.[7] However, if Indian women are to be studied merely as 'representations' or as a 'site' for the play of dominant discourses we are in danger of erasing them completely from history.[8] Indeed, it is ironic that an approach which attempted to critique Orientalist essentialism has done so much to reinforce the image of the passive Indian woman.

The approach adopted here is informed by a conception of agency which is not limited to issues of 'consent' or 'coercion',[9] nor does it reduce autonomy to mere resistance – essentially reactive to the interventions of the colonial state or Indian men.[10] Rather, a much broader view of agency is configured where the focus is on uncovering the intentions and experiences of Indian women as they asserted their rights, addressed social inequalities and rejected tradition in an engagement with the world around them in what amounted to a unique indigenous feminism.[11] These issues are explored in a study of

Maharashtrian women who converted from Hinduism to Christianity from the late nineteenth century onwards. Although the relationship was to become more ambiguous, Christian missions were seen by many scholars as central to the colonialist agenda leading to their exclusion from mainstream histories of South Asia.[12] By treating Indian Christian women as agents it is hoped that a serious gap in Indian historiography will be redressed. Also, in older mission histories women converts were depicted as merely following the dictates of their husbands. However, when the focus shifts to the experiences of women themselves and the process of conversion which they went through, a much more complex picture emerges. This chapter traces the inner struggles which these women went through after the conversion of their husbands, the prolonged resistance which many exhibited and the reasons which they gave for their ultimate conversion. Finally, it will attempt to trace the character of this indigenous feminism and determine whether this consciousness went beyond the question of individual empowerment to encompass a wider conception of women as a group which could be used as the basis for collective action.

The historical context of the missions in Maharashtra

As early as the 1820s, missions from the Scottish Board and the Church Missionary Society had established roots in Bombay and were highly successful in developing high schools, while the American Board prospered at Ahmednagar. Some of the first male converts were from influential Parsi and Brahmin families in Bombay and Ahmednagar. Members of indigenous elites aspiring to a professional education for their children in the 1820s and 1830s had little choice but to send their boys to mission schools. Undoubtedly, the first converts were products of schools run by missionaries. By the last decade of the nineteenth century the missions of the American Board, the Free Church of Scotland, the Church Missionary Society and the Society for the Propagation of the Gospel were firmly established in larger towns like Bombay and Poona and were slowly spreading into smaller towns and villages. Together, they boasted a 'native Christian' population of approximately 60,000.[13]

Not surprisingly, the first female converts were the wives, mothers or sisters of the first Brahmin, Muslim or Parsi converts. However, as early as the 1820s the education of women had been a key strategy of missionary activity. Their programmes rested on the belief that the 'womanhood of India' was 'the protectress and zealous adherent of traditional heathenism'.[14] As grandmothers, mothers and wives Hindu women were thought to plant the first seeds of idolatry and ritual in children. Thus, conversions were unlikely unless the influence of women was combated. These trends were reinforced by developments in Europe and America. In the later half of the nineteenth century the complexion of missionary activity changed with the beginnings of women's movements in the West. Historians have shown how European and American women in their quest for self-definition and alternative roles began to interest themselves in the cause of the 'heathen' woman.[15] More recently Geraldine Forbes, Antoinette Burton and Barbara Ramusack have examined the roles of missionary and non-missionary white women's activities in the colonies.[16] They argue that white women who went to colonies in the nineteenth century constructed and relied on the notion of 'enslaved' Indian women which served the purposes of their own programmes of emancipation. Overseas opportunities not only provided space for the surplus 'genteel' population of white women but empowered them through collaboration in the ideological work of empire.

These developments were soon to have an impact on India. In the 1860s the first women's auxiliary units of various missions such as the Society for the Propagation of the Gospel and the London Missionary Society began to arrive in India. Between 1858 and 1871, according to Richter, there were eight women's auxiliary units of Anglican and American missions in India.[17] Such was the enthusiasm among female circles in England that the Church of England Zenana Missionary Society alone sent 214 women between 1887 and 1894. They brought a new angle to the old missionary enterprise, a concern for the 'desolate plight of Indian womanhood'. Combating *sati* or widow-burning and infanticide, providing refuge homes for deserted wives and widows, educating women in *zenanas* or women's quarters – all these appeared prominently on missionary women's agendas. Missionaries regarded the Bombay Presidency, especially the Marathi-speaking region, as ideal ground for their conversion programmes. In missionary literature typical accounts note that, historically, the region appeared to have been little influenced by Muslim practices. Women having greater freedom of movement and the unveiled Maharashtrian women provided fewer obstacles for the work of Western missionary women.

However, this concern with the woman's question was not cited as a reason for conversion by prominent male converts in Maharashtra. Though individuals like Baba Padmanji expressed concern at the suffering of Hindu widows in his work, just as missionary tracts did, the treatment of women in the various religions was not a major issue for male converts.[18] This was despite the fact that this question had become a major bone of contention for many Hindus, with an increasing number of tracts dealing with the question of the salvation of Hindu women.[19] The emerging Indian intelligentsia in the early half of the nineteenth century was faced with an eclectic culture. On the one hand it was marked by missionary activity, and on the other by the reforming zeal of influential Brahmins who criticised the contemporary state of Hindu society and the practices of a corrupt Brahmin priesthood. Baba Padmanji, a prominent male convert, recorded how he benefited from this eclectic atmosphere:

> The *Dnaynodaya* [Christian newspaper] convinced me of the truth of Christianity and the futility of the claims of the Shastras [Hindu religious books] to divine inspiration; the *Prabhakar* [newspaper edited by a Hindu reformer] destroyed my religious reverence for the Brahmans; and the *Dnyan Prakash* [newspaper concerned with theological questions] had preserved me from falling into the quagmire of atheism.[20]

In a manner similar to Baba Padmanji many educated male converts arrived at an acceptance of Christianity after an intellectual engagement with the religious precepts of Hinduism and Christianity, exhibiting a formidable knowledge of the scriptures of both religions.[21] In short, for Hindu males conversion was born out of a major questioning on abstract theological issues, whether in relation to questions of 'revealed' religion or on the inconsistencies of the Hindu religious texts.

In contrast, while women converts did not simply follow the dictates of their husbands in converting to Christianity, nor was the relative validity and truth of each religion the primary issue for them. For high-caste educated women like Pandita Ramabai, Krupabai Satthianadhan and Soonderbai Powar it was the treatment of women in each religion which emerges as the main issue in their process of conversion and their adherence to Christianity.[22]

Reconstituting Indian womanhood: critiques of Hinduism by high-caste educated women

The earliest signs of the creation of feminist consciousness among Maharashtrian women are discernible in their evaluation of the position of women in various religions and their eventual acceptance or rejection of them. Given the rigours of high-caste oppression, the conversion of low castes to Christianity has been seen as unproblematic. Later, it will be argued that their conversion was a much more complex process than the above generally accepted view implies. For the moment, however, it is important to ask why high-caste educated Hindu women became attracted to Christianity. One of the most vociferous sections of Maharashtrian feminists were converts from Hinduism, not just prominent converts, who, it could be argued, were merely following the dictates of their husbands, but a host of relatively unknown high-caste women who converted of their own volition. Many of these women showed great resistance to conversion, continuing their opposition years after their husbands' initial conversion. Conversion took place after a gendered critique of Hinduism and Christianity in which the former was found wanting.

Even among those women who followed their husbands a certain prioritisation of desires is evident. Wives of male converts usually had the choice of staying with their parents or their extended family. Moreover, they had heard of the great persecution converts were subjected to by Hindus, yet they chose to follow their husbands. In fact, quite a few of them had dramatic escapes from their enraged kith and kin. For example, Ganderbai Powar told the court that she had been imprisoned in her own home and prevented from joining her husband for years.[23] Not all women were successful in resolving conflicts over religious issues and quite a few cases ended tragically. Lakshmibai, another woman, entered a period of intense introspection and remained with her parental family for seven years before deciding to rejoin her husband only to find that he had given up on her and re-married. She died a year later.[24] Anandibai Bhagat, who accompanied Pandita Ramabai on her trip to Wantage, England in 1882, committed suicide.[25] In her case the anxieties of conversion were accompanied by the tensions brought on by her interaction with missionaries.[26] In order to get a complete picture of the conflicts, ambivalences and resolutions of women's struggle to create a social space for themselves we have to look at their experiences of the processes of conversion.

As a first-generation convert, the views of Pandita Ramabai (1858–1922) are crucial and through her writings she provides us with a key to the growing feminist consciousness among women in Maharashtra.[27] Born into a Chitpawan Brahmin family of Mangalore district, Karnataka (South India), her father, Ananta Shastri Dongre, was a priest and taught at the Peshwa's (regional ruler's) court. He taught his wife to read and write and she in turn taught Ramabai. Ramabai was a child prodigy. At the age of twelve she had committed to memory 12,000 verses of the ancient Sanskrit scriptures. Along with her brother, Srinivas, she travelled all over North India and at the age of twenty reached Calcutta. Here she was drawn to the reform circles and in an open competition with male pandits on Hindu theology and philosophy she won the title 'Pandita Saraswati'. In June 1880, she married Bipin Behari Das, a Bengali Kayasth, considered a rebellious act as Maharashtrians viewed Kayasths as low castes. At twenty-two, she was fluent in five Indian languages (she would eventually master Greek, Latin and Hebrew), and in 1882, she learned English with Ramabai Ranade (a prominent Hindu female reformer) and amalgamated the latter's Ladies' Association with other women's groups to form the Arya Mahila Samaj, a premier women's organisation of Maharashtra. Her first book in Marathi,

Stri-Dharma Niti (Prescribed Laws and Duties on the Proper Conduct of Women), earned her funds to travel to England. In England she stayed with the Wantage Sisters and studied Christian theology, converting in 1883. For a while she held the Chair of Sanskrit at Cheltenham, Ladies College. Between 1885 and 1887 she travelled in America and studied the kindergarten system of education. Meanwhile her vision for liberating Indian women had crystallised and she lectured extensively on the pitiable condition of Indian women and the need to emancipate them. Her next book in English, *The High-Caste Hindu Woman*, a powerful feminist tract, caught the imagination of the American public from Quakers to Evangelicals who formed sixty-five 'Ramabai Circles' and pledged to make her projects successful. The circles were coordinated under an elected Board called The American Ramabai Association. Pandita Ramabai was awarded the Kaisar-i-Hind medal by the Indian government in recognition of her services to Indian women.

In her earliest analysis of Hinduism's treatment of women, written for the *Cheltenham Ladies College Magazine* in 1885, she argued that Hinduism gives central importance to men while women's functions were merely to worship their husbands. It was only through her husband that a Hindu wife could secure a place in heaven. It was women's lack of 'personal responsibility' to God which created dissatisfaction within Pandita Ramabai.[28] She quoted the Code of Manu, the ancient Hindu law-giver, to show how a Hindu wife is supposed to obey and worship her husband as a god, however reprehensible he may be. By removing 'personal responsibility' to God, Ramabai argued that there was nothing to sustain a wife unlucky enough to be married to an unworthy husband. A wife in such a position was robbed of the personal dignity which a Christian woman could claim. Hindu women, she reflected, could not reach the 'true dignity of womanhood' since Hinduism did not respect women as independent human beings. This conclusion led Ramabai to investigate the manner in which the unjust treatment of the sexes evolved in the practice of Hinduism. Her sense of acute dissatisfaction with Hinduism in this respect is set out in her autobiographical work – *A Testimony*.[29] She found a common strand linking all the Sanskrit texts of the *Mahabharata*, Dharma Shastras, Vedas, Smritis and the Puranas to the modern poets and popular preachers of the day, which was that:

> women of high and low caste, as a class, were bad, very bad, worse than demons, as unholy as untruth, and that they could not get Moksha as men. The only hope of their getting this much-desired liberation from Karma and its results, viz., countless millions of births and deaths and untold suffering, was the worship of their husbands. The woman has no right to study the Vedas and Vedanta and without knowing Brahma no one can get liberation, i.e., Moksha ... My eyes were being gradually opened, and I was waking up to my own hopeless condition as a woman, and it was becoming clearer and clearer to me that I had no place anywhere as far as religious consolation was concerned. I became quite dissatisfied with myself, I wanted something more than the Shastras could give me ...[30]

Reading the Vedas (an act forbidden to women) only served to increase her discontent. However, it was only in 1883, three years after her husband's death, that she went to England and saw the work of the Wantage Sisters of Fulham (Church of England), among whom her interest in Christian doctrine was awakened.

Pandita Ramabai recognised the work of the Wantage Sisters, through whom she realised that 'fallen women' (prostitutes) could be brought back into society. She contrasted their work with the contemporary Hindu practice of shunning prostitutes as the greatest of all sinners and unworthy of compassion. She asked the Sisters why they cared for prostitutes and learned from them about 'Christ's meeting with the Samaritan woman' and his teachings on the nature of true worship which excluded 'neither male nor female'.[31] It was then that she realised that 'there was a real difference between Hinduism and Christianity', and was convinced that Christ alone, in her words, 'could transform and uplift the downtrodden womanhood of India and every land'.[32] Once again, it is the feminisation of missionary Christianity which appealed to Ramabai. The rhetoric of a religion that did not exclude women had a practical application for Ramabai. On returning to India, she translated into action some of her borrowings from mission Christianity by founding the Kripa Sadan (or Home of Mercy), probably the first home for the rehabilitation of prostitutes in India.

In 1883 Pandita Ramabai was baptised along with her daughter Manoramabai. She records that finally she felt at peace with herself, having found a 'religion which gave privileges equally to men and women; and where there was no distinction of caste, colour or sex in it'.[33] Her rebellion, then, was against Hinduism – a religion she perceived as one that preached inequality between the sexes, which counterposed good and evil respectively in men and women. She rejected the Vedantic or Hindu teachings about the 'unreality' (illusion) of life and showed a preference for a religion which conceived of human life as 'reality' because this philosophy opened a multitude of possibilities, especially the potential to live intensely and with a purpose. Mission Christianity through the practice of 'good deeds' allowed Indian women to participate in public life. In a similar manner to Pandita Ramabai, other Hindu women who had been educated in mission schools embraced Christianity through a learning process. An interesting case was that of Gunabai, who studied at a mission school in Ahmednagar where she was impressed by the 'Christian values' of compassion and mercy. Her daughter Shewatbai recollected that John Bunyan's *Pilgrim's Progress* had such an impact on her that she lost all traces of hesitancy and reserve about the wrath of her family and community and ran away to the mission house and was disowned by her parents.[34] Through missionary discourse Christianity had a profound effect on the perceptions of a certain small but influential section of such literate Maharashtrian women.

Pandita Ramabai's critiques were improved and extended by a second generation of Christian women who concentrated more on the exposition of the role and status of women in Hinduism in their efforts to empower Indian womanhood. Second-generation Christian women were much more systematic in their analysis, addressing men as the original culprits in the vilification of women through their coding and encoding of Hinduism. Soonderbai Powar (1856–1921) was the daughter of first-generation Christians, Ganderbai and Ramachandra. The first booklet she wrote was aimed at encouraging disheartened missionaries and was entitled *Is Zenana Work a Failure?*. She was well known in Britain and India for her involvement in anti-opium and temperance movements. In 1883, she met Pandita Ramabai and became her 'right hand' for seven years. Once she felt confident that Ramabai's work had stabilised she left to open a Zenana Training Home in Poona. This school flourished on funds she had secured from her campaigns in England, Scotland and Ireland. Among her writings, the book *Hinduism and Womanhood* most clearly expressed her views on women's issues.

Like Pandita Ramabai, Soonderbai Powar located women's servitude in Hindu religion and social customs, but she elaborated on Pandita's critique by highlighting the role of men with much greater clarity. Soonderbai described Indian women as 'slaves' who had been forced to merge their personal freedom and individuality in the personality of man.

Through an acute observation of Hindu mannerisms, the expressions used on the birth of a female child, the popular sayings about wives and widows and the offensive language used against women, she tried to show the ways in which woman is devalued by Hinduism, making it impossible for her to be an inspiring companion to her husband or a wise and responsible mother to her children.[35] Weaving a narrative through the life-histories of the students in her Zenana Training Home, she concluded that, if Hindu women were in 'bondage', it was one imposed by selfish men through the rules of a religion which made them perceive woman 'as nothing more than a soulless animal to be used for the pleasure of man'.[36] Dissecting Hindu customs like early marriage, female infanticide, the harsh treatment of widows, the dedication of girls as temple prostitutes and the dowry system, she labelled them as the 'bitter fruits of Hinduism'. Soonderbai claimed that: 'in the name of their religion, Hindus do many wicked things and have many bad customs which cruelly limit or destroy the liberty of the subject, and strangle social and family happiness'.[37] According to Soonderbai, such customs derived sanction from the inviolable principles of their religion and philosophy and Hindu men would do nothing to alter them because they had themselves created them. She felt, therefore, that only the Christian religion could free women from such bondage.

Krupabai Satthianadhan (1862–93), another second-generation Christian woman, went further in her analysis, not only investigating Hindu men's resistance to granting equal rights to women but also showing how Hinduism negatively affected the attitudes and stunted the personalities of Hindu women. Krupabai's parents, Haripant and Radhabai Khisty, were among the earliest Brahmin converts in the Bombay Presidency. Krupabai turned out to be a precocious child and the American mission at Ahmednagar offered her the option of enrolling as a teacher or studying further. Krupabai had made up her mind to be a doctor so she was sent to Madras Medical College, which had opened its doors to women. While in Madras she met a Cambridge-returned Indian Christian, S. Satthianadhan, and married him. In her own time, she was widely known and held a national and international audience for her writings. Her known writings comprise about twenty essays, two novels and many poems. Her novels were compared to Jane Austen's because of her eye for details, satiric tones and for exposing domestic hypocrisies of the time. Of particular note here are her feminist critiques, exposition of white racism and her criticisms of the English-educated Indian middle classes. Due to failing health she was forced to discontinue her studies and died at the age of thirty-one.

Krupabai's critique of the nature of women's oppression in Hindu society and her arguments for the education of women helped women not only to counteract the onslaught of Hindu vilification and contempt for women but, in a larger sense, to help women break through the rigidity of the roles prescribed for them.[38] In the first place she maintained that marriage should not be the only goal of a woman's life. Second, she argued that education led women to develop some freedom of thought and action, to begin to question the social tyranny and injustice they were subjected to, and to become self-reliant. Third, she argued that this process of women's self-realisation was the only way for the Indian nation to progress.

Krupabai began her analysis with the general proposition that the independence of women was anathema to Hindu men. Because of the high status that a man commanded in Hindu society, the minute a male child was born he was treated like a king. As a result of this he grew up to be a 'petted, spoiled despot, or a selfish ease-loving lord'.[39] To his 'inflated, self-satisfied nature' the very idea of an intellectual wife, in any way superior to him, 'will be gall-wormwood'; qualities that he lacked would not be tolerated in his wife.[40]

The second rationale she outlined was a psychological one. Hindus, argued Krupabai, had lost their power as rulers and had been in servitude for centuries, thus, exercising authority at home was an important compensation for the Hindu male which he would never let go willingly. The third reason she gave was the economic necessity of exploiting the labour services of women for the efficient functioning of Hindu joint families. She concluded that if Hinduism entailed inferior status and lack of rights for women, Hindu men were heavily implicated in the process.

The critiques of second-generation Christian women were closely linked to contemporary male discourse on female education. One of the commonest allegations of male progressives was that women were the greatest opponents of education: they preferred to be ignorant; their interests could never rise above petty gossip and trifles; they blocked reform work.[41] Krupabai challenged these arguments by placing responsibility for intrigues and gossip among women on the shoulders of selfish Hindu males. She pointed out:

> How few of our educated men ever trouble themselves about their women – as to how they spend the whole day, whether or not they find the hours hanging on their hands, whether the leading of an idle existence is hateful to them or not! They only look upon the women as mere appendices to their great selves ... They [women] are not to be blamed; they know of no higher mode of existence: there is nothing to occupy their minds; no interest is taken in them: they are treated as toys and play-things, and are humoured and pleased with gilded trinkets or any such trifles.[42]

What we observe here is a rigorous contesting of the knowledge about women claimed by Hindu men. Second-generation women gave a cultural explanation for Hindu women's inferior status, rather than rooting it in a biological theory of the weakness of the 'gentle sex'. If Hindu women were ignorant and bigoted, the reasons were external to them. Krupabai's analysis of the attitudes of Hindu men and the atmosphere in Hindu homes eventually led her to argue that it was only by leaving Hinduism that women could redeem themselves.

Krupabai set up a model of independent/dependent women and opposed it with another binary pairing of Christianity/Hinduism. Her ideas are best expressed in the two novels written by her in the English language in the 1890s, under the titles *Kamala: A Story of Hindu Life* and *Saguna: A Story of Native Christian Life*. Kamala's life is described as 'dark' and a prolonged sadness permeates it. Kamala is a young, beautiful and sensitive girl who is brought up in isolation by her father, a Brahmin pandit who has chosen to be a recluse. Kamala is married early to an English-educated man called Ganesh. The couple's love-life is fractured by the machinations of a jealous mother-in-law and scheming sisters-in-law, a common plot of novels during this period of social reform. Ganesh comes under the influence of Sai, a profligate though accomplished woman, who is described as one 'attached to a dramatic company', probably an actress, a profession which had terrible connotations during the nineteenth century. Ganesh spends less and less time with his wife, who is ill-treated by her in-laws. Eventually, Ganesh dies of cholera and Kamala gives birth to a child which also succumbs to fever. Distraught, Kamala rejects her only choice of happiness, the proposal of her childhood betrothed, Ramachander Row, who is willing to marry her despite her being a widow. The author comments that 'Her religion, crude as it was, had its victory.'[43]

Through the narrative of the novel, we learn of the origins of Kamala's convictions. We are told that Kamala became resigned to her lot, and it was her crude religious convictions that enabled her to do so.[44] Kamala had learned from her father that whether she was good or bad, whether she enjoyed pleasure or suffered pain, she ought not to grumble but accept it meekly, 'for it was her fate'. Caught in a turmoil between her heart, which wished to follow Ramchander, and her mind, which enjoined the duty of a faithful wife, Kamala reasoned that if women like Sita and Savitri – the ideal women from the ancient Hindu past – could not get their due in this world and had to submit to fate, then how could an ordinary mortal like her protest against it? Krupabai's message was that Hindu teachings gave women very little consolation even when it taught them to be resigned to their fate through passive role-models like Sita. Hinduism made women listless, 'feeble in purpose and in will', resulting in their complete non-interest in life as 'life itself was a poor spiritless affair'.[45] No matter how much Hindu women tried to assert and control their lives, Krupabai felt that 'the book of fate would come to pass do what she could to avert it'.[46]

Saguna, the subject of Krupabai's second novel, is presented as a complete contrast to Kamala. Her life is described as 'bright' in comparison to Kamala's 'dark' one. Saguna's life is influenced by the 'new order of things', which Krupabai says is sweeping all over India.[47] The 'new order of things' refers to the introduction of Christianity as a choice for Indians dissatisfied with the old order of life. Saguna's childhood is described as a 'sweet and innocent' one nurtured in domestic peace and quiet, where learning was encouraged and her freedom of speech and action was unchecked. Her eldest sister is treated as an equal and a friend by her father and her brother. Patience and kindness suffuses the Saguna household, and comfort in suffering and contentment in poverty mark their lifestyle. It is suggested that Christian life is of a 'purer faith' and 'higher culture' than Hindu life and that it encourages open-mindedness in those who profess it. Thus, Saguna is given complete choice in pursuing a profession – a freedom unthinkable for Hindu girls of her day except in the most radical circles. Saguna's female friends are allowed to interact freely with young men and choose their own spouses – once again, contrasted with Hindu customs. In the mission school, Saguna meets Christian girls, all of whom had a 'definite work in view' and were receiving training for it.[48] Through the voice of Saguna, Krupabai tries to get across to readers that Christianity held open the possibilities of leading a more independent life.

Saguna is later enthused with the idea of serving and improving the condition of her Indian sisters. She enrols in a medical college to become a doctor. To her, Christianity was the only religion which inculcated the idea of respect for other human beings. This was a more appealing philosophy than a religion which, in her view, reduced the idea of duty solely to the husband, regardless of the latter's worthiness. Krupabai thus focused the entire narrative on the growth of Saguna through Christian influence into a confident and independent 'new woman'. Among Indian Christian women's writings, Krupabai's analysis offers the most intricate link between religion and a woman's identity and role. Although it has been suggested so far that second-generation women's critiques were sharper, a notable continuity with the first-generation converts is their common conviction that Hindu women were helpless and passive due to their adherence to Hinduism.

The 'God of widows and deserted wives': illiterate women and Christianity

A large number of semi-literate women converted to Christianity towards the end of the nineteenth century, many at Pandita Ramabai's Sharada Sadan – the largest school for Brahmin widows in India at the time. In 1892, 12 out of 49 widows and 13 non-widows at Sharada Sadan converted to Christianity. Interestingly, all of them were adult Brahmin women and faced the possibility of ill-treatment (as a result of their conversion) from their relatives and/or guardians. In 1899, only 8 out of the 108 women at Sharada Sadan remained Hindus, while Pandita Ramabai claimed in 1905 (the year she publicly dropped secular teaching) that 1,500 out of 2,000 pupils in her schools were Christians.[49] Because of the highly structured organisational and managerial aspects of her schools, it is unlikely that she had any direct influence on the girls' decisions. The Executive Committee of the American Ramabai Association had drawn up the constitution of Sharada Sadan as a 'secular' institution. It made it clear to Pandita Ramabai that if there was any cause for dissatisfaction, the funding of her school would stop, as it was being supported by an annual grant of about $10,000 drawn from an eclectic American public of all persuasions on the specific understanding that the school would be non-sectarian. Moreover, the Managing Committee, drawn up by the American Ramabai Association, largely consisted of Maharashtrian male Hindu reformers whose list of guidelines allowed the Pandita access to her students only in the lecture rooms.[50] We have to look elsewhere for an explanation of the huge numbers of conversions.

The views of the converts can be constructed from the exhaustive personal interviews with pupils carried out by Judith Andrews, Chair of the American Ramabai Association.[51] Many of the Brahmin widows who converted to Christianity revealed that on their entry into Sharada Sadan they were not compelled to fast or shave their heads, as Hindu society demanded they do. The widows were informed in the classrooms that the spirit of their dead husbands was not linked to the hair on their head, as Hindu practice would have them believe, and for the first time they read about a God who did not believe in persecuting them for so-called lapses in good behaviour.[52] In Ramabai's school they did not have to endure the concepts of pollution of touch and sight associated with widows. The widows quickly attributed their misery to Hindu religious customs and eventually accepted Christianity, as a way of escaping some of the hardships of Hindu strictures. From the interviews it is apparent that mission Christianity was helping them to cope with their everyday existence much better than Hinduism. Thus an extremely pragmatic approach governed their acceptance of Christianity. One of Sharada Sadan's more exceptional students, Nurmadabai, who was removed from the school after the first uproar over the conversion issue in 1893, confirmed the reason for the many conversions. She had attended Sunday school since the age of seven and at the age of ten she was admitted to the Sharada Sadan. It was in this school that she felt for the first time that there was 'something real about this religion'.[53] She told Judith Andrews that a large number of girls had previously experienced no happiness in their own homes but in Sharada Sadan, instead of abuse, they were given affection and kindness.

Part of the explanation for the voluntary acts of conversion can be surmised from Pandita Ramabai's method of instruction. As early as 1886, she had mused that Manu's Code of Law and the earliest Hindu scriptures ought to form part of the syllabus in girls' schools in order to make them realise their true position in Hindu religion and society.[54] Certainly the Puranas (Hindu scriptures) were taught in her schools.[55] It is possible that women were encouraged to think on these issues as a result of her teaching. To many of these illiterate widows from oppressive families, Christ was represented as a 'saviour' of 'deserted wives, prostitutes and widows'.[56] Such a notion had a tremendous appeal to harassed and tormented women. The statistics available for Pandita Ramabai's schools show that two-thirds of the pupils were widows. A significant proportion of the widows who were not bound by any kinship ties or guardians were swift to see the advantages of freeing themselves from caste restrictions such as cooking food prepared by their own hands and from a religion that seemed to offer no comfort for women, especially widows. In 1896 only a handful of women in the Sharada Sadan remained Hindus but they had indicated to Pandita Ramabai that this was only because of pressure from powerful relatives.[57] Ramabai herself was constantly surprised by the behaviour of orthodox Hindu girls, who within a few days of their arrival thought of breaking caste rules. Hindu women, compelled to fast and shave their heads and perform endless rituals in their own homes, once freed of that compulsion, were able to quickly rekindle their aspirations and needs.

A third category of women converts were the wives of the male converts drawn from low castes, such as tanners, carpenters and masons. Their conversions, it appears, were prompted by issues of personal morality. These women initially followed their husbands and agreed to live with them in the belief that a Hindu wife's duty was to serve her husband. However, they remained opposed to their husbands' conversions and expressed disapproval by keeping a separate house, serving separate meals to their husbands and continuing Hindu rituals for several years. The reasons they gave for their eventual conversion are based on the transformation they experienced in their menfolk's attitude and conduct towards them. Ganderbai, for example, narrated that when her husband was a Hindu, he was hot-tempered, petulant and harsh to her but was 'all kindness' after he became a Christian.[58] Women like Sakubai argued that Christianity must be a superior religion since her husband had not remarried in spite of her refusal to live with him for two whole years.[59] Christianity in colonial India was perceived by many women to embody customs that favoured women in contrast to what they saw as the harsh reality of Hinduism.

The category of women who turned to Christianity on the basis of the issue of 'morality' approached it from a subjective point of view. This is better understood when we contrast women's attitudes to male converts who used the 'morality' argument. A well-known male Maharashtrian Christian of the late nineteenth century, Nehemiah Goreh, argued that the monotheist god in Hinduism as described in the most important texts of Hinduism, the Vedas and Upanishads, had sublime attributes yet no sense of morality, being unable to distinguish right from wrong.[60] The Hindu god, according to Goreh, was immoral and adulterous. How can one worship God, he reasoned, if he claims to be immortal but is full of mortal failings? Issues of morality are not considered by Goreh from a subjective point of view but as an abstraction. The question of literacy did not pose a barrier to the conversion of low-caste women. Semi-literate and illiterate women arrived at the same conclusions regarding the 'purer spirit of Christianity' but from a subjective viewpoint rather than through a philosophical exposition. The appeal of an alien religion was thus quite differently perceived and experienced by men and women. In the transition from disapproval to acceptance of Christianity many illiterate or semi-literate women displayed no knowledge of the theological constructs of either religions. But, after their baptism, they were given basic training in Christian doctrines. In the capacities of Bible women and catechists, they were able to relay religious precepts in a simple manner to villagers and thus proved to be some of the most enthusiastic workers in the proselytisation programmes of the missionaries.

Indian women's interaction with missions: conflicts over belief and methods

Despite the sense of liberation which conversion brought to Hindu women, their rejection of Hinduism was never absolute and their relationships with the Western agents of their new religion were not unproblematic. When Indian Christian women forged links with the

West, an important mediator was the white female missionary. The missions of various denominations befriended Indian Christian women and rendered services to them through forming their beliefs, clearing their doubts and helping them in times of financial distress. Indian Christian women readily acknowledged this help.

On arrival in India, as we shall see, these women did not encounter a docile set of Indian Christians who could be manipulated at will. In terms of organisational work Indian women Christians differed in approach and methods of action. Although the various missionary creeds profoundly affected the beliefs of Christian women, this was not an uncritical adoption. The more influential among them filtered these ideas, throwing out what did not suit the interests of their enterprises. The strength of their feminist consciousness is revealed in the cases of Soonderbai and Pandita Ramabai. They were attacked by Western missionaries as well as influential male Indian Christians and were severely criticised throughout their careers for their unconventional religious beliefs. Neither belonged to any church nor did they profess any kind of attachment to a particular denomination. Various accusations were hurled against them and they were called mercenaries exploiting Christian sympathy to promote the welfare of 'high caste Hindu women'.[61] The careful mapping of boundaries by Indian Christian women between themselves and missionaries represented the formation of an indigenous variety of feminism. Although firmly rooted in an alien religion, it held women's issues at the heart of its concerns. Indian Christian women indigenised Christianity because of their woman-centred approach to religion. This stemmed from the belief that any compromises with organised Christianity, apart from their own selective borrowing, would undermine their programmes for the advancement of Indian women.

It is important to explore the reasons why Indian Christian women resisted belonging to any particular creed or sect. All of these women believed that in the spirit of Christ there was neither male nor female. Their feminist critique of Hinduism led to their rejection of it. For them, Hinduism preached inequality between the sexes either as part of Hindu doctrines themselves or through the interpretation of Hindu priests. As Christians they were frequently pressured into accepting a particular church in order to carry on their work. However, Pandita Ramabai was very critical of divisive tendencies within the Church as a whole. Her correspondence on theological questions clearly reveals the reasons behind her opposition. In a letter to Sister Geraldine, in 1885, she wrote: 'I have just with great efforts freed myself from the yoke of the Indian priestly tribe, so I am not at present willing to place myself under another similar yoke by accepting everything which comes from the priests as authorised Command of the Most High.'[62] Obedience to the law and to the Word of God, according to her, were quite different from obedience to priests alone. Soonderbai also conducted her work on non-denominational lines in the belief that allegiance to a particular church meant subordination to mediating agencies. Neither of them wanted any intermediaries between God and themselves. Soonderbai, on her tours in Britain, was constantly asked about her denominational status, to which she wittily replied 'King's Own'.[63]

Christian women critically examined the Indian past with a view to understanding the position of Indian women and their gradual decline in status.[64] Krupabai and Pandita Ramabai attributed this to the gradual ascendancy of the priestly class among Hindus. Nothing, according to them, marked the constitution of Hindu society as much as the power and influence that the Brahmin priesthood commanded over Hindus.[65] In their opinion, it served the priest's interests to keep the Hindu woman as credulous and ignorant as possible, since learned and clever women, especially widows, would be able to manage their own affairs and estates without the aid of the family priest. Thus, the Hindu priest-hood had taken every opportunity to decry women's learning, and blamed learned women for every misfortune that fell upon a family in India. With such an analysis of the role of the Hindu priesthood it was not surprising that Indian Christian women were reluctant to accept church mediation.

Many Indian Christian women, especially those who had visited Britain, discerned the ways in which Victorian values were reinforced by the Church's views on female sexual-ity. Giving allegiance to a particular church entailed an acceptance of Victorian values. Among these were sex segregation and the biological determinist theories which outlined separate spheres for men and women. These issues were of prime importance to Indian Christian women. For someone like Pandita Ramabai, who taught carpentry and masonry to women, the natural division theory was an unacceptable one.[66] On one occasion, as the Professor of Sanskrit at Cheltenham Ladies College, Ramabai offered to teach British offi-cers as part of their preparation for India. However, when she sought permission to do so through the Principal, Dorothea Beale, she was told that the clergy would not allow a woman to teach men because it was a transgression of natural laws. In late-nineteenth-century India, in contrast, rapid changes had not yet crystallised into rigid rules. Women such as Cornelia Sorabji taught for a year at a male college in Ahmedabad while Pandita Ramabai frequently addressed all-male Indian audiences. Any strict conformity to church laws would mean a curtailment of their freedom of speech and action. Likewise, Soonderbai rejected modern interpretations of the Bible and taught her own versions which she felt were closer to the true spirit of the Bible. Indian Christian women had a clear notion of the balance of power between the sexes and it was their belief that in accepting a male intermediary, a necessary condition of belonging to a church, their free-dom of speech and action would be curtailed.

The tensions between Indian Christian women and their Western 'sisters' increased towards the end of the nineteenth century. While bearing the brunt of missionary attacks on their belief and work, Indian Christian women were themselves active in criticising Western missionary attitudes towards Indian culture and Indians. The earliest commen-taries on 'racism' among women were by Indian Christian women. Saguna, Krupabai's literary self, noted, at the age of fourteen, the insolence and arrogance of Western missionaries towards Indians. She recalled her humiliation and anger at the way her mother had tried to console her by saying: 'How can you expect them to be friends. Don't you see the difference, they are white and we are black. We ought to be thankful for the little notice that they take us.'[67] Cornelia Sorabji also called for a 'certain change in the attitude of the mind' if Westerners wanted a genuine interaction with Indians.[68] Indian Bible women also observed the differences between 'old' and 'new' missionaries. The 'new' ones they felt were 'cold, unemotional and kept barriers with supercilious airs', and they predicted that with such attitudes Western missionaries would not convert a Hindu in a thousand years![69]

Indian Christian women were among the first to criticise the 'Orientalist' notions of Western missionaries. Indian women drew attention to the missionaries' tendency to address Indians as 'benighted heathens' and their habit of constantly classifying them. They felt that the contempt and unjustified arrogance of Western missionaries arose through such classifications. Pandita Ramabai insisted that all missionaries who embarked on a voyage to India should study the history and literature of the Hindus.[70] She was con-vinced that Western missionaries were alienating Indians and thus harming the cause of Christianity in India. Further, she argued that St Paul himself, as an apostle, became a Jew to the Jews, and a Greek to the Greeks, and that 'God's method of work' was 'building on the old foundations, keeping that which is good, and destroying only that which is evil, decaying, ready to perish'.[71] She saw no rationale in decrying everything in the Indian scriptures, and expected missionaries to argue with Indians on an intellectual level regarding the particularities of each religion.

Indian Christian women were constantly emphasising 'Indianness' and maintained Indian dress, diet and etiquette.[72] Manoramabai went to the extent of telling missionaries eager to work at her mission at Mukti that they ought to be aware of the fact that Mukti was a 'thoroughly Indian mission' and if they were not prepared to accept this style of life they should not come at all![73] Indian Christian women continued to stress their 'Indianness', and in many books authored by them, careful foreword writers mentioned that the authors had not 'denationalised' themselves. Indian women felt the need to distinguish themselves from Western missionaries in order to be able to work ably in their welfare schemes for women without the negative connotations that Westerners were rapidly acquiring with their racist approach. The immense correspondence between Indian Christian women and missionaries points to the fact that the former considered their emancipatory programmes for women as a 'fledgling' which needed nurturing and sensitive treatment. Towards this end they adopted wholly 'Indian' methods of evangelical work. With this in mind Pandita Ramabai once delivered a *kirtan* (a religious discourse in verse) in a temple to a female audience. She defended her action on the ground that women in small towns were not only shy and timid but had no conception of Western public lectures and meetings. With this in mind she had used the *kirtan* to communicate practical lessons on social philosophy chosen from some of the Puranas and delivered them in a new style of lecture. When she was attacked by the Indian Christian community, she countered by pointing out that missionaries employed means like the 'magic-lanterns shows' and t*amashas* (Maharashtrian folk entertainment) to convey their message and so she felt justified in doing the same.[74] The 'Indianness' which Christian women stressed lay also in the method of worship which they consciously adopted from Hinduism and retained as good practice. Lakshmibai, Soonderbai and Pandita Ramabai believed in the *bhakti* form of worship, an emotional expression of love of God, practised from medieval times in India. In the 1900s a great 'revival' was reported with large numbers of girls and women embracing Christianity. When Western missionaries sharply rebuked these forms of worship as expressions of paganism, Indian Christian women defended them as legitimate forms of female worship forming a crucial part of women's lived realities.

This 'Indianness' must not be read as nascent nationalism or patriotism. In fact, a great number of Christian women were opposed to the nationalist activity carried out by the Indian National Congress. Although the fashioning of identity amongst Christian women was taking place through asserting difference from the West, the rationale for this was not nationalistic. Rather, it was associated with their emancipatory agenda for Indian women. Indian Christian women's growth in consciousness and resistance to organised Christianity was often manifested by quoting the biblical verse 'there is neither male nor female' (Galatians 3:28), stressing the equality between the two sexes. Indian Christian women carved out an indigenous feminism through Christianity within the missions in Maharashtra, which defied the norm of male-dominated missionary enterprises. Women missionaries like Pandita Ramabai were highly influential, with a powerful international standing. In the beginning Western missionaries had attracted many Indian Christian women with the message that women were equal to men. Having experienced and exercised a greater degree of autonomy it was hardly likely that they would give it up. To this end many Christian women in their correspondences to each other expressed the desire to be self-sufficient financially, which would have enabled them to cut their dependence on Western sources of funding.

Conclusions

During the colonial era Indian Christian women developed a strong feminist consciousness on the basis of a critique of the status of women in the two opposing choices of religion – Christianity and Hinduism. By shifting the focus to the analysis of the reasons behind their conversion, it has been demonstrated that these women broke away from the inherited Hindu past and found a new sense of freedom of thought, liberty of action, an avenue for self-definition and self-expression, as well as religious consolation. However, this was not by any means an uncritical acceptance. An analysis of their views illustrates that they selectively chose from the dominant male discourses of the time and sought the independence which would enable them to fashion Christianity in the cause of Indian womanhood, in a way that set them apart from missionary, reformist and nationalist discourses. As such, the actions of these women amounted to more than individual empowerment. Because they displayed a keen awareness of women as a distinct group in society and acted upon this to improve the quality of women's lives, a strong sense of the emergence of a distinct feminist consciousness is clearly discernible. They demonstrated the indigenous roots of Indian feminism by maintaining a cultural distance from European Christianity and by separating themselves from denominational allegiance.

A dynamic women's movement had begun in Maharashtra towards the end of the nineteenth century and Christian women played an important part in this pioneering effort. Their greatest contribution was the crucial support they gave to Hindu women, not only through their institutions but as path-breakers who showed the courage to step beyond accepted boundaries. This movement was marked by the prominence of dynamic Indian Christian women, who in many ways laid its foundations – through their ideology, organisation and entry into the public arena. In the first quarter of the twentieth century, Hindu female leaders like Ramabai Ranade, who had been infused with strength from their Christian counterparts, built on this legacy and continued the movement until the coming of Gandhi. In contrast to the widely accepted view that Indian women were passive and uncritical subjects for the reforming activities of others, it has been established that through their development of a feminist consciousness they were active agents in processes of change at the height of colonial rule.

9

SETTLER ANXIETIES, INDIGENOUS PEOPLES, AND WOMEN'S SUFFRAGE IN THE COLONIES OF AUSTRALIA, NEW ZEALAND, AND HAWAI'I, 1888–1902

Patricia Grimshaw

In the year 1896 American Jessie Ackermann published a book entitled *The World Through a Woman's Eyes*.[1] It was a traveler's tale of unusual interest. This lady traveler had undertaken a journey of almost epic proportions (especially given her much-mentioned propensity to seasickness). Since she had sailed out of San Francisco in the autumn of 1888, she claimed to have covered 150,000 miles in all. Following the track of English explorer James Cook over a century earlier, Ackermann visited Hawai'i, New Zealand, and Australia. She had set foot on every continent of the world—exotic places like China, Japan, Thailand, Java, Burma, India, and South Africa. She claimed unusually close contact with local people: "I was a guest in nearly two thousand homes; all kinds of homes, rich and poor, high and low—from the palace, government house and castle to the thatched cot of the sturdy farmer, the canvas or tin tent of the miner, and the bark hut of the lumber camp."[2] Finally, her tale was unusual because of her strong interest in the position of women across the globe. Alas, she observed, the sentiment that lay behind the poet's tribute, that woman was "the sex whose presence civilizes," was acknowledged for a mere quarter of the world's women. She pointed out that only a short time previously, some of her own countrywomen had had to be released from slavery and "elevated to the dignity of womanhood." It could be done. Now was the time for American women to look outward, beyond their own shores, to take American women's "higher civilization" to influence women's lives everywhere.[3]

While she did not acknowledge it in her book, which doubtless she hoped would be bought for enjoyment by the widest possible readership, Jessie Ackermann's journey had indeed been centrally concerned with the ambition to spread "higher civilization" to foreign women. She visited so many lands not simply from a spirit of adventure or curiosity but as a paid organizer, or, as her employers called it, a "round-the-world missionary," of a large and prominent organization, the World's Woman's Christian Temperance Union (WCTU). Frances Willard, the American temperance leader, had shepherded the foundation of the World's WCTU in 1883 when she forged a strategic alliance with Lady Henry Somerset, president of the British Women's Temperance Association, to further their reform interests internationally. The American reformers thereby gained a higher profile and greater international significance, in addition to privileged access for their evangelists, not only where American commercial or mission activity had taken root but also in the countless sites of Britain's widespread empire.[4]

The World's WCTU missionaries, first Mary Leavitt, who began her work in 1884, and later Ackermann, carried a novel message that combined temperance and other moral reform concerns with the women's rights agenda of the U.S. women's movement, including a claim for political rights for their sex. As recent studies have shown, Willard had skillfully persuaded women, whose politicization initially arose from anger at excessive male drinking and its harmful impact on women and children, that solutions for a nation's ills would be found in promoting women's full entry to public life. Voting in elections and standing for political office were both rights and responsibilities that women, representing the spirit of motherhood, should gladly assume.[5] Few nations, Leavitt and Ackermann were to discover, were particularly interested in enfranchising their male populations, not to mention the female half. It was among British and American expatriate communities that the World's WCTU had its greatest immediate impact, since these were the places where democracy, as Americans described it, was a realistic possibility.[6]

There were women among Protestants of British birth or descent in the six colonies of Australia and the colony of New Zealand, as well as among similar Christians of American birth or descent resident in Hawai'i, who were receptive to ideas of political rights. Leavitt and Ackermann visited all these communities, which since the first white intrusion had gone separate ways politically. Hawai'i in 1888 sustained a fragile indigenous Hawaiian kingdom, with an increasingly assertive American planter and business community. By contrast, Britain had incorporated New Zealand and the Australian colonies into its empire, although settlers had managed to claim a good deal of authority for themselves. In all three places, the two envoys found Christian women conversant with the more radical component of the WCTU's agenda, its bid to mobilize women to political action on the basis of "moral motherhood."[7] Local leaders swiftly took up this cause. In New Zealand and the Australian colonies, they were instrumental in bringing the issue to the fore of public debate in the last decade of the nineteenth and first decade of the twentieth century. The successful passage of women's suffrage in New Zealand in 1893 and in the newly federated Commonwealth of Australia in 1902, distinctly in advance of their northern land of origin, brought temporary fame. By contrast, WCTU women of the American community in Hawai'i unsuccessfully raised the question of the women's vote early in the 1890s. Unlike those in many western states and territories of the United States, women in Hawai'i had to wait for their political emancipation until the passage of the Nineteenth Amendment to the Constitution in 1920.[8]

The events that led to the passage of the women's vote in Australia and New Zealand have been the subject of several studies that have explored the campaign for the vote, its protagonists, and its passage through colonial legislatures.[9] In Hawai'i the failure of the WCTU reformers and other suffragists to achieve the vote at an earlier stage has gone largely unremarked.[10] A new understanding of the success of the suffrage movement in Australia and New Zealand and its failure in Hawai'i can come from bringing these sites into a comparative framework of racial fears and contested colonialism.[11] Doing so indicates the extent to which settler anxieties about indigenous peoples' potential access to political rights influenced the differing political outcomes for women's suffrage campaigns. This article commences with an exploration of the intervention of the WCTU-led suffrage campaigns in the civil status of settler and indigenous men and women in colonial New Zealand and Australia; it then evaluates in this context the stance of WCTU activists on race; and finally it considers the contrasting situation in Hawai'i (as kingdom, republic, and American territory) in the late 1880s and 1890s.

By the later decades of the nineteenth century, the six colonies of Australia and the colony of New Zealand were notable for their many effective exponents of British liberalism. Indeed, the success of colonial liberalism in itself explains much about colonial receptivity to new ideas about women's social position. Many male politicians could quote John Stuart Mill's *The Subjection of Women*, and, in the absence of an entrenched conservative ruling class, the political culture was sympathetic to radical democratic proposals. As was the case in the United States, adult white male suffrage was enacted early in most colonies. The British Colonial Office conceded responsible government to their fledgling British colonies in the 1850s, passing most of the internal affairs to settler legislatures. The British established political rights for certain adult men, enshrining property qualifications for elections and standing for office. Quite quickly, however, the new settler governments moved to broaden the electorate. They initially maintained property qualifications for the upper house, the house of review, but enacted adult male suffrage for the lower, popular house, in which substantial power was invested.[12]

Despite the large farming and rural sector in Australian and New Zealand colonies, small industries flourished, stimulating urban growth in port and regional centers. The urban and rural industries in turn promoted the growth of a sturdy union movement that by the late 1800s had spawned labor representatives in parliaments and social democratic parties in the making.[13] Labor men had no political interests in blocking the women's vote, given universal male suffrage, provided that no property qualifications were added to the acts. Few suffrage supporters in or out of the legislatures argued for such restrictions for long. Some of the factors, therefore, that retarded the progress of suffrage campaigns elsewhere—traditional upper-class conservatism, working-class opposition to suffrage that favored the middle class—did not apply in these colonies.[14] The political climate generated by liberalism and nascent labor movements sustained a relative white male tolerance toward civil rights for white women. In the large cities of Sydney, Melbourne, and Christchurch, small numbers of women associated together to press for the vote. Some were middle-class women supported by the income of spouses, while others had private means. Working women were quick to be aware of the suffrage question, and some found routes to register their interest.[15]

Mary Leavitt and Jessie Ackermann found the colonies also to be fertile soil for the WCTU, as a women's organization that promoted temperance along with women's rights. If these suffragists who were temperance activists had a key anxiety, it was violent white men, irresponsible husbands, and abusive fathers. Male drinking to excess, binge drinking, deaths from drunkenness, male-on-male violence, and domestic violence were rife on these male-dominated frontiers of white settlement. The message of the World's WCTU, which Leavitt brought in the mid-1880s and Ackermann reinforced in the late 1880s and 1890s, made sense to progressive evangelical women already active in parochial reform. The WCTU in New Zealand, which Leavitt inaugurated in 1885, when she formed ten branches between February and August, had within two years appointed a Franchise Superintendent, Kate Wilson Sheppard, who proved astute in adapting various methods of political lobbying to pursue the suffrage cause. The women's vote came close to passing in 1890, 1891, and 1892, and finally won a majority in both houses of the legislature in September 1893. All adult women received the vote and exercised it in large numbers in the general election in November of that year.[16]

The situation in the six Australian colonies was similar in the rapidity with which women's suffrage moved from the first serious mention in public debate to political reality. In the two colonies where women's suffrage was enacted before the end of the century, South Australia and Western Australia, the WCTU was also the major player in the suffrage campaign.[17] South Australia enfranchised women in 1894, and Western Australia did so in 1899. It was the South Australian decision that proved crucial in the decision to give women in the new Commonwealth of Australia the vote eight years later, in 1902.

When senior politicians from the six colonies met during the mid-1890s to draft the federal Constitution, they intended to make the provisions for voting rights for the new Commonwealth Parliament the same as currently held good in each colony. Some objected, however, that, since women could vote in South Australia, this one new state would have an unfair advantage. The writers of the Constitution compromised by protecting South Australian women's voting rights, and subsequently Western Australian women's rights, but anticipated swift legislation in the new Parliament to enfranchise women in all other states.[18] Women in the other four states—New South Wales, Victoria, Queensland, and Tasmania—were similarly enfranchised federally, as promised, under the Commonwealth Elections Act in 1902. The voting rights in those states followed on from the federal legislation: 1902 in New South Wales, 1903 in Tasmania, 1905 in Queensland, and 1908 in Victoria.[19]

One reason for the absence of male opposition to women's suffrage was so pervasive as to go almost unnoticed, then and since. A very real anxiety about the future of their new nations consumed leading settler politicians as the century drew to a close, an anxiety that intertwined with responses to women's political rights. How were the white citizens of New Zealand and Australia to keep their countries white? White colonial politicians were not dealing solely with the rights of indigenous peoples. They faced a dual anxiety, given their fear that Asian peoples—particularly Chinese—might immigrate and outnumber the British population, as the latter had once overwhelmed the Aborigines.

As the Australian colonies moved toward federation, a leader in the federation cause, Alfred Deakin, declared: "The question of white Australia touches all colonists' instinct for self-preservation." No power dissolved divisions among colonists so forcefully, he said, as "the desire that we should be one people, and remain one people, without the admixture of other races."[20] In a situation where white male politicians made such racial distinctions, white women could appear to them very much part of the privileged and beleaguered elite white circle, dissolving divisions based on gender. As one member of Parliament said when debating women's suffrage in Western Australia:

> It is admitted on all sides that, while men are only the progenitors of our race, the women are its saviors; and that on the future of the Anglo-Saxon race to which we are all proud to belong, and on the future of the civilized races of the world, women are exercising a higher influence and playing a more important part and will continue to do so, than men can aspire to do. On these lines I claim the right of woman to have a vote.[21]

Added, then, to a liberal political climate and a strong democratic labor movement pledged to social justice was a racism that drove a desire to keep the colonies white. White women were part of the "Anglo-Saxon race" that the colonies celebrated as they congratulated themselves on pioneering a new land and creating prosperous and progressive societies. These men had created a narrative of success in which white women, when they paused to think about it, were a valued part. White women had endured the hazards of new frontiers, they reminded each other, and they were the honored mothers of future white citizens. Such racialized thinking goes some way toward explaining the absence of effective opposition to women's suffrage once women activists publicly promoted the cause.

There was, however, a major difference in the ways these anxieties were represented in the provisions for the women's vote in New Zealand and the Commonwealth of Australia. In New Zealand the electoral act of 1893 brought in universal adult female suffrage for Maori and white settler women alike. Australia, by contrast, brought in female suffrage for white women only. The Commonwealth Electoral Act of 1902 excluded Aborigines, even if, in the letter of the law, this was not for some states immediately apparent. A clause read: "No Aboriginal native of Australia, Asia, Africa, or the Islands of the Pacific, except New Zealand, shall be entitled to have his name placed on the electoral roll."[22] Section 41 of the constitution, which enshrined federal voting rights for those who voted in the states, should have protected the political rights of Aboriginal men in the south-eastern states, but interpreters of the constitution and bureaucratic implementation removed them. In New Zealand settler fears of men of color had led to the incorporation of Maori men into the mainstream political system; hence, Maori women could readily be incorporated as well when the women's vote was on the agenda. Settler fears of men of color in Australia, however, led to their exclusion from mainstream politics at the very time that women's suffrage was on the national agenda. Aboriginal women inevitably suffered the same fate. We need to consider in some detail the working through of racial politics in each country to understand how the different position of indigenous women and men, compared with white women, occurred.

In New Zealand the difference may be traced to two historical factors: Maori adoption of Christianity and Maori capacity for military defense against settler occupation. The British Crown first assumed political control of the islands of New Zealand in 1840 under the Treaty of Waitangi, when Maori chiefs agreed to concede a degree of sovereignty to the British in the face of the continuing uncontrolled arrival of white people. A people who lived principally by horticulture and fishing, Maori society was highly stratified and dominated by a strong chiefly elite. Previously warlike and feuding, the chiefs with their peoples converted to Christianity after 1814 when missionaries first established their mission stations. Initially, Maori groups were prepared to concede land for sale to settlers. As the governor of the colony, Gore Browne, told settler politicians in 1854, their prudent goal had to be "to preserve and to advance the scale of civilization of the native inhabitants of these Islands," while remaining "the pioneers for its colonization by the Anglo Saxon race." Keeping these dual goals in harmony proved very difficult.[23]

When by the early 1860s many Maori chiefs, alarmed at the pressure of the growing number of white arrivals, became reluctant to alienate additional land, hostilities broke into open warfare, and British troops arrived in considerable numbers to defend their expatriates' interests. When the worst of the fighting was over, the British governor in New Zealand and the Colonial Office in London faced the question of how the defeated Maori should be treated in the representative political system established in the colony. Since Maori held most land in common, seldom individually, few Maori men had qualified to vote or stand for office under the first constitution, which contained a property qualification. As settlers began to press for white adult male suffrage, the governor feared that, if Maori men were excluded, ensuing bitterness might lead to further hostilities. As a leading white politician said in agreement, the New Zealand legislature needed "to use the means at its disposal for allaying any of the angry feeling or excitement that might still remain."[24] But the anxieties of settlers did not end there. Despite the fact that Maori, prone to imported European diseases, were rapidly decreasing as the white population grew, Maori were still numerous enough in some electorates to have a substantial influence on the outcome of an election, harming settler candidates and ultimately the supremacy of white interests in the legislature. The result was a compromise. Under the Maori Representation Act of 1867, Maori were allocated four special seats, three in the North Island and one for the whole of the South Island, on an adult male suffrage basis. Only Maori would be eligible for these seats, though Maori could stand in other electorates as well. Viewed from one perspective, it seemed like a liberal provision: Maori men could vote, and at least four Maori would be members of every Parliament. Proposed as an interim measure, the separate electorates in fact stayed in place into the next century.[25]

When the Parliaments of 1890 to 1893, therefore, considered the women's vote, there was little or no question of excluding Maori women. The electoral settlement had occurred twenty-five years earlier. When the question was put to the House of Representatives, "the voices of the friends of the Maori ladies rose in such a roar" that the matter was settled on voice vote.[26] Maori women's political rights could be accommodated by their allocation to the same four Maori electorates. Universal women's enfranchisement in 1893 thus did not unsettle the system previously designed to protect settlers from potential renewed Maori military aggression and Maori political power. White women did not need to be kept out of the system so that Maori women could be kept out also.

The settlement that white legislators reached in relation to white women's and Aboriginal peoples' political rights at the time of the creation of the Commonwealth of Australia was more complex. The history of each colony was different, as were their interests or reservations about joining the federation. Those colonial politicians who promoted federation needed to counter core objections coming from the separate colonies. Aborigines were most numerous in the north and west. When politicians from Western Australia and Queensland voiced negative opinions of Aborigines' capacity to contribute to white political processes and added fears concerning the potential impact of the Aboriginal vote should they exercise it, their peers in southeastern Australia listened sympathetically, ready to compromise. Brazenly, given an ostensible commitment to democracy, Australian politicians were prepared to let white women in while keeping Aboriginal men and women outside the political system. They had all treated indigenous Australians shamefully. The wish to negate them as a political presence as they had marginalized them socially shaped the electoral provisions.

The British occupation of the Australian continent—or at least those parts of it with sufficient rainfall for white pastoralism—was rapid, after the initial decades of convict settlement. As men with their flocks of sheep and herds of cattle fanned out across the interior, they encountered small bands of hunter-gatherer Aborigines who moved across their tribal territories to pursue game and harvest seasonal plants and fruits. When Aborigines resisted white incursions, retribution by white men on horseback with guns was swift and terrible. As in New Zealand, European diseases took a further toll on a beleaguered people. With no treaties to offer even the semblance of protection, surviving Aborigines were accorded no land to which they had title, and many were forcibly resettled on mission stations and reserves where lives of poverty, minimal education, and draconian state surveillance awaited them.[27]

Nevertheless, Aboriginal men were not debarred from political rights in the first constitutions of New South Wales, Victoria, South Australia, and Tasmania under which the British government handed over responsible government to settlers. Nor, when those colonies moved to manhood suffrage, did they insert such a bar. Most Aborigines were, of course, excluded as "paupers" since the state funded the missions on which so many lived. Western Australia and Queensland governments, where the frontier was not closed until the end of the century, retained a property qualification for Aboriginal men. Given that Aborigines had lost their lands, few if any qualified.[28]

When in the 1890s representatives of the colonies met to write a constitution for a new Commonwealth of Australia, they wanted a uniform franchise for federal elections but faced two obstacles. One was the differences across the colonies in existing political rights for Aboriginal men. The other was the fact that one colony, South Australia, had granted political rights to women. The solution was spelled out in the Constitution adopted in 1901, which marked the launching of the new nation, and in the Commonwealth Franchise Act, which the new federal legislature passed the following year. In effect, different outcomes were chosen for Aborigines and for white women. Aborigines, men and women, were in effect excluded from political rights, along with other people of color whose immigration was severely restricted. All adult white women, conversely, received full political rights.[29] Would it not, asked a Western Australian senator, be "absolutely repugnant" to most people of the Commonwealth that an Aboriginal woman, or man, "should have the same rights simply by virtue of being 21 years of age, that we have, after some debate today, decided to give our wives and daughters?" And the legislators did not do so.[30]

While Aborigines who already had the vote in the southeastern states ought to have retained this state right, the federal exclusion trumped the states. Not until 1962 did the federal government restore political rights to Aborigines.[31] Meanwhile, Australia earned the reputation as a site of progressive policies for women. It was progressive for white women only. Aborigines were declared not to be citizens in the land of their birth and swiftly disappeared from mainstream discussion of rights and entitlements.

There is every reason to expect that most politically aware settler women in New Zealand and the Australian colonies sustained ideas about the political rights of indigenes similar to those of their male counterparts. A question remains, however, about the stance of the suffrage activists of the WCTU. Such women belonged to a humanitarian tradition and were consistently vocal in their concern for the status of women of color abroad. At the second national convention of the Australian WCTU in Sydney in 1894, Jessie Ackermann proudly proclaimed: "Our banner floats in forty-seven lands, and in forty-seven languages can we read our motto 'For God and Home and Every Land.' "[32] Local members more quietly pointed out that the World's WCTU proved above all else that women of varying ethnicities and races could work together for a common cause. In the 1890s and early 1900s, the colonial members were reticent, however, about the political rights of indigenous women. Ackermann herself indicated an explanation for their attitude toward the rights of colonized peoples in *The World Through a Woman's Eyes* when she dedicated it to Richard Pratt, the superintendent of the Indian Industrial School in Carlisle, Pennsylvania, whom she called the founder of the "Greatest Educational and Individualizing Enterprise in the World." She hoped that "the great possibilities of the Red Man may become better known and a deeper interest awakened in the first natives of our land."[33] As Christian evangelicals with a heritage of humanitarianism, the local evangelical activists relied on missionaries to look after indigenous peoples' welfare and protection, and they assessed indigenous women and men on the steps they had made in "progress" toward Western educational, religious, and cultural norms.

The WCTU suffragists might have wanted to "uplift" indigenous peoples; they were not usually resistant, however, to settler narratives that legitimated white colonization and expropriation of others' lands. Ackermann's references to the colonies in her book indicated that she, too, had quickly tuned in to settlers' views of the world. Echoing the patronizing attitude of white New Zealanders, she found Maori "very intelligent, more so I should say than are any of the natives of the South Seas," by which she meant that many Maori had adopted aspects of Western education, religion, dress, and behavior.[34] She describes as a "lawless spirit," "a dangerous character," one chief who had continued to resist white settlement. He had "given the authorities very much trouble"; the new chief, who called himself "King," was, on the contrary, "peace-loving and law-abiding."[35] In her later *Australia Through a Woman's Eyes*, Ackermann's sole reference to Aborigines was a photograph depicting on the left a traditional Aboriginal man in a loincloth, spear in hand, and on the right, an Aboriginal man in Western clothes, standing outside a neat cottage, arm-in-arm with a missionary.[36] *The World Through a Woman's Eyes* similarly describes Ackermann's visit to Tasmania, where she invoked the veil of silence that settlers drew over the disgraceful near-genocide of Tasmanian Aborigines. Instead, she rehearsed a history of Australia's transition from its miserable convict origins to a bright progressive present.[37]

The women's vote also made its appearance in the 1890s in the political life of Hawai'i, and once again Jessie Ackermann's brief observations on her visit and subsequent events are instructive of white colonizers' narratives. The "natives" of Hawai'i, she found, had made "great progress" since their language was first transposed into written form. "Idolatry is now unknown among them, their idols are broken, and their superstitions have given way to enlightenment."[38] She was gratified to find that many Hawaiians were industrious, lived in neat houses with gardens, and dressed appropriately for preserving modesty in a tropical climate. The American missionaries who first established themselves in the islands in 1820 had clearly set native Hawaiians on a path that met this evangelical visitor's approval.[39] Yet Ackermann found a grave problem in the existence of a Hawaiian king, David Kalākaua, whose methods of government—indeed, whose very royal existence—disturbed her American democratic and republican convictions. She was reduced to sarcasm in describing her audience with the king:

> This was my first experience in the presence of real live royalty—a natural-born King—a fellow-creature great because he could not help it—born great. Poor man, how sorry I was for him to be thus burdened! Yet I must nerve myself to gaze upon a sight my eyes had never beheld. How I felt! My democratic, Fourth-of-July principles bore down heavily upon me as I thought of the bowing, scraping and "backing out" from his natural-born mightiness.[40]

Ackermann's impressions of Kalākaua were not good; he was "very unpopular among the whites," she noted, and, "had his days been lengthened, he doubtless would have met the fate of the one who tried to succeed him."[41]

With these words Ackermann explicitly allied herself with the white, largely American-stock community—the haoles—who were at the time of her visit competing with the Hawaiian chiefs for political control. The American camp wanted a special relationship with the United States to protect the sugar trade and business; the chiefs wanted to sustain indigenous political control and respect for Hawaiian dignity and worth. The American residents had recently staged a showdown of power with Kalākaua but backed away from a full-blown coup. In 1893 they abandoned their earlier scruples and, with the help of

American marines brought ashore from a visiting naval vessel, deposed Kalākaua's successor, Queen Lili'uokalani, and established the short-lived Republic of Hawaii.[42] In 1898, already involved in fighting Spain in Cuba and the Philippines, the U.S. Congress agreed to annex Hawai'i as a territory; the promise of a naval base at Pearl Harbor was no small incentive. Ackermann echoed the resident American justification for imperialism, observing that the natives "were becoming well educated, the spirit of progress had taken possession of them." They too were starting to feel that "the old form of government did not meet the demands of the day, and the rulers were behind in the recognition of the rights of the people."[43]

The local WCTU women, nearly all of them descendants of or married to descendants of the first missionaries, similarly declared American progress and liberty good for Hawaiians, and they supported their male counterparts in their assumption of power.[44] The leadership of the Hawaiian WCTU, founded in 1884 under Mary Leavitt's guiding hand, had no doubt where their loyalties lay. Mary Greene, daughter of missionaries and herself the Union Superintendent of Work among the Hawaiians, had applauded the American business group when it challenged Kalākaua in 1887: "The women of this country owe a debt of deepest gratitude to those who so wisely planned and carried out the political reform," she told the WCTU Annual Meeting in 1888. "All honor to the men who stood bayonet in hand ready to defend the cause."[45]

Neither did they have qualms about the 1893 coup, or the "Revolution," as the Americans called it, harking back to an earlier heroic blow for liberty in 1776. All appeared to concur with men such as Sereno Bishop, editor of the evangelicals' paper, *The Friend*. "It has been a grand thing to pass through all this exciting and exalting experience," wrote this descendant of pioneering missionaries. "Our noble citizens of American and European blood have once more paid homage and devotion to the lofty cause of Liberty and Progress."[46] WCTU member Emma Smith Dillingham had the grace to concede in a private letter that "This *must* be the *last* Revolution" (emphasis in original), while she assured her correspondent that the men who had taken over government were filled with "the desire to further the welfare of the people in every particular."[47] She clearly discounted the significance of the Hui Aloha Aina (Hawaiian Patriotic League), which sprang into existence in March 1893 to protest the coup and which had an associated women's branch of over 11,000 members.[48]

The WCTU leaders were swift to grasp that the crisis of the newly proclaimed republic, which would necessitate a rewriting of electoral entitlements, offered an opportunity to gain the vote for women. Having unsuccessfully begged the U.S. government to annex the islands, the provisional government that took power after the coup convened a constitutional convention to establish the legal basis of their new republic. Early in 1894 the WCTU called a series of well-attended women's meetings to publicize arguments in favor of enfranchising women, forming a Woman Suffrage Committee to meet with the male delegates to the convention.[49] The gentlemen were more than chivalrous to the women's concerns, but, they asked, were revolutionary times the most favorable for something as radical as the women's vote? As one convention participant declared: "if all the women who asked for the franchise were of the same class as the committee, there would be no trouble." But, as another delegate pointed out, all women were not like the suffragists who stood before them. "We have all factions and degrees of ignorance in this country," he pleaded. "We are trying to make a constitution to suit all classes." Manhood suffrage had existed in the Hawaiian Kingdom since 1850, and he appreciated that the WCTU now rightly pointed out women's claims to equality. But, as Judge Robertson argued in opposing the suffrage, if women were enfranchised at this critical juncture, the numbers of non-American women would add to the problem of numbers that already existed: "There were about seven Hawaiian women to one white woman here. This would give a big majority of undesirable votes." As another delegate put it more crassly: "It would double up on the ignorant vote."[50]

At this point, the suffrage activists sought a compromise. There was, of course, no question of a racial bar, given that, as humanitarians and evangelicals, they did genuinely believe in the potential equality of all races, once appropriately Christianized, educated, and accepting of American values. The WCTU activists did, however, entertain an educational bar, or a property qualification, which would have admitted almost all white women and the more privileged of the women of color. When the convention rejected even these concessions, the suffrage supporters backed a clause in the new constitution that would enable a government in the future to pass women's suffrage by legislation rather than constitutional amendment. That too was lost. Reporting back to the WCTU, the women consoled themselves with the hope that their actions were "an entering wedge, and at some future time we expect to have the privilege of helping to make laws which will be for the uplifting of the Nation."[51]

This moment was a long time coming. The 1898 Organic Act, which completed the incorporation of Hawai'i as a territory of the United States of America, similarly excluded women from voting for or serving in the Hawaiian Senate or House of Representatives or from serving as territorial delegate to Congress. Susan B. Anthony was watching the process and vented her anger: "I have been overflowing with wrath ever since the proposal was made to engraft our half-barbaric form of government on Hawaii and our other new possessions." She wrote:

> I have been studying how to save, not them, but ourselves, from disgrace. This is the first time the United States has ever tried to foist upon a new people the exclusively masculine form of government. Our business should be to give the people the highest form which has been attained by us.[52]

Not many people were listening. Women in Hawai'i had not received the vote in the 1890s because elite white men feared that doubling the Hawaiian vote would have negative implications on their hope for a prosperous, American, business-oriented future. Despite the strong social position of WCTU leaders in Hawaiian society and their humanitarian convictions on social justice, American pragmatic interests prevailed. The haole women appeared oblivious to the irony entailed in their applause for the republic that removed a queen and other highborn Hawaiian women from positions of authority, while they lamented this same new government's denial of women's suffrage to themselves. Their aim was gender equality within a racial hierarchy.

After their early beginning on the path to suffrage, haole women, Hawaiian women, and other women of color in the Hawaiian Islands did not receive the vote until 1920, through the Nineteenth Amendment to the U.S. Constitution. It is ironic to note Judith Gething's point that in the early Hawaiian kingdom many women from the high-born chiefly elite not only had an equal say in the legislature but also took seats in the upper house, the House of Nobles. Through American influence, they lost their political status, only to be graciously given it back by Americans decades later, in 1920.[53]

Suffrage activists in the new white societies of New Zealand, the Australian colonies, and Hawai'i were liberal in political orientation and heirs to a tradition of evangelical humanitarianism. When they presented their case for women's entry into political rights, they eschewed the racism of many fellow colonists. These women were nevertheless part of a privileged social group who colluded in the creation of an historical narrative that presented colonization in a positive light. It was a version of history that had justified, and continued to justify, differential treatment of indigenous peoples. When the suffragists' cause reached the platforms of those holding political power, politicians made decisions based on not just the supposed outcomes on gender relations but on the vote's implications for the colonial project as a whole. They manipulated women's civil rights in ways that would diminish indigenous people's impact on settlers' political dominance.

Thus New Zealand legislators in 1893 were prepared to admit Maori women as well as white women to the vote because Maori women's influence would be contained within preexisting Maori-only electorates. By contrast, the new Australian Commonwealth legislature proceeded effectively to exclude all Aborigines in the same electoral act that enfranchised white women twenty-one years of age and over. Finally, the American men who wrote the new republican Hawaiian Constitution provided a further contrast when they denied both white women and Hawaiian women the vote for fear of destabilizing a finely balanced political compromise. Colonial suffrage campaigns challenged existing codes of gender, certainly, but the politics of race was never far from the surface in legislative resolutions of this debate.

10

CHALLENGING TRADITIONS

Denominational feminism in Britain, 1910–1920

Jacqueline R. de Vries

The impact of World War I on the progress of women's emancipation in Great Britain has been the subject of much scholarly attention.[1] The standard interpretation has emphasized that the war, while the occasion of women's achievement of the vote, ushered in a period of quiescence in feminist organizing. Susan Kingsley Kent, for example, has argued that within the postwar climate, suffragettes demobilized their "sex war," succumbed to public anxiety about women's political and economic emancipation, and ceased to challenge the dominant gender ideology of separate spheres.[2] Other scholars have argued that the postwar emphasis on maternalist values was neither necessarily a concession to the ideology of separate spheres nor inherently antifeminist.[3] These interpretations, however, tend to focus on feminist attitudes toward such issues as politics, employment, and the family, and include little analysis of postwar (or, for that matter, prewar) feminist attitudes toward religion. Yet, as Sheila Fletcher's biography of the prominent Anglican suffragist A. Maude Royden suggests, the postwar period was characterized by unprecedented progress for women within religious contexts and witnessed the rise of the movement for women's ordination to the Anglican Church.[4] When the category of religion is included in the analysis of the British women's movement, postwar feminism begins to look less quiescent.

This essay will attempt to sketch out the ways in which religious beliefs and contexts helped to shape feminist identity and action before, during, and immediately after World War I. I begin with a general consideration of the place of religion within the context of the prewar suffrage movement as a whole. I then move on to a more specific analysis of feminist activism within the contexts of the Anglican and Roman Catholic Churches. Finally, I consider the ways in which World War I reshaped national attitudes toward religion and consequently sparked new confidence and provided fresh opportunities for those women who advanced their feminist ideals through organizations affiliated with specific denominations. I refer to these women as "denominational feminists"; conversely, I use the term "nondenominational feminist" to refer to those women who worked for the vote exclusively through secular suffrage organizations, even though these women may have considered themselves religious and been members of specific denominations.

British feminism and Protestant culture before 1914

The linkages between religion and national identity have been well established for the British context. Protestantism, as embodied in the Anglican Church, traditionally functioned as a key component in the formation and preservation of British national consciousness and, through its staunch opposition to "foreign" Roman Catholicism, served as a powerful force for national integration.[5] As David Hempton has argued, well into the nineteenth century this "shared Protestantism and Anti-Catholicism did not, of course, dissolve the cultural and historical divisions of the British peoples, but it did offer an easily available and deeply felt principle to rally around."[6] By the late nineteenth century, Anti-Catholicism was in swift decline, in part because the growth of Anglo-Catholicism had discredited the Church of England as a bastion of Protestantism, and in part because of the decline of religion more generally.[7] But Anti-Catholicism did not decline at the same pace among all social classes in all parts of the British Isles.[8] Nor did it affect men and women in the same ways.

The British women's movement was shaped within this everchanging, but still deeply rooted, context of the Protestant nation-state. The earliest participants in the nineteenth-century women's suffrage movement were drawn largely from the Protestant middle classes. Many were strongly influenced by evangelicalism, which as the work of Leonore Davidoff and Catherine Hall has demonstrated, "offered women a life work, which, while subordinate, carried dignity and moral weight."[9] Women who joined the movement rarely chose to reject religion wholesale, and in fact frequently attributed their political work to the expression of devout religious belief.[10] The few women who did leave traditional churches turned most often to alternative forms of religious practice, such as spiritualism or Theosophy, rather than to agnosticism or atheism.[11] Whether orthodox or unorthodox, participants in the nineteenth-century women's movement tended to see religion not only as compatible with feminism, but also as a very real, or at least a potential, catalyst for women's emancipation as they defined it.

By the late nineteenth century, the women's movement in Britain had become increasingly focused on the campaign for women's suffrage at the national level and had begun to attract a membership from a broader social spectrum. Growing numbers of working-class women joined suffrage societies after 1900, drawn in by the efforts of Emmeline Pankhurst and her daughters, Christabel and Sylvia, in the slums of Manchester.[12] Catholic and Jewish women also became active in the suffrage movement, although their numbers initially remained small and were drawn mainly from the middle and upper classes. The movement's increasing class and religious heterogeneity inevitably brought varying perspectives and vocabularies. Many Protestant middle-class suffragists, for example, expressed their demands for the vote in strikingly evangelical terms.[13] Suffrage rallies were consciously modeled after the revivalist meetings popularized by Victorian evangelists, the Salvation Army, and the Labour Church, and thus drew on language and styles that may have been unfamiliar to non-Protestant women.

Nevertheless, the evangelical style of the movement did not prove to be a major stumbling block to cross-denominational suffrage cooperation. As I have argued elsewhere, the spiritual language of the Protestant middle-class suffragists served as a common metaphor, unifying suffragists and suffragettes from diverse class and religious backgrounds in a shared struggle for national regeneration.[14] Yet, differences of perspective remained. Protestant middle-class suffragists, for example, largely took for granted their affinity with British political culture and saw the vote as a means by which they could, by virtue of their gender, make important contributions to national life. In contrast, Catholic women, and women from other dissenting groups, saw the vote as a potential victory for both themselves, as women, and for their minority confessional communities.

In an attempt to express these differences, groups of suffragists and suffragettes established their own denominational suffrage leagues between 1909 and 1912. Representing the Anglican, Free Church, Catholic, Scottish Presbyterian, and Jewish traditions, these suffrage societies strove to articulate their unique perspectives on the suffrage question, as well as to persuade more members of their denominations to support the suffrage cause. In contrast to the religious women's organizations in France and Germany, which were distinctly antisuffragist,[15] each of the religious suffrage leagues was committed to securing political rights for women on an equal basis with men. All apparently were inspired by the militancy of the Women's Social and Political Union (WSPU) and (with the possible exception of the Quakers' Friends' League for Women's Suffrage) saw themselves as sharing common goals with the "fighting women." Furthermore, the religious leagues recognized commonalities in their "religious perspective" on suffrage, and they frequently held joint demonstrations and sponsored educational meetings under the collective known as the "United Religious Leagues."

Choosing between radicalism and respectability: Anglican and Catholic suffragists

The two most active and long-lasting suffrage leagues were the (Anglican) Church League for Women's Suffrage (CLWS) and the Catholic Women's Suffrage Society (CWSS). Both were established in the midst of the suffrage agitation and remained vital organizations after the vote was granted in 1918 to women over the age of thirty. A comparison of these two leagues is particularly useful because, while they were both feminist organizations within male-dominated, hierarchically organized churches, they each had a very different relationship to the predominantly Protestant British national culture. As members of the national church, Anglican feminists struggled to define a place for themselves within a hierarchical church, but they also enjoyed greater security and latitude for action than did Catholic feminists. Consequently, Anglican feminists became much bolder than the Catholics in demanding expanded roles and positions of authority for women within their church's structure. Catholic feminists also worked hard to overcome opposition and apathy within their own confessional community, but they faced the additional challenge of overcoming prejudice toward their religion within the wider English population. Consequently, Catholic feminists shaped their organization into more moderate and respectable directions.

The CLWS was the largest of the religious leagues. In the years between 1909 and 1914, the CLWS attracted more than 5,700 men and women members, representing ninety-one branches across England, Scotland, Ireland, and Wales.[16] The league was democratically organized, with regular annual meetings and a governing structure that allowed all members to vote on policy and strategy. Initially, the guiding force of the CLWS was a group of individuals—Gertrude and Claude Hinscliff, Henry Scott Holland, Margaret Wynne Nevinson, and Mabel and Percy Dearmer—who had been strongly influenced by the Christian Socialist movement of the 1880s and 1890s. They brought to the CLWS a strong belief in the potential of combining progressive social action with Christian faith, as well as the conviction that the Anglican Church was to be the main force in the regeneration of British society.[17] These leaders attracted similarly reform-minded Anglicans, particularly those who had drifted from, or become increasingly critical of, the Anglican Church, but had not entirely given up on organized Christianity. Margaret Nevinson, who had dabbled in spiritualism and explored Christian Socialism in the 1890s, commented that the CLWS drew "back to the church of their baptism many wanderers from the fold."[18] The CLWS also attracted a few aristocratic and more orthodox members, who saw it as a respectable alternative to the more militant societies. Louise Creighton, widow of Bishop Mandell Creighton and formerly a prominent suffrage opponent, publicly announced her support for women's suffrage shortly after the formation of the CLWS. To her, the CLWS offered a much-needed counterbalance to the "wild performances" of the suffragettes.[19] More than five hundred clergy also joined the CLWS. Such prominent figures as the Bishops of Lincoln, Hereford, and Kensington agreed to sit on the executive committee; Bishop Gore of Oxford, Bishop Winnington-Ingram of London, and Bishop Paget of Stepney frequently spoke on CLWS platforms; and the editor of the CLWS monthly newspaper, *The Church League for Women's Suffrage* (hereafter *CLWS*), launched in January of 1912, was the Rev. F. M. Green, Vicar of St. Mark's in north London.[20]

The main aim of the CLWS was to persuade both clergy and laity that a suffrage victory for women would benefit both the Anglican church and the nation as a whole. Leaving to nondenominational leagues the work of lobbying the government, the CLWS concentrated its efforts on influencing attitudes among Anglicans. The organization sought to win over critics who believed that public—and, more specifically, political—roles for women were against God's will.[21] Echoing a point made frequently in the wider movement, CLWS members claimed that women's emancipation and Christianity were both compatible and fundamentally intertwined. Through their work, CLWS members hoped the league would model a broad, socially active form of Anglicanism.

Many who joined the CLWS also saw it as a means through which to achieve more general, and not always exclusively feminist, reform within the Anglican Church. Some hoped, for example, that the CLWS would help facilitate greater lay participation in church governance. Among the chorus of enthusiastic clerical members of the CLWS, some advocated women's suffrage less for its own sake than for the benefits it might bring to the Church and the nation. They equated the advancement of women more with the promotion of public morals and national well-being than with women's own rights and needs. Logically, such an argument would weaken if women did not prove themselves worthy of this lofty goal. Indeed, among some Anglican clergy, support for women's suffrage waned as suffragette militancy made national headlines. The Archbishop of Canterbury, Randall T. Davidson, for example, withdrew his support for the suffrage movement after the WSPU began to foment violence, claiming doubts about women's suitability for participation in national politics. As the head of England's national church, Davidson insisted he could not promote a group of women whose views and actions might have a negative effect on the nation's moral tone.[22] By extension, Davidson was reluctant to support the CLWS, which never formally condemned suffragette militancy.

Some Anglican women were unhappy with the CLWS's male-centeredness and timid policies and sought a more confrontational approach. In 1912, Alice Kidd organized the Suffragist Churchwoman's Protest Committee, which bypassed the CLWS's "educational methods" and encouraged the boycott of churches whose clerics were openly opposed to women's suffrage.[23] The Protest Committee's initial efforts predictably caused much consternation among more conservative CLWS members and especially the clergy. Kidd asserted that the Protest Committee's goal was to demonstrate that women were not merely permanent and submissive members of the Church of England.[24] Some women believed the church boycott was still too passive, and formulated another strategy: they attended worship services but walked out immediately before the sermon, or, even more dramatically, interrupted the sermon with shouts of "votes for women." Introduced in 1913, this tactic was particularly successful in drawing publicity and was soon co-opted by other denominational and nondenominational suffrage leagues. The CLWS executive committee officially distanced itself from these actions, preferring to address suffrage opponents directly (and moderately) on the pages of the *CLWS*.

Like the CLWS, the Catholic Women's Suffrage Society attempted to fashion itself as a feminist organization within a male-dominated, hierarchically organized church. But, in contrast to the CLWS, the CWSS was an all-woman society, free from the constant control of the Catholic hierarchy. The society was adamantly in favor of equal suffrage rights and tried not to let the opinions of the Catholic clergy openly influence its aims or methods. Yet, despite its attempts at autonomy, the CWSS could not escape the implications of its status as a Catholic organization within a predominantly Protestant nation. By the end of the nineteenth century, anti-Catholic prejudices were losing ground in Britain, in part because of the examples of social activism and civic leadership provided by prominent Catholic leaders.[25] By 1910, augmented by both new converts and Irish immigrants, the Catholic community in England was no longer a tiny minority. Nevertheless, many Catholics continued to feel that they occupied a secondary status within the Protestant British nation.[26] The CWSS responded to the uncertainties of this position by guarding the integrity of the Catholic tradition and attempting to champion a model of Catholic political activism.

The CWSS was begun in November of 1910 by two young, single, Catholic women who were sympathetic to the militant suffrage movement but concluded that it did not satisfactorily express the vision of Catholic feminists.[27] Few Catholic women of any class background had joined the nondenominational suffrage societies, and Gabrielle Jeffery and May Kendall hoped that the CWSS would provide Catholic women with a respectable way of becoming active in the suffrage battle. In its early years, however, the CWSS remained small and exclusively middle class. The seven original members of the CWSS executive council were mostly in their twenties, single, and well-educated, and they tended to attract members from similar backgrounds. The CWSS drew some members from the Catholic social and cultural elite—including the acclaimed poet Alice Meynell and the well-known convert Mrs. Virginia Crawford, who was also a London County Council member. But it largely failed to interest and, at least before the war, remained comfortably aloof from the bulk of working-class Catholic women.[28]

The CWSS executive council and the majority of its members preferred to advance the suffrage issue quietly through uniquely Catholic "religious and educational" methods. Members were asked to say one "Hail Mary" and the invocation "Blessed Joan of Arc pray for us" every day. The CWSS colors were selected to signify their loyalty to their tradition: blue, in homage to Mary the Mother of Jesus, and the papal colors of white and gold, to honor their allegiance to the Catholic Church. Only Catholic speakers were to appear on CWSS platforms. According to one pamphlet, the CWSS defined its purposes as, first, "to uphold the definite Catholic teaching on points connected with the position of woman legally, socially and politically" and, second, "to carry on an active propaganda on [women's suffrage], which being political cannot be mentioned in the pulpit."[29]

The official Catholic stance toward the CWSS was one of ambivalence, sometimes bordering on hostility. When first organizing their society, the CWSS women asked Archbishop Bourne of Westminster his opinion on women's suffrage. When he refused to offer one, they interpreted his silence as tacit approval and continued with their plans.[30] Few members of the Anglo-Catholic hierarchy were openly supportive of the suffrage cause, and at times some attacked it outright. In 1912, for example, the CWSS found itself an unwitting target of suspicion and hostility from many segments of the Catholic community after the Jesuit Father Henry Day delivered a series of sermons condemning women's social and political emancipation as "immoral," "a blasphemy," and "anti-racial," by which he meant that the vote would lead to the decline of the British birthrate and consequently the weakening of the Anglo-Saxon race.[31]

Within this uncertain climate, the CWSS struggled to define its feminist vision. In response to Father Day's attacks, for example, one CWSS member, Alice Abadam, retaliated with her own series of speeches in which she defended suffrage militancy as "righteous" and berated Father Day as "a politician."[32] But the CWSS executive was uncomfortable with Abadam's bold style and strident rhetoric, believing that patience and fortitude were the best responses to attacks such as Father Day's. In a private letter, the CWSS press secretary Blanche Smyth-Piggot admitted to her friend Mildred Tuker that she believed Father Day was wrong, yet she also thought that "the safest pose for the Catholic Suffrage Society is that of defending the Church and not exposing it, especially to outsiders." The Catholic hierarchy was not infallible, she readily admitted:

> [But] in the case of us Catholics, we must be so absolutely certain of our facts which is not always possible. One has to be on guard against one's own colouring and prejudices, for a time at any rate we must convince the priests rather than set them all against us.[33]

Smyth-Piggot's comments reveal the underlying lack of confidence that pervaded the CWSS before World War I. Unsure of their place as feminists within the Catholic tradition, CWSS leaders were not prepared to push too far or too confidently their claim that women's emancipation was the fulfillment of Christian ideals—a claim that would require some to rethink their conservative Christian beliefs. Wary of latent Anti-Catholicism, the CWSS was reluctant to openly criticize the opinions of other Catholics. The CWSS never confronted the Catholic Church in the manner of the Anglican Alice Kidd. The vast majority of CWSS members did not challenge the Catholic hierarchy, nor did they work to change church polity in order to expand women's roles. The evidence here suggests that their moderation was at least in part a product of their consciousness of minority status within the Protestant state. The women of the CWSS were aware of their church's vulnerable position and, envisioning themselves as representatives of Catholicism, strove to protect it from outside attack rather than to reshape it from within.

National morality and moral patriotism: the impact of World War I on Christian feminism

World War I brought many changes to the CLWS and the CWSS. Like the larger suffrage societies, they pledged their support for Britain's war effort and ceased most of their suffrage campaigning; and like other British suffrage organizations, they too lost some membership and funds during the 1914–18 conflict. Unlike their secular counterparts, however, members of the CLWS and CWSS emerged from the war years with a greater sense of confidence and purpose, largely because of the war's impact on the place of religion in national public life.

For Anglican feminists, progress came in part because of a crisis of (male) authority within the Church of England. While World War I certainly did not begin the drift away from the Church of England, it revealed—more than ever before—the alienation of a majority of the English male population from the life and practice of the nation's established religious institution.[34] At the same time, however, the war spurred greater concern for spiritual issues, as individuals sought hope and sustenance in the face of an often meaningless situation.[35] Because of this increasing interest in spirituality, which was generally

127

perceived as a "feminine" aspect of religious practice, Anglican feminists found widening opportunities and encountered greater interest in, and respect for, their participation in, and reform of, the Church of England.

The high degree of disillusionment with the Church resulted, in part, from disappointment with Anglican leadership on the home front. When war first broke out, many Anglican clergy had responded with enthusiastic support and used their pulpits to appeal for recruits. But by 1916, war weariness had set in, and ordinary people began to regard the Church of England as both hypocritical and complicit with the government in the war's mismanagement.[36] The gap between clergy and lay members was further exacerbated by the clergy's exemption from the draft.[37] In 1916, in an attempt to reclaim the church's waning influence in the everyday lives of the British people, the Archbishop of Canterbury launched the "National Mission of Repentance and Hope." Plans were laid for revival-style retreats and conferences "through all the cities and towns and villages of the land."[38]

Members of the Council of the National Mission, which included A. Maude Royden, believed that the Mission should take a broad view of the nation's "spiritual needs" and speak forthrightly on the issues that had divided the nation before the outbreak of war. In July of 1916, they adopted a resolution on "Relations with the Women's Movement," which declared in unequivocal terms that "underlying this movement there are moral and spiritual elements which demand the frank recognition and close sympathy of the Church." The statement went on to claim that the women's movement had introduced a "new moral consciousness," which doubtlessly would bring "conflict with such laws and customs, habits and traditions, in the social regime inherited from the past," but which deserved the firm support of the Church.[39] This remarkable document signified a new willingness within the Anglican hierarchy to consider women as valuable members of the Church and nation. But this attitude was not shared by the ultra-cautious Archbishop Davidson, who suppressed the statement because of its apparent partisanship on a "political" issue.

Nevertheless, interest in women's moral leadership remained strong among the Council members. As preparations continued for the National Mission, and the Council faced severe shortages of clergy to help with preparation and speaking at the parish level, it began to consider the possibility of using women to lead local prayer and instructional meetings. News of these deliberations leaked out and provoked a wide public discussion of the propriety of female Anglican priests. Critics asserted a "slippery-slope" argument that the use of women speakers during the Mission would inevitably begin a movement for the ordination of women to the priesthood. In the face of such opposition, several Council members reversed their original support for women speakers and allowed the proposition to die. However, the final decision was reached in such a bumbling fashion that many Anglican parishioners were left confused about the Church's official position toward women speaking and teaching in church.[40]

Within this atmosphere of renewed interest in women's leadership roles (but confusion over the specific parameters), advocates of women's ordination saw their opportunity. The CLWS, which during the first two years of war had largely demobilized its suffrage campaign and redirected its organization toward patriotic work, began to concentrate its efforts on expanding women's influence on Anglican Church policy. The organization revived an effort begun before the war to secure women's representation on Anglican lay church councils and, although it initially avoided an official position on women preachers, the CLWS leadership encouraged individual members to consider the issue prayerfully.[41] By the time the vote came in February of 1918 to women over the age of thirty, the CLWS had lost most of its clerical members to war service; of the remaining membership, most were middle-class women, and many were advocates of women's ordination. They knew their goals for the CLWS extended beyond the franchise victory.[42]

In a symbolic gesture, members voted in January of 1919 to rename the organization the "League of the Church Militant" (LCM) to protest that the Church was "not half militant enough" (an interesting choice of words in light of the recently ended war).[43] The LCM also pledged to work for the "spiritual equality" of men and women, a term which proved hard to define. Rev. F. M. Green, for example, who continued as editor of the CLWS journal, now renamed *The Church Militant*, understood "spiritual equality" to mean that no differentiation of function should exist in lay Church work.[44] Other LCM members defined "spiritual equality" to include non-lay work—that is, the right of women to preach and teach from Anglican pulpits. In May of 1919, the General Council of the LCM voted to make women's ordination to the priesthood a central goal: "We repudiate 'subordination' just as earnestly as we repudiate 'inferiority'; we deny that upon man there is conferred according to the divine intention a permanent and essential headship."[45]

As the LCM attempted to chart a course into the male-dominated territory of the ministry, it tended, at first, to adopt an equivocal tone. Both positive and negative opinions (some claimed too many) on women's ordination were included in *The Church Militant*. The LCM executive explained: "Though we are indignant we are not disloyal . . . and though indignant we are not unreasonable."[46] They did not, for example, urge Bishops to ordain women on their own responsibility, nor did they put pressure on Parliament to vote on Anglican polity. Instead, the LCM appealed directly to church members in the hope that "the truth will prevail." But after mid-1919, when Anglican women were granted the right to equal representation on each of the newly reorganized lay councils, the LCM grew bolder in its campaign for women's ordination. LCM members led study groups and public debates and initiated an educational campaign in schools, colleges, and training colleges, to appeal to the "young, well-educated, and thinking class of women" about the position of women in the Church.[47]

Interestingly, as the war-torn nation struggled to rebuild, the issue of women's ordination drew significant public attention. While some LCM members departed in protest, the organization drew more support than it lost. The number of subscriptions to *The Church Militant* in 1920 was four times larger than in 1914, although donations never regained prewar levels, which suggests that while many were interested in the issue of women's ordination, fewer were willing to give it their wholehearted support.[48] The issue did attract the attention of some prominent suffragists, including Millicent Garrett Fawcett and Emmeline Pethick-Lawrence, who served on a women's ordination advisory committee. Public discussions of women's ordination drew large crowds. "Hundreds" had to be turned away from a debate on women's ordination in June of 1919 between the Rev. A. V. Magee and A. Maude Royden held in the Church House in Westminster.[49]

Interest in expanding women's leadership roles in the Church also came from official quarters. In February of 1920 the Lower House of the Canterbury Convocation defeated by a single vote a statement that would have allowed women to preach at non-liturgical services. Several church newspapers resoundingly condemned the failure to pass the motion.[50] The issue of women's ordination came to a head at the July of 1920 meeting of the Lambeth Conference of Anglican bishops, where, after some discussion, Church leaders avoided an explicit statement condemning women preachers. Instead, the bishops reaffirmed the office of deaconess as the sole order of ministry for women "with apostolic approval," but also indicated that women could, on occasion, be allowed to speak and lead prayer in unofficial capacities.

The war years had changed the contexts of action for Anglican feminists. The National Mission had left the door slightly ajar to the possibility of women preaching in church with official sanction. Such an opportunity, the LCM clearly recognized, would allow women to begin to influence church policy and Christian theology at the highest levels. Throughout the 1920s, the LCM would continue to work toward this goal with energy and conviction.[51]

Like the Anglicans, members of the Catholic Women's Suffrage Society emerged from the war years with a broadened sense of purpose and a clearer understanding of their feminist position within their own tradition. The war offered Catholic feminists an opportunity to articulate more clearly their identity as feminists, Catholics, and British citizens. Throughout the war, CWSS members worked hard to demonstrate loyalty to Britain through patriotic service. As the war continued, Catholic feminists benefited from a gradual decline in anti-Catholic attitudes and an increasing recognition of the important contributions Catholics could make to national public life.

At the beginning of the war, the Roman Catholic Church became a target of much British frustration and outrage. In August of 1914, Pope Pius X had died, and his successor, Benedict XV, remained silent on the war until November of 1914, when he issued a statement that called simply for the war's speedy end. The Pope's failure to place guilt for the war squarely on Germany was regarded by many in England as "studied nullity" and "moral supineness," and rumors circulated that the Holy See was secretly allied with Germany.[52]

Within this uncertain climate, the CWSS began to carve an independent voice for itself. Shortly after the outbreak of hostilities in Belgium, the CWSS issued a statement declaring the war a "calamity." Despite their reluctance to applaud Britain's war effort, CWSS members quickly began patriotic work, believing that support for their country was a moral duty. Initially their war service involved mainly relief work among the Catholic poor. While focused along denominational lines, these activities helped to awaken a sensitivity among the predominantly middle-class CWSS membership to the needs of working-class Catholic women.[53]

The CWSS made a big step toward greater self-definition when it launched in January of 1915 a monthly newspaper, *The Catholic Suffragist*, under the editorship of Leonora de Alberti, a talented writer who worked part-time in the Public Record Office. The paper had been in the planning stages since the end of 1913, but had been delayed by various financial difficulties. The CWSS executive saw the war as a crucial moment to begin a suffrage newspaper representing the Catholic perspective. In the opening essay of the first issue, Catholic author Alice Meynell underscored what the CWSS saw as its unique perspective:

> The production in war time of a new paper dedicated to the cause of Votes for Women should remind us that though thousands are suffering acutely, splendidly, and conspicuously, millions are suffering chronically, inconspicuously, and with little hope, evils against which the whole Suffrage movement has set its face. Crime has been lessened by the War, we hear; but we cannot hope that sin has been lessened. And the difficult and arduous work of the women reformers is essentially and fundamentally a moral work. A Catholic suffragist woman is a suffragist on graver grounds and with weightier reasons than any other suffragist in England.[54]

CWSS women believed that Catholicism provided them with a moral framework within which to exercise their civic and patriotic duties in a way that transcended narrow wartime partisanship. CWSS members continually highlighted the kinds of contributions that Catholic women could make to the moral well-being of the British nation. Through the pages of *The Catholic Suffragist*, the CWSS began to articulate its demand for women's suffrage as a kind of moral patriotism.

Indeed, as CWSS members turned their attention to nursing orphans and visiting the sick, they became more—not less—committed to their feminist ideals. Early in 1915, CWSS Executive member Miss Christopher St. John observed that the country had slid into a "rather primitive state of things. Men are fighting, women are nursing and knitting and enduring." She saw this as particularly worrisome because it was coupled with increasing government restrictions on women's liberties.[55] To combat these slippages, the CWSS began to join with nondenominational women's organizations more readily than it had before the war. When the Plymouth Watch Committee proposed to re-enact the Contagious Diseases Acts, for example, the CWSS joined other suffrage organizations to protest these measures.[56] Such willingness to participate in cross-denominational feminism signaled a bolder attitude among CWSS members and enabled them to widen the range of their feminist interests and involvement.

By 1918, anti-Catholic attitudes in Britain had eased. On the war front, religious differences between Protestants and Catholics had faded in importance as British soldiers fought side by side with French and Belgian Catholics, against a Protestant foe. In a gesture of confidence in Catholics' central place within the British nation, the CWSS changed the name of its newspapers to *The Catholic Citizen* in late 1917, when the vote for women seemed assured. In January of 1918, while many suffrage leagues were dissolving, the CWSS voted to continue its work "for the further extension of the franchise to women on the same terms as it is, or may be, given to men; to establish the political, social and economic equality between men and women; and to further the work and usefulness of Catholic women as citizens."[57]

The CWSS clearly felt empowered by the deepening concern in postwar Britain for public morality and by a growing recognition of the contributions that women—especially religious women—could make to cleaning up the public sphere. CWSS members were also encouraged by evidence of increasing support among their own confessional community for a Catholic society of feminist women. In February of 1917, for example, the Archbishop of Glasgow declared in a pastoral letter that, since witnessing women's war service, he had reconsidered his views on women's "place and value . . . in the world" and concluded that their public roles were "in harmony with the practice and teaching of our religion." He charged women to rise "to the heights of your great vocation" and to work "to purify and ennoble the world," either through childrearing or government service.[58] While in retrospect we can see that more women in the postwar period chose the route of childbearing than of government service, such statistics do not diminish the reality that the CWSS emerged from the war years with a greater sense of its purpose as a Catholic women's society devoted to women's leadership within both the Church and the nation. Significantly, the organization enjoyed the longest existence of any of the religious suffrage leagues, becoming the St. Joan's Social and Political Alliance in 1923, and later in the 1920s expanding into the St. Joan's International Alliance, the name under which it continues today.

Conclusions

Before World War I, both Anglican and Catholic feminists had found themselves shackled by the largely conservative interests of their constituencies. As a result of the war's impact on attitudes toward religious belief and practice, as well as toward the relationship between religion and national public life, denominational feminists found expanding opportunities and greater popular interest in their reform agendas. Both the CLWS and CWSS emphasized the expansion of women's moral influence in national public life. While these two organizations clearly drew from a legacy of Victorian ideals about women's natural moral superiority, they reshaped this legacy and applied it in dramatically new ways. The LCM's postwar campaign for women's ordination to Anglican orders aimed at deeply embedded, culturally rooted, gender stereotypes. Similarly, the CWSS's decision to continue their work furthering Catholic women's citizenship activities constituted a clear victory over both their own doubts and wider prejudices toward British Catholics.

Although Anglican and Catholic feminists may be charged with being overconfident and overly impressed by changes in public attitudes that would ultimately prove "evanescent"—after all women's ordination into the Anglican Church was not achieved until November of 1992—the progress they made during the war in defining their feminist vision was certainly not illusory.[59] Particularly in the case of the Anglicans, the war years weakened the clergy's hold on the CLWS and created spaces for Anglican women to assert their independent voices. While they were not immediately successful in securing women's access to the highest offices of the Church of England, the mere fact that the LCM attempted to do so represents a significant development in Anglican feminists' understanding of the cultural sources of women's subordination. Catholic women did not reach the same conclusion as readily, in part because their position as Catholics within a Protestant nation required them to focus more immediately on defining Catholic citizenship, rather than on challenging their church's structure and doctrine. But the continuing vitality of the CWSS demonstrates that, at least among denominational feminists, the British women's movement was far from "quiescent" after World War I.

132

Part III

BIRTHING INTERNATIONAL FEMINIST INITIATIVES IN AN AGE OF NATIONALISMS AND IMPERIALISMS

Introductory remarks

The comparative history of feminisms becomes far more complex in the nineteenth century, with the advent of nationalist efforts to found new, and often militaristic, sovereign nation-states based on the notion of one "people" (bound by language, culture, or religion) and socialist efforts to challenge capitalism and individual property rights. Imperial European powers successfully implanted themselves not only in regions they had long controlled but also in areas of the Middle East, Asia, and Africa. Added to this, the breaking apart of old and complex empires – in particular, the Austro-Hungarian and Ottoman empires – and Western imperial powers' attempts to create and maintain new ones complicated women's status by generating multiple possible identities and loyalties and, sometimes, wrenching conflicts between family, community or "race," and nation. More often than not, women's aspirations to freedom flew in the face of men's efforts to "protect" them. Comparative findings to date indicate, however, that women's activism develops in a patterned manner, from initial attempts to organize and do good, to recognizing that their social interventions cannot be effective without questioning the very sexual order and demanding decision-making power, to outright attempts to challenge masculine domination.

From the outset of Western democratizing movements both in Europe and the Americas, women and men argued for women's full inclusion in the developing national civil societies. The highly gendered politics of nation-building meant that feminists were not invariably successful, e.g. the case of their exclusion from political life (and military operations) in the fourth year of the French Revolution. Such developments set the stage for many other aspiring nations to stage their own campaigns for national self-determination and sovereignty. These campaigns offered women a tremendous set of opportunities to claim their "rights," including their right to full citizenship, but also circumscribed their actions when times got rough. Only rarely did leaders of independence movements or governors of new nation-states, whether in Europe (the cases of independence movements in Greece,

Romania, and Bulgaria are instructive in this respect), Latin America, or the Near or Middle East (as, for example, Atatürk, in the Turkish Republic) embrace claims for women's rights. More often than not, women's rights activists (both men and women) turned to international efforts at cooperation, sometimes in the face of resistance from their respective nation-states. International collaborations offered feminists the opportunity to form more visible and powerful alliances in seeking change and sometimes allowed them not only to shame their national governments but also to circumvent them. Nation-states whose leaders did not take kindly to women's activism or a feminist agenda sometimes shut down their organizations and publications. Following World War I, authoritarian regimes, whether Communist (the USSR under Stalin), Fascist (Italy under Mussolini and Spain under Franco), or National Socialist (Germany under Hitler), dissolved free-standing women's organizations and amalgamated women's activism into a single national organization, one that the reigning party could control. In fact, led by the USSR, the countries of the Communist bloc founded their own Women's International Democratic Federation in 1945.

The articles selected for Part III represent a small but very significant cross-section of the excellent work currently being done in the area of feminism, internationalism and transnationalism prior to World War II. The authors selected here have researched both the organizing efforts and cross-border activism as well as some of the problems and obstacles feminists encountered in working together in these new national and international arenas. These new cross-border efforts were very fragile, run on a shoestring, and depended heavily upon the energy, dedication, and monetary resources of their participants. Typically, national governments did not support them, though ultimately they did begin to listen to them. To emphasize their shortcomings at the expense of their successes in overcoming obstacles or producing results is to deny credit where credit is due.

Leila J. Rupp examines how early twentieth-century European and American women who were still fighting for their own national citizenship built international alliances that bridged "races, nations, creeds, and classes." She compares the strategies of the three earliest major international women's organizations, the International Council of Women (ICW, founded 1888), the International Woman Suffrage Alliance (IWSA, founded 1902), and the Women's International League for Peace and Freedom (WILPF, founded 1919). Drawing on sociological findings concerning group identity formation in social movements, Rupp emphasizes these women's common beliefs in fundamental sex differences that expressed themselves in terms of conciliation and peacemaking, the centrality of compassionate motherhood, and critiques of men's tendencies toward individual and collective violence. These commonalities, coupled with a deep awareness of injustice, real disenfranchisement, and multiple legal handicaps as wives and mothers, connected all women across boundaries. Symbolic gestures and practices indicative of women's solidarity abounded: even displays of national flags and dress at international meetings were meant to foster solidarity through diversity. The friendships these women formed bridged cultures and countries, though not surprisingly they were predicated on certain commonalities such as personal financial resources, education and linguistic breadth, and initially, the predominance of Protestant Christian women of European background – though they actively (but not always successfully) sought out women of different backgrounds, including Jewish, Muslim, and Asian women. In an age of war and imperialism, these internationalist feminists found that they must put off-limits discussions of controversial, purely national issues, addressing only issues that transcended strictly national political quarrels and could provide common ground for action. As new national women's groups (for example, in Egypt) aspired to join these organizations, their national objectives sometimes collided with the antimilitarist values that groups like WILPF defended.

Approaching the international women's organizations from a continental European perspective, **Susan Zimmermann** demonstrates that the route to organizing internationally for women's emancipation in an era of aspiring nation-states was anything but straightforward. In her comparative study of the organizing strategies of the ICW and IWSA with respect to subordinated proto-national cultures (Czechs, Slovaks, Hungarians, Poles, Ukrainians, Serbians, etc.) embedded in what was, until 1918, still the multinational, multi-ethnic Habsburg monarchy, she addresses a series of important organizational dilemmas [dilemmas that had already been resolved with respect to the Swiss Confederation (1848), the unification of Italian states (1861) and German states (1871), and the Australian Commonwealth (1900)]. How, after all, were "international" entities based on "national" committees or councils to treat with women's groups from non-sovereign territorial and cultural entities such as Bohemia, Galicia, or for that matter Hungary? Should these Habsburg territories be granted more than one set of representatives in international women's organizations? Could a would-be nation in the Habsburg realm ever achieve sovereignty in an imperial context? The IWSA, with its single issue focus on suffrage, found an expansive solution, by inviting in representatives of the aspiring national/regional groups that the ICW, with its strict definition of nationhood as sovereign, was unable to accommodate.

Ellen L. Fleischmann weaves together issues of religion, nationalism, and imperial intrusion as she surveys the comparative development of indigenous women's activism in Iran, Turkey, Egypt, and among Palestinian women living under the British Mandate, the fruits (in the last three cases) of the disassembling of the Ottoman Empire following World War I. Like Molony and Anagol, she raises the question of how to understand what she calls "indigenous feminism" in geopolitical contexts where the Western world did not yet have much resonance; where the women involved might not yet recognize their efforts to center on relations between the sexes; where "women's movements" are more often than not culturally nationalist (and in some cases even defensive of the prevailing patriarchal family form), yet still arrive at a consciousness of disparities and injustice in the gender order. Women from these cultures channeled their efforts into secular "nation"-building, but within an oppositional framework and "women's status became a potent symbol and barometer of a society's modernity." Fleischmann shows how nationalist movements of various kinds could serve as vehicles for women's claims and participation yet also could impose emprisoning limits that could "derail" women's energy from contesting gender barriers into the service of "national" – or socialist – ends promoted by men who still intended to control women. Even in new regimes that were friendly to certain forms of women's emancipation – Turkey under Atatürk and Iran under the Pahlevi dynasty – the state quickly took control of feminist demands, curbed their organizations, and damped down grassroots initiatives. Thus women's active participation in these emerging civil societies was effectively leashed and carefully channeled. "State-feminism" was born. Conversely, though, in Egypt and Palestine (and also Syria and Lebanon), Arab women began to organize across religious boundaries (Muslim and Christian – though not Jewish, because of hostility to Zionist efforts to enlarge the Jewish community in Palestine) to unite women in a secular pan-Arab transnational coalition. Fleischmann's descriptions of these women's early cross-border initiatives mirror efforts underway in other parts of the world.

The history of international politics is another area in which historians of feminism have provided transformative rethinking and revision. **Francesca Miller**'s pioneering research on the "transnational" feminist agency of Latin American women crosses boundaries and bridges cultures in the Spanish- and Portuguese-speaking republics, as she probes their understandings of the nation and patriotism across a shared belief of transnational sisterhood and issues. Miller also challenges previous understandings of their interactions with North American feminists, demonstrating the significance of the contributions by feisty feminists from a variety of relatively new nation-states including Argentina, Brazil, Chile, Cuba, Mexico, and Uruguay. Miller reconstructs the story of feminist participation at a series of Latin American scientific congresses, then in the International Conferences of the American States and the Inter-American Commission (which preceded the founding of the Organization of American States in 1948) and she reveals the activities of the Inter-American Commission of Women from its inception in 1928 through the 1930s. Her findings demonstrate luminously how women's "unauthorized" and persistent advocacy, and in this case their successful promotion of an Equal Rights Treaty at a transnational level, could and did ultimately provoke dramatic change in women's legal status in the national republics of the New World. Beyond this, these New World feminists' specific emphases on political participation (even without the vote), on addressing married women's disadvantages in nationality law, and on peace advocacy contributed significantly to putting women's issues on the world map and, between 1945 and 1949, to embedding women's rights in the founding documents of the United Nations.

Ellen Carol DuBois elaborates on the issue of married women's nationality, briefly treated by Francesca Miller, to examine the impact of two succeeding groups of international feminist lobbyists at the 1930 World Conference for the Codification of International Law, sponsored by the League of Nations at The Hague (Netherlands). This is an aspect of international relations that has been left in the shadows by most earlier historians. The Latin American and North American women associated with the Inter-American Commission of Women (discussed in Miller's article, Chapter 14) deployed an effective series of tactics, including the Equal Rights Treaty just adopted by the Inter-American Commission, to force the male conference delegates' attention to the serious inequities and problems faced by women married with men of another nationality due to existing nationality laws that simply assumed/asserted women's dependence and/or stripped them permanently of their original national citizenship. Although the Hague conference resisted addressing this question, some delegates did persistently raise it, thanks to the pressure exerted through the innovative tactics of this transnational group of feminists. Ultimately, the United Nations would take up the issue, resulting in the Convention on the Nationality of Married Women (1957; ratified 1958). This international convention was but one of the long-term triumphs resulting from incessant feminist lobbying within the framework of the League of Nations during the 1920s and 1930s.

Angela Woollacott investigates feminist international activities around the Pacific Rim by comparing the parallel activism of Australian feminists in two very different post-World War I transnational women's organizations, the British Commonwealth League (BCL), which always met in London, and the Pan-Pacific Women's Association (PPWA), which spread its meetings around the Pacific Rim. Both these organizations of progressive women provided feminists with new possibilities for action and influencing governmental policies. Yet global power relations could not entirely be ignored, despite attempts by Australian feminists to combat their government's White Australia policy by promoting the rights and cause of Aboriginal women and by reaching out to Asian, including Indian, women. Woollacott (building on the research of Leila Rupp and Antoinette Burton) insists on the unmistakably progressive character of the women's groups' campaigns even as she underscores the continuing assumptions of white cultural superiority that marked these feminists' transnationalist rhetoric. Her work illustrates the serious obstacles feminists from "Down Under" faced in their attempts to build bridges between women of vastly different cultures and to step beyond and ahead of existing geopolitical realities. This study recasts our understanding of international relations in the interwar period, as well as the important role played by Anglophone women from outside Europe and North America. Like Patricia Grimshaw, Woollacott also reminds us that a new set of players, the so-called "women of the darker races," has entered the debate.

11

CONSTRUCTING INTERNATIONALISM

The case of transnational women's organizations, 1888–1945

Leila J. Rupp

In a world beset by murderous nationalist conflicts, the ideal of internationalism seems elusive. We face a paradox in the final decade of the twentieth century: as global interdependence intensifies, nationalist forces tear apart existing units—most dramatically in the former Yugoslavia—into ever smaller pieces. Likewise, on the intellectual front, as David Hollinger tells us, the critique of a false universalism in the tumultuous years after 1945 convinced American intellectuals of the need for an "ethnos-centered discourse" emphasizing diverse, identity-based communities. Such fragmentation poses the difficult question, "how wide the circle of the 'we'?"[1] In the face of pervasive divisiveness, is there any hope of making connections across national or other kinds of borders?

The process of creating—or, as Benedict Anderson would have it, imagining—national communities has riveted historians, but the construction of internationalism has merited scarcely a glance.[2] Believing that both global connectedness and the destructiveness of contemporary nationalism cry out for an international alternative, and that we as historians must begin to fashion a transnational history, I turn my attention here to the creation of a collective identity in international women's organizations during the first wave of the women's movement.[3] What drew women together across the borders of nationality? Who fell within the circle of the we? What did it mean to profess ties across national, ethnic, and other identities? If we can understand how one large constituency organized transnationally and struggled to define a group identity in a period marked by two global conflagrations, we can start to consider the limits of and prospects for internationalism.

The concept of collective identity, as developed by scholars of the "new social movements" of the 1960s and 1970s, addresses the question of how groups define "who we are."[4] Collective identity is "the shared definition of a group that derives from members' common interests, experiences, and solidarity," and it is constructed and sustained within social movement communities. I use the framework for analyzing collective identity within social movements developed by Verta Taylor and Nancy Whittier.[5] In their scheme, collective identity consists of three parts: the boundaries that mark off a group; consciousness, or the ways of defining a group's common interests; and the politicization of everyday life, embodied in symbols and actions that challenge received wisdom.

Women began to organize across national borders at the end of the nineteenth century. At first, they gathered in conference without any larger, permanent structures, but soon they gave form to those contacts and, in a flurry of institutionalization, founded bodies based on all sorts of interests.[6] As resource mobilization theorists would say, women created an international "social movement industry."[7] I focus here on the three major international women's organizations, the International Council of Women (ICW), the International Alliance of Women (IAW, originally the International Woman Suffrage Alliance, IWSA), and the Women's International League for Peace and Freedom (WILPF). Standing out from the crowd, these three proclaimed their openness to women of all continents, religions, political affiliations, occupations, and colors, worked for a range of goals, organized large numbers of women from different parts of the globe, and survived over a long span of years.[8]

The first major international women's organization, the International Council of Women, came to life at an 1888 meeting of the U.S. National Woman Suffrage Association.[9] Mobilizing a wide variety of existing women's groups, first organized into National Councils of Women, the ICW claimed to represent 4 to 5 million women by 1907 and 36 million by 1925.[10] Emphasizing inclusivity, the ICW assiduously avoided taking sides on controversial issues, including, in the early years, the fundamental question of women's right to vote. In fact, Lady Aberdeen, longtime ICW president, insisted that anti-suffragists deserved a hearing in a meeting on women's political rights at a congress in 1899, spurring suffragists to organize their own international organization.[11]

Unafraid of taking a strong stance for their right to the ballot, women impatient with the ICW's position came together at the 1904 Berlin congress of the ICW to form the International Woman Suffrage Alliance, composed originally of ten national suffrage associations and growing to twenty-five by 1914. The IAW increasingly expanded its interests beyond suffrage, especially as the roster of nations in which women could vote lengthened dramatically after World War I, and as a result periodically toyed with the possibility of merging with the International Council of Women. But its strong feminist identity posed an insurmountable barrier.

Issues of war and peace, increasingly embraced in the 1920s, provoked a crisis in the International Woman Suffrage Alliance in 1915. When the guns of August shattered the widely shared illusion that civilization and progress had outstripped the barbarism of war, controversy within the IWSA over the propriety of holding a peace conference in wartime resulted in the formation of a new organization. Out of a Congress of Women at The Hague in 1915 came the International Committee of Women for Permanent Peace, which in 1919 adopted the name Women's International League for Peace and Freedom.[12] A progressive—to some observers, even radical—group, the WILPF strove for peaceful solutions to global conflict and equality for women.

International organizing among women lurched slowly into motion in the years before 1914, gathered steam at the end of World War I, and nearly screeched to a halt in 1939, although all three of these organizations survived the wars, reconstituted themselves in the late 1940s, and continue in existence today. In the period between the wars, one sign of vitality could be found in the formation of coalitions composed of representatives from a variety of transnational women's organizations. Within four such coalitions focused on lobbying the League of Nations, women cooperated and sometimes vigorously competed in their work on behalf of peace, suffrage, nationality, labor legislation, and the abolition of prostitution. In Geneva between the wars, one woman remarked, everyone was "getting together" and "all the 'get-togetherers' would 'get-together' once again, centrally and all-embracingly."[13]

In theory, the three major international women's organizations welcomed women from around the globe. The constitution of the ICW, drawn up in 1888 and revised in 1936, presented the organization as "a federation of women of all races, nations, creeds and classes." Carrie Chapman Catt, U.S. Woman Suffrage Alliance president, beseeched members in 1908 to "strike a note in this meeting so full of sisterly sympathy, of faith in womanhood, of exultant hope, a note so impelling, that it will be heard by the women of all lands, and will call them forth to join our world's army." And, at the 1915 Hague Congress, assembled by a "Call to the Women of all Nations," the "women of the world," as the official report told it, "raise our voices above the present hatred and bloodshed, and however we may differ as to means we declare ourselves united in the great ideals of civilization and progress."[14]

Despite such grand pronouncements, all three groups fell far short of their global ambitions, although they did expand their reach in the interwar years. All began with national sections in Europe or the "neo-Europes" (the United States, Canada, Australia, New Zealand),[15] and European-origin, Protestant, and elite women continued to dominate the international structures. Inevitably, the process of constructing an international collective identity reproduced global power relations.

Limitations on participation flowed from the nature of international organizing and from unacknowledged assumptions about the superiority and natural leadership of Euro-American societies. Women had to undertake lengthy and expensive travel to attend meetings, serve as officers, and participate in activities, so only those with independent means or sufficient national or international stature to attract subsidies from organizations or individuals could take part. During the early years of her presidency of the ICW, Scottish aristocrat Lady Aberdeen paid for everything, finally closing the purse strings out of fear of setting a precedent for future officers.[16] American May Wright Sewall, pleading limited resources, refused to succeed Aberdeen until the Executive Committee agreed to pay her traveling expenses. In 1906, the ICW voted to provide travel grants to all its leaders, since "otherwise the choice of Officers would be limited to ladies of independent means."[17] Margery Corbett Ashby's family believed that her ability to pay catapulted her into leadership of the Woman Suffrage Alliance, and Carrie Chapman Catt insisted that "I never received so much as one cent upon my own personal expenses which were heavy in carrying out my obligations."[18] Delegates to the Hague Congress footed their own bills, although later the WILPF paid travel expenses for "those in far-off countries who are not able to pay, if the money question alone would prevent them from attending an important meeting."[19] In discussing the cost of a hotel in Innsbruck booked for a WILPF Executive Committee meeting, Lida Gustava Heymann of Germany wrote Hungarian Vilma Glücklich, "Now I ask you, which of us can pay that? The English and Americans!"[20] In some cases, friends, patrons, or national organizations came through with financial support, but without access to resources a woman could not participate in international activity.[21]

Neither could she take part if she was unable to understand what was going on. The existence of three official languages—English, French, and German—privileged native speakers of those languages and made difficult the participation of women who knew none of these tongues.[22] Even well-meaning attempts to institute an "international language" such as Esperanto overlooked its European basis.[23] Furthermore, trilingual communication itself bogged things down: printed translations cost money the organizations did not have, and the practice of translating speeches and discussions at congresses made the proceedings lengthy and tedious.[24] Lady Aberdeen regularly urged ICW members to learn at least to understand all three official languages, but knowledge of a second, third, or fourth

141

language, more common in some countries than others, assumed educational privilege accessible only to relatively elite women.[25] Those who regularly communicated in languages other than their mother tongues sometimes noted the linguistic disabilities of their colleagues. Giving voice to a common sentiment, Dutch activist Martina Kramers wrote Hungarian Rosika Schwimmer, in German, to tell her that she would translate Schwimmer's piece for publication "because the poor monolingual Americans must also know what is going on with you."[26]

Adding to the problem, international congresses and meetings of officers took place primarily in Europe, and to a lesser extent in North America, discouraging those who hailed from other continents. Suggestions or plans to hold meetings in Australia, Hawaii, Brazil, or even Spain, the Balkans, or Czechoslovakia, provoked shocked outcries that "such a far away place has been chosen."[27] These complaints revealed assumptions about the global distribution of membership, since, as an Australian woman wryly remarked in 1909, "the distance is exactly the same going out to Australia as it is coming [to Europe]."[28] Refusal to travel far from Western Europe both resulted from and helped to perpetuate the over-representation in leadership positions of women from the United States, Great Britain, and Western and Northern Europe. Women in the United States gained added leverage because American money played a crucial role in keeping the organizations afloat.[29]

Finally, despite the prominent leadership of a number of Jewish women, the participation of Catholic women, and the involvement of a few Muslim women, a Protestant tone pervaded the international organizations.[30] The ICW clung to the "Golden Rule," an ethical principle common to Judaism, Christianity, and Islam but presented in its New Testament form (Matthew 7:12), as its basis of action; ICW meetings, in the early years, opened with prayers, provoking criticism that led to their ban, since the practice of public prayer expressed American Protestant values; and both the ICW and the WILPF took regular note of Christmas celebrations. Furthermore, anti-Semitism and anti-Muslim prejudice surfaced within the Protestant-dominated international women's organizations.[31]

After World War I shook the foundations of European world dominance and set in motion the process of decolonization, the international women's organizations faced new challenges. Seeking to become—or at least to appear—what they called "truly international," they added members and national sections in Latin America, Asia, the Middle East, and Africa.[32] Although "feminist orientalism" too often continued to characterize attitudes of European-origin women toward "Third World" women, some members questioned traditional thinking.[33] When the Women's International League sought to recruit Indian representatives to its congress of 1921, the Indian News Service and Information Bureau responded bluntly that they wanted "an Indian delegation entirely independent of the British women."[34] And when the WILPF organizers of the 1932 Grenoble congress asked a Chinese woman living in Berlin to come and speak briefly in Chinese, she responded, in German, that she could not undertake a lengthy interruption of her work "merely to speak for a few minutes in a language that probably all of the congress participants could not understand." She found this an "unreasonable demand that I cannot reconcile with my self-respect" and pointedly refused to be used in that way.[35] Eurocentrism did not go unchallenged.

The limits of inclusion, and challenges to them, shaped the process of creating an international collective identity. Conflict among competing perspectives produced the boundaries, consciousness, and politicization of everyday life of internationally organized women, who often participated in a number of communities that sustained distinct, sometimes overlapping, identities. The increasing movement of women into public life from the turn of the century and the geographical expansion of the international women's organizations in the interwar period contributed to the constant renegotiation of collective identity.

Both by assuming fundamental gender differences and by advocating separatist organizing, women in transnational organizations drew boundaries that separated women from men.[36] Sometimes, they painted the differences in broad strokes: German pacifist Anita Augspurg contrasted the "world of men," "built up on profit and power, on gaining material wealth and oppressing other people," to the "new world" women could build that would "produce enough for all and which would include the protection of children, youth and the weak." Augspurg's life partner, Lida Gustava Heymann, likewise condemned men's "lies and hatred and violence" and lauded the world women wanted to establish based on "love, right and mutual understanding."[37]

Such contrasts came to the fore in discussions of what participants oftentimes considered the male business of war and the female penchant for peace. Of World War I, Mary Sheepshanks of England wrote, "Men have made this war; let women make peace—a real and lasting peace." Hungarian Paula Pogány had never in her life "felt more aversion against everything what [sic] carries the character of manhood." In the interval between the wars, Egyptian feminist Huda Shaarawi proclaimed that, "if men's ambition has created war, the sentiment of equity, innate in women, will further the construction of peace." More bluntly, International Woman Suffrage Alliance leader Carrie Chapman Catt insisted, "All wars are men's wars. Peace has been made by women but war never." In the midst of World War II, she ventured that men had never wanted to end war: "They like to fight, they like the adventure, they like the prestige, and they certainly love conquest."[38]

Underlying such sentiments was a widespread essentialist assumption that women's biological capacity for reproduction made them inherently pacifistic. As Germaine Malaterre-Sellier, a French suffrage leader, maintained, "Women who have given life must always have a horror of war." A German-language appeal to women as mothers of sons asked, "Have you forgotten the hour of his birth? No man can sympathize with that, for he has never with a hundred thousand pains borne a child." Women who had given birth were coming to realize "that it is senseless to continue to give life when this life will surely be annihilated by violence and war."[39] Over and over again, women referred to themselves as "guardians, nurses & preservers," "Mothers of the Human Race," "carriers of life," "MOTHERS OF THE NATIONS," "guardians of the new generations."[40]

Appeals to women as mothers served as a staple of the propaganda issued by international women's organizations.[41] Most echoed the "Call to Women" in 1936 issued by the Rassemblement Universel pour la Paix, a peace campaign mounted by both men and women: "[M]others everywhere feel a growing despair. They tremble at the thought that the children they have borne must undergo the horrors of another war." But motherhood as a basis of solidarity did not have to be essentialist, as illustrated by an appeal in 1920 "To the Women of Palestine Who Love Peace." It called on women as the socializers of children to use their power to help "their sons and daughters grow up free from religious and racial prejudice, free from all that is dwarfing in the wrong kind of patriotism." Motherhood had the potential to unite all women, even those who had not given birth. According to Hungarian pacifist Rosika Schwimmer, "Even women who are not physically mothers, feel all as the mothers of the human race."[42] That appeals to motherhood could be strategic as well as heartfelt is suggested by WILPF leader Emily Greene Balch's comment that "I see value in sentimental appeals to 'the mother heart.' "[43]

Another powerful argument for women's difference targeted wartime sexual violence as a stark boundary separating women from men. The ICW's Peace Committee protested in 1913 against "the horrible violation of womanhood that attends all war." Carrie Chapman Catt revealed her vision of civilization and progress, arguing that the "conditions of war subvert the natural instincts of many men of all races, who temporarily return to the brutal practices of the most savage primitive races."[44] Expressing a gloomier view of "civilized" men's peacetime behavior, Rosika Schwimmer protested that the "victimizing of children, young girls, and women of all ages so common in peaceful times, because under the double standard of morals men are not outlawed for sexual crimes, is multiplied in war time."[45] Picking up the theme of violence, the flyer that announced the upcoming Hague Congress referred circumspectly to rape as one reason women needed to come together internationally: "[T]he moral and physical sufferings of many women are beyond description and are often of such a nature that by the tacit consent of men the least possible is reported. Women raise their voices in commiseration with those women wounded in their deepest sense of womanhood and powerless to defend themselves."[46] Violence against women, like motherhood, had the potential to unite women across cultures.

Not all expressions of boundaries between women and men had such potentially universal appeal. One strand of discourse in the period before World War I called attention to women's social roles in the home. Lady Aberdeen argued that devotion to the home brought women together across the chasms of class and race. Finnish Woman Suffrage Alliance member Annie Furuhjelm saw the "motor force of the whole movement" as the "intuitive comprehension of women that they have to go out of their own individual homes in order to make the big world more of a home." For Mary Sheepshanks, it was the fact that women had for so many generations been isolated in their homes that made their schemes for reform different from men's.[47] As women in industrialized societies moved increasingly into the labor force, and as women of European origin recognized divergent patterns of social organization in different parts of the world, this theme lost salience.

Likewise, the motif of women's disfranchisement or lack of political power would diminish over time.[48] At the founding congress of the ICW, U.S. suffragist Elizabeth Cady Stanton referred to the "universal sense of injustice, that forms a common bond of union" among "the women of all nationalities." When women in the United States still lacked the vote, Carrie Chapman Catt saw Chinese suffragists beholding "the same vision which is arousing the women of all the Nations of the Earth" and, turning her gaze to the Balkans, asserted that there "are wrongs of countries and of classes to be righted, but the wrongs of women are common to all races and nations." Mary Sheepshanks agreed: "Unenfranchised, unequal before the law, suffering from innumerable disabilities and injustices, [women] will preserve the bond of their common sisterhood."[49] But the granting of women's suffrage in the United States, Great Britain, Australia, and many of the European countries around the time of World War I created division between enfranchised and still-voteless women. Although the IWSA congress in Stockholm in 1911 had resolved that the nations with suffrage "feel that their work is not done . . . as long as the women of any country remain disfranchised," women voters seemed increasingly eager to move on to other issues. Public discussion of the future of the organization focused on the fact that many women—especially women of the "East," "probably needing our help more than any others"—remained voteless. Annie Furuhjelm warned that "the Enfranchised Women must take up a line of their own in the Alliance or else drop out of it altogether."[50]

Still, the general lack of political power continued to draw a line between women and men, at least in countries where men had some political rights. Siao-Mei Djang, a Chinese woman writing a pamphlet for the WILPF in 1929, could still refer to "the problems which are universal to womenhood."[51] Enfranchised women tended to focus on the independence of women from traditional political parties. According to Emily Greene Balch, women, "in the main outside of the politics of the past," were "free from bad old political habits and traditions, and free to strike out a new political method, not dominated by party, in which social and moral values shall outweigh all others." When Adolf Hitler came to power, the WILPF issued a "Statement on Fascism" proclaiming that "we women, the greater part of whom are outside all political parties, and consequently not obliged to take the orders of any of them, can understand these events independently, with our simple common sense, and our sense of what is human."[52]

The notion of women's difference from men—whether biologically or socially based—found organizational expression in the separatist nature of the three major international bodies and the coalitions they formed. Although European women most often asserted that single-sex organizing represented a temporary expedient or even expressed a preference for organizing with men, associating separatism with "the New World," none of the bodies changed its policies.[53] The ICW invited men to certain congress functions but kept some meetings for women only. Reflecting the increasing integration of women into public life, the WILPF in the 1920s posed the question of whether or not it should remain a women's organization, but it developed a rationale for the status quo based on the range of positions on women's difference.[54] Perhaps a sign of uneasiness over the old-fashioned associations of single-sex organizing in an increasingly hetero-social world, few women explictly defended the practice. Catherine Marshall's sentiments—"It is always a pleasure to meet *Women fellow workers . . . I do* like women best! Who was it said: The more I see of men the better I think of women!"—stand out in the records of the international women's movement.[55]

Some questioned not only the efficacy of separatist organizing but also the assumption of women's difference, although these were isolated voices. The audience at the Hague Congress hissed down one woman for saying that "the average woman is no more for peace than men are," showing not only the existence of dissent but the emotion invested in the dogma of difference.[56] The disillusionment of World War I and the mounting threats to peace in the 1930s took their toll on some activists. Rosika Schwimmer, in 1934, admitted that she no longer believed in women's natural pacifism.[57] Even those who kept the faith always knew that they were different from the majority of women. They were conscious of their identity as internationalists.

Participants regularly described an international "we." Early in the history of the ICW, Teresa Wilson, the Corresponding Secretary, referred to "us . . . International workers." Of a potential co-worker, Emily Greene Balch noted, "She appears to be of our way of thinking." Dutch Woman Suffrage Alliance leader Rosa Manus expressed satisfaction that Mary Sheepshanks was taking over the editorship of the journal *Jus Suffragii* because she was so "internationally minded." Describing a fellow German WILPF member, Lida Gustava Heymann used the phrase "very much in agreement with our ideas." And the phrase "we international women" occurred twice in one letter of Austrian feminist Helene Granitsch.[58]

Internationally minded women did not all agree on the significance of their collective consciousness for individual national identities. For some, internationalism coexisted with a strong national loyalty, unless the two came into conflict, in which case nationalism took precedence. The very principles governing the functioning of the ICW and the IAW, and to a lesser extent the WILPF, reflected this understanding of priorities. The constitution of the ICW stated from the outset that the international body had no power over its member groups, so that no National Council would "render itself liable to be interfered with in respect to its complete organic unity, independence or method of work." In response to a conflict between the National Councils of Sweden and Norway, the ICW added a new article to its constitution specifically excluding all "political and religious questions of a controversial nature affecting the inter-relationship of two or more countries" from the jurisdiction of the international structure.[59] In 1909, the International Woman Suffrage Alliance adopted a bylaw pledging "absolute neutrality on all questions that are strictly national" and promising to "respect the independence of each affiliated association, and to leave it entirely free to act on all matters within its own country."[60] Both the 1915 Hague Congress and the 1919 Zurich congress that gave birth to the Women's International League for Peace and Freedom barred debate on national responsibility for or conduct of the war.[61] Despite this rule, the WILPF prided itself, in contrast to the other two organizations, on its willingness to meet during World War I, to speak out against fascism in the 1930s, and to take strong positions on the eve of World War II.[62] The ICW reported, with regard to the interorganizational Conference on Prevention of the Causes of War held in 1924, that the WILPF "did not feel able to actively co-operate whith [sic] us when our Board of Officers passed a resolution asking all speakers 'to refrain from mentioning incidents of the last War by way of illustration, or any of the political controversies arising therefrom.' "[63] The fear that transnational organizations might infringe on the autonomy of national sections reflected the continued salience of national identities.

Indeed, during World War I, some women, in a fervor of nationalism, had seemed wholly to abandon internationalism. French women's organizations cut their ties to international groups. Marguerite de Witt Schlumberger wrote in an open letter to "Sisters of the Union" (Union Française pour le Suffrage des Femmes), published in *Jus Suffragii*, that this was no time for feminist demonstrations against the war, that Frenchwomen should show "that we are worthy to help to direct our country since we are capable of serving it."[64] The Central Committee of the Union Française pour le Suffrage des Femmes protested the inclusion of its name on a peace petition presented to U.S. president Woodrow Wilson, pointing out that "those who are fighting for our country and for our homes need all of our encouragement and all of our moral force."[65] And the French groups refused to send delegates to the Hague Congress. When pacifist and feminist Gabrielle Duchêne founded a French affiliate of the International Committee of Women for Permanent Peace, the leadership of the French National Council of Women asked her to resign.[66]

In Britain, Millicent Garrett Fawcett of the mainstream National Union of Women Suffrage Societies and Emmeline Pankhurst of the militant Women's Social and Political Union both refused to support the 1915 Hague Congress, although other British women did answer the call.[67] A Belgian woman who attended but did not vote on the resolution calling for the end of the war explained why: "In spite of the fact that my woman's heart knows that the war cannot continue, we cannot demand peace at any price. First of all, we must be given back our country, our prosperity, our well-being. That is all that I have thought of up to now. I cannot think as all of you do; I am Belgian above all."[68]

On the other side of the battle lines, women also expressed fierce loyalty as members of their nations. The Bund Deutscher Frauenvereine refused to participate at The Hague because, as Gertrud Bäumer explained, "It is obvious to us that during a national struggle for existence, we women belong to our people and *only* to them."[69] The German women who did attend met with frosty disapproval at home.[70] Although women of the belligerent nations sat down together at The Hague, their brave attempt to make peace gave rise to some vigorous expressions of nationalism in conflict with, and superseding, internationalism.

Other women in the international movement agreed that the two identities might clash but sought to replace nationalism with internationalism. Sometimes, as an expression of their international consciousness, they repudiated the policies of their own governments. In contrast to the French and German women who metaphorically wrapped themselves in their respective national flags during and immediately after World War I, others engaged in repeated symbolic displays of bonds of what they called "sisterhood." *Jus Suffragii* published an open letter from German women in December 1914 calling on "our sister-women" to recognize that women in wartime share the same fate.[71] French women—Gabrielle Duchêne among them—who regretted the refusal of their national organizations to support the Hague Congress sent an open letter to German women, prompting a return greeting to "our French sisters."[72] At the postwar Zurich congress of the Women's International League, French women unable to attend addressed their "German sisters," refusing to be enemies: "Because we are the same, because we are a single humanity, because our work, our sorrows and our joys are the same, because our children are the same children, we protest against the murderous invention of a 'hereditary enemy.' "[73] In what became a symbol of the possibilities of internationalism, Lida Gustava Heymann greeted newly arrived French delegate Jeanne Mélin with a bouquet of roses and an outstretched hand, which Mélin clasped in friendship.[74]

Similarly, when the Woman Suffrage Alliance reconvened after the war, Frenchwoman Marguerite de Witt Schlumberger and German Marie Stritt sat side by side as an embodiment of solidarity.[75] Re-creating the scene between Heymann and Mélin, a French woman publicly embraced a German delegate who made a plea for peace at the 1926 IAW congress in Paris.[76] And, in 1931, the French and German sections of the WILPF issued a joint appeal to their governments and to the president of the Disarmament Conference convened by the League of Nations, stating their common desires: "Our peoples want *work* and *bread*. They want *peace* and *justice*."[77] Such displays continued throughout the years between the wars.[78]

Members of the WILPF in particular took great pride in transcending nationalism. Explaining the group's philosophy to an inquiring Cuban woman, secretary Mary Sheepshanks in 1930 recounted tales of the German national section planting trees in devastated areas of France, the French section protesting its government's occupation of the Ruhr, and the British section objecting to the treatment of Ireland. In fact, at the 1919 Zurich congress, German women denounced the invasion of Belgium, and Allied women spoke out against the blockade of Germany. When Japan invaded Manchuria in 1931, the Japanese section apologized to their "Chinese sisters" for their country's actions.[79] It became a "tradition in the Women's International League that, if a wrong has been done, it should be the Section belonging to the country which does the wrong that should appeal for right."[80] In this way, members validated their identity as internationally minded women.

Proposals to do away with nation-based organizing within the WILPF also expressed a strong international consciousness. As early as 1915, a British woman wrote to Aletta Jacobs in Amsterdam to say that she and some of her friends wanted to belong to the WILPF without joining the British section, since there "is always a danger ... of the national side being developed at the expense of the international." In response to this kind of concern, the 1924 congress resolved to organize a World Section.[81] Such a group might simply serve the purpose of including women living in countries of which they were not citizens, individuals from countries with no national section, or women who did not get along with their own national groups. But some advocates hoped to sweep away national boundaries altogether. According to international secretary Madeleine Doty, who sought to get the World Section off the ground in 1930, the WILPF ought "to have a group in its midst who belonged to no nation and called themselves world citizens."[82] Thinking along the same lines, the author of a draft report on a "Suprainternational Republic" proposed what she called a "Mondial association" in the WILPF that might hold regional meetings to facilitate contact but whose sections would be named for geographical features that ignored national boundaries or for "great men who were conspicuously non-nationalistic."[83]

Despite continuing discussion, Catherine Marshall referred in 1935 to the World Section as "a still-born child."[84] Throughout the 1920s, conflict raged within the WILPF over the relationship of national sections to the international structures. A critical issue concerned the method of electing the Executive Committee: one faction sought to maintain election by the international congress, another to institute a system of election by national sections. Advocates of the status quo insisted that the new procedure, by introducing national representation, would "*destroy the international spirit* that has always preserved our League up to now."[85] Like supporters of the World Section, these members raised international consciousness above—even called for the elimination of—national thinking.

Still other women in the international movement maintained both national and international identities without tension, conceptualizing the two as complementary rather than contradictory. Emily Greene Balch, winner of the Nobel Peace Prize in 1946, described "international women" as "lovers of our own lands, . . . citizens of the world." The German member of the preparatory committee for the Hague Congress described the triumphal international gathering: "All of the German women who attended the Congress returned home with the conviction that they served their Fatherland well."[86]

The coexistence of national and international consciousness took on special significance for women from countries newly free from imperialist domination.[87] For them, national liberation was a prerequisite for internationalism, a view that women from long-established and often imperialist nations found hard to understand. Margery Corbett Ashby, for example, the longtime British president of the IAW, found the feminist movements in India and Egypt "intensely nationalist."[88] But women involved in both a struggle for independence and international women's organizations often saw no conflict. A woman from the Philippines wrote that the WILPF was "in keeping not only with the objects most dear to our women hearts but also to the aspirations of my people, to have freedom." An Arab woman at the Istanbul congress of the International Alliance of Women in 1935 warned women from the great powers that "no amount of effort on your part will ever achieve your high aim while imperialism reigns in any corner of the world." And Huda Shaarawi, who served on the board of the Alliance of Women, maintained in 1935 that women from the East, like women from the West, ardently desired peace, "but they want it based on justice and respect for the rights of the people."[89]

How difficult dialogue could be across this chasm is illustrated by a controversy over the admittance of an Egyptian section to the WILPF in 1937. Provisionally accepted in April, this section sent proposals for the upcoming conference in Czechoslovakia, making clear that it could not accept disarmament until Egypt had the capability to defend itself and that the issue of limiting and regulating state sovereignty had different ramifications for Egypt than for Britain. "[T]he great imperialist powers . . . have often abused their state sovereignty to conduct an egoistic politics dangerous to peace," the Egyptian representative asserted.[90]

This position provoked consternation in the Geneva headquarters, since the joint chairmen did not want to discourage the section but could not accept its support of the Egyptian army.[91] In response to a letter from Geneva explaining that if the section advocated armament it would not be in accord with the principles of the WILPF, Egyptian spokeswoman Alice Jacot denied any conflict, insisting that universal disarmament did not mean unilateral disarmament, without regard for whether a country were weak or strong, free or oppressed, aggressive or pacifist.[92]

At the request of the Egyptian section, the Executive Committee took up the question. Anna Tuby explained for Egypt that the Anglo-Egyptian Treaty called, among other things, for occupation by the British until Egypt could itself defend the Suez Canal, leaving Egyptian women with the unpleasant choice of supporting an Egyptian national army or the British occupation. Egyptian women advocated the complete independence of Egypt, which alone would make possible peace and disarmament. In the end, the Executive Committee voted to admit the section.[93] It is clear from this incident that Egyptian women had a very different perspective on the meaning of disarmament, sovereignty, and internationalism than did women from countries with secure national identities and independence.

The expansion of the multinational women's organizations beyond Europe and the "neo-Europes" in the 1920s and 1930s brought new challenges to the formation of an international consciousness. Although women embraced competing frameworks for the relationship of international to national identities, they all shared a common devotion, whether weak or strong, to a bond that stretched across national borders. This consciousness of themselves as internationally minded activists constituted an important aspect of their collective identity.

Because transnationally organized women were not usually in everyday contact with one another, politicization of everyday life (the third component of collective identity) manifested itself primarily during the periodic international congresses sponsored by the different groups. At such gatherings, the cultural displays, organizational symbols, and personal interactions expressed women's international-mindedness.

Two different kinds of cultural practices at congresses created visual images of the merging of discrete national loyalties into an international identity.[94] One was the use of national flags in international ceremonies. At the 1906 International Woman Suffrage Alliance conference, according to the official report, the "international character of the meeting was indicated by little silken national flags which marked the seats of each delegation." The Stockholm hall that sheltered an ICW meeting in 1911 was likewise decked out with flags of the constituent countries in order of affiliation. In an added ritual, each National Council president stood up to speak, accompanied by a rendition of her country's anthem. Much to the horror of the German international secretary, Alice Salomon, who had taken great pains to get everything right, the orchestra struck up the German anthem when the French president arose, a mistake Salomon feared would smack of German chauvinism.[95] Faux pas aside, flags and national anthems at international congresses both expressed national loyalties and symbolized the process of bringing different nationalities together under the umbrella of internationalism.

So, too, did a second variety of cultural display, the sharing of national cultural traditions at global gatherings. One of the most popular forms of entertainment was the performance, in national dress, of a traditional song or dance. Sometimes, the committees organizing international congresses asked delegates to wear national costumes or colors.[96] One woman's description of the 1915 Hague Congress expresses the belief that national cultural forms could promote rather than undermine internationalism: "We have caught a glimpse of a beautiful land of the future where every nation and every individual shall give their tribute to the life of the whole, and get it back enlarged and embellished ..., where every one, every nation, and every individual, is enriched by the riches of all others."[97]

Using national symbols in these ways mirrored the perspectives on internationalism that gave priority to nationalism or saw the two as complementary. So, too, did the creation of organizational badges and banners, although these might also serve as an alternative to conventional national symbols, in a sense elevating international—or organizational—identity. The ICW set up a committee to develop a badge sometime after the congress in 1899 and finally, in 1908, adopted a design of the intertwined letters "ICW" modeled on a brooch of Susan B. Anthony's, passed on at her death to Lady Aberdeen. Throughout the long process, various National Councils submitted and resubmitted designs, while committees evaluated the symbolic, artistic, and practical aspects of each. The badge, intended to convey a sense of harmony arising from diversity, could, president May Wright Sewall argued, serve as an effective means of propaganda if worn by members scattered over the face of the earth.[98] The ICW also created a banner in 1925 to replace an earlier one lost in 1914 with the outbreak of war in Europe. Made of silk in the organizational colors of white, gold, and purple, the new standard displayed the Golden Rule printed in Latin, with sunbeams streaming down from the motto onto a map of the world. According to Anna Backer, who conceptualized and presented the banner, the design symbolized "the unity of women of all nationalities, races and creeds."[99]

The International Woman Suffrage Alliance also worked to find appropriate symbols. Neither the founding congress in 1904 nor correspondence afterward hit upon the perfect embodiment of internationalism, but in 1906 the conference in Copenhagen adopted a badge portraying the figure of justice and the words "Jus Suffragii." "In order that this badge shall be truly international," according to the conference report, which also noted that it would be made of bronze in order to be affordable to all women, "suffragists throughout the world should be encouraged to purchase and to wear it."[100] In 1928, the IAW announced a competition for a new design to reflect its new direction in the aftermath of the war, but ten years later a member of the International Executive Committee argued that "fashions have somewhat changed" and "people do not now buy or wear such things to the same extent as formerly."[101] The WILPF also adopted a badge, this one displaying the word "Pax." The Zurich congress in 1919 voted against a membership symbol, but the 1921 congress accepted it so that, as an Englishwoman argued, "we should then recognise each other in any country as sisters of the W.I.L."[102]

Displaying an organizational symbol at home, in everyday life, provided the opportunity, in theory, for women anywhere in the world to identify with internationalism, but there is no indication in the sources that this happened or that badges played the propaganda function their advocates attributed to them. Such symbolic displays, at least in the early years, did, however, serve as an expression of international identity and organizational membership at the periodic gatherings of women from around the world.

Personal interaction at congresses, meetings, and organizational headquarters solidified the notion that national borders could not separate women committed to internationalism. Although scenes of wrenching conflict, congresses also remained in women's memories as inspiring occasions. German ICW member Marie Stritt recalled the 1899 London congress in a 1927 tribute to Lady Aberdeen: "Almost 30 years have gone by since then; life with its passionate desires and battles lies behind me—but the welcome memory of those wonderful days and weeks in London is today as alive for me as it was then." Irishwoman Louie Bennett, in anticipation of the 1934 WILPF congress, also turned her eyes to the past: "I always look back to our first Zurich Congress as an event—an inspiration—a source of refreshment." Estonian delegate Aino Kallas found the most important thing about the 1925 ICW congress in Washington to be "the personal touch." "The world's map is, so to speak, now peopled for me . . . There are friendly faces in all corners of the World, hands which are ready to help, kind voices calling from everywhere, from Iceland to South Africa." And Karleen Baker, editor of the WILPF journal *Pax*, asserted that "it is these friendships made between members in different countries that can be counted as one of the most fruitful results of any international gathering."[103]

Interaction at congresses or meetings materialized in friendships across the borders of nationality, sometimes expressed in terms of family metaphors. Such relationships extended into women's everyday lives. When Lady Aberdeen died in 1939, the new ICW president, Belgian baroness Marthe Boël, described herself as one of "Aberdeen's daughters." Other members referred to Aberdeen as "Our Grannie." Rosa Manus addressed Carrie Chapman Catt first as "my dearest stepmother" and later as "Mother Carrie." When Manus's mother died, Rosa Manus wrote Catt that "I always thought of you both on the same level and now YOU ARE THE ONLY ONE." Manus faced competition from Bertha Lutz of Brazil, who addressed Catt as "Dear (Step-) mother Mrs. Catt," "My dear (mother) Mrs. Catt," and "My dear mother (not step) Mrs. Catt," and signed herself as Catt's "Brazilian daughter." Lutz pulled no punches when she wrote to Manus: "I am not going to put step-sister, because that either presupposes that you are only a step-daughter, which you won't accept, or that I am, and that I also can not brook. So be 'sister' straight away." Within the WILPF, Jane Addams also took the role of "our beloved mother," the "dear lovable Mother whose children were from every clime and every country."[104]

The "daughters" of revered leaders formed attachments among themselves that tied together an international community, though one almost exclusively composed of women of European origin. Friendships blossomed in common work and in turn prepared the ground for continued progress toward organizational goals. Women addressed each other with terms of endearment ("and for you a sisterly kiss," "a kiss from your Martina"[105]), traveled together on behalf of their organizations, paid visits to each other's homes, worried about each other, and put pen to paper to express the importance of their friendships. After a disagreement, Aletta Jacobs wrote to Emily Greene Balch: "But, my dear, do not you know that only dear friends are scolded? Everyone has the need to scold now and then and if you have a dear husband, you use him for that purpose. But if you have not a wife or a husband you must use your dear friends for it."[106] Like symbolic expressions, transnational friendships and the formation of fictive families challenged the idea that one's closest ties fell within the borders of one's country. In these cases, internationalism, in the form of organizational loyalties, took on greater salience, even rivaling national identities.

The international collective identity that was created and sustained within these organizations—the boundaries, the consciousness of internationalism, and the politicization of everyday life—served as the glue that held together these diverse women. The process of defining "who we are" was a contested one, challenged over time by competing ideas of why and how women were different from men, what the proper relationship between nationalism and internationalism should be, and how best to express a commitment to transcending or complementing national identities. Changes in women's lives in industrialized societies at the turn of the century complicated the process, especially the increasing movement of women into the public world manifested in enfranchisement and the erosion of social sex-segregation, as well as the inclusion of members and national sections from dependent and formerly colonial countries in the 1920s and 1930s.

We can see the ways in which the limitations to universalism that were embedded in the functioning of the international women's movement helped shape collective identity. Euro-American assumptions, based on a specific history of gender differentiation in industrialized societies, underlay both the conceptualization of difference between women and men and the tradition of separatist organizing.[107] The notion of transcending nationalism assumed an independent, secure, and perhaps even powerful national existence. And the chance to partake of symbolic representations and personal interaction depended heavily on the ability to travel, to speak and understand one of the three official languages, and to be accepted as part of the "international family."

Despite the realities of power politics, this international collective identity held the potential for wider appeal. If the extension of political rights to women in some parts of the world around the time of World War I divided rather than united women, and if appeals based on women's social roles in the home struck no chords in societies in which women played central roles in agriculture or trade, women could nevertheless unite through their universal roles as mothers and the reality of worldwide violence against women. The perspectives of women from countries struggling for independence in the interwar period shed fresh light on the meaning of internationalism. The rituals of belonging, especially if congresses broke out of the narrow orbit of the traditional host cities (as they finally did after World War II), could extend far more broadly.

The initial steps in the direction of a more universal collective identity may in themselves have been insignificant, but their potential demands attention. Two aspects seem hopeful. First, in line with the postmodernist and feminist recognition of multiple identities and with Hollinger's proposal for a "postethnic perspective" that attempts to find commonalities among different identity communities, it is clear that these women's international collective identities, based on gender, could coexist with their identities as Germans or Egyptians, pacifists or socialists or feminists, Christians or Jews, professional women or workers.[108] If forging bonds across cultures can build on, rather than challenge, existing loyalties, the task of making international connections does not seem so impossible. Second, if we recognize that all ties among groups of people are constructed, not "natural," we can contemplate ways that transnational actors—organizations, institutions, and governments—can design the means to facilitate the creation of a variety of international collective identities. Women within the ICW, IAW, and WILPF might not have chosen these words to describe what they did, but they recognized that they could foster internationalism through such avenues as the socialization of children, education in the history, culture, and languages of other nations, and the gatherings of women from across the globe. If national hatred could be taught, so, too, they believed, could international understanding and love. Despite the limitations, women's internationalism in the period before World War II points the way to one form of global identity to add to the more parochial views we have of ourselves as we move into the twenty-first century.

12

THE CHALLENGE OF MULTINATIONAL EMPIRE FOR THE INTERNATIONAL WOMEN'S MOVEMENT

The Habsburg Monarchy and the development of feminist inter / national politics

Susan Zimmermann

The late nineteenth and early twentieth centuries witnessed the emergence of an organized international women's movement with strong North Atlantic[1] roots and pursuing definite strategies designed to globalize feminist internationalism and to propel the movement toward social and political reform on this level. The organized international women's movement was built on the idea that self-governing nation states or federal states formed the main foundation of any organization operating at an international level. In a global perspective, however, serious political ambiguities and struggles over the construction of the inter / national plagued the late-nineteenth and early-twentieth century wave of inter / national feminism from the outset. Affiliation in the international women's organizations of this period was largely confined to those parts of the world that were not formally colonies, and to countries and regions considered as part of "occidental civilization."[2]

The organizational relation to those other large world regions subject to some form of colonialism or imperialism, or else ruled through multinational empires, posed a serious challenge to the politics of women's internationalism. Women's international organizations frequently confronted the question of how to deal with political entities that did not conform to the western notion of the nation state. In the period before 1918, organizational and political tension and overt struggle over this problem focused largely on some of the non-core regions of Europe. In this context the multinational Habsburg Monarchy developed into a central locus of struggles over the inter / national after 1899. These struggles foreshadowed the challenge that the "colonial question," and more generally the problem of territorial (re-)configuration in non-European contexts, was to pose to women's international organization in later decades.

This article analyses the debates and strategies characterizing the organizational politics of the two major international women's organizations of the pre-1918 period, the International Council of Women (ICW) and the International Woman Suffrage Alliance (IWSA), towards the Habsburg empire. Conversely, it explores the contribution of women and their organizations from within the Habsburg Monarchy in shaping and changing these strategies. In the first part I introduce principles, practices and some of the historical background of inter / national politics within the ICW and the IWSA, that is, the politics of shaping and reshaping the relationship between the international and the national. Neither the relationship between these two components nor the components themselves carried a historically fixed meaning. By the *inter*national I mean the realm of the transnational and potentially global. When speaking about the *national* alone, I will use the term *proto / national*, as this reflects the fact that this realm was composed of supra-national, sub-national and "truly" national components, actors, or dimensions. In the two main sections of the article I then present a comparative historical analysis of the integration of women's movements and organizations from the Habsburg Monarchy into these two international organizations. I argue that the IWSA, through a more dialogical relationship with women from the Monarchy, and by developing a proactive concern with processes of nation-building, arrived at organizational strategies that did not simply mirror the interests dominating the inter-state system of the time, as was the case with the ICW. At the same time, the policy pursued by the IWSA bore marks of an emerging new world order involving new patterns of global hegemony and international politics. Finally, I evaluate the similarities and differences in the politics of the ICW and the IWSA towards the Habsburg Monarchy against this background of political change on the larger international scale as well as within women's internationalism as a whole.

Women's inter / nationalism and the global geography of nations

Strategies for shaping the realm of the inter / national in the internationalizing women's movement focused on symbolic and political representation of the proto / national – lands, nations, states and empires – on an international level. These strategies constantly created and challenged those organizational units regarded as legitimate and constitutive parts of the newly constructed international women's movement. Both the ICW and the IWSA basically conceptualized the international as a multiplication of the national. According to this principle, each group built some form of federation of the women's organizations of a given country as a nationwide umbrella organization – either the National Councils (ICW) or Auxiliaries (IWSA) – that were to be affiliated with the international women's organizations.[3]

From the beginning, the ICW was built strictly and exclusively on the idea that the national constituted the international. Aspirations to introduce additional forms of representation not based on the national met with considerable resistance and were postponed or diluted time and again. This was especially true of the repeated endeavor by the ICW leadership between 1897 and 1904 to develop a form of admission or representation for international societies.[4] Even those who supported the membership of international societies agreed early on that this goal would have to be based on the admission of "national subdivisions of said international societies."[5] Yet at the Berlin Quinquennial 1904 even a completely "nationalized" version of the original intention to incorporate international societies was unacceptable to the majority of the delegates.[6] This made strikingly clear how widespread the hesitation to opt for any internationalism not based exclusively on the national was.

At the same time, the hostility against any form of representation not based on national grounds hinted at the different understanding of women's internationalism held by the groups and National Councils represented in the ICW. While in the eyes of Anglo-Saxon representatives genuinely "international object[s]" of social reform, or movements that went "beyond national concern" did indeed exist,[7] others cautioned against any type of

Figure 12.1 The Habsburg Monarchy in 1910.

"lofty" internationalism that might take priority over the life of peoples. Similar distinctions surfaced in connection with the ICW's work on peace and international arbitration. While the commitment to these agendas in the International Council was strong and continuous, many women involved in the international work of the ICW found the plea for any institutionalized international definition-power over the relations between nations deeply suspicious.[8]

Similarly, in the case of the IWSA, the national – again in the abstract sense of a geographically distinct element of which the international was composed – was key for defining membership and admissions policy from the beginning. The first constitution of the IWSA stated that the new organization was composed of "National Woman Suffrage Associations." If such a collective organization did not exist in a country, the IWSA also accepted representation through a "National Committee" consisting of local suffrage organizations. In countries where no suffrage organizations existed, "Honorary Associates" could be named whose task was to form a "National Suffrage Committee".[9] The terms "countr[y]" and "nation" were used interchangeably in the official policy of the emerging IWSA.[10] The fact that the constitution adopted in 1904 did not clarify whether one or more "national" organization(s) of a single country should or could be admitted to membership led to substantial conflicts early on.[11] In revising its constitution in 1909 and adopting a related directive in 1911, the Alliance cast its vote firmly in favor of some form of united representation of each country, strongly urging concurrent societies within one country towards "joint representation in the Alliance by means of National Federation for International Purposes." Second and third societies from one country were to be represented together with the respective first Auxiliaries from the same country in the International Meetings of the Alliance.[12]

155

With its politics of building the international on the national, the international women's movement contributed to, and in many cases actively promoted, the country-wide organization of women's associations that had hitherto barely existed, promoting a trend of nationalization through internationalization, or inter / nationalization. "[T]hat is what the Council first does – it gives to its women the sense of nationalism, and out of that comes the sense of Internationalism."[13]

As a result of the particular inter / national character of women's international organizations, the relationship between the international women's organizations and the women's movements of the Habsburg Monarchy caused unease locally as well as internationally early on. In Central and Eastern Europe, the predominance of multinational empires implied the incorporation into imperial statehood of many proto-nations and peoples who did not possess an independent and/or complete state apparatus. Polish men and women, for example, were dispersed between territories ruled by Tsarist Russia, Austria – specifically the Austrian (or Cis-Leithanian) part of the Habsburg Monarchy – and the German Empire. A considerable portion of the Czech population in Austria lived in Bohemia as well as in the Margraviate of Moravia, which each formed separate Crownlands of Cis-Leithania. The "Lands of the Hungarian Crown," which included the Croatian territories (the Kingdom of Croatia-Slavonia), did not belong to Austria as represented in the Imperial Diet. Hungary enjoyed far-reaching autonomy within this framework in the Habsburg Monarchy after 1867.

Given this background, the international women's movement directly faced a number of fundamental tensions inherent in its general approach to inter / national organizing, once expansion into the "other," that is Eastern, half of Europe was put on the agenda. The existing inter-state system with all its hierarchies and asymmetries, as well as a huge variety of proto / national arrangements in many regions, did not correspond to the vision of the global as a standardized relation between the national and the international modeled upon the ideal of western constitutional thinking. While never questioning the model itself or its superiority, the international women's movement sought ways of relating to the existing inter-state system. In building its own landscape of the inter / national, from its very beginnings the movement did not intend to function solely as a (new, women-built) superstructure of the existing inter-state system. On occasion it did question some of the dominant relations and hierarchies involved in this system. In part, however, it based its own politics of the inter / national on these very same dominant relations.

The tensions and dynamics in the politics of the movement, which inevitably went with this double-bind, were rooted in two important historical factors. The first of these was the vision of the global that characterized the movement. There was, on the one hand, mainstream thinking about the global in the long nineteenth century, which perceived the world as divided into "civilized" and "uncivilized" parts, the latter having no substantial potential for progress or dynamic development that would result in their "catching-up" with the "civilized" world. Internationalism based on this type of thinking would exclude large parts of the world – or would allow their representation only as subordinates of a member imperial power. On the other hand, the emerging new spirit of internationalism that was to characterize the "short twentieth century" was based on a much more developmentalist vision of the international system, namely on the idea of assimilation as a precondition of inclusion. This vision no longer excluded, at least in principle, the possibility of expanding "civilization" to all countries of the globe.

The international women's movement was, in part, inspired by this "new" internationalism. In particular the IWSA – or, more precisely, its leadership – perceived the nation state or federal state within the context of the inter-state system as an ideal that was to be promoted for continuously growing parts of the world. IWSA President Carrie Chapman Catt was the only major representative of the international women's movement who explicitly declared her commitment to a truly global developmentalist spirit: "Under the influence of this new spirit we realise . . . that before us stretches the task of emancipating the women of the civilised world. Nay, more, since in the progress of things the uncivilised are destined to become civilised, our task will not be fulfilled until the women of the whole world have been rescued."[14]

This was cautious partisanship for extended nation-building beyond those world regions generally perceived as belonging to the "civilized" world, and this world view was translated into a vision of a new international system. As an argument for extending "the nation's liberty" to those world regions, Catt referred to the potential of women's liberty inherent in such aspirations:

> Men may honestly believe that women should be cloistered and veiled, silent, and subject; but when a national interest arises which needs aid, . . . such men, black, brown, white, or yellow . . . encourage women to plunge their nimble fingers into the nation's fire and to bring out the roasting chestnuts of the nation's liberty. . . Just now Asiatic men, not a whit more selfish than western men have been and will be, are beginning to desire a taste of those chestnuts, and all the surveillance is weakening in consequence. . . . It is our business to encourage these women [of Asia] to demand their share of the chestnuts when they have been won.[15]

May Wright Sewall of the ICW was certainly influenced by a similar spirit when she argued that the "feeling" of a "faith in the unity of humanity" in the women's movement probably had "not yet found its right name," but could be defined as a "spirit which finds no difference between the different nations of the world."[16] Yet Sewall never translated these ideas into concrete political judgments similar to those of Catt.

The new internationalism was deeply rooted in the idea of self-government, which had long been the main justification for the claim to individual rights for women "in the home and the State," including the right to vote. Not surprisingly in its founding document, the "Declaration of Principles," the IWSA cited the U.S.-American spirit of constitutionalism and self-determination dating back to the Declaration of Independence.[17] The emphasis on self-government "in the home and the State" implied, by extension – and in adherence to the same American political tradition – an affirmation of self-determination and self-government for all the peoples of the world. Radical representatives of the new internationalist spirit in the international women's movement of the pre-1918 period increasingly understood this principle as important for the "nations without a state" in the European context. In a global context, the new spirit of internationalism had always been characterized by a certain distance from the European colonial system, which in the course of the short twentieth century was to be replaced increasingly by the more informal patterns of hegemony characterizing the period of rising U.S.-hegemony.

The second, equally important factor responsible for shaping the politics of the international women's movement regarding the proto / national was the political aspirations or endeavors of women's movements and organizations from the non-core zones of the inter-state system. Faced with the model of straightforward inter / national organization as pursued by the international women's organizations, the non-German-Austrian women's organizations in the Habsburg Monarchy, for example, soon developed a pro-active attitude with regard to "national" organization. A number of these groups and organizations increasingly perceived the creation of an inter / national women's movement as an historical opportunity not to be missed. Their representational and affiliation endeavors were at times in tension or outright conflict with policy patterns in the international movement that were based on preconceived normative ideas about the fabric of the inter / national. After 1899, political dynamics triggered by these tensions and conflicts influenced the international women's movement's *realpolitik* toward state, nation, and the proto / national.

From early symbolic politics to the political "realism" of the ICW

Early on in the international women's movement, Central Eastern European women, movements or organizations associated with nations or nationalities without states could quite regularly make use of opportunities for public representation. Especially in the beginning, this was barely related to questions of formal membership or institutional status. "Poland," for example, was represented independently as a member of a first "permanent international committee" established on the occasion of the first International Women's Right Congress, held during the 1878 World Exhibition in Paris.[18] In 1893 the ICW accepted a U.S.-based Czech woman as "Vice-President" for "Bohemia."[19] This position (later to be renamed "Honorary Vice-President") was intended to promote contact to countries not yet formally affiliated with the ICW and to promote the establishment of National Councils in these countries.[20] At the ICW's first Quinquennial in 1893, in the "Foreign Advisory Council" "Bohemia" had seven representatives, "Poland" one, and Austria none at all.[21]

These politics of symbolic representation of the national on the international level mirrored the original idealistic approach to "nation" even in the ICW and its circles.[22] Yet after the turn of the century, deliberations and aspirations related to constructing the inter / national in Central Eastern Europe in the international women's movement (including both its international bodies and the individual member associations) gradually acquired a new shape. It was at this time – when institutionalizing and substantially expanding the geographic scope of the major organizations of the international movement was on the agenda – that questions of formal association and membership of the proto / nations in Central Eastern Europe and especially within the Habsburg Monarchy became central. When it came to institutional issues and formal membership, politics – especially of the ICW – were to prove much less idealistic than in the symbolic field of international representation of subordinated nations.

In the ICW the first and most important period of struggle over strategies of representing the Habsburg Monarchy began in the 1890s and culminated in the years 1903–1904. Prior to its second Quinquennial Meeting in London in 1899, the organization launched a major initiative to promote the establishment and admission of new National Councils. The women's movement(s) of the Habsburg Monarchy were explicitly one of the target groups. The ICW solicited a number of women's associations in the monarchy to form a National Council and to send delegates to London.[23] At this point the ICW leadership was clearly bent on establishing and admitting an all "Austrian" Council – "Austria" here meaning the empire as a whole, including Hungary. In this respect the initial intentions of the ICW clearly corresponded to basic intentions of the important German-Austrian associations. At its executive meeting held in March 1899 in London prior to the Quinquennial, the ICW appointed as an "Honorary Vice President" for "Austria" Marianne Hainisch, the "grand old lady" of the (German-)Austrian women's movement who was to become the president of the *Bund Österreichischer Frauenvereine* (Federation of Austrian Women's Organizations, or BÖFVe) for many years.[24] Hainisch had received her mandate to represent "Austria" in London according to a decision taken at two meetings in Vienna prior to the ICW executive meeting. Her mandate was backed by more than a dozen unions, predominantly located in Vienna, and all clearly German-dominated.[25] Hainisch in these years felt comfortable with her new position to which she herself referred as the "Honorary Vice President for Austria-Hungary," and repeatedly described her mission (at least until 1901) as "making the women of Austria-Hungary familiar with ... [the ICW's] goals and to initiate the formation of an Austrian-Hungarian council."[26] In trying to persuade her readers of the viability of such an enterprise, Hainisch referred to the fact that under specific circumstances the initiative of forming a national council of women could and should be based not on "the entirety of the nation," but on the "congruity of the state."[27]

In her efforts to bring about the formation of an All-Habsburg Monarchy Council, Hainisch by no means distorted the political intentions of the ICW leadership. The 1899 position of the ICW leadership was made particularly clear at one of the meetings in London when, at Hainisch's behest, the possibility was discussed of establishing an "Austrian Council" consisting of a number of sections separately representing (at least some of) "Volksstämme" (ethnic groups, peoples) officially recognized as such or of the important nationalities in the Habsburg Monarchy. Hainisch, while arguing that "owing to the variety of races in her country . . . it would be almost impossible to have one National Council . . . suggested they might have three sections, each section representing one of the principal races."[28] In Hainisch's view it was indispensable to establish a German and a Bohemian section as a "runabout [sic] way of two sections" to represent the Cis-Leithanian part of the Monarchy, as well as a Hungarian section.[29] The president of the ICW categorically refused. If it had been possible, she said, to reduce the number of the imagined sections of the imagined council from "the fourteen different races originally in Austria to three, there was hope that before long they might reduce the three to one, and then form a Council truly national."[30]

It is clear from this bargaining between the ICW and its (German-) Austrian counterpart in 1899 and the more immediate aftermath of the Quinquennial, that the parties involved at this level agreed only insofar as their focus was on establishing an all-empire National Council. At the same time, the disagreement as to whether this Council should be composed of national sections as Hainisch suggested would bring intra-Monarchy politics into play at the top level of the ICW. The politics of the leading group of German-Austrians toward the ICW were obviously informed by a certain minimum of political realism when it came to handling the "national question" back home in the Monarchy. To Hainisch it was already obvious by 1899 that it would be simply impossible to bring about a unified representation of the Habsburg Monarchy as wished for by the ICW. She knew that it was unrealistic to envision representation of Austria-Hungary in the ICW without some form of institutional acknowledgement of the multinational character and the constitutional dividedness of the empire. The developments of the following years make strikingly clear that what was presumably perceived as a minimum of political realism on the side of German-Austrian women, was at the same time also a strategy for reassuring the status quo of "national" affairs in the Monarchy by institutionally transferring it to the emerging women's internationalism. Struggle over the "national" question in this period largely concerned ensuring German-Austrian dominance in Cis-Leithania against the rising tide of struggles for more autonomy by the non-dominant nations and the nationalization of their

way of life. At the same time, formal representation and politics of the Monarchy internationally continued to be based on the idea and constitutional reality of an all-inclusive
"Austria," notwithstanding the far-reaching internal autonomy of the Kingdom of
Hungary. Women's organizations and female activists affiliated to some of the (as compared to the German-Austrians) non-dominant nations in the empire, did not easily sub-
scribe to this status quo. In the first years after 1899, this was largely demonstrated by their
lack of response or open opposition to the energetic initiatives by Marianne Hainisch to
create an "all-Austrian" Council. Calls were sent (presumably in German) to "a number of
Hungarian and to all Cis-Leithanian women's associations," but with no positive result. It
was clear to Hainisch that "national quarrels" were a most important factor hindering
cooperation, not to speak of non-German affiliation to the projected council.[31]

In overcoming this blockade, the compromise that finally emerged faithfully mirrored
constitutional and political realities *within* the Habsburg Monarchy *and* the ICW's inclination to mimic constitutional realities shaping the (male-dominated) international system.
In May 1902 the BÖFVe was founded in Vienna with only about a dozen affiliated organizations. The "non German-speaking-associations ... with the exception of one Slovenian
... and one Polish association ... stayed apart."[32] In the years to come the fundamentally
German-Austrian character of the BÖFVe remained unaltered, while national conflict
within the organization was to surface on several occasions.[33] On the ICW level, the
BÖFVe increasingly suppressed matters related to the Czech women's movement.[34]

From the outset the Executive Committee of the ICW supported the formation of the
BÖVFe and expressed its hope of immediate affiliation.[35] Yet the way to official membership was tied up with continuing anxieties over the "Austrian" issue as transferred to the
international level. Separate formation of the future Hungarian National Council, the
Magyarországi Nöegyesületek Szövetsége (Federation of the Women's Associations of
Hungary, MNSz) came about in 1904.[36] At the same time, the German-Austrians, supported
by the ICW leadership, made every effort in 1903 and 1904 to ensure the future status of
their council in the International Council. In 1903, the leadership of the ICW committed
itself to accept "into membership in advance of their application for certain reasons" the
Austrian Council (together with three other Councils).[37] Confirmation of affiliation of both
Austria and Hungary came about at the Berlin Quinquennial in 1904.[38] After this it still took
the ICW (and the Austrian Council) a little while longer to establish 1903 and 1904 as the
"correct official" order for Austrian and Hungarian affiliation respectively.[39]

A tricky problem for the ICW – not only in view of its relation to Austria-Hungary –
was how to represent nations, especially in relation to pre-existing and changing proto /
national constitutional arrangements in and outside of Europe. Particularly during the first
years of the twentieth century there were a number of other cases that required special
attention. Within Europe, the special focus was on the Swedish-Norwegian question (the
process of establishing Norway as a fully independent state culminated between June and
November 1905) and the Finnish-Russian problem (the autonomous status of Finland was
suspended in 1899 and reinstated in 1906, then, immediately following the October
Revolution, Finland declared its independence in December 1917). Outside Europe, the
Australian Commonwealth – established in 1901 and uniting a (growing) number of relatively autonomous settler colonies under British rule – posed a problem to the politics of
admission and representation as pursued by the ICW.

The ICW had to deal with all of these issues, including the "Austrian" problem, roughly
within the same time period. While these cases posed very different problems in comparison with one another, the methods the ICW developed to deal with the proto / national

160

fused, mixed, and complicated the handling of them. An important juncture marking these dealings in the ICW, as put by these and other cases, was the establishment of a committee on "Races and Nationalities" by decision of the Berlin Quinquennial of 1904. This committee, on which all National Councils were to have a delegate, was "to examine the question of political and racial representation."[40] The immediate background for formulating the problem in this way had originally been the Australian case. Since 1900 Lady Aberdeen had repeatedly expressed her wish for a federation of the councils representing different lands in the Commonwealth of Australia, either affiliated or applying for affiliation. Aberdeen argued that it would be "a violation of the fundamental idea of the Council to give to each of these states independent and separate recognition" in the ICW "now that their states are federated into one nation."[41] It was the difference of opinion on this question that in 1903 triggered the idea that the "question of political and racial representation" should be thoroughly studied.[42] In the ensuing period until the Berlin Quinquennial in June 1904, concern about the Australian question was transformed into much more general debate about the right way to represent nations in the ICW. ICW President May Wright Sewall wished to see "separate but complete" or else "distinct and complete" nationalities represented by "bona fide" National Councils in the ICW.[43] The ICW leadership also discussed the "possible formation of National Councils in countries incorporated in a nation with a different nationality."[44] The final decision about the affiliation of the Hungarian Council and the acceptance of the request for affiliation by the Norwegian Council was made in this context.[45] At the Berlin Quinquennial, the motion to formally establish the committee on "Races and Nationalities" was passed in the midst of complex debate. "Once under way the question was further discussed, especially as a representative for Bohemia – or the Czech nation – had announced herself, and the general meeting was thus required to decide whether a Czech women's federation could be established. . . . Envisioned for the time being as a basic principle is the organization based on pre-existing states [staatlichen Gebilden]."[46]

Against the background of these tensions and events, the newly established committee on "Races and Nationalities" was requested in very general terms "to define philosophically and historically what is a nation" in order to enable "just action" on the part of the International Council. Not unexpectedly, the chair of the committee soon declared herself overburdened in dealing with this "rather ... complex problem." For quite a time, the leadership of the ICW did not take any concrete decision as how to handle the matter.[47]

At the same time, tension and rivalry over how to model "just action" with regard to representation of the proto / national continued to plague the ICW. Conflict over Norway grew in 1905 when the country, already affiliated, was on its way to achieving formal independence from Sweden. In this context, the ICW finally adopted an amendment to its constitution stating that it "excludes from its programme political and religious questions of a controversial nature affecting the inter-relationship of two or more countries."[48] With Finland, the International Council had close connections early on through Alexandra Gripenberg, one of the great international women-networkers of the period, who was appointed "Honorary Vice President" in 1893.[49] But in the period when the country was not "self-deciding as to [its] own affairs," tension with Russia was openly transferred to the international public sphere of the ICW.[50] The newly founded National Council of Finland was to be finally federated with the ICW in 1911, a few years after the country had regained its autonomous status within the Russian empire and after the introduction of universal and equal suffrage for men and women which had followed in 1906.[51]

As for the Habsburg Monarchy, international representation relating to the problem of the proto / national never again developed into such overt tension as in the 1899–1904 period. For Marianne Hainisch, ideas of separate representation for nations without a state were taboo, and she mobilized all her influence in the ICW to block any and all such aspirations. As negotiations on "Races and Nationalities" proceeded in the committee, Hainisch, representing the Austrian Council, presented a resolution in which the committee was to propose to the International Council "that the I.C.W. drop the question of nationalities and continue as heretofore to receive the independent states into membership without taking into consideration the nationality of their citizens. But at the same time we advocate the organisation of national groups whose delegations shall elect common representatives for the I.C.W."[52]

Her suggestion was not approved. Finally, the committee proposed to the ICW at its "Special Session" in Geneva 1908 the establishment of an "Advisory Board . . . to which applications for affiliation from countries forming new National Councils may be referred by the Executive." The Board was designed by the committee to put into practice the "principle of arbitration" within the ICW.[53] This decision was intended to give discretionary power with regard to national representation to top-level ICW leadership. At the same time, there was clear disapproval of possible claims for (greater) autonomy for nationalities in the ICW. The Geneva meeting, for example, accepted a resolution suggesting that the ICW would pledge itself to work for a general international arbitration treaty "which shall cover all cases of dispute between nations, except those of autonomy."[54]

While Hainisch did not oppose this amendment in Geneva, she definitely did so at the Quinquennial in Toronto 1909, only a few months later. Again she insisted that "affiliations ... should be based on states and not on nationalities," and that if the proposed board "does not exist, no country could try to come in unless with a duly constituted National Council" by which she meant Councils based on "states." A very slim majority of delegates sided with Hainisch, and the proposition originally adopted by the special committee in Geneva was dropped.[55]

Retrospectively, the ICW (albeit considering alternative options in the period around 1904 to 1906) had taken a straightforward course of "just action" in its politics regarding the proto / national. In federating Councils from the Commonwealth of Australia (or, earlier, its then separate parts), as well as from Norway, Hungary and Finland – while at the same time denying independent representation for the Bohemian women's movement and for Polish women from the former kingdom of Poland, that is, from the territories ruled by Tsarist Russia – the ICW had clearly followed a kind of "containment" policy. While never defining what was to be perceived as a "nation," the International Council indeed promoted federation exclusively for self-governing nations and countries enjoying a far-reaching autonomous status. As was to become obvious, this marked a considerable difference compared to the IWSA, and politics pursued by the two organizations with regard to the "national question" were closely intertwined. The IWSA was oriented much more strongly towards the ideal of self-government. Accordingly, the IWSA, as will be shown below, made use of the newly established women's international domain to assure, within clear constraints, a forum for women representing nations without states.

The IWSA and the spirit of the short twentieth century

In itself, the decision at the ICW Quinquennial in Toronto to block even the idea that the ICW might at some point consider federation of Councils not based "on states" but "on nationalities," appears to be of very limited relevance to the history of the ICW. But the decision was taken in a wider context of significant shifts in the history of constructing the feminist inter / national, and it was meant to shield the ICW against the winds of change. Only a few weeks earlier, at its London meeting of April/May 1909, the IWSA had come to a crucial and essentially different decision regarding modes of representing the women's movements of the Habsburg Monarchy at the international level. In London, the Alliance had admitted the German-Austrian *Frauenstimmrechtskomitee* (Women's Suffrage Committee) as well as the Czech-Bohemian *Výbor pro volební právo žen* (Committee for Women's Suffrage) separately as new[56] members.[57] In doing so, the IWSA, in a critical conflict between ideal nation and real existing constructions of constitutional law in Europe, had positioned itself differently from the ICW. The Alliance had given space for institutionalized international representation to one of many nations without a state in Central Europe. Moreover, the Alliance had defined this space on an equal footing with a second committee formed by women belonging to the dominant nation in the Cis-Leithanian part of the Habsburg Monarchy. This equality prefigured a status of international representation that the Czechs would achieve in the male-dominated, formal international system only after the disintegration of the Habsburg Monarchy.

The history of this decision of the Alliance dates back to 1904–1906, the period in which the formation and affiliation of a Hungarian Auxiliary to the IWSA was under way. The association that was to become this Auxiliary, the *Feministák Egyesülete* (Association of Feminists, FE), which under the informal leadership of Róza Schwimmer developed into the single most active organization in the Hungarian women's movement, was founded in 1904–1905. Prior to the establishment of the FE in the context of the bifurcation of the international women's movement, and while still working "with steam" for setting up a Hungarian National Council,[58] Schwimmer had been increasingly drawn into preparations for the founding meeting of the IWSA in Berlin 1904. Finally she was asked to represent the "Hungarian political women's movement" at this meeting.[59] In Berlin, Aletta Jacobs and IWSA President Carrie Chapman Catt urged Schwimmer and her associate Vilma Glücklich to form a Hungarian organization affiliated as an Auxiliary with the IWSA, which they did.

In the process of formal confirmation of Hungary's affiliation as an Auxiliary with the IWSA, the Alliance gave the first formal sign of a certain inclination to distance the organizational patterns characterizing the IWSA from pre-existing constitutional arrangements in the inter-state system. At its 1906 convention the IWSA made its first attempt to define the nation for its own purposes. Catt by now was well aware of the difficulties encountered by the ICW. The resolution passed on this occasion served as a basic political guideline for many years to come: "Any country – even if not possessing a wholly independent government – but possessing the power to fully enfranchise its own women citizens, shall be considered a nation . . . , and may organize a National Woman Suffrage Association which may be eligible to membership of the Alliance."[60] This definition, Catt argued, "calls into action the powers of discrimination in the domain of political constitutions of different States, which several of our delegates possess"; and then the discussion compared the "status of ... Hungary, Iceland and the different German lands."[61]

The 1906 resolution, which marked the beginning of a complex process of developing the IWSA's strategy of shaping the inter / national in suffrage politics vis-à-vis regulation of membership, involved a number of issues essential for defining the relation of international suffrage politics to proto / national spaces and constitutional arrangements (not only) with reference to Central Europe. A key element in this strategy was the constant and exclusive focus on questions of political citizenship. Territories "behind" member organizations in the IWSA were always defined along lines of political citizenship or, more precisely, enfranchisement. In 1909, after years of negotiations, the Alliance, in a very carefully considered and prepared major revision of its constitution, for the first time introduced a regulation concerning membership that included a geographic definition.[62] According to this regulation, "in a country possessing the authority to enfranchise its own women ... [o]ne National Woman Suffrage Association, or one Federation of National Woman Suffrage Associations" was eligible to "become Auxiliary to the Alliance."[63] The territorial element in this definition – the "country" – was exclusively defined by reference to suffrage arrangements, while the term "nation" was not defined at all. The new regulation thus differed from the 1906 resolution in sidestepping the construction or presupposition of a clear relationship between a constitutional and/or territorial unit as defined for the purposes of the IWSA, and the geo-historical phenomenon called "nation." In speaking of suffrage organizations "in" countries, the definition also carefully avoided indicating a relation of representation between the Woman Suffrage Association or Federation affiliated to the IWSA and the territory (not to speak of the nation) "behind" it. Finally, as compared to the 1906 resolution, the revised constitution no longer spoke of *full* enfranchisement but only of enfranchisement.

Three important implications went with this decision. First, it allowed the omission of explicit references to the possible lack of full independence of a government in a country from which the Alliance might have wished to affiliate an Auxiliary. Second, it omitted the reference to layers of enfranchisement within a given territory that was implicit in the term "full" enfranchisement used in the 1906 resolution. In referring to "enfranchisement" and "countries," the revised constitution of 1909 left ample space for interpretations taking or not taking into consideration enfranchisement at the level of states, lands, and empires (with municipal and district levels definitely excluded). Third, the new formulation was carefully phrased so as to avoid taking sides for any particular form of constitutional arrangements related to suffrage. "Full enfranchisement" certainly could have been interpreted as a preference at least for universal, if not for universal and equal suffrage, and thus as a clear stance taken on far-reaching parliamentary democracy. Suffrage was obviously of greater political influence and consequence in a parliamentary democracy than in, say, a constitutional monarchy based on restricted political capacities of the parliament and on heavily restricted forms of suffrage. The Alliance indeed pursued, in practical terms, a politics of neutrality in all matters related to constitutional arrangements beyond the question of in/equality with regard to political citizenship between the sexes.[64] Consequently, debate on the political value of suffrage in a given constitutional context was persistently downplayed, while insofar as its ideals were concerned the IWSA already in its "Declaration of Principles" had clearly referred to "self-government in the home and the State" and to "representative ... government."[65] At least for Catt – and for others dedicated to constitutionalism and self-government in the sense of the spirit of the short twentieth century – "the movement for woman suffrage is just a part of the eternal forward march of the human race toward a complete democracy."[66]

As for the Habsburg Monarchy, only the Hungarian part of the complex problem of "nationhood" and constitutional arrangement pertaining to suffrage was fully covered by these definitions of 1906 and 1909. After 1867, the Hungarian parliament certainly possessed the authority to enfranchise its own women, even if Hungary comprised only a "portion"[67] of a bigger constitutional unit.[68] Affiliating a separate Hungarian Auxiliary was therefore indeed in perfect keeping with the IWSA regulations of 1906 and 1909. At the same time the "Austrian question" needed a different form of input. In Cis-Leithania, the retrograde law of associations prohibited female membership in legally recognized political associations and, by implication, the formation of any women's organization focusing explicitly on suffrage. In 1905 the struggle over electoral reform introducing male universal suffrage to the Imperial Diet became the main political issue in Cis-Leithania. German-Austrian, Czech and Polish women formed separate movements to change the law of associations as well as to achieve women's suffrage. For the time being they could not work through formally constituted suffrage associations, while according to the IWSA constitution of 1904 only such organizations were entitled to affiliation.[69] In the Austrian case, this problem coincided with the "nationality question," to which the attention of Alliance President Catt was increasingly drawn after her first trip through the Monarchy in 1906. At this point Catt, while representing the burgeoning spirit of the short twentieth century in the international women's movement, had still confined her Austrian contacts to the German-Austrian women's movement.[70] In the capital city of the Crownland of Bohemia, Prague, where in 1900 more than 90 percent of the population officially declared Czech their "colloquial language," Catt made a public appearance at a meeting held in the German language.[71] Upon arrival in Prague, however, Catt (along with Aletta Jacobs who was accompanying her) was immediately involved in German-Czech tensions and the ensuing separation of Czech and German groups within the women's movement. The day after the German meeting, Františka Plamínková, a leading figure of the Czech-Bohemian *Výbor pro volební právo zen*, which had been founded in late 1905, made a formal visit to the two guests from the IWSA.[72] Plamínková reported the activities and the goals of the Czech-Bohemian suffrage movement and explained why it had boycotted the public meeting. Catt was reportedly "[m]uch interested" in Plamínková's report and deeply impressed by her personality, as well as to have promised on this occasion to come back and pay a second visit to the Bohemian capital.[73]

For the time being, the IWSA remained wrapped in silence with regard to the "Czech question."[74] But Catt used the subsequent period to clarify her understanding of the constitutional arrangements regarding suffrage in the Habsburg Monarchy,[75] and to consciously build the relationship not only with German-Austrian, but also with leading Czech-Bohemian activists. By 1908, Catt was determined to offer representation in the IWSA to both groups on an equal footing. In June of the same year, at the international conference of the IWSA, Plamínková and Marie Stepanková represented the Czech- Bohemian, and Marie Lang the German-Austrian suffrage committees as "fraternal delegates."[76]

In spring 1909, on the eve of the London Quinquennial of the IWSA, Catt again traveled to Prague,[77] this time as a guest of the Czech women's movement. While on her trip, Catt herself wrote mockingly to Aletta Jacobs of "the German and Czech war over the ... international suffrage visitors."[78] Later, Plamínková described the visit in *Jus Suffragii* as a kind of triumph for the Czech suffrage movement.[79] In revising its constitution at the London meeting of 1909 the IWSA adopted a new regulation allowing for the affiliation of suffrage committees from countries where neither national nor local suffrage organizations existed. "Austria" was explicitly named as the point of reference for the creation of this new possibility. The German-Austrian and Czech-Bohemian committees both became "affiliated organizations," equal in status as compared to each other, but unequal in status as compared to regular Auxiliaries from other countries.[80]

This step was of utmost importance in designing an "Austrian politics" for the IWSA, bound to the ideal of the national rather than based on a simple affirmation of existing constitutional arrangements or their political consequences in women's politics. At least retrospectively Catt represented herself as having been openly, if cautiously, in favor of national independence early on. She remembered that already in Berlin 1904 she had answered a question put by Annie Furuhjelm, an eminent representative of the Finnish women's movement, by saying, "All the little countries will surely be free and indepen-dent [after] many years have passed by."[81]

However, all steps designed to promote the ideal national within the bonds of suffrage internationalism were brought into effect by the IWSA under one clearly defined precon-dition: real existing state frontiers and constitutional arrangements shaping the European lands marked the limits of any affirmative action to be taken in service of the ideal national. First of all it was clarified that "national antagonisms" were not to play any role in the IWSA as an organization.[82] Consequently, the constitution of 1909, revised with the "Austrian question" in mind, referred only to the existence or non-existence of formally constituted and legally recognized suffrage organizations.[83] The fact that the phrasing of the new paragraph did not even hint at the intention or possibility of admitting more than one such "Committee" or even a number of "nationality"-based committees from one country – an intention that with reference to Austria had been spelled out and pursued pub-licly at the top level of the IWSA beginning in 1908 – clearly points to the conscious avoidance of open involvement with the "nationality question" in Austria. In the final analysis, therefore, the IWSA utilized the constant reference to the retrograde Cis-Leithanian law on associations as a means whereby women's politics could back the ideal national without explicitly taking sides with respect to tensions or conflicts over "nation-ality" or constitutional arrangements.

Austrian politics as (re-)designed by the IWSA in 1908–1909 should also be read in relation to the additional but never explicitly addressed, context of resolving the problem of multiple affiliations of Suffrage Associations from one and the same country, which was concluded in the same constitutional revision in 1909. The new regulation was to ensure joint representation of all organizations from one country within the IWSA. As opposed to this, the regulation left the requirement for "national federation" to the future for those (exceptional) countries where only a "Committee" could be affiliated. In view of the situation in Cis-Leithania it seems clear that the reluctance to request "national feder-ation" from suffrage "committees" was intended to pave the way for putting into practice the commitment of the Alliance to the ideal nation. The regulation on committees allowed for the visible representation of the existing geographically and nationally divided com-mittees of Cis-Leithania.

The new regulation restricted international representation of committees to one delegate each, resulting in the Austrian case in only two delegates, while full scale Auxiliaries were entitled to twelve delegates each.[84] This was obviously intended to be a precaution against over-representation and even equal representation of countries without duly constituted suffrage organizations on the international level, underlining once again that its new "Austrian politics" were not intended to prefigure or promote territorial and constitutional change in relation to Cis-Leithania or other lands. As usual, Catt built her related argument on straightforward reference to the existing system of political representation as it related to suffrage:

A special amendment to the Constitution was ... adopted which applies to the con-dition in Austria where a law ... prevents the formation of a national association. This clause permits the States of Austria to become independently affiliated with the Alliance until such time as a national association can be formed. Under these provisions the States of Austria and Bohemia have become members; but the two together must be regarded as one nation, since it is the Empire of Austria alone which can grant them the suffrage which they ask.[85]

On the level of tactics, this statement, referring once again to the Austrian law of associations as well as in defining the "States of Austria" as "one nation," was intended to ease any possible worry among representatives of dominant groups in Central Europe such as the Germans and German-Austrians. On a strategic level, the combined regulations for countries possessing and not possessing national suffrage organizations allowed the Alliance to assume a flexible approach with regard to historical developments and events to come. In the IWSA politics promoting the "ideal national" were taken very seriously, while the principle of not openly questioning political frontiers and territorial arrangement always took precedence over more radical attempts to promote such politics.

This became strikingly clear in 1913 when a third woman suffrage committee from Cis-Leithania, which was formed by Polish suffrage activists in the Crownland of Galicia, was admitted. This step implied that the IWSA would not give ground on an organizational level to any politics related to the "Polish nation" that implicitly or explicitly questioned or transgressed existing political frontiers between Austria, the German Empire, and the Kingdom of Poland (subordinated to Czarist Russia).[86] The declared objective of the IWSA was to systematically internationalize the women's suffrage movement. Had the Alliance made room in its own house for political aspirations that disputed existing political frontiers, this undoubtedly would have precipitated those highly explosive potential conflicts that were rightly perceived as countering any internationalist feminist mission and vision. It was, therefore, no coincidence that the Alliance in the 1906–1909 period, while step by step developing a relationship to "nation" that was definitely inspired by the spirit of the short twentieth century, worked out rules of keeping national dispute out of its own house.[87]

At the same time, Catt (at least) was fully aware of the fact that geographic boundaries between the nations and states that formed the basis of the international system at the beginning of the twentieth century were in no way static, but part of a process of historical change: "It was ... proposed that our Organisation should consist of National Associations, yet in the face of the well-known racial and political differences which are constantly changing the geographical boundaries of the world, where was the authority to be found who could define a nation?"[88] From this perspective, it was one of the important obligations and opportunities of suffrage internationalism to develop a position (and to be able to develop such a position) that could keep pace with ongoing historical change on its proto / national basis through a strategy that could be labeled a kind of "active passivity."

Conclusion

In a global and long-term historical perspective, it was not by chance that before 1918 within the international women's movement politics over Central Eastern Europe contributed in important ways to the globalization of strategies that shaped the relation between the international and the national. The present study of these strategies has sought to advance transnational perspectives on the history of women's movements on two levels.

First, the ascent of women's organized internationalism involved change and innovation with regard to the gendered character of the inter / national. Through nationalizing organizational structures of existing women's movements in individual countries, international interest and organization in the women's movement contributed substantially to the development of the "female half" of the nation in general, and to a female and feminist public sphere within nations in particular. At the same time the international women's movement itself functioned, on the international level, as an instrument that compensated for the exclusion and marginalization experienced by women of all nations back home, in the public and political spheres of their own countries. Leading representatives of both the ICW and the IWSA repeatedly described their respective organizations as a kind of superstate or substitute-state, in which the female could and would be foregrounded.[89] Women's internationalism was thought to "help to promote the true brotherhood of Nations" through "the greater recognition of the sisterhood of women workers the world over."[90]

Secondly, I have explored the similarities and differences characterizing the strategies of inter / nationalizing women's movements in their relation to the inter-state system as pursued by the ICW and the IWSA as these organizations expanded into Central Eastern Europe. Both the ICW and the IWSA organized internationally on a nation-by-nation basis. This ideal of internationalism drew on western experience, and on a belief in the progressive nature of western models of state-building. Yet as the two organizations endeavored to integrate territories not belonging to the North-Atlantic core zones of the global inter-state system, they both had to re-negotiate this ideal vis-a-vis the complex relation between empire, statehood, nation, and nation-building.

The analysis of politics developed in this connection demonstrates that organized women's internationalism could and indeed did play an important role in shaping and reshaping not only the inter / national character of women's movements on the ground, but also the inter-state system as such. Between 1906 and 1913, especially, the IWSA developed a politics of cautious support for nation-building and self-government in Central Eastern Europe. This policy of the Alliance was built on reference not to territory, but to political citizenship, and on never openly calling into question pre-existing territorial arrangements. Such tendencies would develop openly only after an additional organizational ramification in the international women's movement – which finally led to the establishment of the Women's International League for Peace and Freedom (WILPF). An outspoken declaration pertaining to the geographic extension of national self-determination was, for the first time, produced at the famous 1915 peace congress, the International Congress of Women in The Hague, by leading radical representatives of the twentieth-century spirit of internationalism, many of whom were closely associated with the IWSA, and future leaders of the WILPF. Developments in Central Eastern Europe, where tension over the "nationality question" had developed into open conflict after the outbreak of the war, formed the decisive background for this resolution.[91]

The ICW, in contrast, acted in a much more reserved manner. In the period between 1899 and 1904, the organization had already arrived at a strategy of suppressing international aspirations of women's movements associated with the nations without states in the Habsburg Monarchy. This politics essentially reconfirmed pre-existing international power relations within the realm of women's internationalism. As national tension intensified in the region in the years preceding World War I, the ICW became even stricter in pursuing the related containment strategy.

These differences between the Central Eastern European politics of IWSA and ICW closely intertwined not only with the politically more or less progressive outlook of the two organizations. They also reflected historical-geographic shifts within the patterns of hegemony in the international system, and these shifting relations, in turn, were mirrored in the relative weight of divergent interest within each organization. The inter / national politics adopted by the IWSA prefigured the inter-state system of the short twentieth century, which was to be based largely on the globalization of the nation state within a framework of western hegemony as gradually shifting from (western) Europe to the United States of America. This political positioning implied not only support for the weaker nations of Central Eastern Europe, but also a certain distance from the colonial system dominated by the strong European powers. Within the IWSA as an organization, this positioning was reflected in close reliance on progressive U.S.-American political culture, strong U.S.-leadership, and visible coalition-building with progressive women from the non-dominant nations of the Habsburg Monarchy. Within the ICW, by contrast, the influence of moderate women's organizations representing the "old" and mostly colonial European powers grew over time, and interest and representation of women's organizations from Central Eastern Europe remained comparatively weak.

Whenever it came to conflict between the capability to sustain women's international organizing and reshaping the gendered dimension of the inter / national on the one hand, and actively contributing to other large projects of the short twentieth century, such as the building of independent nation-states in the "other" half of Europe and beyond on the other hand, both the IWSA and the ICW gave priority to the former. Both organizations, though in different ways and for different reasons, lived with the fact that this decision implied tolerance of persistent hierarchies in the inter / national system for many years to come.

13

THE OTHER "AWAKENING"

The emergence of women's movements in the modern Middle East, 1900–1940

Ellen L. Fleischmann

History, politics, and gender

In 1945, two years before her death, the noted Egyptian feminist Huda Sha'rawi was awarded the highest possible state decoration in Egypt. Leila Ahmed notes that the award

> was a measure not only of the prominence Sha'rawi had attained as leading advocate of women's rights but also of the enormous transformation Egyptian society had undergone in the first half of this century. A society in which women of Sha'rawi's (upper) class were veiled and invisible and could have no presence in the world of public and political activities had become one in which they were visible and active in the public domain, in which their activities were reported in the papers (accompanied by photographs of their unveiled faces), and in which the state and secular-minded politicians, literati and intellectuals of the day recognized women's contributions.[1]

Sha'rawi, unlike her more anonymous and unrecognized peers in other parts of the Middle East, achieved in her lifetime and beyond a high public profile in the region, ultimately embodying the quintessential historic "pioneer" of Middle Eastern feminism. We know much less about the rich history of other Middle Eastern women activists and the women's movements within which they functioned.

Beginning around the turn of the twentieth century, at the same time that upper-class Egyptian women began to write about and promote greater freedoms for women, women in other parts of the Middle East also began to organize women's societies, associations, unions, and federations, which led to the formation of nascent women's movements. Although the impetus for organizing often emanated from national crises, these usually loose associations arose during the first four decades of the twentieth century to constitute various forms of indigenous feminisms. In Iran, women left their homes for the streets during the constitutional crisis of 1906–1911; similarly, Turkish women formed their first women's associations around the time of the 1908 Committee of Union and Progress (CUP) coup and the subsequent reinstitution of constitutional rule; in Egypt, women demonstrated and organized in support of the 1919 Wafdist revolution; and Palestinian women convened a national women's congress and demonstrated against British Mandatory policies in the wake of the Wailing Wall disturbances of 1929.

This essay will trace the historical trajectory of the emergence of Middle Eastern women's movements. . . . The region so defined covers twenty-one countries with "few similarities and as many differences."[2] Yet women in the region – from the middle and upper classes, it should be stressed – perceived themselves as sharing a collective cultural and even political identity that transcended regional, linguistic, and religious differences. On a number of occasions, they saw and sought common cause, coming together and uniting around shared concerns. The histories of the individual women's movements are inextricably embedded within the broader context and narrative of a collective history. This article represents a preliminary attempt to integrate some of those individual histories within that broader collective. . . .[3]

In exploring this history, one is immediately confronted with the question: What is the understanding of "feminism" here, especially within the particular historical and geopolitical context of the Middle East in the first third of the twentieth century? . . . Of pivotal interest to those who study women and gender in the Middle East are critical examinations of . . . feminism being undertaken by Third World feminist scholars. Their task became one of redefining feminism in a way that divests it of its Western particularity and instead constructs new meanings incorporating both its universal aspects and its "historically specific and dynamic"[4] forms in the Third World. For our purposes, the task becomes threefold: theoretically redefining feminism; broadening our understanding of the issues that fall under its rubric; and reexamining the history of feminism in order to recognize that "feminism, perhaps outside the terms and definitions as we know it today, has existed in a variety of forms" within Third World societies throughout history.[5] . . . We need to not only "include" Third World women but also entirely reconceptualize feminism as a plural(istic), heterogeneous set of practices with a long, rich history worldwide. Such reformulations take into account the distinct character of the Middle Eastern women's movements, which responded to political, cultural, and social conditions that were unique in some respects, yet analogous in others to the predicaments facing other women's movements. . . .

Many women activists who became involved in women's movements did not necessarily consider or call themselves feminists.[6] Here, the intricacies of the intersections between feminism, colonialism, and nationalism come into play. In many cases women were not attempting to develop "new" gender relations and social practices so much as protect them from the corrosive effects of European colonial rule, as well as from disruptive social, economic, and cultural transformations caused by other internal and regional developments. The focus of their activism was not necessarily on changing inequitable gender relations in their societies so much as on alleviating their effects on women. Activist women perceived their efforts as defending and strengthening national culture and the family against external threats.

This was particularly the case with those women's movements that focused on national struggles. At its core, nationalism highlights the issue of identity. Women were faced with the question: Gender or nation, which came first? The answer depended upon which was the primary site of attack. One "common theme" among the different ways that women have been drawn into protest activities has been that "for a critical mass within the group the situation has become intolerable and those in power have to be challenged."[7] For many women in the Middle East, it was the national situation that became "intolerable" and national identity that was threatened during the period under study. The question of gender inequity invariably was postponed or considered divisive, and the national issue seen as the priority. This was (and continues to be, in some situations) the case even among activist women, who maintained that women could not achieve "rights" when men did not have them.[8]

Yet women used their entry into public life through that "most honorable door," the nationalist struggle, to push at the boundaries that confined them and to begin to challenge cultural, social, and political norms.[9] By acting at all, they transgressed these norms; as one observer put it, nationalism had a "releasing effect" on women.[10] Through their involvement in nationalism, they developed over time an internal critique of gender relations that was sometimes muted but often implicit. This involvement could only bring to the fore the contradictions of their multiple identities as women and national subjects or citizens, not to mention other sources of identity such as religion, class, and kin relations.

A feminist consciousness or "awareness," however, was not necessarily a preexisting condition in many women who became politically active in the women's movements. Consciousness is developed through experience. The experiences of women – their very act of organizing – constituted feminism, despite a lack of explicit feminist consciousness, which sometimes did or did not develop, depending upon the specific historical circumstances.[11] . . . Thus, the women's movements constructed their political positions through an interactive process in which they identified their opposition, and defined themselves politically, in relation to those they opposed. This kind of process does not necessarily flow one way only, nor is it merely reactive; it allows for constant change and requires adaptability within fluctuating political situations. (The opposition itself – for example, colonial structures of rule – is not static, unified, and unchanging.)[12] The women's movements developed a certain flexibility, an inherent component of this concept of feminism.[13] The *dynamic* of opposition – in all its diverse forms – is the universal dimension that binds heterogeneous feminisms together under the rubric "feminism," taking account of this heterogeneity and universality simultaneously. This framework, grounded in examination of the historical experiences of Middle Eastern women's movements, helps us make sense of their diversity as well as the commonalities of their struggles, strategies, and ideologies. . . .[14]

It is one of the premises of this essay that an understanding of the historical roots of women's involvement is important not only because it informs contemporary struggles, movements, and challenges that confront them but also because these histories merit examination in and of themselves.[15] . . . History is not so easily swept aside. . . . Women's developing their own movements was part of an overall historical process in which changes in women's position and the redefinition of gender relations in Middle Eastern societies were at the heart of searing questions revolving around the nature of culture, national and personal identity, and the meaning of modernity. Such transformations and the furious debates they provoked were rooted in political as well as social and cultural change, no matter how much tradition, religion, and culture have been highlighted. Politics is intricately implicated with the process of change, which affected women and notions of gender. The history of this process and all the constituent parts interwoven with it, and embedded within it, would be incomplete without the history of women's political involvement.

History of the movements

In order to make sense of such a broad, rich, and diverse sweep of history, I make the risky proposition of arranging it into three roughly thematic stages of development, purely as a heuristic device. These stages do not necessarily follow a linear chronology because the progressive development of the individual women's movements varied, with stages overlapping, coinciding, preceding, and following one another, at times obscuring the demarcation lines among them.[16] In some cases, several of these stages occurred almost simultaneously, and in other cases, certain women's movements have yet to experience one or another of these stages. The first stage – the so-called awakening – was that phenomenon whereby women and men began to raise the issue of women's status and question previously unchallenged social practices, but not necessarily the social (or political) structures or institutions that governed them. It was during this stage that reformers and other intellectuals initiated debate on women's status in various forums, including the press. This stage also witnessed the development of myriad social, religious, literary, charitable, educational, and in some cases political, women's organizations. A major characteristic of the second stage was women's adoption of nationalism as a liberating discourse, linking it and their own direct involvement in nationalist movements to female emancipation. The third stage is characterized by women's co-optation by, and collusion and/or collision with, the state-building project, resulting in the evolution of state feminism. Of the movements studied here, only Iran and Turkey experienced this stage of development before 1940.

It seems judicious before discussing the specific historical experiences of the women's movements to clarify the use of the terms "awakening" and "movement(s)" to characterize the heterogeneity of the various women's groups that were established. Discursive references to a "women's awakening"[17] began to appear as early as the late nineteenth century in the Middle East, particularly in the women's press; in the Arabic-speaking parts of the Middle East, the term seems to have been more commonly used in the earlier part of the twentieth century. Many women's organizations used the word in their names.[18] As Beth Baron points out, although the phrase originally referred to a literary movement, "it took on a broader cultural and social resonance."[19] I have chosen to use the word because women's utilization of it demonstrates its significance to them. The danger in using this term, however, is that the word "awakening" "presupposes sleep," an often reiterated but false assumption about women's passivity during the nineteenth century.[20] It also contained political connotations and implicit association with the Arab "awakening," a movement whose history continues to be contested and debated more than a century after its inception. Over time the ubiquity and frequency of the term's utilization approached something of a cliché, with all the generality and stereotyping that implies.[21] For that reason, I use the word advisedly and in quotation marks.

The word "movement"[22] began to be used around the 1920s to refer to a wide range of women's public activities that were taking place throughout the region. Increasingly, it began to replace the word "awakening" in this context. "Movement" at its most elemental level is defined as "a series of organized activities working toward an objective" or "an organized effort by supporters of a common goal."[23] My use of the term is deliberately broad. Although many of the different women's societies, organizations, federations, and unions that were established may not have been working toward commonly shared, explicitly delineated and agreed upon goals, it can be argued that women in each Middle Eastern society that experienced this phenomenon perceived their efforts as part of a broader whole, however ill-defined or assorted the myriad and sometimes discordant groups that formed its constituent parts. The emergence of women's movements in the Middle East during this period was not an isolated occurrence but was part of a broader global phenomenon in almost all parts of the world, including India, the United States, Europe, Latin America, and parts of Africa and Asia. Analogous to their counterparts throughout the world, most of the women's movements in the Middle East shared for the most part a basic "transformational character" that provoked reexaminations of gender roles, whether or not this was a specific goal.[24] Each of these movements, individually (on national or local bases) and collectively (on a regional basis), shared a "common concern with improving the position of women in society," despite often indirect ways of working toward achieving this goal and a lack of cohesive, unified strategies.[25]

The women's movements that arose in the early part of the twentieth century also shared a number of characteristics, demonstrating the links and connections between and among women of the region. Bonds of culture, religion, solidarity, and common political concerns were specifically articulated at a number of regional and international women's conferences attended by Middle Eastern women in the 1930s and 1940s. During crises in individual states, women from all over the region expressed solidarity and support for their "sisters" through demonstrations, telegrams, and various protest actions. The press in the Middle East played a major role in facilitating communication and the spread of information through its coverage of the activities of the different women's movements throughout the region, as well as feminist movements elsewhere.[26] Women activists established local and regional networks through correspondence and personal contacts. Prominent Egyptian women activists such as Huda Sha'rawi and Amina Sa'id made speaking tours and were feted by their cohorts in the Mashriq, for example, during the 1940s. By the end of World War II, a solid network of women's organizations existed throughout the region that had fairly extensive contacts and, in some cases, formal organizational ties to each other.

Stage One: The "awakening"

Most of the commentaries on the women's movements locate their shared intellectual foundations in the different reform movements, secular and Islamist, that arose initially during the late nineteenth century. Male reformers have been highlighted for their role in voicing protests about, and promoting improvements in, women's status. Ironically (and perhaps not surprisingly), it was a man, Qasim Amin, the Egyptian judge and author of the influential *The Liberation of Women* (1899), who was long considered by many (mistakenly, according to Leila Ahmed) the "father of Arab feminism."[27] Historians have not focused much attention on the fact that, although the heated debates that ensued in the literate world during this early period were ostensibly *about* women and frequently *among* men, women themselves, far from being merely the objects of this debate, energetically engaged in these contestations, challenging conservative male polemicists as well as other women. In Egypt, for example, two women battled in the press on opposing sides of the issue of women's suffrage as early as 1892.[28] In Turkey, Fatma Aliye Hanim, provoked by a series of articles promoting polygyny, set forth her views in a monograph entitled *The Women of Islam*, which "predate[d]" (1891) and "foreshadow[ed]" many of Amin's arguments in *The Liberation of Women*.[29]

In the early twentieth century, intellectuals in Iran, Turkey, Egypt, and Greater Syria all debated the issue of women within the context of modernity, which was understood to encompass "technological progress, secularism, the rule of law, women's emancipation, and a monogamous family system."[30] Women's status became a potent symbol and barometer of a society's modernity. The porousness of political boundaries during this period facilitated contact, intellectual exchange, and the sharing of many of these concepts among intellectuals and reformers from all over the Middle East. Amin's writings reached beyond the Arab world, influencing, for example, Iranian intellectuals such as Seyyid Hosein Taqizadeh, a Majles (Parliament) representative and newspaper editor who defended women's right to establish their own associations during the convening of the first Majles in 1907.[31] Although Amin's feminist credentials have been recently subjected to critical reevaluation and his feminism may not stand up to contemporary scrutiny, the influence he had upon his peers cannot be discounted.[32] Reformers began to promote women's education and openly challenge and criticize social and cultural practices oppressive to women. Turkish author Ahmad Mithat Efendi attacked forced marriage, concubinage, and polygamy as "social ills," writing about such subjects in his novels.[33] The Iraqi poet Jamil Zahawi, who appealed to the Ottoman government in Istanbul to open a school for girls in Iraq, was fired from his position as professor of law after writing a newspaper article criticizing veiling and fathers' control over their daughters' marriage decisions.[34]

These intellectuals and reformers were attempting to come to terms with socioeconomic, cultural, and political transformations in the region, including the encroachment of Western institutions and structures of domination, which were beginning to penetrate their societies. Shifts in power between rural and urban elites, increased commercialization of agriculture, the Middle East's accelerating integration into the world market, and the effects of Western industrialization on local economies all affected social practices and political responses. The development and gradually increasing dissemination of education helped to foment an intellectual and cultural critique that looked both internally and externally for solutions to perceived social, cultural, and political ills. Criticism took place within both an Islamist framework and a secular one. Many male reformers "found the plight of women a powerful vehicle for the expression of their own restiveness with social conventions they found particularly stultifying and archaic. 'Modern' men often felt alienated from . . . patriarchal structures which curtailed their own freedom considerably, even though women were the more obvious victims of the system."[35] Others have pointed out how the "woman question" in many respects became "part of an ideological terrain" upon which other concerns – most prominently "questions of cultural and national integrity" – were "articulated and debated."[36]

The status of women and issues of feminism, as Thomas Philipp points out, "touched perhaps more directly than any other aspect of the modernist movement upon the personal life of people. . . . One could proclaim oneself in favor of . . . nationalism, constitutional rule, or the validity of modern sciences without necessarily having to change one's private life very much. But new ideas about the role of woman in society had direct bearing on the private life of each individual."[37] Reformist, Western-oriented men were seeking to modernize *themselves*, albeit through focusing their attention on women. Educated, with experience abroad or in increased dealings with foreigners, they began to perceive their own societies within a broader, international context and reflexively turned their attention to women, targeting them as the backward, atavistic embodiments of all that was wrong with "tradition" and traditional culture and religion. "The main enemy of early reformers was 'backwardness,' rather than 'foreignness'";[38] "backward" women would retard society as a whole. As Amin put it: "The status of women is inseparably tied to the status of a nation. When the status of a nation is low, reflecting an uncivilized condition for that nation, the status of women is also low, and when the status of a nation is elevated, reflecting the progress and civilization of that nation, the status of women in that country is also elevated."[39] In some ways, this placing the burden of the nation's "civilization" upon women is a variant on the honor paradigm, which places another of society's burdens on women – that of male honor, defined by the preservation of *women's* sexual purity.

The primary focus of many of these concerns centered on improving middle-class women's effectiveness in their roles as wives and mothers, particularly as educators of children, the men of the future. Suddenly, women had to be "scientifically" trained and educated to learn how to be modern wives and mothers. A woman could not "run her household well unless she attain[ed] a certain amount of intellectual and cultural knowledge"; likewise, an "ignorant mother" could not "transform her child's personality to include good qualities" if she were unaware of such qualities.[40] As Kumari Jayawardena points out, increasingly, "the new bourgeois man . . . needed as his partner, the 'new woman' who was presentable in . . . society yet whose role was primarily in the home."[41]

Women fought back against some of the criticisms levied against their sex by men, supposedly in the name of elevating the nation. Bibi Khanum, an Iranian intellectual, responded to an essay entitled "The Chastisement of Women" with her own heated and satirical defense of her sex, entitled "The Vices of Men" (1896). "The creators of the misfortunes of society were men," she admonished. "The least they could do . . . was to stop going around advising women" and instead, seek "a remedy for their own corruption."[42]

Yet other women endorsed some of the ideas about "reforming" women. They started to articulate their own views on the subject, particularly through writing in the press. Beginning in the late nineteenth century, women began to contribute articles to general-interest mainstream periodicals, often anonymously.[43] But it was the evolution of a separate women's press, first in Egypt and Turkey and then in Iran and Syria, that marked a significant development.[44] For the first time, an explicitly female voice found its way into print, disseminated to an (admittedly limited) literate public. Egypt led the way, with the publication of the first women's periodical, *The Young Woman (al-Fatāh),* founded by Hind Nawfal in Alexandria in 1892. Turkey's earliest women's publication was *The Ladies Own Gazette (Hanimlara Mahsun Gazete)*, which began publishing in 1895. Appearing twice weekly, it circulated widely throughout the Ottoman Empire and even in Muslim areas of the Russian Empire. In Iran, where the women's press confronted particularly harsh hostility and many obstacles, a woman "oculist," Dr. Kahhal, began publication of the country's first women's magazine, *Knowledge (Danish)*, in 1910. Damascene Mary Ajami founded *The Bride (al-'Arūs)* in 1910; Lebanon's first women's journal was *Girl of Lebanon (Fatāt Lubnān)*, introduced by Salima Abu Rashid in 1914.[45]

These early efforts heralded in an impressive wave of publication "by, for, and about women" with local journals often reaching wider audiences throughout the region.[46] In numerous cases, women's periodicals were founded in association with women's organizations. The quality of writing, range of topics, longevity, and circulation figures varied. Some of the earlier periodicals were constrained in their goals and in what types of subjects they covered; Iranian women were instructed by *Majles*, the journal of the newly established Iranian parliament during the first constitutional crisis (1906–1908), to "keep out of politics and affairs of the government." The Iranian women's paper *Knowledge* published a cautious disclaimer on its masthead stating that it "would only publish issues pertaining to domestic questions and 'under no circumstances discuss politics and the issues of the nation.'"[47] Although most of the women's journals during the early years restricted their coverage to "women's topics" such as the home, domestic work, child raising, education, fashion, and the like, this was by no means the case everywhere. The women's press during the second constitutional period in Turkey (1908–1919) severely criticized men for disregarding their promises to emancipate women once they took power. One woman, Ismet Hakki, wrote an article entitled "The Need to Fight" in which she argued that "rights can only be obtained by fighting and . . . rights obtained through struggle [are] easier to safeguard."[48]

A distinct women's press did not evolve everywhere, being notably absent in those parts of the Middle East that did not have large cities with a minimal number of literate women readers. In Palestine, for example, a women's press never really developed.[49] But women's experience in writing and publishing, be it in their own women's publications or in the general-interest mainstream press, ultimately resulted in their increasing recognition and use of the powerful propagandistic possibilities of the press to articulate their concerns and interests, which over time became more overtly political.

The "new" women themselves took advantage of these fermenting debates. Despite the ambivalent and contradictory roots, motivations, and concepts of female emancipation articulated in reformist discourse, such discourse did provide openings that empowered women to be innovative in their time and place: to organize themselves in associations for a common goal or good, often oriented toward "uplifting" their fellow women. This activity usually took the form of charitable or social welfare organizations, which were established in some parts of the Middle East as early as the mid-nineteenth century. The first women's associations generally focused on improving the status of women through working in such areas as health; the care of poor women, infants, and orphans; vocational training; and literacy. The Sisters of Love in Lebanon, for example, established in 1847, ran a school, a tuberculosis sanatorium, and a home for wayward girls.[50] Palestine's first women's association, the Orthodox Aid Society for the Poor, founded in Acre in 1903, provided clothes and trousseau items for poor young girls to "prevent them from remaining unmarried."[51] Many of the earliest philanthropic projects were founded by individual women motivated by specific crises,[52] but over time women's associations formed explicitly for the purpose of fulfilling social welfare functions.

One of the initial impulses to organize arose from a sentiment of *noblesse oblige* on the part of the wealthy toward the less fortunate, which was based upon a "tradition of public service" among both women and men in Islamic societies[53] and, in the case of Christians, upon notions of Christian charity. Indeed, most of the first efforts were primarily religiously based and segregated by confession, with Muslim and Christian women setting up separate organizations. This soon changed, however, and, as Margot Badran points out, it was women who led the way in "extricat[ing] social service from the exclusive hold of religious (or religiously affiliated) institutions."[54] One of the first such secular philanthropic societies was the Mabarrat Muhammad 'Ali, a dispensary for poor women and children, founded in Egypt in 1909.[55] By the 1920s, many, if not most, of the women's organizations then active – both charitable and otherwise – had members and leadership of mixed religious affiliation, and no longer identified themselves primarily as religious associations.

The historical chronology of these various efforts differed from place to place; in Iran and Turkey, for example, women's establishment of their own organizations followed a different trajectory than that of the Arab countries. In the latter, beginning in the late nineteenth century, religiously based charitable societies were generally founded first, followed in the post-World War I period by more overtly social and political groups. The first women's organizations in Iran, with few exceptions, catapulted themselves immediately into national politics, becoming involved in the first constitutional crisis in 1906. In Turkey, it was in the context of a "new atmosphere of freedom" during the second constitutional period (1908–1919), led by the CUP revolution, that women's societies first formed. "No less than a dozen" women's organizations were founded during this period; the Balkan Wars (1912–1913) also acted as a catalyst for some endeavors. The Red Crescent Women's Center, for example, was founded in 1912, as was another women's "club" that organized a hospital and helped war refugees.[56] This first wave of organizing included both religiously oriented charities and more feminist-oriented women's associations. In 1914 the Society for the Defense of the Rights of Women was founded; listed among its aims were several seemingly conflicting goals, including "to fortify woman in the home"; "to render mothers capable of bringing up their children according to the principles of modern pedagogy"; "to initiate Turkish women into life in society"; and "to encourage women to earn their own living by their own work."[57]

Although women's charitable activities have been dismissed by some as "bourgeois" and politically irrelevant, nonetheless their inauguration marked something new and distinct. Middle- and upper-class women had been benefactors and even supervisors of Islamic trusts (*awqāf*) for centuries,[58] but actively setting up and running charitable organizations required women to employ particular skills and engage themselves in public. These organizations also proved to be eminently suitable training grounds for political organizing. As Beth Baron suggests, elite women perceived the social welfare arena as "fertile ground for building a power base and pushing toward the center of politics."[59] Upper-class women found themselves working for the first time in direct contact with the lower classes,[60] an experience that opened the eyes of many, although not to the extent of including poorer women as peers and leaders among their ranks – something that was ultimately to limit the groups' organizational power, growth, and overall effectiveness.

Women also discovered strength in collective work, and they experienced "self-discovery"; "working towards collective goals tapped wellsprings of creativity that had been quiescent."[61] They learned that they could wield authority and influence from within a group, reducing the isolation and powerlessness they might feel as individuals and creating "new networks and bonds among themselves."[62] They had to develop and use organizational skills, exercise control over resources, and manage their own organizations.

Many women were publicly involved at multiple levels, belonging to a number of different groups and building upon and gaining from these experiences. Although Huda Sha'rawi, as always, is renowned for her numerous involvements, many other, less well-known individuals, such as Palestinian Nahid al-Sajjadi, actively participated in a wide range of activities; starting in the 1920s, al-Sajjadi was a member of the Arab Women's Union, the Red Crescent Society, the Women's Solidarity Society, and (later, during the 1948 war) the Society of the Wounded Fighter.[63] One of the remarkable "pioneers" of Iranian feminism, Sedigheh Doulatabadi, was a founding member of the first women's group in that country, the Women's Freedom Society (1907); a member of the National Ladies' Society; a founder of the Isfahan Ladies Company; the creator of the newspaper *Women's Voice*; and a contributor to the journal *Patriotic Women*, among other things.[64]

The women who were involved in these early efforts were almost all educated and from middle- and upper-class backgrounds, as was the case in women's organizations in other parts of the world during this period. Their educations acted as a catalyst, encouraging them to seek change and giving them the confidence and ability to act.[65] They also had more leisure than the poorer urban and peasant women who constituted the majority of women in most Middle Eastern societies. Class played a major role in influencing their organizing styles, the issues they worked on, and their politics. Although eventually many women came to see themselves as part of a women's movement, their concept of "movement" did not necessarily incorporate the mass of women in their societies. Instead, they tended to treat lower-class women more as clients than as constituents.[66] They generally did not address the "root causes," nor did they develop an explicit "critical awareness" of their societies' "profound social inequities and economic distress."[67] In this, they mirrored many of the attitudes of the male reformers, liberal politicians, and nationalists who were their allies during this period.

On the other hand, women's very recognition of the need for the social welfare services their organizations provided constituted a kind of *tacit* political act and implicit criticism of the deficiencies of prevailing political and social institutions. By stepping in to fill perceived gaps, women were fulfilling functions that, over time, became recognized as the responsibility of the local authorities or governments and, when they eventually came into being, the nation-states. (Later, instead of trying to perform the duties of government themselves, women increasingly turned to demanding that the government fulfill its obligations to provide the services that the women's organizations had initially supported.) Through their involvement with charitable work, women began to interact with governmental and state institutions (where they existed), ultimately gaining political skills such as the ability to negotiate with male officials and work the corridors of power. In the process, some women became more analytic and politicized. However, their focus on the positive role of the nation-state in enacting "reform" and legislating change, which intensified particularly after World War I, was to limit their critical analysis and effectiveness.

Elite women organized not only for the benefit of their poorer sisters but, on another level, for their own personal and intellectual development, forming social clubs, intellectual societies, and literary salons. These efforts provided forums for women to gather and discuss intellectual, social, and political concerns and, in many cases, provided training grounds for public speaking. At some of these gatherings, women delivered formal lectures. Such groups naturally tended to form in the larger cities such as Beirut, Damascus, and Cairo, where the concentration of literate women was higher than in the smaller towns and rural areas. Some of the earliest efforts included a salon established by Mariana Marrash in Aleppo in the late nineteenth century; several Cairo intellectual societies, including the Women's Refinement Union (1914), the Ladies Literary Improvement Society (1914), and the Society for the Women's Awakening (1916); and Nazik 'Abid's Women's Literary Club, founded in Damascus in 1920.[68] In societies where public education was extremely limited, these groups played an educational role for the women – many individually tutored or instructed – who attended them.

Perhaps the most significant contribution, and a major priority, of many of the first women's organizations was the establishment of girls' schools. We have seen how the issues of national progress and women's emancipation were directly linked to education in reformist and intellectual discourses during the late nineteenth and early twentieth centuries. This link was one of the major vehicles for the development of a national consciousness among women. The idea of "lifting" the nation by "lifting" women pervaded the earliest stages of women's "discreet public activism"[69] in the first decade of the twentieth century, and it was in the arena of education where many of the women's groups focused their energies toward this end.[70]

The founder of one of Palestine's first women's associations, the Jaffa Orthodox Ladies Society, explicitly linked education, charity, and the nation in her description of how she and a group of [Christian] Orthodox women "decided to found a national women's association to bring up and educate orphan girls and those in need." She made a point of stating in her memoir that this was "the first *national* women's association founded in Palestine" (in 1910). The society set up a girls' section of the previously all-male National Orthodox School.[71] When the Russian government, during the second constitutional crisis in Iran in 1911, asked Iranian women to compare their status to that of European women, their response was that European women's status was "preferable because they possess skills, but not for any other reasons." The Iranian women directly related their comparative lack of skills to the lack of education for women in Iran.[72]

Government-sponsored public education did not become widely available for girls and women until after World War II in most of the Middle East. In the countries that had been part of the Ottoman Empire, after World War I, European Mandatory governments narrowly expanded female education beyond the Ottoman government's tentative beginnings, which had been initiated on a limited basis in some of the Arab provinces in the late nineteenth century; in Iraq, for example, the first girls' school was established in 1899.[73] In Turkey itself, the first government girls' schools were established in the 1850s as part of the Tanzimat (reforms) of the nineteenth century; a secondary school for girls was founded in 1858, and a vocational school in 1869.[74] In Iran, state-sponsored female education was established for the first time in 1918.[75] Egypt's first public educational establishment for females was the School for Midwives, instituted in 1832 during Muhammed 'Ali's reign; several girls' schools were subsequently founded in the late 1880s and 1890s.[76]

Because government-sponsored schools for girls were extremely limited in number and accessibility, missionary and private schools tended to outnumber public schools in the period under study. Women themselves became early and enthusiastic participants in founding, administering, funding, and teaching in the first schools for girls. The Egyptian Nabawiyya Musa, who experienced many struggles in her career as a teacher and administrator, devoted most of her energy and, indeed, almost her entire life to women's education, founding several schools herself.[77] Many of the first women's organizations focused their efforts on this one particular issue.

One stimulus to women's associations founding of educational establishments was the desire for schools that were independent, and not directly under the control of foreign and missionary institutions. In Lebanon, for example, where women's associations took the lead in establishing schools as early as 1847, two women's societies built and supported "national girls' schools as an alternative to missionary schools."[78] The issue of "national" schools came to the forefront as early as the 1880s in Lebanon, probably because of that country's long history of missionary and foreign involvement in education. Criticism of these schools' deculturizing effects intensified during the Mandate periods in Palestine and Syria/Lebanon,[79] with the result that the establishment of independent schools became imbued with nationalist significance.

Syrian and Lebanese women's groups were prominent in founding many schools, some of whose graduates became renowned in the women's movement in the early twentieth century.[80] Palestinian women, as noted above, established girls' schools in 1910, starting a trend that continued throughout the almost thirty-year duration of the British Mandate; some of the schools opened by women's associations in the 1920s operate to this day. In Iran, although it was individual women who took the initiative in founding girls' schools during the first constitutional period, "the new schools were in close organizational relationship with the women's anjumans (councils)." By 1913, there were sixty-three private girls' schools with a combined enrollment of 2,500 in Iran.[81] Women's associations in Egypt, interestingly, do not seem to have followed this trend; school founders tended to be individuals, such as Nabawiyya Musa. Beginning in the 1920s, women's associations started to focus their efforts on demanding that the state take on the responsibility for educating girls; this became a contentious issue between the associations and the European colonial governments, highlighting even more emphatically the articulation between education, women, and the nation.

Stage Two: Women and nationalism

The history of women's role in national struggles in the Middle East has increasingly begun to attract scholarly interest. Until the late 1990s, women's participation was selectively remembered and celebrated in tales of individual heroism and self-sacrifice, or in scattered references to isolated incidents in which women participated. What has not been methodically studied or recorded is the history of women's organized, sustained efforts on behalf of nationalism. The different women's movements in the Middle East experienced instructive contrasts and parallels in their activities, discourses, strategies, and politics. Nearly all of these movements struggled within the context of a male-defined nationalist agenda, which resulted in their developing complex and ambivalent relationships with the mainstream nationalist movements. As an anonymous Iranian woman, writing in the press in 1907, pointed out, accusingly, to the male leaders of the nationalist movement: "You who talk about the rights of the nation, who talk about law, who speak of honor and zeal – we are also part of this nation, we ask for our share in these rights, too."[82]

Nationalism was not an abstract issue for women; they were directly affected by the changes brought about by nationalist regimes that came to power – such as in Turkey – as well as by the changes taking place in states that experienced direct or indirect forms of colonial rule, which endured in one form or another in the Middle East throughout the 1930s. After the turn of the twentieth century, nationalism became a predominant political trend in the Middle East, as peoples under imperialist forms of control increasingly began to turn the liberalist ideologies of the imperialists against them in order to question the legitimacy of foreign rule. Also, importantly, nationalism constituted a potential unifying force in a world where mass mobilization was becoming a key component of modern political ideologies. In the Mashriq, Arab nationalists began to organize secretly for independence within the framework of the Ottoman Empire; the seeds of Turkish nationalism were sown in the Anatolian heartland during the second constitutional period, which followed the 1908 CUP revolution. The British occupation of Egypt after the 1882 'Urabi revolt contributed to the evolution of Egyptian nationalist sentiment. In Iran, Russia's and Britain's virtual dictatorship over the country's economy and politics, in addition to Russia's military occupation during the second constitutional crisis in 1909–1911, provoked a strong, organized nationalist response.

World War I was a watershed in transforming simmering nationalist sentiment into full-fledged nationalist movements in the Middle East. Postwar settlements, which reinforced European domination in the former territories of the dismembered Ottoman Empire, directly contributed to the development of nationalist movements in the Arab former provinces that were relegated to European Mandatory rule: Palestine, Iraq, Syria, and Lebanon. In the truncated remains of the former empire, Turkish nationalists waged a full-scale war of national liberation against European-imposed restrictions, resulting in the establishment of a new and independent Turkish republic under Mustafa Kemal Atatürk in 1923. Egypt remained under British rule, but not acquiescently; in 1919, the Wafdist revolution flared up, forcing Britain to make nominal concessions to Egyptian national sovereignty.

Women, along with men, became ardent nationalists and actively participated in all of these national movements, albeit in different ways than men. Their reasons for doing so varied. In some cases, women saw nationalism as a survival issue. This was obviously the case in Palestine, where the Arab population confronted a colonialist movement, Zionism, whose express purpose was to make the country its own, reducing the majority indigenous

181

population to minority, second-class status. In other situations, women linked economic survival to the national struggle. This happened during the constitutional crisis in Iran, during which women were prompted to organize against government borrowing from, and subsequent economic dependence upon, foreign powers; women were very active in street protests against food shortages and hoarding, which occurred as a result of these policies.

In many instances, women perceived nationalism as an opportunity. It was indeed the "honorable door" through which women could enter in order to participate at new levels of public life. Nationalism became a legitimizing discourse for women, initially as a means to "justify stepping out of their narrowly prescribed role in the name of patriotism and self-sacrifice for the nation" and, ultimately, as a way to "earn" emancipation.[83] Yet nationalist women were careful to incorporate their feminist demands within the safe confines of nationalist ideology, since this was the only ideology permissible to them. "While it was possible for nationalists to be nonfeminists, it was not tolerated or possible for feminists to be nonnationalists."[84] Although nationalism did facilitate women's integration into society, it also "reaffirm[ed] the boundaries of culturally accepted feminine conduct and exert[ed] pressure on women to articulate their gender interests within the terms of reference set by nationalist discourse." Thus, feminism was effectively relegated a "maidservant to nationalism" through explicit or implicit acceptance of the strategy "national liberation now, and women's liberation later."[85] For Palestinian women, this "two-stage" theory became a kind of tacit pact between themselves and the mainstream nationalist movement. One sees vestiges of this approach in the cautious pronouncement of Zlikha Shihabi, president of the Palestinian Arab Women's Union, who, speaking to reporters after the 1944 Arab Women's Conference in Cairo, stated that Palestinian women would not demand more rights than those granted by Islamic law; that "demanding women's rights was before its time."[86]

Although nationalist women generally took care not to promote feminist demands at the "expense" of nationalist ones, there were public discussions of women's political equality – particularly in the press – and a few efforts to raise the issue of women's suffrage. In Iran, one brave delegate proposed that women be granted the right to vote during the second Majles (in 1911), but the proposal was rejected on the basis that (in the words of the clerical leader and deputy, Mudarris) "God has not endowed them with the ability to be electors. . . . Moreover, in our religion, Islam, they are under supervision: 'Men are in charge of women.' . . . They are in our charge. They will have absolutely no right to elect."[87] During the 1920s and 1930s, while Syria and Lebanon were under French Mandate, women attempted to claim their suffrage rights, which were debated in their respective parliaments, but without success.[88] (It should be noted that women in France had not yet obtained the vote either during this period.) The only Middle Eastern women to gain suffrage before 1940 were Turkish women, a development discussed below.

Feminism, or demands for female emancipation, were considered potentially divisive topics in struggles where concepts of the nation being fought for tended to be articulated in communal terms, in order to unify people and elide sources of potential difference.[89] "National feminists" developed a brand of feminism that did not challenge patriarchal social, cultural, and political norms so much as complement them by presenting women as working "alongside men" to "save the nation" and protect it from external threats. Women's ostensibly essential and innate qualities – such as motherhood and self-sacrifice – were channeled to the national cause, recasting women's traditionally gendered roles as new "'national' actors: mothers, educators, workers and even fighters."[90]

Despite the inherent limitations of nationalist discourse, women's actual experiences did have a "releasing effect." One cannot discount the excitement and the positive sense of empowerment, unity, and purpose that involvement in political movements engenders in individual participants. Women's participation in nationalist movements demonstrated their commitment, courage, strength, and ability, serving as a major source of personal and collective development. Their potential for providing a base of support and source of legitimacy to newly emerging national regimes was to influence the state-building projects that followed independence.

Women's involvement took various forms; by and large, they were mobilized by, or cooperated with, the mainstream (i.e., male-led) nationalist movements in mass activities, but they rarely participated within the actual male-led organizations themselves. The case of Turkey provides the exception. During the national liberation struggle after World War I, a handful of individual women, such as Nakiye Elgün and Halide Edib, were prominently involved within the mainstream nationalist movement. In most instances, however, women formed separate associations and engaged in their own segregated activities, occasionally coordinating with the male-led groups. In Egypt, for example, women formed their own branch of the Wafd Party, the Wafdist Women's Central Committee. In Iran, women founded numerous "patriotic" organizations, beginning with the Patriotic Women's League in 1906. Palestine's major women's organization, the Arab Women's Association (later renamed the Arab Women's Union), organized and led most of the women's nationalist campaigns during the 1930s and 1940s, establishing branches in the major towns and cities.

The leaders of these organizations, as was the case with the women's charitable and social welfare associations, tended to be from the educated, urban, upper and middle classes. They were frequently related to male nationalists or politicians, but this did not necessarily translate into their playing a role as "auxiliaries" to, or rubber stamps for, the male-led nationalist movements. In Palestine, for example, political differences often erupted between husbands and wives who were both active in the nationalist and women's movements. The Wafdist Women's Central Committee, an ardent supporter of the nationalist Wafd Party during the struggles against the British, eventually split from the Wafdist government when it came to power in Egypt over serious disagreements on both nationalist and feminist issues.[91]

One of the earliest, most visible, and most dramatic manifestations of women's nationalist activity was the large-scale demonstration, in which women, either alongside men or on their own, confronted colonial governments or their proxies. These were significant events in societies where urban women's public visibility and mobility were restricted. Sometimes women were killed or wounded in these demonstrations. During the first constitutional crisis in Iran in 1906, women demonstrated against the shah, stoning troops from rooftops, marching in huge crowds, and participating in a three-week-long occupation of the British legation. In one street protest, a woman shot and killed an anticonstitutionalist speaker, and was herself immediately killed by a mob.[92] In Syria, women organized their own nationalist demonstration during the visit of the King-Crane commission to Damascus in 1919.[93] Egyptian women were key participants in the turbulent upheavals that ensued after the British refused to allow Egyptian representation at the post-World War I Paris peace conference in 1919. Palestinian women, who had sporadically taken part in anti-Zionist disturbances in the 1920s, regularly joined men in major demonstrations in Nablus, Jaffa, and Jerusalem in the early 1930s. They also frequently held large, autonomous women's demonstrations, particularly during the 1936–1939 strike and revolt. Women's militancy often exceeded men's. In one incident, Palestinian women were demonstrating and getting arrested for curfew violations while the male leadership was praying at the mosque.[94]

Nationalists, both men and women, manipulated gender for political purposes during mass protests. Men in Iran encouraged their wives to attack foreign consulates and installations, since women were unrecognizable due to their being covered by veils.[95] Separate women's demonstrations drew extraordinary publicity for their novelty, making them effective as propaganda tools. The Arabic press in Palestine, for example, faithfully and closely covered women's demonstrations throughout the region, particularly in Syria, Egypt, Turkey, and Iraq. Palestinian women were aware of this propagandistic potential, using mnemonic devices in their statements to the press and manipulating "traditional" concepts of gender in order to draw attention to their demonstrations.[96]

A common pattern that emerged in this manipulation of gender norms was the manner in which nationalists employed women's presence in mixed-sex demonstrations to achieve a variety of tactical objectives. Women defused violent reactions from the police or troops deployed to put down demonstrations by force. The British in Palestine complained that the tactic of surrounding marching women with men created a buffer between the police and the "mob" during demonstrations in 1933. In Iran, the same objective was achieved in the opposite way; it was women who formed barricades around the men to protect them during the 1906 demonstrations. During the 1922 nationalist demonstrations in Syria, women marched at the head of the crowd, ululating "at an unbearably high pitch, bringing the thousands of men behind them to an explosive roar" and causing the French to balk at using force.[97]

The women's movements played a particularly active role in the economic sector, which soon became an arena for nationalist struggles. Many of the nationalist leaders targeted unfair competition or advantages enjoyed by foreign goods in indigenous economies, issues that directly affected women in their everyday lives. As consumers, women played a pivotal role in supporting and upholding economic strikes and boycotting foreign goods. The women's organizations promoted "national" industries by sponsoring workshops that produced indigenous products and by contributing to national banks and funds. During the constitutional crisis in Iran, women donated funds and jewelry and offered to buy shares in the National Bank in order to alleviate dependence upon foreign loans; similarly, women contributed generously to the National Fund in Palestine during the 1930s. The women's movements saw such activities as within their particular purview, and they organized sustained campaigns focused on bolstering their national economies. They aggressively took the lead, acting as enforcers of boycotts through intimidation or outright coercion. During the 1891 tobacco boycott against British monopolies in Iran, women attacked shops that remained open during a national protest. A group of Palestinian women in Haifa was arrested by the British for smashing the shop windows of a strike-breaking merchant during Palestine's 1936 general strike.[98]

Upper- and middle-class women also played a seminal role in generating external support for nationalist causes, effectively utilizing new forms of communication to reach the wider world. They relied extensively on the press and on telegrams, drawing upon their contacts with other women's movements and even foreign governments to solicit international and regional sympathy and solidarity. Women in Iran sent telegrams of protest to foreign governments during the second constitutional crisis when the Russians delivered an ultimatum forcing the Majles to fire its American adviser or face occupation by force.[99] A veritable barrage of telegrams flew back and forth on the issue of Palestine in the 1930s. The Arab Women's Association exchanged telegrams with the Islamic Union of India; with women's associations in Iran, India, Britain, and the Arab world; and with the governments of Iraq, Egypt, Transjordan, Saudi Arabia, Britain, and Kuwait. They frequently highlighted their protests by publishing their telegrams to the British government in the press.[100]

Beginning in the early 1930s, Arab women began to develop a form of pan-Arab nationalism that extended their efforts beyond their own local national causes, directly supporting each other's nationalist struggles through fund-raising, demonstrating, and writing protest telegrams on each other's behalf. (One of the more interesting examples of the latter is a telegram that Syrian women wrote to the Daughters of the American Revolution on behalf of the Palestinian women's cause!) During 1931 demonstrations in Nablus, the Egyptian Sa'adist Ladies Committee (the successor of the disbanded Wafdist Women's Central Committee) sent greetings to the women of Nablus, congratulating them for their "sacrifice" in the face of oppression. Palestinian women sent telegrams of congratulations to the Syrian "women strugglers" *(mujāhidāt)* when they demonstrated in 1933 against the proposed treaty between France and Syria over the terms of Syria's entry into the League of Nations.[101]

The national struggle in Palestine was the focus of a kind of pan-Arab feminism that also included Muslim women of the "East" and that had the effect of uniting women in the region across national and even religious boundaries, specifically with regard to Christian Arab women. One of the major manifestations of this trend was the convening of the "Eastern" (or "Oriental") Women's Conference in Cairo in 1938, during the height of the 1936–1939 Palestine revolt.[102] At this conference, Arab women established a central, coordinating committee under the leadership of Huda Sha'rawi, formalizing their regional relationships. One of their principal aims was to aggressively combat negative portrayals of the conflict in the international press; they called for the establishment of their own propaganda and information bureau.[103] Separate Women's Committees to Defend Palestine were established in the Arab countries; the Syrian chapter was particularly active, sending money and organizing demonstrations in response to events in Palestine.[104]

Another domain in which women participated was armed conflict, often spontaneously, individually, and secretly, but also within their own organizational frameworks. They concealed and smuggled weapons; spied and conveyed intelligence on troop movements; hid men in their homes; provided medical and food aid to combatants; and, occasionally, took up arms alongside men. The women who directly fought tended to be peasant women; this was the case in Turkey during the war of liberation, in Syria during the 1925 rebellion against the French, and in Palestine during the 1936–1939 revolt. Battles often took place in the countryside, where women were more directly threatened by and involved in the violence. The upper- and middle-class women who worked in organizational structures supported the rebellions through covert support activity such as fund-raising, nursing, and arms smuggling. In some instances, special military units for women were formed, usually noncombatant. Nazik 'Abid, who had been granted the honorary military rank of captain by King Faisal, participated in the resistance against the French occupation of Syria in the battle of Maysalun in 1920, wearing a military uniform and heading a woman's medical unit called the Red Star. During the 1948 war in Palestine, women in the Jaffa area formed a secret nursing troop called the Camomile Flowers *(zahrat al-uqhuwān)*, which also provided the fighters with arms.[105] Women paid a high price for their involvement in armed conflict, no matter what form it took. Palestinian women who smuggled arms and ammunition to the rebels during the 1936–1939 revolt were arrested and sentenced to long prison terms. Women were killed in battles in Iran during the civil war that followed the first constitutional crisis, and in Palestine during the revolt. For the most part, however, women's direct participation in armed conflict was relatively limited.

Although women took part in nationalist struggles as individual members of a national collective, it is important to recognize the autonomous organizational structures within which women also participated. The women's movements that emerged during nationalist eras gained valuable organizing experience, enabling them to consolidate their strength and extend their agendas. In many instances, the fact that these groups were *not* integrated into the mainstream nationalist organizations – particularly the leadership – was a source of vitality and autonomy for their own movements. It is striking that the proliferation of new and independent women's organizations occurred principally during periods when nationalist feelings were at their peak. Some of these groups became politically sophisticated and enduring (unless dissolved by the nationalist regimes that subsequently came to power, as discussed below). During the chaotic interregnum between the second constitutional crisis and the consolidation of Reza Khan's regime (1911–1921) in Iran, for example, the women's movement became more independent, structured, and organized; a veritable efflorescence of organizations and women's periodicals took place, among them left-wing, socialist groups.[106] In Palestine, the turbulent 1920s and 1930s saw the establishment of numerous locally active women's associations affiliated with the larger Arab Women's Association. Most of the new women's groups incorporated their more "traditional" social welfare work within a nationalist framework. Thus, for example, groups that focused on promoting women's employment could cast such employment as a patriotic duty, as was the case in Turkey, where women's organizations attempted to facilitate women's entry into the workplace in order to contribute to the war economy during World War I and the war of liberation.

"Women's work" – whether supporting the nationalist struggle or engaging in social welfare activities oriented toward "uplifting the nation" – has too often been considered auxiliary, conservative, and nonpolitical. Rethinking both feminism and nationalism requires eschewing gendered notions of politics and resistance. In the nationalist context, gendered notions of what was considered meaningful in the way of "active" or "passive" resistance have contributed to obscuring the nature of women's participation. The kind of work women engaged in was crucial to the nationalist struggles; for one thing, the fact that women were involved at all contributed to legitimizing nationalism as a communal, collective, unifying ideology. For another, no movement can endure without the sustenance of daily, mundane "support" activities. The provision of necessities such as food, medicine, and funds; and, on another level, the dissemination and use of information for intelligence and propaganda purposes, are not secondary. History's gendered focus on the "main" struggle – armed battles and rebellions, confrontations between nationalist leaders and colonial powers, diplomatic and political maneuverings – obscures the urgent necessity of the work that takes place in what is perceived as the margins. It is perhaps only because the "marginal" work is performed by women that it is considered the footnote to the nationalist narrative rather than constituting the "real" work in and of itself. A history that expands the central narrative to incorporate the margins and that recasts these limited concepts would allow us to more fully recognize the complete contours of the nationalist narrative in all its richness and complexity.

This complexity would include the mixed legacy that nationalism has left to women. Nationalism was, in many cases, the midwife for feminism in the Middle East, although, as Beth Baron wryly notes, "women have served nationalism, but nationalism, in some respects, has failed women."[107] Deniz Kandiyoti notes the "persistent tensions" between different trends within nationalism: a "modernist" trend, which favored an emancipatory role for women, extending the promise of "rights" and equality, and an "organicist" trend, which concerned itself with "the dilution and contamination of cultural values and identity in a post-colonial context."[108] The problem for nationalist women was that they attempted to harness conservative forms of nationalism – performing their nationalist activities within the culturally prescribed confines of the "organicist" trend – to serve the modernist brand of nationalism. Women were unable to resolve these tensions and ended up, in effect, serving two masters at once.

Women participated enthusiastically in nationalist movements, believing that the culmination of national goals – the achievement of the sovereign nation-state – would inextricably lead to their emancipation as citizens within this newly constituted political entity. A Palestinian activist gives a telling explanation for why the women's movement in Palestine was not as involved in pushing for reforms enhancing women's status as movements in Egypt and Turkey: "Such measures of reform [as women's rights] can only be introduced by National Government, or by persons deriving their authority from the people."[109] Thus, Palestinian women, along with their sisters in the region, explicitly linked their future achievement of rights to a national government that they, perhaps naively, equated with "the people." This concept of "rights" was embedded within and inextricably interwoven with a legalistic notion of citizenship that could only be conferred by a national government; it did not address internal structures and sources of inequities in society. What national feminists did not take into account was the fact that, historically, the mere establishment of a sovereign state did not automatically bestow "rights" on women, that disenfranchised groups had to fight for these rights. Egyptian women learned this almost immediately after the establishment of the Wafd government in 1924, when their efforts on its behalf did not translate into enfranchisement or representation within the new government. "No nationalism in the world has granted women and men the same privileged access to the resources of the nation-state."[110] The faith of women's movements in the benevolence of the nation-state as a "possible resource for more progressive gender politics" was to prove misplaced, as those women who experienced national sovereignty were to discover.[111]

Stage Three: State feminism

Turkey and Iran, unlike the Mashriq and Egypt, became sovereign states after World War I. After Turkey's war of independence resulted in the establishment of a republic, Atatürk effected dramatic transformations in all domains of Turkish society: political, cultural, religious, economic, and social. One of the first of numerous laws enacted by the new republic was the abolition of the Islamic caliphate. In 1926 the family code was secularized, revised, and modified, using the Swiss civil code as its model. Women were enfranchised, after repeated demands from feminist groups, through a gradual process beginning at the municipal level in 1930 and ultimately resulting in equal enfranchisement with men on the national level in 1935. Polygamy was outlawed, Islamic dress and veiling were actively discouraged by the state, and women were encouraged to enter the workforce and public life.

The woman question, it has been suggested, was a "pawn" in Atatürk's struggle to establish a "republican notion of citizenship" through the modernization, secularization, and westernization of Turkish society.[112] Although Atatürk made the issue of women central to these efforts, his goal was not to transform and equalize gender relations so much as to make a complete break with the Ottoman past in order to "catapult Turkey to the 'level of contemporary civilizations' (i.e., Western economies and societies)."[113] Despite the fact that women gained important rights in the changes in family law enacted in the 1926 civil code – such as the rights to initiate divorce and inherit equally with men – they are not equal under the law. Wives remain under patriarchal control in marriage, since only men can have legal status as the head of the household. A married woman must request permission from her husband to work outside the home; she must take her husband's name and follow her husband to a new domicile, since only the husband has the right to determine where the couple lives.[114]

In Iran, a military officer, Reza Khan, took control of the government in a military coup in 1921; events here followed a different yet, in some respects, parallel trajectory. Reza Khan was an admirer of Mustafa Kemal and watched his state-building venture closely.[115] Both politicians embraced the notion of establishing strong, centralized states with authority concentrated at the top; in Turkey, it was the ruling People's Party, controlled by Atatürk, that monopolized power. In Iran, Reza Khan directly consolidated power as the autocratic head of state. In 1925 he became shah, establishing the Pahlavi dynasty; he quickly moved to repress any left-wing political currents. The Bolshevik revolution in neighboring Russia in 1917, the proletarianization of urban society, and the rise of a labor movement had all contributed to creating a "radical political atmosphere ... which resulted in an upsurge of feminism, socialism and communism."[116] Reza Shah banned political parties in 1931, stripped the Parliament of power, censored the press, and exiled, imprisoned, or executed leaders of the liberal opposition and leftist parties. The women's movement was not exempt. The offices of the Patriotic Women's League were destroyed by a mob while the police looked on; the leaders of a pro-communist women's organization, the Messenger of Women's Prosperity, were imprisoned and the organization banned.[117]

In both Turkey and Iran, during the process of consolidating the centralized state, the regimes reined in and controlled the women's movements. In Turkey, the new republican state both "circumscribed and defined [the] parameters" of the feminist movement, stifling and discouraging its independence, as the case of the Women's People Party demonstrates. Formed in 1923, this party aimed to modify "'the consciousness, the negligence, the grave situation' that had made womanhood the lowest class of society in all previous periods."[118] Its first major project, an educational congress, was quickly co-opted by the Ministry of Education, which instead held its own conference on the same topic, forcing the party to cancel its effort. Not long after the party's establishment, the government refused permission for it to incorporate on the grounds that women were not yet enfranchised, suggesting that it instead reconstitute itself as an association. The subsequent Turkish Women's League worked on social welfare and suffrage issues. In 1935, two weeks after Istanbul hosted the Twelfth Congress of the International Alliance of Women [known until 1926 as the International Woman Suffrage Alliance], the government ordered the league to disband. The president of the organization rationalized its closure and the dispersal of its assets by stating that, since its goals (enfranchisement and "complete equality") had been fulfilled, it had served its purpose, and "there was no further justification for its continued existence."[119]

In Iran, the state had a similar program for modernization, secularization, and westernization, but, unlike in Turkey, where part of the state-building project entailed the development of representative institutions that held out the promise of democracy, power in Tehran was firmly controlled by the executive. Reza Shah moved more coercively to force social and economic change, and to control the women's movement. After closing down and banning the independent women's organizations, the shah established a state-sponsored women's association, the Ladies Center, in 1935, under the honorary presidency of one of his daughters. The center's goals were to prop up and reinforce domestic gender roles by educating women in child rearing and housekeeping on a "scientific basis." It held lectures on subjects such as unveiling, women's chastity and virtue, and health issues. One of the main objectives of the founding of the association was to lay the groundwork for women's unveiling, which became compulsory by decree in 1936.[120]

Although the independent women's movement in Iran was virtually obliterated, some of its leaders participated in the Ladies Center. Parvin Paidar's explanation for their co-optation (my word) is that the state-supported association provided them with both financial and personal security (they no longer had to deal with "fanatics"), and legitimacy. Afsaneh Najmabadi warns against considering these women (or Turkish women, for that matter) as "pawns in men's games," however; "these women had their own agendas as well."[121] Many of the shah's policies, such as integrating women into society through increased education and employment, were popular among certain limited segments of the population. His repressive measures against the opposition were also effective in limiting resistance.[122]

The 1931 Iranian civil code, however, left women's legal inequality virtually intact in almost every sphere. Women were not enfranchised, and the one hundred articles that were devoted to the family corresponded almost exactly to previous Islamic law as it had generally been practiced in Iran. Divorce remained the sole prerogative of men, women inherited unequally to men, and polygamy remained legal. Indeed, under the article on *sigheh* marriage, a Shi'i practice, men had the right to marry an unlimited number of women for periods of as short as one hour. "The project followed by Reza Shah . . . was to bring modernity to Iran through the establishment of Iranian 'culture' rather than Islam. Within this project, the familial position of women as advocated in the Iranian 'culture' and 'Islam' happened to be more or less the same."[123]

Women were at the heart of the building of the "modern" nation-state in both Turkey and Iran, particularly during the late 1920s and 1930s. Women's participation in nationalist movements had earned them the prerogative to articulate demands for the rights due them as citizens and members of a national collectivity. But one of the major problems in translating their participation into the achievement of rights was that "women's rights" were not conceived of as "part of the problematic of civil liberties and individual rights," but rather were "formulated within the framework of policies that aim[ed] to serve the 'social good.'"[124] Women themselves rejected notions of "individualistic interpretations of feminism,"[125] stressing the socially redeeming potential of their liberation in order to enable them to "serve the nation." Furthermore, "since the new social order was not based on the individual, defined as male, women seemed part of the collectivity rather than needing to enter it through the principle of individual rights."[126]

In Turkey, scholars postulate that the state's granting women rights without their having to fight for them during the state-building era weakened the women's movement, making it acquiescent and passive.[127] "Feminism" became synonymous with "Kemalism," resulting in dependence upon the state and the development of a "pattern of special interaction between the state and women."[128] The state made decisions from above and discouraged grassroots participation in the decision-making process. Women "internalized the patriarchal system to the extent that going beyond its laws was unthinkable." This is cogently summed up by Nakiye Elgün, who said in 1927, when women's enfranchisement was being discussed in the press: "Why don't we nominate women candidates? Because the law does not permit it. Therefore it is not our time yet. Our government has granted us every right our women deserve, in fact more than deserved."[129]

In both Turkey and Iran, the symbolic value of women's emancipation was more important than the substance, since suffrage and/or women's increased social participation and public visibility bolstered the external image of these states as "modern" nations.[130] Both Turkey's and Iran's membership in the "international society of states" was "fragile," and "full acceptance by the other members as a true equal . . . rated very high on the agenda of nationalists."[131] Thus, seemingly trivial issues such as women's dress, for example, became highly charged and imbued with meaning. Women in the "modern" nation-states of Iran and Turkey had to "look like the civilized women of the world," namely European women, in order for these states to be accepted in this international society of states.[132]

Mervat Hatem makes the point that state feminism was a mixed blessing in that although women benefited from the "state's support of women's rights . . . [the state] transformed gender into a political instrument" used to satisfy state interests, thus undermining women's autonomy.[133] Although independent states were not established in the rest of the Middle East until the 1940s, some form of state feminism would appear in the Arab nationalist regimes that arose in the 1950s and 1960s. Nilüfer Çağatay and Yasemin Nuhoğlu-Soysal observe that women's movements could not develop autonomously because the ideologically heterogeneous nationalist regimes in the Middle East shared at least one "common trait"; a "need to monopolize political power in their effort to mobilize the masses" and to suppress all "autonomous movements once a movement [had] acquired state power."[134]

State feminism undermined women's ability to develop a broad-based feminism that incorporated the interests of women from the lower classes, and particularly women in the rural areas, where the social engineering of the state did not take root. Sirin Tekeli notes that the few women who benefited from "rights" – educated, professional elites – "experienced the excitement of being pioneers . . . so passionately that they could not realize that their own position did not reflect the real conditions of most Turkish women. And so they were led into a tragic 'schizophrenic' illusion: the new identity of these women was not one that they had selected themselves, but an ascribed one. And the ascriber was the state."[135] When the state decreed or forced supposedly emancipatory social change on the population, feminism was discredited because of its association with autocratic, westernizing regimes. And feminism was perceived as a culturally "unauthentic," imported, alienating Western ideology with little relevance to the women of the Middle East. Such associations severely limited feminist agendas and diluted their influence on, and effects in the lives of, the majority of women, making their task more difficult.

Conclusion

Although much of the focus above has been on highlighting the unity and analogousness of women's movements in the Middle East, it is important to recognize their heterogeneity and individual characters. Obviously, the specific historical contexts within which each movement operated are crucial. The Palestinian women's movement, for example, has the dubious distinction among those studied here of still being engaged in the struggle for national sovereignty (at the time of this writing in the 1990s and still in 2010). This fact, and the intractability of the Palestinian struggle, has left the troublesome relationship between feminism and nationalism intact and, often, not closely challenged, leaving a distinctive imprint on the Palestinian women's movement.[136]

Other factors that affected the individual character of each of these women's movements were the complex and variegated male responses to women's pushing the boundaries of prescribed female behavior. Paradoxically, the Iranian women's movement was among the most radical and militant at its inception during the constitutional crisis, yet Iranian women lived under some of the most oppressive restrictions in the region at the time, and male responses to their mobilization were often quite severe.[137] Nonetheless, Iranian women did not hesitate to become involved in violent confrontations. In other countries, such as Turkey and Palestine, men sometimes encouraged and even chastised women to get involved in politics.[138] Women often calibrated their organizing styles in response to men's reactions. But it is safe to generalize that male responses tended to be at least ambiguous and, in some circumstances, strongly opposed to women's increased public participation in political movements. As long as women remained segregated within women's organizations and focused their endeavors on social welfare and support activities oriented toward uplifting the nation, men gave cautious nods of approval to their involvement.

The organizing styles of the movements differed; in Iran, strong, autonomous regional women's associations developed in places like Tabriz and Isfahan as well as in Tehran, whereas in Egypt, the movement was more centralized, limited primarily to a few urban areas, Cairo in particular. This was also the case in Turkey and the Mashriq, where, although local women's organizations formed in the smaller towns and cities, a central association usually dominated the national matrix. This sometimes created a certain amount of tension within the individual movements.[139] The issue of unity within the national frameworks of the movements has not been closely examined in the Arab contexts;[140] in Turkey and Iran, on the other hand, writers have pointed to how competition and divisiveness within the women's movements led to a lack of centralization, coordination, and planning, ultimately weakening them.[141]

Despite the individual characters of the movements, however, one is struck by the common, identifiable patterns in their issues, organizing tactics, and ideological expressions, as well as their strong sense of cultural and regional identity and shared concerns. Women articulated this unity when they wrote for publications or assembled at women's conferences, as illustrated by the following statement delivered at the 1944 Cairo Arab Women's Conference by a Christian Arab woman, who began her speech by saying: "I'm the daughter of one nation, one language, one upbringing, one set of customs, one system of mores and one set of goals."[142]

This unity was not limited to Arab women. The first two Eastern Women's Conferences, held in Damascus and Baghdad in 1932, were attended by women from Iran and Afghanistan. The third Eastern Women's Conference, held in Tehran, reaffirmed support for the resolutions drawn up at the earlier meetings (mostly proposals for reforms in women's legal status), and added its own: (limited) female enfranchisement, the retention of "sound morals" by Eastern women, the avoidance of "evil Western customs and morals," and vocational training for repentant prostitutes.[143] The Tehran conference was "the last semi-independent activity" undertaken by Iranian women before the state hijacked the women's movement by establishing the Ladies Center.[144]

During the 1940s, the paths of the various women's movements in the Middle East diverged more distinctly, continuing a process that had already begun in the 1920s and 1930s, particularly in Turkey and Iran. Different political situations inevitably affected the movements. A pan-Arab trend developed among the Arab countries, as manifested in the women's conferences held in Cairo in 1938 and 1944.[145] Most of the Arab states became independent, subsequently turning toward their own state-building projects. State feminism ultimately became the predominant model in many of these newly independent states, and was solidified in Turkey and Iran.

One question that arises about the history of the women's movements concerns the legacy they left to subsequent generations. How important is this history? Can women learn from it? What is the role of history in relation to current politics? History is not simply something that happened to other people, something we can objectify and look at from a distance. It is something continuously unfolding – something to which we look for the origins of ourselves, our societies, our politics and culture. "The only past we can know is one we shape by the questions we ask; yet these very questions are also shaped by the context we come from, and our context includes the past."[146] It is a cliché that, without learning from history, we are condemned to repeat the mistakes of the past. A critical examination of the history of the women's movements should not be a condemnatory or congratulatory exercise, however, but rather part of a project to expand the contours of Middle East history by asking the unasked questions.

14

LATIN AMERICAN FEMINISM AND THE TRANSNATIONAL ARENA

Francesca Miller

In the early twentieth century, feminists from North and South America took their agenda to the tables of the International Conferences of American States. The history of Latin American women's participation in the inter-American conferences suggests that the transnational arena held a particular appeal for Latin American feminists. There are a number of reasons this was so. Within their national communities, they were disfranchised; and, as elsewhere, the national social and political arenas were characterized by androcracy. Moreover, Latin American female intellectuals were particularly alienated from politics as practiced within their countries, excluded from leadership positions by the forces of opposition as well as by their governments.

The inter-American arena in the first half of this century proved to be an important domain for feminist activity, one in which women activists from throughout the Americas pursued a number of the longstanding goals of international feminism. Two of the themes that emerge in the examination of women's concerns in this period are the push for resolutions that would commit the signatory governments to pursue legal and civil reform and the search for international peace.

Establishing a presence: 1898–1928

Venezuelan novelist Teresa de la Parra, speaking before a conference of Latin American women novelists and authors in Bogotá in 1930, described "la influencia de las mujeres en la formación del alma americana."[1] Teresa de la Parra posited a spiritual empathy among women of "Catholic and Spanish America"; she recalled Isabella I of Castile and Sor Juana Inés de la Cruz as spiritual precursors of the assembled women poets and writers. De la Parra would not have described herself as a feminist; however, in her assumption that Spanish-American women had made a different contribution to the *alma americana* than their male counterparts, she implicitly subscribed to the thesis that the historical experience of women is not perfectly analogous to that of the men with whom their lives are linked.[2]

For de la Parra, women were not only different but also, in matters of the spirit, superior. In consonance with her belief in the uplifting moral influence of women on the American soul, de la Parra insisted that "History and Politics are a banquet for men alone." To her, the realm of politics was a corrupt masculine realm from which women should abstain, and history a record that excluded "the young, the people [*o povo, el pueblo*], and women."[3]

Consider, however, the inherent conflict between what de la Parra was doing and what she was saying: while advising women to abstain from politics, she herself was giving a public speech that was explicitly critical of political practice in states governed solely by men, a fairly universal condemnation but specifically aimed at the nation-states of the Western Hemisphere; surely this was a political act in itself. The conflict between her action and her message vividly demonstrates the ambiguity felt by many of de la Parra's colleagues in, on one hand, their alienation from politics as practiced in their own national governments and, on the other, their desire to effect social, political and economic reform—reform that would bring "the young, the people, and women" into social and political equity and, in so doing, transform the essential patriarchal character of the state.

By 1930 the discussion of whether women should enter the political fray was a moot one: women, and issues of special concern to women, were fully in the arena of public debate. However, the history of Latin American women's participation in and contributions to international feminist discourse in the early twentieth century has been shrouded in historiographic assumptions about the nature and extent of feminist thought in Latin America, assumptions that imply that feminist thought in Latin America is derivative and not sui generis. More concretely, it has been assumed that the creation of the Inter-American Commission of Women at the Sixth International Conference of American States in Havana in 1928 was not a collaborative effort by North and South American women but a response to the pressure tactics of the National Woman's Party of the United States and thus another example of North American hegemony, female-style.

The historical record belies these assumptions. Latin American women's participation in and contributions to international feminist discourse are well illustrated in the proceedings of inter-American conferences held between 1880 and 1948. The examination of the inter-American conferences is of particular significance in the study of Latin American women's contributions, because the precedent for using the international congresses of American states as a forum for the debate of feminist issues was established at the Latin American Scientific Congresses, first sponsored by the Sociedad Científica Argentina, which met in Buenos Aires in 1898, Montevideo in 1901, Rio de Janeiro in 1905, and Santiago in 1908. Their purpose was to discuss "scientific, economic, social and political issues," and, as a later chronicler wrote, "women of the Latin American countries have been identified with these congresses since the first."

The majority of women participants came from Argentina, Chile, Uruguay, and Brazil, and the topics they addressed came under the rubric of "social problems": hygiene, child care, nutrition, maternal welfare. All these topics meshed comfortably with traditional feminine interests within their societies and were matters of concern to scientists and educators of both sexes.

For the Santiago meeting in 1908, the Latin American Scientific Congress was expanded to become the First Pan American Scientific Congress. Over two thousand members gathered from throughout the hemisphere; it was observed by W. R. Shepherd of Columbia University that "women school teachers constituted a large part of the audience, and it must be said that they express their opinions, as well as their difference in opinion, from those held by the other sex, with a freedom and frankness which is quite surprising."[4] It was on the issue of access to education for women that these Latin American female intellectuals found themselves divided from their male counterparts. However, discussion of the education issue was appropriate to the forum and does not represent the breadth of feminist social critique in the Southern Cone republics at the turn of the century.[5]

On May 10, 1910, over two hundred women from Peru, Chile, Uruguay, Paraguay, and Argentina convened in Buenos Aires for the first Congreso Femenino Internacional. The sponsoring groups included the Asociación Nacional Argentina Contra la Trata de Blancas, Asociación Nacional del Profesorado, Centro Socialista Femenino, Escuela Normal de Maestras de Tucumán, Grupo Femenino Unión y Labor, Liga Nacional de Mujeres Librepensadoras, and many more.[6] Dr. Cecilia Grierson presided; the topics discussed ranged from international law to health care to the problems of the married working woman, and reflected the participants' conversance with the international reformist and feminist dialogue of the day.[7] Among the resolutions was one commending the government of Uruguay for passage of a bill of divorce and of one demanding equal pay for equal work: "trabajar porque en la igualdad de circunstancias el trabajo de la mujer no sea menos retribuido de que lo del hombre."[8]

What is of significance for the examination of the inter-American congresses is that the women who spoke at the Congreso Femenino Internacional in Buenos Aires formed the nucleus of the South American women who attended the scientific congresses. The scope of their interests, their feminist perspective, and their critical stance vis-à-vis the status quo in their respective societies are well illustrated in the record of the Buenos Aires meeting. Furthermore, in their talks, many of the speakers foreshadowed the rhetoric that came to characterize the arguments put before the International Conferences of American States in the 1920s, as María Samame did in her speech "Democracy and the Political Personality of the Woman." After citing a number of examples from antiquity, she pointed out that Isabella I of Spain deserved the greatest credit for the discovery of the New World, the birthplace of democracy, and concluded, "In the old monarchies perhaps it would have been unnatural to recognize the right of woman suffrage; but in the democratic republics of America it is an inexcusable anachronism not to do so."[9]

The Second Pan American Scientific Congress was held in Washington, D.C., in 1915–1916. The Washington congress took on far more significance within the context of inter-American relations than the previous scientific congresses had done. In 1915, Europe was at war, and in North America, Mexico was in the throes of revolution. The United States Department of State, aware that the audience of the scientific congress would include the diplomatic representatives of the states of the Western Hemisphere resident in Washington, took the opportunity to put forth its interpretation of hemispheric security and the need to build up defensive power. Thus, the character of the meeting was altered from a collegial exchange of professionals to a facsimile of a full-dress inter-American diplomatic conference. One of the consequences was that, unlike the Congresses that had been held in South America, the Washington congress did not include women among the "savants, scientists, and publicists" invited. The women were relegated to the balconies.

Thus began the second phase of women's efforts to focus attention on issues of their special concern. In response to their debarment from the official Washington meetings, a number of Latin American women, among them educators and other professionals, diplomats' wives and daughters, foregathered with their North American counterparts to form an auxiliary meeting—a meeting that attracted so many participants that the women overflowed the small room they had originally been allotted and were moved to the ballroom of the Mayflower Hotel (this fact was carefully noted in the minutes).[10]

In these early phases of women's involvement at the international level, the women participants were of the same social and economic background as their male counterparts. However, the women had a different agenda. On issues of social welfare, their program often intersected with that of reform-minded males; the split came when the women sought to have equality of rights for their own sex, such as equal access to education and to the ballot box and equality within marriage. It is also significant that the women acting at the international level at this time were not, as the men were, professional diplomats, paid commercial agents, or subsidized scholars. The women were involved because they had issues about which they could agree, despite great diversity in background and personal political orientation.

The agenda drawn up at the Mayflower Hotel in 1916 stated that the purpose of the meeting was not only to "exchange views of the subjects of special interest to women," which included "the education of women, training of children, and social welfare," but also to discuss subjects of Pan-Americanism. In the words of the keynote speaker, "We the women of North and South America, which possess similar conceptions of individual rights and constitutional government, possess a common duty to mankind which we must not ignore."[11]

In the 1920s the early efforts of the women bore fruit in a series of well-attended Pan-American women's conferences. One in Baltimore in 1922 began with the intention of emphasizing the importance of suffrage, but concluded with a platform calling for international peace through arbitration; abolition of the white slave trade; access to education at all levels; the right of married women to control their own property and earnings and to secure equal guardianship; the encouragement of organizations, discussion, and public speaking among women and freedom of opportunity for women to cultivate and use their talents and to secure their political rights; and, finally, the promotion of friendliness and understanding among all Pan-American countries, with the aim of maintaining perpetual peace in the hemisphere.[12] Bertha Lutz, founder of the Federação Brasileria pele Progresso Femenino and one of the Brazilian delegates to the Baltimore conference, contrasted the atmosphere there with her experience in trying to bring the women's programs before the League of Nations:

> We were received in the United States, not as if we were representatives of unimportant countries as happens at the international congresses of the Old World, but with a frank cordiality and with the same consideration that has marked the relations of women of the Americas since the days of our pioneering foremothers.[13]

By 1922, the essential components for an effective, formal international exchange among women of the Americas were in place. A continuing organizational structure with an accumulated history of international activity was established; funding sources had been identified; a communications network was in place. Leaders were emerging. Of the Latin American women, some, like Amanda Labarca of Chile and Flora de Oliveira Lima of Brazil, were veterans of the scientific congresses; others, like Bertha Lutz, Clara González of Panama, and Elena Torres of Mexico, represented a new generation. A political platform had been enunciated and agreed upon; it was a distillation of the issues which had been raised over the past two decades. To the prewar concern for social problems and the belief in the need for education had been added the appeal for peace and for equal rights and, as a means to these ends, the desire for inclusion at the diplomatic council tables.

The sympathetic atmosphere and reformist zeal of the Pan-American women's conference described by Lutz were hardly characteristic of the prewar International Conferences of American States. The early Pan-American meetings, convened between 1881 and 1910, had been primarily devoted to establishing conventions that would enhance inter-American commercial opportunities and exhibited little of the fiery idealism expressed by Simón Bolívar, who had dreamed that "the assembling of a Congress of Panama composed of diplomatic representatives from independent American nations [would] form a new epoch of human affairs," or the hopes of Henry Clay, who in 1828 called Bolívar's proposal the opportunity to establish "a human-freedom league in America."[14]

The invocation of the ideals of Pan-Americanism by the feminists working at the international level added a new dimension to the inter-American conferences of the 1920s. The Fifth International Conference of American States, held in Santiago in 1923, which was the first convened since the onset of World War I, took place in an atmosphere of controversy. The desire of the women to insert feminist issues and matters of broad social reform into the program of the conference paralleled the desire of many in both North and South America, male and female, to use the conferences to challenge United States imperialist activities in Central America and the Caribbean—a political position that was, in turn, fully supported by feminist leaders throughout the hemisphere.[15] A sizable number of "unofficial" female delegates attended the Santiago meeting, which passed a resolution recommending that women be appointed as official delegates to future inter-American conferences.

The next International Conference of American States met in Havana in 1928. There were no official women delegates; nevertheless, women from throughout the hemisphere had traveled to Havana for the conference. And they were not there as interested individuals or spouses. They spoke for the Consejo Feminista Mexicana, the Women's International League for Peace and Freedom, the Federação Brasileira pelo Progresso Feminino, the National Woman's Party of the United States, the Ligue Feminine Haitienne, the Club de Madres of Buenos Aires, and many, many more. They were hosted by the Alianza Femenina Cubana and the Club Femenino de Cuba.

By the end of the conference, these "unofficial" delegates had secured an audience before a plenary session, presented an Equal Rights Treaty for the consideration of the governments of the hemisphere, and successfully lobbied for the creation of an officially designated body, the Inter-American Commission of Women, which was charged with the investigation of the status of women in the twenty-one member states. The IACW was "the first governmental organization in the world to be founded for the express purpose of working for the rights of women."[16]

The Equal Rights Treaty,[17] which was strongly opposed by the United States diplomatic delegation, was eventually ratified by only four member countries and was relegated to obscurity. Nevertheless, the choice of the Pan-American meetings as a forum for the discussion of women's and feminist issues proved politically astute: women had indeed succeeded in bringing "women's issues" to the center of political debate within the hemisphere. The leadership of the Latin American women is clearly illustrated not only in providing the precedent of using inter-American congresses as a forum for the debate of feminist issues but also in the insistence on the inclusion of issues of social justice in the first Pan-American women's platforms, which directly reflected the dominant concerns of Latin American feminists.[18]

In addition to their domestic agenda, through which they hoped to influence their respective national governments to enact laws that would bring women into civil and legal equity with men, the feminists active at the inter-American congresses took strong stands on international issues, supporting the principles of nonintervention, the resolution of conflict through arbitration, and the rights of small nations. In Havana in 1928, the women demonstrated against the United States' occupation of Nicaragua and protested the dismissal of the Haitian representatives.[19]

Many of the Latin American women who attended the Fifth International Conference of American States in Santiago in 1923 and the North and South American women who met at the Sixth IAC in Havana in 1928 were members of the Women's International League for Peace and Freedom. The positions the WILPF took in matters of hemispheric politics are discussed in the report of the Comité de las Américas de la Liga Internacional de Mujeres de la Paz y Libertad:

> La Sección ... ha trabajado por muchos años contra el imperialismo norteamericano, y ha cooperado con resultados favorables por los siguientes fines: Declaración del Gobierno de los Estados Unidos que nunca volverá a intervenir en países extranjeros para protegar la propiedad norteamericana; ... retiro de los marinos de Haiti, Nicaragua, y la República Dominicana; derogación de la Emienda Platt en la Constitución de Cuba. Desde 1926 ha contribuído a mejorar las relaciones entre los Estados Unidos y Mexico. ... Ha tratado de descubrir y aminorar la explotación de trabajadores en Cuba, Bolivia, Chile y otros países.[20]

> [The Section ... has worked for many years against North American imperialism, and has cooperated with good results to the following ends: The Declaration by the Government of the United States that it would never again intervene in foreign countries in order to protect North American property; ... the retirement of the Marines from Haiti, Nicaragua, and the Dominican Republic, and the removal of the Platt Amendment from the Constitution of Cuba. Since 1926 [the Section] has contributed to the improvement of relations between the United States and Mexico ... and has worked to reveal and ameliorate the exploitation of workers in Cuba, Bolivia, Chile and other countries.]

The members of the first IACW were Flora de Oliveira Lima (Brazil), Aida Parada (Chile), Lydia Fernández (Costa Rica), Gloria Moya de Jiménez (Dominican Republic), Clara Gonzáles (Panama), Elena Mederos de González (Cuba), Irene de Peyre (Guatemala), Margarita Robles de Mendoza (Mexico), Juanita Molina de Fromen (Nicaragua), and Teresa Obrogoso de Prevost (Peru). Doris Stevens (USA) was chair. The IACW took up the task of collecting material on the legal status of women from every country in the hemisphere:

> The commission, created in the Sixth Pan American Conference for the purpose of dealing with the Conflict of Laws and Uniformity of Legislation ... took into consideration the resolution adopted in the plenary session of February 18, 1928, for the constitution of an IACW charged with the duty of preparing information, which it might consider useful, of a legal and other nature, to the end that the Seventh International Conference should take up the study of the civil and political equality in the continent.[21]

The first meeting of the IACW was held in Havana, February 17–24, 1930. In addition to the commissioners listed above, Colombia was represented by Alicia Ricode de Herrera, Haiti by Mme Fernand Dennis, El Salvador by proxy, and Venezuela by Cecilia Herrera de Olavarría. The commission drafted a resolution to establish equality in nationality for presentation to the World Conference for the Codification of International Law, to be held at The Hague in March, 1930. The resolution stated, "The contracting parties agree that from the going into effect of this treaty there shall be no distinction based on sex in their law and practice relating to nationality."[22] Other resolutions requested the American governments to appoint the IACW commissioners as plenipotentiaries to The Hague conference, asked financial support for their work, and thanked the Carnegie Endowment for International Peace for its initial grant of five thousand dollars.

The women did their own secretarial work; they had secured a small office space in the Pan American Union building in Washington only after dealing with numerous harassment tactics—when they arrived at their office in the first few months of their existence, they often found that their two desks had been "borrowed" or that all the chairs were missing. Nevertheless, they succeeded in gathering a substantial amount of legal information from throughout the hemisphere, all of which was carefully collated, hand-labeled, and placed in black leather three-ring notebooks.[23] The intention was to be able to have access to the information pertinent to particular issues as they arose. The first of these was the issue of the nationality of married women.

The earliest opportunity to present the Resolution on the Nationality of Women to an international body came at the meeting of the council of the League of Nations at The Hague in 1931. As the women had no official status within the league, the resolution was put forth by male diplomatic representatives from the Americas: Matos of Guatemala, Barreto of Peru, and César Zumeta of Venezuela. The IACW draft urged the American states

> to consider the question of whether it would not be possible 1) to introduce into their law the principle of the equality of the sexes in matters of nationality, taking particularly into consideration the interests of children, and especially 2) to decide that in principle the nationality of the wife should henceforth not be affected without her consent either by the mere fact of marriage or by any change in the nationality of the husband. It is to be noted that there is a clear movement of opinion throughout the world in favor of a suitable settlement of this question.[24]

No action resulted; the resolution was taken under study. James Brown Scott, editor of the published collection of resolutions, added this comment to the document: "In the interest of historical accuracy, it is necessary to record that the initiative of the Council's action came from the IACW. The League's Commission of Women, when created, will concern itself with, and report to, the 1931 Assembly upon a single point: nationality and the status of women."[25] Scott's comment underscores the achievements of the IACW. Not only had the American women been successful in creating an officially recognized commission that became a model for the creation of the Commission of Women at the League of Nations but the IACW was endowed from the beginning with a far broader mandate for action than was the League Council.

Equal rights and peace: 1928–1938

From the early twentieth century, Latin American feminists, like their North American colleagues, were deeply commited to the idea of peace. At the Pan American Women's Auxiliary meeting in Washington in 1916, the Pan American Association for the Advancement of Women's conference in Baltimore in 1922, the International Conference of American States in Santiago in 1923 and in Havana in 1928, the women reiterated their commitment to "maintaining perpetual peace in the hemisphere."[26]

In the decade between 1928 and 1938, the Inter-American Commission of Women operated as an autonomous body within the inter-American organization. The themes of equal rights and peace, both of which were believed to be within the special province of women, mark their efforts. In the words of Nelly Merino Carvallo, who edited the international woman's journal *Mujeres de América* in Buenos Aires from 1930 to 1935: "From its inception, *Mujeres de América* has been dedicated to peace. Yes: it is through the woman that peace will be secured in the world."[27] The idea that women have a special role as peacemakers is persistent, despite evidence that men have in fact been the diplomats who have arbitrated peace agreements and sought international concord. Certainly the male representatives to the International Conferences of American States saw themselves as working toward peace in the hemisphere. But there are a number of factors that differentiate the attitudes and expressions of men and women in the transnational discourse of the period. First, the male diplomatic community recognized force as a legitimate diplomatic tool; they were not pacifists. Second, the male diplomats and representatives to the inter-American conference tables were speaking for their governments, not of their personal convictions. Only a handful of women were members of national delegations. From the beginning, the constituency of the IACW was drawn from women's organizations. The original members of the commission were, in effect, self-appointed. During the 1930s, the IACW solicited, and received, confirmation by individual governments of the women who already were on the IACW.

There is evidence that another factor was crucial, particularly for the Latin American women. In this era, the women active at the international level had little tradition of identifying with the nation-state. To the contrary, they had historically articulated their position as other within the home, the society, and the nation, and looked to the transnational arena as the space where they could find mutual support from one another and publicize their agenda. We are not speaking of all women—some were patriotic, and most were indifferent. We are not speaking of the women of the Liga Patriótica, or of the women who embraced their disfranchisement and inequality as badges of femininity, but of feminists who articulated their position of dissent from the prevailing order and sought change.

The 1930s were a period of powerful nationalist movements in Argentina, Mexico, and Brazil. The iconography of those movements was overwhelmingly masculine, the ideal national figure being a male head of state, who, if not himself a general, a hero of the revolution, or a gaucho, was certainly surrounded by military power. Although women worked for reform and change at home, they had few effective channels for garnering support, and their programs were often dismissed as irrelevant by both government and opposition leaders. Alienation from the political process within the national community should not be construed as obviating love of homeland, of place, of one's historical family; rather, it should be understood as part of the meaning that the transnational arena held for Latin American feminists in this era.

The Seventh International Conference of American States, held in Montevideo in 1933, marked the first inter-American conference at which women had an official presence, both within the Inter-American Commission of Women and as members of national delegations.[28] At that meeting, the Convention on the Nationality of Women was presented to the conference by the Inter-American Commission of Women. The convention stated, "There shall be no distinction based on sex as regards nationality." It was signed by twenty American countries, becoming the first convention on the rights of women to be adopted at an international conference. It served as the model for the Convention on the Nationality of Women that was subsequently adopted by the League of Nations.[29]

The women's work for gender equity did not diminish their commitment to the cause of international peace. Of central concern in the Southern Cone in this period was the conflagration in the Gran Chaco. The dispute between Bolivia and Paraguay over the vast territory of the Chaco, which stretches from the eastern slopes of the Andes to the Paraguay River, began with isolated armed skirmishes in the late 1920s. The conflict flared into a bloody war that ultimately took nearly 100,000 lives and bankrupted the treasuries of the participants before a truce was reached in 1935.

During the war, nationalist passions were high. In this unsympathetic atmosphere, *Mujeres de América* ran a petition initiated by the Círculo Argentino "Pro Paz"[30] and addressed to the delegates at the Montevideo conference. The petition called for arbitration and denounced the participants in the war as tools of international capitalist interests; but most telling of the sentiments of the publication and its audience was the dedication of the July–August 1933 issue to the women of Boliva and Peru, "reviving the spirit of the glorious days of Independence" when the two nations were one.

En la dolorosa tragedia que conmueve las soledades del Chaco, un corazón de americana y defensora de la paz a toda costa, Ilora de dolor y de inquietud fraternales. Y, ante la impotencia de detener esta cruenta tragedia, aspiro por lo menos que *Mujeres de América* vaya formando un nuevo concepto de "patria" que es progreso; "patria" que es paz; "patria" que es unión.

Sí, mujeres bolivianas, amigas mias, unámosnos todas. Trabajemos con fé, con amor, para que en no lejanos días tengamos la patria grande, la patria sin fronteras; la patria fundada en el mejoramiento espiritual.[31]

[In the unhappy tragedy that breaks the solitude of the Chaco, a heart of America and defender of peace at all costs, weeps full of pain and broken brotherhood. And, confronted with the impossibility of halting this cruel tragedy, I hope that at least *Mujeres de América* may help to form a new concept of "patria" that is progress; "patria" that is peace; "patria" that is unity.

Yes, women of Bolivia, my friends, we are one. We are working with faith, with love, for the time where we will be one great country, a "patria" without frontiers; a country founded on spiritual betterment.]

The idea of a "patria" without boundaries is a specifically nonnational vision.[32] The ways in which feminists in Latin America talked and wrote about peace, as but one aspect of their transnational activities, illuminates the ways in which they viewed the nation-state. The idea of sisterhood, of an imagined community of interests based on gender, of the women's insistence on the commonality of the human experience, undermines the idea of nation. This is well illustrated in the subsequent history of the women's platform.

The Eighth International Conference of American States met in Lima in 1938; the main business of the conference was the effort, led by the United States, to unite the hemisphere in the event of war. In the "Declaration of Lima," the American republics reaffirmed their continental solidarity and "determination to defend themselves against all foreign intervention."[33] The Inter-American Commission of Women succeeded in putting forth its resolution that "women have the right to the enjoyment of equal civil status,"[34] but the Lima conference was also the scene of an attempt to disestablish the Inter-American Commission of Women as an autonomous entity. The Inter-American Commission of Women had never enjoyed the support of the United States diplomatic corps, and under the Roosevelt regime, it became a particular target of Eleanor Roosevelt.[35] Its feminist stance had made it a target for attack throughout its existence, and in the atmosphere of the late 1930s the women's platform was seen as secondary to the efforts to unite the hemisphere. The feminist leaders were advised to turn their efforts to the defense of democracy, not to raise divisive issues. Over the protests of the members of the commission itself, the opposition, which came principally from the United

States delegation, succeeded in recasting the Inter-American Commission of Women from an independent women's commission to a subsidiary unit of the inter-American apparatus.[36]

Despite its diminished status, the IACW continued its work, and its legacy is readily apparent in the next decade. At the Chapultepec Conference on the Problems of War and Peace in Mexico on March 8, 1945, the wording of the Lima resolution was directly incorporated into the plans for the United Nations; in October, 1945, in San Francisco, Inter-American Commission of Women representatives Bertha Lutz of Brazil, Minerva Bernadino of the Dominican Republic, and Amalia Caballero de Castillo Ledon of Mexico used the precedent inter-American resolutions on the status of women to insist that the opening paragraph of the Charter of the United Nations include the phrase "the equal rights of men and women." It reads, "We the peoples of the United Nations, determined ... to reaffirm faith in fundamental human rights, in the dignity and worth of the human person, in the equal rights of men and women and of nations large and small."[37] In Bogotá in 1948, again with the leadership of Amalia Caballero de Castillo Ledon, the Comisión Inter-americana de Mujeres was established as part of the Organization of American States.

The Guatemala conference

Legal rights and the appointment of women to the diplomatic tables were only a part of the Latin American and North American feminists' agenda in the pre-World War II period. The women's concerns and those of their like-minded male colleagues on issues of social welfare, education, and the need for economic change were incorporated in the Chapultepec Charter, the Charter of the United Nations, and the newly organized Organization of American States. Women themselves were now part of governmental delegations, and much of their agenda was incorporated into the international agenda.

A number of questions arise. Did women as the counter-voice at the international conferences vanish after 1945, only to reemerge during the United Nations International Year of the Woman in 1975? Did women, once they were the official representatives of their governments, cease to function as a pressure group for change? Did the historical antinationalist position of the first generation of Latin American feminists disappear in the 1940s? Or is there evidence of the continuation of a separatist, explicitly feminist, political strategy within the context of inter-American relations?

By 1947 the attention of the inter-American diplomatic community had shifted from social and economic reform to a focus on opposition to communism, a position embraced by governments throughout the hemisphere. An extraordinary meeting of American foreign ministers and heads of state was convened at the Inter-American Conference for the Maintenance of Continental Peace and Security, in Petropolis, near Rio de Janeiro, from August 15 to September 2, 1947, at the instigation of the Latin American states.[38] The delegates drew up the Treaty of Reciprocal Assistance, known as the Rio Pact, which put into effect the principle that an attack upon one American state would be considered an attack upon all. The emphasis on arming the nation-states of the Western Hemisphere, which has formed the bulk of inter-American assistance in postwar history, dates from this agreement.[39]

Between August 21 and August 27, 1947, the Primer Congreso Interamericano de Mujeres convened in Guatemala City.[40] Women from fifteen American nations attended. They came not as representatives of their governments but as delegates from women's clubs throughout the hemisphere: Zonta International, Sociedade Civica Feminina de Santos, Brasil; Unión Femenina de Colombia; Movimiento Pro Emancipación de las Mujeres de Chile; Asociación Puertorriqueña de Esposas de Masones; La Cruz Blanca de la Paz (Cuba); Federación

Argentina de Mujeres Universitarias; Ateneo Femenino (Bolivia); Asociación de Mujeres Tituladas del Uruguay; Alianza Femenina Colombiana; Comités Populares Femeninos de Guayaquil; Sociedad Unión de Costureras (El Salvador); Ligue Feminine d'Action Sociale (Haiti); Unión Democrática Femenina Hondureña; Ateneo Mexicano de Mujeres; Sección Femenil de Sindicato Nacional de Trabajadores de la Educación (Mexico); Cruzada de Mujeres Nicaragüenses; and Asociación Continental de Intelectuales de América (Panama). Most of the representatives from the United States—who hailed from cities from Minneapolis to San Francisco to Boston to Brooklyn—were members of the Women's International League for Peace and Freedom, as were the Canadian women.[41]

These women were not politically radical within their national communities, but they believed strongly in the need for women to speak out on issues of social and political equality, human welfare, and peace. Their first press release stated:

> The First Inter-American Congress of Women meeting in Guatemala, representing mothers, wives, daughters of our Continent, has resolved in plenary session to denounce the hemispheric armament plan under discussion at the Rio Conference, asking that the cost of the arms program be used to support industry, agriculture, health and education for our people.

The women declared their right to speak on international issues: "We consider that inter-american political problems deserve particular attention on the part of women of the Continent. ... We resolve to ask the Pan American Union and all Pan American associations to enact the following resolutions in the inter-American conferences." Their first concern was that the "American governments meeting in conference in Rio de Janeiro comply in good faith with the Final Act of Chapultepec, which is an instrument of peace, and not give it a militaristic interpretation."[42]

In those weeks of August 1947, the proceedings of the Rio conference were headlined in the world press; The New York Times carried daily page-one coverage. The Primer Congreso Interamericano de Mujeres was also noted in the press. In a number of Latin American papers, including the opposition press in Guatemala, it was accused of communist sympathies. On August 19, The New York Times carried a story—on page 21, in the Food Section of the Women's Pages.

The women were not successful in staying the arming of the Americas, but it is apparent that in the immediate postwar period the women of the Americas continued to look beyond the nation-state to the transnational arena for community, for empowerment, for the opportunity to articulate their ideas and to be heard. The women who met at Guatemala City in 1947 to counter the Rio Pact came together not to buttress the position of their respective nation-states but to protest the aggrandizement of national power through arms at the expense of the citizenry, an issue they saw as within their traditional purview. Nor was their petition based upon an imagined equation between dollars for arms and dollars for aid; the Latin American women, especially, clearly perceived the probability of arms' being used not in defense of the hemisphere but against the populace by the state.[43]

The women were acting within the historical context of a half century of a feminist, pacifist tradition, established by the women of the Americas from the Latin American Scientific Congresses of the 1890s to the Primer Congreso Femenino in 1910 to the creation of the IACW in 1928. In the immediate postwar period, when the formal inter-American community refused to respond to the women's historical commitment to peace and disarmament, the women again looked to a separatist transnational strategy.

15

INTERNATIONALIZING MARRIED WOMEN'S NATIONALITY

The Hague campaign of 1930

Ellen Carol DuBois

In 1930, the League of Nations convened an International Conference for the Codification of Law at The Hague, in the Netherlands. This legal event, which anticipated creating a more systematic supra-national judicial system, became the focus for an extraordinary and far reaching international feminist campaign. Focused on the question of nationality for married women, the women's efforts at The Hague opened up into a prolonged feminist presence in the League of Nations as well as reinvigoration of national movements, especially in the Western Hemisphere. A relatively unexplored dimension of the history of twentieth century feminism, the campaign for equal nationality laws formed one of the activist streams that connected women's rights activities in the post-World War I period through to the 1950s. This article will explore the early phases of these developments.

The 1930 Conference was organized to establish worldwide standards of law on three issues in particular: maritime law, a perennial favorite of international jurists; the responsibilities of nation-states for actions against aliens, an issue of consequence as a result of war and postwar conditions; and finally, universal and non-conflicting terms of nationality. This was the issue which was of greatest concern to women, for women and children were preponderant among those affected by the upheavals in nationality during World War I.

On the one hand, nationality would seem to be a matter of purely national significance: a sovereign state determines the bases of membership within it. And yet, as world war and its aftermath had made abundantly obvious, nationality was part of an international legal order, as states were expected to respect each other's rules of nationality, and as dramatic changes in borders, sovereignty, territory, crumbling empires and new nations shifted and compounded the nationality of individuals with greater frequency and more chaos than ever before. If the world community of nations did not respect a uniform system of the laws of nationality, then these problems of statelessness and multiple citizenships would necessarily arise, and it was with this dilemma in particular that the jurists of the Hague Conference were concerned.[1]

As far as the rules of women's nationality were concerned (and subordinating variation between nation-states in favor of cross-national generalizations) one might say that there were three general categories of national practices: the past, the present and the future. The past treated men and women similarly when it came to nationality, in that both retained their nationality of birth despite shifts in residence and family status.[2] Through the nineteenth century, many nation-states changed their laws to follow the rule of dependent wifehood in establishing distinct terms of nationality for married women.[3] Thus, when a woman of one country married a man of another, she was deprived of her own nationality lest conflicts between nations be imported into the marriage and threaten the all-important principle of "family unity." At the time of the 1930 conference, this might be said to be the present. The Hague Codification Conference was concerned with the incompleteness of this change, with wives who had lost their own nationality but were not incorporated into that of their husbands, or with wives who retained their nationality but were also connected to their husband's, with the consequence having either no nationality or two. The rise in international exchanges, including marriages, made these anomalies increasingly common. As a legal scholar of the period wrote, "There is a romantic ring to the phrase 'a man without a country,' but there is stark realism in the situation of a woman without a country."[4]

It was the inequity of this situation, especially in light of the growing demand of women around the world for substantive citizenship, which brought feminist attention to The Hague. Women's rights activists came there to argue for what they were quite sure was the future: equality between men and women before the law with respect to individual civil and political rights.[5] Their conviction about the historical inevitability of their cause had gained power by virtue of the recent victories of women's enfranchisement across much of Europe and North America. Indeed, the vitality of the campaign for women's legal equality in numerous nations was widely acknowledged, even by opponents, as a major factor in forcing the question of married women's nationality to the fore. What citizenship – and its most important consequence, political enfranchisement – was to the nation-state, so the issue of nationality was to the international order: the system by which individuals became active members of the polity, and accrued the attendant rights and responsibilities.[6] "Citizenship being the expression of the relations between a government and its citizens, it touches the citizens in many respects and many rights and privileges depend upon it," explained Juanita de Molina Fromen, a Nicaraguan nationality activist, in February 1930. "So far rights and privileges have belonged to men and the time has come when equality between men and women in regard to nationality must be realized."[7]

The feminist analysis of nationality demonstrates the centrality of the structures of marriage to the legal inequalities which women suffer. Most of the legal discriminations against women were artifacts of the impact of marriage, which put them in a position of legal subordination to their husbands. In the Anglo-American legal system, this principle of legal subordination of women via marriage was called "coverture." In this property-based system, married women, long deprived of the right to own and dispose of property, became for legal purposes property themselves. Other nations followed systems different in the details yet similar in the overall impact.[8] For example, Dutch women, like Spanish, tended to keep their maiden names, albeit subordinated by hyphen to that of their husbands. Yet, by marrying, a Dutch woman lost her legal autonomy and independence and joined children, the infirm and others in the category of dependent persons.

The impact of nationality laws, whether discriminatory or egalitarian, could vary, depending on the class and/or race of the woman involved. The United States, on the one hand, led in establishing independent nationality for wives, while on the other allowed the law to observe distinctions of class, race and ethnicity.[9] In 1922, the federal "Cable Law" (named after its Senatorial sponsor) undid earlier changes and guaranteed that American women would retain their citizenship when marrying non-Americans. Numerous prominent women, including suffragists Crystal Eastman, Harriot Stanton Blatch and Congresswoman Ruth Bryan Owen, had found themselves severely disadvantaged when marriage to foreigners (in all three cases, Englishmen) deprived them of their citizenship.[10] Such women fought hard for independent nationality for all women regardless of marriage to preserve their political options and property rights as Americans. However, the Cable Law reform specifically excluded those American women who had married non-American men ineligible for citizenship by virtue of race, in particular Chinese, and they continued to be deprived of their citizenship by their marriages.[11] As for the immigrant wives of native or naturalized American citizens, the new principle of independent nationality regardless of marriage was applied to them but worked to their disadvantage, as they could no longer gain American citizenship through their husbands, but had to go through naturalization procedures.[12]

By the 1920s, the leading international women's organizations unanimously supported legal reforms to insure independent nationality for married women.[13] As Margery Corbett Ashby, president of the International Alliance of Women for Suffrage and Equal Citizenship (IAWSEC; before 1926 known as the International Woman Suffrage Alliance), explained, "Women are not more inclined than men to agree on any question but on this one point of nationality we have an amazing agreement. . . ."[14] In 1920, the International Alliance created a "Committee on the Nationality of Women," with participants from the other broad-based international women's federation, the International Council of Women (ICW).[15] At its 1923 meeting in Rome, the International Alliance resolved that "this question of married women's independent nationality could only be adequately dealt with by international agreement."[16]

In 1928, when the League of Nations announced its intention to convene an International Codification Conference in The Hague sometime in the next two years, the women of the Committee on the Nationality of Women sprang into action. These efforts were directed by a group of pioneering women lawyers concerned with the inequities of married women's legal position. Chief among them were the British pacifist and suffragist Chrystal Macmillan, who had been part of the historic international feminist Congress at The Hague fifteen years earlier; Maria Vérone, a leading French feminist lawyer and suffragist; and the Dutch suffragist and parliamentarian, Betsy Bakker-Nort, whose 1914 doctoral dissertation compared married women's legal disabilities across national borders. The Committee on the Nationality of Women drafted international legal standards for married women's independent nationality and forwarded its proposal to the preparatory committee appointed by the League of Nations for the Hague Conference. The committee's position rested on the twin principles that "the nationality of a woman should not be changed by reason only of Marriage" and that "the nationality of a married woman should not be changed without her consent."[17]

To press this case at the Codification Conference itself, the Committee on Nationality arranged a joint meeting followed by a public demonstration to be held in The Hague on Friday 14 March 1930. The timing coincided with the Codification Conference's opening ceremonies the day before, to which the feminists were not invited. An advertisement in the local paper, predicting high attendance, encouraged the audience to arrive early for the evening event.[18] At the Twee Steden, a restaurant two blocks from the main conference site, the IAWSEC and ICW activists welcomed a large audience with short speeches describing the morning's meeting, followed by a procession, a public spectacle adapted from the grand suffrage parades of the past. Women from many nations – young women, it was emphasized, to counteract the obviously middle-aged character of the meeting's organizers – carried their respective countries' flags. Each was dressed to symbolize her country's nationality laws. The closer to the Committee on Nationality's proposed standard of independent nationality for wives, "the more cheerful the colors." White meant complete equality, and was worn by a handful of Western Hemisphere nations. Pink, blue, etc., meant some change in the direction of equality. Black meant that the country was thoroughly discriminatory in its nationality laws: "and therefore," the newspaper reported, "the Dutch dress was pitch black." "It's a rather painful situation," Bakker Nort observed, for the Dutch women to be hosting this event, because "the legal situation of women [here] is still based on the obsolete principle of subjection of women to men."[19]

Even as they paraded around the room, the Council and Alliance women already knew that the Codification Conference intended to ignore their proposal. Despite their extensive preparation, their confidence, and the historic inevitability of their demand, it was clear that they could make no immediate impact on the Codification Conference itself, which was a conservative and circumspect event. National laws had begun to change, planners for the formal conference conceded, but they nonetheless regarded any incorporation of the principle of equality into international law as premature.[20] To the degree that they were prepared to face the proliferation of cases of statelessness and dual citizenship among women and children, the international jurists intended to do so with as little disruption as possible to male headship of marriage. They did not intend to engage with the larger principles that mattered to the women activists, of equality, of choice, of autonomy, and in particular of the disestablishment of male marital authority.

To make matters worse, the chairman of the Codification Conference was a longtime enemy of the Dutch woman suffrage movement. Former Prime Minister Theodorus Heemskerk had been the bane of the existence of Aletta Jacobs, the venerable foremother of Dutch suffragism. Nonetheless, in the midst of the Twee Steden meeting, Chrystal Macmillan excitedly announced that Minister Heemskerk and the official Bureau charged with the administration of the Conference would receive a small deputation of the women the next day (15 March) at the Peace Palace, at which time they would accept a copy of what Heemskerk called their "requests." But this was by no means to affect the general conference. Heemskerk had made it very clear that the women could expect little of substance from him: "we have not met to waste time in futile argument," meaning, of course, over the principle of equality for women.[21] Newspapers quoted him as describing the women's proposals as "the unattainable dream."[22] What he agreed to was a brief, largely courtesy meeting for the women activists before the Codification Conference Subcommittee on Nationality, two weeks hence. Corbett Ashby, Maria Vérone of France, Georgette Ciselet of Belgium, Louise Van Eeghen of the Netherlands (ICW), and Ingeborg Hansen of Denmark formed the joint delegation that waited on the former prime minister and his associates.

In retrospect, it is painful to observe the IAWSEC and ICW women struggling to find cause for celebration in the face of the obvious failure of these efforts. Despite the delegation's awareness of Heemskerk's hostility to their project, newspaper coverage of the event indicates that they were deferential in their meeting with him.[23] In general, they prided themselves on decorous, unified and dignified requests to men in power. Recognizing defeat and adjusting to it was a particular skill of such women, developed over years of frustration. Nevertheless they praised themselves for the breadth of the support that they had demonstrated for the principle of married women's independent nationality. As many of them pioneers in male-dominated professions, they were also genuinely proud at the number of women in the formal delegations to the Codification Conference, for which they had campaigned avidly, although from our perspective, the numbers were still tiny. Among the forty-five national delegations, there were only two regular women delegates and nine other women in subordinate positions as substitute delegates, technical advisers or secretaries.[24]

After the meeting with Heemskerk, according to one woman in the US delegation, the feminist nationality activists "unfortunately . . . thought that they had done all they needed to do, so they went home." Chrystal Macmillan and Maria Vérone were to return two weeks later for the brief formal meeting Heemskerk had promised with the Conference Nationality Subcommittee.[25] A whiff of exhaustion is detectable in their departure; perhaps another group, they hoped, "will be able to start anew with a fresh and new approach."[26] At that point, the distinguished jurists, relieved of having to address the women's demands, turned away from the issue of wives' nationality to the matter that really interested them, further refinements in the international law of the sea.

So far, most of the principals in this muted drama have been European: the men in charge of the Conference, the women who had come to plead with them for recognition of their rights and failed to get a decent hearing. Now enter the Americans, a second, more militant wave of women activists, aided by a small group of male jurists also from the Western Hemisphere who hoped for more from the Codification Conference. Together they succeeded in disrupting the course of Minister Heemskerk's tightly run juridical ship, although not in changing its ultimate direction. By Americans, I mean the United States but also, and indeed more importantly for the purposes of this particular account, Latin Americans. These Western citizens of the new world contrasted themselves to backward looking Europe: let us "see to it," US lawyer Laura Berrien declared in February 1930, "that there shall not be written into the new world law about to be born the old discriminations against women which have existed in the past."[27]

These American militants manifested a very different style than the Council and Alliance women, one that was more modern with respect to women, men, power and politics. Several of them were genuine modernists of literature and art. Some were mistresses of disarming wit, undercutting the familiar charge that feminists were all seriousness, easily ridiculed. With respect to their own sex, they were impatient with the commitment to being ladylike, with the hesitancies and moderation practiced by their immediate predecessors at The Hague. They preferred the tactical agility and boldness of a small group; able to adapt swiftly to changing circumstances, they worked as a cadre. They were also much more comfortable working with men. They liked the straightforward approach to and nearness of power that they found among men. And they also were willing and able to flirt (and sometimes more) and saw no conflict in using all avenues to power and influence, including sexuality, for their ends. With respect to the nationality issue, they were willing to risk more, even to win less. "As to asking for everything at once, on nationality," explained their spokeswoman at The Hague to a British colleague, " . . . we would rather fail the first time to get what we ask for . . . rather than to get any more world wide inequality."[28]

The confident heterosexuality of this militant crowd contrasts with the prior style of women's activism which had long thrived in a separate and parallel woman's world; modern historians have developed the term "homosocial" to describe this ardently woman-centered but not particularly sexual environment. The leading US militant activist at The Hague, Doris Stevens, was particularly well placed and comfortable with men: throughout this story she seems to have been friendly with most of the important figures in the US State Department, up to and including the Secretary, Henry L. Stimson.[29] "In all her activities, male companionship played an important role," observes historian Leila Rupp, "even in her feminist activism."[30] At the time of the Hague Conference, Stevens was married to one man, former Woodrow Wilson aide-de-camp Dudley Malone, and deep into an affair, ultimately a marriage, with another, *New Republic* writer Jonathan Mitchell. A sense of the cultural and stylistic gulf between the two wings of the women's movement is underscored by the suspicion of some IAWSEC women that Stevens' brilliant way with publicity, her ability to turn even the worst of defeats into a public relations opportunity (which we shall see soon on display at The Hague) came from her sexual power over Mitchell and other men of the press.[31]

In addition to Stevens, the militant feminist presence at The Hague relied on the backing of a growing cohort of Latin American women activists. Many of them were part of a coordinated movement for the establishment of what were called "Accion Feminista" organizations around the region, with membership drawn from the growing population of educated and professional women. Among them were Maria Robles de Mendoza, Mexican sociologist and founder of a Hispanic-based pan-American organization, the Union of American Women, and Cuban Blanche Z. De Baralt, author of an important reminiscence of Jose Marti. In Nicaragua, Cuba, Mexico, Chile and elsewhere, such women were affiliated, to one degree or another, with a growing liberal, even socialist, wave that was remaking the politics of the region. These Latin American women are crucial to my story because the vehicle for the militants at The Hague was a pan-American organization, the Inter-American Women's Commission formed in 1928 by a combination of US and Cuban feminists at a Congress of American States in Havana.[32] Without the Inter-American Women's Commission (IAWC) US militants such as Doris Stevens could not have been able to move independently of the IAWSEC/IAW Committee of Nationality within the international diplomatic circuit around the League of Nations, as the United States was not a League member.[33]

Soon after its formation in Cuba in 1928, the leaders of the IAWC set their sights on the Hague Codification Conference and raising the issue of married women's nationality there.[34] Alice Paul, the leading figure in the US militant feminist community, spent two years compiling a massive study of nationality laws, not just in the Americas, but around the world. Immediately before the Hague meeting, from 17 through 25 February 1930, Doris Stevens was back in Havana, getting formal recognition from the Pan American Union for the IAWC's position on equal nationality as a principle of international law. Armed with the official endorsement of the American republics, she returned briefly to the United States and then steamed her way to the Netherlands, arriving on 28 March, two weeks after the conference had begun, and the Alliance and Council women had departed. Stevens was determined to keep the feminist campaign alive. Along with two young French feminists Fanny Bunand-Sevastos and Simone Téry, Stevens set up shop at the Hotel Kastel Wittenburg in the suburbs of The Hague, where many delegates were staying and where lobbying could be done in the halls, in the restaurants, and throughout the grounds.

Stevens was prepared to bring popular pressure to bear on this international conference of jurists, accustomed to contemplating modest changes in legal systems without outside interference, certainly from women. But it was precisely the atmosphere of embattlement, the opposition of traditionalists, which energized militants such as her. "On the one side . . . the delegates of 45 nations armed with the full powers of their governments," she later wrote. "On the other were women leaders whose only weapons were their own convictions and their belief in the justice of their demand."[35] It was the capacity to flush out deep, hidden antagonism from under superficial gentility on which the militant method prided itself and used to justify its confrontational tactics. "Feminists have very little to fear from announced open opposition," Stevens later observed to a Panamanian ally. "It always reacts in favor of the feminists. . . . it does no good to fight in the dark."[36]

This second wave of feminists at the Hague Codification Conference worked closely with a handful of men on the inside. Two Chilean delegates were particularly valuable allies. Miguel Cruchaga, an important liberal economist and former Chilean ambassador to the United States, was the women's leading champion. A Chilean feminist wrote of him, "The feminists had raised . . . [him] as champion of equality and he was confused by the unexpected role of champion; his temperament did not ask for it."[37] Cruchaga agreed to introduce a proposal to substitute for the timid points of discussion that had been allotted to the issue of married women's nationality. His statement was simple and straightforward: "the contracting states agree that . . . there shall be no distinction based on sex in their law and practice relating to nationality."[38] Cruchaga was supported by his Chilean colleague at the Hague Conference, Alejandro Alvarez, one of the great figures of international law in this period, who championed an explicitly and proudly American approach to international law, distinguished from the European by its greater idealism, its openly progressive intent, its capacity to synthesize continental and British legal traditions, its commitment to individual rights, and its lack of taint from the failures of world war. "It is necessary to reconstruct, or for those who are afraid of the word, to renew International Law . . . by taking note of international life as at the present time and in its actual world as it exists," Alvarez wrote in his "Impressions" on the 1930 Hague Conference.[39]

One other male figure should be mentioned here among the American allies of the militant feminists at The Hague: James Brown Scott. Although Scott was not an official member of the US delegation to The Hague, he was the behind the scenes mover and shaker. Scott had met the feminists at Havana in 1928 at the time of the formation of the Inter-American Commission of Women. He immediately took up their cause, championing it at the Pan American Union, at the Institut du Droit International, and before the Carnegie Endowment of Peace, for which he served as Director of the International Law division. He was an absolutely committed feminist. Together with Alvarez, he had formed before the war the American Institute of International Law, an effort to open up a distinctly American – and openly more progressive – division of the community of international jurists.[40] When Doris Stevens observed in 1929 that "we have never made a more valuable friend," if anything she was understating Scott's potential importance to the international feminist project at The Hague.[41]

Cruchaga and Alvarez contacted their embassy in Paris to locate a Chilena with enough composure to speak for their country. And this is where Marta Vergara enters the picture. Vergara was born in 1898 to an "aristocratic but impoverished family," a class identity that later led her to participation in workers' politics and membership in the Chilean Communist party. In 1930, she was a poet and a journalist, who had recently left Salvador to live the expatriate artist's life in Montparnasse. Among other things Vergara is of interest because, unlike the US women with whom she worked so closely in 1930, she eventually combined left-wing socialist politics and a deep feminist sensibility. In the mid-1930s, she became one of the founders of the feminist popular front organization, the Movimento Pro-Emancipation de la Mujeres de Chile (MEMCH).[42] Her important role in the history of Chilean feminism, which involved bringing together advanced women's rights principles with a worker-based politics in the mid-1930s, seems to have been the result of her exposure to international feminism in The Hague in 1930.

Vergara was the first Latin American to join the militant contingent at The Hague. She was summoned to the Netherlands not because of her personal opinions but simply because she was a woman from Chile. Chile was one of only five countries which had enacted nationality laws that did not discriminate against married women; the others were

Uruguay, Paraguay, Argentina, and the Soviet Union, which sent three men to the Conference as non-voting observers. In her autobiography Vergara wrote that she was a "virgin" when it came to feminist matters and agreed to go only because the IAWC would pay her way and she could see the Rembrandts, tulips and windmills. She described her experience as a spokeswoman for women's equality as her "feminist kindergarten" and praised Doris Stevens for her non-condescending and sure-footed mentorship.[43] The episode inaugurated Vergara's career as a feminist and more generally as a political activist of the left.

March 31, the appointed time for the brief meeting of feminist nationality advocates with the Conference Subcommittee on Nationality, to which Heemskerk had agreed two weeks before, was fast approaching. Doris Stevens had convinced the IAWSEC and IAW women to allow the IAWC to participate, in the persons of herself and Marta Vergara but Vergara's arrival from France had been delayed a day. Stevens was insistent that Vergara must attend, and pressed and pressed until the other feminist activists and the chair of the subcommittee on Nationality agreed to a one-day postponement in the hearing until she got there. "As a Chilean woman," Vergara "was most precious," explained Fanny Bunand-Sevastos. Rushed to the Peace Palace, Vergara joined Stevens and the others for their first glimpse of the inner sanctum of the Conference, the Justice Hall of the Peace Palace. Beautiful paintings on the wall, observed Bunand-Sevastos, if "a little conventional," like "the men sitting around the table. . . ."[44]

When we first meet Vergara, on 1 April 1930 at this brief hearing before the Nationality Committee of the Codification Conference, she was not yet a dedicated feminist, and according to her memoirs, she felt the task assigned to her was over her head politically and intellectually. Her assignment was to assure the committee that in a country with equal nationality laws, family life had not fallen apart. "You may be sure that [women's] natural devotion will not be affected by the granting of that right [of nationality]," she duly reported to the Nationality subcommittee delegations.[45] Vergara's speech had been written for her by Benjamin Cohen, Cruchaga's secretary, and it was he who inserted the language that asked for equal nationality "as a favor" – a locution which infuriated Stevens.[46] In a photo taken of Vergara at the time of her arrival, her studied look at the camera is mysterious, postured, the very embodiment of exotic southern femininity. She is barely visible through the fur coat that she clutches around her and the dramatic cloche pulled down over her eyes. In her memoirs she wrote that she had absorbed, from her conventional female education, a prejudice against feminists, whom she identified with a repudiation of femininity.[47]

A second photograph of Vergara only a few weeks later tells a different story, and shows a remarkable change. She stands full face towards the camera, no longer swathed in an exotic fur coat. She smiles. Her face is entirely visible. She is literally beginning to open up. She was enchanted by Stevens and the other feminists she met in The Hague and quickly joined them in their efforts to reverse the Conference's – and with it the League's – stand on married women's nationality. The Hague episode gave Vergara her first experience with the revolutionary spirit in female form. Writing of the days just after the April 1 hearing, she recorded an interview with an unnamed feminist, perhaps Stevens, in which we can certainly hear Vergara's own thoughts: "Feminism absorbs everything . . . life, fortune, health and personal gifts. . . ," she quoted the unnamed feminist. "I have known women in cases of religious madness . . . I have known keen and exalted revolutionaries. But . . . here alone have I felt the deep exaltation that comes from service in behalf of a cause and of an idea."[48] Vergara was describing the thrill of the transcendent experienced in political form in the modern age and so largely prohibited to women, and it was a thrill that she could not resist. The experience remade her life and her priorities.

The pressure from the IAWC succeeded in precipitating an energetic if ultimately futile debate in the Nationality subcommittee, at which some amount of support for the Chilean equality measure was voiced. Several of the handful of women attached to national delegations spoke on behalf of greater equality for women. Ivy Williams, the first woman barrister admitted to the Bar in Great Britain, emphasized the relationship between equal nationality and women's economic position.[49] Marcelle Renson, a Belgian woman lawyer, took the more conciliatory tack of asking the jurists to consider how they would feel, as fathers, if their daughter married improvident men of foreign nationality who squandered their wealth. A male delegate, Chao Chu Wu, former Chinese Minister to the United States, took special pleasure pointing out that the laws regarding married women's nationality in his country were in advance of those in Europe.[50]

Speaking against equality in nationality, the Italian delegate was determined "to safeguard family unity and protect the married woman," not surprising in light of the political turn that Mussolini, once considered a possible champion of women's rights, had taken.

The longest and most elaborate opposition came from the Dutch delegation, delivered by its sole female member, deputy law minister L. C. (Lucy) Schonfeld-Polano. Even though the Dutch law of nationality could cost a wife married to a foreigner her citizenship, "the difficulties involved by independence are more numerous," she insisted. Schonfeld-Polano was backed up by a letter signed by other Dutch women lawyers who contended that the principle of family unity in nationality law was more necessary to protect the sex's "higher social task."[51] The feminist speakers had been warned before the hearing that "no arguments we may advance . . . will give us a single vote."[52] And indeed, when the votes were taken, early the next morning, only the Chileans voted in favor of their equality proposal. All the other delegates duly voted to send the original submissions of the preparatory committee to the final drafting committee.

A more pragmatic group might have stopped there, as these votes in the relevant subcommittee were usually taken to conclude all conference debate. But for the American militant feminists, defeat was inspiring. "Terrific odds, far from discouraging [Doris Stevens], seem only to enhance her pugnacity," wrote Simone Téry, who eagerly joined in the fight.[53] For the next two weeks they publicly challenged the jurists at every stage of the conference process, including at the final session. In published accounts, Vergara described how the women plunged into an energetic round of lobbying with delegates – those staying at the Kastel Wittenburg, in the restaurants and streets of The Hague, and especially in and around the Peace Palace, where they were a regular sight. Vergara reported that Nicholas Politis, the chair of the Nationality Subcommittee and a genteel and dapper Greek diplomat who the previous wave of women activists had regarded as moderately friendly to their cause, reacted with "fury that knew no bounds" when accosted by French writer Simone Téry. "You cannot teach me anything new," she recalled him saying. "Women are not ready to govern."[54]

The militants' combination of feminine and feminist lobbying methods seems to have impressed Vergara and her account helps us to see her in the midst of a sort of political/personal paradigmatic gender shift. "Women defend their right to exist . . . through fair play, although they know very well that generally it is easier to win by foul means," Vergara wrote. "A pair of beautiful eyes constitutes a far better argument than any speech of a solon in skirts when it comes to dealing with men. . . . Yet not even a gown from Lanvin's [she was describing the elegant Bunand-Sevastos] succeeded in softening the tyrant [at The Hague]." Thus her approval of the feminist method: "The Hague is the camp of those who wish to stand on their own feet, courageous and alert, fighting against their destiny, which heretofore has been a series of injustices."[55] Fluent in French as well as Spanish, Vergara joined the lobbying – "indefatigably."[56]

The most spectacular moment of the American militants' campaign is absent from the formal reports of the conference but dominated press coverage and shows both their weaknesses and strengths in high relief. As the date for the final formal vote neared, the women's lobbying, intended to prohibit submission of the treaty for ratification, became more intense. A local journalist reported that:

> The women stood at their posts in the marble corridors of the peace palace [lobbying delegates] . . . They seem to have become part of the landscape…. There is never any news in this conference until the women arrive …[57]

In yet another attempt to get the women off his back, Heemskerk took the unusual step of allowing himself to be photographed with them on the Peace Palace steps. The same Dutch reporter reported the accompanying dialogue:

> *Heemskerk:* This does not mean that I am of the same opinion as you women.
>
> *The women:* No indeed. We know how opposed you are to equality for women.
>
> Editorial comment: "The 78 year old jurist who had already made clear how fanciful their ambitions and expectations for equality are . . . nevertheless finds it pleasant to be in their midst.[58]

By the next day, 8 April, however, Heemskerk had had enough and gave the order to have the women ejected by the Dutch police from the palace grounds. Vergara was on her way to the Peace Palace in a taxi but was barred by the iron gate which was, for the first time in memory, closed to visitors. She was planning to confer with Cruchaga, her countryman, but could not get through the gate to submit her card and be admitted into the Palace. As always, the militants made sure that a photographer was present, who took many pictures of the event. Vergara was impressed at the militants' ability to turn the desperation and mistakes of their opponents to their own benefit: "A half an hour after the women were stopped at the gates, the press of the whole world was being informed of the incident, further strengthened with photographic evidence."[59]

The event even made the Dutch funny papers. A cartoon depicted Heemskerk, a stern God, banishing a bespectacled and nearly naked feminist delegate from the Garden of Eden of the Peace Palace. Hanging from the Tree of Knowledge were the articles of the Codification Treaty.[60] Such ridicule disturbed the ICW and IAWSEC women. Rosa Manus, the IAWSEC's woman on the scene, described the events in a letter to Carrie Chapman Catt, back in the United States:

> They worried the men morning noon and night, until the president told the police that no more women were allowed inside . . . which is of course a very bad thing for the whole movement. But this is the way they always behave.[61]

Martha Vergara was much more pleased by the ruckus. "Thus we have disturbed the quiet town of The Hague," she happily concluded.[62]

Heemskerk's action was a miscalculation. Vergara called it "the last measure of despair" and a "tribute to the feminist campaign" by highlighting his fear that the delegates might "be influenced by the women's arguments." The ban did not deter the women from meeting with delegates outside the grounds; it only brought them the press coverage that they deployed so brilliantly. Reporters were particularly offended that women journalists had been ejected along with the activists. In her autobiography Vergara describes herself as one of these, noting that even once admitted to the Peace Palace, she stayed outside in "solidarity."[63]

Politics and not just male defensiveness were at work. On chairman Heemskerk rested the responsibility for a successful Codification Conference, which in turn was to set the groundwork for the establishment of an international court; but the conference had been a failure on all subjects except for the modest agreements achieved on nationality. "As there can be no world court without a world code," a reporter observed, "the conference was determined to launch one, even at the expense of the women."[64] The proposed nationality treaty "is an offense to the dignity and honor of women all over the world," Stevens declared on 11 April. The men of the Codification Conference, "have repeated the fallacies of the past . . . [and] patched up the old humiliating system of one rule for men and another for women instead of throwing it out."[65]

At the very last day of the conference, when delegations were scheduled to sign on formally to the treaty, the feminists finally achieved a minor victory. The signatory event was at the Riddersaal, where, as Stevens noted,

> knights once frolicked . . . The delegates had dined well and no doubt amply. They were in evening dress. There was exhilaration in the air . . . The nationality convention was . . . the only document to come out of the conference . . . Then all of a sudden David Hunter Miller, head of the US delegation, went to the platform and announced that the USA would not sign.[66]

Even the militant feminists were astonished, since the US delegation had not been particularly helpful to them in earlier votes.

Two forces coincided to produce this outcome. One was that American feminists back in the US brought out the female troops for heavy-duty lobbying. President Herbert Hoover received at least three different delegations, featuring wealthy and prominent Republican women.[67] "What the great miracle to me," wrote Rosa Manus to Catt, "is how they managed to make President Hoover send a cable to the American delegation in which he told them to vote against the resolution. What kind of an influence have they?"[68] But the pressure of these women, however brilliantly mobilized, would not have had any impact had it not been for the substantial anti-League feeling within the US Congress, to which they played remorselessly. For the US Senators who publicly pledged to vote against the Nationality Treaty, the women's protest perversely served as a useful cover for isolationist sentiments in which feminist issues figured not at all.

After the events at The Hague, the IACW continued to press against ratification, and succeeded in getting several Latin American countries to refuse to sign onto the treaty. With the help of the IAWC, Marta Vergara, no longer a virgin in the ways of international politics, was appointed to a regular position on the Chilean delegation to Geneva[69] and served as the major spokeswoman for equal nationality at the League. A US feminist publication noted the audacity of her position: "heretofore women delegates have . . . [never] led a fight against the great powers. Rarely indeed has any man delegate from a small country lifted his voice against the great powers."[70] Doris Stevens paid tribute to her "brilliant work," without which they could not have possibly made the impact that they did.[71] The IAWC was able to delay the adoption of the Nationality Treaty for seven years, long enough to bring its issues to Geneva to be openly debated at the League Assembly. But in the end, the League of Nations was determined to pass the Nationality Treaty, complete with its accommodations to marital inequalities, and so it did.

Vergara and Stevens formed a bond through their feminist activism that endured through many shifts of their respective political positions.[72] In 1933, Vergara wrote from Santiago to tell Stevens that she had fallen in love with Chilean communist Marcos Chamudes, had joined the Communist party, and could no longer work in a pan-American environment, because she now saw that US imperialism would destroy Latin America. Stevens, always the pragmatist, was undaunted and assured Vergara that there must be some way for her to continue to be of use to the feminist cause. Within three years, Vergara was taking a popular front approach in which she was bringing together working-class women and progressive middle-class liberals in a socialist feminist organization – the aforementioned MEMCH. By the mid-1930s, she was once again working with Stevens in the IAWC. They continued to visit and correspond through World War II, after Vergara and Chamudes were ejected from the Communist party and moved to the United States. They shared an appreciation for each other's political skills, a fundamental feminism, and the memory of the events of 1930. In semi-retirement, Stevens wrote affectionately to Vergara, "I came across the photographs at the historic Hague Conference. It brought back many tender memories of your valor."[73]

On a larger canvas, the impact of the feminist nationality campaign in The Hague reached out in several directions. Agitation for equal nationality within the League of Nations opened up into a sustained feminist campaign there. In 1931, in response to a resolution from three Latin American delegations, the League established an official Women's Consultative Committee on Nationality, on which Vergara sat, along with women from Asia and the Middle East as well as Europe, England and the United States.[74] The committee pressed and pressed and eventually secured a resolution committing the League to a systematic study of the status of women in all member nations. But the year was 1937, and, because of the League's inability to condemn members who were waging war on other states, it was faced with collapse. Nonetheless, the notion of women's non-governmental organizations acting as formally recognized consultants to an international body as well as the plans for a formal multinational investigation into the status of women carried over into the early history of women's rights in the United Nations, founded less than a dozen years later.[75]

Looking westward, the Hague episode also invigorated the Inter-American Commission on Women. While the feminists were working in the League to defeat the Nationality Treaty that had been forged at The Hague, they were able to get the principles of equality and women's autonomy written into a Married Women's Nationality Treaty passed by the Pan American Union, at the 1933 Congress of American States in Montevideo, Uruguay. Within a few years all the American states had committed themselves to bringing their nationality laws into line with these principles. By the mid-1930s, the IAWC, which had been led in its first few years by US women, was abandoned by the US government and passed into the hands of Latin American women, many of them, like Marta Vergara, protégés of Doris Stevens. Like the various feminist efforts at the League of Nations, the Inter-American Commission on the Status of Women was a conduit into the United Nations, providing several of its original activists.[76]

Finally, the Hague event helped to invigorate feminism at the national level throughout Latin America. The seeming ability of US women to deal directly and effectively with Congress and the President, to influence their government's position on the Hague Nationality Treaty, impressed the Latin American women with the power of enfranchisement. "Why else should twenty five Senators hasten to cable and assure us of the firm attitude of the United States Senate?" wrote Vergara.[77] "The rest of the nations will receive this action with indifference, but in the United States, one cannot irritate women with impunity," she noted with obvious admiration.[78] After the Hague Convention of 1930, a generation of Latin American feminists worked to build a more aggressive, determined Latin American women's rights movement. The 1930s is the take-off decade for women's equal political rights in Latin America, beginning in 1932 in Uruguay and Brazil, followed by Cuba in 1934. In Chile, MEMCH helped to win voting rights for women at the municipal level in 1934 although it had to wait until 1949 for enfranchisement in federal elections.[79]

The battle for married women's independent nationality did not end soon and was not won easily. Although the issue was high on the list of women's rights interests in the early years of the United Nations, a binding international treaty on the Nationality of Married Women, resting on the premise that the UN was committed to "fundamental freedoms for all without distinction as to sex," was not passed until 1957, though it was quickly ratified in 1958. But as in so many cases, the consequences of this particular battle for women's equal rights must be assessed in terms of the long struggle as well as the final achievement. In the almost three decades after the Hague Conference of 1930, the international movement for independent nationality for married women provoked a multifaceted and sustained campaign for women's rights concerns at the League of Nations and the United Nations, facilitated numerous transnational interactions among women activists, helped to advance feminist movements especially in Latin America, and contributed significantly to a realignment in international feminism in the direction of the Global South. More than virtually any other women's rights struggle, even more than enfranchisement, the battle to disentangle national citizenship and marital status indicates that the achievement of full citizenship and comprehensive rights for women necessitates overriding the framework of national sovereignty and requires collaborating on an international, even transnational stage.

16

INVENTING COMMONWEALTH AND PAN-PACIFIC FEMINISMS

Australian women's internationalist activism in the 1920s–30s

Angela Woollacott

If historicising feminist internationalism is an important way for end-of-the-twentieth-century feminists to grapple with its status, problems and possibilities, seeing both historical patterns and variations from them might be an obvious step. Leila Rupp, in her valuable work on the large European- and American-dominated women's international organisations of the early twentieth century, has posited one pattern for that period. Having 'lurched slowly into motion in the years before 1914, gathered steam at the end of World War I, and nearly screeched to a halt in 1939', according to Rupp, these organisations regrouped after World War II and have continued through the rest of the century.[1] This pattern of historical emergence suggests that, while the years just prior to World War I were a foundational moment, the end of the war and then the interwar period were a time of crucial growth and consolidation for feminist internationalism. In this essay, I propose to interrogate one national cohort of internationalist feminists and their interwar activism, Australian feminists' engagement with two smaller and more specifically defined organisations, the British Commonwealth League and the Pan-Pacific Women's Association, in order to explore dynamics within feminist internationalism in this period.

Basing an essay on one national grouping of feminists may seem a paradoxical, perhaps even wrong-headed, approach to internationalism. However, my purpose is to examine the multivalent and even contradictory currents circulating within Australian feminists' internationalism in this period, and thus to raise questions about the global political views informing their activism. Framing such a study around one national grouping allows me to capture these coexisting, diverse currents. On the one hand, the British Commonwealth League (hereafter the BCL), headquartered in London but in which Australian feminists played leading roles, presents distinct evidence of continuity with the nineteenth- and early twentieth-century British imperial feminism which Antoinette Burton has so astutely analysed.[2] On the other hand, the BCL was very much a product of post-World War I internationalist zeal linked to the League of Nations, and also of changing dynamics within the British Empire and the shifting balance of power both between Britain and the white-settler dominions, and between Britain and India. At the same time, Australian women's involvement with the Pan-Pacific Women's Association (hereafter PPWA) signalled a new field of vision, one in which Australian feminists saw themselves as aligned within a

Pacific-area international context, a context that at least some associated with the future, perhaps thus implicitly seeing British Commonwealth connections as tied to the past. My aims in this essay include outlining the feminist internationalist activism of Australian women in the context of both of these organisations in the interwar period, assessing the global politics involved, considering their stances as white British dominion women in international contexts and in terms of Australia's colonisation of Aboriginal people, and historicising their activism in the broader picture of feminist internationalism.

The BCL and the PPWA share some of the features of the large international organisations which Rupp has studied, the International Council of Women, the International Alliance of Women for Suffrage and Equal Citizenship (formerly International Woman Suffrage Alliance) and the Women's International League for Peace and Freedom. Like them, the BCL and the PPWA relied upon the active membership of privileged women who could afford to pay their own travel expenses to regular meetings in (for Australian women, often very) distant cities, and who had the leisure to undertake the necessary weeks or months away from home. Moreover, the BCL and the PPWA were both, albeit to different extents, dominated by white English-speaking women. But the BCL and the PPWA each presented a significant challenge to the European and American hegemony of the three larger organisations. The BCL, while its conferences were always held in London and in that way it was congruent with the others, was constitutionally designed to spread organisational leadership between the dominions of the British Commonwealth and Britain itself, and also centrally included India.[3] The PPWA represented the global decentralisation of feminist international organisation even further. Consciously established as a regional focus for feminists distant from Europe, other than the mainland USA and Canada its national constituent committees were all outside the boundaries of Europe and North America, and its conferences moved around the Pacific. Rupp argues that, although in the interwar period they sought with measurable success to become 'truly international', and that 'challenges to feminist orientalism mounted', the large international women's organisations remained, at least until World War II, 'heavily Euro-American in composition and leadership'.[4] Looking at the BCL and the PPWA in this same period allows us to consider the ways in which global power relations operated within feminist international organisations that promised to challenge the entrenched Euro-American hegemony of the larger groups.

Rupp's pattern of historical emergence in fact fits the BCL well. During the British suffrage movement's intensive and militant phase, some Australian women, consciously proud of their own already-enfranchised (since 1902) status, participated in feminist activism in London. In 1911, when prominent Australian feminist Vida Goldstein was invited to help the cause through a lecture tour of England, one of the results of her visit was the formation in London of the Australian and New Zealand Women Voters' Committee, which aimed to draw attention to the fact that Australian and New Zealand women, voting citizens at home, suffered disenfranchisement while residing in the imperial metropole.[5] In 1913, the committee proclaimed that one of its objects was to 'help forward the Woman's Movement in every part of the British Empire'.[6] By 1914, as a result of the visits of Harriet Newcomb, from Australia but residing in London and honorary secretary of the committee, to New Zealand, Australia and South Africa, the British Dominions Woman Suffrage Union (BDWSU) was formed in order that those three countries and Canada should join forces as the self-governing dominions of the empire, and that enfranchised Australian and New Zealand women might help Canadian and South African women also attain the vote.[7] During the war, the BDWSU subordinated its suffrage work in favour of organising clothing for poor London children and war refugees, participating in feminist opposition to special wartime police powers over prostitutes, generally promoting communication among activist women in the dominions and Britain, and in particular organising three biennial conferences.[8] Having changed its name to the British Dominion Women Citizens' Union in late 1918 in honour of both British and Canadian women's enfranchisement, for a few years following the war the union organised regular meetings in London to discuss women's and empire issues.

Perhaps partly because of the retirement from BDWCU leadership of Harriet Newcomb and her (also from Australia) partner Margaret Hodge, between 1922 and 1924 the BDWCU was transformed into the British Overseas Committee of the International Woman Suffrage Alliance. In the summer of 1924, when the British Empire Exhibition staged at Wembley attracted women and men from the dominions and colonies to London to participate in this spectacle and largest-ever imperial exhibition, London-based feminists took advantage of the presence of feminists from around the empire to convene various meetings.[9] The British Overseas Committee erected a stand at the exhibition, especially to attract the attention of dominion women to international feminist issues.[10] It was in this context of renewed imperial feminist activism that in early February 1925 the British Overseas Committee convened a half-day conference on the 'whole question of the organisation of women living in the British Empire, whether enfranchised or still without their citizen rights'.[11] Many years later, M. Chave Collisson, originally from Sydney, recalled how she and Bessie Rischbieth, of Perth, Western Australia, plotted together to arrange the meeting because 'We were impressed by the need to rouse fresh interest in the work and needs of women's action overseas, then somewhat overlooked while British women sought to consolidate their position as full citizens'.[12] To an audience including women from South Africa, Australia, New Zealand and Canada, Collisson urged that there ought to be a central organisation in London to represent the interests of 'Empire women', who would benefit from the dissemination of knowledge about conditions throughout the empire, as well as from an organisation that would work for equal franchise and citizenship, and would provide hospitality to 'empire feminists' while in London. Bessie Rischbieth addressed the need for women to know about legislative changes occurring throughout the empire, and to participate in the changing relationship between Britain and the dominions.[13] If rousing British feminists out of their preoccupation with insular issues and their own partial enfranchisement was one motivation, a platform from which to boost the visibility and importance of dominion feminists, and thus overcome their subordinate status as colonials within the imperial metropolis, was very likely another. And both coexisted with strongly held feminist convictions about women's issues across the empire.

From the February conference, in May the British Commonwealth Women's Equality League was inaugurated, with the motto 'To secure equality of liberties, status and opportunities between men and women in the British Commonwealth of Nations'.[14] By July when it convened its first longer conference, the British Commonwealth League had shortened its name and Chave Collisson was its official organising secretary. The two-day conference was held in a venue very familiar to feminists, Caxton Hall in Westminster, with the announced theme of 'The Citizen Rights of Women Within the British Empire'. Significantly for an organisation which in its earlier incarnations had united white women of the self-governing dominions of the empire, the programmed speakers at this first annual BCL conference included two representatives from Bermuda, one from the British West Indies, and one from Kenya, Charlotte Despard who spoke on behalf of Irish women, and six Indians. The sessions were arranged thematically so that, for example, the afternoon on

'Economic Equality' included a speaker each from Britain, Australia, India and the British West Indies.[15] Speaking in the session on 'Political Equality', Atiya Begum Fyzee Rahamin of India began by proclaiming, 'Here we are the sisters of the vast Empire collected in this hall to-day, irrespective of caste and colour, united by a growing force, fired for the one enthusiasm to demand what is our birthright, Freedom and Equality'. At another point in her speech, Rahamin asserted that she thought 'the Conference a real God-send', and 'begged the co-operation of the Western women in convincing the politican that he must facilitate the establishment, socially and nationally, of the position of women'.[16] In the same session, Mrs MacGregor Ross of Kenya 'begged women when getting political liberty, not to forget the other races. Liberty must go beyond the boundaries of sex and race.'[17] This first full conference, then, seemed to signal that the BCL stood for racial and transnational equality among women of the British Commonwealth and Empire.

While white dominion and British women were still very much in control of the BCL, the process in which the League came to be geographically, colonially and racially more inclusive compels scrutiny, particularly for any exploration of early twentieth-century feminist internationalism. In fact, even prior to World War I, the BDWSU had shown interest in India. Antoinette Burton has demonstrated that debate about Indian women featured in the leading British feminist periodical *Common Cause* in the years immediately prior to the war,[18] which suggests that the BDWSU was very much a part of its British suffrage movement context. At its first conference, in July 1914, Carrie Chapman Catt, president of the International Woman Suffrage Alliance, had spoken on the 'Women's Movement among the Races of the East', and a reception at the International Women's Franchise Club was the venue for an address by Sarojini Naidu on 'Ideals of Indian Womanhood'. Yet, in the same year, a request from the Mussoorie Suffrage Society of North India for inclusion in the BDWSU was apparently rejected, suggesting the possibility that, while the union wanted to hear from and about Indian women, they were not then ready to include them fully as equal participants.[19] By 1918, at least partially through the work of Margaret Hodge, the BDWSU had 'draw[n] the women of India into fellowship, and awaken[ed] an interest in Indian affairs', with events such as a series of Indian teas and an address by Dr Rao on 'India's Position in the British Commonwealth'.[20] The BDWSU's biennial conference that year included a speech on women's suffrage in India, and a 'gala evening devoted to India'. *Jus Suffragii*, the organ of the International Woman Suffrage Alliance, editorialised that the 'bringing together of India and the self-governing British Dominions was perhaps one of the most notable achievements of the Conference'.[21] By 1919, the BDWCU boasted 'an Indian section'.[22] In the wake of the April 1919 Amritsar massacre, when hundreds of unarmed Indian people were shot by British troops, in July 1920 the Women's Freedom League convened a protest meeting of both Indian and British people in Central Hall, London, at which Margaret Hodge of the BDWCU presided.[23]

In September 1919 the BDWCU extended its attention in another direction, hosting an address by Solomon T. Plaatje of the South African Native Deputation, on recent land laws in South Africa and their effects on the native population.[24] According to Vida Goldstein, back in London again after attending the 1919 international women's peace conference in Zurich, and very interested in the work of the BDWCU of which she was a member, Plaatje's talk was symptomatic of a changing postwar global mood. Related to the Paris peace talks, in Goldstein's view, 'The condition of subject races in every country is coming to the front as never before; the slogan of "Self-Determination" has given them such hope & inspiration that they have come out of the seclusion of of [sic] their own countries

to London, to Paris, & compelled the attention of the working classes to their own particular grievances against Society & Governments, & to the injustices they share in common
with white workers. This awakening of coloured & other subject races has been one of the
wonders of the war period.'[25]

Goldstein's contention that the war and the global political discussions attendant upon
the Paris peace talks had altered race relations world-wide is valuable contemporary commentary, at least as context for an exploration of the shifting imperial and racial politics
within which the BCL established its Commonwealth feminist programme in 1925.
Particularly given the fact that, at the February 1925 half-day conference where the BCL
was first projected, no mention was made of including women of colour – or indeed of any
issues other than those pertaining to white dominion women – the racial and colonial politics embodied by the BCL and represented at its annual conferences for the rest of the
interwar period, and what those politics can tell us about feminist internationalism in this
era, become complex and telling issues which I shall explore below.

Three years after the formation of the BCL in London, sixteen Australian feminists, representing five Australian states and several national women's organisations, and including
some women actively engaged with the BCL, attended the first Pan-Pacific Women's
Conference in Honolulu in 1928. This first Pacific-rim women's conference included
women from New Zealand, the US, Japan, Canada, China, Hawaii, the Dutch East Indies,
the Philippines, Samoa, and Fiji. In an expanded definition of the Pacific region, India
was represented too: 'India, though not "Pacific," is Asiatic, and no conference which
would include other women of Asiatic countries would omit Indian women'.[26] The conference was held under the aegis of the Pan-Pacific Union, a body which sought to promote Pacific-region communication through topical conferences often in fields of science
or social science. In this connection to a pre-existing organisation, the Pan-Pacific
Women's Conference was not unlike the BCL's efforts to hold women's conferences in
tandem with Imperial Conferences of heads of state in London, such as the 1926 conference which debated the new status of the dominions. Bessie Rischbieth, 'Chairman' of the
Australian delegation to the Honolulu conference and who delivered a plenary address on
'The Influence of Women in Government', later commented that Australian women's participation in the Pan-Pacific conferences was important because 'Australia's opportunity,
and we hope her destiny, in the Pacific, is to help liberate the awakening East to a free part-
nership of nations by freedom of growth', a formulation which posited Australian women
as at once leaders and partners in relation to Asian and Pacific Islands women.[27] Perhaps
it was both the near simultaneity of the foundation of the two organisations, and her perception that Australian women played leading roles in them, that led Bessie Rishbieth in
her 1964 memoir of Australian women's political activism to join the history of the BCL
and the history of the Pan-Pacific Women's Association together in a chapter titled 'Brief
Histories of Two Kindred Societies'.[28]

Subsequent Pan-Pacific women's conferences were held regularly every few years,
until, as Rupp's pattern indicates, World War II caused a major hiatus, from which women
recovered their organising slowly and with difficulty. At the second conference in 1930,
held again in Hawaii, the organisation called the Pan-Pacific Women's Association was
formed; in 1955 at the Manila conference, the name was extended to the Pan-Pacific and
South-East Asia Women's Association. The 1930 constitution spelled out the association's
aims as being 'To strengthen the bonds of peace among Pacific peoples by promoting a
better understanding and friendship among the women of all Pacific countries', and 'to initiate and promote co-operation among the women of the Pacific region for the study and

betterment of existing conditions'.[29] While there were national committees within constituent countries, in fact the association's *raison d'être* was largely to stage its international women's conferences every few years, with papers focusing on women's political
and legal status, women in industry, social welfare and education, and international relations. Delegates to the 1937 conference in Vancouver believed that that conference
marked a significant move away from papers consisting of 'purely factual and statistical
information' and towards 'broad international questions'. Ironically enough, it was
decided in Vancouver that the 1940 conference, which was never held because of World
War II, was to be on 'The Study of Practical Ways and Means of Promoting International
Understanding'.[30]

An obvious similarity between the BCL and the Pan-Pacific Women's Association
(PPWA) is the fact that they both existed largely in order to convene their regular conferences, despite the BCL's annual conferences being held more often. Yet London's unwavering status as metropolitan venue for the BCL conferences suggests an imperial central
grasp on power, which is at odds with the careful geographic mobility of the Pan-Pacific
conferences, the first three of which were held in Honolulu, but which then moved in turn
to Vancouver, back to Hawaii, then New Zealand, Manila, Japan, Australia and so on. One
of the PPWA conference principles was to house the delegates together in one place pur-
posely to build international friendships and understanding,[31] a specific goal that was
never enunciated by the BCL and was perhaps less likely to be achieved at conferences in
London. A slight factor of difference between the BCL and the PPWA is that while both
Australian and New Zealand women were active in both organisations, Australian women
held a more dominant role in the BCL (indeed, Australian women were founders and leaders of the BCL, substantially outnumbered any national representation within it other than
British, and sometimes even outnumbered that[32]), while New Zealand women seem to
have been somewhat more to the fore in the PPWA.[33] Yet Australian women formed their
own Pan-Pacific Conference Women's Committee soon after the first conference in 1928,
and by 1934 an Australian, Dr Georgina Sweet, had become the PPWA's international
president.[34]

Rischbieth, in an article written for the *International Women's News* in 1941 while she
was living in London, described the PPWA conferences in stridently romantic terms captured in her subtitle 'Where East and West Meet'. As a result of the conferences held since
1928, Rischbieth claimed (regardless of the forced cancellation of the 1940 meeting) that:
'As an outcome of contact, women now realise that Eastern and Western cultures, deeply
different as they are, can be made to blend and harmonise. They know that through the
impact of Western Science, coupled with the deeper knowledge of the spiritual laws of the
East, a fuller humanity will arise and develop in the process. They realise that we are living in but half the world's culture, and therefore the next step towards world federation is
to bring about an adjustment in the relationship between East and West.' Rischbieth's
belief in the 'deeper knowledge of the spiritual laws of the East' was based on her commitment to theosophy. Kumari Jayawardena has recently argued that theosophist feminists
interested in South Asia came 'nearer the concept of sisterhood' than did Christians during the colonial period, because they 'stood firm against the colonial policies of their own
governments'.[35] Yet even in this 1941 peroration to feminist internationalism and its possibilities, Rischbieth's conception of internationalism was one in which Western women
continued as leaders and other women as the objects of their attention. In her concluding
exhortation to her readers, she urged: 'I am persuaded that the Pacific is destined to
become the new orientation ground for the splendid work already accomplished by the

indefatigable effort of women in the international field in Europe. The call goes forth then to the organised women of the Western world to turn their attention to the Pacific as a new stepping-off ground for a wider and richer internationalism.'[36]

Eleanor Hinder, an Australian who served as the programme secretary for the first Pan-Pacific conference in 1928, was a member of the delegation to that conference from China, one of three non-Chinese delegates of a five-member delegation. The constitution of this delegation reflects Western nations' intervention in China, particularly in the treaty ports, and the dominant roles of white women resident there in at least some supposedly Chinese women's organisations, such as Hinder's work for the YWCA of China.[37] (In contrast to this Western colonisation of the Chinese delegation, it is worth noting that the fifty-one-member delegation from Hawaii – quite separate from the US mainland delegation – included women of Filipina, Japanese, Chinese, Korean and Hawaiian ethnicity.[38]) Yet Hinder's hopes for the first Pan-Pacific women's conference, expressed in an article written on its eve, were founded on more critical distance from the European- and American-dominated international feminist organisations than Rischbieth expressed. While underscoring the historical significance of the large international women's organisations such as the International Council of Women, the IAW, the Women's International League for Peace and Freedom, and the World's YWCA, Hinder pointed out that three of these were based in London and one in Geneva, which made them remote to women of the Pacific. A Pacific regional international women's organisation, she suggested, could well act as a clearing house for material from these European-based organisations. But, at least as importantly, it would work to inform those organisations about the realities of Pacific women's lives, their concern with basic issues such as education, and the fact that Western-style organisation might not be the only path Pacific-area women envisaged.[39]

Despite Rischbieth's easy assumption of Western women's leadership role, it is important to acknowledge that Australian and New Zealand feminists' serious interest in the Pacific region was unusual in the 1920s and 1930s, and ought at least in part to be read as politically progressive. Although there was overlap between the women who participated in the BCL and PPWA conferences, such as Rischbieth's active role in both, some women chose one international orientation over the other. At a time when Australia's official stance on immigration, the White Australia policy, was explicitly framed to exclude Asians, women who sought to learn more about Asian women's lives and to cooperate with them on women's issues were consciously at odds with their cultural context. Moreover, in developing Australia's connections to Asian and Pacific countries, feminists were engaged in a process of redefining Australia as an Asian and Pacific nation. In the late twentieth century it has become a widely accepted yet profoundly transformative view that Australia is indeed an Asian-Pacific nation; as it is sometimes drily put, Australians have discovered that what they habitually called the Far East is in fact the near north. In the 1920s–30s, such a perspective was transgressive of most Australians' world views, and certainly of Australia's diplomatic and political alignments. In an obituary note on Rischbieth in the *International Women's News* of May 1967, her longtime IAW and BCL British colleague Margery Corbett Ashby wrote: 'To Europeans Australia was a far off member of the British Commonwealth, Bessie Rischbieth showed us Australia as a leading member of the Pan Pacific and later of South East Asia with its deep concern for the women in that vast area. She was ahead of many politicians.'[40] Interwar Australian feminists, including those who were active internationally, represented a spectrum of political views from the left to the conservative, and Bessie Rischbieth fell towards the conservative end.[41] Yet she was a feminist leader on Aboriginal issues within Australia, and regarded as progressive in her advocacy of Australian participation in the Pacific. Further, continuous feminist activism in the Pacific region in this period signalled an internationalist field of vision that broke with the British Empire and Commonwealth mould. Australians involved in the PPWA were developing feminist connections, based not on shared historical ties, but on an assumption that regional commonality could be a basis for overcoming linguistic and cultural obstacles to communication and joint endeavour to improve women's lives.

As Leila Rupp has argued, the interwar period was a crucial time for feminist internationalism. The war had compelled feminists to consider issues of international relations more urgently than before; feminist pacifism (inherently internationalist) had been both challenged and strengthened by it; and in countries where women were enfranchised, internationalist zeal spawned during the war by US President Woodrow Wilson's Fourteen Point Plan, and later by the League of Nations, contributed to women's new definitions of themselves as voting citizens, political actors who could make a difference.

For Australian feminists, postwar internationalism thrived in a significantly altered and evolving national and imperial context. The 'Commonwealth' in the British Commonwealth League's name held doubly resonant significance for Australian women. When the Australian colonies federated into one nation in 1901 they became the Commonwealth of Australia. By 1907 the term 'dominion', which had been applied to Canada since it achieved self-government in 1867, came into use as the official referent for the white-settler components of the British Empire.[42] Yet Australia's particular name continued in such currency that at the 1924 British Empire Exhibition, where the Canadian and Australian pavilions dominated all but the British Palaces of Engineering and Industry, the Canadian pavilion was located on Dominion Way and the Australian on Commonwealth Way.[43] At the same time, the realignments between Britain and its dominions in the immediate postwar years were reflected in the emergence of the term British Commonwealth, to denote the self-governing white-settler dominions in contradistinction to the dependent colonies, whose subordinate status was reflected in their continuing to be called the 'Empire'.[44] These realignments were obvious not only to the dominions and Britain, but to the rest of the world, through such developments as the dominions enjoying separate representation at both the 1919 Paris peace conference, and (as well as India) in the League of Nations; the 1926 Imperial Conference and the resultant Balfour Declaration which laid out the new relationships; and the 1931 Statute of Westminster which elaborated their legalities. To at least some Australian, Canadian, New Zealand and South African feminists, it was of great constitutional significance that, as spelled out in the Balfour Declaration, the United Kingdom and the dominions were now 'autonomous communities within the British Empire, equal in status, in no way subordinate one to another in any aspect of their domestic or external affairs, though united by a common allegiance to the Crown, and freely associated as members of the British Commonwealth of Nations'.[45] Moreover, as relations between the dominions and Britain changed, and new arrangements were devised for intergovernmental consultation, it was important to dominion feminists to support their governments' enhanced voices in Commonwealth and imperial affairs, to ensure their own access to government channels in London and in dominion capitals, and to promote reciprocal arrangements on women's issues such as married women's nationality and maintenance payments to deserted wives.

Bessie Rischbieth recorded in her political memoir that the formation of the BCL as a newly structured organisation for empire women was inevitable in the post-World War I period, because beside the dominions' changing relationship to Britain, the League of

Nations had altered international relations and with them the citizenship status of women subjects of the empire.

> Formerly, all matters of International concern, including those affecting women, had to go through the British Government. Under 'Dominion Status' such matters became the responsibility of the National Governments of the respective Dominions. Therefore, with the emergence of the League of Nations, women had to approach their particular National Government in order to place their views before that body. For this reason it became necessary to reorganise the former Dominion Woman Citizen's Union.

Yet, Rischbieth continued, some women (British rather than dominion) were reluctant to acknowledge the changes in intra-imperial relationships:

> Many women in the United Kingdom held what might be described as the old-fashioned Empire viewpoint, and they were considerably concerned over any suggested Empire change. On the other hand, there were members with a sense of the real value and equality of every part of an evolving British Commonwealth. Their attitude was that the Dominions were really self-governing Nations tied with a very close spiritual tie to the Mother Country.[46]

One way in which the BCL reflected changing intra-imperial relations through Australia's new global recognition as a nation in its own right was Bessie Rischbieth's inclusion in the official Australian delegation to the 16th Assembly of the League of Nations in Geneva in 1935, and the report she made to the BCL in London immediately after the Assembly's conclusion.[47] But there is other evidence, to be found in the reports of the BCL annual conferences, of the ways in which the BCL sought to shape feminist activism in the evolving Empire and Commonwealth.

Just as the history of the BCL's precursors reveals both white dominion women's assertion of their leadership roles, and their desires to embrace Indians and other colonised peoples of the empire, the reports of the BCL's annual conferences from 1925 to the outbreak of World War II suggest that both dynamics continued, at times perhaps despite tensions between them. The 1927 conference had as its primary theme the 'Social and industrial position of Women other than British Race, governed under the British Flag'. The preamble of the conference report claimed that 'More than 200 millions of women of other than British race are governed under the British Flag. Enfranchised women can no longer argue that they have no responsibility.'[48] Thus delineating the special responsibilities of British women who could vote, and Australians, Canadians and New Zealanders as the enfranchised women of the 'autonomous communities' in the newly realigned British Commonwealth of Nations, the conference made clear that these women's responsibilities particularly included the 'native peoples' about whom they passed four resolutions. These resolutions ranged from an assertion that 'natives' should be treated equally before the law, to urging the 'Imperial Government' to arrange for the training of 'native' women in maternity work, to urging that all commissions of enquiry into 'native problems' should include 'suitable women' and that women should be appointed 'as protectors of native women and girls'.[49] Commonwealth feminism (as opposed to imperial feminism), then, suggested that the enfranchised (white) women citizens of the dominions, not just British women, were responsible for their less fortunate imperial sisters. Particularly because

Australian and New Zealand women had been among the first enfranchised in the world, they readily positioned themselves as modern, educated women, in control of their own lives and bodies, and thus definitionally opposite to 'native women', in a fashion similar to the more recent construction of the 'Western woman', in implicit opposition to the 'average third world woman', which Chandra Talpade Mohanty has described.[50] Despite the fact that the conference paper on 'Chinese Women in Hong-Kong' was delivered by Miss Ho-Tung, and a paper on 'Indian Women and Industrialism' by Munshi Iswar Saran, in other papers, such as that by Mrs Rheinallt Jones on 'The Native Woman in S. Africa', white women spoke about and thus ostensibly on behalf of women of colour. Yet some cross-racial commentary proved controversial. Mrs Neville Rolfe's account of her 'Recent Impressions of India' drew immediate criticism from the floor from Dorothy Jinarajadasa of the Women's Indian Association, who asked for and received time on the second day's programme to express her criticism, and from Mrs S. C. Sen, who used some of her own programmed time for her paper on 'Education in India' also to criticise Rolfe's remarks. Rolfe, secretary general of the British Social Hygiene Council, in her comments on prostitution and venereal disease in India, had suggested that Indian religions, ignorance of science and absence of social responsibility for the poor were largely to blame. In response, Sen denied that Indian religions approved of prostitution, and pointed out that in fact it had flourished under British colonial rule. Jinarajadasa contended that Indians had their own traditions of social responsibility, and described Indian women's current activism on the issue of prostitution. Sen and Jinarajadasa obviously swayed the conference: when Rolfe tried to move two resolutions, the conference refused to accept them for discussion.[51] Clearly, for Sen and Jinarajadasa the issue was not just that of a white British woman representing Indian women, but the specific and critical claims she made.

Notwithstanding the hegemonic preponderance of white women on BCL conference programmes, on top of the racial and class skewing inherent to the perennial London venue, the fact that Jinarajadasa and Sen not only voiced their criticism of Rolfe's representations of Indian women, but prevailed, is significant. This incident at the 1927 conference accorded with, and was probably linked to, the BCL's positioning in the *Mother India* debate. Amid the international controversy which broke over Katherine Mayo's book *Mother India* (a polemic against the possibility of Indian self-rule) after its publication in 1927, the BCL convened an evening 'conference' in London in 'response to a general desire among women to hear the opinion of Indian men and women themselves upon the subjects dealt with in the book'. The three speakers, all Indian, included Mrs S. C. Sen.[52] Writing over two years later in *Stri Dharma*, the journal of the Women's Indian Association, Hannah Sen discussed the racial, imperial and anti-colonial nationalist ideological clashes still stirred by the *Mother India* debate. Sen reported, particularly for an Indian readership, on a conference in London in October 1929 on 'Women in India', chaired by MP Eleanor Rathbone. The major provocation at the conference, according to Sen, was a proposal 'for a new and highly paid cadre of Women's Medical Service' to include a research department. The Indian women delegates at the conference 'refused to be drawn into the trap and registered a strong protest against this scheme of exploitation'. Moreover, the Indian women claimed the right to speak for themselves and their societies – which they had not been able to do at the conference – and 'very firmly dissociated themselves from any measure that savoured of patronage or threatened to lead to racial cleavage'. While this whole conference had been an 'unhappy' event in Sen's view, it did produce at least the positive result that some 'British women' and their organisations outspokenly criticised the conference 'in loyal support of the Indian delegates'. One of the three she mentioned by name was

Chave Collisson and the British Commonwealth League.[53] Immediately after the BCL's conference on the *Mother India* debate, Collisson had in fact visited India in order to 'make connections for the League in India at Bombay, Madras and Calcutta' with Indian women's organisations.[54] Arguably, then, while perpetuating some imperial dynamics of white women's assuming a hegemonic leadership role, the BCL was at least sometimes sufficiently concerned to let colonised women speak for themselves for it to be possible to see the Commonwealth feminism they were intent on forging as relatively more egalitarian and inclusive than various stripes of imperial feminism.

The BCL's overarching aim was to build 'strong Woman's Empire Political power to be used for good'.[55] The notion of 'good' clearly left much room for interpretation. But the League's methods were straightforward. The annual conferences aimed to expose activist women to information on imperial issues, as well as to provide a venue for women from different countries to meet and discuss feminist concerns. Taking an example again from the 1927 conference, when Mrs J. D. Rheinallt Jones of Johannesburg had the floor to speak on 'The Native Women of South Africa', she took the opportunity to draw her audience's attention to a bill on the 'Colour Bar' currently before the South African Parliament, which she believed demanded world-wide scrutiny, as well as to urge her audience to inform themselves and to ask critical questions about South African rule in the South West Territory (under League of Nations mandate) and British rule in Basutoland, Swaziland and Bechuanaland.[56] In between annual conferences, the BCL relied firmly on the power of the letter. Chave Collisson as organising secretary would write, for example, to member societies in constituent countries, to inform them of resolutions passed at the conferences, to urge them to lobby their respective governments on specific issues, and to suggest that they in turn write to member societies in other countries to congratulate them on particular achievements or to offer support in current struggles.

One way in which the BCL's interwar Commonwealth feminism differed significantly from older or other versions of imperial feminism was through broadening London feminists' agendas. The slate of issues presented at BCL conferences included topics not previously adopted by metropolitan feminists: while feminist concern with the empire was anything but new, the BCL addressed itself to a range of issues concerning indigenous women. Australian feminists used their foundational and dominant role in the BCL to ensure that conferences repeatedly considered issues concerning Aboriginal women. Papers on Aboriginal women were delivered at the 1927 and 1929 conferences, and every subsequent conference up to and including 1939; speakers included white Australian feminists who were advocates for and had investigated the living conditions of Aboriginal women, Constance Ternent Cooke of South Australia, Mary Montgomery Bennett of Western Australia, and Edith Jones of Victoria. While these speakers gave their audiences broad-ranging information on the numbers, location, employment, health and welfare of both Aboriginal men and women, they drew particular attention to prostitution and sexual abuse of Aboriginal women.[57] At the instigation of Australian feminists, BCL conferences passed resolutions calling for greater Australian federal government intervention on issues of Aboriginal access to land, employment rights, health and welfare, improved cooperation between federal and state governments on Aboriginal issues, and the employment of white women with official responsibility. Fiona Paisley has argued persuasively that, particularly through their papers presented to BCL conferences in the interwar period, Australian feminists presented and publicised a radical critique of Australian government policy on Aborigines, especially Aboriginal women.[58] Bennett, Cooke, and other leading feminists actively concerned with Aboriginal issues, challenged the premise that government policy 'protected' Aborigines. They claimed that it served white rather than indigenous interests, and called instead for national policy which would effectively protect Aboriginal women from the sexual predations of white men, keep Aboriginal families intact and empower women as mothers, and provide Aboriginal people with the benefits of citizenship which were their rights as British subjects but which they were currently denied.[59] In keeping with the imperialist feminist focus on indigenous women's sexual exploitation by indigenous men, Australian feminists did criticise Aboriginal practices such as girls being married to older men, but they were more vocal about sexual exploitation by white men. Among other recommendations, feminists repeatedly urged the Australian government to employ 'suitable' and concerned white women as protectors for Aboriginal women.

In developing and pushing their radical critique of Aboriginal policy, these feminists actively sought to prod the Australian government into responsible action and to effect improvements in the lives of Aboriginal women. At the same time, they were conscious of their own positioning as white women citizens within Australia, and their and Australia's positioning within the Empire and Commonwealth. As is made clear in a July 1929 letter which Collisson, as organising secretary, wrote to the BCL's Australian constituent societies requesting their active support of BCL conference resolutions on these issues, they believed that feminist protest against the sexual exploitation of indigenous women by white men empire-wide would be helped 'if an active and forward policy in regard to the native race under the control of a young white nation, were set afoot'. Moreover, BCL leaders were anxious to push for an Aboriginal policy that was in no way 'contrary to the principles of our feminism', and to do all they could to 'strengthen the hands of the progressive women'.[60] If it is clear that white Australian women activists were claiming an important advisory role for themselves on Aboriginal issues, and hoping to entrench white women in the professional capacity of 'protectors' of Aboriginal women, their activism ought to be seen as more than just self-promotion. In a cultural context in which the belief that Aborigines were dying out was gradually being replaced by calls for their biological and cultural absorption into white society, and government policy was largely based on such racist assumptions so that Aboriginal women rather than white men were penalised for women's sexual exploitation, feminists' work to improve Aboriginal women's lives was both urgent and progressive. In a radical literary departure in the 1920s, white novelists Catherine Martin and Katharine Susannah Prichard depicted the plight of Aboriginal women for the reading public.[61] The very important contribution that Australian feminist activists made on international conference platforms was to take Australian race relations from the obscurity of the nation's backblocks, and place them firmly in the international spotlight. Nevertheless, especially given some evidence that they failed to maximise Aboriginal women's own political power,[62] the implications of their speaking for Aboriginal women demand scrutiny. While by contemporary standards it was a relatively circumspect term, their calling indigenous peoples 'less forward races' immediately indicates their conception of themselves as both superior to and responsible for indigenous women. White Australian feminists sought at once to change Australian government policy to improve conditions for Aboriginal people, to enhance their own power as enfranchised citizens within the Australian Commonwealth, to advance a feminist agenda within the British Empire and Commonwealth, and to underscore their own imperial/international[63] role as white dominion women. As Paisley has recently pointed out, the issue of citizenship was central: white feminists protested Aboriginal women's exclusion from citizenship, because they recognised the importance of their own citizenship that they were actively redefining in national, imperial and world terms.[64] The complexity of these

dynamics both defies easy categorisation and reveals the difficulties in the path of feminist internationalism, especially when that internationalism involved the double layering
of white colonial/dominion women positioning themselves as authoritative imperial and
international voices for women in whose colonisation they were implicated.

For all the internationalist zeal and altered geopolitical international relations of the
interwar period, it is clear that Commonwealth and Pan-Pacific feminisms both shared the
white English-speaking women's hegemony of the larger international women's organisations, and in some ways reconstituted other or older forms of imperial feminism. We can
see, both in the BCL and the PPWA, contradictions similar to those which Antoinette
Burton has identified within nineteenth- and early twentieth-century British feminism: the
promise and rhetoric of international sisterhood, towards which white Western women
assumed they would naturally lead other women.[65] Assumptions of white Western
women's leadership roles saturated the Western-dominated women's international organisations throughout the interwar period, not least the assumption that Western women were
well placed as current or potential experts on the status of indigenous women, and that as
experts they should then speak on colonised women's behalf. For example, at its board
meeting in September 1936 the IAW resolved to work with existing organisations 'for the
protection of native peoples' on the position of 'native women', 'that documents should
be collected on the position of native women from Colonial Institutes or Museums in
Belgium, France, Great Britain and the Netherlands', and 'to suggest to Auxiliaries in
countries with colonial possessions that they should endeavour to get women students to
take as their theses the question of the Position of Native Women'.[66] The BCL was in this
way very much in accordance with its larger internationalist feminist context. By 1930, the
second avowed object of the British Commonwealth League, listed in its constitution, was
'To secure for women of the less forward races within the British Commonwealth the
fullest possible preparation for freedom, while safeguarding them from the operations of
law or custom which degrade them as human beings'.[67] White dominion and British
women thus saw themselves as leaders, advocates and guardians of indigenous women.

When Bessie Rischbieth commented retrospectively in the early 1960s that the annual
BCL conferences in London 'have provided a meeting ground for Dominion women, and
for the many women of all races, creeds and colours living under the British flag', it could
be argued, she was inadvertently revealing that within the BCL some women were more
equal than others.[68] The hegemonic role ascribed to white dominion women is even clearer
in her formulation that: 'Overseas women who had gained [by 1925] this important new
[dominion] status were very conscious of their responsibility to work for the emancipation
and citizenship status of the millions of women who were still living in the Colonies and
Dependencies under the British flag'.[69] In her most revealing reference, in summation of
nearly four decades of BCL work, she alludes to 'the work carried out by the women of
the United Kingdom and women of the Overseas Dominions, working in close co-operation',[70] thus ultimately erasing women of colour from 'the work' altogether, other than as
constituting white women's 'responsibility'.

The BCL reflected changing intra-imperial dynamics of the interwar period in that it
insisted on the equal status with British women of women from the self-governing dominions. In its inclusion of Indian women, and support of their right to speak for themselves,
it also reflected the changing balance of power between Britain and India, as India gained
international recognition through its representation in the League of Nations, and as the
Indian National Congress increasingly gained power within the subcontinent itself. At the
same time, the BCL's vision of a united British Commonwealth, tied together in good part

by joint loyalty to the British Crown, reflected limitations on at least some members' support for anti-colonial nationalism in the non-self-governing colonies or territories of the empire. While interwar proposals for Indian self-rule were often discussed within the framework of dominion status, and thus Indian women were potentially equal partners with white-settler dominion women, the BCL did not adopt Indian nationalism as a cause. The BCL can be seen, historically, as a product of a stage of the British Empire in which progressive-minded loyalists advocated a loosening of imperial bonds in order to maintain imperial and Commonwealth unity.

It is possible to see contrasts between the global politics of the BCL and the PPWA, despite the partial overlap in their constituencies. The BCL, while supporting the continuation of imperial connections, was arguably the more effective of the two organisations in terms of direct advocacy work on feminist issues. Perhaps partly because of the organisation's adherence to an effective central leadership (within which white dominion and British women held sway), the BCL, as mentioned above, relied on directives from the organising secretary in London to urge member societies to lobby their own governments and to support the struggles of societies in other countries. The PPWA, whose organisation consisted of committees within participating countries, and whose conferences, while at first tied to Honolulu, soon moved around the Pacific in a conscious attempt at geographic inclusiveness and international diversity, did not effectively go much beyond the exchange of information and fostering of connections facilitated by its triennial conferences. The PPWA's stronger commitment to internationalism (as opposed to imperial connections) was at least in part a factor of the timing of its birth, in 1928, in contrast to the BCL's roots in its prewar precursor organisations. Ien Ang has recently urged that feminists should not aim to resolve all differences among women, but rather work towards 'a more modest feminism . . . predicated on the fundamental *limits* to the very idea of sisterhood'.[71] In this kind of frame, the PPWA's format of meeting primarily to listen to each others' papers and discussion comments, rather than to hammer out a unified agenda, can be seen as more internationalist and perhaps in that sense potentially more progressive. In these decades, however, while the BCL's feminism was constrained by its assumption that, for most non-white women, white women's speaking on their behalf was an acceptable modus operandi, it probably had more global feminist impact.

Writing in the *International Women's News* at the turn of 1941, Rischbieth directly connected the international spheres of the BCL and the PPWA by asserting that the future lay in the Pacific. Reassuring a readership whom she clearly assumed to be Western, she predicted: 'My own conviction is that the Pacific area is a place of vital destiny in coming events and a likely new focus point for the world . . . [I]t renews my courage to dwell on the possibilities of this British expansion ground "down under". Such expansion, in the new world – possibly a freer world – would be directed by the three British nations set in the Pacific: Canada, Australia and New Zealand . . . Accordingly if the centre of gravity shifts to the Commonwealth and its environs, you may feel assured that it is to an almost wholly British people.'[72] Marilyn Lake has argued that early twentieth-century Australian feminists' concern for Aboriginal women and their links with international women's organisations such as the BCL and the PPWA led them to 'an embarrassed recognition of their own and their country's racism', to an 'active engagement with women from Pacific, Asian and African countries' and to an increasing orientation toward the international arena as their political agenda was thwarted at home.[73] While this positive assessment of interwar Australian feminism has much validity, I contend that we need also to recognise critically the complexity of cross-cultural interactions and to identify the multiple and even contradictory valences in Australian feminists' internationalist activism in this period. The work of the BCL and the PPWA surely did promote international feminist connections, exchange of information and solidarity. To some degree, the BCL decentred imperial feminism and fostered direct representation of dominion and colonial women, albeit at metropolitan headquarters. The PPWA, even more decentring, sought to develop women's cooperation on women's issues across developed/developing, political, racial, religious and cultural divides. And the BCL's concern for direct participation and self-representation by Indian women was racially egalitarian.

Yet few other women of colour spoke at BCL conferences in these decades. Not only were white dominion and British women the self-assured leaders of the BCL, Rischbieth's notion of the Pacific – and thus implicitly the PPWA – as a 'British expansion ground "down under" ' indicates that she believed whiteness and Britishness qualified dominion women for leadership roles in the Pacific region as well as the British Commonwealth. Clearly Commonwealth feminism had at least partly moved away from the direct appropriation, representation and silencing of women of colour by white women that characterised versions of imperial feminism, and Pan-Pacific feminism had come into being with a more egalitarian international framework. The internationalist zeal of the interwar period impelled feminists towards cross-cultural and international discussions of women's issues, and internationalist feminist agendas. But assumptions that some women were inherently suited to lead others had left powerful legacies.

Part IV

RECONCEPTUALIZING HISTORICAL KNOWLEDGE THROUGH FEMINIST HISTORICAL PERSPECTIVES

Introductory remarks

Feminist scholarship has issued important challenges to still-prevailing paradigms of male-centered historical knowledge that have long set the standard for "general" history – political history (with its focus on nation-state formation and national governments); intellectual history, economic, social, cultural, and religious history. By insisting on the centrality of sex and gender to human sociopolitical organization and identity formation, it also challenges the paradigms of an earlier male-centered challenger – Marxist historiography – in which class occupied the central role, and the socioeconomic issues of the proletariat, or working class (mostly male), took center stage.

As feminist scholars in a number of countries challenged conventional accounts of nation-state formation, historians of feminisms have pushed these boundaries even further to illuminate, expand, and transform our understanding of whole areas of conventional historical knowledge. They reveal the extent of the "knowledge wars" that developed in the West when learned men undertook to monopolize authoritative knowledge, professionalized and institutionalized in universities, in which women found themselves unwelcome. They also expose the power of political "party-lines" and factions to shape ostensibly neutral/objective accounts of what happened. It took decades for feminist scholars to recognize that what we needed to do was not only to compile new knowledge about women and feminist campaigns, but also to ask new questions, placing gender relations and interrogations of hierarchy and power at the center of our historical analyses. We also discovered the necessity to query and dispute, as early feminist Biblical critics queried and disputed – the very construction of received wisdom – what is included, what is left out, what is valued and what is not valued. The historical study of feminisms ultimately poses fundamental questions: What do we know? How and why do we know it? And who decides? These four articles in Part IV provide illuminating responses to these questions.

Ann Taylor Allen's article on "Feminism, Social Science, and the Meanings of Modernity" documents the "flowering of feminist intellectual activity" in Europe during the later nineteenth century and into the early twentieth century. By focusing on issues addressed by women intellectuals from a variety of national cultures, reassessing the origins of the family, and challenging male rule and the subordination of women, Allen throws into question the comprehensiveness – and comprehensibility – of the still prevailing male-centered intellectual history of modern Europe. After reviewing the ideas of the canonical male thinkers on the subject, from Bachofen to Engels and Bebel, Tönnies, Simmel, and Weber, Allen turns to an analysis of the feminists' contributions and, crossing borders and languages, shows how these feminist scholars of both sexes absorbed earlier scholarship, especially Bachofen's controversial approach to "mother right," and developed entirely novel and woman-friendly responses. The new knowledge they produced was revolutionary, and it promised to be politically helpful for ending the subordination of women. Indeed, these years of the mid-to-late nineteenth century were the early years of feminist historical scholarship. By exploring the sexual politics of knowledge and focusing on ostensibly "overlooked" topics that did indeed preoccupy important male thinkers, scholars like Ann Taylor Allen demonstrate how much remains to be learned about European intellectual history, and how, by using feminist perspectives to restore gender issues to center stage in our thinking (as they generally are in real life) and to examine debates instead of linear results, feminist scholars can arrive at entirely new understandings, both then and since, that promise to turn the study of intellectual history inside-out.

Rochelle Goldberg Ruthchild's masterful survey of "Women's Suffrage and Revolution in the Russian Empire, 1905–1917," "challenges the standard paradigms about the conditions . . . that favored early woman suffrage breakthroughs." She revises earlier understandings of women's suffrage successes by comparing the important suffrage victories in Finland (1906) where both women and men obtained a parliamentary vote (the first in Europe, and, for the Finns a victory over their Swedish minority) and in Russia (1917) within the context of Russian imperial politics in a time of war, instability, and revolution. "The relatively quick women's suffrage successes there were not won through long struggles within democracies, but by revolutions bursting forth in an autocracy weakened by war," Ruthchild asserts. The Russian empire occupied a huge territory and, like the Habsburg Empire [addressed by Susan Zimmermann in Part III] encompassed many different cultures. It was, as Ruthchild points out, "hardly peripheral" to world-historical concerns; "it was neither stable, nor democratic, nor lacking class tension, but rather a highly stratified multinational empire ruled by an autocratic Tsar." Her reevaluation of the 1906 Finnish suffrage victory within the Russian imperial context (Finland, a semi-autonomous Grand Duchy under Russian control, did not achieve full independence from Russia until 1917) is long overdue as is the revisiting of the feminists' campaigns for suffrage and women's rights in Russia between 1905 and 1917. Ruthchild's careful reconstruction of events in St. Petersburg in 1917 between International Women's Day [February 23; March 8 western calendar] and the October seizure of power by the Bolsheviks, her attention to Russian feminists' contributions to the campaign for votes for the Constitutional Assembly, and her interpretative shift all demonstrate how radically different political history can look when women's participation is taken into account and when the geographic and chronological perspective is expanded beyond the purely national and short-term. Bridging Anglophone and Russian scholarship and sources, Ruthchild's article addresses and supercedes both the Finnish nationalist and the Marxist-socialist interpretative frameworks which so heavily shaped earlier accounts of these complex revolutionary events. Her research restores and rehabilitates feminist enterprise and campaigning, thereby achieving a major rethinking of and a greater appreciation for the feminists' activities.

Like Ruthchild, **Louise Edwards** challenges conventional wisdom about the advent of women's suffrage in China (accorded in 1947, not 1949), while pointing to the "unstated conventions" that underlie the error. Getting the date wrong was only a symptom of deeper problems in the writing of China's political history, where bitterly opposed political factions contended for political authority – in China's case, the Republic of China (ROC, now Taiwan), which enfranchised women in its 1947 Constitution, and the People's Republic of China (PRC, ruled by the Chinese Communist Party), whose leaders (Mao-Tse Tung and Chou En-Lai) ousted the partisans of Chiang Kai-Shek in 1949 and established a one-party authoritarian state in which the vote became meaningless. Drawing on scholarship in Chinese and in English, the author offers an illuminating and sophisticated analysis of the issues surrounding the decades of absence of actual scholarship on the Chinese women's suffrage movement. After sketching the three waves of Chinese women's suffrage activism that began in 1905, she takes a clear-eyed look at some issues that implicitly shape national suffrage narratives in the Western world – such as the very presumption of a democratic nation-state in which women wanted equal access. But that presumption – along with the possibility of closure – becomes problematic, not only in China, but in any setting in which a democratic nation-state was never put in place. Edwards's account offers an object lesson in how political struggles shape history and how the victors (in this case, the PRC) take all to the exclusion of other actors in the story. Her analysis could apply to many other societies, including the emerging nation-states of eastern Europe and central Asia, where scholarship on the suffrage movements and women's activism (in other than party and labor contexts) was deemed politically incorrect by Communist governments and has only begun to emerge since the 1990s.

Marilyn J. Boxer examines the "international career" and political and historiographical consequences of the concept "bourgeois feminism." This term, launched in the 1890s by Clara Zetkin of the German Social Democratic Party, was meant to denigrate and demean the activities of women's rights activists (who had recently claimed the label "feminists") and to discourage socialist women from cooperating with them. In Zetkin's view proletarian women could only emancipate themselves through paid labor; class, not sex, must be the most important political category. Zetkin's polemical perspective not only became the watchword in Marxist-socialist circles for many decades, including the Third International (Comintern) but it also subsequently infiltrated the very language of a more recent generation of socialist-feminists and discouraged research by historians who were wary or supercritical of earlier "bourgeois" feminist movements as a possible area of study. Through an intensive re-reading of sources and historical accounts, Boxer's bold multilingual and cross-cultural comparative challenges this previously dominant paradigm on a number of levels. She demonstrates authoritatively how past quarrels can inadvertently foreclose later research options and how historians themselves can become entangled in polemics that blind them to important and conflicting evidence. "In addition to questioning the class bases on which this long-accepted distinction rests," the author argues, "we need to create new histories of feminism that are no longer encumbered by problematic assumptions about women and putative class interests or by socialist politics of the past." This volume attests to the power scholars can attain when they cast off ideological blinders, ask new questions, and seek out a fuller range of evidence.

17

FEMINISM, SOCIAL SCIENCE, AND THE MEANINGS OF MODERNITY

The debate on the origin of the family in Europe and the United States, 1860–1914

Ann Taylor Allen

Of the year 1913, the Viennese novelist Robert Musil wrote, "The time was on the move . . . But in those days no one knew what it was moving towards. Nor could anyone quite distinguish between what was above and what was below, between what was moving forward and what backwards."[1] This new relationship to time, space, and history pervaded literature, the arts, and the social and natural sciences in Europe at the turn of the twentieth century, from about 1890 until 1914. William Everdell, the author of a recent book on the intellectual history of this era, defines its central theoretical project as "the profound rethinking of the whole mind set of the nineteenth century." This process of rethinking eroded familiar nineteenth-century European and North American paradigms: beliefs in progress and in seamless continuity were shaken by a new emphasis on rupture, randomness, and "ontological discontinuity," and reliance on scientific objectivity by a recognition of the subjective element in all thought and observation. Most of the literature on European and North American intellectual history at the turn of the century emphasizes the problematic and disorienting effects of (as Everdell puts it), "the impossibility of knowing even the simplest things that the nineteenth century took for granted."[2] In fact, the characterization of the period from 1890 to 1914 as an era of pessimism, alienation, and anxiety has become a cliché of intellectual history. In German political thought, Fritz Stern describes a mood of "cultural despair"; for the social sciences, writes Lawrence Scaff, "the central problem appears to be the same in every case: a sense that unified experience lies beyond the grasp of the modern self and that malaise and self-conscious guilt have become inextricably entwined with culture." Eugen Weber remarks that, in France at the turn of the century, "the discrepancy between material progress and spiritual dejection reminded me of my own era."[3] In Britain, the literary critic Terry Eagleton refers to a "cataclysmic crisis of Victorian rationality."[4] In the Austrian Empire, Carl Schorske describes "autumnal pessimism."[5] Even in the still optimistic culture of the United States, according to Daniel J. Wilson, philosophers faced a "crisis of confidence" as their cultural authority was challenged by the natural sciences.[6] In Western European civilization as a whole, Modris Eksteins identifies a spirit of "orgiastic-nihilistic irony" among the essential preconditions for the senseless violence of World War I.[7] The editors of a recent anthology of articles on this period, Mikulas Teich and Roy Porter, criticize the "distinctly simplistic" tendency of many historical accounts to "concentrate on individual as well as social alienation as particularly characteristic of fin de siècle feeling."[8]

"One of the tasks of women's history," wrote Joan Kelly in 1977, "is to call into question accepted schemes of periodization."[9] This article will revise the conventional picture of this era by looking at one of its most important and least recognized developments—the flowering of feminist intellectual creativity that produced some of the first scholarly analyses of the position of women in prehistory, history, and the modern era. The context for such analyses was provided by one of the era's most important intellectual controversies, which concerned the origins of the family, patriarchy, and the subordination of women. The importance of feminist scholarship to the intellectual life of this era has seldom been recognized; indeed, the accounts quoted above base their picture of Western culture at the turn of the twentieth century wholly or chiefly on the experience and ideas of one segment of the population, male academic, literary, and artistic elites. But, as Kelly suggested through the question "Did women have a Renaissance?" accepted characterizations of an era and its culture often do not include the experience of subordinated or silenced groups, and the full consideration of such groups can not only supplement but fundamentally change these characterizations. Recent developments in intellectual history, particularly the "linguistic turn," have encouraged the inclusion of subordinated groups by shifting attention away from prominent authors and their works to the many ways in which texts are read, and meaning is made, within culture. Dominick LaCapra, for example, has pointed out that ideas are created not only by individual authors but also by the many readers, commentators, and critics (or "communities of discourse") who, often over the course of many generations, discuss, revise, and expand on ideas received from the culture's dominant texts.[10] I shall demonstrate the emergence of a feminist community of discourse, and show that these feminist scholars responded to the era's changing theoretical paradigms not, as did some of their male contemporaries, with despair, anxiety, alienation, or a flight into the irrational but with a new sense of optimism and intellectual empowerment.[11]

The article will trace the debate on the origins of the family from its beginnings around 1860 until 1914, with a particular focus on the years after 1890. During the period from 1860 to 1890, the explosive expansion of data on human societies past and present provided the basis for the first evolutionary theories of the origins and development of the family. At first, these theories supported typically Victorian narratives of progress that affirmed Western forms of the patriarchal family as the culmination of human development. But around 1890, a turn to cultural relativism in the social sciences called all such paradigms—including the superiority of Western forms of the family—into question. Most existing accounts of this controversy—including those by feminist scholars—are centered chiefly or only on prominent male thinkers, and thus conclude that its result was the vindication of patriarchy.[12] I will argue that, on the contrary, the very conception of patriarchy as a historical phenomenon, contingent on time and place, provided the basis for the emergence of a feminist critique of male supremacy, in both the past and the present, that has continued throughout the century.

This critique of patriarchy emerged in the context of a much broader discourse, which included male and female, obscure and illustrious, anti-feminist and feminist speakers; the feminists' contribution will be embedded in this context. All of the theorists to be included here came from the Western world, the majority from the German and English-speaking cultures, and some from France, the Netherlands, and Scandinavia. But the significance of their ideas was by no means confined to the West. As the following pages will show, the polarity of male and female was often used as an analogy through which other polar oppositions—such as prehistory and history, civilization and barbarism, reason and emotion, *Gesellschaft* and *Gemeinschaft*—were understood. These concepts became central to the fields of anthropology, sociology, and psychology, through which Western observers interpreted both their own and non-Western cultures. As many of the feminist authors to be quoted acknowledged, their critique of patriarchy would never have been possible without the awareness of cultural variation brought by encounters with other peoples. The impact of the transition to be discussed here, from Victorian myths of progress to cultural relativism, has shaped attitudes toward gender relations and toward non-Western cultures throughout the twentieth century.

The debate on the origins of patriarchy was, of course, not new in 1860. In fact, the seventeenth-century British philosophers John Locke and Thomas Hobbes had recognized the bond of mothers to children as more natural, and thus in a sense more primary and fundamental, than that of fathers. Their conclusion, that the patriarchal family nonetheless had (in Locke's words) a "Foundation in Nature" was not so much argued as asserted on the basis of the male's natural superiority in strength and reason.[13] In the eighteenth century, missionaries such as the Jesuit Joseph François Lafitau reported matrilineal societies among the Iroquois and other Native American peoples and even speculated that this might have been the original form of the human family.[14] French women who belonged to the utopian socialist movements of the 1830s and 1840s were inspired by the Romantic movement's exaltation of nature as a source of moral values to invoke the natural mother-child bond against the injustice of a civil-law system that gave total power in the family to husbands and fathers. One such socialist author passionately asserted (in an 1834 pamphlet), "Woman is the family, and the child should bear her name."[15] But among the problems facing these early socialists was the lack of a historical basis for their challenge to the patriarchal family.

No such basis was provided by the major works on the history and status of women that appeared in the next two decades. For these works (chiefly written by male intellectuals) claimed that patriarchy had existed throughout human history. The French historian Ernest Laboulaye, who was among the first serious scholars of women's history, concluded that existing French laws on the family, as enshrined in the Napoleonic Code, represented the culmination of a history of enlightened reform.[16] Auguste Comte, founder of the field of sociology, asserted authoritatively that the present-day status of women reflected "the natural subordination of woman, which has reappeared under all forms of marriage, in all ages."[17] John Stuart Mill, though strongly dissenting from such views, nonetheless traced women's subjection to "the very earliest twilight of human society," when "every woman . . . was found in a state of bondage to some man," and saw the improvement of women's status as the necessary outcome of a general pattern of progress in Western society.[18]

By 1861, the center of the debate shifted to the new discipline of legal history. In a magisterial work, the British jurist Sir Henry Maine declared that the original basis of society was the patriarchal family, traceable not only to the Old Testament but to the Roman legal tradition that culminated in the conception of *patria potestas*. To Maine, whose chronological framework, based on biblical chronology, traced the age of the earth only to 4004 BCE, these Old Testament and classical societies seemed very close to the origin of humanity. Maine did not intend to defend this form of the family; on the contrary, he criticized current British laws and, in his most famous formulation, advocated the necessary and beneficial progress of the marriage relation "from status to contract."[19] However, even this representative example of the Victorian paradigm of progress also raised unanswerable questions. Maine, whose conception of historical development was based wholly on the decisions of lawmakers, could give no plausible explanation why this development had occurred only in Western societies.

In the middle decades of the nineteenth century, when biologically based theories of behavior had become central to scientific discourse—"for the apotheosis of Reason," remarked Mill, "we have substituted that of Instinct"[20]—such an intellectually based theory of human development could not go unchallenged. The alternative view came from an unlikely source, for the Swiss legal scholar Johann Jakob Bachofen was as far removed from feminist controversy as any conservative patrician could be. Born in 1815 into the mercantile ruling class of Basel, Bachofen studied law in several European countries. In Berlin, he studied under the legal scholar Friedrich Karl von Savigny, the prime exponent of Romantic theories of law as the expression of the history and spirit of a people; in Paris, he may well have been exposed to the work of Laboulaye among other historians; in London, he visited the British Museum. During a scholarly sojourn in Rome, he observed, with great alarm, the revolutionary events of 1848. As democratic movements in Basel threatened the position of his class, Bachofen's youthful liberalism swiftly gave way to disillusionment. In the 1850s, he gave up his university professorship and most of his public offices, withdrew to a comfortable life of independent scholarship, and pursued first medieval and then classical studies in a search for the roots from which he believed that the European civilization of his era had been so calamitously torn.[21]

At the time when Bachofen wrote, the modern fields of archaeology, anthropology, or ethnology hardly existed, and Troy, Mycenae, Knossos, and the cities of Mesopotamia were as yet unexcavated. In his search for the origins of human society, the Swiss scholar was drawn to the earliest period then known to classical scholarship, the archaic period of Greek civilization (about 1000 to 700 BCE), which, in the context of the short biblical chronology, seemed close to the beginning of the human race.[22] Bachofen's source material was limited to the relatively small number of artifacts and texts of that period to which he had access during his visits to Italy, Greece, and the British Museum. His scholarly method, which marked him as a belated representative of the Romantic movement, was regarded by his contemporaries as impossibly outdated and unscientific. This judgment has been affirmed by contemporary feminist scholars, who have criticized Bachofen for mistaking myth for history, as if his interpretation of myth had been simply erroneous or naïve.[23] But in many ways, Bachofen's analysis of mythology as a form of symbolic expression, though it looked backward to the Romantic movement, also anticipated much later insights of psychoanalysis and modern social science. Certainly, he regarded mythology as a valid historical source, though not for a factual history of events—in fact, he regarded the era's positivist historical method with great contempt. His interest, rather, was in the structures of knowledge and consciousness that underlay all events and functioned as "the lever of history."[24] The window into these deeper structures was provided by the symbolic language of mythology, which he interpreted intuitively, through "the shorter path of the imagination, traversed with the force and swiftness of electricity."[25] Bachofen (whose approach somewhat resembled that of present-day deconstructionists) read the texts of the archaic period with particular attention to their gaps, silences, and inconsistencies. These he attributed to an editing process through which traces of a more ancient narrative had been expunged from the historical record.

In a hefty and erudite volume (it contained many quotations in the original Greek) published in 1861, he announced his results: the theory that the earliest form of social organization had been based on what he called *Mutterrecht*, a family and kinship system centered on women. An elaborate evolutionary narrative explained this system's rise, fall, and replacement by patriarchy. The history of the human race, Bachofen generalized, could be understood as a struggle to rise from the material and physical to the abstract and rational level. In its earliest and most "material" stages of development, the human race had lived not in orderly nuclear families but in a state of total sexual promiscuity under the auspices of the goddess of lust, Aphrodite. As fatherhood was not known, inheritance and family structure were matrilineal. The mother-child bond was the first social tie and the basis of the first moral sensibility. "Woman at this stage," states a much-quoted passage, was "the repository of all culture, of all benevolence, of all devotion, of all concern for the living and grief for the dead."[26] The term *Mutterrecht* denoted matrilineal inheritance and family structure, and not necessarily political rule by women; the use of "matriarchate" as a translation was thus often misleading. In fact, Bachofen portrayed this first, Hobbesian stage as one of male dominance and sexual exploitation of women; and he speculated that, although men liked this existence well enough, women found it nasty, brutish, and short. Through the moral authority conferred by motherhood, they forced men to enter into marriage and familial ties, thus initiating a more genuinely matriarchal second, or Demetrian phase, in which the goddess of grain presided over a settled rural culture, marked by a reverence for the earth and for natural processes, piety, hospitality, and solidarity: "an air of tender humanity permeates the culture of the matriarchal world."[27]

But, as Bachofen recounted, this classical period of matriarchy was disrupted by women's resort to arms and violence to defend their rule against male aggression. The female warriors, or Amazons, soon converted to the new cult of Dionysus, phallic god of male fertility, who transported his female votaries into wild ecstasies of drunkenness and lust, "showing how hard it is at all times for women to observe moderation."[28] Such unfeminine excesses doomed the matriarchy, which was soon conquered by the forces of male supremacy. The victory of patriarchy was celebrated in the worship of male gods, such as Apollo, who symbolized the "heavenly light" of rationality. Maternity was a natural, paternity a legal relationship; and thus, Bachofen concluded, "the triumph of paternity brings with it the liberation of the spirit from the manifestations of nature, a sublimation of human existence over the laws of material life."[29]

Bachofen's text can be and (as we shall see) often was read as a classically "Victorian" narrative of progress and seamless development, justifying essentialist notions of male and female nature. Feminist authors of the 1970s rightly criticized his overtly Victorian notions of womanhood: "Bachofen's matriarch is a far cry from today's liberated women," complained the anthropologist Joan Bamberger.[30] However, as LaCapra has pointed out, a reading based only on the author's overt intentions can seldom capture either the complex, sometimes contradictory implications of a text or the many interpretive possibilities it offers.[31] In fact, many aspects of Bachofen's narrative subverted rather than supported the conventional assumptions of his age. Ironically, considering his conservative distaste for the Enlightenment, Bachofen lent scholarly authority to one of that era's most radical ideas: that the dominance of man over woman, like other political arrangements, was not inevitable but was contingent on time, place, and culture.[32] Moreover, this system of domination could never be secure, for the ascendancy of patriarchy depended on an imperfect process of what would later be called sublimation, and was constantly subverted by the forces of irrationality and emotionalism that Bachofen stereotyped as female, or "matriarchal." The history of culture, he wrote, showed "how hard it has been for men, at all times and amid the most varied religious constellations, to overcome the inertia of material nature and to assume the highest calling, the sublimation of earthly existence to the purity of the divine father principle."[33] And Bachofen's tone subverted his overt message, for it was elegiac rather than triumphal—a conservative dislike for modern times spoke through his poetic evocation of the organic, pious, and pacific values of the lost matriarchal world. Finally, Bachofen's picture of women was by no means totally "essentialist," for as a Romantic, he reveled in myth and history as a treasury of the grotesque, marvelous, and fantastic, and lavished his considerable literary skill on pictures of women, not just as decorous matrons but as bloodthirsty warriors, stern despots, crazed Dionysian votaries, lustful sexual predators, even as poetic lesbians. Much material would later be found to fuel the feminist imagination here.

The failure of Bachofen's weighty tome to gain public attention in the 1860s was due chiefly to its Romantic style, so alien to the positivist scholarly methods that were then at the height of their influence. But before his death in 1882, he saw many of his basic ideas affirmed by the new field of anthropology. In the 1860s, a change in chronological orientation, which the historian Thomas Trautmann has called the "time revolution," replaced the short biblical chronology with a greatly lengthened estimate of the age of the earth and of the human race. The authority of biblical and classical texts as sources for the origins of human society was now discredited, and the focus of research shifted to existing non-Western societies, which seemed to offer more reliable insights into the period of human development now known as prehistory.[34] While invalidating Bachofen's scientific framework, however, the new research paradoxically raised his status and visibility as a scholar by affirming some of his ideas, including the variability of forms of the family and the possibility, now confirmed by anthropological evidence, of woman-centered familial and kinship structures. Anthropologists first used this information to reinforce typical Victorian paradigms of progress, which ranked "savage" societies as the lowest and Western civilized societies as the highest stage of human development. "Men in savagery," wrote the American anthropologist Lewis Henry Morgan, had been providentially "left behind to testify concerning the early condition of mankind in general."[35] Morgan, who had studied the Iroquois, asserted in 1877 that family organization everywhere had developed from promiscuity through matriarchy (meaning matrilineal inheritance and an equal position for women in society) to patriarchy. The Scottish anthropologist John Ferguson McLennan reached a similar conclusion even earlier, in 1865.[36] Although they had reached these results before they read Bachofen, Morgan and McLennan subsequently acknowledged the central importance of what Morgan called his "work of vast research."[37]

In the 1880s, both the British anthropologist Edward Burnett Tylor and the German Adolf Bastian, founders of the field in their respective countries, hailed Bachofen as a pioneer and affirmed the transition from matriarchy to patriarchy as an essential and universal stage in cultural development. But the integration of Bachofen's theory into a narrative of progress from "low" to "high" civilization required the anthropologists to ignore, refute, or ridicule the aspects of his theory that questioned conventional beliefs in progress, including his interest in the mythology and legends of cultures that the new generation of scholars considered primitive. Though conceding that women's status might be higher in societies with matrilineal or matrilocal family structures, most ethnologists believed that actual female political dominance, which could not be documented in existing societies, was a fantasy. Most portrayed the period they called "matriarchal" as a brutal and barbarous period and patriarchy, though oppressive to women, as a step forward in the evolution of human culture. Morgan attributed the rise of patriarchy to the accumulation of property in the hands of men, and the British anthropologist Sir John Lubbock likewise to both the rise of private property and the development of familial love, which he identified

242

with the recognition of paternity.[38] As Elizabeth Fee points out, the overt and intentional content of early anthropological works thus certainly confirmed conventional beliefs in male supremacy.[39]

However, the expanded view of human prehistory, which had seen the rise and fall of so many human cultures, also left all essentialist notions of human nature open to contestation. The German-born socialists Karl Marx and Friedrich Engels were voracious readers of anthropological literature, particularly of the works of Morgan.[40] In his treatise *The Origin of the Family, Private Property, and the State*, written in 1884, after the death of Marx but faithful to his ideas, Engels asserted that the age of primitive matriarchy had been marked by gender equality and communal ownership of property, and that the establishment of private ownership in land and slaves had brought the "world-historical defeat of the female sex."[41] The victory of patriarchy had brought the reign not of superior rationality but of inequality and injustice.

Many works of socialist authors, among whom the most widely read was the head of the German Social Democratic Party, August Bebel, shared Engels's conception of the history of the family.[42] Their polemic against bourgeois marriage was based firmly on Bachofen's theory of primordial promiscuity, which Morgan had confirmed. Marriage, argued these socialist theorists, was not a universal aspect of human culture but had arisen only when men sought to ensure orderly inheritance by including women among their ever more numerous possessions. Engels and Bebel certainly did not advocate a return to "mother-right," which they too regarded as a primitive stage of civilization. By placing the struggle of the sexes in prehistory, the socialist theorists effectively removed it from the present; in fact, by subsuming women within the family, they denied them any other interests than those of the men of their class. Nonetheless, socialist theorists firmly insisted that patriarchy was not the culmination of a history of progress but an evanescent stage in human development that would give way to egalitarian forms of marriage and society.[43]

The same questioning about the transition from female-headed to male-headed forms of the family was also carried on in the new field of sociology. The influential Herbert Spencer, founder of the field in Britain, used anthropological data to support his theory of "Social Darwinism," which applied the laws of natural selection to the development of society. The matrilineal family, he asserted, had been inadequate to provide for its offspring; only fathers could adequately protect women and children, and thus prevailing forms of monogamous marriage were "the natural form of sexual relation for the human race."[44] But the assumption that patriarchy meant progress was vigorously challenged by the American sociologist Lester Frank Ward, who devoted much of his career to exposing and contesting Spencer's use of Darwinian theory to justify a complacent acceptance of the economic and political status quo. Ward, a convinced socialist and feminist, argued that evolutionary advantage was conferred by cooperation as well as by competition, and that the evolution of the brain had endowed human beings with the potential for more rational forms of social organization. Ward reversed dominant assumptions about gender by attributing the power to transcend "nature" through rationality to females. He based his "gynecocentric" theory of social evolution on anthropological discoveries, including "the astonishingly extensive researches of Bachofen," the works of Morgan, and on alternative interpretations of Darwinian biology. In all species from insects to human beings, he claimed that the female was the stronger and more essential organism and the male "a mere afterthought of nature."[45] Drawing on Darwin's theory of sexual selection, Ward insisted that in early human beings as in other animal species, females had originally exercised dominance in selecting their male mates as well as in other aspects of life. The matriarchal period, a period of motherly nurture, order, and nonviolence, had been disrupted only by male usurpation of power, from which all social problems, such as war, inequality, and disease, had resulted. Ward envisaged the reconciliation of the sexes through new and egalitarian forms of romantic love.[46]

Thus, by the 1890s, the Victorian narratives of progress that had justified the rise of patriarchy had already been contested, and their erosion provided an opening for some of the first explicitly feminist scholarly interpretations. The very prominent and visible American feminists Elizabeth Cady Stanton and Matilda Joslyn Gage had argued since the 1870s that the Christian churches constituted the major obstacle to the advancement of women.[47] Both Stanton and Gage were thus receptive to Bachofen's thesis, to which Stanton was introduced by the British scientist and active feminist Karl Pearson in 1890.[48] Although unable to read Bachofen's *Das Mutterrecht* in the original (which was not, and in fact has never been, fully translated into English), the American feminists could learn of its central argument from the many English-language scholarly works they used in their research, among which those of Morgan figured prominently.

Their studies resulted in two of the earliest and most significant works of feminist history: Stanton's "The Matriarchate or Mother-Age," first delivered as an address to the National Council of Women in 1891, and Gage's *Woman, Church and State: A Historical Account of the Status of Women through the Christian Ages; With Reminiscences of the Matriarchate*, first published in 1893. Although dependent on the work of male scholars, both authors also specifically contradicted conventional associations of patriarchy with progress. They refused to accept the view of the matriarchal period as a primitive phase; on the contrary, they argued that this system had prevailed in many high civilizations, including that of ancient Egypt.[49] Although Gage denied that matrilineal institutions had their origin in an age of sexual promiscuity, the less conventional Stanton was quite prepared to admit that women had first gained supremacy during a period when "sex relations being transitory and promiscuous, the idea of paternity was unknown."[50] Both portrayed the matriarchate in its period of mature development as a model of female humanitarianism, justice, and equality. And both turned Bachofen on his head; the triumph of patriarchy was not a victory for order and rationality but rather for all kinds of regression. The patriarchate, insisted Gage, "was the rule of men whose lives and religion were based on passions of the grossest kind."[51] The witch burnings of the Christian Middle Ages, both speculated, had brought the final defeat of matriarchal institutions and the descent of a patriarchal dark age.[52]

Feminist scholars not only reversed the still-conventional narrative of progress, but in the process they developed the epistemological perspective that was characteristic of the 1890s: the critique of claims to objectivity and the perception of the subjective element in all knowledge. Gage attributed androcentric theological traditions to "the overheated fires of [male] feeling"; Stanton argued that male historians wrote from their "own true inwardness" and that women must "question all historians, sacred and profane, who teach by examples or precepts any philosophy that lowers the status of the mothers of the race."[53] And for Stanton and Gage, the challenge to objectivity produced not anxiety or doubt but a new optimism and confidence. "The assertion that women have always been physically inferior to men, and consequently have always been held in a subject condition, has been universally believed," Stanton argued. "The worst feature of these assumptions is that women themselves believe them . . . Fortunately historical research has at last proved the fallacy of these assumptions and all the arguments that grow out of them."[54] However, the attempts of Gage and Stanton to gain acceptance for this view of women's history within a mainstream, organized feminist movement failed, for such movements in the United States were dominated by the religious women who would later likewise reject the great project of Stanton's last years, *The Woman's Bible*, which also contained references to the "matriarchate."[55] Perhaps for this reason, the works of Stanton and Gage were seldom cited by the next generation of feminist intellectuals.

In the decade of the 1890s, this view of matriarchy as a universal early stage in the development of human society was increasingly called into question by the newest research in the academic fields of biology, anthropology, and ethnology.[56] Darwinian theory, the social implications of which were first fully explored during this decade, compared the family patterns of human beings to those of other animals.[57] Among the most influential of the Darwinian theorists was the Finnish anthropologist Edward Westermarck. The aspect of Bachofen's and Morgan's theories that Westermarck sought to refute was the assumption, disturbing to the defenders of Christian morality, that the original and therefore perhaps the most "natural" state of human sexuality was promiscuity. Westermarck's widely read book on the origins of the family, first published in 1891, used arguments originated by Darwin to dismiss this possibility and to assert the universality of male dominance. From "what we know of the jealousy of all male quadrupeds, promiscuous intercourse is utterly unlikely to prevail in a state of nature," Westermarck argued.[58] Likewise, the period's most influential work on the origins of religion, James George Frazer's *Golden Bough* (first published in 1890) insisted that, despite the existence of matrifocal kinship systems and mother-goddesses, both marriage and male dominance were universal aspects of culture in past and present.[59]

But the effect of the new research was to introduce new questions rather than to provide answers. By the daunting profusion of his examples, Westermarck had in fact dissolved normative notions about the family and gender relations in what the sociologist C. Wright Mills later called a "lethal bath of facts" showing the immense variation in codes of sexual morality across time and space.[60] Likewise, Frazer, who found the resemblance between "savage" and Christian religious practices disturbingly close, undermined confidence in the moral superiority of Western religion and culture. These works thus dealt a major blow to linear theories of progress and encouraged the turn to cultural relativism, which affected many aspects of social-science research after 1900. As George W. Stocking remarks, this era saw the beginnings of the process of dehistoricization, through which anthropology and other social sciences changed their focus from evolution through time to variety among and within existing cultures.[61] The struggle between "primitive" and "civilized" values was no longer seen as past but as present, played out in contemporary society and, increasingly, in the individual psyche. In this context, Bachofen's work was open to a host of new interpretations. To be sure, the factual accuracy of his picture of primeval matriarchy was largely discredited in the light of more reliable data. But other aspects of his scholarly approach that had been ridiculed by the previous generation, such as his view of mythology and symbolism as windows into human consciousness, were greeted with a new enthusiasm by innovators in such fields as sociology, psychology, and psychoanalysis. Many of Bachofen's central insights—the culture-producing role of women and mothers, patriarchy as imperfect sublimation, gender relations as the basis of symbolic representation—now influenced new theoretical interpretations of contemporary Western society and the psychic forces that drove it.

Among the most important works that drew on Bachofen as well as many other texts was the German sociologist Ferdinand Tönnies' path-breaking work *Gemeinschaft und Gesellschaft* (Community and Society), first published in 1887 but not widely read until the turn of the century. Tönnies held that social bonding arose from human individual psychology and took two forms: *Gemeinschaft*, or community, and *Gesellschaft*, or society. In his preface, Tönnies paid tribute to "the inordinately informative insight with which Bachofen (*Mutterrecht*) and Morgan (*Ancient Society*) have penetrated the history of the family, the community, and institutions in general."[62] The concept of *Gemeinschaft*, or community, was based in part on Bachofen's picture of the matriarchate—it was the organic, traditional, and emotional bond of family, village, and tribe, epitomized by the mother-child relationship. *Gesellschaft*, by contrast, was the impersonal, rational, and legally regulated bond linking members of a commercial or business corporation, state bureaucracy, or other such structure, and its quintessential expression was the contract. These categories, in which all of social life was contained, were gendered; Tönnies designated *Gemeinschaft* as a feminine and *Gesellschaft* as a masculine principle, and sometimes used gender relations as an analogy for other fundamental social oppositions: "as the sexes depend upon living together . . . so stand country and city, the mass of the people and the ruling class, in mutual dependence on each other."[63]

The history of modern society, in Tönnies' analysis, had brought the predominance of *Gesellschaft* over *Gemeinschaft*, and thus the repression of female by male values. Tönnies contested the conventional association of this development with "progress." In the same elegiac tone in which Bachofen had lamented the decline of the matriarchy, he deplored the estrangement of the modern individual from the sustaining energies of home, soil, and family.[64] Tönnies' sociology thus broadened Marx's basic concept of alienation by adding a psychological and sociological dimension to its original economic meaning.[65] However, because he identified the male-stereotyped values of *Gesellschaft* with civilization, he saw little possibility for the return of *Gemeinschaft*, although late in his career he hoped that socialism might bring back some of the lost spirit of community.[66]

The gendered categories of *Gemeinschaft* and *Gesellschaft* became basic to the development of sociology at the turn of the century. Building on Tönnies' concept of alienation, Georg Simmel asserted that modern society had created cultural forms and institutions (objective culture) that, though originally intended to enhance human possibilities, had become detached and estranged from the human spirit that produced them and thus operated to confine and constrain it. Like Tönnies' *Gesellschaft*, Simmel's "objective culture" was distinctively male: "there is no sense in which culture exists in a domain that lies beyond man and woman. It is rather the case that . . . our objective culture is thoroughly male."[67] By suppressing the female, who for Simmel embodied subjectivity, emotional integrity, and a holistic view of reality, male objective culture had cut itself off from the wellspring of its original energies. Simmel, though a feminist, saw little prospect of women's advancement, for, as culture was essentially male, women could not participate in its creation without denying their basic nature.[68] Simmel influenced Max Weber, the most prominent sociologist of the era, who also insisted that the triumph of rationality and calculation over female-identified emotionality was necessary—any reversal of the process would bring disorder—and developed the metaphor of civilization as an "iron cage" to express both the inevitability and the tragedy of this development.[69] These German sociologists gained international prominence as innovators in their field and interpreters of problems that were widely regarded as common to all modern Western societies.

Such prestigious figures as Tönnies, Weber, and Simmel are often taken as representative of an age of anxiety and pessimism; as H. Stuart Hughes remarks of Weber, the vision of the future that they offered "was bleak in the extreme."[70] But in describing alienation as a universally human experience, these sociologists had failed to apply their own critique of objectivity self-reflexively and to recognize the element of subjectivity in their own ideas.[71] By contrast to this male academic elite, whose traditional cultural authority was threatened in the modern world, most feminist intellectuals of this era did not view modernity with such pessimism—though acknowledging that patriarchy was indeed an iron cage, they aspired to escape from it. The many feminist theorists of this era who cited Bachofen's and other similar theories were not primarily interested in proving the historical existence of matriarchy; in fact, many acknowledged that the scientific evidence for such a period was ambiguous. Rather, they used the concepts of matriarchy and patriarchy (as Tönnies had used "community" and "society") as ideal types, or generalized models through which to interpret complex issues. Some of the hottest public debates of the period—centered on such issues as the reform of family law, the rights of unmarried mothers and their children, the support of mothers by the state, and sexual morality—provided the context for feminists' assertions of the importance of motherhood to culture. *Das Mutterrecht* was a useful source because it described various phases of "mother-right," from promiscuity to the orderly, female-headed household, and could thus support varied approaches to sexual morality.

In France, a translation of the introduction to *Das Mutterrecht* was undertaken in 1903 by a small and vocal group of feminists, the French Group for Feminist Studies (Groupe Français d'Etudes Féministes), who focused their efforts chiefly on the reform of marriage law. They translated only Bachofen's ample introduction (the entire volume, they explained, would have been too long and therefore too expensive for most women to buy) and struggled valiantly with the "interminable sentences in which, according to the genius of the German language, the meaning appears only with the very last word."[72] In their introduction, the group's president, Jeanne Oddo-Deflou, remarked specifically on the androcentric bias of supposedly objective male scholarship and noted caustically that the rejection of Bachofen's thesis by male academics was all the more reason for feminists to take an interest in it. She rejected male scholars' association of matriarchy with primitivism and emotionality, and of patriarchy with rationality. Like Stanton, she asserted that the mother-age civilization, in which institutions and government promoted human health and welfare, had been supremely rational. It was patriarchy that had led the human race into irrationality, the prime example of which was the legal primacy given to the rights of fathers over those of mothers; other abuses had followed from this.[73] Even though Oddo-Deflou reveled in aspects of Bachofen's work, such as the exuberantly imaginative portrayal of women that more conventional scholars had dismissed, she was clearly much less interested in the historical accuracy of such images than in their symbolic appeal. She depicted the Amazons as role models for later feminist generations, although she reassured readers that contemporary Amazons aspired to conquer "without helmet or breast-plate . . . in the arena of reason."[74]

In 1905, the Group for Feminist Studies founded a periodical, *L'entente*, which published articles not only on the matriarchate but on many other aspects of women's history. The group became the center of an intellectual avant-garde stressing women's right to higher education and professional development as well as the reform of family law.[75]

French socialist feminists developed a more explicitly Marxist version of this same discourse on prehistory. The prominent theorist Aline Valette harked back to an original female-headed culture that had been destroyed by male expropriation of mothers' rights to their children—a prototype, she asserted, of the later capitalist expropriation of the workers' right to the value of their labor. Both feminist groups envisaged the result of the downfall of patriarchy not as a new mother-age but as an age of gender equality.[76]

In the English-speaking world, where women gained access to academic positions much earlier than their continental counterparts, the feminist challenge to patriarchal bias began to have a substantial impact on some academic disciplines. Among the best known of this first generation of women academics was Jane Ellen Harrison, a distinguished classical scholar and fellow of Girton College, Cambridge. Harrison was a member of a school known as the Cambridge Ritualists (also including such prominent Oxonians as Gilbert Murray), which used methods derived from the social sciences, particularly anthropology, to develop new perspectives on the Greek and Latin classics.[77] Friedrich Nietzsche, who was deeply influenced by Bachofen, had modified conventional pictures of a rational and virtuous Greek civilization by emphasizing the Greeks' emotional and licentious (or Dionysian) proclivities.[78] Harrison cited Bachofen as well as other anthropological literature to argue that the ancient matrilineal society of Greece had revered the forces of life, nature, change, and sexuality through its worship of male and female nature deities such as Dionysus. Later Greek civilizations had replaced these deities with the male-dominated Olympic pantheon (headed by the domestic tyrant Zeus) in order to impose the patriarchal conservatism that still dominated Western civilization. "In the Homeric Olympians," declared Harrison, who had defied her own conventional family to become a scholar, "we see mirrored a family group of the ordinary patriarchal type, a type so familiar that it hardly arrests attention."[79] Thus for Harrison, the idea of a matriarchal past reinforced not essentialized images of womanhood but, on the contrary, a critique of patriarchal religion in the classical past and in contemporary Western society.

Matriarchal theories also inspired many English-speaking feminist theorists of this period; only two prominent examples can be given here. Charlotte Perkins Gilman, among the most scientifically sophisticated and original minds produced by American feminism, was a great admirer of Lester Ward and his gynecocentric theory; "nothing so important to humanity," she insisted, had "been advanced since the theory of evolution."[80] Among the other influences on Gilman as well as on many of her contemporaries was the work of the American anthropologist Otis Tufton Mason, who had concluded from the profuse anthropological data on the role of women in non-Western cultures that women had been the original creators of industry, the arts, government, religion, and most other aspects of civilization.[81] Gilman argued that women had originally been the dominant sex, which needed men only (as in some animal species) for purposes of fertilization. "The woman, the mother," she declared in her treatise of 1911, "is the first coordinator, legislator, and executive."[82] The contemporary "androcentric culture," based on an irrational glorification of the trivial male fertilizing function, had "resulted in arresting the development of half the world."[83] For Gilman, "the matriarchate" functioned much more as an imaginative than as a scientific concept. Her fictional account of an all-female utopia, *Herland*, contested the conventional categories of social science by showing emotion and rationality, community and society as perfectly harmonious rather than in conflict.[84]

The British feminist Frances Swiney, who was the head of the Cheltenham Suffrage Society as well as a widely published author, cited Bachofen, Morgan, Ward, and Mason in support of a central concern of British suffragists of her era—the struggle against venereal disease, prostitution, and child mortality. Swiney was not the first to popularize these authors in Britain, for in the 1890s their theories had been discussed by such prominent reformers as the socialist and biologist Karl Pearson and the feminist author Mona Caird, both of whom were ardent believers in the "mother-age," and the essayist and novelist Olive Schreiner, a skeptic.[85] Swiney glowingly described a golden age when male sexuality had been disciplined by women to serve the needs of orderly reproduction and health. Her best-known treatise, *The Bar of Isis*, lauded the decree of this ancient mother-goddess making sexual intercourse during pregnancy and lactation unlawful. Violation of this decree by the "abnormal and fostered sexuality of the human male," she charged, had undermined the health of women, children, and the population generally and made women's bodies into "the refuse-heap of sexual pathology."[86] The League of Isis, a society Swiney founded in 1907, heralded a new age of empowered motherhood in pamphlets with such titles as "The Mother of the Race."[87] The ideas of both Gilman and Swiney were publicized in the periodicals of the British suffrage and other reform organizations.[88] Most British and American suffragists evoked the matriarchal past in support of what was called the "social purity" argument, which upheld traditional standards of female sexual morality but insisted that men, too, must follow them.[89]

However, matriarchal theories could also be used to challenge such standards, and this was by far their most controversial and notorious application. In the Netherlands and Germany, highly public debates on family law, and especially on the legal status of unmarried mothers and their children, raised questions about patriarchal family organization. Feminist groups attributed the shockingly high rate of infant mortality among "illegitimate" children to laws that in the Netherlands forbade paternity suits altogether and in Germany limited child-support obligations. Whereas most feminists in both countries argued for the enforcement of paternal responsibility, small but vocal groups dissented. Citing Bachofen in support of their contention that matriliny was the oldest and most "natural" form of the family, they argued that unmarried mothers should not be forced to undergo the humiliation of paternity suits but should instead receive financial support and legal recognition from the state.

In the Netherlands, this argument emanated chiefly from a small group who in the period 1893–1895 contributed to the journal *Evolutie*, published by the organization Vrije Vrouwen (Free Women) and edited by Wihelmina Drucker.[90] In Germany, it was most conspicuously advanced by a group founded in 1905, the Bund für Mutterschutz (League for the Protection of Mothers). The group's founder was Ruth Bré (her real name was Elisabeth Bouness), who was herself an illegitimate child. Bré proposed that unmarried mothers should form a matriarchal colony of mothers and children in the countryside, and she called on the state to support this scheme. The league soon attracted prominent figures: bourgeois feminists such as Helene Stöcker, socialists such as Lily Braun and Henriette Fürth, as well as some male sexual reformers. This new leadership rejected Bré's utopian plan on both theoretical and practical grounds. Matriarchy, insisted Helene Stöcker, had been a primitive phase of an evolutionary process that should result in the reconciliation rather than the separation of men and women.[91] Likewise, Drucker and other Dutch feminists declared that parental responsibility should be shared by men and women.

But both the German and the Dutch groups attacked the moral code that sacrificed the rights of mothers and children to those of fathers, and both demanded equal inheritance rights for illegitimate children and the support of single mothers by some form of state-sponsored insurance. A major source of theoretical and practical ideas for the League for the Protection of Mothers was the Swedish reformer Ellen Key. Though not a believer in primeval matriarchy, Key affirmed Bachofen's theory that women's motherly love had been the first form of altruism in human society, and thus the source of all "helpfulness, compassion, far-thinking tenderness, personal love."[92] She was among the first feminist theorists to propose that the state must take some responsibility for supporting children, a provision that would enable women to fulfill their desire for children without dependence on men. Key asserted that mother-headed families, though an offense to conventional notions of morality and propriety, were not contrary to nature, for they replicated "the arrangement which is already found in the lower stages of civilization, the arrangement which nature herself created."[93] Many members of the league went further to affirm what they called the New Ethic: the right of women to choose their own forms of sexual self-expression, within or outside marriage.[94] Many also advocated women's right to control their reproductive lives through access to contraception and to legalized abortion. A vision of motherhood as a creative and life-giving force, free of patriarchal restraint, inspired the program of these sex reformers. "Inviolable and universally valid is not marriage, this contract regulating sexual relations, but motherhood alone," wrote the German socialist Henriette Fürth, "the creative principle underlying all that is."[95]

The New Ethic was supported in the Netherlands only by a few intellectuals and in Germany chiefly by supporters of the League for the Protection of Mothers, which, though its total membership of 3,800 was large for such a radical group, included only a small minority of German feminists. Nonetheless, the influence of these groups on public discourse was out of all proportion to their size. The New Ethic became the fashionable topic of the day, and the German sexual radicals, in particular, influenced debates on sexual morality throughout the Western world.[96] Many members of mainstream feminist movements were alarmed at the implications of the new theories for the institution of marriage, for they feared that the subversion of laws on marriage and the normative status of the two-parent family might have disastrous consequences for the many women who were still dependent on male breadwinners.

Among the most scholarly and thoughtful of such moderate feminists was Marianne Weber, a leader of the mainstream German feminist organization, the Bund Deutscher Frauenvereine (League of German Women's Organizations). As early as 1904, Marianne Weber had warned against the tendency to believe that the matriarchal era was a "lost paradise."[97] Both she and her eminent husband, Max Weber, condemned the League for the Protection of Mothers as (in Max's professorial opinion) "an utterly confused bunch," who advocated "crass hedonism and an ethics that would benefit only men."[98] In her monumental study, *Wife and Mother in Legal History*, published in 1907, Marianne devoted an entire chapter to a refutation of Bachofen and his socialist interpreters. Matrilineal family structures, she argued, had not constituted a universal first stage of civilization, and where they had existed had not ensured a high status for women, who were usually under the control of male relatives. And marriage had not enslaved but, on the contrary, advanced women by guaranteeing the legitimate status of their children.[99] Max, who was likewise concerned about the use or misuse of scholarship to support political agendas, supported these views.[100]

However, Marianne also argued that, just as the family had evolved throughout prehistoric and historic time, it must continue to change in the direction of equality. She advocated not only equal rights for women over property and children but also divorce by mutual consent. And both she and Max, who had engaged in "countless confidential conversations" with their friends concerning personal ethics, admitted that the ideal of monogamous marriage was not attainable by everyone. Marianne emphasized in a speech of 1907 that people who did not live according to this ideal should not therefore automatically be regarded as immoral. As his biographer Arthur Mitzman has noted, Max's idea of "charisma," the revitalizing force that overcomes alienation and restores emotional wholeness, was in many ways informed by this new view of sexual morality.[101]

Another kind of objection, equally important for the future development of feminism, was raised by the French socialist feminist Madeleine Pelletier. As an amateur anthropologist, Pelletier was skeptical about the historical existence of matriarchy.[102] As a clear-sighted and uncompromising critic of gender stereotypes, she saw many dangers in her fellow feminists' high-flown exaltation of the maternal role, which she perceived as confining rather than liberating. Men's respect for motherhood or worship of mother-goddesses had not brought women equality in the past, nor would it in the future. "Future societies may build temples to motherhood," snapped Pelletier, "but only to lock women into them."[103]

Whatever their disagreements, all of these feminist thinkers cited the evolutionary history of the family to support their contention that, like earlier forms of the family, its present-day forms were also destined for extinction. Pelletier militantly advocated the right of women to control or to reject reproduction altogether through legalized contraction and abortion. Along with many other socialists, such as the American Charlotte Perkins Gilman, the Germans Lily Braun and Henriette Fürth, and the British Alice Melvin and H. G. Wells, she envisaged new forms of family organization such as the collective household, where married and single residents would share common kitchen, laundry, and childcare facilities.[104] A particularly controversial contribution to this discussion came from the young American anthropologist and student of Franz Boas, Elsie Clews Parsons, who was also influenced by the French Group for Feminist Studies.[105] In a book entitled *The Family*, which was published in 1906 as a textbook for college courses, Parsons admitted that the existence and extent of the matriarchal stage of family development was "a matter of controversy."[106] But she was in no doubt that present-day forms of male supremacy were subject to the same evolutionary forces that had shaped the family throughout its history. In order to adapt to the social conditions of the present, she argued, the family must change to provide economic independence and reproductive self-determination for women, freedom of divorce and remarriage, and tolerance for premarital sexual relations and temporary "trial marriages." In fact, she speculated, with advancing contraceptive technology, "the need for sexual restraint as we understand it may disappear."[107] "The morality of the barnyard!" fumed the *New York Herald*; "the most revolutionary and indecent performance of anything I have ever heard," agreed the reviewer for the *Evening Sun*.[108]

By 1900, the discussion of the origins and evolution of the family had become so pervasive that it included many diverse groups and provided the basis for a variety of philosophical and literary agendas. Much the best-known and most influential reception of Bachofen was by a predominantly male German avant-garde, located in Munich and clustered around the charismatic poet Stefan George. The George circle, which included many openly homosexual men, so epitomized the intellectual counter-culture of the German Empire that it was known as "das geheime Deutschland" (secret Germany). Many members of this group had connections to other prominent theorists, such as the Webers, Simmel, and the psychoanalyst Carl Gustav Jung.[109] In 1897, a subgroup that called itself the "Cosmic Circle" (Kosmische Runde), and was headed by the philosopher Ludwig Klages, the classical scholar Karl Wolfskehl, and the poet Alfred Schuler, made *Das Mutterrecht* into a cult classic.[110] Even this male-dominated group was not insulated from feminist criticism. The liveliest account of the group is a novel (*Herrn Dames Aufzeichnungen*, or *Mr. Dame's Notes*) written by one of its female members, the Countess Franziska zu Reventlow, who, like her contemporary Thomas Mann, had escaped from a proper North German family to lead a bohemian life in the Munich artists' quarter of

251

Schwabing. "Bachofen is a well-known scholar," Reventlow's protagonist is told when he arrives in Schwabing, "and if you want to live permanently in our neighborhood, you must read him."[111]

For the Cosmic Circle, the world of Bachofen's matriarchy was what Jung would later term the collective unconscious—in the words of Klages, "the original consciousness (*Urbewußtsein*) of the human race"—which had too long been repressed by a now decadent and declining civilization.[112] They proclaimed the imminent return of matriarchy, which would put an end to rationality, Christian ethics, and modern technological and social progress and liberate the bracing and purgative forces of sex, race, and blood. This vision included the "liberation" of women through sexual promiscuity and a matrilineal family structure that made paternity irrelevant. "According to Bachofen, hetaerism [promiscuity] was the earliest life-style," remarks a female character in Reventlow's novel, "and in Wahnmoching [Schwabing] we also think it's just the greatest [*die enormste*]."[113]

The Cosmic Circle, like the rest of George's entourage, rejected all of the goals of feminism along with all other manifestations of modernity. Reventlow became known as the epitome of matriarchal morality through her sexual adventures and her refusal to name the father of the resulting son, but she nonetheless saw the misogynist racist, and generally reactionary implications of the group's agenda. Not only did she poke fun at costume balls at which staid professors appeared dressed as Dionysus and engaged in pompous revelries, but she perceived that this male-defined conception of sexual "liberation" did not, in the end, liberate women: "for most of them," reflects one of her characters, "it's actually a misfortune."[114] And she also saw the cult's most sinister possibility: the creation of a pseudo-scholarly basis for the Aryan racial myth. The Cosmic Circle broke up due to the anti-Semitism of Ludwig Klages, who blamed the Jews for the development of patriarchal religion and thus for all the evils of civilization and turned this vitriolic accusation against his Jewish colleague, Wolfskehl.[115] During the 1920s, anti-Semitic interpretations of Bachofen would reinforce the growth of National Socialist ideology.

Thus in the pre-war era, the disturbing vision of female power evoked by the term "matriarchy" was no longer relegated to prehistory but was used in the present, by feminists and anti-feminists alike, to attack revered ideals of family, gender, and sexual morality. The apprehensions that this critique aroused were powerfully expressed in the visual arts of the era, in which themes from classical mythology were often used to depict the threat to civilization posed by the anarchic force of unchained feminine power.[116] Popular works such as Otto Weininger's *Sex and Character* (1903) likewise warned against the threat to Western culture posed by the growing influence of women, whom Weininger associated with irrationality and sexual disorder.[117] In the immediate pre-war years, the flamboyant and destructive tactics adopted by British militant suffragettes added to these fears. In a widely read novel of 1909, *Ann Veronica*, H. G. Wells strongly suggested that the new theories of prehistory and history encouraged the "bitter vindictiveness" and the "hostility to men" that he embodied in a fictional suffragette, Miss Miniver. "The primitive government was the Matriarchate. The Matriarchate!" she stridently proclaims. "The Lords of Creation just ran about and did what they were told."[118]

Freudian psychoanalysis, one of this period's most influential theoretical projects, was reckoned by its contemporary critics among the symptoms of this sexual disorder, but it can also be understood as an attempt to contain sex through the restabilization of patriarchy. In its fundamental philosophical and psychological assumptions, psychoanalysis owed much to the Romantic movement, and to Bachofen as its belated representative.[119] During the years 1912–1913, the debate on the origin of the family was central to the development of the psychoanalytic movement, as it was shaped by the schism between the followers of Sigmund Freud and those of his former protégé, Carl Gustav Jung. Jung was born in Basel, where Bachofen had become a legend in academic circles, and his works of this era, although they did not cite Bachofen (who was not considered scientifically reputable) clearly showed his influence. The primary attachment to the mother in the individual psyche corresponded, in Jung's system, to the original matriarchal phase of human development.[120] Among the many issues in the Freud-Jung controversy was Freud's theory that the Oedipus complex—the (male) child's incestuous desire for the mother and sexual rivalry with the father—was the universal basis of personality development. In a letter of 1912, Jung asked Freud how the Oedipus complex could have developed during the "early, cultureless period of matriarchy . . . There, the father was purely fortuitous and counted for nothing, so he would not have had the slightest interest (considering the general promiscuity) in enacting laws against the son. (In fact, there was no such thing as a father's son)."[121] During these years, Jung was strongly attracted to the ideas of the Cosmic Circle (to which he was exposed through his colleague and patient Otto Gross); he, too, was determined to overthrow the sexual repression enforced by patriarchal religious and family structure and to return to the more permissive morality he associated with the matriarchal past.[122] Freud's assertion of the universality of patriarchy was at the same time a defense of psychoanalysis against cooptation by the advocates of a sexual radicalism he abhorred. "Many authors regard a primordial state of promiscuity as unlikely," responded Freud to Jung. "Mother-right should not be confused with gynaecocracy . . . Mother-right is perfectly compatible with the polygamous abasement of woman. It seems likely that there have been father's sons at all times."[123]

Freud's treatise of 1913, *Totem and Taboo*, used anthropological data to explore the origins of patriarchy. The theoretical background to this work was the controversy over the origin of the incest taboo, which had been found to be common to all human societies. Among "primitive" peoples, anthropologists such as the British W. Robertson Smith, James George Frazer, and J. J. Atkinson had discovered that rules regulating intermarriage were enforced through the creation of groups who were forbidden to marry among themselves. These groups often imagined a distinctive totem animal as a common father and revered him through ritual feasts.[124] Atkinson started from Darwin's picture of the original human family as a horde ruled by a single dominant male, who had sexual access to all the females and drove away his sons when they became sexual rivals. He speculated that at some point one of the females had managed to prevent the banishment of her sons by inducing them to renounce sexual relations with female members of the group, thus establishing the incest taboo, the totem group, and the law of exogamy.[125]

Freud drew a more bloodthirsty picture: the adolescent sons, mad with desire for the females of the group, had banded together to kill and cannibalize the father. But then, stricken with terrible guilt, they had renounced the rewards of their crime, the sexual possession of the females, and had raised the murdered father to the status of a god (originally the totem), whom they periodically placated through the ritual enactment of the original murder and cannibal feast. Freud conceded that a period of female dominance corresponding to Bachofen's "matriarchy" might have existed after the father's murder, but the creation of a new patriarchal system had soon followed. Thus patriarchy, and its enforcement through the Oedipus complex, had developed from "this memorable, criminal act with which so many things began, social organization, moral restrictions, and religion."[126]

Freud confessed himself at a loss to "indicate the place of the great maternal deities who perhaps everywhere preceded the paternal deities," for he considered that God had always been "at bottom . . . just an exalted father."[127]

Freud's anthropology was soon challenged by experts. However, the Freudian theory of the human personality became immensely important to the culture of the 1920s, and thus has often been identified by historians as a factor in the decline of feminism during that decade.[128] But the implications of Freudian theory for feminism have in fact been more ambiguous. Freud's theory of the Oedipus complex recast Bachofen's narrative: in the life of each individual, an era of maternal love and permissiveness (infancy) is ended through the imposition of patriarchy in the form of the internalized enforcement of the incest taboo, which becomes the basis of the child's entry into the adult world.[129] By reconceptualizing a historical process as a psychic one, Freud did indeed argue that the origins of patriarchy were, and must be, replicated in each individual's development. But he nonetheless retained many aspects of the narrative's original structure as a story of conflict, repression, and sublimation. For Freud, gender consciousness is not entirely an innate characteristic but develops over the life of the individual, partly in response to culture. Thus the Freudian framework has accommodated some important feminist works, including those of Simone de Beauvoir.[130] And Freud himself did not glorify patriarchy but shared some of his con- temporaries' perceptions of its negative consequences: the reign of the father-gods still caused neurosis and misery. "It must be said that the revenge of the deposed and reinstated father has been very cruel," he concluded in *Totem and Taboo*; "it culminated in the dom- inance of authority."[131]

In 1913, in the same year as Freud wrote, the British suffragist and journalist Catherine Gascoigne Hartley told the same story with a more positive outcome to emphasize not the universality but the evanescence of patriarchy.[132] Hartley, who was widely read in femi- nist and other progressive circles, had much the same qualifications (or lack of them) for this intellectual task as her eminent contemporary; she, too, was an amateur in the field of anthropology, and she had read the same body of literature, including Bachofen and Atkinson.[133] Even though she accepted Atkinson's story of the primal family, Hartley crit- icized its highly biased assumption that the women of the group would have played a wholly passive role. On the contrary, she speculated, the first enforcement of the incest taboo must have been due to the agency of the women, who objected to the patriarch's sex- ual molestation of their daughters and banishment of their sons and, through their unity and numbers, were able to oppose his "egoistical" authority. According to Hartley, the col- lective action of the women had initiated the period of matriarchy that Bachofen had so poetically described. This was, however, a transitional period, for the young men and women sought partners from other groups and gradually built up the institution of the nuclear family, in which males gained authority. But the age of patriarchy was also clearly transitional, and contemporary developments, particularly of the women's movement, pointed the way to a new age of gender equality. "We stand in the first rush of a great movement," she concluded in 1914. "It is the day of experiments . . . We are questioning where before we have accepted, and are seeking out new ways in which mankind will go . . . will go because it must."[134]

This article has concentrated on the period from about 1860 until 1914 because these were the years when the historical origin of the family occupied a prominent position in academic and political discourse. During the 1920s, academic social scientists gave up historical for functionalist approaches to human society, which focused on the working of institutions such as patriarchy rather than on their origins.[135] And, as feminist intellectuals aspired to enter the academy, they were under pressure to conform to the norms of academic disciplines. When Mathilde Vaerting, the only woman to gain a professorship of sociology during the Weimar Republic, attempted to revive the theory of primordial matriarchy in a book published in 1921, she was derided by her colleagues for advocating "feminism in the guise of science."[136] Robert Briffault's *The Mothers*, which used the historical development of the family as an argument for the reform of marriage, was rejected as unscientific by the prominent social scientists of the day, especially by Bronislaw Malinowski, then a leading figure in the field of anthropology.[137] However, theories of matriarchal origin continued to influence many fields, including psychiatry, social theory, and political discourse on left and right.

At the dawn of the "new" feminist movement of the 1960s and 1970s, the theories of Bachofen and Engels experienced a brief revival in popular feminist literature. Troubled both by conventional ideas of biological determinism and Simone de Beauvoir's assertion that women had always been "the second sex," some feminist activists responded favorably, as had their forerunners at the turn of the century, to the picture of an age when women ruled; and socialist feminists found a powerful source of inspiration in Engels's theory that connected the oppression of women with the rise of private property and capitalism.[138] But this enthusiasm was short-lived; early texts on the origins of the family, scholars soon charged, had promoted essentialized images of women, and had furthermore been tainted with an outworn and oppressive Victorian confidence in progress and in the superiority of Western institutions.[139]

Such judgments largely ignore both the many feminist participants in the debate and its significance for the intellectual life of the period in which feminist scholarship first flourished. Far from reinforcing Victorian ideals of womanhood and the superiority of Western forms of the family, the discourse ultimately opened these ideas to contestation. Accurate knowledge of the origins of the family, wrote Elsie Clews Parsons in 1906, would sweep away "the most notable survivals of primitive taboo," which serves "the preservation of the group's social customs and traditions."[140] To conventional religious and secular ideals of the family, "that fair Family Tree," exulted Jane Ellen Harrison in 1912, "anthropology, sociology, and psychology have continued to lay the axe."[141] Although Harrison's triumphalism was clearly premature, for new theories of the natural rightness and universality of patriarchy would arise, they now had to be argued for rather than simply assumed. While today's readers can certainly see elements of essentialism in the discourse on the origins of the family, feminists of this era were far more aware of the ways in which it had undermined conventional views of women's nature and potential. In 1922, Mary Ritter Beard, who was in many ways the founder of American women's history, paid tribute in a speech given in Tokyo to the importance of anthropological discoveries for her own evolving view of the active and creative role of women in history. In 1942, Charles and Mary Beard wrote retrospectively that, by contrast to the conventional political history that entirely ignored women, anthropological literature at the turn of the century (specifically, the works of Morgan, Ward, and Otis Tufton Mason) had "found women at the very center of civilization in origin and development—as creators and preservers of the arts and that perennial moral strength of civilization."[142]

During the era from 1890 to 1914, feminist intellectuals used research in the social sciences in order to create new approaches to knowledge and new views of the historical and contemporary roles of women. Our recognition of the significance of this development should modify still-conventional views of the intellectual life of this period, which is usually characterized through terms such as "disenchantment," "cultural pessimism," and "orgiastic-nihilistic irony" and introduced by textbooks under such headings as "Culture and Crisis," "Uncertainty in Modern Thought," "From Optimism to Anxiety," and "Consciousness and Confusion."[143] If seen within the framework of the era's own critique of objectivity and emphasis on multiple perspectives, cultural pessimism represented less a universally human "modern dilemma" than the specific dilemma of male elites who, though sometimes critical of authority structures such as patriarchy, nonetheless regarded their decline as a threat to rationality, order, and civilization itself.[144] Although they shared the same analytic framework, feminist intellectuals did not respond with uncertainty, despair, or nihilism but with a new intellectual confidence; for them, the downfall of patriarchy meant not the destruction but the realization of civilization. Nineteenth-century beliefs in progress and in objectivity had justified male supremacy. The erosion of these beliefs through the new discourses on cultural relativism and historical evolution created a climate in which gender could be recognized not as ordained by divine will or by biological determinism but as constructed by history and culture. And the view of history that these feminists created emphasized not degeneration but renewal, and not the despair of rationality but new access to its empowering potential. In 1909, members of the Actresses' Franchise League, a British group that used theatrical performances to support the suffrage cause, enacted a play by Cicely Hamilton, *The Pageant of Great Women*, commemorating the achievements of women throughout history. "Feeling the riot and rush of crowding hopes," concluded a character identified only as "a woman," " 'Tis good to be alive when morning dawns."[145]

18

WOMEN'S SUFFRAGE AND REVOLUTION IN THE RUSSIAN EMPIRE, 1905–1917

Rochelle Goldberg Ruthchild

The Russian Empire was the site of two of the earliest, quickest, and most complete female suffrage breakthroughs, in Finland in 1906, and in revolutionary Russia in March and July 1917, yet their significance has been largely ignored. Historians of global feminism generally portray the first women's suffrage victories as happening in the Western democracies, colonial and post-colonial states. Some argue that early suffrage gains were won 'in nations most similar to England', 'independent, Western countries with a strong, national women's movement', or 'countries where there was no, or at most minimal, class tension'. Those favouring a more global context argue that women's suffrage first came to states and nations on the periphery, far from Europe but with strong connections to the West, like New Zealand and Australia.[1]

As part of the West or as part of the rest, Russia does not fit these paradigms. At the turn of the twentieth century, Russia was neither stable, nor democratic, nor lacking class tension, but a highly stratified multinational empire ruled by an autocratic Tsar. Although its relation to the West has been contentious, Russia, occupying the largest landmass of any country on earth, was hardly peripheral. Part of the system of European alliances, a major battlefield in Europe's wars, Russia was more central in the early twentieth century than was the United States.[2]

Lists of women's suffrage victories often omit Russia, or attribute suffrage to decrees issued by the Soviet government in the wake of the Bolshevik Revolution.[3] The invisibility of the Russian women's suffrage achievement can partially be attributed to the existing scholarship in Russian history. Most works on the late Imperial period still exclude or marginalise women, despite the fact that the field of Russian women's history has grown enormously in the last decades.[4] Historians of feminism and the Russian women's movement have made significant and path-breaking contributions. But in the prevailing Western interpretations, feminism is portrayed as a failure, its demise well underway before the Bolshevik Revolution. In this narrative, the feminists, usually categorised as 'bourgeois', or 'liberal', deserved to be marginal because their main demand, women's suffrage, was peripheral to the concerns of the female masses. Those who acknowledge the early suffrage victories downplay their significance, arguing that the women's vote changed little and in Soviet Russia was meaningless under the Bolshevik dictatorship. Some, especially post-Soviet Russian women's historians, have made significant contributions in seeking to rehabilitate the feminists, but their work has not received the attention it deserves from Western women's historians.[5]

In this article I argue that an understanding of the multiple paths to women's suffrage cannot be achieved without examining events in the Russian Empire before the October 1917 Bolshevik Revolution. This history shows that the very lack of entrenched democratic institutions could aid the success of the women's suffrage cause. The Tsarist system, based on patriarchal authority and a rigid class system, symbolised the antithesis of representative government. The relatively quick women's suffrage successes there were not won through long struggles within democracies, but by revolutions bursting forth in an autocracy weakened by war.

As has been amply demonstrated, the democratic revolutions of the late eighteenth century were not democratic for women. Both rolled back women's rights and, in France, feminist heads.[6] Nevertheless, by defining rights as based on the individual rather than a class, the American and French Revolutions inspired challenges to restrictions on the full political participation of disfranchised groups.[7]

Hard-fought struggles in the nineteenth century achieved universal male suffrage in most of the West but, despite feminist challenges, democracy remained an almost exclusively male preserve.[8] None of the major Western democracies led in extending the female vote. Left and right opposition proved effective enough to make France (1944) the last major European power to grant women the vote. Indeed, male democracy often hindered the progress of women's suffrage. Gisela Bock, in her survey of European women's history, argues that the procrastination of France and Switzerland (1971) were 'not although they were the oldest male democracies in Europe, but because they were'.[9]

The revolutions in the Russian Empire in the early twentieth century were among the first successfully to include all adult women in their demands for democracy. In the case of Finland, war, revolution, female agency, and a united nationalist movement led to victory. In Russia, two wars and two revolutions broke open the structures barring women from suffrage. Finland's achievement is noted more frequently by women's history scholars, but in both cases the role of revolution in speeding the pace of change is often ignored or downplayed.[10]

Women's suffrage in Finland

The critical factors in Finland's pioneering women's suffrage triumph had much more to do with Finland's peripheral place within the Russian Empire than its location in relation to the heartland of Europe. Ceded from Sweden to Russia in 1809, Finland was a semi-autonomous Grand Duchy. Finnish ministers reported directly to the Tsar, as Finnish Grand Duke, and his appointed Governor-General, thus bypassing the Russian bureaucracy. This autonomy was fragile. Although nominally governed by a Diet of Four Estates (nobles, clergy, peasants, and burghers), only eight percent of the population could vote for this legislature. Factory workers and landless peasants were excluded from the ballot. Real power remained in the hands of the Tsar, as the Diet could not override his vetoes.[11]

Even the trappings of Finnish autonomy, such as its own legislature, currency, postage stamps, challenged the advisors of Tsar Nicholas II, who ascended to the Russian throne in 1896. Severe Russification policies, heavy-handedly implemented by Bobrikov, Nicholas's appointee as Finnish Governor-General, stirred a massive nationalist resistance. Women, already active in women's associations and in revivalist and temperance movements, played an important part in the struggle. Some held especially influential positions. Dr. Tekla Hultin (1864–1943), a member of the *Unioni Naisasialiitto Suomessa* (Finnish

Women's Rights, or Feminist Union), was secretary to the 'father of Finland', Leo Mechelin, Vice-President of the Senate. Mechelin proved a key champion of women's suffrage.[12]

The fight for women's rights became part of not only the nationalist struggle with Russia but also the nationalist and class struggle between Swedish and Finnish speakers within Finland proper. A Bill providing for equal rights for both sexes and for women's suffrage was first introduced in the Diet in 1897. Political instability delayed consideration of the Bill until the end of 1904 and the beginning of 1905. The noble and burgher Estates, dominated by Swedish speakers, opposed the Bill; the clergy rejected women's rights on religious grounds. Only the peasant estate, which had a clear Finnish speaking majority, passed the Bill.[13]

Finland was a largely agrarian society. Almost ninety percent of the population earned their living from the land and many were landless peasants. The word for citizen in Finnish comes from *kansa*, for folk or commoners, not, as in German, from Bürger, the word for town dweller.[14] Male peasants are generally stereotyped as patriarchal and anti-feminist, but in Finland, the structure of rural society aided the fight for women's rights. Peasant traditions of gender collaboration, and women's highly visible participation in the revivalist and temperance movements, contributed to the sense of the unity of both sexes in the public sphere and in seeking national and political rights.[15]

The Finns' achievement owed its immediate impetus to the social upheaval of the 1905 Revolution in Russia, brought on by the outcome of the Russo-Japanese War of 1904–1905, the first defeat in modern history of a European by an Asian power. Finland's southeastern border was about twenty miles from the imperial capital of St. Petersburg; the Russian unrest spread quickly to the Finns. A massive Finnish general strike and demonstrations in October 1905, part of unrest throughout the Russian Empire, demanded democratic reforms, including national autonomy and universal suffrage for both sexes.[16]

Responding to the Finnish strikes, Nicholas II appointed a committee to reform the Finnish Diet and phase in universal male suffrage. In the interim, the social movement supporting women's suffrage gained strength. The first public meeting for women's suffrage attracted more than 1,000 women and marked the beginning of a large-scale petition campaign. By December 1905 the women's movement completely unified when the conservative *Suomen Naisyhdistys* (Finnish Women's Association) abandoned its previous support for limited suffrage, joining socialists and feminists in endorsing universal ballot access. Male politicians more and more viewed women's suffrage as advantageous to such causes as temperance, Finnish linguistic and cultural identity, and fiscal conservatism. In the end, pressured by events on the streets, the committee produced a proposal for a unicameral two-hundred-person legislature, elected by universal male and female suffrage.[17]

Presented with the committee report, the Tsarist bureaucrats were sceptical about the thoroughly radical step of extending the vote to women. Robert Hermanson, the chair of the Finnish committee, opposed such a change. But Leo Mechelin countered their concerns, arguing that: 'The opinion of the nation demands it, and there is no reason to fear that women will not use their vote with the same feeling of responsibility as men'.[18] On 29 May 1906, the Finnish Diet passed proposals that transformed the Finns' highly restrictive system of representation into the most democratic in the world.[19]

The reforms needed the sanction of the Russian monarch to take effect; the Tsar approved them in July 1906. Nicholas's motives had nothing to do with support for women's rights and everything to do with Finland's place in his Empire. Concessions in Finland quieted one area of disturbance, allowing the regime to focus on Russia proper. Yet by the stroke of his pen, the Tsar advanced women's rights further than had any

Western democracy. All Finnish females over the age of twenty-four gained the right to vote and to seek elective office. When the first elections were held in 1907, nineteen women, many of them members of feminist and/or socialist organisations, gained seats in the two-hundred member *Eduskunta*, the Finnish parliament, becoming the world's first female parliamentary representatives.[20]

The Finnish achievement cannot be separated from revolutionary events in the Russian Empire, and it was exceptional for its unity. Finnish-type coalitions of feminists, nationalists, and socialists including women's suffrage in demands for national autonomy and self-determination were rare. In other parts of the Empire, women activists were often stigmatised, and women's issues considered secondary to nationalist or socialist goals. In Ukraine, for example, politically active women had to overcome opposition within the nationalist movement, becoming, as Martha Bohachevsky-Chomiak has observed, 'feminists despite themselves'.[21]

The swiftness of the Finnish victory surprised and electrified international feminist activists. One Finnish feminist leader, the newspaper editor Annie Furuhjelm (1854–1937), credited Carrie Chapman Catt (1859–1947), leader of U.S. suffragists and the President of the International Woman Suffrage Alliance (henceforth the IWSA), with inspiration. Furuhjelm, rebuffed by the International Council of Women (henceforth the ICW) in her attempts to gain recognition for Finland as a separate nation, encountered Catt at the IWSA's founding congress in Berlin in 1904. Catt approved Finland's affiliation with the IWSA and Furuhjelm 'went home a suffragist'.[22] In August 1906, Furuhjelm won an enthusiastic response when she reported to the Second Conference of the IWSA, in Copenhagen. Catt hailed the Finnish achievement, noting in her speech that the attention of feminists had been turned to struggles elsewhere and then, like a bolt from the blue, 'there above us, all the women of Finland stand today. Each wears the royal crown of the sovereignty of the self-governing citizen'.[23]

Russian activists covered the Finnish suffrage struggle in articles in feminist and 'thick journals', and in pamphlets.[24] The Russians participated in the two major international women's organisations, the ICW and the IWSA; feminist periodicals kept their readers informed about events throughout the world. Still, the physical proximity, and ties of blood and political ideals especially linked progressive Finns and Russians. Socialist feminist leader Aleksandra Kollontai (1872–1952) grew up on the estate of her Finnish grandfather. Fluent in Finnish, her first major work was about the working class in Finland. In a telegram to a Finnish social-democratic women's conference, Kollontai 'happily counted herself as Finnish' by virtue of her mother's Finnish blood.[25] The *Vserossiiskii soiuz ravnopraviia zhenshchin* (All-Russian Women's Equal Rights Union) and the Finnish Women's Rights Union, exchanged letters of support at the time of the December 1905 Russian uprising. In October 1906 for the first time a delegation of three socialist feminists, Margarita Margulies, Anna Gurevich (b. 1878), and Evgeniia Rudneva, attended a meeting of the *Sosialidemokraatinen Työläisnaisliito* (Central Organisation of Social Democratic Women) in Viipuri, Finland. Congratulating the Finnish women on their suffrage victory, they hailed them as the 'free women of a free nation', and expressed their hope that the Finnish women's movement would serve as a model for Russian women.[26]

Women's suffrage in Russia

It took one war and one revolution, in 1905, to win suffrage for Finnish women; it would take another war and another revolution for women in Russia to gain their rights in 1917.

The road was harder. Russians did not achieve the unity of the Finns. Initially, key liberal leaders led the opposition to women's suffrage. Socialists attacked feminists as 'bourgeois'; feminists split amongst themselves. And the overall stance of the Tsarist government hardened against extending political rights to women. The collapse of the autocracy, feminist agency, the appeal of equal rights to the urban female masses, and the weakness of the post-revolutionary, Provisional Government, all combined to win suffrage for Russian women in twelve years.

Until 1905, in Russia, political rights were not specifically a woman's issue. The meagre amount of political participation available depended as much on class as on sex. Both female and male property owners could vote in rural and municipal government elections, though the women balloted only through a male proxy.[27]

The issues of women's and men's suffrage in Russia appeared simultaneously with the outbreak of the 1905 Revolution and demands for democratic reforms. Discontent had been brewing for some time but the spark for popular uprisings came on Bloody Sunday (9 January 1905), when troops fired on unarmed worker demonstrators marching peacefully to present a petition to the Tsar. The ensuing revolution compelled Tsar Nicholas II to issue a Manifesto on 17 October 1905, granting a number of democratic reforms, including universal male suffrage. The language of rights filled the air, permeating discussions in all classes. As Kollontai observed in 1905: 'there was no corner in which in one way or another, the voice of a woman speaking about herself and demanding new rights was not heard'.[28] To their dismay and anger, activist Russian women found that demands for 'universal suffrage' and 'equal rights' did not include them. In Saratov, women were called 'excess, unnecessary ballast' at meetings. Attempts to include female suffrage in the platforms of liberal banquets, rural assemblies, and unions of workers, peasants, and professionals were met with smirks, shrugs, or patronising explanations about their untimeliness'.[29]

The leader of the liberal Kadet Party, Paul Miliukov (1859–1943), opposed extending the franchise to women, fearing peasant women's conservatism. Although he had a summer cottage in Finland, and professed great admiration for the pro-women's suffrage nationalist leader Leo Mechelin, Miliukov took his cue from the majority of British and American liberal politicians and opposed women's suffrage.[30] Further to the left, socialist parties included women's suffrage planks in their platforms but did not make women's rights a high priority. Many socialists, male and female, echoed their comrades in the West, citing women's 'backwardness'. Those socialists seeking to organise women often differentiated themselves from the feminists with whom they had much in common in education and class origins. Kollontai, the daughter of a general, bitterly attacked adherents of female suffrage and equal rights as 'bourgeois'.[31]

The hostility or indifference to women's suffrage on the part of leading liberal and socialist male politicians shocked those educated Russian women who believed in the progressive intelligentsia's ideal of egalitarianism. Spurred on by their anger and the opportunities created by the 1905 Revolution with its loosening of Tsarist controls on the formation of political groups, these women and a few male allies formed the first feminist political organisations in Russia, and maintained an organised presence through the repression and reaction which followed the 1905 Revolution.

Three main organisations pressed demands for women's rights; they reflected the diversity of the Russian feminist movement. All three shared a belief in the need for separate women's rights organisations and for suffrage, but they differed on the questions of tactics and ideology. Two were led by physicians. None used the word feminist in their names. The oldest, the *Russkoe zhenskoe vzaimno-blagotvoritel'noe obshchestvo* (Russian Women's Mutual Philanthropic Society, henceforth called the Women's Society), founded in 1895, was heir to the early Russian feminist traditions of philanthropy and education. The two-thousand member organisation, its policies strictly controlled by an executive board dominated by the strong-willed Dr. Anna Shabanova (1848–1932), at first shunned any political involvement. A month after Bloody Sunday, the pioneer feminist leader Anna Filosofova (1835–1912) sought Society members' signatures for a mild petition protesting government repression. Some members hissed at her.[32]

Mutual Philanthropic Society women were accustomed to working through channels and using their connections to gain concessions from the autocracy. Petitions to local governments, officials, and the Council of Ministers went unanswered or were summarily rejected. In May, the Society fully committed itself to the suffrage effort, launching a full-scale campaign and deluging government agencies and officials with thousands of appeals and scores of petitions. Society members' efforts almost equalled those of larger women's rights organisations, all to no avail. Questioned about women's suffrage after the October 1905 Manifesto decreeing the first Russian parliament, or Duma, the relatively enlightened Prime Minister Sergei Witte replied that the issue had not been discussed. At a time when no European country had yet approved women's suffrage, the Tsarist government certainly was not going to be in the vanguard. But Witte was also personally opposed to extending women's rights. He told his Minister of Education I.I. Tolstoi that he considered women the 'chief carriers and inspirers of destructive ideas'. Once women got their first taste of knowledge, asserted the Prime Minister, they felt obliged to be ' "progressive" and the enemies of all "routines" and backwardness'.[33]

To Shabanova, the failure to consider female suffrage amounted to equating women 'with minors, the retarded, or criminals'.[34] Belatedly acknowledging their changing role, Society members in December 1906 voted to establish a separate Suffrage Section. Its enhanced political activism brought the Society greater police harassment, including the cancellation of a talk by the septuagenarian Filosofova. But the most conservative of Russian suffrage groups proved the longest-lived, continuing its activities until 1917.[35]

Russia was the home to one of the first women's political parties in the world. Founded in December 1905 by Dr. Maria Pokrovskaia (1852–1922), the *Zhenskaia progressivnaia partiia* (Women's Progressive Party) reflected her populist concern for the poor, combined with militant feminism. As a municipal doctor in the slums of St. Petersburg, Pokrovskaia had seen firsthand the toll taken by overcrowded living conditions, inadequate diet, inhuman work schedules, and inferior healthcare. As a result, Pokrovskaia's Progressive Party platform included demands not only for civil and political liberties, equal rights, and suffrage, but also for the 'elimination of the unfair distribution of wealth and the just payment of labour'.[36]

The peripatetic Pokrovskaia edited and published the longest-lived Russian feminist journal *Zhenskii vestnik* (Women's Herald) from 1904 to 1917 on a shoestring.[37] Pokrovskaia's positions were closest to radical feminism. Women, she wrote, 'have the fewest rights and are the most deprived part of the population'. In her view, the events of 1905 only confirmed the political selfishness of men and their need to maintain the economic dependence of women. No male-dominated party, she argued, could really champion the interests of women. Like many Western feminists, Pokrovskaia argued that women were morally superior to men and therefore better suited to the practice of politics.[38]

The largest and most heterogeneous feminist organisation was the *Soiuz ravnopravnosti zhenshchin* (Women's Equal Rights Union, henceforth the Women's Union). Founded in late February 1905 by a group of about thirty *intelligentki*, the Women's Union emphasised its ties to the Liberation movement, insisting that: 'the struggle for women's rights is a part of the struggle for the political liberation of Russia'. The organisation's platform, approved in May 1905, included standard Liberationist demands for a constituent assembly, civil rights, the abolition of capital punishment, and national autonomy within the empire. Membership was open to men. Nikolai Chekhov (1865–1947), an active suffrage supporter, prominent educator, and husband of the staunch feminist educator Maria Chekhova (1866–1934), won election to the Union's Central Bureau. Though separate, the Union was not separatist.[39]

In relation to women, the group's platform reflected the twin goals of suffrage and equal rights as well as advocacy for proletarian and peasant women. Planks supported equal access to jobs and education, equality for peasant women in all future agrarian reforms, an end to legalised prostitution, equality for married women, and protective legislation and compulsory insurance for women workers. On suffrage, the Union adhered to the standard 'four-tail' formula (a universal, direct, equal, and secret ballot) with the clarifying three wags (without regard to sex, nationality, and religion).[40]

A loose coalition of local chapters with considerable autonomy, the Women's Union never sought legal sanction from the government, and by 1906 claimed eight thousand members. Union members came almost entirely from the female intelligentsia. They were not among the most oppressed of women, but those who had the greatest experience of equality. There is not much information about the organisation's rank and file, but what is available indicates that they were relatively young (twenty to forty), urban, students or graduates of the women's higher or medical courses. A number worked as writers, translators, teachers, or doctors.[41]

Union chapters reflected a range of political perspectives. Some were dominated by socialists, others by the liberal Kadets, others by women with less clear political affiliations. Teachers Union activists, such as Maria Chekhova, Nikolai Chekhov, Emiliia Vakhterova (b.1863), and Olga Kaidanova, were prominent, as were the sisters or wives of leading Kadets, such as Anna Miliukova (1861–1935), Ekaterina Shchepkina (1854–1938), Zinaida Mirovich (1865–1913), and Liudmila Fon-Ruttsen. The Socialist Revolutionary (henceforth SR) Olga Vol'kenshtein, the Mensheviks Dr. Margarita Margulies and Zoia Shadurskaia (Kollontai's childhood friend), and the Bolshevik Anna Gurevich, also attended meetings. At this time, the SRs, the Mensheviks, and some Bolsheviks favoured work in the professional, labour, national, and peasant unions, which comprised the Union of Unions, the spearhead of the Liberation movement, as a means of creating a broad-based democratic opposition coalition.[42]

The chief achievement of the feminists in this period was the conversion of recalcitrant liberal men to the women's rights banner and intensive lobbying for women's rights among all the left and liberal Unions and parties. By the beginning of 1906, largely as a result of feminist lobbying, representatives of the rural and urban local governments, the professional, trade, and peasants unions had included women's suffrage planks in their platforms. After emotional debates highlighted by one of the rare instances anywhere of open political disagreement between spouses (Anna Miliukova and Paul Miliukov), the Kadets finally capitulated in January 1906, making a woman's suffrage plank mandatory for all members.[43]

Women's suffrage in the Russian parliament: high hopes and dashed expectations

With their victories at the party level, feminists now turned to the first modern Russian parliament, the 'Duma of popular hopes', which opened on 27 April 1906. They were not alone in expressing great expectations for the Duma. Milukov called 27 April the 'First day of Russian political freedom!'.[44] For the feminists, there was good reason for optimism. In the Duma, delegates from left and centre parties predominated. If they combined forces, the Kadets and the *Trudovaia gruppa* (Labour group), or Trudoviks, had a clear majority. At the Kadet Party's Third Congress, held to discuss tactics five days before the opening of the Duma, the first point on the list of proposals to be brought before the new legislative body was 'the realisation through legislative norms of . . . the equality of all citizens—without distinction of nationality, religion, class and sex—and freedom; the introduction of universal, equal, direct and secret voting, without distinction of sex, in both in national and local elections'.[45] This was to be accomplished, according to the second point of the tactical programme, even if such a strategy led to 'an open break with the government'.[46]

Beginning the lobbying campaign, the Women's Society sent a 5,000-signature petition to the Duma on its first workday. The petition, noting that several government decrees in 1905 barred the participation of women in the electoral process, protested the exclusion of one half of the population from the political sphere.[47] But once again, liberal politicians were quick to jettison women's rights. The 'woman question' surfaced immediately and intensely in the short-lived First Duma, but key liberal politicians showed little enthusiasm for it. The first major agenda item for the new parliament was the response to the Tsar's address from the throne,[48] viewed as setting the political tone and priorities of the fledgling body.[49] The Duma response gave short shrift to women, calling for universal suffrage, but omitting explicit mention of women's suffrage and equal rights, despite the majority vote in favour of these demands at the Kadet Party's January 1906 Congress and the resolutions at the Kadet's Third Party Congress.[50]

The Trudoviks, second in numbers only to the Kadets, proved the strongest advocates of women's rights.[51] As in Finland, the standard image of the ultra-conservative patriarchal male peasant proved more complex. An amalgam of populist intellectuals and peasant representatives, the Trudoviks had, without a struggle, included women's equal rights in the first line of their 1906 programme.[52] It was the Trudovik Ryzhkov who first explicitly raised the issue of women's rights in this Duma in a forceful and well-received speech at the 2 May session, urging support of female suffrage: 'We forget in this first Russian parliament about Russian women, who fought shoulder to shoulder with us for freedom. We forget that the son of a female slave cannot be a citizen'.[53]

The Duma deputies were the focus of concerted lobbying by women's rights advocates. Kadet Central Committee member and feminist activist Ariadna Tyrkova observed that: 'Women still didn't have the vote, but they developed such energy that they considered the deputies their representatives, and acted as if the Tauride Palace was their home or club'.[54] The lobbying seemed at least partially rewarded when, on 15 May, the issue of women's rights once again arose in the Duma. The Kadets presented a proposal reflecting their strategy of embedding the question of women's rights into the general question of equal rights, and addressing discrimination based on nationality, religion, and class, as well as sex. Noting that one law could not sweep away all the barriers to equality, the proposal called for the creation of a committee composed of thirty-three Duma deputies, to begin the massive work of investigation and compilation necessary to make equal rights at least a legal reality.[55] The proposal passed easily.[56] On 7 July, the committee presented the completed document, scheduled for Duma debate on 10 July. On 7 July 1906, at the time that he gave final approval to the sweeping democratic reforms in Finland, the Tsar dissolved the First Russian Duma.[57]

This was as far as any comprehensive package on women's equal rights would get in any Duma. The Second Duma was more radical than the First, but although proposals and petitions on women's suffrage were presented by the Trudoviks, these were not considered before the Duma was dissolved on 3 June 1907.[58] As the autocracy regained its footing, it curbed the concessions made in reaction to revolution. The backlash intensified with the electoral law of 3 June 1907, called the Stolypin coup d'état after the Tsar's new conservative Prime Minister. By increasing representation, especially by large landowners and ethnic Russians, Stolypin ensured that the Third Duma would be more conservative and nationalist than its predecessors. Trudovik representation decreased to thirteen; the Kadets and their allies were down from one hundred and eight to fifty-four.[59]

Paul Miliukov and fifty-two of the Kadets on 27 June 1908 introduced a limited women's suffrage proposal to the Third Duma. This proposal sought to grant universal suffrage to all Russian citizens over the age of twenty-one and legally resident in a city for more than six months, but it died in committee.[60] The failure of the Kadet proposal simply underlined the obvious. The Duma, greeted with such enthusiasm two years before, was now the graveyard of hopes for quick realisation of women's political equality. The Tsarist government, back in control, sought to curtail rights, not expand them. As Pokrovskaia noted: 'The optimistic expectations of women for equal rights, called forth by the First Duma, had already begun to fade by the Second. The Third Duma destroyed them completely'.[61]

Those women still carrying the tattered banner of equal rights took stock of their dwindling resources and the change in the country's political climate and sought new strategies. The editors of *Soiuz zhenshchin* (Women's Union), in the anomalous position of publishing a journal for an organisation that did not exist, addressed the issue of their much weakened tactical position. They compared the situation to the period before 1905. Then, a series of congresses had served to keep opposition elements together and renew energy. Now, a women's congress could serve the same purpose. Such a congress, they wrote, should have a three-fold significance: 'organisational for women in general; agitational for society as a whole; and educational and theoretical for people specially working on the woman question'.[62]

In the three years since a feminist political movement had arisen in Russia, much had been done. The Women's Union, in its brief tenure, through its pamphlets, public meetings, and petition gathering, had publicised women's rights issues. Union members, particularly dedicated to recruiting peasant and proletarian women to their cause, brought the message of women's rights to remote villages in the countryside and teeming sweatshops in the cities. Although the feminist rank and file had diminished, the cadre of leaders who emerged in 1905 remained largely intact and active. This situation was not unlike that of other liberal and left parties, which had had in the changing conditions, to rely on committed cadres of activists rather than a larger mass movement. Two of the three feminist organisations, the Women's Society and the Progressive Party, continued to meet. The feminist journals *Zhenskii vestnik* and *Soiuz zhenshchin* still appeared, despite censorship.

The Women's Union may have died, but between 1908 and 1917 the issues of women's suffrage and women's rights did not. Outside the Duma, supporters of women's rights clashed furiously over the best approaches to emancipate women. The conflicts among and between the various feminist and socialist factions surfaced in the First All-Russian Women's Congress, held from 10–16 December 1908. The Women's Congress reflected what remained of the hopes and dreams of Russia's women's rights movement. Through the Congress, feminist leaders sought to revive a movement weakened by government repression, uniting all factions in a National Council of Russian Women. The Congress attracted over one thousand delegates, mostly from the female intelligentsia, but also including a small group of women workers affiliated with the social democrats. It was an urban gathering; peasant women were conspicuously absent. Ironically, at this gathering it was on the rocks of the suffrage issue that the feminist ship foundered.[63]

The Congress failed to achieve the objectives of its organisers. The delegates were unable to agree on a general set of demands and unite to form an umbrella Russian women's organisation. The issue that symbolised the lack of unity was not economic; the delegates actually agreed on the resolutions that stressed the economic oppression of women. Instead, suffrage proved most divisive, and it was the women workers group that was most militant, presenting a resolution calling for universal suffrage. The women workers were primed to walk out at some point, but they were also leaderless. Kollontai, who had most actively recruited worker delegates to the Congress, attended the first four days of the gathering before eluding police capture. Successfully fleeing abroad, she did not return to Russia until March 1917.[64]

The workers group was split among the chief factions, the Mensheviks and Bolsheviks. Given the lack of strong leadership, it is significant that the workers took their stand on the issue of suffrage, showing that this issue continued to have resonance among them. Indeed, on suffrage, the workers more closely represented the views of the majority of the delegates, who supported universal suffrage. Feminists allied with the Kadets, claiming to fear that the police would immediately close the Congress, substituted at the last minute a resolution for limited suffrage, angering many delegates. At this Congress, the ballot, not a piece of bread, ultimately symbolised the continued conflicts over the best approach to liberating women. Workers argued for universal suffrage 'as one of the chief weapons in women's struggle for complete liberation', and Kadet activists supported limited suffrage. The same women who had earlier challenged the male leaders of their party for bowing to political expediency now made expedient arguments themselves.[65]

Limited suffrage and equal suffrage

In the aftermath of the 1908 Congress, a new organisation, the *Liga ravnopraviia zhenshchin* (League for Women's Equal Rights, henceforth the Women's League), led the rights' fight. The League drew up one more suffrage proposal for the Third Duma. It simply stated that: 'persons of the female sex enjoy equal rights with men to choose and be chosen for the State Duma'.[66] Introduced by the Trudovik Bulat on 15 February 1912, it bore the signatures of a total of forty deputies, mostly Trudoviks and Kadets.[67]

Among the Tsar's Ministers, Ivan Shcheglovitov, the Minister of Justice, famous for his role in instigating the anti-Semitic murder trial of Mendel Beilis in 1912, most articulately expressed the hard-line government position on women's rights. Shcheglovitov had years earlier supported admitting women to the full practice of law,[68] but his opinion of the place of women in society significantly changed in 1908, after the uncovering of an abortive assassination plot against him involving some women students.[69] In opposing the Bulat bill, Shcheglovitov raised the spectre of female radicalism. In the West, female suffrage might be a conservative force, but in Russia, danger came from 'the admiration of women for revolutionary ideals'.[70] Let loose in the public sphere, such revolutionary passion was so uncontrollable that it threatened the state.[71] On 9 April 1912, the Council of Ministers rejected the Bulat proposal. The message was clear: there would be no progress on women's suffrage under any Tsarist government.[72]

Women's suffrage in the Fourth Duma

Stymied by autocratic intransigence, Russia's liberals articulated their vision of a modern democratic state, explicitly including women. With the words, 'Gentlemen, it is our turn, it is Russia's turn', Paul Miliukov became the chief spokesman for a universal suffrage proposal submitted as part of a package of bills seeking to extend civil rights and civil liberties to the Fourth Duma. Miliukov presented the suffrage bill for the Kadets on 27 February 1913, a date sandwiched between evidence of the new, ten days after the first International Women's Day celebrations in Russia, and a reminder of the old, six days after the commemoration of the three-hundredth anniversary of the Romanov dynasty.[73] In the Duma debates on 8 and 13 March 1913, Miliukov noted that Finland, Norway, and most recently Denmark, had legalised votes for women; he sought to place Russia 'also in the ranks of these northern countries'. Specifically, he acknowledged the success of Finnish women's suffrage.[74] Women's participation, especially their 'agitation' on the questions of education, alcoholism, unemployment, and housing, he argued, were essential to the development of democracy.[75] If male peasants and others were 'infected' by prejudice, this must be combated, not accepted.[76] Pokrovskaia found his turnabout 'astonishing'.[77] Defeated by a vote of 206–106,[78] this was the last suffrage proposal to be discussed in the Duma.[79]

Despite the Duma defeats, women's rights supporters could console themselves with anecdotal evidence that attitudes were changing towards greater acceptance of gender equality. Respected cultural figures like the artist Ilya Repin, the writer Maksim Gorkii, even Leo Tolstoi, announced their support of women's suffrage.[80] Male peasants were often considered the most adamant supporters of patriarchy, yet members of the Trudovik peasant party remained the most consistent supporters of women's rights. In 1911, a Trudovik deputy announced in the Duma that letters from peasants in different parts of the country overwhelmingly supported women's suffrage.[81] Male workers also responded to inquiries about the female vote. In 1912, the Club of the Women's Progressive Party placed a questionnaire in the form of an ad, in a number of newspapers. One hundred and forty-two people responded, and again the overwhelming majority, one hundred and twenty-six, favoured female suffrage. The heaviest response came from readers of the two Bolshevik papers, *Pravda* (Truth), the official party paper, and *Nevskaia zvezda* (Nevskii star). Forty-three, mostly men, responded; only two opposed suffrage.[82]

International Women's Day and women's suffrage

Despite evidence of changing attitudes, the struggle over women's suffrage continued especially fiercely on the left. Socialist women were caught between the Scylla of their male comrades' sexism and the Charybdis of successful feminist appeals to proletarian women. Angered at some male socialists omitting women's suffrage from their platforms, socialist feminist Clara Zetkin (1857–1933) first proposed a socialist women's holiday at the women's conference of the Second International in Copenhagen in 1910. The date of the holiday, 8 March, originated from a 1908 New York City demonstration by female Jewish needle trade workers for both unionisation and the vote. Zetkin strongly supported suffrage as a democratic reform advantageous to the female proletariat; she proposed to the Copenhagen conference that a women's holiday be celebrated world wide, with its chief demand 'universal suffrage'. The presence of three Finnish socialist parliamentary representatives, among the first women in the world to win elective office, further underscored the socialist commitment to female suffrage. Aleksandra Kollontai was the only Russian delegate to the conference, representing St. Petersburg textile workers. She was thus quite familiar with the holiday's goals.[83]

From the start, the celebration of International Women's Day in Russia sparked conflict as activists across the feminist-socialist spectrum claimed the holiday. In naming the celebration, Zetkin had used the word women, and not women workers, acknowledging that women were a separate organising category.[84] The first Russian celebration took place on 17 February 1913.[85] Although the official date for the holiday was 8 March, the Russian organisers of the celebration, fearing police interference, set their commemoration earlier.[86] To underline the importance of the holiday, special issues of both the Bolshevik *Pravda* and the Menshevik *Luch* (Ray) appeared. The six-page *Pravda* contained articles about women workers, the significance of the socialist movement and of the holiday. In all, celebrations took place in five cities—St. Petersburg, Moscow, Kiev, Samara, and Tbilisi.[87]

International Women's Day was also embraced by feminists, who emphasised the holiday's original demand for women's suffrage. In 1913, feminists lobbied the Duma to designate International Women's Day a holiday. By 1914, a feminist Women's Day meeting organised by the Women's Progressive Party in St. Petersburg featured lectures on women's suffrage and participation in local government.[88] In Moscow, the Women's League was able to win approval for a celebration. In 1915 and 1916, despite the war and a government ban, the day was commemorated by small meetings and celebrations.[89]

The appearance in 1914 of socialist journals specifically for women workers further showed some change in social democrats' opposition to separate organisation among women, but also demonstrated continued apprehension about such a strategy. The Menshevik effort, *Golos rabotnitsy* (Voice of the Woman Worker), lasted for only two issues.[90] The Bolshevik *Rabotnitsa*, which owed its origins in part to the popularity of the special women's page inaugurated by *Pravda* in 1913, proved more successful. Its first issue, which appeared despite the arrests of the editorial board in March 1914, contained a lead article by Nadezhda Krupskaia, Lenin's wife, explaining the raison d'être of the journal. Matching hostility to 'bourgeois' feminism with anxiety about the loyalty and political maturity of women workers, Krupskaia referred to most women workers as 'backward'. Women were a problem; they needed to be organised, to be as active as were their male comrades. Women workers' 'backwardness' consisted also in their attraction to feminist appeals, in failing to distinguish between class and gender interests. They had to understand the distinction between the socialist and feminist approaches to women's rights, for the 'struggle for women's rights with the opponents of those rights—men—this is the resolution of the "woman question" among the bourgeoisie'.[91]

Such was the situation for women's rights in Russia on the eve of war. Feminists remained divided over the issues of limited or universal women's suffrage. Liberals articulated a democratic vision for Russia that fully included women. Socialists argued that only they could truly liberate 'backward' women. There was no hope for any major change in the status of women as long as the Tsarist government ruled. Nicholas II's concession to Finnish women was certainly not to be duplicated in the rest of the Russian Empire as long as he remained in power.

War and revolution, 1914–1917

The World War brought about especially great social and economic changes for Russian women. The mobilisation of men to the front brought women into the labour force in growing numbers.[92] Assuming greater responsibilities and new roles in the fields and the factories, women became agents of political change. As the war dragged on, and the Tsarist government demonstrated its incompetence both on the battlefield and the home front, popular discontent grew.[93] Women, responsible for feeding their families, were largely the ones who stood in the breadlines, and these lines became organising points where women could share their discontent.[94]

It is generally accepted that the street demonstrations that led to the collapse of the Tsarist regime began on 23 February, International Women's Day. Contemporary observers set the stage for later accounts, relegating women's entry into the public arena to the category of unorganised 'angry women', or spontaneous food rioters, and then moving on to the real revolutionary actors, be they the organised vanguard male workers, revolutionary activists, or peasant soldiers.[95] Alexander Kerensky, for example, speaking in the Duma on 23 February, referred to the demonstrators repeatedly as 'hungry and wild women'.[96]

The demonstrations were planned. On 23 February, there were organised demonstrations in several parts of the city, involving both socialists and feminists, to commemorate International Women's Day. Bolshevik worker Anna Kostina, for example, remembered that a list of speakers for International Women's Day events had already been prepared and requests to have them address workers meetings were funnelled through the apartment of a Bestuzhev women's higher courses student named Tolmacheva.[97]

The crowds took city officials by surprise; their composition suggests cross-class co-operation as well. Feminists joined in protesting economic conditions, notably the lack of bread. The Petrograd governor, A.P. Balk, described several lively groups of 'many ladies, and even more poor women, students, and fewer workers compared to previous demonstrations'. They gathered in the centre of the city, on Znamenskaia Square, Nevskii Prospekt, and at the City Duma, as well as in the workers districts. In the beginning, these crowds were well-behaved, laughing, talking to each other, but also chanting in a restrained, plaintive way, 'Bread, Bread'. Balk had no idea why the groups had gathered on that day, and why there were so many women in the crowds.[98]

The demonstrations surprised and displeased social-democratic leaders. They did not want to start anything on International Women's Day, preferring to wait until 1 May to initiate a revolution. To the leaders, the women who marched were 'ill-behaved', meaning that they did not listen to the orders of male party leaders. Accounts by party leaders in the Vyborg district, a Bolshevik stronghold, emphasise the female planners' insubordination. On 22 February, for example, when a group of women workers met to plan the celebration, V.N. Kaiurov of the Bolshevik Petrograd Committee instructed them to avoid strikes or other isolated actions.[99] According to Trotsky and other observers, on 23 February, 'despite all directives, the women textile workers in several factories went on strike'.[100]

Women workers were still suspect, as 'backward' elements of the proletariat susceptible to feminist siren songs of sex solidarity; they were not a high socialist organising priority. Only one International Women's Day leaflet was printed by any socialist group. The leaflet shows the ways in which International Women's Day had been redefined by many on the Russian left over the course of the seven years from its inception. To emphasise its class character, the holiday's name, International Women's Day, became 'Woman Workers Day (*Zhenskii rabochii den*)', or the 'Woman's "May Day" '. The holiday's original chief demand, women's suffrage, was not mentioned at all. The emphasis was entirely on class struggle; the appeal was to women workers to follow the lead of their proletarian brothers.[101]

The condescending tone of the leaflet is especially ironic in light of the actual events of 23 February and the days after. The leaflet highlights the backwardness of women workers who 'only recently became part of the family of workers', and who 'often still are afraid, and don't know, what and how to make demands'. The bosses, it continues, exploit the 'darkness and timidity' of the women workers. Exhibiting ongoing anxiety about the loyalties and potential power of women workers, the leaflet urges them: 'and comrade women workers, don't hold back your remaining male comrades, but join with them in simultaneous struggle with the government and factory owners'.[102] The passive women, then, were urged to join the fight already initiated by the male workers.

Women predominated in 23 February demonstrations and actions, and women laid the groundwork for the subsequent events leading to the triumph of the Revolution. Encouraged or harassed by women, male workers laid down their tools, public transport ground to a halt, and troops and Cossacks refused to fire on crowds. Such action or inaction aided the spreading demonstrations that brought down the Tsarist government.[103] Accounts from the time credit the crucial role of women in sparking the revolutionary events and moving them forward. The Bolsheviks, in *Pravda*, on the front page of its 7 March edition, specifically hailed women, who 'were the first to come out on the streets of Petrograd on their Women's Day'.[104] Feminists joined in the euphoria. Pokrovskaia wrote: 'Long live freedom! Russia has suddenly turned a new page in her history and inscribed on it: Freedom!' But she also added a sober note. This was only the first step; the old regime had tumbled, but the establishment of real freedom still lay ahead, and it would be difficult.[105]

From the chaos of the February Revolution, two competing forces emerged to lead the country. Both came into existence at the same time, several days before the Tsar officially abdicated on 3 March. The Petrograd Soviet (Council) of Workers and Soldiers Deputies was created on 27 February, led by members of the revolutionary intelligentsia. The Provisional Government, composed of liberal and left members of the Duma, formed on 28 February. Both met in the same building, the Tauride Palace, where the Duma had convened. In these early post-revolutionary days, the leaders of both the Soviet and the Provisional Government were in frequent contact.[106]

Women initiated the fall of the Romanovs, but once in power, liberal and left politicians ignored them. Neither the Provisional Government nor the Soviet would officially affirm women's equal rights. The Soviet quickly passed and published a resolution calling for the convocation of a Constituent Assembly elected by universal, secret, equal, and direct suffrage, but with no mention of women. The first Provisional Government programme of 3 March 1917 also said nothing about women. Miliukov, Minister of Foreign Affairs in the first Provisional Government, and the advocate for women's rights in the Fourth Duma, was silent on the issue. Immediately women's groups bombarded the government with petitions and demands for the inclusion of women in its programme.[107] Although the new Minister of Justice, Alexander Kerensky, the only socialist in the initial Provisional Government cabinet, had earlier said: 'I am a partisan of complete equality of rights for women and will defend it within the Government', he would not give a firm guarantee. At a meeting of the *Moskovskii komitet obshchestvennykh organizatsii* (Moscow Committee of Public Organizations), Maria Chekhova, the Moscow Women's League delegate, questioned Kerensky about the Provisional Government's commitment to extend the vote to women. Kerensky replied that the government had not yet had time to decide the matter but promised his strong support.[108]

The Russian calendar differed from the Western calendar by thirteen days; the International Women's Day demonstrations that sparked the Revolution were on 23 February, 8 March by the Western calendar. The calendar discrepancy gave Russian feminists two opportunities to mark International Women's Day. Following up on her interchange with Kerensky, Chekhova raised the issue of his response and the Provisional Government's policy at a Women's League meeting on 8 March (by the Russian calendar) commemorating International Women's Day. Those present voted to have Chekhova send a follow-up telegram to Kerensky on that day, stating in respectful but firm language that they would continue to demand full female suffrage and that the Women's League stood ready to mobilise the necessary 'womanpower' to accomplish that goal for the Constituent Assembly elections. It was clear that on their own, the new leaders of Russia would not act quickly on women's suffrage. Kerensky's response was not noted by Chekhova, but interviewed on 11 March he stated that women's suffrage would have to wait until the Constituent Assembly, that this was too vast a change to undertake immediately.[109]

Most historians of Russian women argue that suffrage was an issue of interest only to privileged women, of those who wore the 'hats', not the 'kerchiefs', the traditional head covering of the female masses.[110] But in the days and weeks after the revolution, demands for full suffrage and women's rights resonated among all levels of the population, both women and men, as part of the widespread fervour for implementing democratic reforms. This was a time before the return to Russia of Lenin, Krupskaia, Kollontai, and other socialist leaders. The spontaneous demands for women's rights demonstrate how deeply the feminist message had penetrated the working class. Workers attending the Narva Evening Classes decided to spend the rest of their term discussing contemporary political and social questions, including women's rights. On 5 March, a meeting of twelve hundred credit union employees, after heated debate, passed four resolutions, the second of which called for Constituent Assembly elections based on universal suffrage 'without distinction of sex'.[111] The *Rabochaia gazeta* (Workers Gazette) reported that on 8 March 'a vast army of working women from factories in the Moskovskii and Porokhovaia districts . . . appeared at the City Duma to declare their demands for women's electoral rights'. Interest in equal rights was not confined to the revolutionary capital. An Irkutsk meeting of 3,000 women and men sent a telegram to the Provisional Government demanding full electoral rights for women in the Constituent Assembly. Women workers in Kostroma and Iaroslavl joined equal rights organisations.[112]

Demonstrations by women workers in early March included demands for suffrage. On 5 March, women from four factories held a meeting at which they called for their sisters to unite with their proletarian brothers and fight for women's rights, among other issues. On 8 March, a large group of women workers demonstrated in front of the State Duma with banners demanding female suffrage.[113] And on 9 March, the Executive Committee of the Petrograd Soviet published a statement supporting women's suffrage in the upcoming Constituent Assembly elections.[114]

Suffrage had appeal even to those who condemned feminists. Votes for women was an issue in the Vyborg district, a Bolshevik stronghold and the origination point for the main socialist International Women's Day demonstration in February. A 12 March rally of eight hundred Petrograd women workers adopted the Bolshevik programme for women and stated its opposition to the 'bourgeois women's movement'. But the rally also had as its first demand full voting rights for women.[115] The popularity of women's rights demands among the female masses concerned Kollontai. The soldatki, the soldiers' wives who had played an important role in the February Revolution, alarmed her by their support for and alliance with feminist groups.[116]

Articles in socialist newspapers used women's prominence in the February Revolution as conclusive evidence for the female vote. The first post-revolutionary issues of *Pravda* reflected the democratic hopes inspired by the February Revolution. The Bolshevik paper reported on women workers' demands for equal rights and linked them to the Revolution. On 10 March, Anna Ulianova, Lenin's sister, using the pseudonym Olga Bobyleva, linked the history of Russian women and women workers' development from 1905 to 1917 with the struggle for suffrage. She took pains to emphasise the great strides made by working women, the 'light of consciousness' awakened by the 1905 Revolution and carefully included the usual exhortations to women workers to join with their male comrades in common struggle. But she noted that more and more women no longer just followed men, or joined hands with them, but 'independently, on their own initiative, began to work in the revolution, to learn on their own'.[117] To Ulianova, by initiating the February Revolution, women demonstrated their revolutionary credentials. Each woman 'needs the right to participate equally with men in elections, the right to be elected to the Constituent Assembly, to city councils and to district and rural organisations. She needs the right to study and hold all government positions for which she is qualified and to receive equal pay'.[118] Granting women equal rights would complete the revolution.

Dissatisfaction over the Provisional Government's failure to act led to the second large foray of women into the public arena in 1917. Organised by the Women's League, it was the largest women's demonstration yet in Russia, larger than the February International Women's Day marches. An estimated 35,000 to 40,000 women took part. Those marching for women's rights were led by women who might be considered more well-behaved. They had explicitly rejected the militant behaviour of the English suffragists, and were not about to imitate their tactics, or those of Chinese suffrage supporters who smashed the windows of their parliament in 1912.[119] They were asking Provisional Government leaders for the vote, not demanding it as their right.

The march began at the City Duma on Nevskii Prospekt, in the heart of the city, and headed toward the State Duma, at the Tauride Palace. Its cross-class character was immediately apparent. For this kind of a mass demonstration could not have been composed exclusively or even largely of the female intelligentsia from which most feminist activists came. The number of educated professional women in all of Russia at that time was still quite small, nowhere near the number participating in the march.

The feminist writer Liubov Gurevich (1866–1940) described: 'an endless orderly column, with red banners unfurled and placards: thousands, tens of thousands of women'. The crowd included women of the professional and working classes: 'factory workers and women doctors, hospital nurses and writers, maids and students, telegraph operators and sisters of mercy'. The organisers clearly sought to identify their cause with that of the non-party left. The revolutionary heroine Vera Figner (1852–1942) rode in the lead car, flanked by 'Amazons' on white horses. Many marchers carried banners and placards with such slogans as 'Hail Women-Fighters for Freedom', 'A Place for Women in the Constituent Assembly', 'Women Workers Demand a Voice in the Constituent Assembly', and 'Without the Participation of Women Suffrage is not Universal'.[120]

The crowd waited until Nikolai Chkeidze and Matvei Skobelev, President and Vice-Presidents of the Soviet appeared, but they were non-committal. Finally, the conservative

President of the Duma, Mikhail Rodzianko, appeared. Dr. Poliksena Shishkina-Iavein (1875–1947), President of the Women's League, addressed them, citing the egalitarian traditions of the Russian revolutionary struggle: 'women were your faithful comrades in the gigantic struggle for the freedom of the Russian people'; and calling for full citizenship for women: 'the Constituent Assembly in which only one half of the population will be represented can in no way be regarded as expressing the will of the whole people'.[121]

In a rare show of unity, the leaders of the Soviet and Provisional Government, Chkeidze and Rodzianko, quickly capitulated, and the crowd received assurance from Prince L'vov, Head of the Provisional Government, that he would approve women's suffrage for the upcoming elections.[122] Two days later, on 21 March, a delegation of women from Petrograd and Moscow met with Prince L'vov. The feminist factions were now unified; the delegation included Figner, Shabanova of the Women's Society, Shishkina-Iavein of the Women's League, Miliukova and Tyrkova of the Kadets, Olga K. Nechaeva of the Russian Union of Democratic Women's Organisations, Pokrovskaia of the Women's Progressive Party, Countess Sofia Panina, the philanthropist and the only female in the Provisional Government cabinet, A.N. Rinkevich, A.M. Kalmykova, an early patron of Legal Marxism, and Dr. M.I. Nikol'skaia and E.V. Gorovits, representatives of Moscow women. No women workers were among the delegates. In other words, the group represented a cross-section from the intelligentsia, members of the non-party left, and liberals. Figner presented L'vov with a brief statement about women's rights and asked for a clarification of the Provisional Government's position on the issue. L'vov assured the delegation that the Provisional Government ministers unanimously favoured female suffrage and that a law providing full equality for women was being drafted. The women were jubilant. Exulted Maria Pokrovskaia: 'Long live the free and equal citizeness!'[123]

But this was not the end of the story. The decree giving women suffrage was finally issued as part of the general Electoral Law, with a strong helping hand from Ekaterina Kuskova (1869–1958), the non-party socialist, who capitalised on her connections within the Provisional Government to hold its leaders to the promises they had made at the 19 March women's rights demonstration. Published on 20 July 1917, the law granted full suffrage and the right to run for elective office to all women and men aged twenty and over.[124]

What had begun as a movement of educated women, and then gained a following among urban workers and soldiers' wives, now spread to the peasant majority in the countryside. Although the Bolsheviks overthrew the Provisional Government in November, they allowed the Constituent Assembly elections to proceed. In the pre-election campaigns and the actual voting, the issue of women's participation in the public sphere affected all parts of the country. Women took their new rights seriously. In urban areas, their participation rate totalled fifty-four percent, compared to forty-seven percent for men. In rural areas, some peasant men forbade women to vote. A peasant assembly in Tomsk province decreed that: 'Under no circumstances are women to vote; in each family the head should vote for the entire family'.[125] But despite all the obstacles to their voting in the countryside, peasant women's turnout was also high. The percentage of female voters reached seventy percent; the male total was seventy-seven percent. Among non-Russian nationalities, the turnout was even higher. In urban areas like Baku, the percentage of Muslim women voting reached seventy-seven percent, with overwhelming majorities for the Muslims of Russia list.[126] These figures compare favourably with those for the U.S. in 1920, the first election in which women voted. In that year's presidential election, the female turnout averaged about thirty-seven percent, compared to the male rate of about fifty-five percent.[127]

The majority of all votes in the 1917 Constitutent Assembly election went to the Socialist Revolutionaries. A feminist slate, including Shishkina-Iavein,[128] Yefimenko, Chekhova, Kuskova, E.N. Shchepkina, and Kalmykova, received a modest 7,676 votes.[129] On 5 January 1918, the Constituent Assembly convened, with ten women sitting amidst the 767 deputies. The Socialist Revolutionary deputies included such revolutionary heroines as Ekaterina Breshko-Breshkovskaia, Vera Figner, and Maria Spiridonova, along with M.D. Perveeva, Anastasia Sletova-Chernova, and O.A. Matveevskaia. The Bolshevik women deputies included Kollontai, Evgeniia Bosh, Elena Rozmirovich, and Varvara Iakovleva.[130] After the first day, the Bolsheviks dispersed the Constituent Assembly.[131] The Assembly election was the only relatively free national election in which women participated until after the collapse of the Soviet Union in 1991.

Conclusion

Women's suffrage (the vote and the right to hold elective office) is one of the great democratic reforms of the twentieth century. If suffrage did not achieve as much as had been hoped for, this should not diminish the significance of the struggle.[132] It was not war alone, but war and revolution that won the vote for Finnish and Russian women. In Finland, Russia's defeat in the Russo-Japanese War weakened the forces at the disposal of the Tsar and caused him to make concessions in Finland to preserve his power in Russia proper. In Russia, the First World War dramatically weakened support for the Tsarist government, making it possible for a series of street demonstrations to escalate into the collapse of the regime. There is a direct link between the events of February 1917, when Petrograd women took to the streets on International Women's Day to spark the revolution, and the suffrage march and the electoral law that granted full democratic rights to Russian women. Russian feminists thus achieved their chief goal before the Provisional Government was swept away by the October Bolshevik Revolution. Indeed, women's suffrage is among the few lasting achievements of the Provisional Government.[133]

In comparison to their sisters in other countries, the Finns and Russians won their rights in a remarkably short time. American women struggled for seventy-two years, French women one-hundred-fifty-one years—from Olympe de Gouges's first feminist Declaration during the French Revolution to Charles de Gaulle's proclamation in 1944. Finland's revolution made it the first in Europe to win suffrage and the right to vote for women. Russia became the first major world power to grant its women the right to vote, one year before Germany, three years before the United States, eleven years before Great Britain, and twenty-seven years before France.

In Finland, women's rights became part of the nationalist struggle against the Russian Empire, uniting most of the population. Finnish peasant traditions of gender co-operation as well as the strong female presence in revivalist and temperance movements strengthened support for women's rights. In Russia, a strong tradition of egalitarianism among the progressive elite combined with anger at the betrayal and indifference of male political leaders spurred feminist activism. Two new female social groups, industrial workers, and women with formal education, both of which emerged in the nineteenth century, proved crucial to the success of women's rights movements in many countries, including Russia. Women activists from both groups, joining together, ensured that the early twentieth century revolutions in Russia ultimately defined democracy to include women. Making visible this path to the female vote provides a fuller understanding of the multifaceted history of the global suffrage movement.

WOMEN'S SUFFRAGE IN CHINA

Challenging scholarly conventions

Louise Edwards

In their 1994 survey of women's suffrage around the globe, Caroline Daley and Melanie Nolan erroneously identified 1949 as "the year" Chinese women gained suffrage rights.[1] Most scholars working in Chinese studies also hold this misconception, since 1949 marks the ascension to power of the Chinese Communist Party (CCP).[2] In fact, Chinese women won suffrage rights in 1947 with the implementation of the Constitution of the Republic of China. This error reflects more than a simple problem of historical method. It reveals two key unstated conventions of the scholarly narrative underpinning studies of women's suffrage around the world. First, the error highlights the importance of temporal closure in our scholarly practice—the narrative of women's suffrage is inscribed along a linear path that ceases at a particular year/month/day when suffrage was won. Second, the mistake points to the dependency of our current research style on geopolitical closure—the history of women's suffrage relies heavily on the existence of a stable nation-state with prescribed national borders and consistent government systems. These narrative conventions pose particular difficulties for scholars working on histories of the "developing" world and have contributed to the dearth of research on non-Western suffrage struggles.[3] As Carol Pateman has pointed out, "We know remarkably little about how women won the vote around the world. . . . How important are cultural differences, or differences in political regimes?"[4]

Identifying geopolitical and temporal closure is comparatively unproblematic in the histories of the European and American suffrage struggles. However, in China and many other non-Western countries, the notions of "nationhood" and "government" were fraught with complications at the very time their suffrage movements were active. During the period when the Woman's Christian Temperance Union (WCTU) espoused the internationalism of the women's suffrage movement,[5] the tensions produced by struggles against imperialism or colonialism and by nationalist campaigns for economic and social reconstruction were of preeminent concern in many parts of Asia and Africa. For the suffrage activist in Asia during the first half of the twentieth century, the pressing questions included the following: "Which 'government' do we lobby for suffrage?" "What should be the relationship between nationalist and feminist struggles?" "What are the borders of our nation, and who are the 'national women' we represent?" These questions were crucial in the formation of the non-Western suffrage struggles.

The exploration of the Chinese women's suffrage movement provides several opportunities: first, to rediscover one of the world's important women's suffrage campaigns; second, as part of this process, to bring into sharp relief the unstated narrative conventions that have sustained excellent writing on Western suffrage movements;[6] third, to explore the problem China poses for imperatives of geopolitical closure; fourth, to analyze the role histories of suffrage can perform in the enunciation of a national narrative of legitimate governance; and fifth, to reveal the tensions inherent in the current conception of the existence of a necessary division between nationalist and feminist causes.

Three waves of Chinese women's suffrage activism

In contrast to the decades of work carried out on the Western experience, the history of the Chinese women's suffrage movement remains largely unexplored, and, as a consequence, misconceptions abound.[7] Prime among these is that China had no suffrage movement worth examining. In fact, women waged a very successful and sustained struggle over the course of four decades, not only to win gender equality in political rights but also to gain a guaranteed minimum quota of seats for women in parliament. Despite the difficulties presented by political repression, economic instability, and war, Chinese women suffrage activists continued their struggle, changing tactics, shifting speaking positions, and invoking different ideological weapons to suit the changing times. The flexibility of tactics and continuing change in the sociopolitical context conspired to diminish recognition of the women's suffrage movement in China over the long term. The ideological battles for legitimacy waged between the People's Republic of China (PRC) and the Republic of China (ROC) on Taiwan have also played an important role in suppressing scholarly work on, and popular awareness of, the Chinese women's suffrage movement. Not only does the Chinese women's suffrage movement fit less readily into the Western conventions of suffrage history writing, but suppression of awareness about the movement has served both ROC and PRC political interests well.

The Chinese women's suffrage movement commenced with the anti-Qing, pro-Republican movement in the first decade of the twentieth century. Women proponents of a republican government believed that women would have equal rights within the future republic. They had been active in the main anti-monarchy group, the Revolutionary Alliance, from its formation in 1905, undertaking a full range of revolutionary activities including bomb-making, forming assassination squads, publishing, and lobbying.[8] Li Yu-ning has argued that the Revolutionary Alliance was attractive to women largely because it was "the first major political party in China to recognize the principle of equality between men and women."[9] Gender equality was thus an explicit goal within their involvement in the anti-monarchy movement. One prominent woman publisher and anti-Qing activist of the time, Luo Yanbin, made the founding premise of her magazine, *China's New Woman's World*, the notion that women were citizens equal in every respect to men.[10] China's women's suffrage activists staunchly opposed the Qing monarchy (1644–1911) primarily because they considered the establishment of a democratic republic to be a prerequisite for women's participation in politics.

In 1911 the Qing monarchy was overthrown, and Asia's first republic—the Republic of China—was formed. Women political activists assumed that the advent of democracy meant democracy for women as well as men. However, male revolutionaries betrayed their female counterparts in the process of dividing power. To both conservatives and radicals, women's suffrage was a useful but expendable bargaining piece in realizing their broad political goals.[11] The constitution of 1912 and its accompanying electoral laws excluded women from participating politically in the new Republic of China.

China's suffragists embarked upon an intense and tumultuous campaign to reassert their "natural rights" to equality and liberty as human beings. Their invocation of Jean-Jacques Rousseau's "natural rights" was a continuation of the rhetoric used to rally support for the republican movement against the Qing monarchy and carried currency among a broad spectrum of China's politically active population—even the conservative republicans.[12] The women's suffrage activists engaged in extensive lobbying, protests, and parades. On March 20, 1912, in frustration at the continued resistance to women's suffrage by China's provisional parliamentarians, women stormed the parliamentary chambers, demanding a fair hearing on their proposed constitutional amendment. After being forcibly expelled, the women returned to smash the windows of the parliament in direct and conscious imitation of recent actions by British suffragettes.[13] Opposition to their cause stiffened over the next few months. The Revolutionary Alliance merged with more conservative parties in August 1912 to form the GMD (Nationalist Party, also known as KMT), and the clause advocating sexual equality was not included in the new party manifesto. Despite these considerable setbacks, the campaign continued unabated for more than a year. It terminated only when a broad range of democratic political activities was prohibited under the repressive presidency of Yuan Shikai. In November 1913, Yuan banned the main women's organization, the Women's Suffrage Alliance, marking the end of the "first wave" of suffrage activism.

The small number of women involved in first wave activism were mostly educated members of gentry families. Almost all had studied in Japan before the formation of the Republic and had joined anti-Qing groups while overseas.[14] Many had parents or brothers who supported their study abroad and their political activities. A notable exception to this general rule is the revolutionary martyr Qiu Jin (1877–1907). Leaving an unhappy marriage, Qiu Jin sold her possessions, left her children, and went to Japan to join the anti-Qing revolution to the end of liberating China's women. This cause eventually led her back to China, where she established a school for women, a women's army, and a radical newspaper for women. Her anti-Qing activities marked her as a traitor; she was captured and executed in 1907.[15] Among Qiu Jin's women friends in the Chinese community in Japan was the recently widowed Tang Qunying (1871–1937). Tang's studies in Japan were initially self-funded, but she later won a scholarship from the Hunan Provincial Government. On her return to China, she led the women's suffrage cause throughout the first wave of activism from her position as president of the Women's Suffrage Alliance. She is considered one of China's foremost women's suffrage activists.[16] China's first suffragists were few in number and, like the men who were active in politics during this time, almost exclusively from elite families. These women regarded their participation in the republican movement as emblematic of the roles that all of China's women would play in their imagined republican nation of the future.

With the termination of democratic activities by Yuan Shikai, China entered a period of chaos. Most prominent women's suffrage campaigners went into hiding or fled to Japan. The nation disintegrated into several rival pieces as warlords fought their way back and forth across the country, forging and breaking alliances with the remnants of the republican government, which itself was split between the north and the south.[17] By the 1920s some of China's provinces reestablished military and political order and declared themselves "independent." Heading these independent provinces were democratically inclined provincial governments. In the absence of a stable national government, these new provincial governments became the focus of the "second wave" women's suffrage movement. Consequently, during the early 1920s four of China's most important provinces passed constitutions that guaranteed gender equality in political rights—Hunan, Guangdong, Zhejiang, and Sichuan.[18] These constitutional changes were in direct response to the activism of women who were "second wave" suffragists.

In contrast to the women's suffrage activists of the first wave, the women who worked to change the provincial constitutions represented a slightly broader cross-section of China's population. They were still overwhelmingly educated women, some with overseas training—largely in the United States rather than Japan—but increasing numbers of the expanding urban middle class were also involved. China's educational and commercial infrastructure in urban areas had expanded since the establishment of the republic. The schools, in particular, provided fertile ground for the women's suffrage movement. The major influence on these women was the radical social and cultural transformation that had taken place in China in the aftermath of World War I. Called the May Fourth Movement or the New Culture Movement (1915–1925), this social revolution highlighted the importance of Western-style science and democracy for the rejuvenation of China, and it promoted women's rights as a major key to improving China's prospects. The considerable support that male, reform-minded intellectuals provided for the notion of sexual equality and women's liberation was important to the success of the second wave of women's suffrage activism. As Wang Zheng notes, "The feminist movement was viewed by these men as a necessary stage in the development of human society. It was a sign of modernity."[19] Magazines and journals on the woman question flourished at this time, and many of the articles were written by and for a male readership.[20]

The main groups that formed during this phase included the Beijing-based Women's Rights League and the Progressive Association for Women's Participation in Politics. The more effective groups were the various United Women's Associations (UWA) that were located in the urban centers of such provinces as Hunan, Zhejiang, and Guangdong. It was the UWAs that won the crucial sexual equality guarantees in the provincial constitutions mentioned above. The two Beijing groups not only faced very conservative governments but were themselves riven with factional disputes.[21] Beijing women gained equality only when the national constitution was promulgated two decades later. In Shanghai the local UWA branch was supported by the WCTU and led by Liu Wang Liming—a dedicated suffrage activist with the strong international links associated with the WCTU. In many respects Liu Wang is representative of the "second wave" activist. Her widowed mother supported the family on needlework, and the children gained education through an American missionary school. An excellent student, Liu Wang became a Christian and joined the WCTU while only a middle school student. She was awarded a scholarship to study at Northwestern University in Illinois in 1916. During her time in the United States, Liu Wang studied science and intensified her links with the WCTU. She returned to China after graduating in 1920, and, from this point on, her life revolved around philanthropic and political activities related to women's rights and welfare and human rights in general.[22]

The tactics employed by the second wave activists were much like those of their predecessors, apart from the terrorism of the anti-Qing feminists. Street marches, rallies, petitions, publishing, lobbying, pamphleteering, and storming parliamentary sessions were standard tactics during these first two phases of the Chinese women's suffrage campaigns. Newspapers published special sections on women in politics, and vigorous debates between pro- and anti-women's suffrage advocates appeared in print. The Chinese women activists were acutely aware of parallel movements in Europe and the Americas through their international connections like the WCTU. In contrast to both the U.S. and British movements, China's suffragists did not embark on hunger strikes to indicate their strength of purpose. The most likely reason is that, during the Qing dynasty, chaste widows who starved themselves to death on the passing of their spouses had been honored as "exemplary women" in official reports and with the construction of memorial arches.[23] So hunger tactics held quite different connotations in the Chinese context.

As soon as a national government was formed in 1928 with the unification of China under the GMD, suffrage activists targeted the new national government. Its democratic pretensions and the precedents set by the provincial governments as well as the United States and the United Kingdom, where women had already won suffrage rights, suggested that duplicating these victories at a national level in China would be relatively straightforward. Indeed, when the draft constitution of 1936 was announced, women's suffrage activists took great delight in noting its declaration that "Delegates to the People's Congress shall be elected by universal, equal, and direct suffrage."[24] This victory was to remain theoretical until the promulgation of an amended draft in 1946 (implemented January 1, 1947), but it did guarantee women participation in the various semidemocratic parliaments, government committees, party planning, and electoral processes in the interim. The delay between the passing of the draft in 1936 and the promulgation of the document in 1946 resulted because of the invasion by Japan in 1937 and the ensuing war, but also because President Chiang Kai-shek grew increasingly hostile to the idea of democratic rule and repeatedly delayed elections.

In the decade between 1936 and 1946, China's women's suffrage activists made a strategic, philosophical shift in their public activism. In this "third wave," they embarked upon a campaign to win a set minimum number of seats for women in the national legislature, premised on the notion that women required special protection to enhance their participation in politics.[25] The campaign to ensure that gender equality was enshrined in the constitution prior to 1936 had openly rejected the idea that men and women were different, having built its case on the inherent and natural rights of *all* human beings to equality and liberty. After 1936, the suffragists altered their campaign rhetoric and stressed differences between men and women. This evolution of the women's suffrage rhetoric was a strategic success, because, when the Constitution of the Republic of China was promulgated, the women of China not only had suffrage rights, they also had a guaranteed 10 percent minimum quota of seats.

Many of the women from the "second wave" groups, like the UWAs, served as leaders in this "third wave" of activism. Moreover, women from both major political parties were involved. The split between the GMD and the CCP made nonpartisan feminist activity dangerous, but many women, like Liu Wang Liming, persevered with support from feminists within the two main parties. During the war against Japan, China established a semidemocratic, multiparty forum called the People's Political Council (PPC), and some of China's prominent feminists were appointed or elected to this advisory body. During the protracted debates on the constitution (which repeatedly included calls for Chiang Kai-shek to hold elections), the women representatives successfully argued for the allocation of minimum quotas for women. The participation of women in the PPC demonstrated the effectiveness of China's women politicians in furthering women's opportunities in China.

China and temporal and geopolitical chaos

Thus, the "correct year" for women's suffrage in China should be 1947. However, the search for a "year"—a temporal closure—that pinpoints the success of the women's suffrage movement remains problematic in the case of China because of the lack of closure in "national" geopolitical structures. From 1946 until 1949, the country slipped into civil war as the ruling GMD fought to suppress the rising power of the CCP. Once the Communists won the war, they ignored the rulings of the previous government and instead set about creating their own constitution. In this process of deleting one government's history and propagating another's, 1949 has been hailed as the year Chinese women were guaranteed equality with men. Since then, the history of China's women's movement has been consistently subordinated to the histories of the two major political blocks. The historiographical re-creation of CCP control of China as an inevitable end point reflects a clear ideological goal on the part of the CCP, which aimed to legitimize its rule. It demonstrates the ready compliance of Western historians with this version of historical events as a logical progression stretching back from and serving to justify the present. It also derives from the narrative conventions of studies of the history of women's suffrage that have sought a firm and uncomplicated date within a firm and continuing nation-state.

The People's Republic of China's historical narrative of the Chinese women's movement centered on the role of the CCP in liberating Chinese women from centuries of oppression.[26] It consequently suppressed the contribution of the non-CCP affiliated women's movement of the first half of the century through the maintenance of a hegemonic "grand narrative."[27] The common history of the women's rights movement of the first half of the century traces the CCP's initiative in improving the status of women from the 1930s, making no mention of the women's suffrage activism that led to the proclamation of gender equality in both Hunan and Guangdong provinces in 1921. At that time, the CCP consisted of a mere handful of radical intellectuals, while the women's suffrage movement had been active for over a decade. Instead of the history of the women's suffrage groups, we read of the CCP's supposed skill in teaching organizational skills to a previously ineffective, elitist suffragist movement.[28] We are also encouraged to learn of the CCP's Jiangxi Soviet where the constitution guaranteed sexual equality in 1931—despite its geographical and numerical insignificance for most of China.[29] Communist heroines are thus celebrated, and the nonpartisan feminists of the first, second, and third wave of suffrage activism are ignored or dismissed. Wang Zheng describes this CCP project as the "construction of a public memory."[30]

The stability of government and nation in China since 1949 has provided such a degree of consistency to this version of China's women's movement that the "year" of 1949 has been accepted almost universally. Other than Bernice Lee's 1975 doctoral work, few people recognize the extent of the Nationalist Government's legislative reforms in relation to women's status in society.[31] Until the 1980s equally little was known about the women's movement in China in the Republican period, and it was routinely dismissed as a branch of the male-dominated political debates. The works of Christina Gilmartin, Wang Zheng, and Ono Kazuko have been particularly significant in promoting this new scholarship to the Western academy.[32] In China, the work of the All China Women's Federation in its establishment of Women's History Centers during the late 1980s has served the same purpose.[33]

However, the opportunities provided by the rupture of foreign invasion and civil war for radical reinvention of the recent past by a government sensitized to the power of propaganda do not fully explain the absence of research on the women's suffrage movement in China. Equally important are the historical conventions that have sought narrative closure in writing suffrage histories. These have the tendency to underrate the activities of women in nondemocratic systems of government. Women in the PRC, and until 1987 the ROC, had not yet "achieved" democracy in the Western sense of the word. Constitutional guarantees of sexual equality in political participation on the part of the PRC government could be perceived as meaningless by scholars on the right and more than slightly embarrassing by scholars on the left. How can 1949 be "the year" for celebrating women's suffrage when Chinese people—women and men alike—lived in a one-party state where elections were highly contrived, stage-managed events? Free and fair elections were not a feature of the one-party states of the post-civil war Chinas. The existence of these dictatorships in the ROC and the PRC had the effect of negating the importance or recognition of the women's suffrage movement in China. Because there was no democracy, there could be no closure. However, failed women's suffrage movements and "theoretically" successful suffrage movements remain worthy of exploration. Indeed, they may illuminate not only the influence of different cultural formations on the suffrage movement but also the foundations required for democratic systems of governance to emerge.

Women's suffrage for the sake of the state

A further factor inhibiting scholarship on the history of the women's suffrage movement in China is the limited utility of the narration of the movement for the contemporary project of "imagining" the Chinese nation. In democratic nations, the history of the women's suffrage movement can be depicted as part of the process of nation-building. This is less readily achieved in the PRC where the CCP maintains its right to rule without the electoral processes the women's suffrage activists upheld. In Western democracies, on the occasions where the women's suffrage movement is recognized or celebrated (e.g., by the erecting of statues or the funding of commemorative conferences), such rituals *are* able to perform the function of confirming the virtue of the current political and social system. This is possible because women suffrage activists were fighting to be included *within* the system that later provides the financial support to build the monuments, *not* fighting to overthrow it. The existence of the women's suffrage movement thus serves to affirm the contemporary nation-state and its notions of governance. This role is unavailable to Chinese women's suffrage activists because the political philosophy of the current government of the PRC is premised on the destruction of the capitalist system and the party politics form of democracy that the women's suffrage movement aimed to penetrate.

In China, the CCP regarded the women's suffrage movement as a useful vehicle for mobilizing middle-class women to its cause in the 1920s and early 1930s, but fundamentally the CCP saw the suffrage campaign as a distraction from what it considered to be the real struggle—the class struggle—to liberate the people.[34] The ascendancy of a Marxist party to power in China has therefore severely limited the extent to which women's suffrage activists could be "inherited" as heroes of nation-building as they have been in the last several decades in countries such as Australia, New Zealand, and the United States.[35]

Even in these Western democracies, the emergence of women's suffrage activists as heroes required a certain shifting of emphasis by governments and by those historians who used these figures for nationalist ends. Too frequently the details of the women's suffrage campaigns have been ignored on the fiction that the government administration in power bestowed upon women equal political rights in an enlightened and benevolent fashion. In her path-breaking work on the New Zealand women's suffrage movement, Patricia Grimshaw noted that the role of the women's movement in winning the vote was routinely understated, and the enlightened leadership of the current administration was as routinely exaggerated.[36] Audrey Oldfield revealed the same in her study of the Australian case in an aptly titled volume, *Woman Suffrage in Australia: A Gift or a Struggle?*[37] As Grimshaw and Oldfield demonstrate, this is a distorted version of events. In the writing of New Zealand and Australian history then, the key tension revolves around the correct apportioning of glory for the policy change that all agree to have been a noble initiative. Women's suffrage, in the Western historical consciousness, is unambiguously progressive and positive.

On the rare occasions that the China's women's suffrage movement has been officially acknowledged, it has faced a similar "reorientation." Li Ziyun's comment, "With one flourish of the pen, Chinese women acquired the right to vote, something their sisters in the West had spent decades, even centuries fighting for," erroneously suggests that Chinese women did not fight for their suffrage rights. It suggests that the CCP simply gave political rights to women in 1949. The campaign for set minimum quotas for women has been similarly transformed from a successful and sustained period of lobbying by women activists into a benevolent act by an otherwise dictatorial GMD government. Chien Tuan-sheng, in his seminal work on China's political history, described the 1946–1947 constitution where the 10 percent quota was enshrined as follows: "the reference to women is intended to give them stimulus to seek elective offices."[38] In fact, many women had lobbied long and hard to win these quotas, and there was no shortage of likely candidates for parliament. These women were wisely attempting to ensure that political party wrangling was prevented from eliminating women during preselection battles.

While both Western and Chinese histories reinterpreted the suffrage movements and reapportioned credit, a crucial difference remains between these historical traditions. In the case of the Marxist government of the PRC, women's suffrage activists are seen as women who sought to participate in a form of government and leadership that the CCP regards as seriously flawed, corrupt, and biased in favor of the elite. In the 1920s, when China's suffrage activists were enjoying their first successes, the CCP's prominent woman revolutionary, Xiang Jingyu, dismissed their efforts as diversions that prolonged the misery of the broad mass of the Chinese population. She declared that the Chinese parliaments were so corrupt and venal that women would simply be sullied by participation and, moreover, would gain nothing as a result of this degrading participation. In a 1924 article published in the influential "bourgeois" journal, *The Ladies Journal* (Funü zazhi), Xiang published a particularly scathing appraisal of the women's suffrage movement:

> If the suffrage movement is successful then it simply means that a whole bunch of women will enter the pigsties of the capital and the provinces where together with the male pigs, they can preside over the nation's calamities and the people's misfortunes.[39]

Ironically, her notion that participation in the political process was polluting echoed those conservatives who opposed suffrage on the grounds that it would sully feminine purity. However, unlike the conservatives, she opposed participation in parliament by men as well.

Xiang provided a comprehensive critique of the women's suffrage movement—caustically referring to it as the "movement to become officials" (*zuo guan yundong*)—in a 1923 article responding to one by Wang Bihua, President of the Zhejiang UWA. Wang had advocated the importance of women's participation in the political process as a key method of ensuring that women's legal rights were equal to those of men. First, Xiang highlighted the class-specific nature of Wang's concerns. So what if women get equal inheritance and property rights with men? This is only a cause for celebration among the women whose families had property to distribute. Second, she argued that women's involvement in the present corrupt political process would simply corrupt those who entered parliament, since their lives as officials would cause their commitment to principles of women's rights to wither. These women, she insisted, would "enter [government] white and exit black." She summarized her arguments about the sullying effects of political participation saying: "In reality, the movement to become an official is like immersing a mud Buddha in water." Third, Xiang astutely raised the point that the current political situation in China was so chaotic and prone to rapid change that it was very doubtful that any legislative gains would ever be implemented. Would they not merely be reduced to nominal reforms of "black words on white paper?" She then went on to draw the reader's attention to the effects of women's rights activists in parliament by raising doubts about the effectiveness of the presence of Wang Changguo (1880–1949) in the Hunan Provincial Assembly. Wang was one of China's few elected women parliamentarians in the 1920s. To Xiang Jingyu, women's participation in the parliamentary system was destined to be ineffectual and, worse still, would have a negative effect on the personal lives and ideological commitment of the women involved.[40]

This historical antipathy to the women's suffrage movement on the part of the CCP has reduced the scope for the reinvention of women's suffrage activists as national heroes. They were not struggling to build the current (CCP) system of government and, still more problematically, could even be seen as foreunners of the democracy movement that so annoys the current Chinese leadership. The absence of a democratic culture within which the nation's suffrage struggles can be positively invoked provides new challenges for those scholars aiming to research these campaigns. These challenges are not easily met within the dominant conventions of writing on women's suffrage with its dependency on temporal and geopolitical closure.

Searching for authenticity: nationalist or feminist?

Suffrage campaigns in the non-Western world have often been intertwined with natio-nalist liberation movements. As we shall see below, this dual political focus has called into doubt the extent of suffrage activists' "feminist" credentials. Are these women fundamentally nationalists who just happen to be female? Or are they feminists who are deploying nationalist rhetoric to further feminist goals? These questions ignore the fact that geopolitical closure, in the form of a stable democratic system of government, created the space for the emergence of feminist movements that could be discretely identified as "authentic." In geographic regions where democratic self-rule was nonexistent or unstable, suffrage activists were often dismissed as not really thorough-going suffragist feminists because they were often also involved in nationalist struggles against imperialism, colonialism, or despotism.

Historians of the Chinese suffrage movement contend with this dilemma because, for the most part, China's suffrage activists were simultaneously members of various pro-Republic democratic parties as well as women's suffrage groups. For example, the leading women's suffrage activist of the first wave from 1911 to 1913, Tang Qunying, was an active member of Sun Yatsen's Revolutionary Alliance as well as the leader of the Women's Suffrage Alliance.[41] In the 1920s women's suffrage activists in the UWAs were routinely members of the GMD. Similarly, women involved in the Women's Rights League were often active members of the CCP. Among left-leaning critics wanting to claim the tradition of women's activism for the class struggle, the suffrage activists' commitment to "feminism" as well as "nationalism" has often been read as diminishing their feminism. For example, in 1942 Song Qingling, wife of Sun Yatsen, declared "from the very start, our women fought not under the banner of a barren feminism but as part and parcel of the democratic movement as a whole."[42] Later Western scholars such as Roxanne Witke concurred: "A remarkable trait of politically motivated Chinese women was that the most avant-garde would not be arrested at the feminist stage of struggle for suffrage and women's rights."[43]

The concern to establish a juncture between the nationalist and the feminist in the search for either the "true nationalist" or the "authentic feminist" is problematic in the case of China—and indeed many other non-Western nations. The establishment of a democratic system of government was a vital prerequisite for women's suffrage and clearly most politically minded women were likely to be involved in the broad struggle to establish such a governing system as part of their agenda. This should not diminish or be constructed as diluting their commitment to the women's suffrage cause. To the contrary, their participation in nationalist struggles was regarded as an important first step in demonstrating their right to equality. By fighting for republicanism or national independence, such women were staking their claim for full access to the rights and privileges of the "imagined" republic that they expected to result from their efforts. Failure to act in the nationalist struggles would have been seen as proof of women's inability to contribute to public life. As Ono Kazuko notes, "For the women who took part in the military arena [fighting against the Qing to establish a republic], their demand for rights—the franchise—as citizens of a republic, was something self-evident."[44]

Among the first political groups to form after the collapse of the Qing was the Women's Suffrage Comrades' Alliance, many of whose members had been active in the anti-Qing rebellion. On November 12, 1911, only weeks after the collapse of the Qing forces, one of China's most prominent female anti-Qing rebels, Lin Zongsu, called women together in Shanghai to form a lobbying group to press for gender equality within any future constitution. Lin had an impressive record of feminist activism within the anti-Qing movement. She had written the preface for China's first feminist treatise—Jin Songcen's 1903 *A Tocsin for Women*—and had been active in publishing revolutionary material while studying in Japan.[45] She is recognized as China's first woman journalist and proved to be an astute political player on the issue of women's suffrage.[46] Lin was simultaneously a member of the Revolutionary Alliance and the Socialist Party during these years. Only five days after the establishment of the provisional parliament, Lin had an audience with provisional president Sun Yatsen to seek his support for women's suffrage. Sun's theoretical and philosophical support for women's suffrage was forthcoming, and Lin promptly published her version of their conversation in her journal, *Women's Times* (Funü shibao). According to her article, Sun had stated,

> In the future, women's right to vote will surely be affirmed. Women too should gain knowledge of law and politics and strive to understand the truth about freedom and equality. Of course, opponents of women's suffrage may appear, but I will intervene on your behalf. I recognize that your association represents women comrades from the entire nation, and I fully respect your objectives.[47]

Other daily papers reprinted the article, and Sun found himself the object of criticism from the conservatives in his interim parliament.[48] Lin Zongsu's intention was to undermine potential conservative opposition to women's suffrage by invoking the support of Sun as "father" of the revolution. In February 1912 Lin merged her Women's Suffrage Comrades' Alliance with five other feminist groups to form the Women's Suffrage Alliance with Tang Qunying at its head. The unification of the women's movement under one banner was an attempt to create a more effective feminist lobbying voice during the crucial period when the national constitution was being discussed. For later critics to diminish the contribution of women such as Lin and Tang to the suffrage cause, on the grounds that they had fought for a democratic government as part of a nationalist struggle, is untenable. In part, this mistaken conception has been made possible by the conventions of scholarship on the women's suffrage movement that are better suited to nations privileged with the geopolitical closure possible in more stable democratic political systems.

In the case of China, the first women's suffrage activists were linked with anti-Qing revolutionaries and later with the GMD or CCP. In subsequent years, the political history of China has been dominated by the histories of these parties. The interparty and intraparty alliances formed by women's suffrage activists to enhance women's participation in politics have been lost in the process. The subsuming of the feminist movement into the nationalist cause effectively diminished the feminist contribution and made these Chinese feminists less worthy of "inheritance" in the history of the women's movement. They were, according to the nationalist reading, less "authentically" feminist. This logic would render all women's movements in the colonial or postcolonial geopolitical regions as "compromised feminism," all of which had to negotiate with other political movements because their own success was contingent upon the success of national independence or republicanism. In this regard, the absence of geopolitical closure challenges scholars writing on the Chinese women's suffrage movement to find paradigms suitable for conceptualizing postcolonial women's suffrage that do not rely on discrete boundaries between nationalism and feminism.

Conclusion

The narrative conventions dominating academic writing about women's suffrage have served the histories of Western women's movements well. But these methods and styles are not entirely applicable to the histories of the women's movement in the nations of Asia. The imperative of national independence or national rejuvenation dictated by decades of imperialism or colonialism required a different set of allegiances and strategies on the part of the women's suffrage activists. The process of reformulating and rebuilding the nation, required as a direct consequence of Western colonial and imperial endeavors, similarly necessitates a different scholarly approach. The identification of a "year" of victory needs to be recognized as having multiple problematic political implications in newly "imagined" nations. Within non-Western political cultures, the creation of an "affirming" rediscovery of women's enthusiasm for "democracy" is often undercut by suspicions of such a celebration of a Western-style democracy. Finally, recognition of the inevitability of the integration between nationalist and feminist struggles is needed. This task requires academics working in the histories of Asia's women's suffrage movement to untangle complex connections between feminists and other political lobbyists.

20

RETHINKING THE SOCIALIST CONSTRUCTION AND INTERNATIONAL CAREER OF THE CONCEPT "BOURGEOIS FEMINISM"

Marilyn J. Boxer

On Bastille Day 1889, German socialist Clara Zetkin announced to delegates from twenty countries assembled in Paris on the centennial of the French Revolution that "the emancipation of women, together with that of all humanity, will take place only with the emancipation of labor from capital." Zetkin assured these founders of the Second International that they need not fear losing "proletarian" women to others who were claiming to advance their interests, especially the women's rights groups who held their own international congresses in the French capital that summer. Despite her own comfortable origins as the daughter of a schoolteacher and a doctor's widow who had herself co-founded a women's rights organization, Zetkin denounced the nonsocialist "bourgeois women's movement" as a vain effort "built upon sand . . . [with] no basis in reality." While challenging her overwhelmingly male audience to recognize women's need for paid work to ensure their economic independence, she emphasized in this speech that "bourgeois" women offered no solution to the "woman question." Speaking at a women's rights congress in Berlin in 1896, she startled participants by declaring herself their "adversary [*Gegnerin*]."[1]

Zetkin's message would reverberate far and wide and last into the twenty-first century, bolstered in its long life by New Left and feminist activists and scholars, including historians of the 1970s generation. In 2004, anthropologist Kristen Ghodsee, assessing the condition of women in postsocialist Eastern Europe, asserted that "not much has changed since 1907," and quoted Zetkin's speech at the First International Congress of Socialist Women, held that year in Stuttgart: "There cannot be a unified struggle for the entire [female] sex . . . No, it must be a class struggle of all the exploited without differences of sex against all exploiters no matter what sex they belong to." Socialists must not, Zetkin had stressed, collaborate with "bourgeois feminists," even on issues of common concern. Drawing on this speech, Ghodsee suggests that the development of educational and advocacy institutions modeled on those created by women in "the West" threatens postcommunist Eastern European women with a new kind of "cultural feminism" that, like the earlier "bourgeois feminism" to which she likens it, is inappropriate to their real interests. Other scholars attest to the persistence of this concept.[2]

"Bourgeois feminism," however, is a slippery term that relies on a notion of "class" that has been substantially "reworked" in light of cultural studies and gender analysis. Historians today point to multiple ways in which gender and class work together, showing, for example, how wives *sans profession* became in the nineteenth century a marker of upwardly mobile masculinity. The binary distinction between public and private that underlay both scholarly and popular notions of gender has similarly been challenged, and the "public sphere" itself is seen to have been constructed so as to exclude women.[3] But no one has yet looked critically at how earlier, dichotomous notions of class and gender relationships have affected women's movements and their historians.

The construct that Zetkin and socialists of her era developed to distance themselves from burgeoning women's rights movements had its origins in European class politics at the turn of the twentieth century.[4] That construct was redeployed by leftists in a later period of feminist militancy, and historians had a role in passing along the politics and rhetoric of the earlier age to a new generation of students and activists. In addition to questioning the class basis on which this long-accepted distinction rests, we need to create new histories of feminism that are no longer encumbered by problematic assumptions about women and putative class interests or by socialist politics of the past. Such a reinterpretation might also shed light on the limitations of the European Left and its lost opportunities in the long process that Geoff Eley has termed "forging democracy."[5]

The origins of the concept "bourgeois feminism" lie deep in the early history of Marxian socialism. Both Marx and Engels portrayed the working-class woman as a victim of (industrial) capitalism, Marx offering a detailed portrait of the death of a twenty-year-old milliner from overwork, and Engels reporting his observation in England that "most of the prostitutes of the town had their employment in the mills to thank for their present situation." In his landmark book *The Origin of the Family, Private Property and the State* (1884), Engels famously declared that "within the family, he is the bourgeois and the wife represents the proletariat," but neither he nor Marx showed sympathy for organized feminism. For Marx, it represented "false women's emancipation"; he declared that "German women should have begun by driving their men to self-emancipation." Engels wrote to an American correspondent in 1891 that, thanks to efforts to organize socialist women, "the antiquated semi-bourgeois women's rights asses will soon be ordered to the rear."[6]

The most widely read of the male socialists on the woman question, however, was the German leader August Bebel. In the introduction to his classic work *Woman under Socialism* (1883), Bebel noted that "the hostile [*feindliche*] sisters have . . . a number of points of contact, on which they can, although marching separately, strike jointly [with socialists]." While the extent of Bebel's support for nonsocialist women's movements is disputed, early in his career he did assist his countrywoman Louise Otto-Peters in creating a women's emancipation organization, and he also acknowledged that "working-class women have more in common with bourgeois women or aristocratic women than do working-class men with men of other social classes."[7]

On women's issues, however, the most influential socialist activist of the time was Zetkin, who articulated and strenuously maintained what became the orthodox Marxist-socialist position on women's rights movements. Her 1889 Paris speech became what German women's historian Ute Frevert terms "the manifesto of the proletarian women's movement."[8] Although early in her career Zetkin expressed strong support for many goals of the women's rights movement, she came to view it as a "serious, dangerous power of the counter-revolution" that must be stopped. She sincerely believed that the condition of women, to whom she once referred as "slaves," would be remedied only through socialist revolution.[9] Zetkin prescribed a "clean break [*reinliche Scheidung*]" between proletarian parties and other political movements. Despite continuing to advocate some feminist goals, she expressed "extreme animosity" toward the idea of sisterhood, using derisory language such as "stupid feminist dreams about harmony" to describe feminist politics, and calling feminists "muddle-headed, wishy-washy, weak." By the mid-1890s, she had set in motion a worldwide movement to pillory nonsocialist women's rights efforts. Her biweekly journal, *Die Gleichheit* [Equality], addressed to women workers and party members, "untiringly differentiated between socialist and bourgeois women, socialist and bourgeois tactics," Jean Quataert has said. Her rejection of "bourgeois feminism" was "ostentatious," commented her French contemporary, the socialist and feminist activist Madeleine Pelletier. Women's historians have termed it "savage" and "vicious." It was also enormously effective.[10]

Who were these "bourgeois feminists" who posed such an alleged danger to working women? Prevailing marriage and property laws in late-nineteenth-century Europe ensured that *bourgeoises* rarely enjoyed the privileges and power of the capitalist *bourgeois*. Some rejected the values of the marketplace, and many continued women's traditional philanthropic work to aid poor women. Increasingly, however, daughters of bourgeois families also worked for pay. As teachers, postal or sales clerks, and low-level administrators, they in no way fit the image of the socialist ideal, the laborers in "the great virile trades . . . heroes who brought about the second industrial revolution," as Michelle Perrot puts it. Nevertheless, they were assumed by socialists to be, in Rosa Luxemburg's inimitable phrase, "the parasites of the parasites of the social body."[11]

In linking the words "feminism" and "bourgeois," socialists drew on a well-developed terminology laden with negative affect. Beyond "bourgeois classes," myriad usages abound: bourgeois deviation, bourgeois family, bourgeois individualism, bourgeois morality, bourgeois respectability, and, of course, bourgeois feminism—but rarely bourgeois socialism. But what does "bourgeois" mean? An imaginary other, a negative stereotype, even a mod way to say *passé*—"so last year"? Once a marker of residence or legal order, by the late decades of the nineteenth century it had become merely a pejorative epithet.[12] Heavily influenced by Marxist notions of a "bourgeois revolution," it was (and is) used to denigrate not only individuals but, through a kind of conceptual and linguistic slippage, also the ideas and aims of a political movement, namely feminism.[13]

But the term has long been contested. In 1968, Canadian historian Shirley Gruner, examining its usage in France in the 1830s, declared, "The word 'bourgeoisie' has never had the good fortune to be defined in any strict sense." It was associated with several social theories, including Saint-Simonianism and Marxism, of course. Definitions at that time ranged from "a small capitalist elite" to "the immense majority of the population." It was used confusingly by Fourierists "both to mean the mass of small craftsmen and artisans and to mean the neo-feudal capitalists." Gruner wondered if it had any further usefulness. Two decades later, studying the "bourgeois experience" in nineteenth-century Europe, Peter Gay found "a Babel of definitions." He points out that it could refer to the vast majority who were neither nobility nor peasants, but also that in mid-century, "Parisian proletarians used *bourgeoise* to designate respectable, sober working-class housewives whose husbands were afraid of them." Penned by writers such as Gustave Flaubert, Arthur Schnitzler, and Émile Zola, the word became an insult. Flaubert, who named himself "bourgeoisophobus," told George Sand, "Axiom: Hatred of Bourgeois is the beginning of all virtue."[14]

More recently, Sarah Maza has ascribed the French bourgeoisie to a "social imaginary." After its prerevolutionary use as a legal category disappeared, she states, the "bourgeoisie" became a negative, a way to describe "what *someone else* was." It carried a taint inherited from the old regime, implying both "unearned privilege and cultural deficiency."[15]

Bourgeoisophobia persisted; generations later, some leftist students even initially "dismissed the civil rights movement as 'bourgeois'; ... since the blacks sitting in at Woolworth lunch counters were college students, it meant that they were middle class and not the workers or sharecroppers of revolutionary prediction."[16]

Today it appears that Zetkin's position rested less on any clear socioeconomic distinction among women than on ideology, political strategies, and perhaps personal rivalries.[17] It also depended, as Eley importantly points out, on relationships among labor, socialist, and liberal parties that, in each national context, set the parameters within which women could act.[18] While many profound differences marked the lives of working-class and leisured women, Zetkin's stance ignores the extent to which many members of the reviled bourgeois class stood closer in social background and political outlook to the socialists themselves than to the "parasites." Her position reflected the socialist leaders' fears of diverting attention away from class struggle and of alienating the artisanal core of their working-class support, who for the most part held traditional views about women.[19] Zetkin adamantly refused all invitations to collaborate; in one notable incident in 1895, she even engaged in a published dispute with her socialist colleagues after declining to serve on a proposed cross-class commission—a "mishmash commission," she said—to study working conditions for women factory workers, a project they thought she should support.[20]

In her efforts to uphold her vision of class struggle and to avoid cross-class collaboration, Zetkin moved away from Bebel and his criticism of the limits imposed on women by motherhood, domesticity, and traditional gender roles. As the primary voice on women's issues of German Social Democracy (the SPD), Europe's largest and dominant socialist party; as founder and leader of the socialist women's international; and as longtime editor (1891 to 1917) of the socialist women's journal, Zetkin had broad and profound influence. Following her lead, working-class leaders everywhere were "haunted," in Quataert's view, by concern lest "their" women "be intimidated by their bourgeois sisters to pursue purely feminist goals." They strove incessantly to repudiate those who sought to breach the class divide.[21] Zetkin's ideas recur in the works of well-known socialist women in several other countries, notably Eleanor Marx in England, Alexandra Kollontai in Russia, and Louise Saumoneau in France—the latter two of whom became Zetkin's devoted younger followers, and each of whom exerted significant influence in her own country. All agreed on the importance, in Eleanor Marx's words, of "organis[ing] not as 'women' but as *proletarians*; not as female rivals of our working men but as their comrades in struggle." (Still, less separatist than the others, Marx proposed that "where the bourgeois women demand rights that are of help to us, we will fight together with them."[22])

Kollontai's major contribution to the theory of "bourgeois feminism," a lengthy 1908 "antifeminist polemic," was written expressly to undermine potential class collaboration. Under her influence, socialist women attacked women suffragists aggressively, appearing at feminist meetings to harass speakers and disrupt proceedings. Although her personal history contradicted her words, the nobly born Kollontai exaggerated the feminists' "selfish class character." She wrote, "Between the emancipated woman of the intelligentsia and the toiling woman with calloused hands, there was such an unbridgeable gulf, that there could be no question of any sort of point of agreement between them." One biographer describes Kollontai as the "scourge of the bourgeois feminists."[23] Ironically, she developed one of the most radical critiques of women's roles in family and sexuality of her era, for which she was criticized by Lenin and rejected by many others.[24]

In France, the first published call to establish a separate female constituency for Marxist socialism appeared in 1899. It initially expressed ambivalence toward feminism. The conveners, who termed themselves "socialist feminists," acknowledged the "legitimacy of [feminist] claims, regarding them as reforms whose realization would improve the situation of women," and declaring, "we will defend them as such." This appeal reappeared without change for at least five years, but its authors, who included Saumoneau, soon dropped the f-word and increasingly emulated Zetkin's strident opposition to "bourgeois feminism." Aiming "to tear socialist and proletarian women away from feminist confusionism," Saumoneau "adhered to the letter" of Zetkin's caution against cross-class cooperation.[25] Like her mentor, she attacked her opponents' character, describing them as "naïve, deranged and hysterical." Historian Charles Sowerwine states that "Saumoneau not only broke with the feminist movement, but also prevented the socialist women's movement from putting any emphasis on the struggle for equality between the sexes and even from taking into account the problems of women in recruiting them to the party. Women would come into the social-ist party as citizens, like the men, or they would not come at all." In France, even after World War I, "socialist women simply continued to repeat Saumoneau's arguments," says Paul Smith. "Saumonisme" prevailed, says Christine Bard, referring to 1936, when, with a social-ist government in power, socialist women opted not to press for the right to vote. Saumoneau "continued as a destructive power behind the scenes," says Helmut Gruber, ensuring that female participation was limited to those few willing to join the overwhelmingly male party and brave the inhospitable masculine ambience of local meetings.[26]

A fourth socialist woman of this era who strongly voiced similar suspicion of nonso-cialist feminists was the Dutch leader Henriëtte Roland Holst-Van der Schalk. In 1898, when Dutch feminists organized a national exhibition on women's work, Roland Holst urged working-class women to boycott it, publishing a pamphlet in protest.[27] In hostile lan-guage that vied with Zetkin's invective, Roland Holst called the exhibition leaders "hyp-ocritical, fork-tongued, cowardly . . . middle-class feminists." At a preliminary meeting called to inform working women of exhibition plans, she expressed "great anger, the speaker stamping her feet and her eyes 'ablaze with hatred and scorn,' while she shouted insults at the president herself."[28]

How much influence these socialist women had outside leadership circles and beyond major cities is uncertain.[29] What is clear is that, while maintaining many different positions on other issues, most other socialist parties adopted the Second International's and the SPD's party line of anathematizing "bourgeois feminism."[30] Some leaders, despite per-sonal ambivalence, divorced themselves from nonsocialist feminist groups, although few expressed opposition in such vituperative language as Zetkin, Kollontai, Saumoneau, and Roland Holst.[31] In fact, many socialist women distinguished between formal, organiza-tional collaboration and cooperation among individuals. This point was recognized in 1900 at the first conference of German socialist women, where it was agreed to leave it to individuals to decide whether to "occasionally or temporarily work alongside 'women's righters' and other bourgeois elements." In many cases, especially at the local level, they did collaborate.[32] The "clean break" policy advocated by Zetkin, and reinforced by the socialist leadership, however, forced many left-leaning women to choose. A Dutch inter-nationalist lamented in 1911 that "the SD [Social Democratic] women refuse to take a leaflet from the hands of a woman with the badge of the suffragists, although it is an appeal written by Bebel . . . himself."[33]

Rivalry over organizational power and resources played a major role in shaping the con-flict. Socialist parties had access to substantial resources unavailable to women's groups. Lily

Braun, who vied with Zetkin for leadership in Germany, noted that working-class women's opportunity to ally with a large, powerful party meant that "proletarian women . . . had the potential of being politically effective; bourgeois women did not." When a new socialist women's group was formed in Paris in 1913, Pelletier predicted sarcastically that "it will leave feminism behind to please the men in the party." An Austrian socialist, describing her colleagues, noted, "Beginners in the class struggle, they were anxious to maintain their prestige vis-à-vis their male comrades."[34] Criticism by socialist women of "bourgeois feminism" was at the least a shrewd strategy.

The socialists' ardent castigation of "bourgeois feminism" persisted through the interwar period, despite male socialists' participation in so-called bourgeois governments during the Popular Front of the 1930s. It was most influential where socialist parties adhered closely to the principles and politics of the Second International, less so, for example, in Great Britain. It appeared as far away from its origins as China in the 1920s and Vietnam in the 1930s.[35] It was, of course, affected by the rise of welfare states, with support from nonsocialists and socialists alike, and by changing communist policies. "Feminism," however, had come to signify "bourgeois feminism." The legacy of class division persisted, so that, as Mineke Bosch comments about the Dutch women's movement, when feminism reemerged in the 1970s, conflicts between a "bourgeois" women's movement and a "proletarian" movement were taken entirely for granted by activists.[36] They soon made their way into the academy as well.

After World War II, claims for women's rights on the left reemerged with the founding by French communists in 1945 of the Women's International Democratic Federation, to pursue the fight against fascism and to represent working-class women. Caught up in Cold War politics, the WIDF, Leila Rupp states, "continued the well-worn socialist tradition of hostility to the bourgeois women's movement," contending with older international women's organizations for representation at the United Nations.[37] A short collection of excerpts from writings by Marx, Engels, Lenin, and Stalin, published in 1951 as *The Woman Question*, offered as an appendix a selection by Zetkin from her famous 1920 interview with Lenin, including Lenin's counsel to "draw a clear and ineradicable line of distinction between our policy and [bourgeois] feminism." Reprinted in 1970, this publication appeared that year on the reading list for the first course in women's history taught in the first women's studies program in the United States.[38]

By the time that feminism reappeared as a highly visible movement, many of its demands had been achieved in the countries where "first wave" feminists had been most active. Believing, mistakenly, that their predecessors had limited their quest to the vote, some "second wave" feminists distinguished between what they called "equal rights feminism" and "women's liberation." Their new demands included elimination of many restrictions on women's lives that they associated with "bourgeois" society, including "bourgeois morality" and sexual repression. Given the experience of many new leaders in New Left movements, it is no surprise that dichotomous thinking about the relationship between feminism and socialism reemerged, along with criticism of the "bourgeois character" of the woman suffrage movement by activist author Kate Millett and others. The "bourgeois feminist movement" of the suffragists constituted a "trap," wrote Robin Morgan in the emblematic text of 1970, *Sisterhood Is Powerful*.[39]

Class issues infused the politics of women's liberation from its beginnings. Many activists perceived capitalism as an obstacle to the equality of women as well as of the working classes. In Britain, the women's liberation journal *Red Rag*, in its inaugural issue of 1972, announced its support for "revolutionary change in society, for ending capitalism and establishing socialism." In France, where anti-bourgeois sentiment was particularly strong and feminism subject to "aggressive" ridicule, feminists of the 1970s were, in historian Florence Rochefort's words, "profoundly anchored in the new left and the extreme left."[40] By linking feminism to socialism, activists could show their recognition that women's liberation intended far more than relieving Betty Friedan's unhappy housewives of "the problem that has no name."[41]

Two of the earliest and most influential activist-scholars, Juliet Mitchell and Sheila Rowbotham, emerged from leftist groups in England, where the new feminism was closely related to the labor movement. The new women's movement on the left is sometimes dated from the appearance in 1966 of Mitchell's article "The Longest Revolution" in the *New Left Review*, which reminded readers of the Marxian legacy and the socialist failure to solve the problem of women's subordination. What held women back, in Mitchell's analysis, was the "traditional," that is to say, the "bourgeois" family. But Mitchell also cautioned against too early a class division among the new feminists. "Perhaps in the future, the biggest single theoretical battle will have to be that between liberationists with a socialist analysis, and feminists with a 'radical feminist' analysis. But that future has come too soon. The conflict is premature because neither group has yet developed a 'theory.' The practice which is that theory's condition of production has only just begun." Mitchell avoided using the term "bourgeois feminism," preferring instead to identify feminists who believed that equality could be won without a socialist revolution as "liberal."[42]

Sheila Rowbotham, a "worker student" in history whose pioneering 1972 book, *Women, Resistance, and Revolution*, linked women to the cause of socialist revolution, employed the term "bourgeois feminist" only in the final sentence of her introductory chapter. But she intended it in no derogatory sense, simply as an attribute of women who had very early challenged the status quo in women's roles. She also offered a revisionist reading of socialist policy, arguing that feminist "changes will not follow a socialist revolution automatically but will have to be made explicit in a distinct movement now, as a precondition of revolution, not as its aftermath."[43]

Writing retrospectively, Rowbotham noted the extent to which leftist movements of the late nineteenth and early twentieth centuries had caricatured feminists and made feminism into a "dreaded bogey." These "over-simplified caricatures of 'bourgeois feminism' which concertina-ed several kinds of feminism into one grotesque creature . . . have been taken too much at face value by socialist women writing history." She herself had failed, she said, to problematize the relationship between socialism and feminism sufficiently, or to challenge an "uncritical acceptance of a simple polarity between socialism and feminism." "It was not," she wrote in a subsequent book, "a simple question of reactionary middle-class feminists versus enlightened working-class socialists."[44]

The new women's history was strongly influenced by developments in labor history. Both Mitchell and Rowbotham had studied with E. P. Thompson, the famous British activist-scholar who helped to bring about new perspectives on working-class and socialist history.[45] But by neglecting women in his classic work *The Making of the English Working Class* (1963), he sensitized female activist-scholars to the "cult of masculinity" greatly admired by the left. In a perceptive account of Thompson's influence and the difficulties arising from it, titled *What's Left?*, Julia Swindells and Lisa Jardine state the problem: "What is admissible within the Thompson enterprise of retrieving working-class consciousness as a 'suitable' topic for historians is going to be a problem for subsequent radical history, particularly when social history belatedly remembers the women. The 'value' of working-class men's experience is authorized by culture, and in that account the women provide the 'virtue' via the family. But in that case, the women will always appear in the account *as* bourgeois."[46]

Similar problems arose in radical movements in North America, France, Germany, Italy, and elsewhere. As women turned "personal" into "political" issues in the politics of 1960s radical movements, they often found themselves shoved aside and belittled. "We are trashed as bourgeois feminist irrespective of the political position we take," commented Dorothy E. Smith, a Canadian Marxist feminist activist-scholar. "If you are working-class they'll humiliate you with your sex and class ignorances, if you're middle-class they'll call you a petty bourgeois deviationist," complained Rowbotham.[47] This rejection of leftist women's perspectives contributed substantially to shaping the new women's movement, in which women on the left played a formative role.

Two developments of the 1970s brought increased prominence to the assumption of a deep class division among activist women, in which use of the word "bourgeois" to casti-gate nonsocialist feminists continued. One was a self-identified socialist feminist move-ment whose adherents began a search for new theory to remedy flaws in the work inherited from nineteenth-century socialists.[48] The second movement, also heavily influenced by nineteenth-century socialist thought, was the academic field of women's studies. The ter-minology and the legacy of disdain for "bourgeois feminism" appear often in the literature of both movements.

Socialist feminists drew on Engels to legitimize women's claims; some cited Mitchell; most assumed a socialist revolution essential to women's liberation. While factional poli-tics split women's movements, numerous theorists tried to integrate socialism and femi-nism by developing materialist explanations that, unlike Marxism, included human reproduction and linked the systems of "patriarchy" that governed family life with rela-tions of production. Others inveighed against "bourgeois feminism." "Today we polemi-cize with 'bourgeois' and 'petty-bourgeois' feminists," said Mary-Alice Waters in 1972. "Many of us are dissatisfied with a strict bourgeois feminism," wrote Charnie Guettel in 1974. "Bourgeois and proletarian women confront each other in the labor market, and bourgeois women are one of the instruments used to undercut the wages of proletarian women . . . today [just as] in Clara Zetkin's day," wrote Marlene Dixon in 1977. Like their predecessors in the Second International, these women assured their male colleagues of their commitment to socialist revolution and of their rejection of nonsocialist feminisms.[49]

Aiming to reduce the conflict, theorist Lise Vogel noted that Zetkin, in an 1896 speech, did not propose a simple dichotomy but divided women into groups, separating out the "ruling-class women of the Upper Ten Thousand" from the lower and middle bourgeoisie who constituted the core of the bourgeois women's movement, and whose demands she then considered "entirely justified." In Vogel's view, Zetkin's later intransigent opposition to nonsocialist women reflected her resistance to reformism within the socialist movement as well as her pragmatic politics. ("Most revisionists and at least some reformists in the SPD were, in fact, closely allied to bourgeois feminism," as they more generally favoured collaboration with liberals, states Richard J. Evans.[50])

During the later 1970s and the 1980s, as feminism faded from the public eye, it reap-peared in rapidly spreading women's studies programs, where, from the beginning, the influence of socialist thought was strong.[51] Academic feminism drew heavily on the liter-ature that informed the radical movements of the 1960s and early 1970s. Whatever the course discipline, many reading lists included works in which students encountered discussion of socialism's relationship to feminism. Engels's *Origin of the Family* appeared on many of the first syllabi in women's studies, along with Simone de Beauvoir's *The Second Sex* (1952) and Kate Millett's *Sexual Politics* (1970), both of which rely on Engels. Essays by socialists Margaret Benston, Marlene Dixon, and Roxanne Dunbar that linked women's liberation to socialist revolution appeared repeatedly.[52] The first women's studies textbooks, which generally included some effort to explain the origins of women's "oppression" and concomitant proposed solutions, tended to define women's movements using oversimplified terms. As Michèle Barrett and Anne Phillips write, "1970s feminism assumed one could specify a *cause* of women's oppression . . . [one that] lay at the level of *social structure* . . . In the taxonomies so beloved of the period—as of many commentators subsequently—feminisms were divided into their liberal, socialist, and radical varieties." The notion of "bourgeois feminism" (sometimes identified as "liberal feminism") found a place alongside socialist feminism and radical feminism as one of the "Big Three" frequently cited by historians and feminist theorists.[53]

Not only did this practice confuse class origins and class outlook, it defied the reality that feminism's constituency persisted in cutting across alleged class borders. It obscured the fact that feminism also transcended racial lines. Even though, as Zillah Eisenstein points out, "The 'bourgeois' woman has not really been identified yet in terms of a class analysis specifically pertaining to women," she was readily targeted for dismissal. The founders of the women's studies program at San Diego State chastised themselves and others associated with the university for their "petit bourgeois" biases. In 1974, when the African American Combahee River Collective, identifying its politics as socialist, published the first book on "black women's studies," it rejected support for a leading black feminist group, the National Black Feminist Organization, for its "bourgeois-feminist stance." Introducing a reprint of Clara Zetkin's work in 1984, activist Angela Davis opined that "bourgeois feminists today . . . have a great deal to learn from Zetkin's analysis."[54]

Historians, meanwhile, set out to recover the heritage of socialist women and feminist socialists. As a research topic, the relationship between feminism and socialism offered several attractions. It provided entrée for young historians into the popular subfield then dubbed the "new social history." It offered attractively untrodden ground, including virtually untouched archival materials. It also offered a chance to contribute to the wider movement for social change. History, at least on the left, seemed to allow for "making a statement." Perhaps it also offered what Virginia Woolf described as "the glamour of the working class and the emotional relief afforded by adopting its cause."[55] No one snickered at the idea of working-class history, and, of course, no one wanted to be "bourgeois."[56] Like earlier feminists who applauded the socialists for their stance on women's rights, the new historians of women also appreciated the recognition that socialist parties had afforded women's causes—"the first in all countries," as the secretary-general of the National Council of French Women, Mme. Avril de Sainte-Croix, declared in 1907.[57]

At that time, however, one could read basic texts about socialism without encountering a single reference to women.[58] The focus was on ideology and organizations, political parties and trade associations, strikes and protest marches; the rhetoric was dominated by the language of class, and the working class was embodied in the artisan, factory hand, or miner, its "quintessential worker" clearly male.[59] Sources included organizational records, proceedings of party congresses, party platforms, personal papers of party leaders, and periodical publications supported by party funds. Labor history told of men and organizations.

As Beatrix Campbell wrote (of Britain), "The socialist movement . . . [was] swept off its feet by the magic of masculinity, muscle and machinery," and its historians failed to challenge this perception.[60]

Despite New Left influences, the initial challenge to consensus history did not extend to women's interests. French labor historian Michelle Perrot, who became one of the founders of French women's history, tells a revealing story of resistance by Trotskyist, Maoist, and other radical students. In 1973, when sociologist Andrée Michel introduced analysis of the family into the first women's history course in France, she "was reproached . . . They said they did not want to hear about family models; the family was bourgeois."[61] The historiography also reflects the long dominance in the academy of structuralism. In this heyday of the "longue durée," not only was biography all but banished from the historical profession, it was doubly suspect on grounds of elitism. The term "women worthies" took on a pejorative cast, while women workers and women on the left attracted disproportionate scholarly interest.[62]

Rowbotham introduced her readers to Anna Doyle Wheeler, Flora Tristan, Eleanor Marx, Alexandra Kollontai, Angelica Balabanoff, Emma Goldman, and many other socialist women.[63] Werner Thönnessen's 1969 study (which appeared in English in 1973) of the SPD's stance toward women brought prominence to Clara Zetkin and her German party. Thönnessen charged "the [bourgeois] women's movement . . . [with its] problem-ridden aim of legal equality" with responsibility for society's ability to "liquidate the proletarian women's movement." He credits "bourgeois feminism," along with "proletarian anti-feminism" and the SPD's turn to reformism ("revisionism"), for having "banished women's liberation once and for all into the realm of utopia."[64] Another pioneer of German women's history, Amy Hackett, quoting Zetkin's view of sisterhood as "sentimental simpering about harmony," wrote in 1972 that "the deepest split in German feminism was between Social Democratic and bourgeois women."[65]

Although France occupied a much lesser place in the story, as the nation whose history had long attracted more Anglophone historians than any other non-English-speaking country, it also gained considerable notice in the 1970s. Russia's revolutionary history and the prominence of its radical women likewise drew attention to links between socialism and feminism. Between 1975 and 1979, several unpublished dissertations and at least seven monographs and collections of essays appeared in English, focusing on socialist women and highlighting the division between "bourgeois feminism" and "socialist feminism."[66] Generalizations based on three national histories, featuring Zetkin, Saumoneau, and Kollontai, soon found their way into women's history and women's studies courses, and greatly affected interpretations and evaluations of women's movements.

Important works of this period include Berenice Carroll's 1976 anthology, offering two chapters on socialism and feminism, one on Engels (and Marx) and another on the "bourgeois" women's movement in Germany and its association with liberalism.[67] The same year, *The Socialist Register* published an aptly titled article, "Marxist Women versus Bourgeois Feminism," that included in translation important primary sources by Bebel (including his reference to "the enemy sisters") and Zetkin as well as Rosa Luxemburg, and also brought Eleanor Marx into the "war" fought by German Marxist women "to counteract the influence of bourgeois feminism."[68] That year also, Richard J. Evans published the first of a series of works through which he helped to establish Germany as the paradigmatic case of socialist relations with feminism. Taking as a starting date 1894, the year that marked the formation of a national federation of German women's organizations and their (contested) vote to exclude socialist women's groups (though not working women),

Evans called attention to the class antagonism that made alliance "impossible," despite what he calls their "wide agreement of aims."[69]

Studying the socialist-feminist connection in France, Sowerwine in 1978 also pointed to signal events in the early years of the two movements. During a struggle for dominance among socialist factions at a formative meeting of the French Workers' Party (POF) in 1880, feminist leader Hubertine Auclert and her group chose to support a Proudhonist-influenced group that envisioned only traditional roles for women, over their Marxist-oriented, and theoretically more feminist, rivals. Sowerwine attributes the choice to the power of private property over feminist claims in their scale of values (and generalizes from it to "bourgeois feminists"). Other possible readings of this event (including my own) suggest alternative explanations, including personal rivalries and loyalties as well as the differing definitions of socialism and feminism that divided factional leaders and their followers. Auclert's biographer points out, importantly, that even before the contentious meeting, the collectivist group had already rejected allying with the advocates of women's rights.[70]

A second event that affected relations between socialist and feminist women occurred during the International Congress on the Condition and Rights of Women in Paris in 1900. In a debate over the scope of proposed labor legislation, a dispute arose over whether to include domestic servants, as socialist participants advocated. The controversy itself, while brief, led to an extended, bitter, and highly personalized argument between two founders of the newly formed "socialist feminist" group and a nonsocialist leader of the conference, and it supposedly soured relations between women's groups permanently. Following Sowerwine, Robert Stuart, a historian of the POF, views the "notorious" conflict as "emblematic of the irreconcilable class conflict dividing militant French women."[71] But a rereading of the conference proceedings raises the question of whether this confrontation outweighs an important proposal, termed "minor" by Sowerwine, by the "bourgeois" journalist and conference convener Marguerite Durand. This plan called for minimum piecework rates, female labor inspectors, and extension of labor legislation to domestic workers and commercial employees (categories that included the vast majority of women workers). Without denying that some feminists did oppose socialism, this history could also be written to highlight the efforts of "bourgeois" women to improve conditions for working-class women.[72]

"Bourgeois" women, for example, were not always dismissive of domestic servants. Just two years earlier, at the summer-long exposition on women's work organized by Dutch "bourgeois" women at the Hague, servants were offered free entrance and were included as speakers in an extensive, embedded conference on domestic service. Lily Braun, cast out of German Social Democracy as too "bourgeois," suggested that a domestic servants' union be organized, and called on servants "to strike against the semi-feudal relationship under which they work." In 1899, when she formally proposed the inclusion of female servants in labor legislation under consideration at the Reichstag, "her party comrades discouraged her, arguing that maids were not genuine proletarians." Braun's efforts on behalf of household workers elicited the charge that she was "deflecting the working class from its struggle for power." In Russia, following the Revolution of 1905, feminists organized a union for domestic workers; they also encouraged peasant women to claim access to land and voting rights, and drew many working women into their suffrage efforts.[73]

These complexities notwithstanding, in 1978, when Jean Quataert and I published a collection of essays about socialist women in five European countries, we inadvertently contributed to the revival of class-based categorical thinking about feminism. In our introduction, we defined the terms "socialist feminism" and "bourgeois feminism" primarily in terms of ideological heritages. Although we described many of the socialists as artisans or employees of small shops, even as intellectuals, rather than as prototypical "proletarian" factory workers, and noted that the feminists labeled "bourgeois" included teachers and white-collar workers as well as leisured women, we did not delve further into class identity. Nor did we criticize the solidly "bourgeois" (if not upper-class) origins of most of the socialist leaders. We tended to categorize our subjects just as the socialists of that era had done.[74]

The unexamined definition of "bourgeois feminism" and the alleged gulf that lay between its adherents and the socialists found their way into women's history also through textbooks. The first and for a decade the only text designed specifically for survey courses in European women's history, *Becoming Visible* (1977), offered chapters on modern France, England, Russia, Germany, and Spain, all with a leftist slant; and in its second and third editions (1987, 1998) it included a selection by Sowerwine on socialism and feminism that passed along the unexamined use of "bourgeois feminism." While admirably summarizing the origins and significance of the socialist response to socioeconomic changes wrought in working-class women's lives, this chapter also exaggerated the depth of the division between women's groups, as well as the success of socialist parties in attracting women workers.[75]

What, for instance, if the nonsocialists had been described by historians not as "bourgeois" but as "liberal" feminists or "suffrage" feminists; or, following German and Russian usage, as "equal rights feminists"; or, for the French case, as Karen Offen did some years ago and Carolyn Eichner and Florence Rochefort have done more recently, as "republican feminists"? Gisela Bock points to some feminists who avoided the ambivalent word "bourgeois," which in German refers to citizenship as well as class status, by referring to the "civic women's movement." Jean Quataert now prefers "reform feminist" to her earlier usage. For socialists and some historians of the 1960s and 1970s, however, to borrow from Rochefort, "the [feminist] movement was just as pejoratively 'bourgeois' as it had been for their predecessors near the end of the nineteenth century."[76]

For the generation of activist-historians who began professional careers in the early 1970s, the emphasis on socialist women leaders and their opposition to "bourgeois feminism" served a political purpose. Claire Moses observes that these "constructions" of women's history allowed the new feminists "to stake out a position more radical than that of [their] grandmothers ... [and their] mothers." "We therefore reclaimed the Socialist women for feminism, denying their self-naming," she adds.[77] "The dichotomies—Women and Labour, Sex and Class, Feminism and Socialism have been the intimate inhabitants of both my psyche and my intellectual work (if the two can be separated)," Sally Alexander recalls.[78]

It seems curious now that, given the influence of E. P. Thompson, more studies of socialism and feminism in the 1970s did not emphasize the impact of culture on the formation of consciousness for socialist and feminist activists in the earlier period. By the mid-1980s, however, following Joan Scott's influential challenge to apply gender analysis to historical studies and the flowering of cultural studies, new perspectives on individual identity and class consciousness began to dissolve old dichotomies. Where the 1982 English edition of Sowerwine's book bears the title *Sisters or Citizens?*, Evans's 1987 study of feminism, socialism, and pacifism in Europe features inclusion in its title, *Comrades and Sisters*. In this work, Evans notes that the doctrine of a sharp separation between working women and "bourgeois feminists" promulgated by Zetkin, Saumoneau, and Kollontai was "by no means an inevitable extrapolation of the fundamentals of Marxism."[79]

Evans's point reappears with emphasis in a biography of Bebel that appeared in 2000. Examining Zetkin's ascendancy over Bebel in shaping Marxist thought on collaboration with nonsocialist women, Anne Lopes and Gary Roth note, "Until Zetkin, no one had implied [that to 'cross class'] was unmarxist. The marxian legacy, as it has come to be known in the subsequent historiography, is largely a fiction created by Zetkin herself . . . The social democratic outlook already included the gamut of bourgeois feminist interests and mostly did so with greater consistency and fervor." In the eyes of these authors, historians who deemphasized Bebel's feminism "merged the history and the historiography."[80]

In fact, there was a long history of efforts to link socialism and feminism. In the pre-Marxist era in France, the definition of the "feminine" that shaped romantic socialist conceptions encompassed all women. From the Saint-Simoniennes of the 1830s, through the revolutionaries of 1848 and the Communardes of 1871, "proletarian" women collaborated with "bourgeois" women. Many women identified as "bourgeois feminists" considered themselves socialist and participated in socialist organizations.[81] Some socialist women, even in Zetkin's own party, rejected her policy of absolute noncooperation. Some working-class women joined "bourgeois" groups, and many in the latter ranks worked to improve working-class women's employment skills and educational opportunities. Indeed, in many instances, nonsocialist feminism grew out of women's work to aid impoverished and abused women.[82] Common goals, such as winning the vote, opposing militarism, or resolving the "motherhood dilemma," sometimes elicited collaboration, sometimes "parallel wars."[83] Even the alleged "litmus test" of class loyalty, protective legislation, on close examination by historians from nine European countries as well as Australia and the United States, turns out to be anything but. Trade union women, fearing loss of employment, often opposed it, and division appeared in socialist and nonsocialist women's groups alike. Rather than a clear-cut struggle between "bourgeois feminists" and defenders of women workers, positions on restricting female labor ran the gamut among adherents of all political persuasions.[84]

Largely since the 1990s, new historical scholarship has emerged from Northern and Eastern Europe and far beyond that shows the global purchase of the concept "bourgeois feminism," while also blurring the dichotomous lines it suggests.[85] In Denmark and Sweden, where socialists collaborated with liberals to achieve democratic parliamentary institutions, barriers between "bourgeois" and socialist women's groups were often breached.[86] In Ukraine, the Galician leader Natalia Ozarkevych Kobrynska, portrayed by Martha Bohachevsky-Chomiak, argued explicitly against Zetkin, advocating linkages between the two social movements and rejecting the socialist denigration of feminism as "bourgeois."[87] In Hungary, where in the early twentieth century socialists "nervously guard[ed] their charges against any 'bourgeois influence,' " Judith Szapor notes that some socialists nevertheless formed alliances with "bourgeois" feminists to campaign for the vote, and even tried to put into practice Lily Braun's proposals to resolve domestic servants' problems by creating communal households. Although Hungarian feminism later became what Andrea Pető terms "an isolated stream" echoes of an antifeminist heritage persisted in post-1989 Hungary. "Feminists were considered aliens by conservative Christians, and bourgeois by the labor movement."[88] In Bulgaria, according to Krassimira Daskalova, ideological divisions over class collaboration split the socialists in 1903 and left "feminism" stigmatized as "bourgeois," while also stereotyped as opposing " 'traditional Bulgarian values' of love, marriage, and family."[89] In Poland, states Jill Bystydzienski, "State propaganda successfully managed to belittle the feminist cause and to plant almost unanimous disdain for western feminism presenting it as a bourgeois preoccupation of well-to-do, disaffected, mainly American women." Any emerging feminism today must define itself as neither "Western" nor communist.[90]

Disdain for feminism reached Asia as well. In China, Bebel was translated in the early 1920s, and the Chinese Communist Party adopted the advancement of women as a basic tenet. But despite party work undertaken to improve the condition of women, Chinese leaders found it useful to denigrate "feminism"; the word itself, as Wang Zheng shows, became a negative term, usually accompanied by the adjective "bourgeois" and often qualified as well by "Western."[91] Kumari Jayawardena writes that when feminism arose in South Asia in the 1970s, "The Left brought out the old quotations on the Woman Question, while dismissing feminism as a dangerous Western import."[92]

These examples serve to show that, as the editors of a 1989 collection of globally ranging essays on women and socialism state,

> The enduring power of these early debates should be underlined. They have resonated through every socialist movement in the twentieth century without exception . . . From China to Nicaragua, this nineteenth-century model has been consciously adopted, even when its appropriateness was, at the least, open to question. While other aspects of the Marxist-Leninist program . . . have been adapted to national conditions, this element has remained remarkably unchanged, whether the country deploying the theory was Asian, Southeast Asian, African, European, or Latin American.[93]

Phrases such as "capitulation to bourgeois feminism" and "knuckled under to bourgeois feminism" were commonly employed, and the term "bourgeois feminism" was used to label behavior deemed to favor "individualism" or to defy traditional strictures about female conduct.[94]

The concept "bourgeois feminism" rested on reductionist constructions of class status and political interests that are a poor fit for the realities of women's lives. In an era when level of skill and control over production served to define male workers' identity, and in turn profoundly affected the ideology and language of class, women were assumed to have no work-derived identity. Instead, most women became "proletarian" or "bourgeois" on the basis of their relationships to men.[95] But, as Rochefort concludes, "The women designated by socialists as 'bourgeoises' were for the most part situated well to the left on the political spectrum." In her view, the socialist attack on feminism in the Second International "did not bring about a major schism within the [French] feminist movement; for feminists it remained possible to have a twofold commitment."[96] Studies from postcommunist Eastern Europe also show that "many women . . . seemingly identified as both feminists and socialists without much effort."[97]

Class ascription also reflected a gendered double standard. While socialists adopted working-class identities for themselves and ignored the "bourgeois" class origins of men whose views they approved, they labeled women of similar background with the term of opprobrium. This practice did not go unnoticed. Maria Grever and Berteke Waaldijk cite a Dutch journalist who argued in 1898 that "the proletariat judged rich women more harshly than rich men, while capitalists victimized poor women more than poor men."[98] In 1907, French feminist Nelly Roussel said, "Two women of the opposite classes may have more common interests, more similar sources of revolt, consequently more terrain for entente than have a man and a woman belonging to the same milieu . . . There are no 'managerial classes' among us."[99] In her 1936 memoir, Jeanne Bouvier, a working-class Frenchwoman, also complained, recalling that "feminists are all treated as 'bourgeoise,' but the husbands of these feminists, if they are members of a political or philosophical party of the left, are not 'bourgeois.' " In contrast, as Christine Bard points out, "Economically, teachers, especially when single, belong to the working-class . . . [But because] their educational level allowed them to participate in intellectual circles, *voire 'bourgeois,'* " a designation they denied. Although historians and sociologists long ago recognized the nature and significance of the "new class" into which so many working women were drawn, these insights eluded most socialist leaders and early historians of socialist and feminist relationships.[100]

Studies of the class backgrounds of socialist women and of nonsocialist feminists drawn from British, Bulgarian, Dutch, German, Spanish, and Swedish history of the early twentieth century suggest further confusion. Few socialist women worked for pay; they were socialists by sympathy but not "proletarian." Fewer performed labor that produced "surplus value." In Bulgaria, France, Germany, the Netherlands, Spain, and Sweden, most were stay-at-home wives of socialist men. Many British feminists came from working-class origins, but typically worked in service occupations, especially as teachers. In the British suffrage movement, those who held dual commitments to labor movements and to feminism tended to be undercounted. In the Netherlands, few feminists were wealthy women.[101] It is not clear that the class backgrounds of socialist women and feminists were "very different," as Sowerwine has alleged.[102] Given a paucity of data, mixed reports, generational shifts, and national differences, as well as multiple varieties of socialism and of feminism, assertions about feminists' and women socialists' "class" backgrounds seem at best to be premature. In any case, Marxist class definitions and categories offer little insight.

Rhetoric masked the reality that party allegiance did not parallel class differences among women. As a political movement, feminism has never been "bourgeois" in the sense that Marxists proposed. "Bourgeois feminism" was invented by socialist women and did not exist as a discrete, identifiable, class-based women's movement. Nor was there as absolute a class divide between women's groups as socialist leaders and some of their historians asserted. This allegation allowed a strategic shift in socialist perspectives on the woman question to take place, from the more collaborative views of August Bebel and others to Clara Zetkin and her followers, who portrayed feminism as if it were the complaint of a special interest group. The socialists, says Quataert, "promoted their own gendered form of identity politics." As a political strategy for rejecting feminism, it helped socialists claim "proletarian" values for themselves, while it masked the motivations of its formulators and their failure to create a woman-centered socialism that might effectively attract women workers.[103]

If the purpose, conscious or unconscious, of the enemies of "bourgeois feminism" was to squelch any potential for unity among women's movements, they succeeded, probably beyond what they could have imagined. The concept spread around the globe, and it persisted for a century as a means to discredit nonsocialist women activists. Feminism fell into a double bind. It was suspect as "bourgeois," but also came to be rejected, especially in formerly communist countries after 1989, for its association with socialism.[104] In the 1980s, as identity politics and the language of race and ethnicity replaced class as a central focus, "bourgeois" lost its place as the epithet of choice, but left behind a divisive

300

residue. The dichotomizing concept also owes its long life to the scholars, myself included, who employed the term, and failed to challenge its validity. Today, however, received ideas and inherited dichotomies elicit criticism. Comparing nineteenth-century women's emancipation movements, the editors of a 2004 volume conclude, "There was more crossing of borders between feminism and socialism than the long-established image of the 'hostile sisters' would lead us to suppose. Historiography has also exaggerated the rift between the two wings of the women's movement for political reasons."[105]

Feminism is one of the most misunderstood movements of modern times, and historians have contributed to the misjudgment. The "most lasting legacy" of the socialist rejection of feminism as "bourgeois" was not, as Sowerwine asserted, "the development of separate organization for working-class women and a consequent articulation of their distinct concerns."[106] Whether the latter ever happened is debatable. What is certain, in my view, is that the most far-reaching legacy for women was the socialists' success in spreading disdain for feminism, on the ideological grounds that to be a practicing feminist was to be "bourgeois." The association between socialism and feminism was, as Karen Offen declares, "a lethal relationship . . . From a feminist perspective, organized socialism in Europe—and more broadly, the social democratic left—has a lot to answer for."[107] Geoff Eley states, "Socialist parties' claims to be the vanguard of democracy, rallying all progressive causes to their banner, foundered on this gender neglect."[108] The socialist stance toward feminism hindered both movements in achieving mutually desired goals.[109]

The history of the European Left's relationships with women and feminism is an important part of political history that needs reassessment. Historians today might begin by opening previously closed categories and replacing organizational approaches with thematic, women-centered frameworks.[110] With a reconceptualized question that employs gender as a category of analysis and redefines politics to include sexual politics, identifies the many positive contributions of nonsocialist feminists to the lives of women workers, and examines such neglected topics as the impact on socialist politics of concepts of motherhood and the population question, understanding of historical relationships between socialist and feminist movements and their consequences for democratic movements and society would be clarified and enriched. This revision would recognize the importance of feminism's history to the history of the left and to modern history as a whole, with new appreciation for how categorical class thinking and political commitments affected both its history and historians.

SUGGESTED FURTHER READING

This list of suggested further reading is organized for each selection, containing more recent articles and books recommended by the authors or the editor that do not appear in their endnotes. More recent contributions have less supplementary bibliography. Additional references to salient works on feminisms and nation-state formation, and pertinent theme volumes not mentioned elsewhere appear at the end.

1 Was Mary Wollstonecraft a feminist? (Karen Offen)

Falco, Maria J., ed. *Feminist Interpretations of Mary Wollstonecraft*. University Park, PA: Penn State University Press, 1996.

Goldsmith, Elizabeth, and Dena Goodman, eds. *Going Public: Women and Publishing in Early Modern France*. Ithaca, NY: Cornell University Press, 1996.

Gordon, Felicia, and P. N. Furbank. *Marie Madeleine Jodin, 1741–1790: Actress, Philosophe and Feminist*. Aldershot: Ashgate, 2001.

Hesse, Carla. *The Other Enlightenment: How French Women Became Modern*. Princeton, NJ: Princeton University Press, 2001.

Knott, Sarah, and Barbara Taylor, eds. *Women, Gender, and Enlightenment*. Houndmills: Palgrave Macmillan, 2005.

Mellor, Anne K. *Mothers of the Nation: Women's Political Writing in England, 1780–1830*. Bloomington, IN: Indiana University Press, 2000.

Offen, Karen. "Reclaiming the European Enlightenment for Feminism: Or, Prologomena to any Future History of Eighteenth-Century Europe," in *Perspectives on Feminist Thought in European History: From the Middle Ages to the Present*, ed. Tjitske Akkerman and Siep Stuurman. London: Routledge, 1998, pp. 85–103.

Offen, Karen. *European Feminisms, 1700–1950: A Political History*. Stanford, CA: Stanford University Press, 2000.

Offen, Karen. "Challenging Male Hegemony: Feminist Criticism and the Context for Women's Movements in the Age of European Revolutions and Counterrevolutions, 1789–1860," in *Women's Emancipation Movements in the Nineteenth Century: A European Perspective*, ed. Sylvia Paletschek and Bianka Pietrow-Ennker. Stanford, CA: Stanford University Press, 2004, pp. 11–30.

Smith, Hilda L., ed. *Women Writers and the Early Modern British Political Tradition*. Cambridge: Cambridge University Press, 1998.

Smith, Hilda L. *All Men and Both Sexes: Gender, Politics, and the False Universal in England 1640–1832*. University Park, PA: Penn State University Press, 2002.

Smith, Theresa Ann. *The Emerging Female Citizen: Gender and Enlightenment in Spain*. Berkeley, CA: University of California Press, 2006.

Stuurman, Siep. "L'Égalité des sexes qui ne se conteste plus en France: Feminism in the Seventeenth Century," in *Perspectives on Feminist Political Thought in European History,* ed. Tjitske Akkerman and Siep Stuurman. London: Routledge, 1998, pp. 67–84.

Taylor, Barbara. *Mary Wollstonecraft and the Feminist Imagination.* Cambridge: Cambridge University Press, 2003.

Todd, Janet M. *Mary Wollstonecraft: A Revolutionary Life.* London: Weidenfeld & Nicolson, 2000.

Tomaselli, Sylvana. "The Most Public Sphere of All: The Family," in *Women, Writing, and the Public Sphere 1700–1830,* ed. Elizabeth Eger et al. Cambridge: Cambridge University Press, 2001, pp. 239–256.

2 Re-rooting American women's activism (Nancy A. Hewitt)

Boylan, Anne M. *The Origins of Women's Activism: New York and Boston, 1797–1840.* Chapel Hill, NC: University of North Carolina Press, 2002.

Dorsey, Bruce. *Reforming Men and Women: Gender in the Antebellum City.* Ithaca, NY: Cornell University Press, 2002.

Ginzberg, Lori D. *Untidy Origins: A Story of Woman's Rights in Antebellum New York.* Chapel Hill, NC: University of North Carolina Press, 2005.

Isenberg, Nancy. *Sex and Citizenship in Antebellum America.* Chapel Hill, NC: University of North Carolina Press, 1998.

Jones, Martha. *All Bound Up Together: The Woman Question in African American Public Culture, 1830–1900.* Chapel Hill, NC: University of North Carolina Press, 2007.

Offen, Karen. "Women and the Question of 'Universal' Suffrage in 1848: A Transatlantic Comparison of Suffragist Rhetoric" (with documents in French and in English translation), *NWSA Journal,* 11:1 (1999), 150–177.

Paletschek, Sylvia, and Bianka Pietrow-Ennker, eds. *Women's Emancipation Movements in the Nineteenth Century.* Stanford, CA: Stanford University Press, 2004.

Passet, Joanne. *Sex Radicals and the Quest for Women's Equality.* Urbana, IL: University of Illinois Press, 2003.

Sklar, Kathryn Kish, and James Brewer Stewart, eds. *Women's Rights and Transatlantic Antislavery in the Era of Emancipation.* New Haven, CT: Yale University Press, 2007.

Sneider, Allison L. *Suffragists in an Imperial Age: U.S. Expansion and the Woman Question, 1870–1929.* New York: Oxford University Press, 2008.

Vapnek, Lara. *Breadwinners: Working Women and Economic Independence, 1865–1920.* Urbana, IL: University of Illinois Press, 2009.

Wellman, Judith. *The Road to Seneca Falls: Elizabeth Cady Stanton and the First Woman's Rights Convention.* Urbana, IL: University of Illinois Press, 2004.

Zaeske, Susan. *Signatures of Citizenship: Petitioning, Antislavery and Women's Political Identity.* Chapel Hill, NC: University of North Carolina Press, 2003.

3 Liberty, equality, morality (Anne Summers)

Daggers, Jenny, and Diana Neal, eds. *Sex, Gender, and Religion: Josephine Butler Revisited.* New York: Peter Lang, 2006.

Jordan, Jane, and Ingrid Sharp, eds. *Josephine Butler and the Prostitution Campaigns.* 5 vols. New York and London: Routledge, 2002 and Curzon, 2003.

Summers, Anne. "Gaps in the Record: Hidden Internationalism," *History Workshop Journal,* no. 62 (Autumn 2006), 215–231.

Summers, Anne, ed. Special issue: "Gender, Religion, and Politics: Josephine Butler's Campaigns in International Perspective (1875–1959)," *Women's History Review,* 17:2 (April 2008).

Van Drenth, Annemieke, and Francisca de Haan. *The Rise of Caring Power: Elizabeth Fry and Josephine Butler in Britain and the Netherlands*. Amsterdam: Amsterdam University Press, 1999.

4 "To educate women into rebellion" (Sandra Stanley Holton)

Adickes, Sandra. "Sisters not Demons: The Influence of British Suffragists on the American Suffrage Movement," *Women's History Review*, 11:4 (2002), 675–690.

Bolt, Christine. "British and American Feminism: Personal, Intellectual, and Practical Connections," in *Women's Emancipation Movements in the Nineteenth Century: A European Perspective*, ed. Sylvia Paletschek and Bianka Pietrow-Ennker. Stanford, CA: Stanford University Press, 2004, pp. 283–300.

Boussahba-Bravard, Myriam, ed. *Suffrage Outside Suffragism: Women's Vote in Britain, 1880–1914*. Houndmills: PalgraveMacmillan, 2007.

Davis, Sue. *The Political Thought of Elizabeth Cady Stanton: Women's Rights and the American Political Tradition*. New York: New York University Press, 2008.

Delap, Lucy. *The Feminist Avant-Garde. Transatlantic Encounters of the Early Twentieth Century*. Cambridge: Cambridge University Press, 2007.

DuBois, Ellen Carol. *Harriot Stanton Blatch and the Winning of Woman Suffrage*. New Haven, CT: Yale University Press, 1997.

Fletcher, Ian Christopher, Laura E. Nym Mayhall, and Philippa Levine, eds. *Women's Suffrage in the British Empire: Citizenship, Nation, and Race*. London: Routledge, 2000.

Holton, Sandra Stanley. "From Anti-Slavery to Suffrage Militancy: The Bright Circle, Elizabeth Cady Stanton and the British Women's Movement," in *Beyond Suffrage: International Feminist Perspectives*, ed. Caroline Daley and Melanie Nolan. Auckland: Auckland University Press, 1994, pp. 213–233.

Holton, Sandra Stanley. *Suffrage Days. Stories from the Women's Suffrage Movement*. London: Routledge, 1996.

Rendall, Jane. "Recovering Lost Political Cultures: British Feminisms, 1860–1900," in *Women's Emancipation Movements in the Nineteenth Century: A European Perspective*, ed. Sylvia Paletschek and Bianka Pietrow-Ennker. Stanford, CA: Stanford University Press, 2004, pp. 33–52.

Rupp, Leila J. *Worlds of Women: The Making of an International Women's Movement*. Princeton, NJ: Princeton University Press, 1998.

5 Women's rights, feminism, and suffragism in Japan, 1870–1925 (Barbara Molony)

Bardsley, Jan. *The Bluestockings of Japan*. Ann Arbor, MI: University of Michigan Press, 2007.

Hiratsuka, Raichō. *In the Beginning, Woman Was the Sun: The Autobiography of a Japanese Feminist*, translated and annotated, with an Introduction by Teruko Craig. New York: Columbia University Press, 2006.

Lowy, Dina. *The Japanese "New Woman": Images of Gender and Modernity*. New Brunswick, NJ: Rutgers University Press, 2007.

Mackie, Vera. *Feminism in Modern Japan: Citizenship, Embodiment and Sexuality*. Cambridge: Cambridge University Press, 2003.

Mackie, Vera. "Embodied Subjects: Feminism in Imperial Japan," in *Japanese Women: Emerging from Subservience, 1868–1945*, ed. Hiroko Tomida and Gordon Daniels. Folkestone, Kent: Global Oriental, 2005, pp. 95–118.

Molony, Barbara. "Citizenship and Suffrage in Interwar Japan," in *Women's Suffrage in Asia: Gender, Nationalism, and Democracy*, ed. Louise Edwards and Mina Roces. London: RoutledgeCurzon, 2004, pp. 127–151.

Molony, Barbara. "The Quest for Women's Rights in Turn of the Century Japan," in *Gendering Modern Japanese History*, ed. Barbara Molony and Kathleen Uno. Cambridge, MA: Harvard University Asia Center, 2005, pp. 463–492.

Molony, Barbara. "Ichikawa Fusae and Japan's Pre-War Women's Suffrage Movement," in *Japanese Women: Emerging from Subservience, 1868–1945*, ed. Hiroko Tomida and Gordon Daniels. Folkestone, Kent: Global Oriental, 2005, pp. 57–92.

Ogawa, Manako. "'The White Ribbon League of Nations' Meets Japan: The Trans-Pacific Activism of the Woman's Christian Temperance Union," *Diplomatic History* 31:1 (2007), 21–50.

Orii, Miyako, and Hiroko Tomida. "*Shin Fujin Kyōkai* (The Association of New Women) and the Women Who Aimed to Change Society, in *Japanese Women: Emerging from Subservience, 1868–1945*, ed. Hiroko Tomida and Gordon Daniels. Folkestone, Kent: Global Oriental, 2005, pp. 232–257.

Sato, Barbara. *The New Japanese Woman: Modernity, Media, and Women in Interwar Japan*. Durham, NC: Duke University Press, 2003.

Silverberg, Miriam. *Erotic Grotesque Nonsense: The Mass Culture of Japanese Modern Times*. Berkeley, CA: University of California Press, 2007.

Tomida, Hiroko. *Hiratsuka Raichō and Early Japanese Feminism*. Leiden: E. J. Brill, 2004.

Ueno, Chizuko. *Nationalism and Gender*, transl. Beverley Yamamoto. Melbourne: Trans Pacific Press, 2004.

Yasutake, Rumi. "Men, Women, and Temperance in Meiji Japan: Engendering WCTU Activism from a Transnational Perspective," *The Japanese Journal of American Studies* 17 (2006), 91–111.

Yoneda, Sayoko. "Hiratsuka Raichō's Idea of Society: Nature, Cooperation and Self-Government," in *Japanese Women: Emerging from Subservience, 1868–1945*, ed. Hiroko Tomida and Gordon Daniels. Folkestone, Kent: Global Oriental, 2005, pp. 21–39.

6 Feminism and Protestantism in nineteenth-century France (Florence Rochefort)

Gubin, Eliane, Catherine Jacques, Brigitte Studer, Florence Rochefort, Françoise Thébaud, and Michelle Zancarini-Fournel, eds. *Le Siècle des féminismes*. Paris: Éditions de l'Atelier, 2004.

McMillan, James F. "Wollstonecraft's Daughters, Marianne's Daughters and the Daughters of Joan of Arc: Marie Maugeret and Christian Feminism in the French Belle Epoque," in *Wollstonecraft's Daughters : Womanhood in England and France, 1780–1920*, ed. Clarissa Campbell Orr. Manchester: Manchester University Press, 1996, pp. 186–198.

The following pertinent publications by Florence Rochefort are listed in chronological order:

Rochefort, Florence. "La séduction résiste-t-elle au féminisme?," in *Séduction et Sociétés: approches historiques*, ed. Cécile Dauphin and Arlette Farge. Paris: Seuil, 2001, pp. 214–243.

Rochefort, Florence. "From Women's Rights to Feminism in Europe 1860–1914," in *Political and Historical Encyclopedia of Women*, ed. Christine Fauré. New York: Routledge, 2003, pp. 315–326. [Translated from the French.]

Rochefort, Florence. "Contrecarrer ou interroger les religions," in *Le Siècle des féminismes*, ed. Eliane Gubin, Catherine Jacques, Florence Rochefort, Françoise

Thébaud, Brigitte Studer, and Michelle Zancarini-Fournel. Paris: Atelier, 2004, pp. 347–363.

Rochefort, Florence. "The French Feminist Movement and Republicanism, 1868–1914," in *Women's Emancipation Movements in the Nineteenth Century: A European Perspective*, ed. Sylvia Paletschek and Bianka Pietrow-Ennker. Stanford, CA: Stanford University Press, 2004, pp. 77–101.

Rochefort, Florence. "Laïcisation des mœurs et équilibre de genre, le débat sur la capacité civile de la femme mariée (1918–1938)," *Vingtième Siècle: Revue d'histoire*, no. 87 "Laïcité, séparation, sécularisation 1905–2005" (July–September 2005), 129–141.

Rochefort, Florence. "Religions, genre et politiques laïques en France, XIXᵉ–XXᵉ siècles," *French Politics, Culture and Society*, 25:2 (Summer 2007), 19–33.

Rochefort, Florence. "Vers une sacralité du féminin au sein des discours de la différence," in *Le sacré hors religions*, ed. Françoise Champion, Sophie Nizard, and Paul Zawadski. Paris: L'Harmattan, 2007, pp. 139–154.

Rochefort, Florence. *Hier les femmes.* Paris: Aubanel-La Martinière, 2007.

Rochefort, Florence, ed. *Le pouvoir du genre. Laïcités et religions 1905–2005.* Toulouse: Presses Universitaires du Mirail, 2007.

Rochefort, Florence. "The Abolitionist Struggle of Pastor Tommy Fallot: Between Social Christianity, Feminism and Secularism (1882–1893)," *Women's History Review*, 17:2 (2008), 179–194.

7 From Fredrika Bremer to Ellen Key (Inger Hammar)

Andersen, Mie, and Bente Rosenbeck, "Ligestilling, ægteskab og religion [Equality, marriage and religion]," *Kvinder, køn og forskning*, no. 4 (2006), 17–31.

Andreason, Tayo, Anette Borchorst, Drude Dahlerup, Eva Lous, and Hanne Rimmen Nielsen, eds. *"Moving On: New Perspectives on the Women's Movement."* Acta Jutlandica 67:1, Humanities Series 66. Aarhus: Aarhus University Press, 1991.

Blom, Ida. "Modernity and the Norwegian Women's Movement from the 1880s to 1914: Changes and Continuities," in *Women's Emancipation Movements in the Nineteenth Century: A European Perspective*, ed. Sylvia Paletschek and Bianka Pietrow-Ennker. Stanford, CA: Stanford University Press, 2004, pp. 125–151.

Herman, Sondra. "Feminists, Socialists, and the Genesis of the Swedish Welfare State 1919–1945," in *Views of Women's Lives in Western Tradition*, ed. Frances Richardson Keller. Lewiston, NY: The Edwin Mellen Press, 1990, pp. 472–510.

Manns, Ulla. "Gender and Feminism in Sweden: The Fredrika Bremer Association," in *Women's Emancipation Movements in the Nineteenth Century: A European Perspective*, ed. Sylvia Paletschek and Bianka Pietrow-Ennker. Stanford, CA: Stanford University Press, 2004, pp. 152–164.

Manns, Ulla. *Upp systrar, vapnen er? Kon och politik i Svensk 1800 – Talsfeminisms* [To Arms, Sisters: Sex and Politics in Nineteenth-Century Sweden]. Stockholm: Atlas Akademi, 2005.

Manns, Ulla. "Upplyft kvinnan och hon ski upplyfta mänskligheten [Uplift the Woman and She will Elevate Humanity]," in *Fredrika Bremer – föregångare och förebild*, ed. Anita Widen. N.p., Gidlunds, forthcoming.

Manns, Ulla. "Fredrika Bremer. A Preacher on the Borders of Religion," in *Women's Everyday Religion*, ed. Marja-Liisa Keinänen. Stockholm: Stockholm University Press, 2009.

Markkola, Pirjo, ed. *Gender and Vocation: Women, Religion and Social Change in the Nordic Countries, 1830–1940.* Helsinki: SKS, 2000.

Markkola, Pirjo. *Synti ja siveys. Naiset, uskonto ja sosiaalinen työ Suomessa 1860–1920* [Sin and Morality. Women, Religion and Social Work in Finland, 1860–1920]. Helsinki: Finnish Literature Society, 2002.

Markkola, Pirjo. "Nordic Gender Models and Lutheranism. A Historical Perspective," in *Gender, Religion, Human Rights in Europe*, ed. Kari Elisabeth Børresen and Sara Cabibbo. Rome: Herder, 2006, pp. 28–38.

Markkola, Pirjo. "Lutheranism, Women and the History of the Welfare States in the Nordic Countries," in *På kant med historien. Studier i køn, videnskab og lidenskab tilegnet Bente Rosenbeck på hendes 60-årsdag*, ed. Karin Lützen et al. Copenhagen: Museum Tusculanums Forlag, 2008, pp. 90–105.

Melby, Kari, Anu Pylkkanen, Bente Rosenbeck, and Christina Carlsson Wetterberg, eds. *The Nordic Model of Marriage and the Welfare State*. Copenhagen: Nordic Council of Ministers, 2001.

Ulvros, Eva Helen. *Sophie Elkan: hennes liv och vänskapen med Selma Lagerlöf*. Lund: Historiska media, 2001.

Wikander, Ulla, and Ulla Manns, eds. *Det Evigt kvinnliga: En historia med förändring*. Stockholm: Tidensforlag, 1994.

8 Indian Christian women and indigenous feminism, *c*.1850–*c*.1920 (Padma Anagol)

Anagol, Padma. *The Emergence of Feminism in India, 1850–1920*. Aldershot: Ashgate, 2006. See especially Chapter Two titled "Discriminating Converts: Christian Women's Discourse and Work."

Basu, Aparna. "Mary Ann Cooke to Mother Theresa: Christian Missionary Women and the Indian Response," in *Women and Missions: Past and Present Anthropological and Historical Perceptions*, ed. Fiona Bowie, Deborah Kirkwood, and Shirley Ardener. Oxford: Berg, 1993, pp. 187–208.

Cox, Jeffrey L. *Imperial Fault Lines: Christianity and Colonial Power in India, 1818–1940*. Stanford, CA: Stanford University Press, 2002.

Flemming, Leslie. *Women's Work for Women: Missionaries and Social Change in Asia*. Boulder, CO: Westview Press, 1993.

Laxmibai Tilak. *Sketches from Memory*, transl. Louis Menezes. Delhi: Katha Publications, 2007. [A poignant memoir of a high caste Hindu woman's account of her husband's and her own conversion to Christianity. A classic in Indian literature of the nineteenth century.]

Pargament, Kenneth. *The Psychology of Religion and Coping: Theory, Research and Practice*. New York: Guilford Press, 1997.

Ramabai, Pandita. *Pandita Ramabai Through Her Own Words: Selected Works*, transl. and ed. Meera Kosambi. New Delhi: Oxford University Press, 2000. [A first generation high caste Hindu convert's experiences in translation.]

Robinson, Rowena, and Clarke Sathianathan. *Religious Conversion in India: Modes, Motivations, and Meanings*. Oxford: Oxford University Press, 2003.

Shourie, Arun. *Missionaries in India*. Delhi: South Asia Books, 1998.

9 Settler anxieties, indigenous peoples, and women's suffrage in the colonies of Australia, New Zealand, and Hawai'i, 1888–1902 (Patricia Grimshaw)

Brookes, Barbara, and Patricia Grimshaw. "Maori and Aboriginal Women's Activism in a Decade of Assimilation: New Zealand and Victoria, Australia, in the 1950s," in *Intersections: Gender, Race and Ethnicity in Australasian Studies*, ed. Margaret Allen and R. K. Dhawan. New Delhi: Prestige Books, 2007, pp. 10–22.

Evans, Julie, Patricia Grimshaw, David Philips, and Shurlee Swain. *Equal Subjects, Unequal Rights: Indigenous Peoples in British Settler Societies.* Manchester: Manchester University Press, 2003.

Grimshaw, Patricia. "White Men's Fears and White Women's Hopes: The Victorian Equal Suffrage Act," *Victorian Historical Journal*, 79:2 (November 2008), 185–209.

Grimshaw, Patricia. "Colonialism, Power and Women's Political Citizenship in Australia, 1894–1908," in *Suffrage, Gender and Citizenship: International Perspectives on Parliamentary Reforms*, ed. Irma Sulkunen, Seija-Leena Nevala-Nurmi, and Pirjo Markkola. Cambridge: Cambridge Scholars Press, 2009, pp. 34–55.

Sneider, Allison L. *Suffragists in an Imperial Age: U.S. Expansion and the Woman Question, 1870–1929.* New York: Oxford University Press, 2008.

10 Challenging traditions (Jacqueline R. de Vries)

Clark, Elaine. "Catholics and the Campaign for Women's Suffrage in England," *Church History*, 73:3 (2004), 635–665.

de Vries, Jacqueline, R. "Rediscovering Christianity After the Postmodern Turn," *Feminist Studies*, 31:1 (2005), 135–155.

de Vries, Jacqueline R., and Sue Morgan, eds. *Women, Gender and Religious Cultures in Modern Britain, 1800–1940.* London: Routledge, 2010.

Dixon, Joy. *Divine Feminine: Theosophy and Feminism in England.* Baltimore, MD: Johns Hopkins University Press, 2001.

Gullace, Nicoletta F. *The Blood of Our Sons: Men, Women, and the Renegotiation of British Citizenship During the Great War.* London: Palgrave Macmillan, 2004.

Morgan, Sue, ed. *Women, Religion and Feminism in Britain, 1750–1900.* London: Palgrave, 2002.

Summers, Anne. *Female Lives, Moral States.* Newbury: Threshold Press, 2000.

Yeo, Eileen Janes. "Protestant Feminists and Catholic Saints in Victorian Britain," in *Radical Femininity: Women's Self-Representation in the Public Sphere*, ed. Eileen Janes Yeo. Manchester: Manchester University Press, 1998, pp. 127–148.

11 Constructing internationalism (Leila J. Rupp)

Anderson, Bonnie S. *Joyous Greetings: The First International Women's Movement, 1830–1860.* New York: Oxford University Press, 2000.

Berkovitch, Nitza. *From Motherhood to Citizenship: Women's Rights and International Organizations.* Baltimore, MD: Johns Hopkins University Press, 1999.

D'Itri, Patricia Ward. *Cross Currents in the International Women's Movement, 1848–1948.* Bowling Green, OH: Bowling Green State University Press, 1999.

DuBois, Ellen Carol. "A Momentary Transnational Sisterhood: Cuban/US Collaboration in the Formation of the Inter-American Commission on Women," in *An Intimate and Contested Relationship: The United States and Cuba*, ed. Alessandra Lorini. Firenze: Firenze University Press, 2006, pp. 81–95.

"Féminisme international," special issue of *Sextant: Revue du Groupe interdisciplinaire d'Études sur les Femmes* (Brussels), double issue no. 23–24 (2007).

Gerhard, Ute. "The 'Long Waves' of Women's Movements from an International Perspective," paper given at the Nordic Conference in Iceland, 10–12 June 2004. Online at: www.nikk.uio.no/arrangementer/konferens/island04/papers_pdf/Gerhard/

Gubin, Eliane, and Leen Van Molle, eds. *Women Changing the World: A History of the International Council of Women, 1888–1988.* Brussels: Editions Racine, 2005.

Jonsson, Pernilla, Silke Neunsinger, and Joan Sangster, eds. *Crossing Boundaries: Women's Organizing in Europe and the Americas, 1880s–1940s*. Stockholm: Uppsala Universitet, 2007.

McFadden, Margaret, H. *Golden Cables of Sympathy: The Transatlantic Sources of Nineteenth-Century Feminism*. Lexington, KY: University Press of Kentucky, 1999.

Offen, Karen. *European Feminisms, 1700–1950: A Political History*. Stanford, CA: Stanford University Press, 2000.

Vellacott, Jo. "Feminism as if All People Mattered: Working to Remove the Causes of War, 1919–1929," *Contemporary European History*, 10:3 (2001), 375–394.

12 The challenge of multinational empire for the international women's movement (Susan Zimmermann)

Blackwell, Joyce. *No Peace without Freedom: Race and the Women's International League for Peace and Freedom, 1915–1975*. Carbondale, IL: Southern Illinois University Press, 2004.

Crawford, Neta C. *Argument and Change in World Politics: Ethics, Decolonization, and Humanitarian Intervention*. New York: Cambridge University Press, 2002.

De Haan, Francisca, Krassimira Daskalova, and Anna Loutfi, eds. *A Biographical Dictionary of Women's Movements and Feminisms: Central, Eastern and South Eastern Europe, 19th and 20th Centuries*. Budapest: Central European University Press, 2006.

Feinberg, Melissa. *Elusive Equality: Gender, Citizenship, and the Limits of Democracy in Czechoslovakia, 1918–1950*. Pittsburgh, PA: University of Pittsburgh Press, 2006.

Ferree, Myra Marx, and Aili Mari Tripp, eds. *Global Feminism. Transnational Women's Activism, Organizing, and Human Rights*. New York: New York University Press, 2006.

Fisch, Jörg. *Die europäische Expansion und das Völkerrecht. Die Auseinandersetzungen um den Status der überseeischen Gebiete vom 15. Jahrhundert bis zur Gegenwart*. Stuttgart: Steiner, 1984.

Gunning, Isabella R. "Arrogant Perception, World-Travelling and Multicultural Feminism: The Case of Female Genital Surgeries," *Columbia Human Rights Law Review*, 23:2 (1992), 189–248.

Koskenniemi, Marti. *The Gentle Civilizer of Nations. The Rise and the Fall of International Law 1870–1960*. Cambridge: Cambridge University Press, 2002.

Midgley, Clare, ed. *Gender and Imperialism*. Manchester: Manchester University Press, 1998.

Naples, Nancy A., ed. *Community Activism and Feminist Politics. Organizing Across Race, Class, and Gender*. New York: Routledge, 1996.

Narayan, Uma. *Dislocating Cultures. Identities, Traditions, and Third World Feminism*. New York: Routledge, 1997.

Orford, Anne. *Reading Humanitarian Intervention: Human Rights and the Use of Force in International Law*. Cambridge: Cambridge University Press, 2003, esp. pp. 38–71, 158–185.

Robinson, Fiona. *Globalizing Care: Ethics, Feminist Theory, and International Relations*. Boulder, CO: Westview Press, 1999.

Rodríguez-Piñero, Luis. *Indigenous People, Postcolonialism, and International Law: The ILO Regime (1919–1989)*. New York: Oxford University Press, 2005.

Sarkar, Mahua. *Visible Histories, Disappearing Women. Producing Muslim Womanhood in Late Colonial Bengal*. Durham, NC: Duke University Press, 2008.

13 The other "awakening" (Ellen L. Fleischmann)

Ahmed, Leila. *Women and Gender in Islam: Historical Roots of a Modern Debate*. New Haven, CT: Yale University Press, 1992.

Amin, Camron Michael. *The Making of the Modern Iranian Woman: Gender, State Policy, and Popular Culture, 1865–1946*. Gainesville, FL: University Press of Florida, 2002.

Badran, Margot. *Feminists, Islam, and Nation: Gender and the Making of Modern Egypt*. Princeton, NJ: Princeton University Press, 1995.

Baron, Beth. *Egypt as a Woman: Nationalism, Gender, and Politics*. Berkeley, CA: University of California Press, 2005.

Çakir, Serpil. "Feminism and Feminist History-Writing in Turkey: The Discovery of Ottoman Feminism," *Aspasia: International Handbook of Central, Eastern, and Southeastern European Women's and Gender History*, 1 (2007), 61–83.

Fleischmann, Ellen L. *The Nation and Its "New" Women: The Palestinian Women's Movement, 1920–1948*. Berkeley, CA: University of California Press, 2003.

Izraeli, Dafna N. "The Zionist Women's Movement in Palestine 1911–1927," *Signs: Journal of Women in Culture and Society*, 7:1 (Autumn 1981), 87–114.

Paidar, Parvin. *Women and the Political Process in Twentieth-Century Iran*. Cambridge: Cambridge University Press, 1995.

Pollard, Lisa. *Nurturing the Nation: The Family Politics of Modernizing, Colonizing and Liberating Egypt (1805–1923)*. Berkeley, CA: University of California Press, 2005.

Rowe, Victoria. "Armenian Writers and Women's-Rights Discourse in Turn-of-the-Twentieth-Century Constantinople," *Aspasia: International Handbook of Central, Eastern, and Southeastern European Women's and Gender History*, 2 (2008), 44–69.

Thompson, Elizabeth. *Colonial Citizens: Republican Rights, Paternal Privilege, and Gender in French Syria and Lebanon*. New York: Columbia University Press, 2000.

14 Latin American feminism and the transnational arena (Francesca Miller)

Dore, Elizabeth, and Maxine Molyneux, eds. *Hidden Histories of Gender and the State in Latin America*. Durham, NC: Duke University Press, 2000.

Franceschet, Susan. "State Feminism and Women's Movements," *Latin American Research Review*, 38:1 (2003), 3–40.

Friedman, Elisabeth Jay. "The Reality of Virtual Reality: The Internet and Gender Equality Advocacy in Latin America," *Latin American Politics and Society*, 47:4 (2005), 209–211.

Hallum, Anne Motely. "Taking Stock and Building Bridges: Feminism, Women's Movements and Pentacostalism in Latin America," *Latin American Research Review*, 38:1 (2003), 169–186.

Miller, Francesca. "Women in the Transformation of Latin America and the Caribbean," in *Capital, Power and Inequality in Latin America and the Caribbean*, ed. Richard L. Harris and Jorge Nef. New York: Rowman and Littlefield, 2008, pp. 174–195.

Mujeres Latinoamericanas en Cifras. 1992 (this is an ongoing publication, there are later editions) Facultad Latinoamericana de Ciencieas Sociales con la colaboracion del Servicio Nacional de Mujer (SERNAM). Sixteen books, each edited within the country under study. Editado por el Instituto de la Mujer, Madrid, and FLASCO, Chile.

Pan American Health Organization (PAHO). 2005. *Gender, Health and Development in the Americas: Basic Indicators, 2005*. Washington, DC: PAHO, Gender, Ethnicity and Health. Online at: www.paho.org

Vargas, Virginia. "Las nuevas dinamicas feministas en el nuevo milenio." Centro de la Mujer Peruana Flora Tristan, March 2007. Online at: www.flora.org.pe/pdfs/gina_nue-vadinamicas.pdf

Wamsley, E. Sue. "Constructing Feminism Across Borders: The Pan American Women's Movement and the Founding of the Inter-American Commission of Women," in *Crossing Boundaries: Women's Organizing in Europe and the Americas, 1880s–1940s*, ed. Pernilla Jonsson, Silke Neunsinger, and Joan Sangster. Uppsala: Uppsala University Press, 2007, pp. 51–71.

15 Internationalizing married women's nationality (Ellen Carol DuBois)

DuBois, Ellen Carol, and Katie Oliviero, eds. Introduction to special issue: "Circling the Globe: International Feminism Reconsidered, 1920 to 1975," *Women's Studies International Forum*, 32:1 (January–February 2009), 1–3.

16 Inventing Commonwealth and Pan-Pacific feminisms (Angela Woollacott)

Lake, Marilyn. *Getting Equal: The History of Australian Feminism*. St Leonards, NSW: Allen & Unwin, 1999.

Paddle, Sarah. "'For the China of the Future': Western Feminists, Colonisation and International Citizenship in the Inter-war Years," *Australian Feminist Studies*, 16:36 (November 2001), 325–341.

Paddle, Sarah. "The Limits of Sympathy: International Feminists and the Chinese 'Slave Girl' Campaigns of the 1920s and 1930s," *Journal of Colonialism and Colonial History*, 4:3 (Winter 2003). Article accessed online in HTML at: muse.jhu.edu/journals/jcch/

Paisley, Fiona. *Loving Protection? Australian Feminism and Aboriginal Women's Rights, 1919–1939*. Carlton South, Victoria: Melbourne University Press, 2000.

Paisley, Fiona. "Cultivating Modernity: Culture and Internationalism in Feminism's Pacific Age," *Journal of Women's History*, 14:3 (Autumn 2002), 105–132.

Paisley, Fiona. "Performing New Zealand: Maori and Pakeha Delegates at the Pan-Pacific Women's Conference, Hawaii, 1934," *New Zealand Journal of History*, 38:1 (2004), 22–38.

Paisley, Fiona. "Glamour in the Pacific: Women's Internationalism and Maori Politics at Pan-Pacific Women's Conferences in the 1950s," *Pacific Studies*, 29:1–2 (March–June 2006), 54–81.

Paisley, Fiona. *Glamour in the Pacific: Cultural Internationalism and Race Politics in the Women's Pan-Pacific*. Honolulu: University of Hawaii Press, 2009.

17 Feminism, social science, and the meanings of modernity (Ann Taylor Allen)

Allen, Ann Taylor. "Patriarchy and its Discontents: The Debate on the Origins of the Family in the German-speaking World," in *Germany at the Fin-de-Siècle: Culture, Politics, Ideas*, ed. David Lindenfeld and Suzanne Marchand. Baton Rouge, LA: Louisiana State University Press, 2004, pp. 81–101.

Allen, Ann Taylor. *Feminism and Motherhood in Western Europe, 1890–1970: The Maternal Dilemma*. New York: Palgrave-Macmillan, 2005.

Eller, Cynthia. *The Myth of Matriarchal Prehistory: Why an Invented Past Won't Give Women a Future*. Boston, MA: Beacon Press, 2000.

Fuchs, Rachel Ginnis. *Contested Paternity: Constructing Families in Modern France*. Baltimore, MD: Johns Hopkins Press, 2008.

Gossman, Lionel. *Basel in the Age of Burckhardt: A Study in Unseasonable Ideas*. Chicago: University of Chicago Press, 2000.

Kern, Kathi. *Mrs. Stanton's Bible*. Ithaca, NY: Cornell University Press, 2001.

Offen, Karen. *European Feminisms, 1700–1950: A Political History*. Stanford, CA: Stanford University Press, 2000.

Ruether, Rosemary Radford. *Goddesses and the Divine Feminine: A Western Religious History*. Berkeley, CA: University of California Press, 2005.

18 Women's suffrage and revolution in the Russian Empire, 1905–1917 (Rochelle Goldberg Ruthchild)

Edmondson, Linda. *Feminism in Russia, 1900–1917*. Stanford, CA: Stanford University Press, 1984.

Edmondson, Linda. "Women's Rights, Gender and Citizenship in Tsarist Russia, 1860–1920: The Question of Difference," in *Women's Rights and Human Rights*, ed. Patricia Grimshaw, Katie Holmes, and Marilyn Lake. Houndmills: Palgrave, 2001, pp. 153–167.

Edmondson, Linda. "Feminism and Equality in an Authoritarian State: The Politics of Women's Liberation in Late Imperial Russia," in *Women's Emancipation Movements in the Nineteenth Century: A European Perspective*, ed. Sylvia Paletschek and Bianka Pietrow-Ennker. Stanford, CA: Stanford University Press, 2004, pp. 221–239.

Goldberg (Ruthchild), Rochelle Lois. "The Russian Women's Movement, 1859–1917." PhD dissertation, University of Rochester, 1976.

Muravyeva, M.G., N.L Pushkareva, and N. V. Novikova, eds. *Gendernoe ravnopravie v Rossii. Materialy mexhdunarodnoi nauchnoi konferentsii, posviashchennoi 100-letiiu Pervogo Vserossiiskogo zhenskogo S"ezda 1908 goda. 21–23 marta 2008 goda* [Gender Equality in Russia. Materials of the International Conference, Commemorating the 100th Anniversary of the 1908 First All-Russian Women's Congress, March 21–23, 2008]. St. Petersburg: Aleteia, 2008.

Offen, Karen. *European Feminisms, 1700-1950: A Political History*. Stanford, CA: Stanford University Press, 2000.

Ruthchild, Rochelle Goldberg. "Writing for Their Rights. Four Feminist Journalists: Mariia Chekhova, Liubov' Gurevich, Mariia Pokrovskaia, and Ariadna Tyrkova," in *An Improper Profession: Women and Journalism in Late Imperial Russia.*, ed. Jehane Gheith and Barbara Norton. Durham, NC: Duke University Press, 2001, pp. 167–195.

Ruthchild, Rochelle Goldberg. *Equality and Revolution: Women's Rights in the Russian Empire, 1905–1917*. Pittsburgh, PA: University of Pittsburgh Press, 2010.

Stites, Richard. *The Women's Liberation Movement in Russia: Feminism, Nihilism, and Bolshevism, 1860–1930*. Princeton, NJ: Princeton University Press, 1978, rev. ed. 1991.

Yukina, Irina. *Istoriia zhenshchin Rossii: Zhenskoe dvizhenie i feminizm v 1850–1920-e gody. Materialy k bibliografii* [The History of Women in Russia: The Women's Movement and Feminism from 1850–1920. Bibliographical Materials]. St. Petersburg: Aleteia, 2003.

Yukina, Irina. *Russkii feminizm kak vyzov sovremennosti* [Russian Feminism as a Call to Modernity]. St. Petersburg: Aleteia, 2007.

Yukina, Irina I., and Guseva, E. Iu. *Zhenskii Peterburg: Opyt istoriko-kraevedcheskogo putevoditelia* [Women's Petersburg: An Historical Guidebook of Local Lore]. St. Petersburg: Aleteia, 2004.

19 Women's suffrage in China (Louise Edwards)

Dong, Madeleine Yue. "Unofficial History and Gender Boundary Crossing in the Early Republic: Shen Peizhen and Xiaofengxian," in *Gender in Motion: Divisions of Labor and Cultural Change in Late Imperial and Modern China*, ed. Bryna Goodman and Wendy Larson. Lanham, MD: Rowman & Littlefield, 2005, pp. 169–189.

Edwards, Louise. "Co–opting the Chinese Women's Suffrage Movement for the Fifth Modernisation – Democracy," *Asian Studies Review*, 26:1 (September 2002), 285–307.

Edwards, Louise. "Narratives of Race and Nation in China: Women's Suffrage in the Early Twentieth Century," *Women's Studies International Forum*, 25:6 (November–December 2002), 619–630.

Edwards, Louise. "Chinese Women's Campaigns for Suffrage: Nationalism, Confucianism and Political Agency," in *Women's Suffrage in Asia: Gender, Nationalism, Democracy,* ed. Louise Edwards and Mina Roces. London: RoutledgeCurzon, 2004, pp. 59–78.

Edwards, Louise. *Gender, Politics and Democracy: Women's Suffrage in China.* Stanford, CA: Stanford University Press, 2008.

Glosser, Susan. *Chinese Visions of Family and State, 1915–1953.* Berkeley, CA: University of California Press, 2003.

Goodman, Bryna. "The Vocational Woman and the Elusiveness of 'Personhood' in Early Republican China," in *Gender in Motion: Divisions of Labor and Cultural Change in Late Imperial and Modern China*, ed. Bryna Goodman and Wendy Larson. Lanham, MD: Rowman & Littlefield, 2005, pp. 265–286.

Huang, Philip C. C. "Women's Choices under the Law: Marriage, Divorce and Illicit Sex in the Qing and Republic," *Modern China* 27: 1(2001), 3–58.

Judge, Joan. "Citizens or Mothers of Citizens? Gender and the Meaning of Modern Chinese Citizenship," in *Changing Meanings of Citizenship in Modern China*, ed. Merle Goldman and Elizabeth J. Perry. Cambridge, MA: Harvard University Press, 2002, pp. 23–43.

Tran, Lisa. "Concubines under Modern Chinese Law." PhD dissertation, University of California, Los Angeles, 2005.

Wang Zheng. *Women in the Chinese Enlightenment: Oral and Textual Histories*. Berkeley, CA: University of California Press, 1999.

20 Rethinking the socialist construction and international career of the concept "bourgeois feminism" (Marilyn J. Boxer)

Boxer, Marilyn J. "'Communist Feminism' as Oxymoron? Reflections of a 'Second-Wave' Feminist Historian of European Socialism and Feminism," *Aspasia: International Handbook of Central, Eastern, and Southeastern European Women's and Gender History*, 1 (2007), 241–246.

Boxer, Marilyn J. "Linking Socialism, Feminism, and Social Darwinism in Belle-Époque France: The Maternalist Politics and Journalism of Aline Vallette." Paper given at the 2007 Conference of the International Federation for Research in Women's History.

Boxer, Marilyn J., and Jean H. Quataert, eds. *Socialist Women: European Socialist Feminism in the Nineteenth and Early Twentieth Centuries.* New York: Elsevier North-Holland, 1978.

Callahan, Kevin J. "The 'True' French Worker Party: The Problem of French Sectarianism and Identity Politics in the Second International, 1889–1900," in *Views from the Margins: Creating Identities in Modern France*, ed. and introd. by Kevin J. Callahan and Sarah A. Curtis. Lincoln, NE: University of Nebraska Press, 2008, pp. 158–188.

Gruber, Helmut, and Pamela Graves, eds. *Women and Socialism / Socialism and Women: Europe between the Two World Wars.* New York: Berghahn, 1998.

General

International feminism/women's movements/comparative

Allen, Ann Taylor, Anne Cova, and June Purvis, eds. Special issue: "International Feminisms," *Women's History Review* (forthcoming 2010).

Bader-Zaar, Birgitta. "Zur Geschichte der internationalen Frauenbewegungen: Von transatlantischen Kontakten über institutionalisierte Organisationen zu globalen Netzwerken," in *Internationalismen: Transformation weltweiter Ungleichheit im 19. und 20. Jahrhundert*, ed. Karin Fischer and Susan Zimmermann. Vienna: ProMedia Verlag, 2008, pp. 107–128.

Bader-Zaar, Birgitta. *Die Einführung des Frauenwahlrechts: Grossbritannien, Deutschland, Österreich, Belgien, und die USA im Vergleich* [The Introduction of Women's Suffrage: Great Britain, Germany, Austria, Belgium and the USA in Comparison], *L'Homme, Schriften 3*. Cologne: Böhlau, 2010.

Blom, Ida, Karen Hagemann, and Catherine Hall, eds. *Gendered Nations: Nationalisms and Gender Order in the Long Nineteenth Century*. Oxford: Berg, 2000.

Bock, Gisela. *Women in European History*. The Making of Europe Series. Oxford: Blackwell, 2002. [English translation, by Allison Brown, of *Frauen in der europaischen Geschichte: Vom Mittelalter bis zur Gegenwart*. Munich: C. H. Beck, 2000]

Cohen, Yolande, and Françoise Thébaud, eds. *Féminismes et identités nationales: Les processus d'intégration des femmes au politique*. Lyon: Centre Jacques Cartier, 1998.

Cova, Anne, ed. *Comparative Women's History: New Approaches*. Boulder, CO: Social Science Monographs, Columbia University Press, 2006. [Also published in Portuguese and French.]

Cova, Anne. "The National Councils of Women in France, Italy and Portugal: Comparisons and Entanglements 1888-1939," in *Gender History in a Transnational Perspective: Biographies, Networks, Gender Orders*, ed. Oliver Janz and Daniel Scholpflug. Oxford: Berghahn Books, forthcoming 2010–2011.

DeHaan, Francisca, et al., eds. Special issue : "Women's Movements and Feminisms," *Aspasia : International Handbook of Central, Eastern, and Southeastern European Women's and Gender History*, vol. 1 (2007).

DuBois, Ellen Carol, and Robert Cherny, eds. Special Issue: "Woman Suffrage: The View from the Pacific," *Pacific Historical Review*, 69:4 (November 2000).

DuBois, Ellen Carol, and Katie Oliviero, eds. Special issue: "Circling the Globe: International Feminism Reconsidered, 1920 to 1975," *Women's Studies International Forum*, 32:1 (January–February 2009).

Fauré, Christine, ed. *Encyclopédie politique et historique des femmes*. Paris: Presses Universitaires de France, 1997. [In English translation as *Political and Historical Encyclopedia of Women*. New York: Routledge, 2003.]

Fell, Alison S., and Ingrid E. Sharp, eds. *The Women's Movement in Wartime: International Perspectives, 1914–1919*. Houndmills: Palgrave Macmillan, 2007.

Gehmacher, Johanna, Elisabeth Harvey, and Sophia Kemlein, eds. *Zwischen Kriegen: Nationen, Nationalismen und Geschlechterverhältnisse in Mittel- und Osteuropa, 1918–1939*. Osnabrück: Fibre, 2004. [A publication of the German Historical Institute, Warsaw.]

Gerhard, Ute, ed. *Feminismus und Demokratie: Europaische Frauenbewegungen der 1920er Jahre*. Königstein: Ulrike Helmer, 2001.

Gubin, Éliane, Valérie Piette, and Catherine Jacques. "Les Féminismes belges et français de 1830 à 1914: Une approche comparée," *Le Mouvement social*, no. 178 (January–March 1997), 36–68.

Gubin, Éliane, Catherine Jacques, Florence Rochefort, Brigitte Studer, Françoise Thébaud, and Michelle Zancarini-Fournel, eds. *Le Siècle des féminismes*. Paris: Les Éditions de l'Atelier, 2004.

Guy, Donna J. "The Politics of Pan-American Cooperation: Maternalist Feminism and the Child Rights Movement, 1913–1960," *Gender & History*, 10:3 (November 1998), 449–469.

Hagemann, Karen, Sonya Michel, and Gunilla Budde, eds. *Civil Society and Gender Justice: Historical and Comparative Perspectives*. New York: Berghahn, 2008.

Hecht, Dieter Josef. "Die Weltkongresse jüdischer Frauen in der Zwischenkriegszeit: Wien 1923, Hamburg 1929," in *Religion, Geschlecht und Engagement: Die jüdischen Frauenbewegungen im deutschsprachigen Raum*, ed. Margarete Grandner and Edith Saurer. *L'Homme: Schriften* 9. Vienna: Böhlau Verlag, 2005, pp. 123–156.

Huber-Sperl, Rita, with Kerstin Wolff, eds. *Organisiert und engagiert: Vereinskultur bürgerlichen Frauen im 19. Jahrhundert in Westeuropa und den USA*. Königstein: Ulrike Helmer Verlag, 2002.

Jacques, Catherine. 2004. "Construire un reseau international: l'exemple du Conseil international des Femmes (CIF)," Chapter 7 in *Le Siècle des féminismes*, ed. Gubin, et al. Paris: Les Éditions de l'Atelier, 2004, pp. 127–141. [See above, under Gubin.]

Koven, Seth, and Sonya Michel, eds. *Mothers of a New World: Maternalist Politics and the Origins of Welfare States*. New York: Routledge, 1993.

Lavrin, Asunción. *Women, Feminism, and Social Change in Argentina, Chile, and Uruguay, 1890–1940*. Lincoln, NE: University of Nebraska Press, 1995.

McCune, Mary. *"The Whole Wide World, Without Limits": International Relief, Gender Politics, and American Jewish Women, 1893–1930*. Detroit, MI: Wayne State University Press, 2005.

Paisley, Fiona. *Glamour in the Pacific: Cultural Internationalism and Race Politics in the Women's Pan-Pacific*. Honolulu: University of Hawaii Press, 2009.

Paletschek, Sylvia, and Bianka Pietrow-Ennker, eds. "Women's Emancipation Movements in Europe in the Long Nineteenth Century: Conclusions," in *Women's Emancipation Movements in the Nineteenth Century*. Stanford, CA: Stanford University Press, 2004, pp. 310–333.

Pierson, Ruth Roach, and Nupur Chaudhuri, eds., with Beth McAuley. *Nation, Empire, Colony: Historicizing Gender and Race*. [International Federation for Research in Women's History, 1995 Conference, Montreal]. Bloomington, IN: Indiana University Press, 1998.

Saurer, Edith, Margareth Lanzinger, and Elisabeth Frysak, eds. *Women's Movements: Networks and Debates in post-communist Countries in the 19th and 20th Centuries*. *L'Homme, Schriften* 13. Cologne: Böhlau Verlag, 2006.

Schöck-Quinteros, Eva, Anja Schüler, Annika Wilmers, and Kerstin Wolff, eds. *Politische Netzwerkerinnen: Internationale Zusammenarbeit von Frauen 1830–1960*, vol 10 in Schriften des Hedwig Hintze-Instituts Bremen. Berlin: Trafo Verlag, 2007. [Articles in English and German.]

Sinha, Mrinalini. "Suffragism and Internationalism: The Enfranchisement of British and Indian Women under an Imperial State," *The Indian Economic and Social History Review*, 36:4 (1999), 461–484.

Sinha, Mrinalini, Donna J. Guy, and Angela Woollacott, eds. Special issue: "Feminisms and Internationalism," *Gender & History*, 10:3 (November 1998).

Tyrrell, Ian. *Woman's World, Woman's Empire: The Woman's Christian Temperance Union in International Perspective, 1880–1930*. Chapel Hill, NC: University of North Carolina Press, 1991.

Van Goethem, Geert. "An International Experiment of Women Workers: The International Federation of Working Women, 1919–1924," *Belgisch Tijdschrift voor Filologie en*

Gescheidenis/Revue Belge de Philologie et d'Histoire, 84:4 (2006), 1025–1047. Online at: www.globallabour.info/en/2008/09/the_international_federation_01.html

Ward, Margaret. "Nationalism, Pacifism, Internationalism: Louie Bennett, Hanna Sheehy-Skeffington, and the Problem of 'Defining Feminism'," in *Gender and Sexuality in Modern Ireland*, ed. Anthony Bradley and Maryann Gialannella Valiulis, Amherst, MA: University of Massachusetts Press, 1997, pp. 60–84.

Wikander, Ulla. "International Women's Congresses, 1877–1914: The Controversy over Equality and Special Labour Legislation," in *Rethinking Change: Current Swedish Feminist Research*, ed. Maud L. Eduards, et al. Uppsala: HSFR, distributed by Swedish Science Press, 1992, pp. 11–36.

Wikander, Ulla. "Political and Economic Citizenship in the International Women's Movement at the Turn of the 20th Century," in *Demokratie und Geschlecht/Démocratie et sexes: Interdisziplinäres Symposium zum 150jährigen Jubiläum des Schweizerischen Bundesstaates*, ed. Birgitte Christensen. Zurich: Chronos Verlag, 1999, pp. 53–72.

Wikander, Ulla. *Feminism, Familj och Medborgarskap: Debatter på internaionella kongresser om nattarbetsförbud for kvinnor 1889–1919* [Feminism, Family and Citizenship: Debates at International Congresses on Night Work for Women 1889–1919]. Göteborg: Makadam Förlag, 2006.

A sampling of other pertinent publications
on feminism in proto-national and national state (religious or secular)
settings not addressed in this volume

Avdela, Efi. *Le Genre entre Classe et nation: Essai d'historiographie grecque.* Paris: Editions Syllepse, 2006.

Baumann, Ursula. "Religion, Emancipation, and Politics in the Confessional Women's Movement in Germany, 1900–1933," in *Borderlines: Genders and Identities in War and Peace 1870–1930*, ed. Billie Melman. London: Routledge, 1998, pp. 285–306.

Cano, Gabriela. "Revolución, feminismo y ciudadanía en México (1915–1940)," in *Historia de las mujeres en Occidente,* ed. Georges Duby and Michelle Perrot. Madrid : Taurus, 1993, vol. 10, pp. 301–311.

Capel Martinez, Rosa, ed. *Historia de una conquista; Clara Campoamor y el voto femenino.* Madrid: Ayuntamiento de Madrid, Dirección General de Igualdad de Oportunidades, 2007.

Chang, Doris T. *Women's Movements in Twentieth-Century Taiwan.* Urbana, IL: University of Illinois Press, 2009.

Cheschebec, Roxana. "Feminist Ideologies and Activism in Romania (approx. 1890s–1940s): Nationalism and Internationalism in Romanian Projects for Women's Emancipation." PhD dissertation in history, Central European University, Budapest, 2005.

Cremer, Douglas J. "The Limits of Maternalism: Gender Ideology and the South German Catholic Working-Women's Associations, 1904–1918," *Catholic Historical Review*, 87:3 (July 2001), 428–452.

Daskalova, Krassimira. "Bulgarian Women in Movements, Laws, Discourses (1840s–1940s)," *Bulgarian Historical Review*, nos. 1-2 (1999), 184–200.

Daskalova, Krassimira and Georgeta Nazerska. *Women's Movements and Feminisms in Modern Bulgaria (1850s–1940s).* Sofia: Bulgarian Association of University Women, 2006.

Emmert, Thomas A. "Ženski Pokret: The Feminist Movement in Serbia in the 1920s," in *Gender Politics in the Western Balkans: Women and Society in Yugoslavia and the Yugoslav Successor States*, ed. Sabrina P. Ramet. University Park, PA: Pennsylvania State University Press, 1999, pp. 33–49.

Kark, Ruth, Margalit Shilo, and Galit Hasan-Rokem, eds. *Jewish Women in Pre-State Israel: Life History, Politics, and Culture*. Waltham, MA: Brandeis University Press and University Press of New England, 2008. [English translation of a volume of essays originally published in Hebrew in 2001.]

Lake, Marilyn. *Getting Equal: The History of Australian Feminism*. Sydney: Allen & Unwin, 1999.

Paletschek, Sylvia, and Bianka Pietrow-Ennker, eds. *Women's Emancipation Movements in the Nineteenth Century*. Stanford, CA: Stanford University Press, 2004. [Many essays on women's organizing efforts throughout Europe.]

Planert, Ute, ed. *Nation, Politik und Geschlecht: Frauenbewegungen und Nationalismus in der Moderne*. Frankfurt: Campus, 2000.

Ray, Bharati. *Early Feminists of Colonial India*. New Delhi: Oxford University Press, 2002.

Ryan, Louise, and Margaret Ward, eds. *Irish Women and Nationalism: Soldiers, New Women and Wicked Hags*. Dublin: Irish Academic Press, 2004.

Sinha, Mrinalini. *Specters of Mother India: The Global Restructuring of an Empire*. Durham, NC: Duke University Press, 2006.

NOTES

1 Was Mary Wollstonecraft a feminist? (Karen Offen)

1 For "the mother of English feminism," see Irene Coltman Brown, "Mary Wollstonecraft and the French Revolution, or Feminism and the Rights of Man," in *Women, State and Revolution: Essays on Power and Gender in Europe since 1789*, ed. Siân Reynolds (Amherst: Univ. of Massachusetts Press, 1987), 6; For "the best known feminist of the 18th century," see Jane Rendall, *Origins of Modern Feminism* (New York: Schocken Books, 1984), 55.

2 *A Vindication of the Rights of Woman, with Strictures on Political and Moral Subjects* (1792). All page references cited in this article are to the 1967 Norton Library edition, with an introduction by Charles W. Hagelman.

3 Karen Offen, "Sur l'Origine des Mots 'Féminisme' et 'Féministe'," *Revue d'histoire moderne et contemporaine* (Paris), 34, no. 3 (July–Sept. 1987): 492–96. English version, "On the French Origin of the Words 'Feminism' and 'Feminist'," *Feminist Issues*, 8, no. 2 (Fall 1988): 45–51.

4 See Karen Offen, "Defining Feminism: A Comparative Historical Perspective," *Signs: Journal of Women in Society and Culture*, 14, no. 1 (Autumn 1988): 119–57. An abbreviated English version appears in *Equality and Difference: Gender Dimensions in Political Thought and Morality*, ed. Gisela Bock and Susan James (London: Routledge, 1992). See also Karen Offen, "Liberty, Equality, and Justice for Women: The Theory and Practice of Feminism in Nineteenth-Century Europe," *Becoming Visible: Women in European History*, ed. Renate Bridenthal, Claudia Koonz, and Susan Stuard, 2nd revised ed. (Boston: Houghton-Mifflin, 1987), 335–73.

5 See the *Collected Letters of Mary Wollstonecraft*, ed. Ralph Wardle (Ithaca, N.Y.: Cornell Univ. Press, 1979) and *The Works of Mary Wollstonecraft*, ed. Marilyn Butler and Janet Todd. 7 vols. 1989. Note also the following biographies: Ralph Wardle, *Mary Wollstonecraft: A Critical Biography* (Lawrence, Kans.: University of Kansas Press, 1951; republished University of Nebraska Press, 1967); Eleanor Flexner, *Mary Wollstonecraft: A Biography* (New York: Coward McCann, 1972; Baltimore, Md.: Penguin Books, 1973); and Claire Tomalin, *The Life and Death of Mary Wollstonecraft* (New York: Harcourt Brace Jovanovich, 1974). For a discussion of these works, see Janet M. Todd, "Review Essay: The Biographies of Mary Wollstonecraft," *Signs*, vol. 1, no. 3, part 1 (1976): 721–34, and the brief Twayne biography by Moira Ferguson and Janet M. Todd, *Mary Wollstonecraft* (Boston: Twayne Publishers, 1984).

6 The British case has been extensively studied, e.g., Hilda Smith, *Reason's Disciples: Seventeenth-Century English Feminists* (Urbana, Ill.: University of Illinois Press, 1982); Katharine M. Rogers, *Eighteenth-Century English Feminism* (Urbana, Ill.: University of Illinois Press, 1983); and Alice Browne, *The Eighteenth Century Feminist Mind* (Brighton: Harvester Press, 1987). For Continental European texts in translation, see Susan Groag Bell and Karen Offen, eds., *Women, the Family, and Freedom: The Debate in Documents*, vol. 1 (Stanford, Calif.: Stanford University Press, 1983), Part 1, and supplementary documents prepared by Karen Offen for NEH seminars 1989 and 1992.

7 Including the most recent, Virginia Sapiro, *A Vindication of Political Virtue: The Political Theory of Mary Wollstonecraft* (Chicago: University of Chicago Press, 1992); the major exception is Tomalin's biography (see note 5), which infers more than it proves about Wollstonecraft's French connections.

8 G. J. Barker-Benfield, "Mary Wollstonecraft: Eighteenth-Century Commonwealthwoman," *Journal of the History of Ideas*, 50, no. 1 (Jan.– March, 1989), 95–115.

9 To date I have encountered no record of its critical reception in France. Copies of the Paris edition exist at the Bibliothèque Nationale, the Bibliothèque Marguerite Durand, and in the Gerritsen "History of Women" microfilm collection. The introduction by M.-F. Cachin to the 1976 reprint (Paris: Payot) provides no further illumination on this point.

10 Charles-Maurice de Talleyrand-Périgord, *Rapport sur l'instruction publique, fait au nom du Comité de constitution, à l'Assemblée nationale, les 10, 11, et 19 septembre 1791 [Projet de décrets sur l'instruction publique]* (Paris, 1791), pp. 115–120 passim. Unpublished transl. by KMO in NEH documents.

11 Marie-Jean-Antoine-Nicolas Caritat, marquis de Condorcet, "Sur l'Admission des femmes au droit de cité," *Journal de la Société de 1789*, 3 July 1790, and reprinted in Condorcet's *Oeuvres*, X; English translation, "Condorcet's Plea for the Citizenship of Women," by John Morley, *Fortnightly Review*, 13 (1 June 1870), 719–24, and reproduced in Bell & Offen, *WFF*, I, doc. 24.

12 Talleyrand, *Rapport*.

13 See Phyllis Stock, *Better than Rubies* (New York: G. P. Putnam's Sons, 1978) for an overview of women's education in Europe, and especially chap. IV on the eighteenth-century debate. See also Samia I. Spencer, "Women and Education," in *French Women and the Age of Enlightenment*, ed. Samia I. Spencer (Bloomington: Indiana University Press, 1984), 83–96.

14 Quote from General Introduction, Karen Offen book ms., "The Woman Question in Modern France," pp. 2–3.

15 On the controversy over Marie-Antoinette, see Chantal Thomas, *La Reine scélérate: Marie-Antoinette dans les pamphlets* (Paris: Editions du Seuil, 1989); Elizabeth Colwill, "Just Another Citoyenne? Marie-Antoinette on Trial, 1790–1793," *History Workshop*, no. 28 (Autumn 1989): 63–87; and Lynn Hunt, "The Many Bodies of Marie-Antoinette: Political Pornography and the Problem of the Feminine in the French Revolution," in *Eroticism and the Body Politic*, ed. Lynn Hunt (Baltimore: Johns Hopkins University Press, 1991). For the discussion on women and luxury in eighteenth-century political and economic thought, see Tjitske Akkerman, *Women's Vices, Public Benefits: Women and Commerce in the French Enlightenment* (The Hague: Het Spinhuis, 1992). Some of these concerns date back to Fénelon, even to Vivès, writing in sixteenth-century Spain.

16 On the more favorable views of harem culture and Islamic women's "liberty" construed as sexual freedom (e.g., you can go anywhere in the veil without being discovered) by eighteenth-century British women writers, see Billie Melman, *Women's Orients: English Women and the Middle East, 1718–1918, Sexuality, Religion, and Work* (Houndmills, Basingstoke: Macmillan and Ann Arbor: Univ. of Michigan Press, 1992), 77–98.

17 E.g., "She refuses to grapple honestly with the limits [modesty, chastity] may impose on women's public role." Joan B. Landes, *Women and the Public Sphere in the Age of the French Revolution* (Ithaca, N.Y.: Cornell University Press, 1988), 131. "Take for instance, the moralizing tone...," Christine Fauré, *Democracy without Women* (Bloomington: Indiana University Press, 1991), 3.

18 The concept of "passionlessness" was developed by Nancy F. Cott, "Passionlessness: An Interpretation of Victorian Sexual Ideology, 1790–1850," *Signs*, 4, no. 2 (1978), 219–36.

19 By contrast, Barbara Taylor makes much of Wollstonecraft's "wild wish." See "Mary Wollstonecraft and the Wild Wish of Early Feminism," *History Workshop Journal*, no. 33 (Spring 1992), 197–219. I am arguing here that Wollstonecraft's text is far more grounded in acceptance of sexual difference than interpretations such as Taylor's would indicate.

20 The works of Montesquieu and John Millar convey these themes. See especially Rendall, *Origins*, chap. 1, and Paul Bowles, "John Millar, the Four-Stages Theory, and Women's Position in Society," *History of Political Economy*, 16, no. 4 (Winter, 1984), 619–638.

21 The controversy over whether friendship can exist between the sexes, and particularly between husband and wife, originates in the texts of Greco-Roman antiquity, and continues from Montaigne to Mill, via Daniel Defoe, Hester Chapone, and many others. It was a live issue in late eighteenth-century Anglo-American society; see, for example, Edith B. Gelles's chapter on Abigail Adams's friendship with James Lovell in *Portia: The World of Abigail Adams* (Bloomington: Indiana University Press, 1992).

22 Compare Josefa Amar y Borbon, *Importancia de la instruccion que conviene dar a las mugeres* (Zaragoza, 1784), transl. by Margarita Parreno, in NEH documents.

23 Edith B. Gelles, work in progress critiquing the U.S. historiography on "republican motherhood."

24 The usual comparison is with Olympe de Gouges's "Droits de la femme" (see below, note 29). See Joan B. Landes, *Women and the Public Sphere in the Age of the French Revolution*, chap. 4, and Brown, "Wollstonecraft" (note 1 above).

25 "Petition of Women of the Third Estate to the King, 1 January 1789," in *Women in Revolutionary Paris*, ed. Darline Gay Levy, Harriet B. Applewhite and Mary Johnson (Urbana: Univ. of Illinois Press, 1979), 18–21. The following discussion is taken from Offen, "Women and Politics in the French Revolution," unpublished ms. [Ed. This material has since been published as chap. 3 of Karen Offen, *European Feminisms, 1700–1950: A Political History* (Stanford, Calif.: Stanford University Press, 2000).]

26 Cahier des doléances et réclamations des femmes, par Madame B***B***, Pays de Caux, 1789, reprinted in *Cahiers de doléances des femmes en 1789 et autres textes* (Paris: EDHIS, 1981), I, 47–51. Karen Offen translation, NEH documents.

27 "Requête des dames à l'Assemblée Nationale (1789)," reprinted in *Cahiers de doléances....* Karen Offen translation, NEH documents.

28 Etta Palm, "Adresse des citoyennes françoises à l'Assemblée Nationale, " (July 1791); Karen Offen translation in *WFF*, I, doc. 25.

29 Olympe de Gouges, *Les Droits de la femme* (Paris, 1791); NC/KO transl. by Nupur Chaudhuri, with Susan Groag Bell and Karen Offen, in *WFF*, I, doc. 26.

30 Karen Offen, "Feminism," *Encyclopedia of Social History*, ed. Peter N. Stearns (New York: Garland Publishing Co., Inc., 1994); see also Offen, "Defining Feminism...," pp.150–53.

31 Mitzi Myers provocatively lays out the substantive parallels between Wollstonecraft and More in "Reform or Ruin: 'A Revolution in Female Manners'," in *Studies in Eighteenth-Century Culture*, ed. Harry C. Payne, vol. 11 (1986).

2 Re-rooting American women's activism (Nancy A. Hewitt)

The author wishes to thank Claire Moses, Beverly Palmer, Vivien Rose, Bonnie Anderson, Nancy Isenberg, and Gabriella Hauch for their insights and encouragement and the faculty and graduate students at Rutgers University (December 1997), the participants at the American Historical Association session on 1848 in Seattle, Washington (January 1998), and the participants at the International Federation for Research on Women session on 1848 in Melbourne, Australia (June 1998) for their challenging questions and comments. For inclusion in this collection, the author and editor have made a few minor editorial corrections.

1 Eleanor Flexner, *Century of Struggle: The Woman's Rights Movement in the United States* (Cambridge, Mass: Belknap Press, 1959); Elizabeth Cady Stanton, Susan B. Anthony, and Matilda Joslyn Gage, eds., *History of Woman Suffrage*, 6 vols. The original two-volume history covered 1848–1880 and was published in New York by Fowler & Wells in 1881. Succeeding volumes were published between then and 1922, the last volume being completed by Gage alone following the deaths of Stanton and Anthony.

2 Some of those most important works in this area are Rosalyn Terborg-Penn, "Discrimination Against Afro-American Women in the Woman's Movement, 1830–1920," in *The Afro-American Woman: Struggles and Images*, ed. Rosalyn Terborg-Penn and Sharon Harley (Port Washington, NewYork: Kennikat Press, 1978): 17–27, and *African American Women and the Struggle for the Vote, 1850–1920* (Bloomington: Indiana University Press, 1998); Paula Giddings, *When and Where I Enter: The Impact of Black Women on Race and Sex in America* (NY: William Morrow, 1984); Yamila Azize, "Puerto Rican Women and the Vote," reprinted in *Unequal Sisters: A Multicultural History of Women in the United States*, ed. Ellen DuBois and Vicki Ruiz (NewYork: Routledge, 1994); Joan Jensen, "'Disfranchisement is a Disgrace': Women and Politics in New Mexico, 1900–1940," in *New Mexico Women: Intercultural Perspectives*, ed. Joan M. Jensen and Darlis Miller (Albuquerque: University of New Mexico Press, 1990); Ellen Carol DuBois, "Working Women, Class Relations, and Suffrage Militance: Harriet Stanton Blatch and the New York Woman Suffrage Movement, 1894–1909," *Journal of American History* 74 (June 1987): 34–58.

3 See, for instance, the treatment of woman's rights and suffrage in Sara Evans, *Born for Liberty: A History of Women in America* (New York: The Free Press, 1989), which is widely used as a text in American Women's History courses across the country, and which is particularly sensitive to race and class differences among women.

4 Elizabeth Cady Stanton, *Eighty Years and More: Reminiscences, 1815–1897* (New York: T. Fisher Unwin, 1898). The version sketched below, based on Stanton's autobiography, comes from Anne Firor Scott, *Natural Allies: Women's Associations in American History* (Urbana: University of Illinois Press, 1992), p. 54. She bases her version on Ellen C. DuBois, *Feminism and Suffrage: The Emergence of an Independent Women's Movement in America, 1848–1869* (Ithaca, New York: Cornell University Press, 1978), chap. 1. This version parallels that found in most women's history and American History texts. For two articles that suggest a more complex origin for the Seneca Falls Convention, and woman's rights more generally, see Judith Wellman, "The Seneca Falls Woman's Rights Convention: A Study of Social Networks," *Journal of Women's History* 3 (Spring 1991): 9–37; and Nancy A. Hewitt, "Feminist Friends: Agrarian Quakers and the Emergence of Woman's Rights in America," *Feminist Studies* 12 (Spring 1986): 27–49.

5 Wellman, "The Seneca Falls Woman's Rights Convention;" Nancy Isenberg, *Sex and Citizenship in Antebellum America* (New York: University of North Carolina Press, 1998); and Hewitt, "Feminist Friends."

6 Beverly Palmer of Pomona College in California is currently working on a collection of Mott letters, sermons and speeches. [See Palmer, ed., *Selected Letters of Lucretia Coffin Mott* (Urbana: University of Illinois Press, 2002)] For biographical information on Mott, see Anna B. Hallowell, ed. *Life and Letters of James and Lucretia Mott* (Boston: Houghton, Mifflin, 1884); and Margaret Hope Bacon, *Mothers of Feminism: The Story of Quaker Women in America* (San Francisco: Harper & Row, 1986).

7 *Proceedings of the Woman's Rights Convention, held at Syracuse, New York, September 8, 9, and 10, 1852* (Syracuse: J.E. Masters, 1852), p. 1.

8 See Mary Robbins Post to Isaac and Amy Post, Sept. 12, 1848, in which she cites an earlier letter from Amy Post, Isaac and Amy Post Family Papers, University of Rochester, Rochester, New York.

9 On Mott's travels in western New York, see Lucretia Mott to Edmund Quincy, published in *The Liberator*, October 6, 1848.

10 See especially Frederick Douglass's *North Star*, which had just begun publication in early 1848 and covered events in Europe extensively during that spring and summer.

11 See Bonnie Anderson, *Joyous Greetings: The First International Women's Movement, 1830–1860* (New York: Oxford University Press, 2000) for a pathbreaking analysis of these early international connections.

12 *Proceedings . . . Syracuse, 1852*, quote p. 35; letter pp. 32–35.

13 On the life of Jeanne Deroin, see Claire Goldberg Moses, *French Feminism in the Nineteenth Century* (Albany: State University of New York Press, 1984); and Moses and Leslie Wahl Rabine, eds, *The Word and the Act: French Feminism in the Age of Romanticism* (Bloomington: Indiana University Press, 1992).

14 Lucretia Mott, "Law of Progress," in *Lucretia Mott: Her Complete Speeches and Sermons*, ed. Dana Greene (New York: Edwin Mellen Press, 1980), p. 75. Thanks to Bonnie Anderson for bringing this speech to my attention.

15 The *North Star* provided lengthy coverage of the upcoming Emancipation Day celebration in its July 14, 1848 issue, the same issue in which the announcement of the Seneca Falls Woman's Rights Convention appeared.

16 Mott to Quincy, *The Liberator*, Oct. 6, 1848.

17 See Moses, *French Feminism*; Catherine M. Prelinger, "Religious Dissent, Women's Rights, and the *Hamburger Hochshule für das weibliche Geschlecht* in Mid-Nineteenth-Century Germany," *Church History* v. 45 (1976): 42–55; and Hewitt, "Feminist Friends."

18 On the political vision of the Friends of Human Progress (also known as the Congregational Friends and the Progressive Friends), see Yearly Meeting of Congregational Friends, *Proceedings of the Yearly Meeting of Congregational Friends, Held at Waterloo, N.Y., from the Fourth to the Sixth of the Sixth Month, Inclusive, with an Appendix, 1849* (Auburn, N.Y.: Oliphant's Press, 1849); and Yearly Meeting of Congregational Friends, *Proceedings . . . . 1850* (Auburn, N.Y.: Henry Oliphant, 1850).

19 See, for instance, Mary Robbins Post to Dear All [Isaac and Amy Post], May 5, 185[1], Post Family Papers.

20 On Rochester Convention, see Report, "Rochester Woman's Rights Convention," August 2, 1848, Phoebe Post Willis Papers, Rare Book and Manuscript Room, University of Rochester, Rochester, New York; and Hewitt, "Feminist Friends."

21 Material in this paragraph is taken from Terborg-Penn, *African American Women and the Struggle for the Vote,* chap. 2; and Benjamin Quarles, "Frederick Douglass and the Woman's Rights Movement," History 2000 Occasional Papers Series, No. 1-1993 (Baltimore, Md: Morgan State University Foundation, 1993).

22 These campaigns to end segregated schooling in the North have not been widely covered in the secondary literature. Information on them can be found in the *North Star*; the *History of Woman Suffrage*, vol. 1; and *The Liberator*.

23 On black women's antislavery activity, see Dorothy Sterling, ed. *We Are Your Sisters: Black Women in the Nineteenth Century* (NY: WW Norton, 1984), Part II; and Julie Roy Jeffrey, *The Great Silent Army of Abolitionism: Ordinary Women in the Antislavery Movement* (Chapel Hill: UNC Press, 1998), chap. 4.

24 Described in Sterling, *We Are Your Sisters*, pp. 62–64.

25 Elsa Barkley Brown, "Negotiating and Transforming the Public Sphere: African American Political Life in the Transition from Slavery to Freedom," *Public Culture* (Summer 1994): 107–146.

26 See Isenberg, *Sex and Citizenship*, p. 48.

27 Isenberg discusses these protests in *Sex and Citizenship*, pp. 69, 139–40. Her analysis should encourage additional work on the scope and language of these protests.

28 Magoffin quoted in Janet Lecompte, "The Independent Women of Hispanic New Mexico," *Western Historical Quarterly* 22:1 (1981):17–35.

29 Ibid.

30 For an overview of Seneca women's status, see Joan M. Jensen, "Native American Women and Agriculture," in *Women and Power in American History*, ed. Kathryn Kish Sklar and Thomas Dublin, vol. 1 (Englewood Cliffs, NJ: Prentice-Hall, 1991), pp. 8–23. See also Sally Roesch Wagner, *The Untold Story of the Iroquois Influence on Early Feminists* (Aberdeen, South Dakota: Sky Carrier Press, 1996); and Harriet S. Clarke Caswell, *Our Life Among the Iroquois Indians* (Boston and Chicago: Congregational Sunday School and Publishing Society, 1892), especially pp. 79–80 on the new 1848 constitution; and Mott to Quincy, *The Liberator*, Oct. 6, 1848.

31 For a detailed account by a Quaker missionary of Seneca Indian life, see Caswell, *Our Life Among the Iroquois Indians*.

32 For a discussion of this interest and ambivalence about Indian women in the women's movement, see Dolores Janiewski, "Giving Women a Future: Alice Fletcher, the 'Woman Question' and 'Indian Reform,'" in *Visible Women: New Essays on American Activism,*ed. Nancy A. Hewitt and Suzanne Lebsock (Urbana: University of Illinois Press, 1993), pp. 325–44.

3 Liberty, equality, morality (Anne Summers)

1 The research for this article formed part of a project on the international networks of Josephine Butler, based at the Women's Library, London Metropolitan University, and financed by the Leverhulme Trust between 2004 and 2007. The project sponsored an internet listing of Butler's manuscript letters in European archives (now to be found at www.thewomenslibrary.ac.uk/butler) and two international colloquia. The author and editor have made a few editorial corrections and clarifications in this version.

2 Annemieke van Drenth and Francisca de Haan, *The Rise of Caring Power. Elizabeth Fry and Josephine Butler in Britain and the Netherlands* (Amsterdam: Amsterdam University Press, 1999). There is no widely available reference work on the history of the Federation. Josephine Butler's anonymously published work, *The New Abolitionists: a Narrative of a Year's Work* (1876) was supplemented by her *Personal Reminiscences of a Great Crusade* (first published in 1896), carrying the narrative up to 1880. The Federation published many pamphlets and reports: its organs in Britain were *The Shield* (1870–1886, 1897–1970) *The Dawn* (1888–1896) and *The Storm-Bell* (1898–1900); its headquarters in Switzerland published the *Bulletin Continental* (1875–1901), continued as *Revue Abolitionniste*. Affiliated publications which flourished in the 1880s but on which I have been unable to find further bibliographic details included *La Coscienza Pubblica* (Italy), *Der Korrespondent* (Germany), *Bulletin de la Société de la Moralité Publique* (Belgium), *Het Maanblad* (Netherlands), and *Maanedsblad* (Denmark).

3 Anne Summers, 'Gaps in the Record: Hidden Internationalisms,' *History Workshop Journal* 52, (2001), pp. 217–27.

4 Aya Takahashi, *The Development of the Japanese Nursing Profession. Adopting and Adapting Western Influences* (London: Routledge Curzon, 2004), p. 120.

5 See Judith R. Walkowitz, *Prostitution and Victorian Society: Women, Class and the State* (Cambridge: Cambridge University Press, 1980). Jane Jordan, *Josephine Butler* (London: John Murray, 2001) is the latest biographical treatment.

6 Bibliothèque Publique et Universitaire de Genève, Manuscrits français 6933 ff. 82–83, letter of J. Butler (to Frédéric Passy?) April 1871.

7 See *Prophylaxie Internationale des Maladies Vénériennes . . . [MM. Crocq et Rollet] . . . Rapport fait au nom de la Commission nommée par le Congrès Medical International de Paris de 1867* (Lyon, 1869), pp. 13–19; Sheldon Amos, *A Comparative Survey of the Laws in Force for the Prohibition, Regulation and Licensing of Vice in England* (London, 1877), pp. 1–2; Anon., *De la Police des Mœurs* (Brussels : A. Lefevre, 1880), pp. 10–16.

8 Jordan, *Josephine Butler*, p. 279, states that in 1895 'Recent members of the Federation in Europe seemed not to know who Josephine was'; the work of Philippa Levine, in particular *Prostitution, Race and Politics: Policing Venereal Disease in the British Empire* (London/New York: Routledge, 2003), has done much to focus attention on the imperial dimensions of the abolitionist campaign.

9 At the time this article was written, the project had not yet extended to a sixth country, Italy. On the relative failure of abolitionism to implant in Italy, see Bruno Wanrooij, 'Josephine Butler and Regulated Prostitution in Italy,' followed by Marjan Schwegman, 'Comment: Amazons in Italy; Josephine Butler and the Transformation of Italian Female Militancy' in *Women's History Review* 17:2 (April 2008), pp. 153–79. See also Mary Gibson, *Prostitution and the State in Italy, 1860–1915* (Columbus OH: Ohio State University Press, 1986).

10 James Stuart, *Reminiscences* (London, 1912), pp. 215–16. See Regula Zürcher, 'Marie Goegg-Pouchoulin (1826–1899): Politisches Engagement im Spannungsfeld von dualistischer Geschlechterordnung und feministischem Programm,' in Rita Huber-Sperl (ed.), *Organisiert und engagiert. Vereinskultur bürgerlicher Frauen im 19. Jahrhundert in Westeuropa und den USA* (Königstein: Taunus, 2002).

11 The activities of the Amies de la Jeune Fille are recorded in *Journal du Bien Public*, issued for many years with the *Bulletin Continental*. The online *Historisches Lexicon der Schweiz* notes of Betsy Cellérier: 'Die Bekanntschaft mit Josephine Butler führte sie zur Sittlichkeitsbewegung'; see http://www.dhs.ch/externe/protect/deutsch.html. Emma Hess, as a good French-speaker, was asked by friends in Zurich to attend the Lausanne conference of the Federation in 1887; she gained her first experience of addressing large assemblies when she reported on the Federation's activities. I am grateful to the Gosteli-Stiftung, Worblaufen, near Bern, for the opportunity to find this information in its collection of press-cuttings and biographical ephemera.

12 On Pieczynska and von Mülinen, see Anne-Marie Käppeli, *Sublime Croisade. Ethique et politique du féminisme protestant, 1875–1928* (Geneva, 1990). Interesting early sources on nineteenth century Swiss feminists include Emilie Benz, 'Die Geschichte der Frauenbewegung in der Schweiz,' in: Helene Lange and Gertrud Bäumer (eds.), *Handbuch der Frauenbewegung*, vol. I (Berlin, 1901), pp. 189–210, and Annie Leuch-Reineck, *Le Féminisme en Suisse* (Lausanne, 1929).

13 On the links between Dutch abolitionism and feminism, see van Drenth and de Haan, *Caring Power*, especially chap. 6 and the Chronological Appendix; Martina Kramers, 'Die Geschichte der Frauenbewegung in Holland,' in Lange and Bäumer, *Handbuch*, vol. I, p. 215: 'Ohne die Weigerung des Vorsitzenden, weibliche Mitglieder aufzunehmen, würde die niederländische Frauenbewegung heute einen grossen eifrigen Verein weniger zählen'. Mme Edith de Falloise, president of the Foyer Lilla Monod in Brussels (originally established by Butler's supporters as a home for prostitutes wishing to start a new life), has pointed out that in Belgium, the membership of the respective committees involved many married couples, so that mixed meetings took place in private if not in public!

14 On Isala van Diest, see references in F. De Bueger-Van Lierde, 'La Ligue belge du Droit des femmes,' *Sextant* 1 (1993), p. 15 (which gives, however, an incorrect date for her medical qualification). Van Diest contributed the chapter on Belgium in Theodore Stanton (ed.), *The Woman Question in Europe* (London/New York/ Paris 1884; reprinted New York, 1970), which is prefaced, pp. 364–65, by the editor's interesting biographical notice.

15 For an exploration of the different strands in women's and purity organisations in Germany, see Ursula Baumann, *Protestantismus und Frauenemanzipation in Deutschland 1850 bis 1920* (Frankfurt/New York, 1992); and L. Sauerteig, 'Frauenemanzipation und Sittlichkeit. Die Rezeption

des englischen Abolitionismus in Deutschland,' in: R. Muhs, J. Paulmann and W. Steinmetz (eds.): *Aneignung und Abwehr. Interkultureller Transfer zwischen Deutschland und Grossbritannien in der 19ten Jahrhundert* (Bodenheim, 1998). On Bebel's interest, see *Woman in the Past, Present and Future* [first English translation of the work which became *Die Frau und der Sozialismus*], (London, 1885), pp. 95–96. Bebel's sympathy for the movement continued through the 1890s; see *Mrs Butler's Plea for an Interest in the Abolitionist Work on the Continent of Europe* (1893), p. 5, and *A Revolting Injustice: what Deputy Bebel says on the State Regulation of Vice* (1896).

16 See above, note 12.

17 *Congrès International du Droit des Femmes, Paris 25.7–9.8.1878* [Proceedings published as a supplement to: *Le Droit des Femmes*, ed. Léon Richer (Paris, 1878–79)] pp. 114, 124–29. On the chronology of French abolitionism see Alain Corbin, *Women for Hire* (Cambridge, MA: Harvard University Press, 1990), chaps. 5 and 7.

18 *Congrès International des oeuvres et institutions féminines, 12–18 July 1889* (Paris, 1889), pp. 65, 125–26, 150, 291–94. On the history of this split, see Florence Rochefort 'The French Feminist Movement and Republicanism, 1868–1914,' in: Sylvia Paletschek and Bianka Pietrow-Ennker (eds.): *Women's Emancipation Movements in the 19th Century* (Stanford, CA: Stanford University Press, 2004), pp. 88–89.

19 Quotation from 'Visages du Féminisme Réformiste,' online catalogue of the Centre des Archives du Féminisme, University of Angers (http://bu.univ-angers.fr). For Sainte-Croix's interwar role in formulating League of Nations policy, see Carol Ann Miller, 'Lobbying the League: Women's International Organizations and the League of Nations,' unpublished D.Phil. thesis, University of Oxford, 1992, chap. 5; and Karen Offen, 'La plus grande féministe de France. Mais qui est donc Madame Avril de Sainte-Croix?,' in: *Bulletin* no. 9, *Archives du Féminisme*, 2005; 'Intrepid Crusader. Ghénia Avril de Sainte-Croix Takes on the Prostitution Issue,' in: *Proceedings of the Western Society for French History, Colorado Springs conference, Oct. 2005* (2006), and 'Madame Ghenia Avril de Sainte-Croix, the Josephine Butler of France,' *Women's History Review*, 17:2 (2008), pp. 239–55.

20 On Butler's 'lineages', see Anne Summers, *Female Lives, Moral States. Women, Religion and Public Life in Britain 1800–1930* (Newbury: Threshold, 2000), pp. 124–27.

21 Women's Library, 3/HJW (Henry J. Wilson Archive), Box 286, 'Federation file II, 1875–1879'; item 320, letter from G. Stutzer, Director Brunswick State Asylum for Idiots (translated copy), 8 May 1875. Emphasis in the original.

22 Butler, *Personal Reminiscences of a Great Crusade*, pp. 284–86.

23 Women's Library, 3/HJW (Henry J. Wilson Archive), Box 286, 'Federation File 1896–June 1898'; printed extracts from Butler's correspondence: letter of 26 February 1897.

24 The Federation met at Neuchâtel in 1882, Basel in 1884, Lausanne in 1887, Geneva in 1888, Bern in 1892 and 1896 and Geneva again in 1899 (the last Congress to be attended by Josephine Butler in person).

25 *Journal du Bien Public* IX, 8 (1884), p. 66.

26 *Journal du Bien Public* IX, 3 (1884), p. 33; IX, 10 (1884), p. 81; *Bulletin Continental* IX, 8 (1884), p. 66.

27 Bibliothèque Publique et Universitaire de Genève, Manuscrits français 4790, ff. 60–61v, J. Butler to Marie Sandoz, 13 April 1888.

28 Amsterdam University Library, Réveil Archiv item 0799, J. Butler to H. Pierson, 6 July 1896.

29 In 1899 the Appenzell branch was circulating a journal, *Heimathglocken*, edited in Berlin, and indignantly repudiating the reproach 'de n'avoir pas un ton assez suisse et républicain': Archives d'Etat de Genève, Archives privées, l'Association du Sou pour l'Oeuvre du relèvement moral 57.5 (10) (iv). On the split, see 57.5. (10) (vi), *l'Association du Sou, Marche de l'Oeuvre –1901* (Genève, Bureau du Secrétaire Général de la Fédération, 1902).

30 Marie Fischer-Lette was a novelist and a daughter of Wilhelm Adolf Lette, founder (1866) of the 'Verein zur Förderung der Erwerbstätigkeit des weiblichen Geschlechts' in Berlin – commonly referred to as the Lette-Verein.

31 *Durch Kampf zum Sieg! Dem Andenken der Frau Josephine E. Butler gewidmet von ihrer treuen Mitarbeiterin Marie Fischer, geb. Lette* (Hamburg: Kommissions-Verlag der Agentur des Rauhen Hauses, 1907), pp. 14, 16, 17, 19.

32 Internal communication of Butler to the Federation Executive: *Gossipping Letter* No. 1. 31.8.1894.

33 It was reported of 'Miss Lungstrass' work at Bonn' that she had 'had a conflict of three hours' duration with M. Stoecker, the well-known opponent of the Jews . . . She is filled with a horror

for the whole thing, worthy of an Anglo-Saxon woman': Federation report over Butler's name in: *New Abolitionist Work throughout the World* (1885), pp. 28–29.

34 I am grateful to Pfarrer Dr. J. Grashof, author of *Geschichte des Evangelischen Kirchenkreises Gladbach* (diss., B-Verlag Rödingen) for bringing this aspect of Weber's career to my attention. On Stöcker's politics, see P. J. Pulzer, *The Rise of Political Anti-Semitism in Germany and Austria* (New York, 1964; Cambridge, MA.: Harvard University Press, 1988).

35 Landesarchiv Berlin, Helene-Lange-Archiv, B Rep. 235-13 MF-Nr. 3458, Butler to Pappritz 18 Feb., Cheltenham, n.d. (1901–02?).

36 Bibliothèque Publique et Universitaire de Neuchâtel, Fonds Felix Bovet, Ms 2098/86, 223, Butler to Felix Bovet 12 July 1896.

37 International Information Centre and Archives for the Women's Movement (IIAV), Amsterdam, Correspondence of the Rev. Hendrik Pierson, letter of Butler to Pierson, 30 April 1895.

38 IIAV, Correspondence of the Rev. Hendrik Pierson, letter of Butler to Pierson, 19 August 1896.

39 See, among others, Corbin, *Women for Hire*; Annet Mooij, *Out of Otherness. . . . the Dutch venereal disease debates 1850–1990* (Amsterdam, 1998); Petra de Vries, *Kuisheid voor mannen, vrijheid voor vrouwen. De reglementering en bestrijding van prostitutie in Nederland 1850–1911* (Hilversum, 1997); A. Cairoli, S.Engel, *Le Déclin des Maisons Closes. La prostitution à Genève à la fin du XIXe siècle* (Carouge, 1987).

40 For a general survey, see, for example, René Rémond, *Religion and Society in Modern Europe* (Malden, MA, 1999). On France, see Florence Rochefort, 'La prostituée et l'ouvrière: Approches protestantes et catholiques du féminisme sous la IIIe République,' in F. Lautman, ed.: *Ni Eve ni Marie. Luttes et incertitudes ...*(Geneva, 1997), p. 221.

41 Van Drenth and de Haan, *Caring Power*; Jean Bauberot, *Le retour des Huguenots* (Paris, 1985), pp. 118, 120–22; Butler, *The New Abolitionists* (London, 1876), pp. 14–20.

42 British Continental and General Federation, report, *Troisième Congrès International, La Haye, 17–22 septembre 1883*, pp. 45–47.

43 Bibliothèque Publique et Universitaire de Genève, Manuscrits français 4790, ff. 54–55v; Butler to Marie Sandoz, 7 July 1887.

44 Bibliothèque Publique et Universitaire de Genève, Manuscrits français 5774/3, Hanna Bieber-Böhm, 'La Fédération et le mouvement pour le relèvement de la moralité publique en Allemagne', n.d. (original article in: *Neue Bahnen*, 1 March 1899). For a summary of Bieber-Böhm's campaigns, see Lange and Bäumer, *Handbuch*, vol. II, pp. 172–79.

45 Helene von Mülinen, *Eine Vielumstrittene Frage. Referat gehalten an der Konferenz der Fédération Abolitionniste in Genf, 19 Sept. 1899, ...*(Geneva, 1900), pp. 9, 11.

46 The same, pp. 4–5. At the Geneva Congress of 1899 the French journalist Marcel Huart had spoken in favour of free love: for some of the repercussions, see the letter of H. J. Wilson in *The Shield*, October 1899, p. 63; Minutes of the Executive Committee, 22 February 1900; and A. de Morsier, *Lettre familière aux Membres du Comité-Exécutif de la Fédération Abolitionniste Internationale,* March 1900.

47 Lange and Bäumer, *Handbuch*, vol. II, p. 163.

48 See note 45.

49 Lange and Bäumer, *Handbuch*, vol. I, p. 150; E. Lüders, *Minna Cauer. Leben und Werk* (Stuttgart, 1925), pp. 114–15.

50 See Luders, *Minna Cauer*. See also Mundaneum (Mons), Fonds Léonie La Fontaine 66, file, 'Lettres diverses': letter of J. Butler to the 'ladies of die Frauenbewegung,' 29 October 1898; letter of J. Butler to 'Dear Friend' (Minna Cauer), n.d.; and Landesarchiv Berlin, Helene-Lange-Archiv, B Rep 235-01, Mf-Nr 3218, typed copy of Butler's letter of 29 October 1898, with annotations by Cauer; Mf-Nr 2234, printed copy of the same letter in Bund Deutscher Frauenvereine leaflet, February 1899.

51 J. Butler, *Truth Before Everything* (July 1897); see also Jordan, *Josephine Butler*, pp 278–81.

52 See note 11 on Emma Hess. Clara Maria Dutoit-Haller, one of the earliest 'Amies de la Jeune Fille' (Freundinnen Junger Mädchen) in the Bern region of Switzerland, organised an all-female event in the 1880s which her obituarist described as 'einer unerhörter Neuheit . . . sogar die Begrüssungsrede am Bankett hielt eine Dame!'; Burger-Bibliothek Bern, *Mitteilungen der Neuen Madchen Schule,* Bern, Dezember 1916, 'Nekrolog,' p. 125.

53 Lange and Bäumer, *Handbuch*, vol. I, p. 152; vol. II, p. 189.

54 See note 2.

4 "To educate women into rebellion" (Sandra Stanley Holton)

I would like to thank the University of Adelaide and the Australian Research Council for awarding me research fellowships in 1990 and 1992, allowing me the freedom to undertake the research presented here, and also the Australian Academy of the Humanities, the Australian Research Council, the Ian Potter Foundation, and the University of Adelaide, each of which during this period provided support for the necessary travel. Earlier versions of this article were presented at the 1992 conference of the Australian and New Zealand American Studies Association in Adelaide, and the "Suffrage and Beyond" conference in Wellington in 1993, held to mark the centennial of the enfranchisement of women in New Zealand.

1 Elizabeth Cady Stanton was in England from October 1882 to November 1883, from November 1886 to March 1888, and from March 1890 to August 1891. Elizabeth Cady Stanton, *Eighty Years and More: Reminiscences, 1815–1897* (1898; rpt. edn., New York, 1970), chaps. 12, 16, 27, recounts these visits; and see also *Elizabeth Cady Stanton, as Revealed in Her Letters Diary and Reminiscences*, Theodore Stanton and Harriot Stanton Blatch, eds., 2 vols. (New York, 1922), 2: 196–213, 233–50, 262–79, which reproduces extracts from her diary for these periods. I look at some other aspects of her friendship with the Bright circle in my essay "From Anti-Slavery to Suffrage Militancy: The Bright Circle, Elizabeth Cady Stanton and the British Women's Movement," in *Suffrage and Beyond: International Feminist Perspectives*, Caroline Daley and Melanie Nolan, eds. (Auckland, 1994).

2 I have deliberately not applied the term "conservative" here to denote opposition to the Radical-Liberal approach to suffrage. Although there were prominent British suffragists who might rightly be so described, for example, Emily Davies and Frances Power Cobbe, the conflicts discussed in this article were fiercest *among* liberal suffragists, and so I adopt the terms "radical" and "moderate" to indicate points on a continuum of advanced opinion, while "Radical-Liberal" is used to indicate affiliation to a particular current within liberal opinion. For a detailed comparison of some leading conservative and liberal suffragists, see Barbara Caine, *Victorian Feminists* (New York, 1991).

3 Millicent Garrett Fawcett, "England," in *The Woman Question in Europe*, Theodore Stanton, ed. (New York, 1884), 1–29; Helen Blackburn, *Women's Suffrage: A Record of the Women's Suffrage Movement in the British Isles, with Biographical Sketches of Miss Becker* (London, 1902); and "Great Britain: Efforts for the Parliamentary Franchise," in Susan B. Anthony and Ida Husted Harper, *History of Woman Suffrage*, vol. 4 (1886; rpt. edn., New York, 1970), 1012–25; Millicent Garrett Fawcett, *Women's Suffrage: A Short History of a Great Movement* (London [1912]). Occasional references to members of the Bright circle as individuals are to be found in each of these standard histories, especially those who maintained good relations with the moderate leaders, such as Priscilla Bright McLaren and Lilias Ashworth Hallett, but Bertha Mason, *The Story of the Women's Suffrage Movement* (London, 1912), suggests more clearly their existence as a coherent circle that provided significant leadership to the movement at various times. More recently, Patricia Hollis, *Ladies Elect: Women in English Local Government, 1865–1914* (Oxford, 1987); and Philippa Levine, *Feminist Lives in Victorian England: Private Roles and Public Commitment* (Oxford, 1990), both note the existence of this circle of women reformers.

4 E. Stanton, *Eighty Years*; T. Stanton and Blatch, *E. C. Stanton*; Ida Husted Harper, *Life and Work of Susan B. Anthony*, 3 vols. (Indianapolis, 1898–1908); Harriot Stanton Blatch and Alma Lutz, *Challenging Years: The Memoirs of Harriot Stanton Blatch* (New York, 1940). Most of the correspondence between Elizabeth Cady Stanton and members of the Bright circle drawn on here is in the form of transcripts bound together as "Elizabeth Cady Stanton Correspondence" in the Mabel Smith Douglass Library, Douglass and Smith Colleges, the State University of New Jersey, Rutgers (hereafter, ECSC), and I am grateful to the library for allowing me to quote from and cite this collection and to Keith Jones for background information concerning it. Patricia Holland of the Elizabeth Cady Stanton–Susan B. Anthony microfilm project originally located this material for me and provided the photocopies from which I worked. I am also grateful to Patricia Holland for reading an earlier version of this article and alerting me to some errors. My attention was first drawn to this topic when researching the Millfield Papers, in the private Clark family archive, C. and J. Clark, Street, Somerset, UK (hereafter, MP), where letters from Elizabeth Cady Stanton to some of her British network came to light, copies of which have since been deposited with the microfilm project. I am grateful to Richard Clark for permission to research in and draw upon this collection and to Jean Brook of the Museum and Archives, C. and J. Clark, for her help in this work.

5 Radicals formed a loose grouping on the left of the Liberal Party between the 1860s and 1890s, held together by their commitment to the ideas of John Stuart Mill. They had some significant links with popular radicalism, especially with republicans and freethinkers, and were a notable presence within the early organizations of the British women's movement, although, again, their presence as a distinct, coherent current of opinion has been largely ignored. See Sandra Stanley Holton, "Free Love and Victorian Feminism: The Divers Matrimonials of Elizabeth Wolstenholme and Ben Elmy," *Victorian Studies*, 37 (Winter 1994): 1–25. For background on the Radicals, see Roy Jenkins, *Sir Charles Dilke: A Victorian Tragedy* (London, 1958); Edward Royle, *Radicals, Secularists and Republicans: Popular Free-Thought in Britain, 1866–1915* (Manchester, 1980); Eugenio F. Biagini, *Liberty, Retrenchment, and Reform: Popular Liberalism in the Age of Gladstone, 1860–1880* (Cambridge, 1992).

6 Carole Pateman, *The Sexual Contract* (Stanford, Calif., 1988), esp. ix, 3–6, and chaps. 5–6; compare with the accounts of nineteenth-century analyses of marriage in Levine, *Feminist Lives*, chap. 3; Susan Kingsley Kent, *Sex and Suffrage in Britain, 1860–1914* (Princeton, N.J., 1987), chap. 3. Lee Holcombe, *Wives and Property: Reform of the Married Women's Property Law in Nineteenth Century England* (Toronto, 1983); Mary Lyndon Shanley, *Feminism, Marriage and the Law in Victorian England 1850–1895* (Princeton, N.J., 1989); and Holton, "Free Love," all emphasize the importance of the question of coverture for the nineteenth-century suffrage movement.

7 Because all the early histories were written from the moderate perspective, the works of Helen Blackburn, Millicent Garrett Fawcett, or Bertha Mason, for example (see n. 2), offer no detailed analysis of this major source of discord among British suffragists and occasionally may even mislead; for example, Fawcett, "England," 5, gives the impression that the suffrage movement in Britain held continuously to the simple equal rights formulation supported by J. S. Mill, although in fact from 1874 the national leadership repeatedly retreated to a more limited formulation that explicitly excluded married women.

8 It is noteworthy that E. Stanton, *Eighty Years*, chap. 14, devotes a whole chapter to marriage in relation to women's rights, while the early histories of the British movement by Blackburn, Fawcett, and Mason (see n. 2), written from the perspective of the moderate leadership, completely ignore the Women's Franchise League, and subsequent historians have in general made at most a passing reference to its existence. E. Sylvia Pankhurst gives it the greatest prominence in her autobiographical work *The Suffragette Movement: An Intimate Account of Persons and Ideals* (1931; rpt. edn., London, 1977), when discussing the role of her parents in the nineteenth-century movement. The most substantial recent account is David Rubinstein, *Before the Suffragettes: Women's Emancipation in the 1890s* (Brighton, 1986), 143–45, which focuses on its first few years and somewhat underestimates the actual lifetime of the league.

9 This aspect of the twentieth-century suffrage campaign is discussed in more detail in Sandra Stanley Holton, *Feminism and Democracy: Women's Suffrage and Reform Politics in Britain 1900–1918* (Cambridge, 1986).

10 Ellen Carol DuBois, "Woman Suffrage and the Left: An Internationalist Socialist-Feminist Perspective," *New Left Review*, 186 (1991): 20–45, esp. 20, 22. DuBois explores other aspects of these links between the British and American movements in "Working Class Women, Class Relations, and Suffrage Militance: Harriot Stanton Blatch and the New York Woman Suffrage Movement, 1894–1909," in *Unequal Sisters: A Multicultural Reader in U.S. Women's History*, Ellen Carol DuBois and Vicki L. Ruiz, eds. (New York, 1990), 176–94; and DuBois, " 'Spanning Two Centuries': The Autobiography of Nora Stanton Barney," *History Workshop*, 22 (1986): 131–52.

11 This visit was also especially significant for the formation of an organized movement for women's rights in America, since it marked the beginning of the friendship between Elizabeth Cady Stanton and Lucretia Mott, which resulted in the Seneca Falls convention of 1848. See Elizabeth Cady Stanton, Susan B. Anthony, and Matilda Joslyn Gage, *History of Woman Suffrage*, vol. 1 (1881; rpt. edn., New York, 1976), 50. Kathryn Kish Sklar, " 'Women Who Speak for an Entire Nation': American and British Women Compared at the World Anti-Slavery Convention, London 1840," *Pacific Historical Review*, 59 (1990): 453–99, provides an illuminating comparison of the effect of this event on the formation of a women's movement in both countries. DuBois, "Woman Suffrage," 25, suggests that a radicalizing influence on Elizabeth Cady Stanton was her introduction to Chartism during her first visit to Britain.

12 See, for example, Mary Priestman to Anna Maria Priestman, October 15, 1846; Alice Clark to Priscilla Bright McLaren, August 2, 1897, July 11, 1901, and to the Priestman sisters, May 19, 1907, and August 30, 1910, Boxes 14 and 75 respectively, MP. Priscilla Bright McLaren and a

close friend of the Priestman sisters, Mary Estlin, were also among the early supporters of Garrison in Britain. See Duncan Rice, *The Scots Abolitionists 1833–61* (Baton Rouge, La., 1981), 48, 178–79.

13 George Macaulay Trevelyan, *The Life of John Bright* (London, 1913), 34–43; John Travis Mills, *John Bright and the Quakers*, 2 vols. (London, 1935), 1: 383–94; Keith Robbins, *John Bright* (London, 1979), 19–27. The importance of the Anti–Corn Law League as a training ground for women's rights campaigners is a commonplace in the British literature; see, for example, Ray Strachey, *The Cause: A Short History of the Women's Movement in Great Britain* (1928; rpt. edn., London, 1978), 32, although it has yet to receive detailed investigation.

14 Although the importance of Quaker women is routinely acknowledged in the standard histories of the British women's movement, it has not received the same detailed analysis given to the American case. It is likely that there are some major points of difference between the two countries. Elizabeth Cady Stanton, for one, found English Quakers far more conservative than their American counterparts, especially in comparison with Hicksite Quakers such as Lucretia Mott, who was received with notable reserve by leading British Quakers in 1840 but met with a sympathetic response among British Unitarians; see E. Stanton, *Eighty Years*, 82–86; *James and Lucretia Mott: Life and Letters*, Anna Davis Hallowell, ed. (Boston, 1884), 170–79, 187–90; *Mary Howitt: An Autobiography*, Margaret Howitt, ed. (1889; London, 1891), 151–52. On the attitude of the London Yearly Meeting to the Hicksites, see Edwin B. Bronner, *"The Other Branch": London Yearly Meeting and the Hicksites 1827–1912* (London, 1975). The Chartist Quaker and suffragist Anne Knight provides a notable exception to this picture; see Gail Malmgreen, "Anne Knight and the Radical Subculture," *Quaker History*, 71 (1982): 11. For a more general account of British Quakers in this period, see Elizabeth Allo Isichei, *Victorian Quakers* (Oxford, 1970). Compare with the role of Hicksite women in radicalizing the American women's rights movement detailed in Nancy A. Hewitt, *Women's Activism and Social Change: Rochester, New York, 1822–1872* (Ithaca, N.Y., 1984); and "Feminist Friends: Agrarian Quakers and the Emergence of Woman's Rights in America," *Feminist Studies*, 12 (1986): 27–49; Blanche Glassman Hersh, *The Slavery of Sex: Feminist-Abolitionists in America* (Urbana, Ill., 1978), 131–32, 145–48.

15 Ursula Mellor Bright herself was not a Quaker, and the advanced liberal outlook of her husband, Jacob Bright, led him to resign from the Society of Friends. Priscilla Bright McLaren was disowned for not marrying according to the practices of the Quakers, but this judgment was rescinded after the death of her husband. In naming the women of this circle, I follow the form that the individual concerned appears to have preferred. Some chose, like their American friends, to combine their single name with their husband's name, Helen Priestman Bright Clark even retaining also her mother's single name, while others did not follow this practice. Ursula Mellor Bright tended to use the polite form of the day, "Mrs Jacob Bright," in public, while usually signing herself Ursula M. Bright in letters.

16 Ellen Carol DuBois, *Feminism and Suffrage: The Emergence of an Independent Women's Movement in America 1848–1869* (Ithaca, N.Y., 1978), 39.

17 Blackburn, *Women's Suffrage: A Record*, 64, notes that in the 1886 Parliament she had a husband, two sons, two brothers, and a nephew in the House of Commons; T. Stanton and Blatch, *E. C. Stanton*, 2: 196–213; E. Stanton, *Eighty Years*, 352–75.

18 Elizabeth Cady Stanton to Miss Priestman, January 30, postmark 1883; Elizabeth Cady Stanton to "Dear Widow and Spinsters," October 30 [1883], Box 23, MP.

19 Elizabeth Cady Stanton to Miss Priestman, January 30, postmark 1883, Box 23, MP; E. Stanton, *Eighty Years*, 361. Among the leadership of the early women's movement in Britain, both Barbara Leigh Smith Bodichon and Bessie Rayner Parkes, for example, were raised within that current of British radicalism that had supported the American Revolution. Their forebears had been among those who incorporated into their radicalism a notion of the "freeborn" Briton, a "patriot" identity that only began to be captured from the 1860s on by an imperialistic jingoism of the Right. See Hugh Cunningham, "The Language of Patriotism," in *Patriotism: The Making and Unmaking of the British National Identity*, Raphael Samuel, ed., 3 vols. (London, 1989), 1: 57–89; E. J. Hobsbawm, *Nations and Nationalism since 1780: Programme, Myth, Reality* (Cambridge, 1990), 120–25.

20 E. Stanton, *Eighty Years*, 372, 397; see T. Stanton and Blatch, *E. C. Stanton*, 2: 206–07, for an account of Elizabeth Cady Stanton's visit to Helen Priestman Bright Clark, when it was feared that she "had shocked all the saints and clergy" in expressing to a local clergyman her forthright

views on the meaning of the Bible; Ursula Bright to Elizabeth Cady Stanton, September 18 [1886?]; Priscilla Bright McLaren to Elizabeth Cady Stanton, November 12, 1886, both ECSC, Douglass Library; see also Elizabeth Cady Stanton to Anna Maria Priestman, November 8 [1886], and to Mary Priestman, October 21, 1895, both Box 23, MP. The latter mentions Ursula Bright and her niece Kate Thomasson in connection with the *Woman's Bible*.

21 E. Stanton, *Eighty Years*, 398; Priscilla Bright McLaren to Elizabeth Cady Stanton, July 17, 1883, ECSC, Douglass Library.

22 Quoted in David Rubinstein, *A Different World for Women: The Life of Millicent Garrett Fawcett* (Columbus, Ohio, 1991), 202; see also Fawcett, "England," 4.

23 Elizabeth Cady Stanton to "Saint Margaret [Tanner], Saint Anna [Maria Priestman], Saint Mary [Priestman]," October 13 [1890], Box 23, MP.

24 Harper, *Susan B. Anthony*, 2: 546, 565; see also 2: 553–79, which recounts how during this visit Susan B. Anthony also formed an extensive friendship network in Britain among leading suffragists there.

25 Joan Hoff, *Law, Gender, and Injustice: A Legal History of U.S. Women* (New York, 1991), 121–35, and Appendix One, which explains that although the end of coverture began much earlier in the United States, it was nonetheless a complex and uneven process that took a century to complete.

26 Jane Rendall, "Citizenship, Culture and Civilization: The Languages of British Suffragists, 1866–1874," in Daley and Nolan, *Suffrage and Beyond*. In particular, Rendall shows the significance for suffragism of a new emphasis on social altruism within late nineteenth-century liberalism. Pateman, *Sexual Contract*, 51–59, 108–12, 156–82, 191–92, 202–03, explores the meaning of the loss of property in their own persons by married women.

27 For more detail on the various disputes among suffragists in these early years, see Barbara Caine, "John Stuart Mill and the English Women's Movement," *Historical Studies*, 18 (1978): 52–67; and "Feminism, Suffrage and the Nineteenth Century English Women's Movement," *Women's Studies International Forum*, 5 (1982): 537–50; Andrew Rosen, "Emily Davies and the Women's Movement, 1862–67," *Journal of British Studies*, 19 (1979): 101–21; A. P. W. Robson, "The Founding of the National Society for Women's Suffrage 1866–1867," *Canadian Journal of History*, 8 (1973): 1–22.

28 Lydia Becker's role in the British suffrage movement still awaits historical assessment, but see Joan Parker, "Lydia Becker: Pioneer Orator of the Women's Movement," *Manchester Region History Review*, 5 (1991): 13–20. Blackburn, *Women's Suffrage: A Record*, 23–43, provides an uncritical portrait by a close colleague, while Pankhurst, *Suffragette Movement*, 34–52, gives a more equivocal account. To begin with, Lydia Becker was an ally of the Radical-Liberal suffragists, supporting Jacob and Ursula Bright, for example, in their dispute with John Stuart Mill and his stepdaughter, Helen Taylor, over combining suffrage campaigning with agitation for the repeal of the Contagious Diseases Acts, the legislation that had introduced the compulsory medical surveillance of prostitutes. Even though he also opposed this legislation, Mill was hostile to the determination of those he called the "Bright and Becker set" to mix the two issues. See Caine, "John Stuart Mill," 60.

29 A. Grenfell to Anna Maria Priestman, and sent on to Mary Priestman, May 3, 1874, Box 17, MP.

30 Elizabeth Wolstenholme Elmy, a Manchester headmistress, played a leading role in every major women's rights campaign in this period; see Ellis Ethelmer, "A Woman Emancipator: A Biographical Sketch," *Westminster Review*, 145 (1894): 424–28; Pankhurst, *Suffragette Movement*, 31–34; Dora Montefiore, *From a Victorian to a Modern* (London, 1927), 42–43, for short portraits. DuBois, "Woman Suffrage," 27, places Elmy alongside Elizabeth Cady Stanton as one of the few figures who maintained the "radical suffragist tradition" within the women's movement. Shanley, *Feminism, Marriage and the Law*, provides an extensive and stimulating analysis of the interconnection of these various campaigns in the activities of figures such as Elmy.

31 Lydia Becker to "Dearest" [Elizabeth Wolstenholme, whose own annotations identify her as the recipient], March 1, 1874, E. Sylvia Pankhurst Archives, International Institute of Social History, Amsterdam (hereafter, ESPA). I am grateful to the institute for providing me with photocopies from this archive.

32 Reported in Mary Priestman to Helen Priestman Bright Clark, September 16, 1877, Box 14, MP. See Pateman, *Sexual Contract*, 181–82, for a fuller discussion of the significance of this vow. On the Elmys' marriage, see Holton, "Free Love"; on that of the Pankhursts, see Pankhurst, *Suffragette Movement*, 55.

33 From Susan B. Anthony's firsthand account, quoted in Harper, *Susan B. Anthony*, 2: 567–68, which also makes it clear that she herself stayed aloof from the controversy and believed her old friend's involvement in it to be misjudged: "I contend it is not in good taste for either of us to counsel public opposition to the bill before Parliament"; Ursula Bright to Elizabeth Cady Stanton, July 2 [1883], ECSC, Douglass Library.

34 T. Stanton and Blatch, *E. C. Stanton*, 2: 208–09; Priscilla Bright McLaren to Elizabeth Cady Stanton, July 17, 1883, ECSC, Douglass Library. For a concise analysis of the issues involved in this controversy, see Elizabeth Wolstenholme Elmy's article on Woodall's Bill in the serial *Personal Rights Journal*, March 15, 1886.

35 Mrs. Jacob Bright, "Letter of Mrs Jacob Bright . . . " (n.d. [*circa* 1883]); for the response of other Radical-Liberal suffragists, see, for example, Alice Scatcherd to Anna Maria Priestman, November 11, 1882, Box 22, MP; and compare with the leadership's view, as expressed in Helen Blackburn to Anna Maria Priestman, August 19, 1886, Box 19, MP, which refers to "our extremist friends" whom she hopes may be persuaded to "a wiser direction." On the increasingly bitter feelings among suffragists at this time, see Margaret Bright Lucas to Anna Maria Priestman, January 10, 1884, and Priscilla Bright McLaren to Helen Priestman Bright Clark, January 19, 1884, which refers to the "cat and dog work" between Ursula Bright and Lydia Becker, Boxes 23 and 36 respectively, MP. Priscilla Bright McLaren, as so often, attempted to play a conciliatory role within the movement, maintaining her friendships with Lydia Becker and Millicent Garrett Fawcett and remaining an important channel of communication between the Radical-Liberal suffragists and the moderate leadership; see, for example, her letter to Helen Priestman Bright Clark, March 13, 1884, Box 36, MP.

36 Helen Blackburn to Anna Maria Priestman, November 15, 1883, Box 19, MP; Priscilla Bright McLaren to Helen Priestman Bright Clark, February 2, 1884, Box 36, MP, reporting a letter from Lydia Becker that presented the proposal as indicative of a growing split in the British movement and commenting, "I am not quite sure that Aunt Urlie [Ursula Bright] may not be using this as an annoyance—but there is no real proof yet." It is possible that there was also some jealousy of the Americans' leadership in this initiative. Priscilla Bright McLaren in this same letter, like a number of other British suffragists, remarked privately on Lydia Becker's envy of any prominence achieved by other figures in the movement.

37 Only the American chronicles tell the story of this international initiative, and the histories produced by the British movement remained parochial, although Blackburn, *Women's Suffrage: A Record*, does include a "Supplementary Chapter on Colonial Progress." Anthony and Harper, *History of Woman Suffrage*, 4: 124–42, credits the idea to Elizabeth Cady Stanton, but she herself subsequently acknowledged that her original conception of "intellectual cooperation" among suffragists around the world had not been fully realized through the International Council of Women that grew out of this initiative. The members of this body soon found the suffrage issue too contentious to pursue. Nonetheless, she maintained that it had met another of her aims in achieving suffragist "power over popular thought," E. Stanton, *Eighty Years* 412–14. It should also be noted that Theodore Stanton's editor's introduction to *The Woman Question*, v–vi, suggests that the adoption of a leadership stance toward movements in other parts of Europe was based on some shared sense of ethnic superiority among Anglo-American suffragists.

38 The old Vigilance Association with which many Radical-Liberal suffragists had long been closely linked now became the Personal Rights Association, and it took a critical stand on many of the repressive policies and activities for which the National Vigilance Association was known. See Judith R. Walkowitz, *City of Dreadful Delight: Narratives of Sexual Danger in Late-Victorian London* (Chicago, 1992), 22–24, 82–83, 102–05; Lucy Bland, " 'Purifying' the Public World: Feminist Vigilantes in Late Victorian England," *Women's History Review*, 1 (1992): 397–412; Deborah Gorham, " 'The Maiden Tribute of Modern Babylon' Re-examined: Child Prostitution and the Idea of Childhood in Late-Victorian England," *Victorian Studies*, 21 (1978): 357–79, 366–68.

39 T. Stanton and Blatch, *E. C. Stanton*, 2: 235, 270; Priscilla Bright McLaren to Elizabeth Cady Stanton, November 17, 1887, ECSC, Douglass Library; E. Stanton, *Eighty Years*, 399, 422–23.

40 E. Stanton, *Eighty Years*, 408; Elizabeth Cady Stanton to the Priestman sisters, February 21 and 26, 1888, Box 23, MP.

41 See Elizabeth Cady Stanton to Helen Taylor, March 6 [1888], and Priscilla Bright McLaren to Helen Taylor, January 21, 1888, vols. 12 and 13 respectively, the Mill-Taylor Papers, Archives of the British Library of Political and Economic Sciences, the London School of Economics, to which my thanks for allowing me to read in these papers; Helen Taylor to Susan B. Anthony,

March 7, 1888, HM10610, Harper Collection, Huntington Library, Los Angeles, with thanks to the Huntington Library for permission to draw on this and other correspondence in its Western Historical Manuscripts collection; E. Stanton, *Eighty Years*, 410, which provides also a sympathetic portrait of May Dilke.

42 The previous few years had seen a rapid formation of Women's Liberal Associations, first founded in Bristol in 1881 by Anna Maria Priestman at least in part out of her frustration with the national suffrage leadership. This rapid growth, however, reflected the growing importance of women as election workers, following the passage of the Corrupt Practices Act of 1883. In 1887, the associations were brought together in the Women's Liberal Federation (WLF), for control of which suffragists waged a long struggle. See Sandra Stanley Holton, "The Strange Death of Liberal Feminism: Anna Maria Priestman and the Origins of the Women's Liberal Federation," paper delivered to the "Wollstonecraft 200" conference, University of Sussex, December 1992. For further discussion of the WLF, see Leslie Walker, "Party Political Women: A Comparative Study of the Liberal Women and the Primrose League, 1890–1914," in *Equal or Different: Women's Politics 1800–1914*, Jane Rendall, ed. (Oxford, 1987), 165–91; Claire Hirshfield, "Fractured Faith: Liberal Party Women and the Suffrage Issue in Britain, 1892–1914," *Gender and History*, 2 (1990): 173–97.

43 The "new rules" society called itself the Central National Society for Women's Suffrage (CNSWS), while the new "old rules" organization somewhat confusingly called itself the Central Committee of the National Society for Women's Suffrage (CCNSWS). Each was sometimes also more conveniently referred to by the address of its central offices, as, respectively, the "Parliament Street" society and the "Great College Street" society.

44 Lydia Becker's editorial in *Women's Suffrage Journal*, 20 (1889): 48, describes the split and argues that the married women's claim for the vote was an "uncalled for and gratuitous obstruction" to the main demand. *Personal Rights Journal*, April 1889, records the dissidents' intervention at the first annual meeting of the CNSWS, an episode again generally ignored in the standard histories of the suffrage movement for this period.

45 Women's Franchise League, "Report of Proceedings at the Inaugural Meeting, London July 25th 1889" (London [1889]), 3, 6, in the Fawcett Library, London Guildhall University, gives Richard Pankhurst's generous recognition of these others' role in its formation. Sylvia Pankhurst's account in *Suffragette Movement*, 95, serves to emphasize the role of her parents at the expense of those who actually undertook this task, while Harriot Stanton Blatch in *Challenging Years*, 73, emphasizes the role of Ursula Bright, recalling that "Mrs Pankhurst and I, burdened as we were by young children and domestic cares, were the admiring neophytes of the circle." Ursula and Jacob Bright, in fact, initially kept aloof from the new society for reasons that remain unclear; see Elizabeth Wolstenholme Elmy to Harriet McIlquham, May 9, 1889, June 5, 1890, September 19, 1904, September 27, 1904, Additional Manuscripts 47449 and 47454, the Elizabeth Wolstenholme Elmy Papers, British Library (hereafter, EWEP), with my thanks to the British Library for permission to quote from this correspondence.

46 T. Stanton and Blatch, *E. C. Stanton*, 2: 288 n. 4. Elizabeth Cady Stanton's endorsement of the league and involvement in its business in 1890 is evident also in the "Programme for the Women's Franchise League International Conference, 16–17 July 1890," proof copy in Harriet McIlquham Papers, Fawcett Library, London Guildhall University. My thanks for permission to draw on its collections and more particularly to David Doughan for providing photocopies of some of the printed material cited above and below. The conference was apparently conceived as a successor to a similar event in Paris the previous year and to the original Washington meeting in 1888. Little information on these events appears to have survived, but see *Personal Rights Journal*, July 1890. Elizabeth Cady Stanton was also during this period exchanging ideas on methods of activism with Alice Scatcherd, with whom Harriet Stanton Blatch was working closely in the Women's Liberal Federation as well as in the Women's Franchise League; see Alice Scatcherd to Elizabeth Cady Stanton (fragment), enclosed in Elizabeth Cady Stanton to Alice Clark, October 20, 1890, Box 75, MP. Similarly, Elizabeth Wolstenholme Elmy spent the summer of 1890 in Basingstoke with the two American suffragists as she tried, unsuccessfully, to retain her role in the league's leadership; Elizabeth Wolstenholme Elmy to Harriet McIlquham, October 27, 1890, Additional Manuscripts 47449, EWEP.

47 Women's Franchise League, "Inaugural Proceedings," 25–26. Among the league's early leaders were also Clementia and P. A. Taylor, whose radicalism went back to the 1840s Anti–Corn Law League and abolition, and whose home, Aubrey House, where the first women's suffrage petition

had been pasted up in 1866, had also provided the gathering place for Radical-Liberal circles in London in that period. Also included were Josephine Butler, who had led the campaign against the Contagious Diseases Acts from 1870 until repeal in 1886, and Emmeline Pankhurst and Florence Fenwick Miller, from among a second generation of radical suffragists.

48 For example, she encouraged the efforts of Alice Clark in this respect; Elizabeth Cady Stanton to Alice Clark, October 20 [1890], Box 75, MP.

49 Women's Franchise League, "Report of Meeting in Support of 'The Women's Disabilities Bill' " (London [1889]), M50/2/32/3, Manchester Public Library Archive. I thank the City of Manchester Arts and Leisure Council for permission to draw on this material; Women's Franchise League, "Inaugural Proceedings," 22, Fawcett Library, London Guildhall University. For a further account of the league's platform, see Florence Fenwick Miller, "On the Programme of the Women's Franchise League" (London, 1890), also Fawcett Library, London Guildhall University.

50 T. Stanton and Blatch, *E. C. Stanton*, 2: 262; Elizabeth Wolstenholme Elmy to Harriet McIlquham, May 26, 1890, June 5, 1890, October 27, 1906, Additional Manuscripts 47449 and 47455, EWEP. Her letters at this time also indicate tensions with Alice Scatcherd and Florence Fenwick Miller over her position as paid secretary. Pankhurst, *Suffragette Movement*, 96, presents a different interpretation, which is misleading both in terms of the timing of these events and in wrongly suggesting a change of position on the inclusion of married women in the suffrage demand by Elmy.

51 Minutes, July 25, 1890, Women's Franchise League, in the Special Collections Department, Northwestern University Library, Evanston, Illinois (hereafter, WFL Minutes). I am grateful to R. Russell Maylone, Curator, for providing me with a microfilm copy of this minute book, and for permission to draw on this source here. Elmy's departure from the league was followed shortly afterward by the resignation of McIlquham, and the two together subsequently formed the Women's Emancipation Union, which continued to support the women's suffrage bill Elmy herself had drafted for the league but which, in a noteworthy addition, also campaigned for the legal recognition of rape in marriage. See "Women's Emancipation Union: An Association of Workers to Secure the Political, Sexual, and Economic Independence of Women" (Congleton, November 1891). Anna Maria Priestman was among those who gave her support to this new organization. For accounts of the WEU, see Rubinstein, *Before the Suffragettes*, 144–45; Lucy Bland, "The Married Woman, the 'New Woman' and the Feminist: Sexual Politics of the 1890s," in Rendall, *Equal or Different*, 141–64.

52 WFL Minutes, April 23 and May 29, 1891; also November 24, 1890, January 2, 1891, February 2, 1891, March 18, 1891, December 4, 1891, April 25, 1893, May 18, 1893, March 16, 1894, June 9, 1894, for examples of its international links and orientation toward radical and working-class organizations. Other sources for the activities of the league include a few pamphlets, which survive in the archives of the Manchester Public Library and in the Fawcett Library, London Guildhall University; also, some letters of Ursula Bright to Emmeline Pankhurst, in ESPA, and occasional irregular reports and correspondence in the *Personal Rights Journal*, the *Women's Gazette and Weekly News*, the *Women's Herald*, the *Women's Penny Paper*, and the *Women's Signal*. The last provides the only documentary source I have been able to identify for the league's final years.

53 For example, WFL Minutes, September 15, 1890, February 2, 1891, February 3, 1892, May 18, 1892, June 9, 1894.

54 WFL Minutes, February 2, 1891, March 18, 1891 (which suggests that its income for the previous year was a little over £350), May 4, 1891, November 11, 1891, [April 12] 1894; and see also Elizabeth Wolstenholme Elmy to Harriet McIlquham, October 27, 1889, Additional Manuscripts 47449, EWEP.

55 WFL Minutes, September 15, 1890, February 2, 1891, March 18, 1891, April 23, 1893. In keeping with a Garrisonian tendency to a loose and unhierarchical organization, the role of chair of the executive meetings rotated among its members, whose attendance could also be very irregular.

56 Mrs. Jacob Bright, "The Origins and Objects of the Women's Franchise League of Great Britain and Ireland," *The World Congress of Representative Women*, May Wright Sewall, ed. (Chicago, 1894), 415–20, esp. 416, 418.

57 Bright, "Origins," 416, 417, 420.

58 Women's Franchise League, "Inaugural Proceedings," 22.

59 For example, May Dilke's response to the Anti-Suffragists "Appeal," *Nineteenth Century*, 26 (1889): 97–103, mobilizes just such a conception of citizenship to counter the militaristic account of citizenship often used as an argument against votes for women. She asserted, for example, that

women in childbirth put their lives at risk equally with men called on to do battle, insisting that the maintenance of society rested not on warfare but on labor in all its forms. Although much of women's labor went unpaid, it was "quite as fundamental a part of civilized life as the paid labour of men." Moreover, she argued, women were also increasingly entering the paid work force and therefore needed their own voice in the making of laws that controlled the paid labor market.

60 This perspective is evident also in Richard Haldane, "Some Economic Aspects of Women's Suffrage," *Contemporary Review*, 58 (1890): 830–38. Haldane was at this time a rising young Liberal politician and in 1889 and 1890 introduced into Parliament the Women's Franchise League's Women's Disabilities Removal Bill.

61 Recalled in Blatch and Lutz, *Challenging Years*, 79. See also Anthony and Harper, *History of Woman Suffrage*, 4: 310–11, which gives the text of part of her paper "Woman and the Economic Factor" presented to the National-American Convention in Washington in 1898. Compare also Diane Kirkby's discussion of "industrial feminism" in the United States in the early twentieth century, *Alice Henry: The Power of Pen and Voice; The Life of an Australian-American Labour Reformer* (Cambridge, 1991), which also examines the international exchange of ideas among suffragists, most especially through the WTUL (Women's Trade Union League).

62 WFL Minutes, May 2, 1892, August 5, 1892, September 28, 1892, October 19, 1892. Elizabeth Wolstenholme Elmy's account of the affair differs significantly from that of the league demonstrators and is to be found in her letter to Harriet McIlquham, May 18, 1892, Additional Manuscripts 47449, EWEP.

63 WFL Minutes, May 23, 1892; and compare with the discussion of a subsequent compromise in Elizabeth Wolstenholme Elmy, "Women's Suffrage," *Shafts*, April 1897.

64 See Pankhurst, *Suffragette Movement*, 116–18, for a fuller discussion of this event and its meaning. Walter McLaren, son of Priscilla Bright McLaren, was the member of Parliament who secured government agreement to this amendment after tense and complex negotiations, while Ursula Bright and her supporters exerted pressure to ensure that the government did not back down on its agreement. See Walter McLaren to Millicent Garrett Fawcett, November 26, 1893, December 2, 1893, January 8, 1894, January 11, 1894, January 13, 1894, Manchester Public Library Archives, M50/2/1/206–210; Ursula Bright to Emmeline Pankhurst, November 25, 27, and 28, 1893, ESPA.

65 Pankhurst, *Suffragette Movement*, 120, suggests that after the success of the Local Government Act in 1894, Ursula Bright drifted away from politics to theosophy, while the Pankhursts were increasingly drawn into socialist politics and away from their former Liberal circles. Reports in the *Women's Signal*, May 27, June 3, January 7, 1897, however, provide evidence that Alice Scatcherd kept the league alive at this time and that it participated in the consultations that preceded the eventual reunification of the movement within the National Union of Women's Suffrage Societies. It continued, too, to find occasion for the expression of the Radical-Liberal perspective, organizing its own Jubilee address to Queen Victoria of "representative women," among whom members of the Bright circle were much in evidence. This called for "one royal word of sympathy" for—"one expression of gracious confidence" regarding—equal civil rights for women, while Millicent Garrett Fawcett organized an altogether more respectful address from the CNSWS. *Women's Signal*, April 15 and July 1, 1897.

66 Blatch and Lutz, *Challenging Years*, 73. Another account of this period, Montefiore, *From a Victorian*, 41, similarly recalled "continuous signs that a breaking away of more urgent spirits was imminent," singling out the Union of Practical Suffragists for special mention. This body had been formed by Anna Maria Priestman in 1896 to work within the Women's Liberal Federation and encourage a stronger commitment to women's suffrage. Its executive committee included Ursula Bright and Harriot Stanton Blatch, as well as Mary Priestman and Eva McLaren from among the Bright circle; see Union of Practical Suffragists, "Leaflet No XII" (n.d. [*circa* 1898]); and *Women's Signal*, May 27, 1897, for a report of its first annual meeting.

67 The classic example of this approach remains George Dangerfield's extremely influential account in *The Strange Death of Liberal England* (London, 1935); see also Andrew Rosen, *Rise Up Women! The Militant Campaign of the Women's Social and Political Union, 1903–1914* (London, 1974). More recent alternative approaches to suffrage militancy are to be found in Brian Harrison, "The Act of Militancy," in his *Peaceable Kingdom: Stability and Change in Modern Britain* (Oxford, 1982); Martha Vicinus, *Independent Women: Work and Community for Single Women 1850–1920* (Chicago, 1985), esp. chap. 7; Liz Stanley with Ann Morley, *The Life and Death of Emily Wilding Davison* (London, 1989); Sandra Stanley Holton, " 'In Sorrowful Wrath': Suffrage

Militancy and the Romantic Feminism of Emmeline Pankhurst," in *British Feminism in the Twentieth Century*, Harold L. Smith, ed. (Aldershot, 1990), 7–24.

68 See, for example, Dora Montefiore's letter on tax resistance in *Women's Signal*, June 17, 1897, together with the editor's response, August 5, 1897. Her account in *From a Victorian*, 72–83, makes such tactics central to early conceptions of militancy and suggests that the subsequent rejection of the tactics of civil disobedience was one of the sources of the first splits among the early leadership of the Women's Social and Political Union.

69 Mutual endorsement and exchange of views evidently remained important to these transatlantic friends in Elizabeth Cady Stanton's declining years. When Helen Priestman Bright Clark visited her in New York in 1900, she was again characteristically advised not to be "too afraid of over-stepping the conventionalities." T. Stanton and Blatch, *E. C. Stanton*, 2: 351. The Bright circle also arranged for an address from thirty of its members on the occasion of their American friend's eightieth birthday; see *New York Tribune*, November 12, 1895; and see also the Women's Franchise League's address to the NAWSA (National American Woman Suffrage Association) convention 1891, reported in *Women's Journal*, March 14, 1891.

70 Quoted in Gail Parker, "Introduction," to E. Stanton, *Eighty Years* (1898; rpt. edn., New York, 1971), xix; and DuBois, "Woman Suffrage," 28.

71 T. Stanton and Blatch, *E. C. Stanton*, 1: xviii.

5 Women's rights, feminism, and suffragism in Japan, 1870–1925 (Barbara Molony)

The author wishes to thank the Suntory and Toyota International Centres for Economics and Related Disciplines at the London School of Economics and Political Science for permission to use material contained in her article, "State and Women in Modern Japan: Feminist Discourses in the Meiji and Taishō Eras," in Janet Hunter, ed., *Japan: State and People in the Twentieth Century* (London, 1999).

1 The relationship of women to the Japanese state has been the object of much discussion in English-language Japanese studies. Some scholars look at women as the target of government policies; see, e.g., Sharon H. Nolte and Sally Ann Hastings, "The Meiji State's Policy toward Women, 1890–1910," in Gail Lee Bernstein, ed., *Recreating Japanese Women, 1600–1945* (Berkeley, 1991), 151–174; Janet Hunter, "Factory Legislation and Employer Resistance: The Abolition of Night Work in the Cotton-Spinning Industry," in Tsunehiko Yui and Keiichirō Nakagawa, eds., *Japanese Management in Historical Perspective* (Tokyo, 1989), 243–272; Yoshiko Miyake, "Doubling Expectations: Motherhood and Women's Factory Work under State Management in Japan in the 1930s and 1940s," in Bernstein, ed., *Recreating Japanese Women*, 267–295; Sharon L. Sievers, *Flowers in Salt: The Beginnings of Feminist Consciousness in Modern Japan* (Stanford, Calif., 1983). Some works examine women as agents of some part of the state; see, e.g., Sumiko Otsubo, "Engendering Eugenics: Feminists and Marriage Restriction Legislation in the 1920s," in Barbara Molony and Kathleen Uno, eds., *Gendering Modern Japanese History* (Cambridge, Mass., 2005); Barbara Molony, "Citizenship and Suffrage in Interwar Japan," in Louise Edwards and Mina Roces, eds., *Women's Suffrage in Asia: Gender, Nationalism, and Democracy* (London and New York, 2004), 127–151); Kathleen Uno, *Passages to Modernity: Motherhood, Childhood, and Social Reform in Early Twentieth-Century Japan* (Honolulu, 1999). Some are interested in women in organized or institutionalized politics or movements; see, e.g., Vera Mackie, *Creating Socialist Women in Japan: Gender, Labour, and Activism, 1900–1937* (Cambridge, Eng., 1997); Helen M. Hopper, *A New Woman of Japan: A Political Biography of Katō Shidzue* (Boulder, Colo., 1996); Yukiko Matsukawa and Kaoru Tachi, "Women's Suffrage and Gender Politics in Japan," in Caroline Daley and Melanie Nolan, eds., *Suffrage and Beyond: International Feminist Perspectives* (New York, 1994). Some works study women in groups that articulate with state power; see, e.g., Sheldon Garon, "The World's Oldest Profession? Prostitution and the State in Imperial Japan, 1900–1945," *American Historical Review*, 93 (1993), 710–733; Garon, "Women's Groups and the Japanese State: Contending Approaches to Political Integration, 1890–1945," *Journal of Japanese Studies*, 19 (1993), 5–41. Others look at the discourses about women and the state. For some works in English, see, e.g., Barbara Molony, "The 1986 Equal Employment Opportunity Law and the Changing Discourse on

Gender," *Signs*, 20 (1995), 268 302; Kathleen Uno, "The Death of Good Wife, Wise Mother?" in Andrew Gordon, ed., *Postwar Japan as History* (Berkeley, 1993), 293–322; Laurel Rasplica Rodd, "Yosano Akiko and the Taishō Debate over the 'New Woman,' " in Bernstein, ed., *Recreating Japanese Women*, 175–198.

2 Although the term "feminism" (*feminizumu*) was introduced in Japan in a 1910 article in *Hōgaku Kyōkai zasshi* [Journal of the Law Association], I shall use the term to refer to a broad range of discourses, beginning in the early Meiji period, that supported women's rights or the improvement of women's condition or status. See Sōgō Joseishi Kenkyūkai, ed., *Nihon josei no rekishi* [Japanese women's history] (Tokyo, 1993), 192–193, for more on the introduction of the term "feminism."

3 Susan Mann has written persuasively that "contemporary Western feminism may remain parochial in its insistence that its own telos of freedom and agency be at work in every record of women's lives." See Mann, "The History of Chinese Women before the Age of Orientalism," *Journal of Women's History*, 8 (1997), 174. In the case of discussions about rights, advocates were explicit about the quest for women's rights; the historian need not project her own feminist hopes of finding calls for agency.

4 George M. Wilson, *Patriots and Redeemers in Japan: Motives in the Meiji Restoration* (Chicago, 1992), offers an insightful treatment of Tokugawa anti-authoritarianism. See also Matsumoto Sannosuke, "The Idea of Heaven: A Tokugawa Foundation for Natural Rights Theory," in Tetsuo Najita and Irvin Scheiner, eds., *Japanese Thought in the Tokugawa Period* (Chicago, 1978).

5 John Stuart Mill's *On Liberty* was translated into Japanese very early—in 1868. This translation was followed in the 1870s and early 1880s by translations of works by other Western political theorists. Jean-Jacques Rousseau's *Social Contract*, though translated later (1882) than Mill's work, was highly esteemed by activists in Japan's People's Rights movement. See Masaaki Kosaka, ed., *Japanese Culture in the Meiji Era: Thought* (10 vols., Tokyo, 1958), 8: 115, 146.

6 Wendy Brown, *States of Injury: Power and Freedom in Late Modernity* (Princeton, N.J., 1995), 4.

7 For more on Rousseau's ideas, see, e.g., Carole Patemen, *The Sexual Contract* (Stanford, Calif., 1988), passim.

8 See, e.g., Sievers, *Flowers in Salt*, 52; Yasukawa Junosuke and Yasukawa Etsuko, *Josei sabetsu no shakai shisōshi* [Intellectual and social history of discrimination against women] (Tokyo, 1993), chapter 1.

9 On "fraternity," see, e.g., Donald Roden, *Schooldays in Imperial Japan: A Study in the Culture of a Student Elite* (Berkeley, Calif.,1980).

10 Suzuki Yūko, *Nihon josei undō shiryō shūsei: Shisō, seiji* [A collected history of the Japanese women's movement: Thought and politics] (11 vols., Tokyo, 1996), 1: 18.

11 "Subjectivity" refers here to personhood endowed with the ability to think, feel, and reason, accompanied by some degree of individual agency.

12 Patrilineality is effectively problematized by Kathleen Uno in "Questioning Patrilineality: On Western Studies of the Japanese *Ie*," *positions*, 4 (1996), 569–594. She argues convincingly that scholars have often distorted the historical roles of patrilineality. Meiji women's rights advocates also strongly contested what they saw as continuing patterns of women's subordination through patrilineality and its ties with the other "p's" of patriarchy, prostitution, and polygamy.

13 For a comparison with the United States, see Gayle Gullett, "Constructing the Woman Citizen and Struggling for the Vote in California, 1896–1911," *Pacific Historical Review*, 69 (2000), 573–593.

14 See, e.g., Sievers's discussion of the Women's Reform Society. Sievers, *Flowers in Salt*, 87–114.

15 "Citizenship" is a complicated term in this period. See Atsuko Hirai's insightful commentary on terms translated as "citizen" in "State and Ideology in Meiji Japan—A Review Article," *Journal of Asian Studies*, 46 (1987), 89–103.

16 Barbara Molony, "Women and the State in Modern Japan: Feminist Discourses in the Meiji and Taishō Eras," in Janet Hunter, ed. *Japan: State and People in the Twentieth Century* (London, 1999), 32–38.

17 Mackie, *Creating Socialist Women*, 92, finds this stance problematic, noting that these feminists "unwittingly reinforced the notion that the normal relationship between the State and individual women is one of 'protector' and 'protected.' "

18 Hiratsuka Raichō, *Hiratsuka Raichō jiden: Genshi josei wa taiyō de atta* 3 [Autobiography of Hiratsuka Raichō: In the beginning, woman was the sun] (Tokyo, 1973), 41; Hiratsuka Raichō, *Watakushi no aruita michi* [The path I walked] (Tokyo, 1955), 195.

19 Mackie, *Creating Socialist Women*, 62–63.

20 Ichikawa Fusae, *Ichikawa Fusae jiden: Senzen hen* [Autobiography of Ichikawa Fusae: Prewar volume] (Tokyo, 1974), 53.

21 Hiratsuka, *Genshi josei*, 86. For a detailed analysis of Hiratsuka's focus on eugenics, see Otsubo, "Engendering Eugenics."

22 Rōdōshō Fujinshonenkyoku, ed., *Fujin no ayumi sanjūnen* [Thirty years of women's progress] (Tokyo, 1975), 28–29. Under the terms of the Civil Code, women enjoyed virtually no equal rights or privileges. Subject to strict supervision by the head of the "house" (*ie*), women became legally incompetent after marriage.

23 Ichikawa, *Jiden*, 53. As Otsubo notes, Hiratsuka's advocacy of marriage restriction, influenced by the thinking of Ellen Key, was inspired as much by eugenics (albeit a gender-based variety of eugenics) as by women's rights thought. Because Ichikawa focused more on rights, however, this study will emphasize the rights aspect of the NWA's work in the area of sexually transmitted disease.

24 Hiratsuka, *Genshi josei*, 71–73.

25 "Good wife, wise motherism" is treated by a number of scholars, most notably Uno, whose numerous works on this subject cover the Meiji era to the present.

26 Nolte and Hastings, "Meiji State's Policy," 156.

27 Hiratsuka, *Genshi josei*, 82. This argument was not unique to Japan. In the United States, venereal disease was viewed as destructive to the family, but, it was believed in the first decades of the twentieth century, a man's secret infection should not be revealed to his relatives by his physician, lest he lose his dominance in the family. See Allan Brandt, *No Magic Bullet: A Social History of Venereal Disease in the United States since 1850* (New York, 1985), 18–19. As in Japan, U.S. feminists were infuriated with "men for infecting women and destroying the lives of children." See Lois Rudnick, "The Male Identified Woman and Other Anxieties: The Life of Mabel Dodge Luhan," in Sara Alpern, Elisabeth Israels Perry, Ingrid Winther Scobie, and Joyce Antler, eds., *The Challenge of Feminist Biography: Writing the Lives of Modern American Women* (Urbana, Ill., 1992). Otsubo, in "Engendering Eugenics," notes that Hiratsuka, in justifying the legislative petition's focus on restricting only men's access to marriage, emphasized the importance of eugenics to the Japanese race and nation as well as to wives and children (the latter being the feminist emphasis).

28 Hiratsuka Raichō, "Karyūbyō danshi kekkon seigenhō ni kansuru seigan undō" [The petition movement for a law to limit marriage for men with venereal disease], *Josei dōmei*, 1 (Oct. 1920), 35.

29 Hiratsuka, *Genshi josei*, 117; Ichikawa, *Jiden*, 75.

30 Tabuchi Toyokichi, "Fujin no seijiteki jiyū o shuchō Tabuchi-shi no enzetsu" [Mr. Tabuchi's speech in which he insisted on women's political freedom], *Josei dōmei*, 3 (Dec. 1920), 8–9, 16. *Josei dōmei* published Tabuchi's speech in its entirety.

31 "Fujimura Yoshirō-shi no chikei kaikin hantairon hihan" [A criticism of Mr. Fujimura's opposition to revising the Police Law], *Josei dōmei*, 8 (May 1921), 5. Fujimura's stress on the greater importance of women's role in the household is similar to that espoused by the Home Ministry fifteen years earlier; as Nolte and Hastings, "Meiji State's Policy," 156, put it, "the state's claim on the home pre-empted women's claims on the state."

32 Ichikawa Fusae, "Sōritsu yori josei dōmei hakkan made (2)" [From founding to the publication of Josei Dōmei], *Josei dōmei*, 2 (Nov. 1920), 46. It appears that Ichikawa's initial fears about the NWA's image, at least as far as the government was concerned, were unfounded. Although the NWA and other women's groups formed in later years gave high priority to acquiring political rights for women, their existence was not considered a violation of Article 5, Clause 1, which prohibited women's participation in political associations; a political association was usually considered one composed of individuals capable of exercising political power, which women were unable to do without the vote. Women were more likely to have been closely supervised for violation of Clause 2, which prohibited attendance at political rallies and meetings.

33 Hiratsuka Raichō, "Shakai kaizō ni taisuru fujin no shimei" [The mission of women in social reconstruction], *Josei dōmei*, 1 (Oct. 1920), 10.

34 This demand appears, along with the other two petitions, in the opening pages of several issues of the organization's bulletin. See *Josei dōmei*, 3 (Dec. 1920), 2.

35 This changed in the following decade, when Ichikawa became a principal supporter of the Mother-Child Protection Law of 1937. Barbara Molony, "Equality versus Difference: The Japanese Debate over 'Motherhood Protection', 1915–1950," in Janet Hunter, ed., *Japanese Women Working* (London, 1993), 131.

36 Ichikawa Fusae, "Chian keisatsuhō daigojō shūsei no undō (1)," *Fujin Kōron* 5 (Dec. 1920), 24.
37 Ichikawa Fusae, "Zettaiteki danjo byōdō? [Absolute male-female equality?] *Josei kaizō* (Apr. 1924), 28–36, reprinted in Ichikawa Fusae Kinenkai, ed., *Ichikawa Fusae-shū* [Collected works of Ichikawa Fusae], vol. 1 (Tokyo: Nihon Tosho Sentaa, 1994), 264–274.
38 Ichikawa, "Zettaiteki danjo byōdō?" 36.
39 Yamakawa Kikue's May Day manifesto, cited in Mikiso Hane, ed., *Reflections of the Way to the Gallows: Rebel Women in Prewar Japan* (Berkeley, Calif., 1988), 126–127.
40 This seems a rather weak critique of imperialism, given all we know today about the gender oppression that characterized Japanese imperialism in the 1930s and 1940s. But the comfort women would appear after Yamakawa wrote these criticisms of imperialism. And the socialist-feminist theorizing about imperialism widely available today would have seemed heretical in a 1920s context in which only class mattered.
41 Yamakawa Kikue, "Shin Fujin Kyōkai to Sekirankai," *Taiyō*, 27 (July 1927).
42 Ibid., 135–137.
43 Mackie, *Creating Socialist Women*, chapter 6.
44 Yoshimi Kaneko, *Fujin sanseiken* [Women's suffrage] (Tokyo, 1971), 153.
45 Yamakawa defended her actions in the March 1928 issue of *Rōnō*. Quoted in Ichikawa, *Jiden*, 147, and in Kaneko Shigeri, *Fujin mondai no chishiki* [Scholarship on women's issues] (1934; Tokyo, 1982), 218.
46 Ide Fumiko and Eisashi Akiko, *Taishō demokurashii to josei* [Taishō democracy and women] (Tokyo, 1977), 257–260; see also Shidzue Ishimoto, *Facing Two Ways: The Story of My Life* (1935; Stanford, Calif., 1983; reissue of original edition, with new introduction and afterword by B. Molony), 254.
47 Kaneko Shigeri, *Fujin mondai no chishiki*, 218.
48 Yamataka (Kaneko) Shigeri, "Watakushi no rirekisho" [My resume], *Nihon keizai*, Nov. 20, 1975; Chino Yūichi, *Kindai Nihon fujin kyōikushi* [A history of women's education in modern Japan] (Tokyo, 1979), 242.
49 Kubushiro Ochimi, *Haisho hitosuji* [Focus on abolishing licensed prostitution] (Tokyo, 1973), 169; Izuma Tsuko, "Fusen jisshi no kekka o yosōshite" [Anticipating the results of implementing women's suffrage] in *Fujin mondai to fujin no yōkyū* [Women's issues and women's demands] (Tokyo, 1929), 121.
50 Cited in Kirisutokyō Fujin Kyōfūkai, ed., *Nihon Kirisutokyō Fujin Kyōfūkai hyakunenshi* [100-year history of the Japan Christian Women's Reform Society] (Tokyo, 1986), 526–527; see also Ichikawa, *Jiden*, 144; and Kubushiro, *Haisho*, 170–171.
51 Ichikawa, *Jiden*, 150.
52 The Peace Preservation Law passed in 1925 was directed against groups and individuals who advocated a change in the "national polity" (*kokutai*) or who advocated the abolition of private property. Ambiguities in the law would later make it possible to increase the number of offenders and to increase government pressure on the women's movement. See Richard Mitchell, *Thought Control in Prewar Japan* (Ithaca, N.Y., 1976), 63.
53 Ichikawa, *Jiden*, 150; Yoshimi, *Fujin sanseiken*, 155.
54 Kirisutokyō Fujin Kyōfūkai, ed., *Nihon Kirisutokyō Fujin Kyōfūkai*, 528.
55 *Tokyo asahi shinbun*, citations of March 10, 1925, quoted in Ichikawa, *Jiden*, 152.
56 For more on the activities of Diet supporters, see Murata Shizuko, "Daigishi Yamaguchi Masaji to fujin sanseiken undō" [Representative Yamaguchi Masaji and the women's suffrage movement], *Rekishi hyōron*, 517 [History critique] (May 1993), 83–99.
57 Ichikawa, *Jiden*, 155. It is believed that legal expert Hozumi Shigeto was the first to use the word *fusen* to apply to women in 1924. See "Fusen mondai" [The women's suffrage issue], *Fusen*, 1 (March 1927), 10.
58 Ide Fumiko, "Nihon ni okeru fujin sanseiken undō" [The women's suffrage movement in Japan], *Rekishigaku kenkyū* [Historical studies research] (Nov. 1956), 18–19.
59 Works on feminists' actions and discourse in the remainder of the interwar period abound. See, for example, Garon, "Women's Groups and the Japanese State"; Mackie, *Creating Socialist Women*; Molony and Molony, *Ichikawa Fusae*; Hopper, *A New Woman of Japan*.
60 Molony, "Equality versus Difference," 129–130.
61 See, e.g., Fujime Yuki, "Zen Kansai Fujin Rengōkai no kōzō to tokushitsu" [Structure and characteristics of the All-Kansai Women's Federation], *Shiron*, 71 [Historical discourse] (1988), 71–100; Sheldon Garon, "Women's Groups and the Japanese State."

62 Fujita Taki, "Fusen undō hitosuji ni" [Focusing on the women's suffrage movement], in Ichikawa Fusae to Iu Hito Kankōkai, *Ichikawa Fusae to iu hito* [The person called Ichikawa Fusae] (Tokyo, 1982), 122.

6 Feminism and Protestantism in nineteenth-century France (Florence Rochefort)

Translated from the French by Karen Offen; updated and elaborated for an English-language audience in collaboration with the author. Florence Rochefort would particularly like to thank Karen Offen for the present translation, for her pioneer work on the history of feminism in France, and especially for her continuous encouragement (since our first meeting in the 1980s) to continue research on this subject.

1 Maïté Albistur and Daniel Armogathe, *Histoire du féminisme français du Moyen Age à nos jours* (Paris: Éditions des femmes, 1977); Michèle Riot-Sarcey, *La démocratie à l'épreuve des femmes* (Paris: Albin Michel, 1994); Laurence Klejman and Florence Rochefort, *L'Égalité en marche: Le féminisme sous la Troisième République* (Paris: Presses de la FNSP/Éditions des femmes, 1989); Christine Bard, *Les filles de Marianne: Histoire des féminismes 1914–1940* (Paris: Fayard, 1995); François Poullain de la Barre, a one-time French Catholic theology student turned Cartesian philosopher who converted to Protestantism and moved to Geneva, proposed, notably in his *De l'égalité des deux sexes* (1673), that women have access to every career, from the pulpit to the highest ranks of the army. For the *Jeunes Femmes* movement, see Sylvie Chaperon, "Le Mouvement Jeunes Femmes, 1946–1970: de l'Evangile au féminisme," *Bulletin de la Société de l'Histoire du Protestantisme Français*, vol. 146 (Jan.–March 2000), pp. 153–183.
2 Jean Bauberot conducted a seminar on this subject in 1982 at the École Pratique des Hautes Études, but his work has never been published in its entirety. See the short entries on "feminism" in Jean Bauberot, *Éncyclopédie du protestantisme* (Paris and Geneva: Labor et Fides, 1995), p. 570; Jean Bauberot and Jean-Paul Willaime, *Le protestantisme* (Paris: MA editions, 1987); Janine Garrisson-Estèbe, *L'homme protestant* (Paris: Hachette, 1980); Florence Rochefort, "La prostituée et l'ouvrière: Approches protestantes et catholiques du féminisme sous la IIIe République," in Françoise Lautman, ed., *Ni Eve ni Marie: Luttes et incertitudes des héritières de la Bible* (Geneva: Labor et Fides, 1997), pp. 211–229; on Switzerland, see Anne-Marie Käppeli, *Sublime croisade: Éthique et politique du féminisme protestant, 1875–1928* (Geneva : Éditions Zoé, 1990).
3 In her introduction, Liliane Crété, *Le protestantisme et les femmes: Aux origines de l'émancipation* (Geneva: Labor et Fides, 1999), presents some Protestant feminist personalities of the nineteenth and twentieth centuries as the very archetypes of Protestant women, which seems excessive.
4 Jean Bauberot, "La femme protestante," in Georges Duby and Michelle Perrot, *Histoire des femmes*, vol. IV: *Le XIXe siècle* (Paris: Plon, 1991), pp. 199–214.
5 Christine de Pizan, *La Cité des Dames* (Paris: Stock/Moyen Age, 1996); in English as *The Book of the City of Ladies*, transl. by Earl Jeffrey Richards (New York: Persea Books, 1982).
6 The term "féminisme" (which began to spread in its current meaning from 1882 on) can be used in a retroactive fashion to designate this aspiration to the equality of the sexes, the application of which is anticipated in the short term or longer term and in a wide variety of applications. See Karen Offen, "On the French Origins of the Words Feminism and Feminist," *Feminist Issues*, 8:2 (Fall 1988), 45–51.
7 Florence Rochefort, "L'antiféminisme à la Belle Époque, une rhétorique réactionnnaire," in Christine Bard, ed., *Un siècle d'antiféminisme* (Paris : Fayard, 1999), pp. 133–147; Michelle Perrot, *Femmes publiques: Entretiens avec Jean Lebrun* (Paris : Textuel, 1997). The *tricoteuses* – literally, the women who knit – was the label given to women who sat on the French revolutionary assemblies to partake of political discussions, before the British novelist Charles Dickens immortalized them (in his novel *The Tale of Two Cities*, published in 1859) as the impassive knitters who attended the guillotining of revolutionary dissidents under the Terror.
8 André Encrevé, *Les Protestants en France de 1800 à nos jours: Histoire d'une réintegration* (Paris : Stock, 1985); *Protestants français au milieu du XIXe siècle* (Geneva: Labor et Fides, 1986).
9 On Eugénie Niboyet, see Michèle Riot-Sarcey, *Démocratie à l'épreuve des femmes*, Evelyne Lejeune-Resnick, *Femmes et Associations (1830–1880)* (Paris: Publisud, 1991) ; Fernand Rude,

"Eugénie Niboyet," in Stéphane Michaud, ed., *Un fabuleux destin Flora Tristin* (Dijon: EUD, 1985), pp. 120–143; Eugénie Niboyet was the granddaughter of a pastor, not the daughter – as is sometimes alleged. On the Saint-Simonian women, see Claire Goldberg Moses, "'Difference' in Historical Perspective: Saint-Simonian Feminism," in Claire Goldberg Moses and Leslie Wahl Rabine, *Feminism, Socialism, and French Romanticism* (Bloomington: Indiana University Press, 1993), and the accompanying documents in translation.

10 Letter from Eugénie Niboyet to Enfantin, 2 December 1831, as cited by Evelyne Lejeune-Resnick, *Femmes et associations*, p. 56.

11 In Lyon Niboyet founded *Le Conseiller des femmes*, which appeared from 2 Nov. 1833 to 6 Sept. 1834, then the more literary *La Mosaïque lyonnaise* which lasted several months (no. 1, 11 Oct. 1834).

12 The *Société de la morale chrétienne* gave a prize to Niboyet's publications, which included *De la nécessité d'abolir la peine de mort* (1836), *Des aveugles et de leur éducation, De la réforme du systeme pénitentiaire en France* (1838), and *Dieu manifesté par les œuvres de la Création* (1842).

13 Jean Bauberot and Jean-Paul Willaime insist on Protestantism as a culture and as an "ethos." Anne-Marie Käppeli uses the expression "ethic of devotion" to characterize Protestant feminism.

14 "Comité des dames de la société de la morale chrétienne pour l'amélioration morale des femmes detenues," see Lejeune-Resnick, *Femmes et associations*, p. 163. At the Saint-Lazare prison Eugénie Niboyet founded a school for children in the wetnurses' quarters; see Riot-Sarcey, *Démocratie à l'épreuve*, p. 165.

15 Eugénie Niboyet, *Le Vrai livre des femmes*, p. 27, cited in Michèle Riot-Sarcey, "Histoire et autobiographie 'Le Vrai livre des femmes' d'Eugénie Niboyet," *Romantisme*, no. 56 (1987), pp. 59–68.

16 This argument was prefigured in the work of an earlier sixteenth-century radical, Agrippa de Nettesheim.

17 Jenny P. d'Héricourt, *La Femme affranchie: Réponse à MM. Michelet, Proudhon, E. de Girardin, A. Comte et autres novateurs modernes*, 2 vol. (Paris/Brussels, 1860). Deceived by her "libertine" and "hypocritical" husband, Jenny left him and returned to live with her mother, wrote two novels – one against adultery, the other against the death penalty – even as she studied medicine and homeopathy. She obtained a midwife's diploma from the Paris Faculty of Medicine and set herself up as an intellectual, notably in the salon of Madame Fauvety. See Karen Offen, "Qui est Jenny P. d'Héricourt? Une identité retrouvée," *Bulletin de la société d'histoire de la révolution de 1848 et des révolutions du XIXe siècle*, no. 3 (1987), 87–100 ; subsequently, Alessandra Anteghini, *Socialismo e femminismo nella Francia del XIX secolo: Jenny d'Héricourt*. Quaderni dell'Istituto di Scienza Politica, Università di Genova (Genoa: ECIG, 1988), and Caroline Arni and Claudia Honegger, "Jenny P. d'Héricourt (1809–1875): Weibliche Modernität und die Prinzipien von 1789," in *Frauen in der Soziologie: Neun Porträts* (Munich: C. H. Beck, 1998), pp. 60–98.

18 d'Héricourt, *Femme affranchie*, vol. 2, p. 217.

19 *Femme affranchie*, pp. 10–11.

20 Jenny P. d'Héricourt, "Le christianisme et la question des femmes," *Revue philosophique et religieuse*, 1857, p. 43.

21 *The Revolution*, 28 October 1869, cited by Karen Offen, "Qui est Jenny P. d'Héricourt?," p. 97, note 12.

22 Charles Fauvety, "Mme J.-P. d'Héricourt," *L'Avenir des femmes*, 7 February 1875.

23 d'Héricourt, *Femme affranchie*, vol. 2, p. 12.

24 Gabriel Monod, *Madame Edmond de Pressensé: Souvenirs et lettres inédites* (Paris: Fischbacher, 1904), p. 61.

25 Monod, *Pressensé*, p. 15.

26 It seems likely that Elise de Pressensé had been influenced by her friend André Léo not only on social questions but also on the woman question. See Rémi Fabre, "Une grande dame du protestantisme: Élise de Pressensé," *Bulletin de la SHPF*, vol. 132 (Jan.–March 1986), pp. 35–61.

27 Julie Siegfried, *La guerre et le role de la femme*, cited by Françoise Blum and Janet Horne, "Féminisme et Musée social (1916–1939)," *Vie Sociale*, no. 8–9 (1988). Julie Siegfried, the daughter of pastor Puaux, had been raised in the strictest possible Protestant orthodoxy, but had evolved toward religious liberalism. Married to the deputy and industrialist Jules Siegfried in 1869, she and her husband quickly became active in social work, first in Le Havre and then in Paris. She served as a member of the organizing committee for the *Congrès des oeuvres et*

institutions féminines in 1889, and ultimately as the second president of the *Conseil national des femmes françaises*.

28 On this passage, see Evelyne Diebolt, "Les associations face aux institutions: Les femmes dans l'action sanitaire, sociale et culturelle 1900–1965," dissertation for the doctorat d'État, University of Paris VII-Jussieu, and her article, "Femmes protestantes face aux politiques de santé publique (1900–1939)," *Bulletin de la SHPF*, vol. 146 (Jan.–March 2000), pp. 91–132.

29 Alain Corbin, *Les filles de noces, misère sexuelle et prostitution aux XIXe et XXe siècles* (Paris: Aubier Montaigne, 1978) ; Florence Rochefort, "La prostituée et l'ouvrière… ".

30 Anne-Marie Käppeli, *Sublime croisade.*

31 The *Union des amis de la jeune fille* was founded following the 1877 congress of Butler's *Fédération britannique et continentale*, in Geneva. Its headquarters were in Neuchâtel, Switzerland. The Parisian section organized in 1884.

32 Annie Stora-Lamarre, *L'Enfer de la IIIe République: Censeurs et pornographes (1881–1914)* (Paris: Imago, 1990).

33 Caroline de Barrau, née Coulomb, was the daughter of a banker, married to a Protestant aristocrat from the southwest of France. Her younger sister Marie d'Abbadie d'Arrast, who followed the religious instruction of the liberal pastor Athanase Coquerel, became a leading participant in the *Conseil national des femmes françaises* (founded in 1901).

34 Isabelle Bogelot, née Cottiaux, came from a family in the Pas-de-Calais. There is still much to be learned about her links to Protestantism. She may have been influenced by her marriage, in 1864, to Auguste Bogelot. The French journalist Jane Misme characterizes her as being intimately linked to the Protestant milieu without actually belonging to it. See Isabelle Bogelot, *Trente ans de solidarité 1877–1906* (Paris: Imprimerie Doumeme & Co, 1908).

35 Ed. Shuré, "Introduction à Émilie Morsier," *La Mission de la femme* (Paris: Fischbacher, 1897), p. 1; Tommy Fallot, *Madame Caroline de Barrau de Muratel* (Dole : Impr. Blind-Franck, 1889); "Isabelle Bogelot," *Encyclopédie Larousse* (1896 edn).

36 Caroline de Barrau ceded her place as president of the *Oeuvre des libérées de Saint-Lazare* to Isabelle Bogelot in 1887 in order to found, with Pauline Kergomard, *l'Union française pour le sauvetage de l'enfance* [Union for the rescue of little children].

37 In 1885 the *Oeuvre des libérées* obtained from the French government "recognition as a public utility," which had earlier been refused, and it was represented at the penitentiary congress of 1895. See Émilie de Morsier, *Mission de la femme* , and Isabelle Bogelot, *Trente ans de solidarité.*

38 Émilie de Morsier, *Mission de la femme*, pp. 16–17.

39 Émilie de Morsier, *Mission de la femme*, p. 153.

40 Émilie de Morsier, "Intervention au congrès pénitentiaire de Paris," July 1895, *Mission de la femme*, p. 184.

41 "Programme," *Revue de morale progressive*, no. 1 (June 1887); on this publication, see Anne-Marie Käppeli, *Sublime croisade.*

42 Jean Bauberot, *La morale laïque contre l'ordre moral* (Paris: Seuil, 1997).

43 Isabelle Bogelot attended as a delegate from the *Oeuvre des libérées de Saint-Lazare.*

44 Colette Bec, *Assistance et République* (Paris: Éditions de l'Atelier, 1994). Some civil rights demands specifically concerned single women, notably the demand for the right to testify in court and the right to serve as a witness to formal documents attesting to birth, marriage, and death (known in France as *actes d'Etat civil*).

45 Sarah Monod was the daughter of the celebrated revivalist Adolphe Monod. She became the head of an organization of deaconesses shortly before the war of 1870 and served as an *ambulancière* (ambulance assistant) during the war. See Julie Siegfried, "Mademoiselle Sarah Monod," *Christianisme social* (Feb. 1913), pp. 91–94.

46 Florence Rochefort, "La prostituée et l'ouvrière…", in Lautman, *Ni Eve ni Marie* (see note 2).

47 *En mémoire de Mme de Witt-Schlumberger*, commemorative brochure published by the Musée social in 1924 (p. 28). Marguerite de Witt-Schlumberger served as president of the UFSF from 1913 to 1924, and also presided over the *Union féminine pour la Société des Nations*. She was also the only woman named to the *Conseil supérieur de la natalité*. See Christine Bard, *Filles de Marianne.*

48 As reported by Cécile Brunschvicg and quoted in *La Française* (2 October 1939); cited in Françoise Blum and Janet Horne, "Féminisme et Musée social (1916–1939)," *Vie sociale*, nos. 8–9 (1988).

49 Concerning this tension at the heart of Protestantism, see Jean-Paul Willaime, *La précarité protestante: Sociologie du protestantisme contemporain* (Geneva: Labor et Fidès, 1992).

50 Bertie Albrecht, from a Protestant family in Marseille, discovered the birth control movement in London and tried to implant it in France during the 1930s. See Christine Bard, *Filles de Marianne*, p. 244.

51 Claude Langlois, *Le catholicisme au féminin* (Paris: Cerf, 1984).

52 As, for example, in the action of Marie du Sacré-Coeur; see Emile Poulat, "Le rêve contrarié d'une religieuse enseignante: L'Affaire Marie du Sacré-Coeur," *Liberté-laïcité, la guerre de deux France et le principe de modernité* (Paris: Cerf/Cujas, 1987), pp. 269–282.

53 See especially Jean-Noël Luc, *L'invention du jeune enfant au XIXe. De la salle d'asile à l'école maternelle* (Paris : Belin, 1997).

7 From Fredrika Bremer to Ellen Key (Inger Hammar)

1 Under the pressure of social changes, religious legislation from the middle of the nineteenth century began to prepare the way for a secularized state. Gradually the grip of the Swedish-Lutheran unified state embodied in the 1686 Church Law was broken. In 1858 saw the repeal of the Conventicle Act of 1726 that forbade independent gatherings without the presence of a priest. With the Dissenters' Acts of 1860 and 1873, the terms "Swedish" and "Lutheran" ceased to be synonymous. On obtaining specific permission from the king, Swedish citizens were allowed to form non-Lutheran congregations, and were also allowed to become members of religious denominations that did not have state approval. With the Religious Freedom Act of 1951, Swedish citizens were given the right to abstain from membership of the Christian churches. In 2000 the Church of Sweden was disestablished.

2 For further discussion of the Nordic state and church in the nineteenth century see for example Dag Thorkildsen, "Religious Identity and Nordic Identity," in Øystein Sørensen and Bo Stråth (eds.), *The Cultural Construction of Norden* (Oslo–Stockholm–Copenhagen–Oxford–Boston: Scandinavian University Press, 1997) and Henrik Stenius, "The Good Life is a Life of Conformity: The Impact of Lutheran Tradition on Nordic Political Culture," in ibid. For religious discourse in public debate in the Nordic countries see Tarald Rasmussen, "Kristelig og borgerlig offentlighet i Norge på 1800-tallet," in Tarald Rasmussen and Trygve Wyller (eds.), *Kristelig og borgerlig offentlighet i Norge* (Oslo: Norges forskningsråd, 1996).

3 Gustaf Wingren, *Luthers lära om kallelsen* (Lund: Gleerup, 1942), in English, *The Christian's Calling. Luther on Vocation*, translated by Carl C. Rasmussen (Edinburgh: Oliver and Boyd, 1958), 34 f.

4 The pioneering generation of feminists belonged to the cream of Swedish society, and were able to gain a hearing from their liberal friends in the economic, political, cultural, and religious elite. Working-class women, on the other hand, had few opportunities before 1900 to unify or develop emancipatory views on equal terms with upper-class women; they found themselves instead the object of the philanthropic enthusiasms of the leading feminists, intent on raising the proletariat's moral and social status.

5 On the Reformation and gender construction see for example Lyndal Roper, *The Holy Household. Women and Morals in Reformation Augsburg* (Oxford: Clarendon Press, 1989), 2, where she argues that the Reformation gave legitimacy to the subordination perspective. Compare Steven Ozment, *When Fathers Ruled. Family Life in Reformation Europe* (Cambridge, Massachusetts: Harvard University Press, 1983), who counters that the Reformation's focus on marriage was a condition for a strong women's role. Between them one finds Merry E. Wiesner, *Women and Gender in Early Modern Europe* (Cambridge: Cambridge University Press, 1993). See also Merry E. Wiesner, "Spinning Out Capital: Women's Work in the Early Modern Economy," in Renate Bridenthal, Claudia Koonz and Susan Stuard (eds.), *Becoming Visible. Women in European History*, 2nd edn. (Boston: Houghton Mifflin, 1987); and William Monter, "Protestant Wives, Catholic Saints, and the Devil's Handmaid: Women in the Age of Renaissance" in ibid. Another scholar to argue that the Protestant tradition was favourable to the emancipation process was the sociologist Olive Banks, *Faces of Feminism. A Study of Feminism as a Social Movement* (Oxford: M. Robertson, 1981). She identifies the evangelical Christian women's efforts as one of the three branches of the emancipation movement (the others being the ideas drawn from the French Revolution and from Socialist ideology). Even if in the middle of the nineteenth century relations between the sexes were still marked by inequality and belief in disparate gender spheres was intact, argues Banks, the same period saw Protestant women intensifying their demands for liberation. See also Susan Hill Lindley, "*You Have Stept Out of*

Your Place." A History of Women and Religion in America (Louisville, Kentucky: Westminster Knox Press, 1996) 366, who, like Banks, merely mentions the Lutheran tradition in passing. For an overview of the relationship between emancipation and theological reflection, see Susan A. Ross, "The Women's Movement and Theology in the Twentieth Century," in Gregory Baum (ed.), *The Twentieth Century. A Theological Overview* (Maryknoll, New York: Orbis Books, 1999).

6 For further discussion of Luther and his life, see for example Martin Brecht, *Martin Luther Shaping and Defining the Reformation 1521–1532* (Minneapolis: Philadelphia Fortress Press, 1990); on Scandinavian Protestantism see for example Nicholas Hope, *German and Scandinavian Protestantism 1700–1918* (Oxford: Clarendon Press, 1995).

7 The term "calling" – *vocatio* – was traditionally reserved for members of religious orders.

8 On Luther and marriage see Olof Sundby, *Luthersk äktenskapsuppfattning. En studie i den kyrkliga äktenskapsdebatten i Sverige efter 1900* (Lund: Stockholm Diakonistyrelsens förlag, 1959), 65 ff.

9 Wingren 1942, 33 ff.

10 Wingren 1942, 14 ff.; Carl-Henric Grenholm, *Arbetets mening. En analys av sex teorier om arbetets syfte och värde* (Uppsala: Stockholm Almqvist and Wicksell International, 1988), 151 ff.

11 Grenholm 1988, 159 ff.; Bengt Hägglund, *Teologins historia. En dogmhistorisk översikt* (Malmö: Gleerups förlag Lund, 1956), 204 ff.

12 Compare Lars Österlin, Book Review, *Kyrkohistorisk årsskrift* 1962, 283 ff. The editions of the Bible used in this article were: BIBLIA, Thet är All then Helga Skrift på Swensko; Efter Konung KARL then Tolftes Befalning, (Stockholm: 1709); and the Authorised Version, or King James Bible, (London: 1611).

13 Genesis 1:27. For Jewish feminist views on the traditional interpretation of the Creation, see Rachel Adler, "The Jew who Wasn't there. Halakhah and the Jewish Woman," in Susannah Heschel (ed.), *On being a Jewish Feminist* (New York: Schocken Books, 1983).

14 For a more detailed analysis of the patriarchal tradition's views on humanity from St. Augustine to Luther, see Rosemary Radford Ruether, *Sexism and God-Talk. Towards a Feminist Theology* (Boston, Massachusetts: SCM Press Ltd, 1993), 93; for discussion of St. Augustine and Thomas Aquinas see also Kari Elisabeth Børresen, *Subordination and Equivalence. The Nature and Role of Women in Augustine and Thomas Aquinas* (Mainz: Matthias-Grünewald-Verl., 1995). For contemporary views on Biblical passages and exegesis in the nineteenth century as discussed by Frances Willard and Elizabeth Cady Stanton, see Carol Newsom and Sharon H. Ringe, *The Women's Bible Commentary* (London: SPCK, 1992), in particular their introduction to the field.

15 Genesis 2:20.

16 Genesis 2:22–23.

17 Genesis 3:16–19.

18 See for example Lyndal Roper, *Oedipus and the Devil. Witchcraft, Sexuality and Religion in Early Modern Europe* (London: Routledge, 1994), 18.

19 Jane Dempsey Douglass, "The Image of God in Women as Seen by Luther and Calvin," in Kari Elisabeth Børresen (ed.), *The Image of God. Gender Models in Judaeo-Christian Tradition* (Minneapolis: Fortress Press, 1995), 236–257, argues that according to Luther "the whole human situation" was altered by the Fall. Eve is punished severely, but Adam also faces change: "He must contend with raging lust. His duty to support and govern his family as well as to rule over the world is a great burden" (p. 247). Like Ruether, Douglass sees Luther as a representative of the patriarchal tradition that denied woman equal standing with man in *imago Dei*.

20 Martin Luther, *Doctor Martin Luthers Betraktelser öfwer de Första Menniskornas Lefnad. (I Mos. 2–10 kap.) Till underwisning och uppbyggelse för Evangeliska Christna, utgifwen af Carl Georg Hermes, Evangelisk predikant i Kroppendorf wid Magdeburg* (Falun: 1860), 23.

21 Martin Luther, *Doctor Martin Luthers Råd till Föräldrar och Uppfostrare jemte ett Tillägg för äkta Makar. En kostelig Gåfva för hwarje Hus. Af J. G. Kelber* (Stockholm: 1852), 97.

22 For example, Alison Milbank suggests that Josephine Butler, "a worshipping Anglican and wife of a cleric," believed that she had been given her mission to fight prostitution and regulation by God himself: "The significance of her experience is two-fold; it gave her unassailable authority, cutting across the hierarchy of male structures of authority, and it also kept her outside those structures." Alison Milbank, "Josephine Butler: Christianity, Feminism and Social Action," in Jim Obelkevich, Lyndal Roper, and Raphael Samuel (eds.), *Disciplines of Faith. Studies in Religion, Politics and Patriarchy* (London: Routledge and Kegan Paul, 1987), 155.

23 Merry E. Wiesner, "Luther and Women: The Death of Two Marys," in Obelkevich, Roper and Samuel 1987, 299. For the argument that Christianity was "a highly sophisticated construction to reduce femininity to maternity," see Julia Kristeva, *Stabat mater och andra texter i urval av Ebba Witt-Brattström* (Stockholm: Natur och kultur, 1990), 33. As a result of the Lutheran tradition's emphasis on motherhood, the Virgin Mary lost much of the standing she had held in the Catholic church, see Wiesner 1987, 302 ff.

24 For emancipation within a Protestant context, see for example Ruether 1993, 99 ff.

25 Lucy Bland, "'Purifying' the Public World: feminist vigilantes in late Victorian England," *Women's History Review* 1:3 (1992), 396. Bland sees the late nineteenth-century term "public woman" as "interchangeable with the terms prostitute, streetwalker and actress" in England. See also Lucy Bland, *Banishing the Beast. English Feminism and Sexual Morality 1885–1914* (New York: Penguin, 1995), 118; Mary P. Ryan, *Women in Public. Between Banners and Ballots 1825–1880* (Baltimore: Johns Hopkins University Press, 1990), 4 ff.; Joan B. Landes, *Women and the Public Sphere in the Age of the French Revolution* (New York: Ithaca Cornell University Press, 1988), 3; and Judith R. Walkowitz, *City of Dreadful Delight. Narratives of Sexual Danger in Late-Victorian London* (London: Virago, 1992), 20 ff.

26 There is evidence that a good many women were cautious about participating in organized lobbying, feeling that women should act discreetly. On female philanthropy in the Nordic area, see for example Birgitta Jordansson and Tinne Vammen (eds.), *Charitable Women. Philanthropic Welfare 1780–1930. A Nordic and Interdisciplinary Anthology*, (Odense: Odense University Press, 1998); and Karin Lützen, *Byen tæmmes. Kernefamilie, sociale reformer og velgørenhed i 1800-tallets København* (Copenhagen: Hans Reizels Forlag, 1998).

27 For further discussion of public philanthropy in a Lutheran context, see Inger Hammar, "Den problematiska offentligheten. Filantropi, kvinnokall och emancipation," *Scandia* no 2 (1996), 305 ff.; and Inger Hammar, "Den svårerövrade offentligheten. Kön och religion i emancipationsprocessen," *Kvinnovetenskaplig tidskrift* no 2 (1998), 19 ff.

28 Gunnar Qvist, *Kvinnofrågan i Sverige 1809–1846. Studier rörande kvinnans näringsfrihet inom de borgerliga yrkena* (Göteborg: Göteborg Elander, 1960), 13 ff. For women's standing in the Enlightenment and the French Revolution, see Elizabeth Fox-Genovese, "Women and the Enlightenment" and Darline Levy and Harriet Applewhite "Women and Political Revolution in Paris," in Bridenthal, Koonz and Stuard (eds.), *Becoming Visible. Women in European History* (see note 5), pp. 251–277 and 297–306 respectively.

29 Lars Österlin, "Kvinnouppfattningen i Sverige under 1800-talet som kyrkohistoriskt problem," *Svensk Teologisk Kvartalskrift* 38 (1962), 259 ff.

30 Edvard Rodhe, *Den religiösa liberalismen. Nils Ignell – Viktor Rydberg – Pontus Wikner* (Uppsala: Svenska kyrkans diakonistyrelses förlag Stockholm, 1935), 230.

31 Rodhe 1935, 7 ff.

32 *Strauss och Evangelierna, eller Jesu Lefnad af D. F. Strauss. För Tänkande Läsare af alla Stånd bearbetad af en Evangelisk Theolog. Öfversättning* (Stockholm: L. J. Hiertas förlag, 1841); D. Fr. Strauss, *Das Leben Jesu kritisch bearbeitet*, I–II (Tübingen: 1835).

33 Rodhe 1935, 14 ff.

34 There has been considerable interest in Bremer. For an overview of recent research in English, see for example Brita. K. Stendahl, *The Education of a Self-Made Woman – Fredrika Bremer 1801–1865* (Lewiston, New York: The Edwin Mellen Press, 1994); and Laurel Ann Lofsvold, *Fredrika Bremer and the Writing of America* (Lund: Lund University Press, 1999).

35 For more on Bremer's childhood as depicted by her sister, Charlotte Quiding, see Fredrika Bremer, *Sjelfbiografiska anteckningar, bref och efterlemnade skrifter jemte en teckning af hennes lefnad och personlighet, utgifne af Ch. B-r* (Örebro: Abr. Bohlin, 1868), published in English in the same year, Fredr. Milow, *Fredrika Bremer: Life, Letters and Posthumous Works* (New York: Hurd and Houghton, 1868).

36 Bremer 1868, 33. See also Fredrika Bremer, *Fredrika Bremers brev samlade och utgivna av Klara Johansson och Ellen Kleman, del I–IV* (Stockholm: P. A. Norstedt & Söner, 1915–1920) II, letter to F.M. Franzén 29 March 1842.

37 Bremer 1916, letter to Ebba Hildebrandsson née af Wirsén 23 January 1845. See also ibid. 1917, letter to Fredrika Limnell 1 December 1860.

38 See for example Bremer 1915, letters to Charlotte Bremer 13 June 1828, Charlotte Bremer née Hollström 25 October 1831, Frances Lewin 24 November 1831, and P.J. Böklin 20 July 1832.

39 Bremer 1915, letter to P.J. Böklin 11 October 1832. The father died in 1830.

40 Thaly Nilsson, "Fredrika Bremer och riksläsaren," in *Svenska Dagbladet* 11 December 1999, quoting a letter from Bremer to Carl Gustaf von Brinkman 17 December 1831.

41 Bremer 1916, letter to P.J. Böklin 27 October 1842, supplement. On Bremer's preference for common sense over emotion in theological matters, see also ibid. 1917, letter to Hans Martensen 20 December 1847.

42 Bremer 1916, letter to Frances v. Koch 9 March 1839.

43 Fredrika Bremer, *Morgon-väckter. Några ord i anledning af "Strauss och evangelierne"; Trosbekännelse* [Morning Watches: A Few Words on Strauss and the Gospels. The Confession of Faith of Fredrika Bremer] (Stockholm: L. H. Hjertas förlag, 1842).

44 S. L-D Adlersparre and Sigrid Leijonhufvud, *Fredrika Bremer. Biografisk studie* (Stockholm: Norstedt, 1896), I.

45 Erik Petzäll, *Straussdebatten i Sverige. En kyrkohistorisk undersökning* (Lund: Svenska kyrkans diakonistyrelses bokförlag Stockholm, 1936), 306 ff. See also Gustaf Fredén, *Arvet från Fredrika Bremer* (Malmö: Gleerups förlag Lund, 1951), in particular the chapter on *Morgonväkter*.

46 On Bremer's views on literal interpretation of the Bible, see for example Bremer 1916, letter to F.M. Franzén 3 March 1842, and letter to P.J. Böklin 22 January 1847.

47 Fredrika Bremer, *Tvenne efterlämnade skrifter jämte några bref af Fredrika Bremer utgifna af Anna Hierta-Retzius* (Stockholm: O. E. Fritze's Kongl. Hofbokhandel, 1902), 7, "Några inre erfarenheter". For an international perspective on contemporary educational ideals and the literature available to middle-class women see for example Jane Rendall, *The Origins of Modern Feminism: Women in Britain, France and the United States* (Hampshire/London: The MacMillan Press Ltd, 1993), in particular the chapter "Educating Hearts and Minds".

48 Fredrika Bremer, *Brev. Ny följd, tidigare ej samlade och tryckta brev utgivna av Carina Burman. Del I–II* (Stockholm: Gidlunds förlag, 1996), I; letter to Sophie Bolander 20 November 1844.

49 Bremer 1902, 85 (see also Bremer 1917) letter to Lars Johan Hierta 23 November 1848.

50 Bremer 1996 I, letter to Sophie Bolander 20 November 1844.

51 Ibid.

52 Ibid.

53 Bremer 1996 II, letter to Mathilda Foy 14 October 1858.

54 Ibid.

55 Sten Carlsson, *Fröknar, mamseller, jungfrur och pigor. Ogifta kvinnor i det svenska ståndssamhället* (Uppsala: Stockholm Almqvist and Wicksells förlag, 1977).

56 Bremer 1996 II, letter to Henriette Wulff 31 May 1855.

57 Fredrika Bremer, *Hemmen i den nya verlden. En dagbok i bref, skrifna under tvenne års resor i Norra Amerika och på Cuba I–III* (Stockholm: P. A. Norstedt, 1853–54), published in translation as *Homes of the New World. Impressions of America I–II* (New York: Harper and Brothers, 1854). On criticism of the book, see Sigrid Laurell, *Rosalie Roos. Resa till Amerika 1851–1855. Brev utgivna av Sigrid Laurell* (Uppsala: Almqvist and Wiksell, 1969), 139 and 164 f.

58 Bremer 1996 II, letter to Henriette Wulff 14 December 1855.

59 Bremer 1996 II, letter to Mary Howitt 7 March 1856.

60 Bremer, *Hertha, eller en själs historia. Teckning ur det verkliga lifvet* (Stockholm: Adolf Bonniers förlag, 1856).

61 Quoted in Gunnar Qvist, *Fredrika Bremer och kvinnans emancipation* (Göteborg: Akademiförlaget, 1969), 176.

62 Bremer 1920, letter to Fredrika Limnell 15 December 1865.

63 Bremer 1996 I, letter to P.J. Böklin 1–2 January 1842.

64 Bremer 1920, letter to Fredrika Limnell 24 November 1860.

65 Bremer's negative attitude towards the Old Testament dated back to her youth. See for example Bremer 1916, letters to P.J. Böklin 7 December 1839 and 31 May 1840, and to F.M. Franzén 29 March 1842.

66 Bremer 1916, letters to Malla Silfverstolpe 22 July 1843, Eva Hammarén 30 May 1844, and H.C. Andersen 19 October 1841.

67 See for example Bremer 1917, letters to P.J. Böklin 1 October 1847, 2 November 1847, and 22 August 1861.

68 See for example Bremer 1917, letter to P.J. Böklin 22 January 1847. In Bremer 1920, letter to P.J. Böklin 22 January 1858, she wrote from Rome "all honour to our noble Luther and his work."

69 Margret Howitt, *Ett år hos Fredrika Bremer* (Stockholm: 1867, reprint 1984), 26.

70 See Bremer 1920, letter to P.J. Böklin 22 August 1861.
71 She was therefore convinced of the importance of religious freedom, and considered the United States, Britain, and Switzerland to be models in this respect (Bremer 1920, letter to P.J. Böklin 1 January 1861).
72 Bremer 1917, letter to Martensen 1 June 1853.
73 *Tidskrift för hemmet* (hereafter abbreviated to *TfH*) 1866, 22. See also *Dagny* 1888, 3 f.
74 *TfH* 1866, 333.
75 Laurell 1969, 218. See also Qvist 1969, 150, 170, and 173 ff.
76 Laurell 1969, 218 ff.
77 See for example Howitt 1867, 80 ff.
78 Bremer 1920, letters to P.J. Böklin 22 August 1861 and to Sophie Leijonhufvud 1 December 1862.
79 Leijonhufvud, "Karin Sophie Leijonhufvud-Adlersparre," signed article in *Svenskt Bibliografiskt Lexikon*.
80 Sigrid Leijonhufvud, *Sophie Adlersparre (Esselde). Ett liv och en livsgärning* I (Stockholm: Norstedt, 1922), 73. See Bremer 1996 II, letter to Stanislas Barnekow 25 February 1864, in which Bremer described her as "the pleasant, clever Miss Sophie Leijonhufvud, publisher of the periodical: 'reading in the home'."
81 *TfH* 1865, 227 f.
82 *TfH* 1883, 288 f.
83 Laurell 1969, 150.
84 Kungliga biblioteket Stockholm (hereafter KB) Sophie Adlersparres samling Dagbok I a 7 d: 4 d.
85 For an outline of the periodical's views on the education of women, see *TfH* 1859, 4 ff and 179 ff; *TfH* 1860, 3 ff and 177 ff.; *TfH* 1861, 176 ff.
86 The founder of the high school for girls in the United States where Roos taught for a period had as its motto "Better schooling for girls – better mothers – a better society" (Laurell 1969, 60).
87 Christina Florin and Ulla Johansson, "*Där de härliga lagrarna gro ...*". *Kultur, klass och kön i det svenska läroverket 1850–1914* (Stockholm: Tiden, 1993). See in particular the chapter "Mandom, mod och morske män" where the authors argue that the image of man was constructed to counter that of woman.
88 *TfH* 1864, 6. In 1851 Roos wrote from America to her father that her "desired aim" was to achieve "an independent financial position." (Laurell 1969, 68).
89 *TfH* 1861, 260, f.
90 See *Protokoll hållna hos Högloflige Ridderskapet och Adeln, Högvördiga Preste-Ståndets Protocoll, Protokoll hållna hos Välloflige Borgareståndet och Hedervärda Bonde-Ståndets Protokoll vid Lagtima Riksdagen i Stockholm år 1865–1866.*
91 *TfH* 1866, 35 f.
92 Laurell 1969, 218.
93 *TfH* 1866, 46 ff.; *TfH* 1866, 49.
94 From 1868 *Tidskrift för Hemmet* was dedicated to "Nordic women" (Leijonhufvud 1922, 132 ff.).
95 See for example *TfH* 1875, 321 ff., a thorough review of the English theologian S.A. Brooke's book *Christ in Modern Life*. The passage on p. 333, in which he denounced the "false understanding of femininity" that demanded submission from women at all times, was singled out for special praise. See also *TfH* 1875, 90, where Adlersparre discussed the value of new scientific fields, and how they problematized the generally accepted interpretation of the Creation myth, noting that the latter "is not to be understood literally; or, as we would put it, that it can be understood as literal, but by no means as real."
96 *TfH* 1873, 172.
97 *TfH* 1868, 173 ff.; *TfH* 1869, 174.
98 *TfH* 1869, 39.
99 *TfH* 1868 Tilläggsblad, III ff.
100 *Dagny* 1893, 34.
101 *Dagny* 1893, 33 ff.; *Dagny* 1893, 112.
102 *TfH* 1872, 109.
103 *TfH* 1876, 125 ff.
104 *TfH* 1882, 65 ff.
105 For earlier discussion of morality, see *TfH* 1865, 202 ff, and Supplement, 12 f; *TfH* 1866, 308 ff; *TfH* 1867, 276; and *TfH* 1873, 25.

106 For those areas of women's lives that were bound up with morality, the source material is understandably thin. The lack of explicit statements on the most intimate moments of their private lives poses an almost insurmountable problem for an analysis of the reasons for their engagement in this debate. Diaries and letters give little information, and one is forced to depend on passing comments or even to read between the lines. The risk of stretching the evidence to the point of misinterpretation is considerable. The situation is much the same with memoirs and biographies. It was principally those who felt the need to stress the good in domestic life who described their family circumstances; almost without exception, the published material that describes homes noted for their Christianity shows them in a positive light. To unravel the thought processes that lay behind the feminist pioneers' commitment to moral reform, one must instead consider the public debate that arose towards the end of the nineteenth century. By using a theological perspective and focusing on the Christian views of humankind, I believe it is possible to increase our understanding of the early women's movement. For further discussion of the fear of openness in sexual matters in this period in Sweden see Anna Jansdotter, "På turné för sedligheten. Nathalie Andersson-Meijerhelms resa i södra Sverige våren 1883," in Åsa Bergenheim and Lena Lennerhed (eds.), *Seklernas sex. Bidrag till sexualitetens historia* (Stockholm: Carlssons förlag, 1997), 162 ff.

107 See Ulla Manns, *Den sanna frigörelsen. Fredrika-Bremer-förbundet 1884–1921* (Stockholm/Stehag: Symposium, 1997), in particular the third chapter, "FBF tar form 1884–1895".

108 Many have since succumbed to the temptation of seeing the early feminists' engagement as an expression of conventional views and (or) sexual frustration. Few have seen it as a revolt against women's subordinate position in society. For the view that Bremer was a victim of sexual frustration, see Åsa Arping, "Att mäta kvinnligheten. Fredrika Bremer och den sexualiserade litteraturbeskrivningen," *Tidskrift för litteraturvetenskap* 3–4 (1996). International research has had greater success in analysing the pioneer's commitment to moral reform. See for example Susan Mendus and Jane Rendall, *Sexuality and Subordination. Interdisciplinary Studies of Gender in the Nineteenth Century* (London: Routledge, 1989), 1 ff. and 89 ff.; and Sheila Jeffreys, *The Spinster and her Enemies. Feminism and Sexuality 1880–1930* (London: Pandora, 1985), 1 ff. and 86 ff. For Nordic research, see in particular Gro Hagemann, "Seksualmoral og samfunnsmoral. Konkurrerende diskurser i sedelighetsdebatten," in Tarald Rasmussen and Trygve Wyller (eds.), *Kristelig og borgerlig offentlighet i Norge* (Oslo: Norges forskningsråd, 1996). On the relationship between religion and sexuality see for example John Maynard, *Victorian Discourses on Sexuality and Religion* (Cambridge: University Press, 1993), particularly the chapter "Sexual Christianity: Charles Kingsley's Via Media."

109 For an account of the role the morality debate played in the background to Strindberg's early plays see Ulf Boïthius, *Strindberg och kvinnofrågan till och med Giftas 1* (Stockholm: Prisma, 1969), especially the section "Sedlighetsfrågan".

110 *TfH* 1884, 337.

111 *TfH* 1885, 70.

112 *Dagny* 1886, 250.

113 Ulla Manns, "Kultur och kön. Fredrika-Bremer-förbundet i sedlighetsdebatten," in Marianne Liljeström, Pirjo Markkola and Sari Mäenpää (eds.), *Kvinnohistoriens nya utmaningar: Från sexualitet till världshistoria* (Tampere: 1994).

114 During the 1870s, Ellen Key had written in *Tidskrift för hemmet*, arguing strenuously against the cultural decadence that less scrupulous writers expressed. In her eyes, it had a devastating effect, and she was extremely critical of those who welcomed the new spirit of the age. For Key, by far the worst was when writers took it on themselves to make light of virtue and morality, and the fact that such perverted opinions could make any headway proved that there was a general falling off in religious standards (*TfH* 1875, 121).

115 Ulf Wittrock, *Ellen Keys väg från kristendom till livstro* (Uppsala: Appelbergs, 1953), 205; *Dagny* 1887, 21 f. Key did not disguise her sympathy for several of the writers whom Adlersparre disliked, nor could she accept the periodical's reverent enthusiasm for David af Wirsén (KB Sophie Adlersparres samling I a 7 a: 2 Ellen Key to Sophie Adlersparre 11 May 1882, 4 July 1882, 10 July 1883, and 6 December 1885; ibid., I a 7 a: 4 Sophie Adlersparre to Thérèse Gyldén 7 February 1887).

116 *Dagny* 1887, 20. Strindberg, "naturalism's standard-bearer" as Sophie Adlersparre called him, had gone "as far back as Rousseau, whose theories are preached as a kind of gospel of the flesh, with particular application to adolescence."

117 For Key's religious development, see Wittrock 1953, and in particular the section "Den antikristna omvändelsen"; on her views on women, see Ronny Ambjörnsson, *Samhällsmodern. Ellen Keys kvinnouppfattning till och med 1896* (Göteborg: 1974); Ronny Ambjörnsson, "Förord," in Ellen Key, *Hemmets århundrade. Urval och inledning av Ronny Ambjörnsson* (Stockholm: Aldus, 1976); and Ronny Ambjörnsson, "'Qvinnofrågan.' Familj, individ och samhälle," in *Familjeporträtt. Essäer om familjen, kvinnan, barnet och kärleken i historien* (Stockholm: Gidlund, 1978); see also Ulla Manns, "Kvinnofrigörelse och moderskap. En diskussion mellan Fredrika-Bremerförbundet och Ellen Key," in Ulla Wikander (ed.), *Det evigt kvinnliga. En historia om förändring* (Stockholm: Tiden, 1994). On Key and Spencer see Inga Sanner, *Att älska sin nästa såsom sig själv. Om moraliska utopier under 1800-talet* (Stockholm: Carlssons förlag, 1995), 125 ff.

118 See Ellen Key, *"Missbrukad kvinnokraft" och "Naturenliga arbetsområden för kvinnan". Tvenne föredrag* (Stockholm: 1896).

119 For a critique of the term "secularization" in the context of twentieth-century ideological change, see Harvey Cox, "The Myth of the Twentieth Century. The Rise and Fall of 'Secularization'," in Gregory Baum (ed.), *The Twentieth Century. A Theological Overview* (Maryknoll, New York: Orbis Books, 1999).

120 Qvist 1960. See also Gunnar Qvist, "Policy towards Women and the Women's Struggle in Sweden," *Scandinavian Journal of History* 5 (1980), 54 f, 62, and 65 f. Cf. Ida Blom, "The Struggle for Women's Suffrage in Norway, 1885–1913," *Scandinavian Journal of History* 5 (1980).

121 Qvist 1960, 48; Qvist 1969, 273; Gunnar Qvist, *Konsten att blifva en god flicka. Kvinnohistoriska uppsatser* (Stockholm: Liber förlag, 1978), 15 and 32. See also Eva Åsbrink, *Genom portar II. Studier i den svenska kyrkans syn på kvinnans ställning i samhället åren 1809–1866* (Uppsala: Almqvist and Wicksell, 1962).

122 Inger Hammar, "Några reflexioner kring 'religionsblind' kvinnoforskning," *Historisk tidskrift* no 1 (1998); Inger Hammar, *Emancipation och religion. Den svenska kvinnorörelsens pionjärer i debatt om kvinnans kallelse ca 1860–1900* (Stockholm: Carlssons förlag, 1999), 32 ff. For further discussion, see Ulla Manns, "Den religionsblinda kvinnorörelseforskningen – en kommentar till Inger Hammars kritik," *Historisk tidskrift* no 2 (1998), 197 f; and Hanne Rimmen Nielsen, "Religionsblindhed. En debat i svensk og nordisk kvindehistorie," *Den jyske historiker* (December 1998).

8 Indian Christian women and indigenous feminism, *c*.1850–*c*.1920 (Padma Anagol)

I owe an enormous debt to the staff of Mukti Mission, especially Ms Johnstone, who made valuable primary source material on Indian Christian women available to me, especially the Annual Reports of the American Ramabai Association, without which this chapter could not have been written. I have also benefited from the comments of participants at the Annual Conference of the British Association of South Asian Studies, 1992, where it was presented. I would like to thank Patrick McGinn, Geraldine Forbes and Jeffrey Cox, who took the trouble of reading early versions of this chapter and whose detailed criticisms helped me greatly to revise it.

1 For a broad historiographical survey see B. Ramusack, 'From symbol to diversity: the historical literature on women in India', *South Asia Research*, 2 (1990), pp. 139–57, and A. Basu, 'Women's history in India: a historiographical survey', in K. Offen *et al.* (eds), *Writing Women's History: International Perspectives* (Basingstoke, Macmillan, 1991), pp. 181–210.

2 See for example the collection of essays in K. Sangari and S. Vaid (eds), *Recasting Women: Essays in Colonial History* (New Delhi, Kali for Women, 1989), and J. Krishnamurthy (ed.), *Women in Colonial India: Essays on Survival, Work and the State* (New Delhi, Oxford University Press, 1989).

3 M. Sinha, *Colonial Masculinity: The 'Manly Englishman' and the 'Effeminate Bengali' in the Late Nineteenth Century* (Manchester, Manchester University Press, 1996).

4 The task of recovering women's voices has begun through the translations of autobiographies and through emphasis on lesser-known women who have written unique texts questioning gender relations. For a sample see S. Mazumdar, *Memoirs of an Indian Woman*, ed. G. Forbes

Armonk, Sharpe, 1989); T. Shinde, *For the Honour of my Sister Countrywomen: Tarabai Shinde, the Critique of Gender Relations in India*, ed. R. O'Hanlon (New Delhi, Oxford University Press, 1995); and the anthologies edited by S. Tharu and K. Lalitha, *Women Writing in India, 600 B.C. to the Present*, Vols I and II (New York, Feminist Press, 1991).

5 See for example C. Heimsath, *Indian Nationalism and Hindu Social Reform* (Princeton, Princeton University Press, 1964), and David Kopf, *British Orientalism and the Bengal Renaissance: The Dynamics of Indian Modernization* (Berkeley, University of California Press, 1969).

6 Until recently the focus has been on Bengal and representative works are: M. Borthwick, *The Changing Role of Women in Bengal, 1848–1905* (Princeton, Princeton University Press, 1984), and G. Murshid, *Reluctant Debutante: Response of Bengali Women to Modernisation* (Rajshahi, Sahitya Sansad, 1983).

7 Sample studies in a growing field are: L. Mani, 'Contentious traditions: the debate on *sati* in colonial India', in Sangari and Vaid (eds), *Recasting Women*, pp. 88–126; P. Chatterjee, 'Colonialism, nationalism and colonialised women: the contest in India', *American Ethnologist*, 17:1 (1989), pp. 622–33.

8 One of the more extreme positions is that of Gayatri Spivak, who has argued that the subaltern woman cannot speak and cannot be heard: 'Can the subaltern speak?', in C. Nelson and L. Grossberg (eds), *Marxism and the Interpretation of Culture* (Urbana and Chicago, University of Illinois Press, 1988), pp. 271–313; and 'The Rani of Sirmur: an essay in reading the archive', *History and Theory*, 24 (1985), pp. 247–72.

9 The historiography on the subject of *sati* provides a good example of the process by which female agency has been reduced to simplistic notions of volition. For a recent critique on the literature see A. Loomba, 'Dead women tell no tales: issues of female subjectivity, subaltern agency and tradition in colonial and post-colonial writings on widow immolation in India', *History Workshop Journal*, 36 (1993), pp. 209–27.

10 For a conception of agency as resistance see the essays in the collection by D. Haynes and G. Prakash (eds), *Contesting Power: Resistance and Everyday Social Relations in South Asia* (Berkeley, University of California Press, 1991).

11 The complexities of an emergent feminist consciousness of Maharashtrian women between 1850 and 1920 is studied in greater detail in my monograph, *The Emergence of Feminism in India, 1850–1920* (Aldershot and Burlington, Ashgate, 2006).

12 J. Cox has pointed out that South Asian Christians are victims of the critiques of imperialism/colonialism, wherein missionaries are portrayed as imperialists, reducing Indian Christians to 'collaborators' and Pakistani Christians to 'heretics': 'Audience and exclusion at the margins of Imperial History', *Women's History Review*, 3:4 (1994), pp. 501–14.

13 S. Satthianadhan, *Sketches of Indian Christians Collected from Different Sources* (London, Christian Literature Society for India, 1896), pp. 188–9.

14 J. Richter, *A History of Missions in India* (Edinburgh, 1908), p. 329.

15 N. Cott, *The Bonds of Womanhood: 'Woman's Sphere' in New England, 1780–1835* (New Haven, 1977), especially chapter 4.

16 G. Forbes, 'In search of the "Pure Heathen": missionary women in nineteenth century India', *Economic and Political Weekly*, 21:17 (1986), pp. 2–9; A. Burton, '"The White Woman's Burden": British feminists and Indian women, 1865–1915', *Women Studies International Forum*, 13:4 (1990), pp. 295–308; and B. Ramusack, 'Cultural missionaries, maternal imperialists, feminist allies: British women activists in India, 1865–1945', ibid., pp. 309–21.

17 Richter, *A History of Missions*, p. 342.

18 It was only after his conversion that Baba Padmanji wrote a novel, *Yamuna Paryatan* (Yamuna's Rambles) (Marathi) (Bombay, 1937), in which he highlighted the problems of Hindu widows through the trials of the heroine Yamuna.

19 For a sample of this literature see B. H. Khare, *How is Woman Treated by Man and Religion?* (Bombay, 1895); B. R. Row, *Women's Right to Salvation* (Madras, 1887).

20 B. Padmanji, *Once Hindu, Now Christian: The Early Life of Baba Padmanji, an Autobiography*, trans. J. Murray Mitchell (London, 1890), p. 71.

21 Nilakantha Goreh for example was a Brahmin priest who had begun by refuting Christian doctrines and ended as a staunch Christian. See his *A Rational Refutation of the Hindu Philosophical Systems*, trans. Fitz-Edward Hall (Calcutta, 1862).

22 Keeping in mind that nineteenth-century Christianity in colonies embodied certain aspects of cultural imperialism, I use the term 'Christianity' in a qualified sense, i.e., representations of Christianity.

23 H. S. Dyer's Preface in S. Powar, *Hinduism and Womanhood* (London, n.d.), p. 6.

24 Padmanji, *Once Hindu*, p. 136.

25 Anandibai's letter to the Head of the Mission School in Bombay reveals the turmoil caused by the major changes in her life and her unhappiness and fear of having displeased her patron, Mrs Mitchell, a prominent missionary. See her undated letter in A. B. Shah (ed.), *The Letters and Correspondence of Pandita Ramabai* (Bombay, 1977), pp. 11–14.

26 Anandibai's case is similar to the traumatic experiences of Lily Moya recounted in S. Marks (ed.), *'Not Either an Experimental Doll': The Separate Worlds of Three South African Women* (London, The Women's Press, 1987).

27 Scholarship on Pandita Ramabai has expanded considerably in recent years. However, many scholars still consider her coming to consciousness within a religious framework. For example, A. B. Shah labels her a 'rebel in religion' in 'Pandita Ramabai: a rebel in religion', in A. B. Shah (ed.), *Religion and Society in India* (Bombay, Somaiya, 1981), pp. 196–224; Ram Bapat calls her a 'religious revolutionary' but 'certainly not a feminist': see 'Pandita Ramabai: faith and reason in the shadow of the East and West', in V. Dalmia and H. V. Stietencron (eds), *Representing Hinduism: The Construction of Religious Traditions and National Identity* (New Delhi, Sage, 1995), pp. 224–52; and Leslie Flemming argues that both Pandita Ramabai and Krupabai 'found their primary identities in religious communities': see her article, 'Between two worlds: self-construction and self-identity in the writings of three nineteenth century Indian Christian women', in N. Kumar (ed.), *Women as Subjects: South Asian Histories* (New Delhi, Stree, 1994), pp. 108–24. The variety and richness of her writings are accessible in the English language, see S. M. Adhav, *Pandita Ramabai* (Madras, Christian Literature Society, 1979), and A. B. Shah (ed.), *The Letters and Correspondence of Pandita Ramabai* (Bombay, Maharashtra State Board Publications, 1977).

28 P. Ramabai, 'Account of the life of a Hindoo woman', *Cheltenham Ladies College Magazine*, 12 (Autumn 1885), p. 143, Institutional Collection of Mukti Mission (hereafter ICMM).

29 In a personal communication Saraswathi Bhat informed me that this book is given as a gift to female children in South Karnatak Christian families to this day on their attaining the skills to read and write. I would like to thank Meena Siddharth for introducing me to the Christian community of S. Karnatak.

30 P. Ramabai, *A Testimony* ([1907] Kedgaon, 6th edn, 1964), p. 8.

31 P. Ramabai, *A Short History of the Kripa Sadan, or Home of Mercy* ([1908] Kedgaon, 1964), p. 2.

32 Ibid., pp. 2–3.

33 Ramabai, *A Testimony*, p. 13.

34 Recollections of Shewatbai, Mistress of Epiphany School, Poona, on her mother's conversion, *Magazine of Panch Howd*, St Mary Convent (Poona, 1892), n.p. (ICMM).

35 Powar, *Hinduism and Womanhood*. An earlier version of this book was published by her, probably in the 1890s, under the title *The Bitter Fruits of Hinduism* (details unknown).

36 Ibid., p. 31.

37 Ibid., p. 18.

38 Krupabai develops these themes in four consecutive essays: 'Women's influence at home', 'Home training of children', 'Female education' and 'Hindu social customs', in *Miscellaneous Writings of Krupabai Satthianadhan* (Madras, Srinivas Varadachari and Co., 1896), pp. 1–33.

39 Krupabai, 'Female education', p. 18.

40 Ibid., p. 19.

41 This view is echoed by a great number of Hindus whether revivalists or reformers. Vernacular literature and contemporary press writings are replete with this viewpoint.

42 Krupabai, *Miscellaneous Writings*, p. 21.

43 K. Satthianadhan, *Kamala: A Story of a Hindu Life* (Madras, 1895), p. 207.

44 Ibid., p. 57.

45 Ibid., p. 57.

46 Ibid., p. 58.

47 This is a semi-autobiographical novel and Krupabai can be seen clearly in the role of Saguna here: K. Satthianadhan, *Saguna: A Story of Native Christian Life* (Madras, 1895).

48 Ibid., p. 166.

49 A huge controversy broke out in Maharashtra among Hindus over the issue of conversions in Pandita's school. Most of the turmoil took the form of rumours and allegations regarding her supposedly pernicious influence over students. The vernacular press active in denouncing her was

chiefly led by B. G. Tilak, a prominent Hindu conservative who turned the Age of Consent debate from a feminist to a nationalist one. Pandita was accused of dishonesty and even received death-threats from orthodox Hindus.

50 It is therefore hardly possible to see any direct coercion by her of her students. Disturbed by the furore caused over the conversions, the American Ramabai Association sent their President Mrs Andrews to investigate the matter in 1893. After a fact-finding tour lasting six months, she submitted an extensive report describing the allegations against Ramabai as 'baseless fabrications'. Ramabai, however, conceded to Mrs Andrews that she may have had indirect influence over her students through her lifestyle. *Annual Report of the American Ramabai Association*, 11 March 1894, pp. 16–19 (ICMM).

51 The guardians of students were also requested to send their opinions. D. K. Karve, an important Hindu male social reformer who married Ramabai's first pupil, reported that in her four-year training at the school his wife had never been coaxed or cajoled into embracing Christianity and had remained a Hindu. See his letter to Mrs Andrews dated 2 Feb. 1894, *Annual Report*, 1894, pp. 27–9.

52 Explanations offered in popular Hinduism in order to comfort and provide a rationale for regarding the austere life ahead of them.

53 In 1893 when Nurmadabai was removed from Sharada Sadan she refused to go to any other school and after two years, seeing her conviction and obstinacy, her parents allowed her to go back to Ramabai's school. From Nurmadabai's Address at the Annual Meeting of the American Ramabai Association, *Annual Report*, 1903, pp. 40–2.

54 Ramabai, 'Account of the life of a Hindoo woman', p. 146.

55 *Mukti Prayer Bell* (Magazine of Mukti Mission), Dec. 1904 and Oct. 1905 (ICMM).

56 'The story of Jivi and others', typed manuscript, n.p. (ICMM).

57 P. Ramabai to Dr Donald, President of American Ramabai Association, 13 Sept. 1902 (ICMM).

58 K. Storrie, *Soonderbai Powar: A Noble Worker for Indian Womanhood* (London, n.d.), pp. 6–7.

59 A. Hastings, in his work on the ambiguities of the impact of missions on African women, notes a similar trend: 'Were women a special case?', in F. Bowie, S. Ardener and D. Kirkwood (eds), *Women and Missions: Past and Present* (Oxford, Berg, 1993), pp. 109–24.

60 N. Goreh, *Four Lectures Delivered in Substance to the Brahmos in Bombay and Poona* (Bombay, 1875), pp. 1–11.

61 S. M. Adhav, 'Pandita Ramabai', paper read at Church History Association of India, Western India Branch, 12 March 1978, p. 1 (ICMM).

62 P. Ramabai to Sister Geraldine, 12 May 1885, in Shah (ed.), *Letters and Correspondence of Pandita Ramabai*, p. 59.

63 Storrie, *Soonderbai Powar*, p. 45.

64 For further elaboration of Christian women's critiques of the Indian past, see my book, *The Emergence of Feminism in India, 1850–1920*.

65 K. Satthianadhan, 'Female education', *Miscellaneous Writings*, pp. 16–17; P. Ramabai, Stri-Dharma Niti: *Prescribed Laws and Duties on the Proper Conduct of Women* ([1882] Kedgaon, 33rd edn, 1967), pp. 40–5.

66 P. Ramabai to Rev. Dr Pentecost, 6 Dec. 1892, in *Pandita Ramabaicha Chikat Pustak* (Notebook of Pandita Ramabai) (Marathi, Rajas Dongre Collection).

67 Satthianadhan, *Saguna*, p. 108.

68 C. Sorabji, 'Social relations', *Pan-Anglican Papers*, pp. 1–4 (ICMM).

69 Satthianadhan, *Saguna*, pp. 132–40.

70 P. Ramabai, 'Indian religion', *Cheltenham Ladies College Magazine*, 13 (Spring 1886), pp. 106–18 (ICMM).

71 Ibid., p. 107.

72 Lakshmibai notes how in dress, Indian Christian women rejected the trailing gowns and skirts of Western women and instead wore a modified version of the Indian sari and a blouse. It differed from Maharashtrian Hindu women's dress in that the sari was not divided and drawn between the legs and tucked at the back but fell loosely like the pleats of a skirt and the blouse was modified to the extent of having wristlength sleeves. They also wore no ornaments except two bangles on each wrist. L. Tillak, *I Follow After: An Autobiography*, trans. J. Inkster (London, Oxford University Press, 1950), p. 168.

73 'Notes to a would-be worker abroad', *Manoramabai's Papers* (ICMM).

74 P. Ramabai's letter, 25 July 1889, *Dnyanodaya* (Marathi).

9 Settler anxieties, indigenous peoples, and women's suffrage in the colonies of Australia, New Zealand, and Hawai'i, 1888–1902 (Patricia Grimshaw)

1 Jessie Ackermann, *The World Through a Woman's Eyes* (Chicago, 1896).

2 Ibid., 19.

3 Ibid., 22.

4 Ian Tyrrell, *Woman's World, Woman's Empire: The Woman's Christian Temperance Union in International Perspective* (Chapel Hill, N.C., 1991).

5 See Janet Zollinger Giele, *Two Paths to Women's Equality: Temperance, Suffrage, and the Origins of Modern Feminism* (New York, 1995); Ruth Bordin, *Frances Willard: A Biography* (Chapel Hill, N.C., 1986); Suzanne M. Marilley, *Woman Suffrage and the Origins of Liberal Feminism in the United States, 1820–1920* (Cambridge, Mass., 1996).

6 For general histories, see Stuart Macintyre, *A Concise History of Australia* (Melbourne, 1999); James Belich, *Making Peoples: A History of the New Zealanders* (Auckland, 1996); Gavan Daws, *Shoal of Time: A History of the Hawaiian Islands* (Honolulu, 1968).

7 See Peggy Pascoe, *Relations of Rescue: The Search for Female Moral Authority in the American West, 1874–1939* (New York, 1990).

8 See Marjorie Spruill Wheeler, ed., *One Woman, One Vote: Rediscovering the Woman Suffrage Movement* (Troutdale, Ore., 1995).

9 For histories of the women's movement in these places, see Audrey Oldfield, *Woman Suffrage in Australia: A Gift or a Struggle?* (Melbourne, 1992): Marilyn Lake, *Getting Equal: The History of Australian Feminism* (Sydney, 1999); Patricia Grimshaw, *Women's Suffrage in New Zealand* (Auckland, 1987).

10 Judith R. Gething, "Christianity and Coverture: Impact on the Legal Status of Women in Hawaii, 1820–1920," *Hawaiian Journal of History*, 11 (1997), 188–220.

11 For histories of colonialism, see Belich, *Making Peoples*; Patrick Wolfe, *Settler Colonialism and the Transformation of Anthropology: The Politics and Poetics of an Ethnographic Event* (London, 1999).

12 See Beverley Kingston, *The Oxford History of Australia, 1860–1990: Glad Confident Morning* (Melbourne, 1988); Keith Sinclair, *A History of New Zealand* (Harmondsworth, Eng., 1980).

13 Stuart Macintyre, *Winners and Losers: The Pursuit of Social Justice in Australian History* (Sydney, 1985).

14 See Caroline Daley and Melanie Nolan, eds., *Suffrage and Beyond: International Feminist Perspectives* (Auckland, 1994).

15 See Lake, *Getting Equal;* Judith Allen, *Rose Scott: Vision and Revision in Feminism* (Melbourne, 1994); Susan Margarey, *Unbridling the Tongues of Women: A Biography of Catherine Helen Spence* (Sydney, 1985).

16 Grimshaw, *Women's Suffrage in New Zealand*; Patricia Grimshaw, "Women's Suffrage in New Zealand Revisited: Writing from the Margins," in Daley and Nolan, eds., *Suffrage and Beyond*, 25–41.

17 Oldfield, *Woman Suffrage in Australia*, 17–58.

18 Patricia Grimshaw, "A White Woman's Suffrage," in Helen Irving, ed., *A Woman's Constitution? Gender and History in the Australian Commonwealth* (Sydney, 1996), 77–97.

19 Oldfield, *Woman Suffrage in Australia*, 17–58.

20 Patricia Grimshaw, Marilyn Lake, Ann McGrath, and Marian Quartly, *Creating a Nation* (Melbourne, 1994), 192. See also Stuart Macintyre, ed., *"And Be One People": Alfred Deakin's Federal Story* (Melbourne, 1995).

21 *Western Australian Parliamentary Debates, 1898*, 12 (1898), 1200.

22 See Pat Stretton and Christine Finnimore, "Black Fellow Citizens: Aborigines and the Commonwealth Franchise," *Australian Historical Studies*, 25 (1993), 521–535. The amazing point is that, while Australians were excluding their own indigenous people, they were prepared to let New Zealand Maori who were resident in Australia vote. Australia still hoped that New Zealand would join their federation; hence they did not want to alienate Maori.

23 *New Zealand Parliamentary Debates, 1854 and 1855* (Wellington, 1885), 13.

24 *New Zealand Parliamentary Debates, Second Session of the Fourth Parliament, 1867* (Wellington, 1885), 336.

25 See Alan Ward, *A Show of Justice: Racial "Amalgamation" in Nineteenth Century New Zealand* (Auckland, 1995); Keith Sinclair, *Kinds of Peace: Maori People After the Maori Wars, 1870–1885*

(Auckland, 1987); Claudia Orange, *The Treaty of Waitangi* (Wellington, 1987); W. K. Jackson and G. A. Wood, "The New Zealand Parliament and Maori Representation," *Historical Studies: Australia and New Zealand*, 2 (Oct. 1964), 26.

26 *Auckland Star*, Aug. 9, 1893, p. 2.

27 See Henry Reynolds, *Frontier: Aborigines Settlers and Land* (Sydney, 1987); and Reynolds, *Fate of a Free People* (Melbourne, 1995).

28 Patricia Grimshaw and Katherine Ellinghaus, "White Women, Aboriginal Women and the Vote in Western Australia," *Studies in Western Australian History*, 19 (1999), 1–19.

29 Grimshaw, "A White Woman's Suffrage." See also Helen Irving, *To Constitute a Nation: A Cultural History of Australia's Constitution* (Melbourne, 1997).

30 *Commonwealth Parliamentary Debates*, 1902, sections 111580–111581.

31 See John Chesterman and Brian Galligan, *Citizens Without Rights: Aborigines and Australian Citizenship* (Cambridge, Eng., 1998); Russell McGregor, *Imagined Destinies: Aboriginal Australians and the Doomed Race Theory, 1880–1939* (Melbourne, 1997).

32 WCTU of Australia, *Minutes of the Second Triennial Convention* (Sydney, 1894), 36. See also Patricia Grimshaw, "Gender, Citizenship and Race in the Woman's Christian Temperance Union of Australia, 1890 to the 1930s," *Australian Feminist Studies*, 13 (1998), 199–214.

33 Ackermann, *The World Through a Woman's Eyes*, dedication page.

34 Ibid., 76.

35 Ibid., 77.

36 Jessie Ackermann, *Australia From a Woman's Point of View* (London, 1913), photo insert between pages 120 and 121.

37 Ackermann, *The World Through a Woman's Eyes*, 92–98.

38 Ibid., 51.

39 See Patricia Grimshaw, *Paths of Duty: American Missionary Wives in Nineteenth Century Hawai'i* (Honolulu, 1989).

40 Ackermann, *The World Through a Woman's Eyes*, 55.

41 Ibid., 59.

42 See Daws, *Shoal of Time*; Ralph S. Kuykendall, *The Hawaiian Kingdom, 1874–1893: The Kalākaua Dynasty* (Honolulu, 1967).

43 Ackermann, *The World Through a Woman's Eyes*, 59.

44 See Barbara B. Peterson, ed., *Notable Women of Hawaii* (Honolulu, 1984); Hawaiian Mission Children's Society, *Missionary Album: Portraits and Biographical Sketches of the American Protestant Missionaries to the Hawaiian Islands* (Honolulu, 1984); J. Linnekin, *Sacred Queens and Women of Consequence* (Ann Arbor, Mich., 1990).

45 WCTU of the Hawaiian Islands, *Third Annual Report 1888* (Honolulu, 1888), 8–9

46 *The Friend*, Feb. 1893, p. 9.

47 Emma Smith Dillingham to (cousins) Samuel and Emily, Feb. 21, 1895, Hawaiian Mission Children's Society Library, Honolulu.

48 Noenoe K. Silva, "Ku'e! Hawaiian Women's Resistance to the Annexation," in *Women in Hawaii Sites, Identities and Voices*, special issue of *Social Process in Hawaii*, 38 (1997), 4–5.

49 WCTU of the Hawaiian Islands, *Tenth Annual Report 1894* (Honolulu, 1894), 9–10.

50 Mary Whitney, Scrapbook, 1894–1898, newspaper clipping, June 21 [1894], Hawaiian Mission Children's Society Library, Honolulu.

51 WCTU of the Hawaiian Islands, *Tenth Annual Report 1894*, 10.

52 Quoted in Gething, "Christianity and Coverture," 213.

53 Ibid., 197.

10 Challenging traditions (Jacqueline R. de Vries)

1 See, for example, Sandra Gilbert, "Soldier's Heart: Literary Men, Literary Women, and the Great War," in Margaret Higonnet et al., eds., *Behind the Lines: Gender and the Two World Wars* (New Haven, 1989); Susan Kingsley Kent, *Making Peace: The Reconstruction of Gender in Interwar Britain* (Princeton, 1993); and Susan Pedersen, "Gender, Welfare, and Citizenship in Britain during the Great War," *American Historical Review* 95, no. 4 (1990): 983–1006.

2 A succinct statement of Kent's argument can be found in her article, "The Politics of Sexual Difference: World War I and the Demise of British Feminism," *Journal of British Studies* 27 (July

1988): 232–53. For a sharp critique of Kent's work, see Jo Vellacott's review of *Making Peace* in *The American Historical Review* 100, no. 3 (June 1995): 903–4.

3 See in particular Seth Koven and Sonya Michel, eds., *Mothers of a New World: Maternalist Politics and the Origins of Welfare States* (London and New York, 1993), who argue that maternalist rhetoric and politics did not originate during the war.

4 Sheila Fletcher, *A. Maude Royden: A Life* (Oxford, 1989).

5 For an introduction to these ideas, see Linda Colley, *Britons* (New Haven, 1993); David Hempton, *Religion and Political Culture in Britain and Ireland* (Cambridge, 1996); Keith Robbins, *History, Religion and Identity in Modern Britain* (London and Rio Grande, 1993); and John Wolffe, *God and Greater Britain: Religion and National Life in Great Britain and Ireland, 1843–1945* (London, 1994).

6 Hempton, *Religion and Political Culture*, 147.

7 D. G. Paz, *Anti-Catholicism in Mid-Victorian England* (Stanford, 1992).

8 Hempton, *Religion and Political Culture*, 150.

9 Leonore Davidoff and Catherine Hall, *Family Fortunes: Men and Women of the English Middle Class, 1780–1850* (London, 1987), 111.

10 See, for example, Barbara Caine, *Victorian Feminists* (Oxford, 1992); Philippa Levine, *Feminist Lives in Victorian England: Private Roles and Public Commitment* (Oxford, 1990), 31. Josephine Butler is the most prominent example.

11 Diana Burfield, "Theosophy and Feminism: Some Explorations in Nineteenth-Century Biography," in Pat Holden, ed., *Women's Religious Experience* (London, 1983), 27–55; Alex Owen, *The Darkened Room: Women, Power and Spiritualism in Late Victorian England* (Philadelphia, 1990).

12 Jill Liddington and Jill Norris, *One Hand Tied Behind Us: The Rise of the Women's Suffrage Movement* (London, 1978).

13 Andrew Rosen, *Rise Up, Women! The Militant Campaign of the Women's Social and Political Union, 1903–1914* (London, 1974), 199–200; Martha Vicinus, "Male Space and Women's Bodies: The Suffragette Movement," in idem, *Independent Women: Work and Community for Single Women* (Chicago, 1985). For the rather different gender ideals among England's immigrant Jewish population, for example, see Rickie Burman, "'She Looketh Well to the Ways of Her Household': The Changing Role of Jewish Women in Religious Life, c.1880–1930," in Gail Malmgreen, ed., *Religion in the Lives of English Women, 1760–1930* (London, 1986).

14 Jacqueline R. de Vries, "'A New Heaven and Earth': Feminism, Religion and the Politics of Identity in England, 1890–1925" (Ph.D. diss., University of Illinois at Urbana, 1996), esp. chap. 3. The term "suffragist" is commonly used to describe nonmilitant suffrage campaigners, while "suffragette" is reserved for those who used militant methods or belonged to a suffrage society that advocated them.

15 Steven C. Hause, with Anne R. Kenney, *Women's Suffrage and Social Politics in the French Third Republic* (Princeton, 1984); see also Ursula Baumann, "Religion, Emancipation, and Politics in the Confessional Women's Movement in Germany, 1900–1933," in Billie Melman, ed., *Borderlines: Genders and Identities in War and Peace, 1870–1930* (London, 1998), 285–306.

16 *Church League for Women's Suffrage Fifth Annual Report* (Mar. 1915), i. Little has been written about the CLWS. The most comprehensive account can be found in Brian Heeney, *The Women's Movement in the Church of England, 1850–1930* (Oxford, 1988).

17 Edward Norman, *The Victorian Christian Socialists* (Cambridge, 1987).

18 As quoted by Claude Hinscliff in "The Story of the CLWS," *Church League for Women's Suffrage*, Oct. 1913, 299–300.

19 Louise Creighton, *Memoir of a Victorian Woman: Reflections of Louise Creighton, 1850–1936*, ed. James Thayne Covert (Bloomington, 1994), 145–46.

20 The most complete list of clerical CLWS members can be found in the CLWS *Fourth Annual Report* for 1913, 45–53.

21 See Brian Harrison, *Separate Spheres: The Opposition to Women's Suffrage in Britain* (London, 1978).

22 See, in particular, Randall T. Davidson's letter to Agnus Gardiner, 1 Mar. 1907, Papers of Randall T. Davidson, Lambeth Palace.

23 Suffragist Churchwoman's Protest Committee flier, Arncliffe-Sennett Collection, Volume 21, British Library.

24 Alice M. Kidd, letter to the *CLWS*, Dec. 1912, 133; Alice M. Kidd, letter to Archbishop Randall Davidson, 25 Mar. 1912, Papers of Randall T. Davidson, Lambeth Palace.

25 Edward Norman, *The English Catholic Church in the Nineteenth Century* (Oxford, 1984); Owen Chadwick, *The Victorian Church, Part II*, 2nd ed. (London, 1972), 411–22.

26 Chadwick, *The Victorian Church, Part II*, 401ff; Norman, *The English Catholic Church*, 16ff. Between 1851 and 1911, the Catholic population in England and Wales had grown from approximately 900,000 to 1,710,000. Robert Currie, Alan Gilbert, and Lee Horsley, *Churches and Churchgoers: Patterns of Church Growth in the British Isles since 1700* (Oxford, 1977), 153–54.

27 The one scholarly account of the CWSS is Francis M. Mason's "The Newer Eve: The Catholic Women's Suffrage Society in England, 1911–1923," *The Catholic Historical Review* 72, no. 4 (Oct. 1986): 620–38. Two other, rather anecdotal accounts of the CWSS are Leonora de Alberti, "A History of the Catholic Women's Suffrage Society," *Catholic Citizen*, 15 Oct. 1928, 77; and Nancy Stewart Parnell, *A Venture in Faith* (London, n.d.).

28 Parnell, *Venture in Faith*, 6. In late 1913 the CWSS had attracted about one thousand members, representing thirteen branches across England and Scotland.

29 "Why do we want a Catholic Suffrage Society?" (CWSS pamphlet, n.d., Fawcett Library, London).

30 Parnell, *Venture in Faith*, 5.

31 Day's sermons were widely publicized in both the Catholic and secular press. See, for example, *The Tablet*, 26 Oct. 1912 and 2 Nov. 1912. Day uses the term "race" to denote nationality.

32 For the conservative Catholic response to Abadam's speeches, see "The Abadamites," *Universe*, Dec. 20, 1912.

33 Blanche Smyth-Piggot to M. A. R. Tuker, 30 Dec. 1912, M. A. R. Tuker Papers, Fawcett Library, London.

34 Alan Wilkinson, *The Church of England and the First World War* (London, 1978); Alan Marrin, *The Last Crusade: The Church of England and the First World War* (Durham, NC, 1974).

35 J. M. Winter, "Spiritualism and the First World War," in R. W. Davis and R. J. Helmstadter, eds., *Religion and Irreligion in Victorian Society: Essays in Honor of R. K. Webb* (London, 1992), 185–200.

36 Wilkinson, *Church of England*, 131.

37 In March of 1918, after the all-out German offensive, the clergy exemption was abolished; but six days later the Government reversed this decision. Ibid., 39–40.

38 Ibid., 72.

39 These statements can be found in *National Mission Paper No. 11: Women and the National Mission* (London, 1916).

40 For one account of the haphazard decision-making process, see Fletcher, *A Maude Royden*, 145–51.

41 Since its inception in 1903, women were denied the right to sit on the Representative Church Council, the Church of England's body of lay representatives. Women's sole official means of influencing church policy was through attendance at the annual Church Congresses. These bodies, however, were non-authoritative—no votes were taken, or decisions made, on any ecclesiastical issues. See Heeney, *The Women's Movement in the Church of England*, 94ff.

42 Membership figures in the postwar period are elusive. Twenty-one of the more than ninety CLWS branches dissolved, and only one new branch was begun, during the war. But the remaining members appeared more tightly organized and committed to advancing feminist reform within the Church of England.

43 "Title and Objects," *The Church Militant*, Feb. 1919, 12.

44 Rev. F. M. Green, "The Functions of Women as Lay Members of the Church," ibid., Nov. 1918, 109–111.

45 "Women and the Priesthood," ibid., May 1919, 36.

46 Ibid.

47 "Educational Campaign," ibid., Dec. 1919, 91.

48 "Annual Report of the Executive Committee," published in *The Church League for Women's Suffrage*, Mar. 1915, and *The Church Militant*, Jan. 1921.

49 For a full transcript of the debate, see "Women and the Priesthood," *The Church Militant*, July 1919, 50–56.

50 Including *The Guardian*, *The Church Family Newspaper*, and *The Challenge*. *The Church Times* withheld comment, which might be interpreted as a silent protest.

51 In 1928 the LCM dissolved itself, leaving advocacy of women's ordination to the "Anglican Group for Bringing the Subject of the Admission of Women to the Priesthood Before the Next Lambeth Conference" (which occurred in 1930).

52 Marrin, *The Last Crusade*, 223–24.

53 For example, the CWSS's Liverpool branch assumed leadership of a club begun by the Women's Patriotic League, through which CWSS members provided relief, entertainment, and educational

classes for wives of soldiers and sailors. "Suffrage Work in War-time," *The Catholic Suffragist*, 15 Sept. 1915, 76–77.

54 Alice Meynell, "The Catholic Suffragist," ibid., 15 Jan. 1915, 1.

55 Christopher St. John, "Sursum Corda!" ibid., 15 Feb. 1915, 9–10.

56 The original Contagious Diseases Acts had been passed in Britain in the 1860s to establish regular health inspections of prostitutes. Mid-Victorian feminists such as Josephine Butler viewed the CDA as state-sanctioned vice, and worked long and hard for their repeal, which came in 1886. See Judith Walkowitz, *Prostitution and Victorian Society: Women, Class, and the State* (Cambridge, 1980) and chap. 3 in this volume.

57 CWSS minutes, Jan. 24 1918, Fawcett Library.

58 As quoted in *The Catholic Suffragist*, 15 Mar. 1917, 28–30.

59 Steven C. Hause has concluded that this was the case for French feminists in his article, "More Minerva Than Mars: The French Women's Rights Campaign and the First World War," in Higonnet et al., eds., *Behind the Lines*, 103.

11 Constructing internationalism (Leila J. Rupp)

I presented part of this article at the American Historical Association conference in San Francisco, January 1994. For their sage advice on this and previous versions, I would like to thank Ken Andrien, Michael Les Benedict, Mineke Bosch, Carole Fink, Susan Hartmann, Maggie McFadden, Karen Offen, Verta Taylor, Ian Tyrrell, Ulla Wikander, and two anonymous reviewers for *The American Historical Review*. In addition, Michael Berkowitz, Victoria Brown, Anene Ejikeme, Carter Findley, Irina Livezeanu, Mala Mathrani, Carla Pestana, Lynn Stoner, Sue Wamsley, and Edith Wynner contributed to my thinking in various ways, and Irene Ledesma, Jutta Liesen, and Ayfer Karakaya Stump provided research assistance. I am also indebted to the American Council of Learned Societies for a 1992–1993 fellowship, and to the Ohio State University Office of Research and Graduate Studies, College of Humanities, Department of History, Center for Women's Studies, and Mershon Center for financial support for this project.

1 David A. Hollinger, "How Wide the Circle of the 'We'? American Intellectuals and the Problem of the Ethnos since World War II," *AHR*, 98 (April 1993): 317–37.

2 Benedict Anderson, *Imagined Communities: Reflections on the Origin and Spread of Nationalism*, rev. edn. (London, 1991). The literature on nationalism is, of course, extensive and has long recognized that there is no universal basis for nationalism; recent works include John A. Armstrong, *Nations before Nationalism* (Chapel Hill, N.C., 1982); Partha Chatterjee, *Nationalist Thought and the Colonial World: A Derivative Discourse?* (1986; rpt. edn., Minneapolis, 1993); Ernest Gellner, *Nations and Nationalism* (Oxford, 1983); Liah Greenfeld, *Nationalism: Five Roads to Modernity* (Cambridge, Mass., 1992); Harold R. Isaacs, *Idols of the Tribe: Group Identity and Political Change* (Cambridge, Mass., 1975); Kumari Jayawardena, *Feminism and Nationalism in the Third World* (London, 1986); William Pfaff, *The Wrath of Nations: Civilization and the Furies of Nationalism* (New York, 1993); Anthony D. Smith, *The Ethnic Origins of Nations* (New York, 1986).

3 See the call for such a history in Ian Tyrrell, "American Exceptionalism in an Age of International History," *AHR*, 96 (October 1991): 1031–55. Other cases of transnational movements built around collective identities include the Socialist Internationals, the labor movement, and the peace movement. See, for example, F. S. L. Lyons, *Internationalism in Europe, 1815–1914* (Leiden, 1963); James Joll, *The Second International, 1889–1914*, rev. edn. (London, 1974); George Novack, Dave Frankel, and Fred Feldman, *The First Three Internationals: Their History and Lessons* (New York, 1974); Susan Milner, *The Dilemmas of Internationalism: French Syndicalism and the International Labour Movement, 1900–1914* (New York, 1990); Sandi E. Cooper, *Patriotic Pacifism: Waging War on War in Europe, 1815–1914* (New York, 1991); W. H. van der Linden, *The International Peace Movement, 1815–1874* (Amsterdam, 1987). See also Robert O. Keohane and Joseph S. Nye, Jr., *Transnational Relations and World Politics* (Cambridge, Mass., 1971).

4 See William A. Gamson, "The Social Psychology of Collective Action," in Aldon Morris and Carol McClurg Mueller, eds., *Frontiers in Social Movement Theory* (New Haven, Conn., 1992), 53–76. Gamson's discussion of collective identity focuses on Alberto Melucci, *Nomads of the Present: Social Movements and Individual Needs in Contemporary Society* (Philadelphia, 1989).

On "new social movements," see Bert Klandermans and Sidney Tarrow, "Mobilization into Social Movements: Synthesizing European and American Approaches," in Bert Klandermans, Hanspeter Kriesi, and Sidney Tarrow, eds., *From Structure to Action: Comparing Social Movement Research across Cultures* (Greenwich, Conn., 1988).

5 Verta Taylor and Nancy E. Whittier, "Collective Identity in Social Movement Communities: Lesbian Feminist Mobilization," in Morris and Mueller, *Frontiers in Social Movement Theory*, 104–29. Taylor and Whittier, in "Analytical Approaches to Social Movement Culture: The Culture of the Women's Movement," in Hank Johnston and Bert Klandermans, eds., *Social Movements and Culture* (Minneapolis: University of Minnesota Press, 1995), 163–87, use the term "politicization of everyday life" to replace what is called "negotiation" in the original model. Emphasis on the social construction of collective identity is central to new social movement theorists.

My thinking on the process of constructing a collective identity has also been influenced by the literature on the emergence of the category and identity "lesbian" at the end of the nineteenth century; see, for example, George Chauncey, Jr., "From Inversion to Homosexuality: Medicine and the Changing Conceptualization of Female Deviance," *Salmagundi*, 58–59 (1982–83): 114–46; Lisa Duggan, "The Trials of Alice Mitchell: Sensationalism, Sexology, and the Lesbian Subject in Turn-of-the-Century America," *Signs*, 18 (Summer 1993): 791–814; Esther Newton, "The Mythic Mannish Lesbian: Radclyffe Hall and the New Woman," in Martin Duberman, Martha Vicinus, and George Chauncey, Jr., eds., *Hidden from History: Reclaiming the Lesbian and Gay Past* (New York, 1989), 281–93; Carroll Smith-Rosenberg, "Discourses of Sexuality and Subjectivity: The New Woman, 1870–1936," in Duberman, *et al., Hidden from History*, 264–80; Jennifer Terry, "Theorizing Deviant Historiography," *differences*, 3 (Summer 1991): 55–74.

6 Maggie McFadden, in "Weaving the Cloth of International Sisterhood," unpublished paper presented at the National Women's Studies Association conference, Minneapolis, June 1988, and in "Weaving the Delicate Web: The Origins of Women's International Networks, 1820–1880," unpublished paper presented at the Berkshire Conference on the History of Women, New Brunswick, N.J., June 1990, categorizes the sources of women's early international connectedness, including organizations, intentional communities, the press, travel, translation, migration, and correspondence. Looking at conferences sponsored by organizations and at independent congresses, Laurence Klejman, in "Les Congrès féministes internationaux," *Mil neuf cent: Cahiers Georges Sorel; Revue d'histoire intellectuelle*, 7 (1989): 71–86, suggests that independent congresses, especially in France, rarely transcended the national context; in general, international congresses facilitated the exchange of information but did not stimulate debate or develop plans of action. On international women's congresses, including "general women's congresses," and the debate over special labor legislation for women, see Ulla Wikander, "International Women's Congresses, 1878–1914: The Controversy over Equality and Special Labour Legislation," in Maud L. Eduards, *et al.*, eds., *Rethinking Change: Current Swedish Feminist Research* (Uppsala, 1992), 11–36. On the first international congress, the 1878 Congrès International du Droit des Femmes in Paris, see Laurence Klejman and Florence Rochefort, *L'égalité en marche: Le féminisme sous la Troisième République* (Paris, 1989), 54–56.

7 A "social movement industry" consists of all the organizations associated with a particular social movement; see John D. McCarthy and Mayer N. Zald, "Resource Mobilization and Social Movements," *American Journal of Sociology*, 82 (1977): 1212–41.

8 The very first international women's organization, the Association Internationale des Femmes, founded in Geneva in 1868, did not survive long. See Richard J. Evans, *The Feminists: Women's Emancipation Movements in Europe, America and Australasia 1840–1920* (London, 1977), 247–48; and Barbara Schnetzler, *Die frühe amerikanische Frauenbewegung und ihre Kontakte mit Europa (1836–1869)* (Bern, 1971). Some bodies organized around a single issue (as did the International Woman Suffrage Alliance in its early years): these included the Union Mondiale de la Femme pour la Concorde Internationale, a peace group centered in Geneva; Open Door International, devoted to the fight against special labor legislation for women; Equal Rights International, which worked for passage of an Equal Rights Treaty; the World Woman's Party, an organization also devoted to equal legal rights for women that merged with Equal Rights International in 1941; and the Comité Mondial des Femmes contre la Guerre et le Fascisme, a Communist-inspired group organized during the Popular Front period of the mid-1930s.

Groups open only to certain categories of women included those clustered by region: the Inter-American Commission of Women (see Francesca Miller, "The International Relations of Women of the Americas," *Americas*, 43 [October 1986]: 171–82; Francesca Miller, "Latin American Feminism and the Transnational Arena," in Emilie Bergmann, *et al.*, eds., *Women, Culture, and Politics in Latin America* [Berkeley, Calif., 1990], 10–26), the Pan-Pacific Women's Association, and the All Asian Women's Conference (see Aparna Basu and Bharati Ray, *Women's Struggle: A History of the All India Women's Conference 1927–1990* [New Delhi, 1990]; Mala Mathrani, "Nationalism or Internationalism? Indian Women and Their International Connections, 1880s–1947," dissertation in progress, Ohio State University). Other bodies organized around religion: the World Woman's Christian Temperance Union (see Ian Tyrrell, *Woman's World, Woman's Empire: The Woman's Christian Temperance Union in International Perspective, 1880–1930* [Chapel Hill, N.C., 1991]), the World Young Women's Christian Association (see Nancy Boyd, *Emissaries: The Overseas Work of the American YWCA, 1895–1970* [New York, 1986]), the Ligue des Femmes Juives, the International Union of the Catholic Women's Leagues, and St. Joan's International Alliance, a group of Catholic feminist women. The Socialist Women's International, which opposed cooperation with bourgeois women's organizations, brought women together on the basis of politics (see Ellen Carol DuBois, "Woman Suffrage and the Left: An International Socialist-Feminist Perspective," *New Left Review*, 186 [March–April 1991]: 20–44). Other groups used occupation and status as an organizing principle, running the gamut from housewives to industrial workers to professional women: the International Women's Co-Operative Guild (see Naomi Black, *Social Feminism* [Ithaca, N.Y., 1989], chap. 8), the International Federation of Working Women, the International Council of Nurses, the Ligue Internationale des Mères et Educatrices pour la Paix, the International Federation of University Women, and the International Federation of Business and Professional Women (see Lena Madesin Phillips, "Unfinished History of the International Federation of Business and Professional Women," folder 249, carton 9, Phillips Papers, Schlesinger Library, Radcliffe College, Cambridge, Massachusetts). Finally, one group, the International Council of Women of Darker Races of the World, organized by color, although it seemingly never organized outside the United States (see Cynthia Neverdon-Morton, *Afro-American Women of the South and the Advancement of the Race, 1895–1925* [Knoxville, Tenn., 1989], 198–201).

Rebecca L. Sherrick, "Toward Universal Sisterhood," *Women's Studies International Forum*, 5 (1982): 655–61, raises provocative questions about the nature of women's international organizing. For a comprehensive guide to international women's organizations, see Bob Reinalda and Natascha Verhaaren, *Vrouwenbeweging en Internationale Organisaties 1868–1986* (Nijmegen, 1989).

9 National Woman Suffrage Association, *Report of the International Council of Women, 1888* (Washington, D.C., 1888); International Council of Women, *Report of Transactions of Second Quinquennial Meeting Held in London July 1899*, Countess of Aberdeen, ed., vol. 1 (London, 1900), 4; "The Birth of the I.C.W.," 1957, box 1, ICW Papers, Sophia Smith Collection [hereafter, SSC], Smith College, Northampton, Massachusetts; May Wright Sewall, *Genesis of the International Council of Women and the Story of Its Growth, 1888–1893* (Indianapolis, 1914); Elizabeth Cady Stanton, "Reminiscences," *History of Woman Suffrage*, vol. 3, Elizabeth Cady Stanton, *et al.*, eds. (Rochester, N.Y., 1886), 922–53. On the ICW, see Edith F. Hurwitz, "The International Sisterhood," in Renate Bridenthal and Claudia Koonz, eds., *Becoming Visible: Women in European History* (Boston, 1977), 325–45; and *Women in a Changing World: The Dynamic Story of the International Council of Women since 1888* (London, 1966).

10 "Presentation of an Address to the Second Peace Conference, held at The Hague, 1907," ICW *Annual Report*, 1906–07; "To Speak and Act for 36,000,000 Women," *Christian Science Monitor*, January 13, 1925, Woman's Rights Collection, Schlesinger Library.

11 "Political Enfranchisement of Women," *Women in Politics, Being the Political Section of the International Congress of Women*, ICW, *Report of Transactions of the Second Quinquennial Meeting Held in London, July 1899*, Countess of Aberdeen, ed., vol. 5 (London, 1900), 115–41; May Wright Sewall, "President's Memorandum" [August 19, 1903], ICW, *Report of Transactions during the Third Quinquennial Term Terminating with the Third Quinquennial Meeting Held in Berlin, June, 1904* (Boston, 1909), vol. 1, describes the 1902 meeting as a direct result of the 1899 Quinquennial; in "The Council and Political Equality for Women," ICW, *Report of Transactions during the Third Quinquennial*, vol. 2, Sewall attributes the Washington

conference to the work of the ICW International Committee that she established; IWSA, *Report of Second and Third Conferences, Berlin, Germany, June 3, 4, 1904, Copenhagen, Denmark, August 7, 8, 9, 10, 11, 1906* (Copenhagen, 1906); Carrie Chapman Catt, "The History of the Origin of the IAW," box 7, Carrie Chapman Catt Collection, Rare Books and Manuscripts Division, New York Public Library [hereafter, NYPL], Astor, Lenox and Tilden Foundations, New York City; Regina Deutsch, *The International Woman Suffrage Alliance: Its History from 1904–1929* (London, 1929). On the IWSA, see Mineke Bosch, with Annemarie Kloosterman, eds., *Politics and Friendship: Letters from the International Woman Suffrage Alliance, 1902– 1942* (Columbus, Ohio, 1990) (page 7 reports the role of Heymann and Augspurg in the founding of the IWSA); and Arnold Whittick, *Women into Citizen* (London, 1979).

12 Aletta Jacobs to "Dear Friends," August 16, 1914, *Jus Suffragii*, 8 (September 1, 1914); Chrystal Macmillan to "Dear——," December 12, 1914, box A–50, Schwimmer-Lloyd Collection, Rare Books and Manuscripts Division, New York Public Library, Astor, Lenox and Tilden Foundations; Aletta Jacobs to Rosika Schwimmer, December 29, 1914, box A–52, Schwimmer-Lloyd Collection; in addition to Jacobs, Hungarian feminist and pacifist Rosika Schwimmer and English suffragist Emmeline Pethick-Lawrence were both working feverishly for peace in the United States, and German pacifists Heymann and Augspurg appealed to Swiss women to call a conference of women from the neutral countries as an expression of solidarity: see Carrie Chapman Catt to Aletta Jacobs, November 13, 1914, Jacobs Papers, International Informatiecentrum en Archief voor de Vrouwenbeweging [hereafter, IIAV], Amsterdam; Anna Howard Shaw to Aletta Jacobs, January 4, 1915, Jacobs Papers, IIAV; Ute Gerhard, *Unerhört: Die Geschichte der deutschen Frauenbewegung* (Reinbek bei Hamburg, 1990), 310; International Committee of Women for Permanent Peace, *International Congress of Women, The Hague—April 28th to May 1st 1915: Report*. On the Hague Congress and the WILPF, see Gertrude Bussey and Margaret Tims, *Women's International League for Peace and Freedom, 1915–1965* (London, 1965); Lela B. Costin, "Feminism, Pacifism, Internationalism and the 1915 International Congress of Women," *Women's Studies International Forum*, 5 (1982): 301– 15; Catherine Foster, *Women for All Seasons: The Story of the Women's International League for Peace and Freedom* (Athens, Ga., 1989); Jo Vellacott, "Feminist Consciousness and the First World War," *History Workshop: A Journal of Socialist and Feminist Historians* 23 (1987): 81–101; Jo Vellacott, "A Place for Pacifism and Transnationalism in Feminist Theory: The Early Work of the Women's International League for Peace and Freedom," *Women's History Review*, 2 (1993): 23–56; and Anne Wiltsher, *Most Dangerous Women: Feminist Peace Campaigners of the Great War* (London, 1985).

13 B. P., "Farewell to Mary Dingman," November 12, 1939, box 1, Dingman Papers, Schlesinger Library. The ICW convened the first coalition, the Joint Standing Committee of the Women's International Organisations, in 1925 to push for the appointment of women to the League of Nations. The League of Nations itself called together the Women's Consultative Committee on Nationality in 1931 to provide advice on the thorny question of the nationality of women married to foreign men. During World War I, the practice of bestowing a husband's nationality on his wife in such cases had led to some women finding themselves enemy nationals in the land of their birth. After the war, attempts by individual nations to remedy this situation caused some women, deprived by their own countries of their nationality but not granted that of their husbands', to become stateless. The 1930 Hague Conference on the Codification of International Law, despite intense lobbying by women, maintained the principle of a woman's nationality following that of her husband, provoking international women's organizations to take up a fight against ratification of the convention. It was in this context that the League of Nations appointed the Women's Consultative Committee. On the nationality question, see Dorothy P. Page, " 'A Married Woman, or a Minor, Lunatic or Idiot': The Struggle of British Women against Disability in Nationality, 1914–1933" (Doctoral dissertation, University of Otago, Dunedin, New Zealand, 1984). The last two coalitions, the Liaison Committee and the Peace and Disarmament Committee, also formed in 1931. See also chaps. 14 and 15 in this volume.

14 "The Constitution and Standing Orders of the ICW," box 1, ICW Papers, SSC; Carrie Chapman Catt, "President's Message," IWSA, *Report of the Fourth Conference of the IWSA, Amsterdam, Holland, 1908* (Amsterdam, 1908), 60–73; "Call to the Women of All Nations" [February 1915], box A–53, Schwimmer-Lloyd Collection, NYPL; Emily Hobhouse, "Foreword," and "Preamble and Resolutions Adopted," International Committee of Women for Permanent Peace [hereafter, ICWPP], *Report*, ix, 35.

15 Alfred W. Crosby, *Ecological Imperialism: The Biological Expansion of Europe, 900–1900* (New York, 1987), uses the term "neo-Europes" to refer to areas of similar climate where European settler colonies succeeded.

16 "Treasurer's Report" and "Minutes of Council Meeting," ICW, *Report of Transactions of Second Quinquennial Meeting*, 1: 91, 162–64; Lady Aberdeen to Presidents of National Councils of Women, August 1897, box 3, ICW Papers, National Council of Women—Great Britain headquarters [hereafter, NCW-GB HQ], London; May Wright Sewall, "Introduction to Volume I," ICW, *Report of Transactions during the Third Quinquennial Term* (Boston, 1909), vol. 1.

17 "Report of the Executive Committee," July 5, 1898, ICW Executive Minute Book, ICW headquarters [hereafter, ICW HQ], Paris; "The Meeting of the I.C.W. Executive Committee in Paris" (June 15–18, 1906), ICW *Annual Report*, 1905–06. See also "Resolutions Passed at the Quinquennial Meeting of the ICW," September 8–18, ICW *Annual Report*, 1920–22.

18 Charles Corbett to his brother, December 18, 1922, box 477, Margery Corbett Ashby Papers, Fawcett Library [hereafter, FL], London Guildhall University; Carrie Chapman Catt to Lena Madesin Phillips, August 11, 1937, carton 5, Phillips Papers, Schlesinger Library.

19 Mabel L. Sippy to Rosika Schwimmer, March 14, 1915, box A–55, Schwimmer-Lloyd Collection, NYPL; Minutes, WILPF Chairmen's Meeting at Zurich, March 24, 1936, reel 33, WILPF Papers, microfilm edition, Microfilming Corporation of America. See also Emily Greene Balch to Jane Addams, April 7, 1920, reel 12, Jane Addams Papers, microfilm edition, University Microfilms International; Edith Pye to Camille Drevet, March 16, 1933, reel 2, WILPF Papers; Yella Hertzka to Mary Sheepshanks, October 24, 1930, reel 2, WILPF Papers.

20 Lida Gustava Heymann to Vilma Glücklich [in German], June 4, 1925, reel 2, WILPF Papers.

21 See, for example, Rosika Schwimmer to Lola Lloyd, August 4, 1915, box A–60, Schwimmer-Lloyd Collection, NYPL; Rosika Schwimmer to Mien Palthe, December 3, 1917, box A–95, Schwimmer-Lloyd Collection; Marthe Larsen to Emily Greene Balch, April 15, 1920, reel 36, WILPF Papers; Aletta Jacobs to Lucy Anthony, July 13, 1920, box 18, Dillon Collection, Schlesinger Library; Clara Ragaz to Myrrha Tunas [German], April 24, 1924, reel 2, WILPF Papers; Emma Ender to Alice Salomon [German], March 22, 1926, 84–331(7), Helene-Lange-Archiv, Landesarchiv Berlin [hereafter, LB]; Jane Addams to Madelaine [*sic*] Doty, June 5, 1926, reel 18, Addams Papers; Gabrielle Duchêne to Madeleine Doty [French], June 25, 1926, F Rés. 207, Dossiers Duchêne, Bibliothèque de Documentation Internationale Contemporaine [hereafter, BDIC], Universités de Paris, Nanterre; Rosa Manus to Josephine Schain, January 2, 1935, box 6, Schain Papers, Sophia Smith Collection; C[lara] Ragaz to [Cor] Ramondt [German], November 26, 1936, reel 3, WILPF Papers; Rosa Manus to Carrie Chapman Catt, August 20, 1938, reel 4, Catt Papers, Library of Congress [hereafter, LC], Washington, D.C.

22 Spanish became a "semi-official" language of the ICW in 1930. This meant that Spanish-speaking members could correspond in Spanish with the ICW and that a Spanish version of the *Bulletin* would be published when enough subscriptions had been gathered.

23 All three of the international organizations considered the use of Esperanto; see "Business Session of the ICW," June 22, 1909, ICW, *Report of Transactions of the Fourth Quinquennial Meeting*, Countess of Aberdeen, ed. (London, 1910); Editorial, "An International Language," *Pax*, 1 (February 1920); Minutes, WILPF Executive Committee, June 1920, reel 9, WILPF Papers; Minutes, ICW Congress, September 16, 1920, ICW, *Report on the Quinquennial Meeting*, Marchioness of Aberdeen and Temair, ed. (Aberdeen, 1921); Emily G. Balch to Helena Swanwick, December 13, 1920, reel 1, WILPF Papers. Anderson, *Imagined Communities*, and Hollinger, "How Wide the Circle of the 'We,' " both make the point that Esperanto is an international language only in a limited sense.

24 See "International Woman Suffrage Alliance," box 22, Dillon Collection, Schlesinger Library; Ishbel Aberdeen, "President's Memorandum regarding the Quinquennial Meeting of the ICW at Rome 1914," box 1, ICW Papers, SSC; "Report of Business Sessions," ICWPP, *Report*, 74, 77, 92–93, 106, 156–57. The ICW *Bulletin* regularly published separate editions in the three languages. *Jus Suffragii*, the journal of the IAW, appeared mainly in English with, at various times, articles or columns or sections in French and occasionally German. WILPF published *Pax* in three separate editions until the Depression made that financially impossible; thereafter, only an English edition, with occasional articles in French and German, appeared.

25 See, for example, I. A. & T. [Ishbel Aberdeen and Temair], "President's Notes," ICW *Bulletin*, 6 (June 1928).

26 Martina Kramers to Rosika Schwimmer [German], May 31, 1907, box A–12, Schwimmer-Lloyd Collection, NYPL.

27 Annie Furuhjelm to Aletta Jacobs, February 12, 1920, box 1, Jacobs Papers, IIAV; see also Alice Salomon, "Character Is Destiny," 106–07, Salomon Papers, Memoir Collection, Leo Baeck Institute [hereafter, LBI], New York; Marie Popelin, "Impressions et souvenirs du Canada," Countess of Aberdeen, Ishbel Gordon, *Our Lady of the Sunshine and Her International Visitors* (London, 1909), 76–81; Marguerite Gobat to Gabrielle Duchêne [French], March 7, 1927, Fol Rés. 206, Dossiers Duchêne, BDIC; Minutes, WILPF International Executive Committee, March 21, 1928, reel 9, WILPF Papers; Carrie Chapman Catt to Bertha Lutz, May 6, 1936, reel 12, National American Woman Suffrage Association [hereafter, NAWSA] Papers, Library of Congress; Minutes, WILPF International Executive Committee, September 10–14, 1936, reel 11, WILPF Papers; Gertrud Baer to Lola Hanouskova [German], February 8, 1937, reel 21, WILPF Papers.

28 "Business Session of the ICW," June 22, 1909, ICW, *Report of Transactions of the Fourth Quinquennial.*

29 ICW presidents included Millicent Garrett Fawcett, England, who was elected in 1888 but refused to serve; Lady Aberdeen, Scotland, 1893–99, 1904–20, 1922–36; May Wright Sewall, United States, 1899–1904; Pauline Chaponnière-Chaix, Switzerland, 1920–22; and Baroness Marthe Boël, Belgium, 1936–47. The Woman Suffrage Alliance was headed by Carrie Chapman Catt, United States, 1904–23, and Margery Corbett Ashby, England, 1923–46. Jane Addams, United States, served as president of the WILPF from its birth to 1929 and until her death held the title of honorary president; Emily Greene Balch, United States, became honorary president when Addams died in 1935, and the leadership fell to a series of joint chairs, all from the United States, England, Germany, the Netherlands, or Switzerland.

In the early years of the ICW, the United States bore the expense of the organization, and dues from U.S. members later made up a significant part of the budget. A legacy from the Leslie Commission, administered by Carrie Chapman Catt, supported the work of the IAW for years. Jane Addams regularly raised money to support the work of the WILPF and contributed much of her Nobel Peace Prize money to the organization. See ICW, *Report of Transactions*, 1899, vol. 1, 38; Margery Corbett Ashby to Carrie Chapman Catt, July 25, 1923, reel 10, NAWSA Papers, LC; Interview with Margery Corbett Ashby, November 23, 1976, conducted by Brian Harrison, cassette 8, Ashby Papers, FL; "Central Bureau Notes," *International*, 3 (January–March 1918); C[or] Ramondt-Hirschmann to Friends, February 16, 1931, reel 22, Addams Papers; "To the Sections" [1931], reel 10, WILPF Papers.

30 Although international Catholic and Jewish women's organizations participated in coalition efforts, there was friction between the major international women's organizations and what was referred to as the Catholic women's movement; furthermore, the fact that the coalitions sought out the involvement of Catholic and Jewish groups, while such organizations as the World Woman's Christian Temperance Union and the World Young Women's Christian Association were charter members, is revealing.

31 On anti-Semitism in the Woman Suffrage Alliance, see Bosch, *Politics and Friendship*, 219–24. On Rosika Schwimmer, a prominent Jewish activist, see Rosa Rauther, "Rosika Schwimmer: Stationen auf dem Lebensweg einer Pazifistin," *Feministische Studien*, 3 (1984): 63–76; and Beth S. Wenger, "Radical Politics in a Reactionary Age: The Unmaking of Rosika Schwimmer, 1914–1930," *Journal of Women's History*, 2 (Fall 1990): 66–99. See also Martina Kramers to Rosika Schwimmer [German], August 31, 1907, box A–13, Schwimmer-Lloyd Collection, NYPL; Salomon, "Character Is Destiny," Salomon Papers, LBI, in which Salomon discusses the opposition to her potential presidency of the ICW; on Rosa Manus as a Jew, see Mia Bossevain, tribute to Rosa Manus, Rosa Manus Papers, International Informatiecentrum en Archief voor de Vrouwenbeweging; Rosa Manus to Carrie Chapman Catt, July 31, 1939, reel 4, Catt Papers, LC, in which Manus discusses a conflict over Palestine with Egyptian feminist Huda Shaarawi. On Shaarawi, see Huda Shaarawi, *Harem Years: The Memoirs of an Egyptian Feminist (1879–1924)*, Margot Badran, ed. (New York, 1987).

32 See, for example, Carrie Chapman Catt, "India" [part 2], *Jus Suffragii*, 6 (July 15, 1912); Stenographic report of Second Congress, October 24, 1921, folder 6, International Federation of Working Women Papers, Schlesinger Library; "Second Annual Convention of the International Association of Medical Women," *Jus Suffragii*, 16 (September 1922); "India," *Jus Suffragii*, 19 (March 1925). I am grateful to Anene Ejikeme, who first noted the use of the term "truly

international" for a later period in " 'One Big Family': Nigerian Women and WILPF, 1950–70" (M.A. thesis, Ohio State University, 1992).

33 See Joyce Zonana, "The Sultan and the Slave: Feminist Orientalism and the Structure of *Jane Eyre,*" *Signs*, 18 (Spring 1993): 592–617. See also Margot Badran, *Feminists, Islam, and Nation: Gender and the Making of Modern Egypt* (Princeton, N.J., 1994); Antoinette Burton, "The Feminist Quest for Identity: British Imperial Suffragists and 'Global Sisterhood,' 1900–1915," *Journal of Women's History*, 3 (Fall 1991): 46–81; Catherine Candy, "Margaret Cousins, 'Mother India' and the Ideal 'Femaculine': An Irish Orientalist Feminist in India," unpublished paper presented at the American Historical Association Annual Meeting, Chicago, December 1991; Barbara N. Ramusack, "Cultural Missionaries, Maternal Imperialists, Feminist Allies: British Women Activists in India, 1865–1945," in Nupur Chaudhuri and Margaret Strobel, eds., *Western Women and Imperialism: Complicity and Resistance* (Bloomington, Ind., 1992), 119–36.

34 Agnes Smedley for the Secretary, Pandurgang Khanko, to Emily Greene Balch, April 28, 1921, reel 1, WILPF Papers; see also [Emily Greene Balch?] to [Marguerite] Gobat [German], May 6, 1921, reel 1, WILPF Papers; Marguerite Gobat to Anna Wössner [German], May 10, 1921, reel 1, WILPF Papers.

35 Chiyin Chen to Anne Zueblin [German], May 14, 1932, reel 20, WILPF Papers.

36 There is an enormous scholarship on the history of "difference" versus "sameness" assumptions and arguments in women's organizing. See, for example, Black, *Social Feminism*; Nancy F. Cott, "What's in a Name? The Limits of 'Social Feminism'; or, Expanding the Vocabulary of Women's History," *Journal of American History*, 76 (December 1989): 809–29; Alice Echols, *Daring to Be Bad: Radical Feminism in America, 1967–1975* (Minneapolis, 1989); Karen Offen, "Defining Feminism: A Comparative Historical Approach," *Signs*, 14 (Autumn 1988): 119–57; Joan W. Scott, "Deconstructing Equality-versus-Difference: Or, the Uses of Poststructuralist Theory for Feminism," *Feminist Studies*, 14 (Spring 1988): 33–50. This is also a critical issue for contemporary feminist theorists: see, for example, Linda Alcoff, "Cultural Feminism versus Post-Structuralism: The Identity Crisis in Feminist Theory," *Signs*, 13 (Spring 1988): 405–36; Hester Eisenstein, *Contemporary Feminist Thought* (Boston, 1983); Carol Gilligan, *In a Different Voice: A Psychological Theory and Women's Development* (Cambridge, Mass., 1982); Elizabeth V. Spelman, *Inessential Woman: Problems of Exclusion in Feminist Thought* (Boston, 1988).

37 Minutes, WILPF International Congress, September 3–8, 1934, reel 20, WILPF Papers; Speech of Lida Gustava Heymann, WILPF Zurich Congress [1919], reel 17, WILPF Papers.

38 Mary Sheepshanks, "Peace," *Jus Suffragii*, 13 (December 1918); Paula Pogány to Mary Sheepshanks, February 8, 1915, box A–54, Schwimmer-Lloyd Collection, NYPL; "L'Orient et l'Occident en coopération," *La République*, April 20, 1935, box 484, Ashby Papers, FL; "Man Made Wars," *Pax*, 6 (May 1931); Carrie Chapman Catt to Margery Corbett Ashby and Katherine Bompas, June 16, 1942, box 3, Catt Collection, NYPL.

39 "A Call to the Congress," *Jus Suffragii*, 20 (March 1926); "Die Waffen nieder! Aufruf an alle Frauen der ganzen Erde," n.d., reel 9, WILPF Papers; "Women's Organisations for World Order" [German], n.d., reel 110, WILPF Papers.

40 Quotations from Milena Rudnycka, "The National Question and Its Peaceful Solution," August 26, 1929, reel 19, WILPF Papers; Ishbel Aberdeen and Temair, "A New Year's Message from the I.C.W. President," January 1925, ICW *Bulletin*, 3 (January–February 1925); "International Manifesto of Women," *Jus Suffragii*, 8 (September 1, 1914); Minutes, Internationaler Frauenkongress, May 12–17, 1919, reel 17, WILPF Papers; Aletta Jacobs to Rosika Schwimmer, August 18, 1914, box A–41, Schwimmer-Lloyd Collection, NYPL; Gertrude G. Bussey and Marie Lous-Mohr to Secretary-General of the United Nations, September 9, 1946, reel 4, WILPF Papers. Similar expressions can be found in Emily Hobhouse, "To Women throughout Europe," n.d., box A–51, Schwimmer-Lloyd Collection; Skandinavische Vorbereitungskom. to "Werte Frau" [August 1917], box A–91, Schwimmer-Lloyd Collection; Marie Hoheisel to Ishbel Aberdeen, ICW *Bulletin*, 13 (December 1934).

41 "Die Waffen nieder! Aufruf an alle Frauen der ganzen Erde"; Emily Hobhouse, "An die Frauen in ganz Europa," n.d., box 118, Fannie Fern Andrews Papers, Schlesinger Library; "Aufruf an die Mütter!" [October 1918], box A–101, Schwimmer-Lloyd Collection, NYPL; "Message of the WILPF to the Women of Japan" [1924], reel 2, WILPF Papers; "To All Mothers—to All Women," call to Women's World Congress for Peace and Liberty, Cuba, October 1939, reel 11, WILPF Papers.

42 "A Call to Women" [1936], nr. 24, Rassemblement Universel pour la Paix Papers, Internationaal Institut voor Sociale Geschiedenis [hereafter, IISG], Amsterdam; "To Women of Palestine Who Love Peace," September 1920, reel 1, WILPF Papers; Rosika Schwimmer, "War and Women" [1914], box A–48, Schwimmer-Lloyd Collection, NYPL. See also Louise C. A. van Eeghen, "Address Given at the Prague Conference of the World Alliance for Promoting International Friendship through the Churches," ICW *Bulletin*, 7 (December 1928); Marie Hoheisel, "The World Needs 'Mothering,' " ICW *Bulletin*, 14 (February 1936).

43 Emily Balch to Elisabeth Waern-Bugge, December 12 [1934], reel 2, WILPF Papers.

44 "Memorandum of the Meeting of the Executive and Standing Committees," May 20–27, 1913, ICW *Annual Report*, 1912–13; "The Atrocities of War," *Jus Suffragii*, 9 (October 1, 1914). Catt pressured Mary Sheepshanks to collect evidence of "wrongs done to women" by any of the belligerents during the war. See Mary Sheepshanks to Rosika Schwimmer, December 15, 1914, box A–50, Schwimmer-Lloyd Collection, NYPL.

45 Rosika Schwimmer, "The Women of the World Demand Peace" [September 1914], box A–42, Schwimmer-Lloyd Collection, NYPL. Schwimmer reported to a colleague on the rape of Hungarian women by Russian soldiers and the rape of French women by German soldiers. See Schwimmer to Florence Holbrook, January 26, 1915, box A–53, Schwimmer-Lloyd Collection.

46 "An International Conference of Women" [1915], reel 16, WILPF Papers. The issue of rape also came up with regard to the Japanese invasion of China (Muriel Lester to Clara Ragaz, April 1, 1938, reel 3, WILPF Papers) and World War II (Carrie Chapman Catt to Margery Corbett Ashby and Katherine Bompas, June 16, 1942, reel 11, NAWSA Papers, LC).

47 "The Presidential Addresses Delivered by the Countess of Aberdeen during the Visit of the I.C.W. Executive Committee to Paris," June 1906, ICW HQ; Annie Furuhjelm, "Our Alliance," *Jus Suffragii*, 8 (May 1, 1914); M[ary] Sheepshanks, "What Women Want," *Jus Suffragii*, 8 (July 1, 1914).

48 Tyrrell, *Woman's World*, points out that Katharine Anthony, in *Feminism in Germany and Scandinavia* (1915), asserted that disfranchisement was responsible for an "unconscious internationalism" among women.

49 National American Woman Suffrage Association, *Report of the International Council of Women* (Washington, D.C., 1888), 33; Carrie Chapman Catt to the Editor, New York *Sun*, January 11, 1913, box 1, Catt Collection, NYPL; Carrie Chapman Catt, "Congress Announcements," *Jus Suffragii*, 7 (February 15, 1913); Mary Sheepshanks, "Is Internationalism Dead?" *Jus Suffragii*, 10 (June 1, 1916).

50 "International Woman Suffrage Alliance," typescript, n.d., box 22, Dillon Collection, Schlesinger Library; Millicent Garrett Fawcett, "The Future of the I.W.S.A.," *Jus Suffragii*, 14 (December 1919); Annie Furuhjelm to Aletta Jacobs, February 12, 1920, box 1, Jacobs Papers, IIAV.

51 Siao-Mei Djang to M[ary] Sheepshanks, July 30, 1929, reel 19, WILPF Papers. Bosch, *Politics and Friendship*, argues persuasively that the model of "universal sisterhood" was largely an American construction. See also Sherrick, "Toward Universal Sisterhood."

52 E[mily] B[alch], "Our Work," *Pax*, 1 (February 1920); International Executive Committee, "Statement on Fascism," April 11–15, 1933, reel 10, WILFP Papers.

53 On the idea of separatism as a temporary expedient, see Ishbel Aberdeen, "Presidential Address," ICW, *Report of Transactions of Second Quinquennial Meeting*, vol. 1; Interview with Margery Corbett Ashby, September 21, 1976, conducted by Brian Harrison, cassette no. 6, Ashby Papers, FL; on the preference for working with men, see Elizabeth Baelde, "Impressions of the visit of the I.C.W. to Canada," Countess of Aberdeen, *Our Lady of the Sunshine and Her International Visitors*, 31–34; Eline Hansen to Rosika Schwimmer, March 12, 1915, box A–55, Schwimmer-Lloyd Collection, NYPL; "Report of Business Sessions," May 1, 1915, ICWPP, *Report*, 162–63; Minutes, Disarmament Committee, January 15, 1932, Peace and Disarmament Committee Papers, Swarthmore College Peace Collection, Swarthmore College, Swarthmore, Pennsylvania; Eva Fichet to Emily Greene Balch [French], August 19, 1934, reel 20, WILPF Papers; Rosika Schwimmer to Gabrielle Duchêne [1934], reel 20, WILPF Papers.

54 "Report of the Meeting of the Committee of Arrangements," July 6, 1898, ICW Executive Minute Book, ICW HQ; "What Is This League?" pamphlet [1920–21], reel 9, WILPF Papers; see also "From Letter from Mrs. Spencer," April 1, 1920, and "From Letter from Eleanor M. Moore," June 12, 1920, reel 1, WILPF Papers; "Circular Letter to Executive Committee," April 30, 1920, reel 9, WILPF Papers; Emily Balch to Jane Addams, January 8, 1921, reel 13, Addams

Papers; Emily Balch to Jane Addams, June 29 [1922], reel 14, Addams Papers; Minutes, 8th International Congress, September 3–8, 1934, reel 20, WILPF Papers.

55 Catherine E. Marshall to Vilma Glücklich, May 14 [1923], reel 15, Addams Papers.

56 "Report of Business Sessions," ICWPP, *Report*, 128–29.

57 Rosika Schwimmer to Gabrielle Duchêne [1934], reel 20, WILPF Papers. See also M. Slieve McGowan, "Women and Politics," *Jus Suffragii*, 17 (February 1923), a challenge to the idea that women's nature is "differently organized" than men's; a protest raised at the WILPF congress of 1932 to the idea that men led the world into war and only women could stop it, Minutes, WILPF Congress, May 15–19, 1932, reel 20, WILPF Papers; Bertha Lutz's comment that "women are not really feminists and still less, pacifists," Lutz to Carrie Chapman Catt, August 25, 1933, reel 12, NAWSA Papers, LC.

58 Teresa Wilson to Anna Simson, December 1, 1898, 83–328(1), Helene-Lange-Archiv, LB; Emily Greene Balch to Jane Addams, February 16, 1921, reel 13, Addams Papers; Rosa Manus to Clara Hyde, October 8, 1923, reel 4, Catt Papers, LC; Lida Gustava Heymann to Vilma Glücklich [German], March 18, 1925, reel 2, WILPF Papers; Helene Granitsch to Helen Archdale [German], June 18, 1931, box 334, Equal Rights International Papers, Fawcett Library.

59 1888 Constitution, printed in Sewall, *Genesis of the ICW*; "Memorandum of the Meeting of General Officers," July 26–27, 1905, ICW *Annual Report*, 1904–05; "The Meeting of the I.C.W. Executive Committee in Paris" [June 15–18, 1906], ICW *Annual Report*, 1905–06. Lady Aberdeen responded to the publication and distribution by the National Council of Women of Norway of a pamphlet explaining the situation between Sweden and Norway by writing to constituent councils: "I am sure that I need not remind you that it would be undesirable for any of our Councils to pass a resolution, or express an opinion, regarding the internal political affairs of any Country." Lady Aberdeen to Marie Stritt, July 11, 1905, 80–309(2), Helene-Lange-Archiv, LB. Likewise, in 1932, when the Greek National Council of Women sent out a letter about the Cyprus situation, Aberdeen wrote all presidents of National Councils to remind them of the constitutional ban on involvement with such conflicts. Lady Aberdeen to Presidents [German], February 17, 1932, 85–334(1), Helene-Lange-Archiv.

60 Minutes, May 1, 1909, IWSA, *Report of the Fifth Conference and First Quinquennial, London, England, 1909* (London, 1909).

61 ICWPP, *Report*. See the proposal for this policy in Chrystal Macmillan to "Dear—," December 12, 1914, box A-50, Schwimmer-Lloyd Collection, NYPL. On the 1919 congress, see [Emily Balch] to [Matilda] Widegren, November 27, 1919, reel 1, WILPF Papers.

62 See, for example, Jane Addams to Kathleen Courtney, August 15, 1932, reel 24, Addams Papers; Olga Misar to Camille Drevet, September 13, 1932, reel 10, WILPF Papers; Minutes, International Executive Committee, August-September 1934, reel 10, WILPF Papers; "Replies from International Organisations to W.I.L.P.F. Proposal re Campaign in Support of Initiative on the Lines of President Roosevelt's Message" [1939], reel 11, WILPF Papers.

63 "President's Report," ICW, "Combined Third and Fourth Annual Report of the Seventh Quinquennial Period," 1922–24, ICW Papers, ICW HQ.

64 "French Suffragists and the War," letter from de Witt Schlumberger to Sisters of the Union, *Jus Suffragii*, 8 (September 1, 1914). At the same time, Schlumberger objected to the portrayal of French women as opposed to international collaboration; see copy of extract from "La Revue," September 15, 1915 [French], Dossier de Witt Schlumberger, Bibliothèque Marguerite Durand, Paris.

65 Le Bureau du Comité Central, l'Union Française pour le Suffrage des Femmes to Carrie Chapman Catt [French], December 23, 1914, reel 20, NAWSA Papers, LC. Catt refused to take this protest seriously; Carrie Chapman Catt to Mme. Schlumberger, January 15, 1915, reel 20, NAWSA Papers. Anna Howard Shaw thought the Frènch women were making a mountain out of a molehill; Shaw to Aletta Jacobs, February 15, 1915, box 2, Jacobs Papers, IIAV.

66 "Some Letters from Those Not Adhering to the Congress," ICWPP, *Report*; Mme. Pichon Landry, "French Women and the Hague Congress," *Jus Suffragii*, 9 (June 1, 1915); on Duchêne, see Klejman and Rochefort, *L'égalité en marche*, 192.

67 Millicent Garrett Fawcett, "Ought There to Be an International Congress of Women in the Near Future," *Jus Suffragii*, 9 (January 1, 1915); "Mrs. Pankhurst Won't Go," *New York Times*, April 8, 1915. Italian women also objected to the congress. See Elma Solens to Rosika Schwimmer [French], March 20, 1915, box A-56, Schwimmer-Lloyd Collection, NYPL; Gabriella Spolletti Rasponi to Lady Aberdeen [French], May 5, 1915, box 10, ICW Papers, NCW-GB HQ.

68 "Report of Business Sessions" [French], April 30, 1915, ICWPP, *Report*, 136. Jane Brigode, from the Fédération Belge pour le Suffrage des Femmes, was offended by Aletta Jacobs' invitation to the Hague Congress; Aletta Jacobs to Jane Brigode, January 1919, reel 36, WILPF Papers. The exchange of letters is printed in *Internationaal*, 4 (January–February–March 1919).

69 Gertrud Baümer, April 4, 1915, "Some Letters from Those Not Adhering to the Congress" [German], ICWPP, *Report*, 306–10. See also Marie Stritt and Alma Dzialoszynski, "Answer by the Deutscher Verband für Frauenstimmrecht to the Christmas Greeting from English Women," *Jus Suffragii*, 9 (April 1, 1915). Gerhard, *Unerhört*, discusses German women's responses, 311.

70 "Internationaler Frauenkongress 1915" [German], reel 1, WILPF Papers. Austrian women also refused to participate. See Ernestine von Fürth, "Opinions of Some Who Refused to Participate," *Jus Suffragii*, 9 (June 1, 1915).

71 "To the International Woman Suffrage Alliance," *Jus Suffragii*, 9 (December 1, 1914).

72 "Copy of Letter of the French Committee to German Women" [French, 1915], reel 110, WILPF Papers; Lida Gustava Heymann and Anita Augspurg, "Antwort des Deutschen Komitees auf einem Schreiben des Französischen Komitees, No. 1," August 20, 1915, box 30, Andrews Papers, Schlesinger Library; Frida Perlen, "Reply on Behalf of the German Committee to the Letter of the French Committee, No. 2" [1915], box A–62, Schwimmer-Lloyd Collection, NYPL. See also "Greetings from Suffragists," *Jus Suffragii*, 10 (February 1, 1916); Helene Lecher-Rohthorn to Aletta Jacobs, April 1916, *Internationaal*, 1 (May–June–July 1916); "Deutsche Frauen an französischen Frauen," May 1916, *Internationaal*, 1 (May–June–July 1916); "Schwestern in den kriegführenden Ländern!" [1916], box A–84, Schwimmer-Lloyd Collection. English women addressed an open Christmas letter to the women of Germany and Austria in 1915, and *Jus Suffragii* published both the original letter and a reply; see "Open Christmas Letter to the Women of Germany and Austria," *Jus Suffragii*, 9 (January 1, 1915); and 9 (March 1, 1915).

73 "Extract from the Forthcoming Report of the International Congress of Women" [French], May 12–17, 1919, reel 17, WILPF Papers; "Zum Internationalen Frauenkongress" [1919], reel 17, WILPF Papers.

74 "Sechster Verhandlungstag" [1919], reel 17, WILPF Papers; "Compte rendu de la conference internationale des femmes à Zurich" [1919], reel 17, WILPF Papers.

75 Jacqueline Van Voris, *Carrie Chapman Catt: A Public Life* (New York, 1987).

76 Alice Park, diary entry, June 3, 1926, box 25, Park Papers, Hoover Institution, Stanford University, Stanford, California; Extract from letter of Editha Phelps to Rosika Schwimmer, June 7, 1926, Mien van Wulfften Palthe-Broese van Groenau Papers, International Informatiecentrum en Archief voor de Vrouwenbeweging.

77 "Communiqué," Section Française de la Ligue Internationale des Femmes pour la Paix et la Liberté [1931], F Rés. 296, Dossiers Gabrielle Duchêne, BDIC.

78 See, for example, "Letter Sent by the French Section to the Women of the German Section," *Bulletin*, January and February 1923, reel 110, WILPF Papers; Andrée Jouve [French], "Messages of Europe, Christmas 1924," reel 18, WILPF Papers; "Geneva Headquarters," *Pax*, 1 (October 1926); Matilda Widegren to Jane Addams, July 25, 1927, reel 19, Addams Papers, which refers to a plan of Heymann's to form a permanent committee of French and German women; "The International Executive Committee," *Pax*, 6 (May 1931); "Germany to France," *Pax*, 6 (August 1931); "Appeal of German and French Women to Their Governments," *Pax*, 8 (February 1933); Gabrielle Duchêne, "Frida Perlen," *Pax*, 9 (February 1934).

79 [Mary Sheepshanks] to Marie Ursule Ferrari [French], August 13, 1930, reel 21, WILPF Papers; "Towards Peace and Freedom," August 1919, reel 17, WILPF Papers; "Women and War in the Far East," *Pax* 7 (May 1932); see also Tomi Wada Kora to Jane Addams, December 1, 1931, reel 22, Addams Papers; Edith Pye to Jane Addams, December 10, 1931, reel 22, Addams Papers.

80 "A New Peace: Report of the International Conference of Women at the Hague, 7 to 9 December, 1922," reel 9, WILPF Papers.

81 Sophie Sturge to Aletta Jacobs, November 8 [1915], reel 9, WILPF Papers; Minutes, WILPF Executive Committee Meeting, Swarthmore, April 25–29, 1924; and Washington, May 8, 1924, reel 9, WILPF Papers; Vilma Glücklich to Jane Addams, October 8, 1924, reel 16, Addams Papers; M[yrrha] T[unas], "National Sections: 1924," reel 2, WILPF Papers; "The World Section," *Pax*, 2 (November 1926).

82 Madeleine Z. Doty, "The W.I.L. World Section," *Pax*, 5 (January 1930). See responses from Lida Gustava Heymann, "The World Section of the W.I.L.," *Pax*, 5 (March 1930); and from Irma Gladys Kerp, "The World Section of the W.I.L.," *Pax*, 5 (April 1930).

83 "Suprainternational Republic," n.d., reel 8, Emily Greene Balch Papers, microfilm edition, Scholarly Resources.

84 Minutes, International Executive Committee, London, March 25–30, 1935, reel 11, WILPF Papers. See also Minutes, 8th International Congress, Zurich, September 3–8, 1934, reel 20, WILPF Papers; "World Section," *Pax*, 9 (October–November 1934).

85 "Raisons pour lesquelles nous restons fermement attachées à la constitution actuelle" [1927], Fol Rés. 206, Dossiers Gabrielle Duchêne, BDIC.

86 See Mercedes M. Randall, *Improper Bostonian: Emily Greene Balch* (New York, 1964), 7; Anita Augspurg, Lida Gustava Heymann, Frida Perlen, and Elise von Schlumberger, "Internationaler Frauenkongress 1915" [1915], reel 1, WILPF Papers.

87 I am indebted to Mala Mathrani, whose Ohio State dissertation in progress, "Nationalism or Internationalism?" explores this relationship in the Indian context, for first bringing to my attention the possibility of viewing nationalism and internationalism as complementary.

88 Margery Corbett Ashby to Josephine Schain, February 5, 1935, box 4, Schain Papers, SSC; Ashby also described Huda Shaarawi (referred to in IAW documents as "Hoda Charaoui") as "terrifically nationalist"; Ashby to Carrie Chapman Catt, June 9, 1926, reel 11, NAWSA Papers, LC.

89 Sofia R. de Veyra to Emily Greene Balch, June 3, 1920, reel 1, WILPF Papers; "Delegates and Friends," carbon copy of speech at Istanbul Congress, 1935, box 1, International Alliance of Women Papers, Sophia Smith Collection; "L'Orient et l'Occident en coopération," *La République*, April 20, 1935, box 484, Ashby Papers, FL.

90 A[lice] Jacot to "Madame" [French], April 15, 1937, reel 3, WILPF Papers; Egyptian section, "Propositions pour le Congrès de Luhacovice" [April 1937], reel 2, WILPF Papers.

91 Lotti Birch to Clara Ragaz and Cor Ramondt-Hirschmann [German], May 1, 1937, reel 3, WILPF Papers; Cor Ramondt-Hirschmann to Lotti Birch [German], May 7, 1937, reel 3, WILPF Papers; Clara Ragaz to Alice Jacot [French], May 12, 1937, reel 3, WILPF Papers; Lotti Birch to Congress Committee [German], May 12, 1937, reel 21, WILPF Papers; Cor Ramondt-Hirschmann to Clara Ragaz [German], May 20, 1937, reel 3, WILPF Papers.

92 Alice Jacot to Clara Ragaz [French], May 22, 1937, reel 3, WILPF Papers.

93 Clara Ragaz to Cor Ramondt-Hirschmann [German], June 24, 1937, reel 3, WILPF Papers; Minutes, Executive Committee Meeting, July 26–August 3, 1937, reel 21, WILPF Papers.

94 Bosch, *Politics and Friendship*, 18–19, describes the IWSA congresses as "cultural manifestations of the political ideal of international sisterhood," emphasizing that the romanticization of difference supported the idea of an essential unity and equality of women. Tyrrell, *Woman's World*, 49–50, also emphasizes the use of hymns, emblems, slogans, badges, flags, and banners to strengthen the notion of women united in temperance work around the globe.

95 "Arrangements for the Conference," *Report, Second and Third Conferences of the International Woman Suffrage Alliance* (Copenhagen, 1906); Salomon, "Character Is Destiny," 129–30, Salomon Papers, LBI. The 1925 ICW congress in Washington also opened with a ceremony in which each national representative came onto the platform accompanied by her national flag; see Eva Perry Moore to Madame President, December 20, 1924, 84–331(6), Helene-Lange-Archiv, LB.

96 Longtime Dutch IWSA activist Rosa Manus, for example, first came to the attention of IWSA leadership when she participated in a dance in Dutch costume at the 1908 Amsterdam conference; see Carrie Chapman Catt to Friends of Rosa Manus, July 10, 1942, Catt Papers, IIAV. Other examples include a lecture-recital on Irish music at the 1926 WILPF congress in Dublin, "Fifth Biennial International Congress of the WILPF," July 8–15, 1926, reel 19, WILPF Papers; an evening of Austrian folk songs and folk dances at the ICW Quinquennial in Vienna in 1930, "Vienna Conference News," ICW *Bulletin*, 8 (March 1930); a program of Sinhalese and Indian folk songs and other cultural forms at the IWSA Istanbul congress in 1935; "Savitri," program of Istanbul Congress, 1935, box 484, Ashby Papers, FL; a performance by Danish dancers and exhibition of Danish arts and crafts at the 1939 Copenhagen IWSA Congress, Minutes, meeting of International Committee, London, July 8–9, 1938, International Alliance of Women Papers, Fawcett Library [hereafter, IAW, FL].

The Swedish auxiliary of the IWSA asked delegates to wear the colors of their country to the 1911 congress, *Jus Suffragii*, 5 (April 15, 1911); Rosa Manus requested that the presidents of national groups wear a ribbon in the colors of their country for a peace meeting on the last evening of the 1926 Paris IWSA congress, Rosa Manus to Presidents, *Jus Suffragii*, 20 (January 1926); the Irish section of WILPF asked delegates to wear national costume or a white dress with a ribbon in the colors of their country to the 1926 Dublin congress, [Madeleine Doty] to

Delegates to Congress, June 10, 1926, reel 19, WILPF Papers; the Joint Standing Committee proposed to ask representatives to wear national costumes at a future dinner, Minutes, Joint Standing Committee, September 7, 1928, Liaison Committee Papers, IISG.

97 Hilma Bovelius, "What an International Congress Means," *Jus Suffragii*, 9 (April 1, 1915).

98 "Editor's Preface to the Minutes of the Hague Executive" [1901], "Minutes of Executive Committee," July 10–12, 1902, "Minutes of Third Day's Meeting" [August 19, 1903], May Wright Sewall, "The Report on Council Insignia" [August 17–19, 1903], Minutes, adjourned business meeting of ICW, June 13, 1904, May Wright Sewall, "Introduction to Volume I," all in ICW, *Report of Transactions during the Third Quinquennial Term*, vol. 1; Minutes, ICW Executive Committee, August 18, 1903, 80–319(2), Helene-Lange-Archiv, LB; May Wright Sewall to Co-Workers, December 31, 1903, 83–329(5), Helene-Lange-Archiv; Ishbel Aberdeen, "President's Report," ICW *Annual Report*, 1905–06; "The Delegates at Hotel Wittsburg" [informal Executive Committee meeting, June 1907], ICW *Annual Report*, 1906–07; May Wright Sewall to Marie Stritt, August 14, 1908, 84–330(2), Helene-Lange-Archiv; "Business Transacted at the Special Session of the ICW," September 1–5, 1908, ICW *Annual Report*, 1907–08; ICW *Annual Report*, 1913–14.

99 Minutes, first business meeting of the Quinquennial Council, May 6, 1925, "Report on the Quinquennial Meeting," Marchioness of Aberdeen and Temair, ed., ICW HQ. See also "Editorial Notes," ICW *Bulletin*, 3 (November–December 1924); and Ishbel Aberdeen and Temair, "President's Memorandum," ICW *Bulletin*, 3 (June–July 1925).

100 IWSA, *Report, Second and Third Conferences of the International Woman Suffrage Alliance*. See also Carrie Chapman Catt to Vilma Glücklich, September 29, 1905, box A–7, Schwimmer-Lloyd Collection, NYPL; *Jus Suffragii*, 4 (October 15, 1909).

101 "Competition for a New Alliance Emblem," *Jus Suffragii*, 22 (June 1928); Minutes, IAW International Committee, July 8–9, 1938, IAW Papers, FL.

102 Minutes, Third International WILPF Congress, July 10–16, 1921, reel 18, WILPF Papers. See also Eleanor M. Moore to Rosa Manus, March 3, 1917, reel 17, WILPF Papers; *Internationaal*, 3 (January–February–March 1918); "Resolutions Passed at the Third Congress of the WILPF," July 10–17, 1921, reel 18, WILPF Papers.

103 Marie Stritt to Lady Aberdeen [German], December 3, 1927, 78–315(1), Helene-Lange-Archiv, LB; Louie Bennett to Gertrud [Baer], May 8, 1934, reel 20, WILPF Papers; "Gleanings from the Council Meetings," ICW *Bulletin*, 3 (June–July 1925); Karleen Baker, "Ninth International Congress of the W.I.L.P.F.," *Pax*, 12 (October 15, 1937).

104 Marthe Boël, "A Message of Goodbye," ICW *Bulletin*, 17 (May 1939); Karen M. Glaesel, "Our Grannie," ICW *Bulletin*, 17 (May 1939); Rosa Manus to Lucy Anthony, December 26, 1920, box 18, Dillon Collection, Schlesinger Library; Rosa Manus to Carrie Chapman Catt, April 5, 1932, reel 4, Catt Papers, LC; Rosa Manus to Carrie Chapman Catt, October 5, 1932, reel 4, Catt Papers, LC; Rosa Manus to Carrie Chapman Catt, February 21, 1939, reel 4, Catt Papers, LC; Bertha Lutz to Carrie Chapman Catt, August 25, 1933, reel 12, NAWSA Papers, LC; Bertha Lutz to Carrie Chapman Catt, February 12, 1934, reel 12, NAWSA Papers; Bertha Lutz to Carrie Chapman Catt, April 12, 1936, reel 12, NAWSA Papers; "Birthday Memorial Book," 1929, Catt Papers, IIAV; Bertha Lutz to Carrie Chapman Catt, July 29, 1931, reel 12, NAWSA Papers; Bertha Lutz to Rosa Manus, November 20, 1928, Manus Papers, IIAV; Marguerite Gobat to Jane Addams, October 3, 1929, reel 20, Addams Papers; "Messages of Europe, Christmas 1924," reel 18, WILPF Papers.

105 Aletta Jacobs to Rosika Schwimmer [German], November 18, 1903, box A–4, Schwimmer-Lloyd Collection, NYPL; Martina Kramers to Rosika Schwimmer, October 17, 1911, box A–27, Schwimmer-Lloyd Collection.

106 Aletta Jacobs to Emily Greene Balch, August 10, 1919, reel 36, WILPF Papers. Bosch, *Politics and Friendship*, provides extensive coverage of such relations within the International Woman Suffrage Alliance. The records of all of the organizations are replete with discussions of friends traveling together to proselytize around the globe (the most renowned was the "world tour" of Carrie Chapman Catt and Aletta Jacobs in 1911–12), invitations, thank-yous, and reminiscences about visits, inquiries about each other's health and well-being, and direct expressions of the meaning of international friendships.

107 My thinking on these issues has been much influenced by the scholarship of U.S. women of color who have critiqued the Eurocentric bias of these aspects of feminist thought and practice. See, for some of the classic statements, The Combahee River Collective, "A Black Feminist Statement," in Gloria T. Hull, Patricia Bell Scott, and Barbara Smith, eds., *All the Women Are*

White, All the Blacks Are Men, But Some of Us Are Brave: Black Women's Studies (Old Westbury, N.Y., 1982), 13–22; bell hooks, *Feminist Theory from Margin to Center* (Boston, 1984); the essays in Cherríe Moraga and Gloria Anzaldúa, eds., *This Bridge Called My Back: Writings by Radical Women of Color* (Watertown, Mass., 1981); Barbara Smith, "Notes for Yet Another Paper on Black Feminism, Or Will the Real Enemy Please Stand Up?" *Conditions: Five* (1979): 123–27.

108 Hollinger, "How Wide the Circle of the 'We,' " 328–37. For a lucid discussion of the issue of identity from a cultural studies perspective, see Duggan, "Trials of Alice Mitchell."

12 The challenge of multinational empire for the international women's movement (Susan Zimmermann)

I am grateful to A. Mevis, B. Bader-Zaar, F. de Haan, M. John, L. Kontler, and G. Melinz for their help at various stages of the research. Two anonymous readers made valuable comments on the earlier version of this article. M. Bosch drew my attention to biographical information on Carrie Chapman Catt and made other important comments. The Österreichische Akademie der Wissenschaften (Vienna), the Central European University (Budapest), and the Wissenschaftskolleg zu Berlin have supported research for this study. All translations into English are mine. The author, in collaboration with the volume editor, has made light revisions in this version; see especially material added to notes 11 and 12.

1   I use the terms "North-Atlantic" and "North Atlantic core zone" in a geographical-political sense. These terms are meant to indicate that in the period at least up to World War I, organized internationalism by the women's movement(s) was dominated organizationally by Western European and US-American women's movements. In collaboration and exchange reaching well beyond these regions, personalities and aspirations rooted and/or located in the North-Atlantic core zones and/or ascribing organizational and thematic leadership to women's endeavors first developed in these zones played a dominant role. For context see Leila J. Rupp, "Challenging Imperialism in International Women's Organizations, 1888–1945," *National Women's Studies Association Journal* 8 (1996): 8–27.

2   Formal (and formally equal) federation and affiliation for women's organizations with the new international organizations remained largely confined to the North-Atlantic region, to the rest of Europe, and to the white settler colonies and large dominions (especially Australia and Canada). Affiliation dates are compiled in Leila J. Rupp, *Worlds of Women. The Making of an International Women's Movement* (Princeton, NJ: Princeton University Press, 1997), 16–18, Table 1.

3   The first constitution of the IWSA used the term "auxiliary" as a *terminus technicus* only. May Wright Sewall, comp., *Genesis of the International Council of Women and the Story of its Growth 1888–1893.* (n.p., n.d.), 19–20; and *Report. Second and Third Conferences of the International Woman Suffrage Alliance.* Berlin, Germany, June 3, 4, 1904. Copenhagen, Denmark, Aug. 7, 8, 9, 10, 11, 1906 (Copenhagen: Bianco Luno, 1906), 116–17.

4   See "Women of Canada. Standing Orders for the Executive Committee of the ICW," microfiche 3255, Bund Deutscher Frauenvereine B 235-01, hereafter B 235-01, Helene Lange Archiv, Landesarchiv Berlin, hereafter HLA-LAB; microfiche 3206 "Minutes of the Meeting of the Executive Committee, London, July 1897," 5–6, B 235-01, HLA-LAB; International Council of Women, *Report of Transactions of the Second Quinquennial Meeting held in London, July 1899* (London: T. Fisher Unwin, 1900), 192–93; and International Council of Women, *Handbook of International Council* (n.p., n.d. [1899]), 122.

5   "ICW: Memorandum to the Presidents of National Councils 1902," 15, microfiche 3176, B 235-01, HLA-LAB.

6   International Council of Women, *Report of Transactions During the Third Quinquennial Term Terminating with the Third Quinquennial Meeting held in Berlin, June, 1904* (Boston: n.p., 1909), 186–87.

7   Sewall to Stritt, 24 July1903, microfiche 3262, B 235-01, HLA-LAB.

8   Sewall to Stritt, 15 April 1900, microfiche 3260, B 235-01, HLA-LAB; Circular letter Sewall to presidents n.d., 3–4, microfiche 3264, B 235-01, HLA-LAB; Circular letter Sewall 19 November 1904, 7, microfiche 3264, B 235-01, HLA-LAB; "Centralblatt 15.05.1899," microfiche 2234, B 235-01, HLA-LAB; Stritt to Sewall, 30 May 1907, microfiche 2234, B 235-01, HLA-LAB; and Stritt to Sewall, n.d., microfiche 2282, B 235-01, HLA-LAB.

9 *IWSA Report 1904–1906*, 117–18.

10 See, for example, *Report. First International Suffrage Conference held at Washington, U.S.A., February 12, 13, 14, 15, 16, 17, 18, 1902* (New York: International Woman Suffrage Headquarters, n.d.), 17.

11 The conflict originally had been triggered by the fact that a second society from the Netherlands had applied for affiliation in 1907. Catt on this occasion recognized "to [her] amazement" that it was not the case that the Constitution "especially forbade two societies in any country from entering the Alliance." Catt to Aletta Jacobs, 2 April 1907, no. 61, Aletta Jacobs Papers, Archives, International Information Center and Archives for the Women's Movement, hereafter AJP-IIAV; see also no. 68, Circular letter Catt to presidents, 27 June 1908, AJP-IIAV.
The general problem raised by this specific case was resolved within the framework of a major alteration of the IWSA constitution in 1909. In the highly controversial process of adopting the related new regulations, the IWSA finally granted extended decision powers to its leadership (the Admissions Committee and the Executive Board), combining this with a strong intention to push concurrent societies of one country towards "joint representation in the Alliance by means of National Federation for International Purposes." By enlarging the influence of the top level of the IWSA on the combination and construction of the elements from which the national was (to be) composed in relation to the international, the *Alliance* tried to prevent quarrels over representation from one country being transferred to the international level.

12 There was no definite regulation for the (hypothetical) case of federation for international purposes failing even after mediation by the Executive Board of the Alliance. Already in 1911 a new society from Denmark and two new societies from Finland were admitted to the Alliance according to the new scheme. These new societies were expected to represent their country together with the respective Auxiliaries from the same country admitted earlier by jointly filling the delegate positions for that country, according to a specific distribution key in all International Meetings of the *Alliance*. At the same time the number of delegates fully entitled to represent a country at all international meetings of the IWSA was enlarged from six to twelve. In a sense, the politics of "national federation for international purpose" came down to restricting voting power of the first, second and third national associations forming a national federation to the same level as it would be if only a single "National Woman Suffrage Association" were admitted from one country. Apart from this directive as to numbers, "National Woman Suffrage Associations" represented through "federation" were often referred to and presented separately (often even as separate *Auxiliaries*) within the orbit of the IWSA. They would also present their separate reports etc. in the international publications of the IWSA. See Constitution of the IWSA (typescript, n.d.), A18, A Series: Rosika Schwimmer Papers, hereafter A, 18, Schwimmer-Lloyd Collection, New York Public Library, hereafter SLC-NYPL; Alterations in the wording of the constitution of the IWSA (typescript, n.d.), A 458, SLC-NYPL; International Woman Suffrage Alliance, *Report of Sixth Congress. Stockholm, Sweden, June 12, 13, 14, 15, 16 & 17, 1911* (London: Women's Printing Society, n.d.), hereafter *IWSA 1911*, 25, 36–37; see also *IWSA 1904–1906*, 116; *Report of the Fourth Conference of the International Woman Suffrage Alliance. Amsterdam, Holland, June 15, 16, 17, 18, 19, 20, 1908* (Amsterdam: F. van Rossen, 1908), hereafter *IWSA 1908*, 38–39; International Woman Suffrage Alliance, *Report of Fifth Conference and First Quinquennial, London, England. April 26, 27, 28, 29, 30, May 1, 1909* (London: Samuel Sidders & Co., 1909), hereafter *IWSA 1909*, 54, 139, 145–56; International Woman Suffrage Alliance, *Report of Seventh Congress, Budapest, Hungary, June 15, 16, 17, 18, 19, 20, 21, 1913* (Manchester: Percy Brothers, n.d.), hereafter *IWSA 1913*, 15–16.

13 International Council of Women, *Report of Transactions of the Fourth Quinquennial Meeting held at Toronto, Canada, June, 1909* (London: Constable & Co., 1910), hereafter *ICW Quinquennial 1909*, 87.

14 *IWSA Report 1909*, 63.

15 *IWSA 1913*, 89. In a private letter to Aletta Jacobs dated December of the same year, Catt, in view of developments in the Philippines, made her position with regard to national self-government much more explicit. "The Philippinos are full of hope that the democrats now in power will grant freedom to those islands"; those "officers," who had lost their position since the visit of Catt and Jacobs, Catt continued, were now lecturing in the US, and "of course no one of them advocates independence, yet it is possible that it may come about. If it does, I imagine it will have a most significant influence upon the entire Asiatic question." No. 106, AJP-IIAV.

16 Sewall in "The Bulletin of the International Council of Women (1904), no. 3," 24, microfiche 3172, B 235-01, HLA-LAB; and International Council of Women, *Reports and Addresses given at the Third Quinquennial Reunion held in Berlin, June, 1904* (Boston: n.p., 1909), 21–23.

17 *Suffrage Report 1902*, 4; for a later, slightly revised version see *IWSA 1904–1906*, 4.

18 *History of Woman Suffrage*, vol. 3, 1876–1885, ed. Elizabeth Cady Stanton, Susan B. Anthony and Matilda Joslyn Gage (New York: Fowler & Wells, 1887), 898.

19 This function was preserved for countries where a National Council did not yet exist. "ICW, List of Officers elected at Chicago, 1893," 7, microfiche 3157, B 235-01, HLA-LAB.

20 ICW, *Handbook*, 121–22; *Constitution of the ICW and Resolutions passed in London 1899 and Berlin 1904* (n.p, n.d.), 2–3.

21 *The World's Congress of Representative Women Convened in Chicago on May 15, and Adjourned on May 22, 1893, Under the Auspices of the Woman's Branch of the World's Congress Auxiliary* (Chicago: Rand, McNally & Co, 1894), 2: 934, 939.

22 This approach was characteristic also for some of the major internationalist publications of the time. *The Woman Question in Europe. A Series of Original Essays*, ed. Theodore Stanton (London: Sampson Low & Co, 1884); *History of Woman Suffrage*, vol. 3; and *Handbuch der Frauenbewegung*, vol. 1, ed. Helene Lange and Gertrud Bäumer (Berlin: Moeser, 1901), esp. 350–60.

23 We possess no compact list of those women's associations in the Habsburg Monarchy to whom the ICW addressed its solicitation in 1899. International Council of Women, *Histories of Affiliated National Councils* 1888–1938 (n.p., n.d.), 145; and *Frauenbewegung, Frauenbildung und Frauenarbeit in Österreich: Hg. im Auftrag des Bundes Österreichischer Frauenvereine* (Vienna: Bund Österreichischer Frauenvereine [1930]), 20–21, 39–41.

24 "Der Frauenweltbund. Denkschrift. (Zweite Denkschrift des dritten Quinquenniums) 1900," 36, microfiche 3218, B 235-01, HLA-LAB.

25 Information diverges with regard to details in *Dokumente der Frauen* 1 (1899/1900): 38, 46, 130; and *ICW 1899*, 130–31.

26 *Bericht über den International Council mit einem Rückblick auf die österreichische Frauenbewegung an der Jahrhundertwende erstattet am 29. März 1901 von Marianne Hainisch* (Vienna: published by Marianne Hainisch [1901]), 3.

27 *Bericht über den International Council*, 4, 6.

28 *ICW Report 1899–1904*, 5–6.

29 Hainisch in her country report on "Austria" to the London Quinquennial. *ICW Report 1899*, 131.

30 This number obviously was intended to refer to the number of nationalities or nations in the Habsburg Monarchy and included more than the "Volksstämme" officially handled as such in Cis-Leithania plus the Hungarians and the Slovaks. *ICW 1899–1904*, 6. At a meeting of the ICW Executive held in London, the possibility was openly discussed of organizing Hungary and Austria as separate National Councils. President Sewall on this occasion, while insisting on the establishment of one common "National Council of Austria," consented to the idea of having "three sections – Austria, Hungary, and Bohemia." Yet at the quinquennial meeting Berta Engel "from Hungary" was registered as a simple delegate without official function, while Marianne Hainisch was present as an "Honorary Vice President" for "Austria." *ICW 1899*, 32, 81, 200; see also Martha Bohachevsky-Chomiak, *Feminists Despite Themselves* (Edmonton: Canadian Institute of Ukrainian Studies Press 1988), 268.

31 *Bericht über den International Council*, 3. *ICW Quinquennial Report 1904*, 84; *Handbuch der Frauenbewegung*, vol. 1, 187. Tension and conflict had long been acute between German-Austrian and Czech currents in the women's movement. See Katherine David, "Czech Feminists and Nationalism in the Late Habsburg Monarchy: 'The First in Austria,'" *Journal of Women's History*, 3 (1991): 26–45.

32 ICW, *Histories of Affiliated National Councils*, 146. See also *Neues Frauenleben* 14, no. 5 (1902): 16–17.

33 *Rechenschaftsbericht 1905–1907 erstattet in der IV. Generalversammlung des Bundes Öesterreichischer Frauenvereine. Wien ... Mai 1907*, 1, 13–16; [Rechenschaftsbericht 1907–1909], 11–13; *Rechenschaftsbericht 1909–1911 erstattet in der VI. Generalversammlung des Bundes Österreichischer Frauenvereine zu Wien, ... Mai 1911*, 2–3, 12–14; *Der Bund. Zentralblatt des Bundes Österr. Frauenvereine* 4, no. 7 (1909): 6; Rechenschaftsbericht 1909–1911, no. 4 (1910): 4–5; and International Council of Women, *Report for 1905–1906* (Aberdeen: Rosemount Press 1906), 118–20.

34 The fact that in the ICW an Honorary Vice President for "Bohemia" was appointed (at some point between 1899 and 1906), implies that the leadership viewed the idea of some form of more or less separate representation of the Czech women's movement as feasible and important. Another Honorary Vice President was named for "Poland." International Council of Women, *Report for 1907–1908*, (Aberdeen: Rosemount Press 1908), 147–48; International Council of Women,

Fourth Annual Report of the Fifth Quinquennial Period 1912–1913 (n.p., n.d.),165; International Council of Women, *Fifth Annual Report of the Fifth Quinquennial Period 1913–1914* (n.p., n.d.), 142–43; Aberdeen to Stritt, 18 November 1904, microfiche 3264, B 235-01, HLA-LAB; Aberdeen to Stritt, 23 November 1904, microfiche 3264, B 235-01, HLA-LAB; Aberdeen to Stritt, 24 March 1905, microfiche 3264, B 235-01, HLA-LAB; "Der Frauenweltbund: Die Ansprachen der Vorsitzenden Gräfin von Aberdeen bei Gelegenheit der Tagung des Vorstandes in Paris, im Juni, 1906," 2, microfiche 3137, B 235-01, HLA-LAB.

35 "Minutes of Executive Committee Meeting, Copenhagen, July 1902," microfiche 3204, B 235-01, HLA-LAB.

36 For a detailed account of intra-monarchy developments in their relation to international action, see Susan Zimmermann, "Reich, Nation, und Internationalismus: Konflikte und Kooperationen der Frauenbewegungen der Habsburgermonarchie," in *Frauenbilder, feministische Praxis und nationales Bewusstsein in Österreich-Ungarn 1867–1918*, ed. Waltraud Heindl, Edit Király, and Alexandra Millner (Tübingen, Basel: A. Francke Verlag, 2006), 119–67. Whenever details of intra-Monarchy developments are referred to in the following, references are contained in this article.

37 These "reasons" were said to be the wish that the Councils in question "should enter the international prior to the next Quinquennial term." "Minutes of Executive Meeting Dresden August 1903," microfiche 3204, B 235-01, HLA-LAB; "M. W. Sewall. To the members of the Executive of the ICW 31.12.1903," 22, microfiche 3263, B 235-01, HLA-LAB; and "M. W. Sewall. To the Presidents of the National Councils" [n.d.], 7, microfiche 3264, B 235-01, HLA-LAB. See also *ICW 1899–1904*, 121.

38 At the executive meeting held on the eve of the quinquennial, Austria was greeted together with Hungary as one of those countries that had officially submitted an application. *ICW Report 1899–1904*, 165.

39 *Der Bund* 1, no. 1 (1905): 1; Letterhead on letter to Minna Cauer, 28 December 1903, microfiche 3237, B 235-01, HLA-LAB; Letterhead on letter to Stritt, August 1904, microfiche 3237, B 235-01, HLA-LAB; *ICW 1899–1904*, 168.

40 ICW, *Report 1905–1906*, 15, 176–77. This formula was translated into German as "Vertretung nach politischen und nationalen Gesichtspunkten."

41 *ICW 1899–1904*, 91–92; "Der Frauenweltbund. Denkschrift. (Zweite Denkschrift des dritten Quinquenniums),"14, microfiche 3172, B 235-01, HLA-LAB; and "Copy of extracts from a letter to Lady Aberdeen commenting on Memorandum of the Hague Conference," microfiche 3204, B 235-01, HLA-LAB.

42 Ensuring the federation of the BÖVFe as the single Austrian Council was on the agenda at the same meeting of the executive. "Minutes of the Executive Committee Meeting Dresden August 1903," 13–14, microfiche 3204, B 235-01, HLA-LAB. The Australian case was finally resolved years later. *ICW 1899–1904*, 117, 129, 165–66, 177, 215; ICW, *Report 1905–1906*, 129–33, 167–69; ICW, *Report 1907–1908*, 22–23, 180–82, 187–88, 197; *ICW Quinquennial 1909*, 79–80, 256; "Memorandum of the Meeting of the Executive and Standing Committees, The Hague, May 1913," 15–16, microfiche 3208, B 235-01, HLA-LAB.

43 Sewall to Members of the Executive of the International Council, 31 December 1903, 11–16, microfiche 3263, B 235-01, HLA-LAB; see also Teresa Wilson to Stritt, 13 February 1904, microfiche 3263, B 235-01, HLA-LAB; Stritt to Sewall, 30 March 1904, microfiche 3263, B 235-01, HLA-LAB.

44 *ICW Report 1899–1904*, 166.

45 An Honorary Vice President for Norway had been appointed already in 1899. "Der Frauenweltbund. Denkschrift. (Zweite Denkschrift des dritten Quinquenniums) 1900," 36, microfiche 3218, B 235-01, HLA-LAB; and "Meeting of the Delegates of the N.C.W.'s held in London March 1905," microfiche 3204, B 235-01 HLA-LAB; and *ICW 1904*, 88.

46 No traces of this part of the story can be found in the official records of the Quinquennial proceedings. Yet it was keenly reported by the well-known representative of the German-Austrian women's movement, Adele Gerber, in *Neues Frauenleben* 16, no. 6 (1904): 8.

47 In 1906 the chair of the committee had proposed that "the fact of possessing the organs of all national life – namely, a *Constitution* and a *Parliament* – characterizes a nation, . . . no matter whether this nation be enjoying a full autonomy or whether it have only a limited autonomy, being incorporated within a large nation and not recognized as an independent diplomatic member." ICW, *Report 1905–1906*, 49–50, 159.

48 ICW, *Report 1905–1906*, 160–62; *ICW Quinquennial 1909*, 417–18; International Council of Women, *First Annual Report of the Fifth Quinquennial Period 1909–1910* (n.p., n.d.), 12;

"Memorandum of the Meeting of General Officers, London July 1905," 76–77, microfiche 3177, B 235-01, HLA-LAB; Lady Aberdeen to Stritt, 11 July 1905, microfiche 3204, B 235-01, HLA-LAB; and Ida Blom, "The Struggle for Women's Suffrage in Norway, 1885–1913," *Scandinavian Journal of History* 5, no. 1 (1980): 17–18; see also Rupp, *Worlds of Women*, 112.

49 "Der Frauenweltbund. Denkschrift. (Zweite Denkschrift des dritten Quniquenniums) 1900," 36, microfiche 3218, B 235-01, HLA-LAB; "Teresa Wilson, What the Women of Europe are Doing towards Forming National Councils ... . Ottawa 1896," 3–4, microfiche 3172, B 235-01, HLA-LAB; and Margaret H. McFadden, *Golden Cables of Sympathy. The Transatlantic Sources of Nineteenth-Century Feminism* (Lexington: University Press of Kentucky, 1999), 17, 30, 148, 176–81.

50 The related – typical – statement on this occasion was: "As to Peace there is nothing to say for Finland. The position of our country makes it impossible to organize any moral peace work." *ICW Quinquennial Report 1904*, 136.

51 The ICW had invited Finnish women for affiliation after the introduction of female suffrage in 1906. Yet the foundation of a National Council was "delayed owing to political reasons" until 1911. These difficulties had to do with the split in Finland between the Finnish Women's Association (founded in 1884, and closely related to the Old Finn tradition) and the Feminist Union, founded in 1892, and closely related to the Young Finns). While the National Council seems to have been dominated by the group around Gripenberg, who had been the founder of the Association, the Union with Annie Furuhjelm as its leading figure was affiliated with the IWSA from 1908. ICW, *Histories of Affiliated National Councils*, 216; International Council of Women, *Third Annual Report of the Fifth Quinquennial Period 1911–1912* (n.p., n.d), 7, 115–16; Riitta Jallinoja, "The Women's Liberation Movement in Finland: The social and political mobilization of women in Finland, 1880–1910," *Scandinavian Journal of History* 5, no. 1 (1980): 40–44, 46. See also Rochelle Ruthchild's article in Part IV of this volume.

52 ICW, *Report 1907–1908*, 181–82.

53 ICW, *Report 1907–1908*, 182, 184, 187; and "ICW, Resolutions passed at Special Meeting in Geneva 1908," microfiche 3208, B 235-01, HLA-LAB.

54 Attachment of letter to Ogilvie Gordon, 27 November 1908, 4, microfiche 3269, B 235-01, HLA-LAB.

55 Instead some kind of board was established that added little to the pre-existing formal decision-making patterns. *ICW Quinquennial 1909*, 113–14, 256; and "Beschlüsse gefaßt auf der Generalversammlung des Internationalen Frauenbundes in Toronto, Canada, von 8. bis 25. Juni 1909" [fragment], 5, microfiche 3242, B 235-01, HLA-LAB.

56 After admission of the German-Austrian *Frauenstimmrechtskommitee*, the IWSA treated provisional cooperation with German-Austrians in the period prior to 1908 as non-existent.

57 *IWSA Report 1909*, 3, 26, 84–88.

58 Róza Schwimmer to "Werte Frau" [Stritt] March [?] 1903, microfiche 3262, B 235-01, HLA-LAB.

59 Here Anita Augspurg to Schwimmer, 14 May 1904, A5, SLC-NYPL; and Adelheid v. Welyczeck to Schwimmer, n.d., A5, SLC-NYPL.

60 *IWSA Report 1904–1906*, 30. The Report of the Seventh Congress of the IWSA in 1913 reprinted this resolution together with four others under the heading "Resolutions defining the policy of the Alliance." *IWSA 1913*, 172.

61 *IWSA Report 1904–1906*, 30.

62 Catt and the group around her worked for months on this "tedious task." On the eve of the London convention of 1909, Catt, in order "to avoid difficulty," even arranged for a "private meeting" devoted to "preliminary consideration of the constitution." Circular letter Catt to presidents, 2 February 1909, A19, A5, SLC-NYPL; see also Anna H. Shaw to Jacobs, 14 December 1908, no. 322, AJP-IIAV.

63 The ICW never gave a definition of the term "country." *IWSA Report 1909*, 25, 33–43, 145; see also *IWSA Report 1908*, 20; and Rupp, *Worlds of Women*, 112.

64 It was a long journey for the Alliance to clarify its position in this regard. Finally, a resolution passed at the Stockholm convention in 1911 stated that "the wording of the [1908, SZ] resolution," namely demanding the franchise for women "on the same terms as it is now or may be exercised by men," had been "misconstrued on the one hand as an expression of hostility to universal suffrage, and on the other hand as a pledge to support universal suffrage." As compared to this, it was repeated now in a different wording, the "sole object" of the Alliance was "to establish the principle that sex should not be a disqualification." *IWSA Report 1913*, 172; and *IWSA Report 1909*, 139–40.

65 *IWSA Report 1904–1906*, 4.

66 Catt in this context explicitly referred to the history of the "American colonies," where "only a very small proportion of the men could vote," and to still existing restrictions of the franchise for men "in most foreign countries." Her references to the "foreign countries" were much more careful in international contexts. "Carrie Chapman Catt, Do you know,? New York 1916," 10, box 3/1, Series III, Carrie Chapman Catt papers, Sophia Smith Collection, Smith College Library, Northampton, MA.

67 This term was used by Catt in the 1906 debate. *IWSA Report 1904–1906*, 30.

68 It was also the Hungarian parliament that elected the Hungarian representatives to the "delegations," which had to handle the "common affairs" in the Monarchy.

69 These had to be either "National Woman Suffrage Associations" or "National Committees" composed of "local" suffrage associations. *IWSA Report 1904–1906*, 116.

70 Catt's efforts to establish substantial relationships with German-Austrian suffragists in 1904/1906, however proved to be unsuccessful. Catt to Vilma Glücklich, (n.d. [1904]), A4, A5, SLC-NYPL; Catt to Schwimmer, 29 September 1905, A7, A5, SLC-NYPL; and Catt to Schwimmer, 24 April 1906, A9, A5, SLC-NYPL.

71 No Czech association was mentioned by Catt while preparing her trip. Catt to Jacobs, 26 September 1906, no. 56, AJP-IIAV; and Catt to Jacobs, 2 October 1906, no. 57, AJP-IIAV.

72 A substantial study on the history of Czech suffrage feminism is Jiří Kořalka, "Die Wahl einer Frau in den böhmischen Landtag im Jahre 1912," in Margret Friedrich and Peter Urbanitsch, *Von Bürgern und ihren Frauen* (Vienna: Böhlau Verlag 1996), 165–78.

73 Jacobs and Catt's biographer Mary Gray Peck recalled the events somewhat differently. Mary Gray Peck, *Carrie Chapman Catt. A Biography* (New York: H. W. Wilson Co., 1944), 152–54; and Aletta Jacobs, *Memories: My Life as an International Leader in Health, Suffrage, and Peace* (New York: The Feminist Press at the City University of New York, 1996), 60–61.

74 The travel report in the international journal of the IWSA, *Jus Suffragii*, did not mention any of the related events, and until 1908 there is no single mention of the Czech-Bohemian suffrage movement in the journal. See *Jus Suffragii* 1, no. 3 (1906/1907): 5.

75 Catt to Schwimmer 26 May 1908, General Correspondence, Copy of Carrie Chapman Catt Papers [Library of Congress, Washington D.C.], Archives, International Information Center and Archives for the Women's Movement, hereafter CCC-IIAV.

76 *IWSA Report, 1908*, 10, 81–82, 84–87. No other reports of non-affiliated organizations were read to the conference.

77 "I must go to Prague," Catt had already written to R. Schwimmer in August 1908. Catt to Schwimmer, 28 August 1908, General Correspondence, CCC-IIAV.

78 11 March 1909, no. 68, AJP-IIAV.

79 *Jus Suffragii* 3 (1908/1909): 64–65.

80 *IWSA Report 1909*, 3, 26, 29, 84–88, 145–46.

81 Catt to T. O. Vaherwuori, 17 December 1941, General Correspondence, CCC-IIAV. Finland was to be federated with the IWSA in 1908. See also fn. 51 above, and Rupp, *Worlds of Women*, 113, 136.

82 Catt in 1908, *IWSA Report 1908*, 72. Already in 1906 it had been resolved that allusions to recent political conflicts between nations were to be avoided.

83 The revised constitution simply said that, "In any country where no Woman Suffrage organization exists[,] a Committee ... which gives evidence of its intention to form a National Woman Suffrage Association, may become Auxiliary to the Alliance." *IWSA Report 1909*, 146.

84 *IWSA Report 1909*, 145–46.

85 *Jus Suffragii* 3 (1908/1909): 69.

86 The related discussions can be found in *IWSA Report 1904–1906*, 34; and *IWSA 1909*, 51, 149. For a detailed account of the Galician-Polish politics of the IWSA and the related developments within the Habsburg Monarchy, see Zimmermann, "Reich, Nation."

87 *IWSA Report 1909*, 51, 149.

88 Catt in her London Presidential speech in *IWSA Report 1909*, 61.

89 ICW President May Wright Sewall spoke of the ICW as a world republic within which the "woman ... without an army, ... without a parliament, without independent wealth" fulfilled her duty. *ICW Quinquennial Report 1904*, 25. For an analogous view expressed by Catt see *IWSA 1909*, 64.

90 Aberdeen to Stritt, 2 June 1905, microfiche 3265, B 235-01, HLA-LAB.

91 The resolution urged "autonomy" for all peoples and requested that any "transference of territory" be based on "the consent of the men and women residing therein." See *International Congress of Women: The Hague, 28th April–May 1st 1915*, ed. International Women's Committee of Permanent

Peace (Amsterdam: International Women's Committee for Permanent Peace, n.d.), esp. XLVI, 36–37, 104–11, 166–68, 230–34.

13 The other "awakening" (Ellen L. Fleischmann)

I would like to thank Afsaneh Najmabadi, Elizabeth Thompson, and Chris Toensing for their comments on earlier drafts of this essay; Lisa Pollard for support and advice; and Camron Amin and Afsaneh Najmabadi for helpful linguistic and other information. I take responsibility for conclusions drawn and any mistakes made. Some endnotes have been updated.

1 Leila Ahmed, "Between Two Worlds: The Formation of a Turn-of-the-Century Egyptian Feminist," in *Life/Lines: Theorizing Women's Autobiography*, ed. Bella Brodzki and Celeste Schenck (Ithaca, NY: Cornell University Press, 1988), 156.
2 Marnia Lazreg, *The Eloquence of Silence: Algerian Women in Question* (New York and London: Routledge, 1994), 7. In the interests of feasibility and scope, this essay will primarily be limited to literature in English and restricted to the Mashriq (the Arab East), Egypt, Turkey, and Iran; in the 1990s, there was very little literature on women's movements in North Africa during this period.
3 [Ed.: Significant cuts have been made in this section, which raise questions about the meaning of "feminism," the intersections of feminism, colonialism, and nationalism, and the issues involved in extending what many considered a "Western-based" concept to non-Western societies. Some aspects of these debates are addressed in the Editor's Introduction for this volume, but readers who want to revisit the state of the debate in the mid-1990s should consult the original version of Fleischmann's essay, published in *Women and Gender in the Middle East*, edited by Margaret L. Meriwether and Judith E. Tucker (Boulder: Westview Press, 1999). In consequence of these cuts, the notes below and in the rest of the essay have been renumbered.] Of particular importance for this discussion are: Sharon Sievers, "Six (or More) Feminists in Search of a Historian," in *Expanding the Boundaries of History: Essays on Women in the Third World*, ed. Cheryl Johnson-Odim and Margaret Strobel (Bloomington: Indiana University Press, 1992), and Margot Badran, *Feminists, Islam, and Nation: Gender and the Making of Modern Egypt* (Princeton: Princeton University Press, 1995).
4 See Chandra Talpade Mohanty, "Cartographies of Struggle: Third World Women and the Politics of Feminism," in *Third World Women and the Politics of Feminism*, ed. Chandra Talpade Mohanty, Ann Russo, and Lourdes Torres (Bloomington: Indiana University Press, 1991), 6. See also Chela Sandoval, "U.S. Third World Feminism: The Theory and Method of Oppositional Consciousness in the Postmodern World," *Genders* 10 (Spring 1991): 1–24, and Anne McClintock, "'No Longer in a Future Heaven': Women and Nationalism in South Africa," *Transition* 51 (1991): 104–123. Also important are the points made about feminism(s) in the plural by Marnia Lazreg, "Feminism and Difference: The Perils of Writing As a Woman on Women in Algeria," *Feminist Studies* 14 (Spring 1988): 101.
5 Janet Afary, *The Iranian Constitutional Revolution, 1906–1911: Grassroots Democracy, Social Democracy, and the Origins of Feminism* (New York: Columbia University Press, 1996), 10.
6 For this reason, I have deliberately used the phrase "women's movements" in the title of this essay. I have chosen to respect women's ambiguity, or historically different concepts about their own activism, despite the fact that *I* would consider their acts as feminist. Although it may seem both contradictory and a fine distinction, I believe there is a difference between women's own conception of their experiences and how we historians retrospectively categorize and name them. We should be explicit and self-conscious about this difference. Furthermore, neither Arabic nor Persian has a specific word for "feminist" or "feminism," making the issues of language, meaning, and intent even more problematic.
7 Guida West and Rhoda Lois Blumberg, "Reconstructing Social Protest from a Feminist Perspective," in *Women and Social Protest*, ed. Guida West and Rhoda Lois Blumberg (Oxford: Oxford University Press, 1990), 15.
8 This theme has been continually reiterated by Palestinian women throughout history. See my "The Nation and Its 'New Women': Feminism, Nationalism, Colonialism, and the Palestinian Women's Movement, 1920–1948," Ph.D. dissertation, Georgetown University, 1996. Published as Ellen L. Fleischmann, *The Nation and its "New" Women: The Palestinian Women's Movement 1920–1948* (Berkeley: University of California Press, 2003).

9   Huda Sha'rawi, *Mudhakkirāt ra'idāt al-'Arabiyya al-haditha* [Memoirs of a modern Arab woman pioneer], introduced by Amina al-Sa'id (Cairo: Dar al-Hilal, 1981), 322, quoted in Badran, *Feminists*, 88.

10 Ruth Woodsmall, *Moslem Women Enter a New World* (New York: Round Table Press, 1936), 363.

11 This is not to say that all women in this historical period did not have or develop feminist "consciousness." Clearly such women existed, as has been amply documented by scholars such as Badran and Parvin Paidar, in *Women and the Political Process in Twentieth-Century Iran* (Cambridge: Cambridge University Press, 1995). On the other hand, the threat to national identity and even survival was so overwhelming an issue in some cases, such as the Palestinians', that feminist consciousness was much more muted and not as overtly articulated as in, say, the Egyptian women's movement.

12 For more on the contradictory, conflicting, and contentious interests *within* colonialist structures of power, see Ann Laura Stoler, "Rethinking Colonial Categories: European Communities and the Boundaries of Rule," *Comparative Studies in Society and History* 31 (1989): 134–161.

13 It should be noted that some women's movements failed to creatively adapt, undermining their effectiveness. This was the case with the Palestinian women's movement during the 1940s, when it was unable to develop a broader base beyond its narrow middle- and upper-class constituency. See Fleischmann, "The Nation and Its 'New' Women," 348–349.

14 [Author: Most of the citations in this note refer to the state of these fields as of the time the article was first published, in 1999]. Pertinent earlier scholarship in other fields than history includes: Julie Peteet, *Gender in Crisis: Women and the Palestinian Resistance Movement* (New York: Columbia University Press, 1991); Sondra Hale, *Gender Politics in Sudan: Feminism, Socialism, and the State* (Boulder: Westview Press, 1996); Haideh Moghissi, *Populism and Feminism in Iran: Women's Struggle in a Male-Defined Revolutionary Movement* (London: St. Martin's Press, 1994); Guity Nashat, ed., *Women and Revolution in Iran* (Boulder: Westview Press, 1983); Nermin Abadan-Unat, ed., *Women in Turkish Society* (Leiden: E. J. Brill, 1981); and Sirin Tekeli, ed., *Women in Modern Turkish Society: A Reader* (London: Zed Press, 1995).

    With the exceptions of book-length works by Badran, *Feminists, Islam, and Nation*, and Paidar *Women and the Political Process*, up to the late 1990s, treatments of women's political and social activism by historians usually took the form of a chapter or passing reference in a book, article, or anthology devoted to contemporary women's movements. See, for example, Leila Ahmed, "Feminism and Feminist Movements in the Middle East, a Preliminary Exploration: Turkey, Egypt, Algeria," *Women's Studies International Forum* 5, no. 2 (1982): 153–168, and her "Early Feminist Movements in the Middle East: Turkey and Egypt," in *Muslim Women*, ed. Freda Hussain (New York: St. Martin's Press, 1984); Nashat, *Women and Revolution in Iran*; Abadan-Unat, *Women in Turkish Society*; and Deniz Kandiyoti, ed., *Women, Islam, and the State* (Philadelphia: Temple University Press, 1991). Kumari Jayawardena's valuable book *Feminism and Nationalism in the Third World* (London: Zed Press, 1986) has chapters devoted to the Turkish, Egyptian, and Iranian women's movements.

    Far more was published concerning Egypt. In addition to Badran's *Feminists*, see her articles, including "Dual Liberation: Feminism and Nationalism in Egypt, 1870s–1925," *Feminist Issues* 8, no. 1 (1988): 15–34; "Competing Agenda: Feminists, Islam, and the State in Nineteenth and Twentieth Century Egypt," in *Women, Islam, and the State*, ed. Kandiyoti (cited above); "Independent Women: More Than a Century of Feminism in Egypt," in *Arab Women: Old Boundaries, New Frontiers*, ed. Judith E. Tucker (Bloomington: Indiana University Press, 1993); and "From Consciousness to Activism: Feminist Politics in Early Twentieth Century Egypt," in *Problems of the Middle East in Historical Perspective*, ed. John Spagnolo (London: Ithaca Press, 1992). See also Mervat Hatem, "Egyptian Upper- and Middle-Class Women's Early Nationalist Discourses on National Liberation and Peace in Palestine (1922–1944)," *Women and Politics* 9, no. 3 (1989): 49–70; Selma Botman, "The Experience of Women in the Egyptian Communist Movement, 1939–1954," *Women's Studies International Forum* 11, no. 2 (1988): 117–126; Thomas Philipp, "Feminism and Nationalist Politics in Egypt," and Afaf Lutfi al-Sayyid Marsot, "The Revolutionary Gentlewomen in Egypt," both in *Women in the Muslim World*, ed. Lois Beck and Nikki Keddie (Cambridge MA: Harvard University Press, 1978); and Beth Baron, "Mothers, Morality, and Nationalism in Pre-1919 Egypt," in *The Origins of Arab Nationalism*, ed. Rashid Khalidi et al. (New York: Columbia University Press, 1991).

    On Iran, see, for example, Paidar (cited above) and Afary (cited above), and Afsaneh Najmabadi, "Zanhā-yi millat: Women or Wives of the Nation?" *Iranian Studies* 26, nos. 1–2 (1993): 51–72. Some earlier writings include: Janet Afary, "On the Origins of Feminism in Early Twentieth-Century

Iran," *Journal of Women's History* 1, no. 2 (Fall 1989): 65–87; Eliz Sansarian, *The Women's Rights Movement in Iran: Mutiny, Appeasement, and Repression, from 1900 to Khomeini* (New York: Praeger, 1982); Simin Royanian, "A History of Iranian Women's Struggles," *RIPEH* 3, no. 1 (Spring 1979): 17–29; and Mangol Bayat-Philipp, "Women and Revolution in Iran, 1905–1911," in *Women in the Muslim World*, ed. Beck and Keddie (cited above).

On Palestine there has been a burgeoning body of literature on women's participation in the resistance movement of the 1960s–1970s and, later, the *intifada*, that sometimes includes glancing references to the past. A partial list includes: Peteet, *Gender in Crisis* (cited above); Orayb Najjar with Kitty Warnock, *Portraits of Palestinian Women* (Salt Lake City: University of Utah Press, 1992); Soraya Antonius, "Fighting on Two Fronts: Conversations with Palestinian Women," *Journal of Palestine Studies* 8 (1979): 26–45; Rita Giacaman and Muna Odeh, "Palestinian Women's Movement," in *Women of the Arab World*, ed. Nahid Toubia (London: Zed Press, 1988); Nuha Abu Daleb, "Palestinian Women and Their Role in the Revolution," *Peuples méditerranéens* 5 (1978): 35–47; Hamida Kazi, "Palestinian Women and the National Liberation Movement: A Social Perspective," in *Women in the Middle East*, ed. the Khamsin Collective (London: Zed Press, 1987); and Islah Jad, "From Salons to Popular Committees: Palestinian Women, 1919–1989," in *Intifada: Palestine at the Crossroads*, ed. Jamal R. Nassar and Roger Heacock (Birzeit and New York: Birzeit University Press and Praeger, 1991). Up to the late 1990s, to my knowledge, the only work that focused on pre-1948 women's activity was my own writing, which includes "Jerusalem Women's Organizations During the British Mandate, 1920s–1930s" (Jerusalem: Palestinian Academic Society for the Study of International Affairs, 1995); and "The Nation and Its 'New' Women."

As of the late 1990s, the only work in English that dealt with the Lebanese and Syrian women's movements was Elizabeth Thompson's "Engendering the Nation: Statebuilding, Imperialism, and Women in Syria and Lebanon, 1920–1945," Ph.D. dissertation, Columbia University, 1995, since published as *Colonial Citizens: Republican Rights, Paternal Privilege, and Gender in French Syria and Lebanon* (New York: Columbia University Press, 2000). Works in Arabic exist, but are also limited.

There was little written in English or Arabic on the Iraqi women's movement by the late 1990s. One of the few examples is Doreen Ingram's *The Awakened: Women in Iraq* (London: Third World Center, 1985). Since then, Nogra Efrati's "The Other 'Awakening' in Iraq: The Women's Movement in the First Half of the Twentieth Century' has appeared in the *British Journal of Middle East Studies* 31, no. 2 (November 2004), 153–173.

Historical studies focused on family, law, Islam, but not on political participation, as of the late 1990s, included: Judith E. Tucker, *Women in Nineteenth-Century Egypt* (Cambridge: Cambridge University Press, 1985); Nikki Keddie and Beth Baron, eds., *Women in Middle Eastern History* (New Haven: Yale University Press, 1992); Leila Ahmed, *Women and Gender in Islam: Historical Roots of a Modern Debate* (New Haven and London: Yale University Press, 1992); Leslie Peirce, *The Imperial Harem: Women and Sovereignty in the Ottoman Empire* (New York: Oxford University Press, 1993); Beth Baron, *The Women's Awakening in Egypt: Culture, Society, and the Press* (New Haven: Yale University Press, 1994); Lazreg, *Eloquence of Silence* (cited above); Denise Spellberg, *Politics, Gender and the Islamic Past: The Legacy of 'A'isha bint Abi Bakr* (New York: Columbia University Press, 1994); Amira E. Sonbol, ed., *Women, the Family, and Divorce Laws in Islamic History* (Syracuse, NY: Syracuse University Press, 1996); and Judith E. Tucker, *In the House of the Law: Gender and Islamic Law in Ottoman Syria and Palestine* (Berkeley: University of California Press, 1998).

15 [Ed.: In the paragraphs omitted here, Fleischmann points to three problems of perception that had hampered historical research on women's movements into the 1990s: first, the prevailing understanding that the "political" was equated with the "national" campaigns; second, the accompanying assumption that these campaigns were gendered male and the relegation of women's public activities to the "social" sphere, which erased the political character of what they were doing, and which remained unquestioned for so long; and, third, the tenacity with which Islam had become "an overarching explanatory paradigm" within earlier scholarship, which precluded examining other important factors.]

16 For a slightly different "historical typology" of Arab (not Middle Eastern) feminism, see Margot Badran, "Feminism As a Force in the Arab World," in *Contemporary Arab Thought and Women* (Cairo: Arab Women's Solidarity Association, 1990), 56.

17 The phrase that was widely used in Arabic was *al-nahda al-nisā'iyya*. (*Nahda* can also be translated as "resurgence," "revival," or "Renaissance," but "awakening" has been the most commonly

rendered translation.) "Awakening" was also used in the Turkish and Iranian contexts. See, e.g., Badr ol-Moluk Bamdad, *From Darkness into Light: Women's Emancipation in Iran*, ed. and trans. F. R. C Bagley (Hicksville, N.Y.: Exposition Press, 1977); and Sanasarian, *Women's Rights Movement*, 33. More research needs to be done to more accurately trace the historical etymology of the use of the term.

18 E.g., the *Ladies Awakening* (*nahdat al-sayyidāt*) in Beirut (no date); the *Women's Revival* (*al-nahda al-nisā'iyya*, founded in 1924 by Ibtihaj Qaddura and Julia Dimashqiyya), also in Beirut; the Society for the Women's Awakening (*jam'iyyat al-nahda al-nisā'iyya*, f. 1916) in Cairo; the Women's Awakening Club in Iraq (f. 1923); and Women's Awakening (*nahzat nisvan*) in Iran (originally the Association of Revolutionary Women, changed to the Women's Awakening by order of the Shah c. 1927). The state feminism project initiated by the Pahlavi regime in Iran in the 1930s was also called the Women's Awakening. Baron, *Women's Awakening*, 20; Thompson, "Engendering the Nation," 91; Badran, *Feminists*, 55; Ingrams, *The Awakened*, 92; Sanasarian, *Women's Rights Movement*, 36–37; and Camron Amin, personal correspondence, 26 May, 1997.

19 Baron, *Women's Awakening*, 2.

20 This is Lisa Pollard's cogent observation. Personal communication, 1 March 1997.

21 The word continues to resonate today, as indicated by its recurrence in the contemporary Iranian women's press, for example. See Afsaneh Najmabadi, "Feminism in an Islamic Republic: 'Years of Hardship, Years of Growth'," in *Islam, Gender, and Social Change*, ed. Yvonne Yazbeck Haddad and John L. Esposito (Oxford: Oxford University Press, 1998), 71–72.

22 During the Mandate period in Palestine, for example, the press frequently referred to women's organized activity as a "movement" (*haraka*). See, e.g., the Palestinian newspapers *Filastīn*, *Sirāt al-Mustaqīm*, *al-Difā'* in the years 1927–1948 for frequent use of the word "movement." As with "awakening," more research needs to be done on the historical uses of the word.

23 *Webster's Ninth New Collegiate Dictionary* (Springfield, Mass.: Merriam-Webster, 1988), 776; and *The American Heritage Dictionary of the English Language*, 3rd ed. (Boston: Houghton Mifflin, 1992), 1182.

24 Mary Fainsod Katzenstein and Carol McClung Mueller, *The Women's Movements of the United States and Western Europe* (Philadelphia: Temple University Press, 1987), 5, quoted in Diana Rothbard Margolis, "Women's Movements Around the World," *Gender and Society* 7, no. 3 (September 1993); 379.

25 Myra Marx Ferree, "Equality and Autonomy: Feminist Politics in the United States and West Germany," in *The Women's Movements of the United States and Western Europe,* ed. Katzenstein and Mueller, 173; quoted in Margolis, "Women's Movements," 379.

26 For example, starting in the 1920s, the Palestinian newspaper *Filastīn* began to publish articles on Turkish women and their "awakening," the women's "awakening" as articulated in the Egyptian and Lebanese women's press, and the women's "awakening" in Iran. See *Filastīn*, "Ladies Magazine," 17 December 1921; "The Turkish Woman," 1 August 1924; "Turkish Ladies in the New Civil Law," 9 November 1926; "Woman's Rights and Her Duties," 4 March 1927; "Women's Awakening in Turkey," 5 April 1930; "The Women's Awakening and Unveiling [in Iran]," 27 May 1932; and "The Women's Awakening in Egypt," 5 June 1932. The Egyptian Feminist Union published articles – in French – on other women's movements in its house organ, *L'Égyptienne* (see, e.g., "Lettre de Palestine," November 1932; and "Le progrès de la femme palestinienne," August 1932). Sanasarian notes that "an interesting feature of feminist periodicals in Iran were translations and articles about the status of women in other countries" (*Women's Rights Movement*, 38). Coverage and support of women's rights was not limited to the women's press in Iran; proconstitutionalist periodicals also "wrote about the accomplishments of women in other nations of the East such as Japan, China, India, Turkey, and Egypt." Afary, *Iranian Constitutional Revolution*, 200.

27 Ahmed, *Women and Gender*, 162–163. As Margot Badran points out, due to history's reliance on "conventional questions, methods and sources," the history of feminism in Egypt (and one can safely extrapolate this to include the Middle East) has been "largely the history of men's feminism written within the framework of men's history." Margot Badran, "The Origins of Feminism in Egypt," in *Current Issues in Women's History*, ed. Arina Angerman, Geerte Binnema, Annemieke Keunen, Vefie Poels, and Jacqueline Zirkzee (London and New York: Routledge, 1989), 154.

28 Hanna' Kawrani, a Syrian Christian, took a position against, while Zaynab Fawwaz, a Muslim, published an article in support in the *Newspaper of the Nile*. See Badran, *Feminists*, 15.

29   Deniz Kandiyoti, "End of Empire: Islam, Nationalism, and Women in Turkey," in *Women, Islam, and the State*, ed. Deniz Kandiyoti (Philadelphia: Temple University Press, 1991), 26–27; and Elizabeth Brown Frierson, "Unimagined Communities: State, Press, and Gender in the Hamidian Era," Ph.D. dissertation, Princeton University, 1996, 76.

30   Paidar, *Women and the Political Process*, 27.

31   Paidar, *Women*, 98. Taqizadeh edited the pro-Revival Party newspaper, *Kaveh*, in which he "praised the efforts of the Islamic reformers such as Qasim Amin to change the 'pathetic position of Muslim women'." According to Paidar (45), Iran did not experience Islamic reformism similar to that in Egypt, where attempts were made to "bring Islamic theory into line with modern social relations while maintaining its authority as a religious system"; instead, reformist movements typically involved either pre-Islamic or antiestablishment Islamic concepts, since Islam was conceived of as an "imported" religion. But the influences from other Islamist movements affected Iran.

32   See Ahmed, *Women and Gender*, 155–165. Amin's influence and arguments continued to resonate in the Middle East long after the publication of his books. (He published a second book, *The New Woman*, in 1900.) Palestinian intellectuals, for example, were still citing him in debates on the "woman question" in the Palestinian press during the 1920s. See Fleischmann, "The Nation and Its 'New' Women," esp. chap. 3.

33   Kandiyoti, "End of Empire," 26.

34   Ingrams, *The Awakened*, 81.

35   Kandiyoti, "End of Empire," 26.

36   Deniz Kandiyoti, "Slave Girls, Temptresses, and Comrades: Images of Women in the Turkish Novel," *Feminist Issues* 8, no. 1 (1988): 35.

37   Thomas Philipp," Women in the Historical Perspective of an Early Arab Modernist (Gurgi Zaidan)," *Die Welt des Islams* 18, nos. 1–2 (1977): 66.

38   Deniz Kandiyoti, "Identity and Its Discontents: Women and the Nation," *Millennium* 20, no. 3 (1991): 431, quoting Sami Zubaida, "Islam, Cultural Nationalism and the Left," *Review of Middle East Studies*, no. 4 (1988): 7.

39   Qasim Amin, *The Liberation of Women*, trans. Samiha Sidhom Peterson (Cairo: American University in Cairo Press, 1982), 6.

40   Amin, 12, 26.

41   Jayawardena, *Feminism and Nationalism*, 12.

42   Paidar, *Women and the Political Process*, 48–49.

43   Nükhet Sirman, "Feminism in Turkey: A Short History," *New Perspectives on Turkey* 3, no. 1 (Fall 1989): 5; and Baron, *Women's Awakening*, 59–60.

44   The following discussion of the women's press reflects the sketchy state of research in the later 1990s, which has since significantly improved.

45   Frierson, "Unimagined Communities," 71; Afary, "On the Origins," 70; and Thompson, "Engendering the Nation," 285–286.

46   Beth Baron, "Readers and the Women's Press in Egypt," *Poetics Today* 15, no. 2 (Summer 1994): 218. Baron reports that an Egyptian woman editor translated and used selections from the Turkish women's press, and that there was even a bilingual Turkish-Arabic journal published by Sa'diya Sa'd al-Din in Alexandria in 1901. Baron, *Women's Awakening*, 61.

47   Afary, "On the Origins," 70.

48   Sirman, "Feminism in Turkey," 7, n. 10. This interesting article provides rich quotations from some very feisty women writers in the press during this period.

49   What did transpire during the British Mandate, however, was women's extensive use of the mainstream press to articulate their political concerns, which happened to dovetail neatly with the male-run press's own politics, particularly in the nationalist arena. The mainstream press devoted a considerable amount of coverage to women's political activities. A number of Palestinian women became prominent journalists, writing for the major newspapers, sometimes in special women's pages. They usually covered "women's topics" as columnists. Notable among them are Mary Shihada, Sadhij Nassar (who coedited the paper *al-Karmil* with her husband), Fa'iza 'Abd al-Majid, and Asma Tubi. See my "The Nation and Its 'New' Women," chap. 3 and 272–277.

50   Thompson, "Engendering the Nation," 369.

51   Asma Tubi, *Abīr wa Majd* (Beirut: Matba'at al-Qalalat, 1966), 122–123.

52   For example, during the Italian invasion of Libya in 1911, Malak Hifni Nasif founded a relief society and a nurses' training center. Badran, *Feminists*, 50.

53 Marsot, "Revolutionary Gentlewomen," 264.
54 Badran, *Feminists*, 50.
55 Ibid.
56 Sirman, "Feminism in Turkey," 6; Kandiyoti, "End of Empire," 29; Yesim Arat, *Patriarchal Paradox: Women and Politicians in Turkey* (Cranbury, NJ: Fairleigh Dickinson Press, 1989), 26; and Margaret Smith, "The Women's Movement in the Near and Middle East," *Asiatic Review* (April 1928), 189.
57 Smith, "Women's Movement," 190.
58 On women and *waqf*, see Mary Ann Fay, "Women and Waqf: Toward a Reconsideration of Women's Place in the Mamluk Household," *International Journal of Middle East Studies* 29, no. 1 (February 1997): 33–51; Carl Petry, "Class Solidarity Versus Gender Gain: Women As Custodians of Property in Later Medieval Egypt," in *Women in Middle Eastern History*, ed. Nikki Keddie and Beth Baron (New Haven: Yale University Press, 1992), 122–142; and Gabriel Baer, "Women and Waqf: An Analysis of the Istanbul Tahrir of 1546," *Asian and African Studies* 17, nos. 1–3 (1983): 9–28.
59 Baron, *Women's Awakening*, 171.
60 Badran, *Feminists*, 51.
61 Anne Firor Scott, *Natural Allies: Women's Associations in American History* (Urbana: University of Illinois Press, 1991), 2.
62 Badran, *Feminists*, 51.
63 Fleischmann, "The Nation and Its 'New Women," 176.
64 Paidar, *Women and the Political Process*, 68–69, 93, 96. Doulatabadi was an indomitable feminist. Paidar reports that after her organization and newspaper were banned and she was exiled from Isfahan, the Isfahan chief of police told her, "You have been born a hundred years too early," to which she replied, "I have been born a hundred years too late, otherwise I would not have let women . . . become so enchained by men today." Paidar, *Women and the Political Process*, 93, quoting Pari Sheykholeslami, *Zanan Ruznamehnegar Va Andishmand Iran* [Women journalists and free-thinkers of Iran] (Tehran: Chapkhaneh Mazgraphic, 1972), 97. It was Doulatabadi's wish that, after her death, no veiled woman participate in her burial ceremony or visit her grave, which was subsequently attacked "by a fanatic mob" shortly after the 1979 revolution. Sanasarian, *Women's Rights Movement*, 33.
65 Selma Botman makes this same point in describing Egyptian women involved in left-wing politics; Botman, "The Experience of Women," 125.
66 Indeed, one can discern uneasiness, fear, and a deep-seated conservatism among some of these pioneering feminists on the issue of class. Matiel Mogannam, a participant in the Palestinian women's movement, commented that Zionism imported "Bolshevik principles" into the country, producing an "effect on the population, not by its propaganda only, but by the genuine uneasiness which it inspired amongst the Arabs, especially amongst the poorer classes." Matiel Mogannam, *The Arab Woman and the Palestine Problem* (London: Herbert Joseph, 1937), 217.
67 Baron, *Women's Awakening*, 175.
68 Badran, *Feminists*, 55; and Thompson, "Engendering the Nation," 370.
69 Badran, *Feminists*, 47.
70 Indeed, the idea continued to resonate into the late twentieth century, as demonstrated by the following comments of the president of the World Bank, James Wolfensohn, delivered at a women's conference on 22 May 1997: "The single best investment is in a girl's education. If you educate a boy, you educate a boy. If you educate a girl, you educate a family or a nation." Nora Boustany, "Diplomatic Dispatches," *Washington Post*, 23 May 1997.
71 Adele 'Azar, unpublished personal memoir, 1965 (kindly provided to the author by Hana Nasir; emphasis mine). (The word "national" in this passage is used for the original Arabic *watani*.) In Palestinian history, there is a tendency to attribute "nationalist" motivations retroactively to many activities; for an exploration of this subject, see Ted Swedenburg, *Memories of Revolt: The 1936–1939 Rebellion and the Palestinian National Past* (Minneapolis: University of Minnesota Press, 1995).
72 Paidar, *Women and the Political Process*, 60.
73 Ingrams, *The Awakened*, 81. Specific information about female education in the Arab countries under Ottoman rule is difficult to come by, because serious studies of the subject have yet to be published. I have been unable to ascertain definitively the dates of establishment of the first government girls' schools anywhere else.

74 Kandiyoti, "End of Empire," 28.

75 Paidar, *Women and the Political Process*, 92–93.

76 Badran, *Feminists*, 8–9.

77 Badran, *Feminists*, esp. 38–48, 56–60.

78 Thompson, "Engendering the Nation," 369.

79 A writer in the Palestinian press questioned the nature and goals of the education girls received in missionary establishments, since they did not learn about their own history, national heroes, or language. She called upon girls to demand their rights to an education that included learning about Arabic culture and language, and upon parents to support national schools. Su'ad Khuri, "Schools and Woman," *al-Difā'*, 22 July 1935.

80 Thompson, "Engendering the Nation," 369–370.

81 Afary, *Iranian Constitutional Revolution*, 184.

82 Anonymous letter, *Tamaddun*, 17 April 1907, 3–4, quoted in Najmabadi, "Zanhā-yi millat: Women or Wives of the Nation?," 66.

83 Kandiyoti, "Identity and Its Discontents," 432.

84 Paidar, *Women and the Political Process*, 76.

85 Kandiyoti, "Identity and Its Discontents," 432; McClintock, "'No Longer in a Future Heaven'," 122; and Giacaman and Odeh, "Palestinian Women's Movement in the Israeli-Occupied West Bank and Gaza Strip," 61.

86 *Filastīn*, 13 December 1944.

87 Quoted in Najmabadi, "Zanhā-yi millat," 55.

88 See Thompson, "Engendering the Nation," 346–368, for a discussion of the battle for women's suffrage in Syria and Lebanon during the French Mandate period.

89 Nilüfer Çağatay and Yasemin Nuhoğlu-Soysal, "Comparative Observations on Feminism and the Nation-Building Process," in *Women in Modern Turkish Society: A Reader*, ed. Sirin Tekeli (London: Zed Press, 1995), 267.

90 Kandiyoti, "Identity and Its Discontents," 432–433.

91 See Fleischmann, "The Nation and Its 'New' Women," 243–248; and Badran, *Feminists*, 80–88.

92 Paidar, *Women and the Political Process*, 53–54, 58.

93 Thompson, "Engendering the Nation," 351.

94 Fleischmann, "The Nation and Its 'New' Women," 218–219. Women sometimes defied the male nationalist leadership by holding their own demonstrations against the latter's wishes. *Al-Karmil*, 8 November 1933.

95 Paidar, *Women and the Political Process*, 54.

96 See Fleischmann, "The Nation and Its 'New' Women," 272–287.

97 Fleischmann, "The Nation and Its 'New' Women," 271; Janet Afary, "The Debate on Women's Liberation in the Iranian Constitutional Revolution, 1906–1911," in *Expanding the Boundaries of History: Essays on Women in the Third World*, ed. Cheryl Johnson-Odim and Margaret Strobel (Bloomington: Indiana University Press, 1992), 104–105; and Philip Khoury, *Syria and the French Mandate: The Politics of Arab Nationalism, 1920–1945* (Princeton: Princeton University Press, 1987), 124. It should be noted that the presence of women in the Syrian demonstration did not deter the French from ultimately shooting three demonstrators dead and wounding others, including women.

98 Paidar, *Women and the Political Process*, 51; and Fleischmann, "The Nation and Its 'New' Women," 219. Among the Haifa women was the notorious activist Sadhij Nassar, secretary of the Haifa Women's Union, who was later imprisoned by the British without charges for seventeen months during the 1936–1939 revolt.

99 Paidar, *Women and the Political Process*, 59.

100 Many were published in the newspaper *Filastīn.*

101 Fleischmann, "The Nation and Its 'New' Women," 304–305.

102 A series of regional "Oriental" women's conferences were held in the 1930s in Beirut, Damascus, Baghdad, and Tehran.

103 *Al-mar'a al-'Arabiyya wa qadiyyat Filastīn* (Cairo 1938: Conference publication), 173. For more on the conferences and pan-Arabism, see Fleischmann, "The Nation and Its 'New' Women," 300–319, and Badran, *Feminists*, 223–250.

104 This can be partially explained by the fact that during the revolt, much of the Palestinian national leadership was in exile in Syria. Furthermore, the ties between Syrians and Palestinians were close on many levels; there were frequent intermarriages, for example, and some people owned property in both countries.

105 Nermin Abadan-Unat, "Social Change and Turkish Women," in *Women in Turkish Society*, ed. Nermin Abadan-Unat (Leiden: E. J. Brill, 1981), 9 no. 13; Thompson, "Engendering the Nation," 351–352; and Khadija Abu 'Ali, *Muqaddimāt hawla al-waqi'a al-mar'a wa tajribatiha fi al-thawra al-Filastiniyya* (Beirut: General Union of Palestinian Women, 1975), 47.
106 Paidar, *Women and the Political Process*, 91.
107 Baron, "Mothers, Morality, and Nationalism," 272.
108 Kandiyoti, "Identity and Its Discontents," 429.
109 Mogannam, *The Arab Woman*, 53.
110 McClintock, "'No Longer in a Future Heaven'," 105.
111 Kandiyoti, "Identity and Its Discontents," 429.
112 Kandiyoti, "End of Empire," 33, 38, 42.
113 Çağatay and Nuhoğlu-Soysal, "Comparative Observations," 269 (quoting Atatürk's speeches).
114 Abadan-Unat, "Social Change and Turkish Women," 14.
115 The Shah visited Turkey in 1934 and was particularly impressed by women's visible participation in work, education, and politics. Paidar, *Women and the Political Process*, 104. Houchang Chahabi describes how Reza Shah developed an attitude of "Keeping up with the Joneses at an international level" in the relationship between the two countries. Atatürk was to return the visit, and Reza Shah did not want him to witness Iran's "comparative 'backwardness'." See Houchang E. Chehabi, "Staging the Emperor's New Clothes: Dress Codes and Nation-Building Under Reza Shah," *Iranian Studies* 26, nos. 3–4 (Summer–Fall 1993): 215.
116 Paidar, *Women and the Political Process*, 92–93.
117 Paidar, *Women and the Political Process*, 101–102.
118 Kandiyoti, "End of Empire," 42; Ayşegül C. Baykan, "*The Turkish Woman*: An Adventure in History," *Gender and History*, 6, no. 1 (April 1994): 108.
119 Kandiyoti, "End of Empire," 42. Feminists from other parts of the world, who often expressed admiration for Atatürk's positions on women, were clearly puzzled by this move and at a loss to explain it. See Woodsmall, *Moslem Women*, 359–360.
120 Paidar, *Women and the Political Process*, 104–105. For a detailed account of how coercive the unveiling and other dress code decrees were during Reza Shah's reign, see Chehabi, "Staging the Emperor's New Clothes."
121 Afsaneh Najmabadi, personal correspondence, 19 January 1998.
122 Paidar, *Women and the Political Process*, 105–106.
123 Paidar, *Women and the Political Process*, 109–110, 113–114.
124 Çağatay and Nuhoğlu-Soysal, "Comparative Observations," 265.
125 Baykan, "*The Turkish Woman*," 112; and Parvin Paidar, "Feminism and Islam in Iran," in *Gendering the Middle East: Emerging Perspectives*, ed. Deniz Kandiyoti (Syracuse, NY: Syracuse University Press, 1996), 52
126 Baykan, "*The Turkish Woman*," 112.
127 Abadan-Unat, "Social Change and Turkish Women," 12.
128 Sirin Tekeli, "Emergence of the Feminist Movement in Turkey," in *The New Women's Movement: Feminism and Political Power in Europe and the USA*, ed. Drude Dahlerup (London: Sage Publications, 1986), 193.
129 Tezer Taşkiran, *Comhuriyetin 50: Yilinda Türk Kadin Haklari* [Turkish women's rights in the fiftieth year of the republic] (Ankara: Başbakanlik Basimevi, 1973), 125; quoted in Arat, *Patriarchal Paradox*, 22.
130 Ibid., 112; Arat, *Patriarchal Paradox*, 30.
131 Chehabi, "Staging the Emperor's New Clothes," 222.
132 Ibid., quoting Hesam al-Din Ashna, ed. *Khoshānat va farhang: asnād-e mahramāneh-ye kashf-e hejāb* (1313–1322) (Tehran: National Archives, 1992), 249.
133 See Mervat F. Hatem, "Modernization, the State, and the Family in Middle East Women's Studies," in *Women and Gender in the Middle East*, edited by Margaret L. Meriwether and Judith E. Tucker (Boulder: Westview Press, 1999), 78.
134 Çağatay and Nuhoğlu-Soysal, "Comparative Observations," 267.
135 Tekeli, "Emergence," 185.
136 This has begun to change in recent years, however, as Palestinian feminists have started to problematize the relationship. See, e.g., Giacaman and Odeh, "Palestinian Women's Movement"; and Penny Johnson and Rita Giacaman, "The Palestinian Women's Movement in the New Era," *Middle East Report*, no. 186 (1994): 22–25.

137 The journal *Zaban-i Zanan*, for example, faced such dire threats that its editor, Sedighgh Doulatabadi, was forced to close it down and move from Isfahan to Tehran, where the political and religious climate was less conservative. Afsaneh Njmanbadi, personal correspondence, 19 January 1998.

138 Fleischmann, "The Nation and Its 'New' Women," 147; and Kandiyoti, "End of Empire," 39.

139 This was the case in Palestine, for example. See Fleischmann, "The Nation and Its 'New' Women," 249–261.

140 Arab women who have written about their experiences in the movements during this period tend to stress their unity, whereas my own research, at least, has revealed contradictions in some of these portrayals. See, e.g., 'Anbara Sallam al-Khalidi, *Jawla fī al-dhikrayyāt bayna Lubnān wa Filastīn* (Beirut: Dar al-nahar lil-nashr, 1978).

141 See, e.g., Baykan, "*The Turkish Woman*," 108; and Sanasarian, *Women's Rights Movement*, 40.

142 Mrs. Munir Khuri, *Filastīn*, 15 December 1944.

143 Fleischmann, "The Nation and Its 'New' Women," 301–303.

144 Paidar, *Women and the Political Process*, 102.

145 Related to this trend was the development of a minor conflict over the naming of the 1938 Eastern Women's Conference in Cairo. Akram Zu'aytir, a Palestinian nationalist who helped organize the 1938 conference, argued with Huda Sha'rawi to change its name to the Arab Women's Conference, but Sha'rawi refused. (Only two non-Arab women attended this conference, which focused on the Palestine problem.) See Fleischmann, "The Nation and Its 'New' Women," 309 n. 42.

146 Carolyn Bynum, "Why All the Fuss About the Body? A Medievalist's Perspective," *Critical Inquiry* 22 (Autumn 1995); 30.

14 Latin American feminism and the transnational arena (Francesca Miller)

1 Teresa de la Parra, *Tres conferencias* (Bogotá: 1930).

2 Karen Offen, "Toward an Historical Definition of Feminism" (Paper presented for the Western Association of Women Historians, May, 1985); Francesca Miller, "Problems and Concerns of Women in Latin America: Historical and Contemporary Perspectives," *Conference Group in Women's History Newsletter* (Winter 1976).

3 De la Parra, *Tres conferencias*.

4 Francesca Miller, "The International Relations of Women of the Americas," *The Americas: A Quarterly Review of Inter-American Cultural History* (Fall 1986): 174.

5 Asunción Lavrin, "The Ideology of Feminism in the Southern Cone, 1900–1940," Latin American Program Working Papers 169 (Washington, D.C.: Wilson Center, Smithsonian Institution, 1986).

6 *Congreso Femenino Internacional* (Buenos Aires: 1910).

7 Teresa González Fanning, "Educación doméstica y social de la mujer," *Congreso Femenino Internacional*, 280.

8 Ibid.

9 J. María Samame, "La democracia y la personalidad política de la mujer," *Congreso Femenino International*, 374.

10 "The Second Pan American Scientific Congress," *Bulletin of the Pan American Union* 45, 8 (December 1915): 762.

11 There is good reason for this ideological diversity, which within the Pan American Women's Central Committee in the 1920s ranged from Wilsonian democrat to Trotskyite. I suggest that it is inherently related to the historical development of a feminist critique of society in the American states. For example, María del Carmen Feijóo writes of the Argentine feminists, "Puede considerarse con certeza que es a partir de 1890 cuando se empiezan a desarrollar de manera sistemática los esfuerzos dirigidos al esclarecimiento de la cuestión femenina y los primeros intentos organizativos. En nuestro pais, son las anarquistas quienes se anticipan en las discusión sistemática del problema" (*La Vida de Nuestro Pueblo* 9, *Las Feministas* [1982]: 7). See also K. Lynn Stoner, "From the House to the Streets: Women's Movement for Legal Change in Cuba, 1898–1958" (Ph.D. diss., University of Illinois, 1983); Shirlene Soto, *The Mexican Woman: A Study of Her Participation in the Revolution, 1910–1940* (Palo Alto, Calif.: R&E Research Associates, 1979); Alicia Moreau de Justo, *El socialismo y la mujer* (Buenos Aires: Editorial La Vanguardia, 1931).

12 "Delegates to the Pan American Conference of Women," *Bulletin of the Pan American Union* 54, 4 (April 1922): 350–351. See also "A Permanent Pan American Association of Women" (n.p., n.d.), Alice Park Collection, Archives of the Hoover Institution on War, Revolution, and Peace, Stanford University.

13 Bertha Lutz, *Homenagem das Senhoras Brasileiras a Illustre Presidente da União Inter-Americana de Mulheres* (Rio de Janeiro: 1926).

14 James Brown Scott, *The International Conferences of American States, 1889–1928* (New York: Oxford University Press, 1931), vii.

15 Papers of the Comité de las Americas de la Liga Internacional de Mujeres de la Paz y Libertad, 1947, Archives of the Hoover Institution.

16 *CIM Inter-American Commission of Women, 1928–1973* (Washington, D.C.: General Secretariat, Organization of American States, 1974), 1.

17 The Equal Rights Treaty was drafted by Alice Paul of the National Woman's Party of the United States and presented to the Havana Conference by Doris Stevens.

18 "Declaration of Lima in Favor of Women's Rights, 1938," *CIM Inter-American Commission of Women, 1928–1973*.

19 Alice Park, 1928 diary, Alice Park Collection, Archives of the Hoover Institution.

20 Papers of the Comité de las Americas.

21 Scott, *International Conferences*, 507.

22 Ibid.

23 Uncollated MS, Doris Stevens Collection, Arthur and Elizabeth Schlessinger Archives of the History of Women, Radcliffe College.

24 Scott, *International Conferences*, 507.

25 Ibid.

26 "The Second Pan American Scientific Conference," *Bulletin of the Pan American Union* 45, (December 1915): 762.

27 Nelly Merino Carvallo, editorial, *Mujeres de América* 1, 5 (September–October 1933). ix. I am grateful to Gwen Kirkpatrick for providing me with a number of copies of this journal.

28 Three women were members of national delegations.

29 Scott, *International Conferences*, 507.

30 Pro Paz was organized by "associaciones femeninas y estudantiles" in Argentina; the signatories of the petition included many men's and women's associations, as well as individuals. Ibid.

31 Ibid.

32 Mary Louise Pratt, "Women, Literature, and National Brotherhood," in *Women, Culture, and Politics in Latin America,* ed. Seminar on Feminism and Culture in Latin America (Berkeley: University of California Press, 1990). Pratt addresses the ideas put forth by Benedict Anderson in *Imagined Communities: Reflections on the Origin and Spread of Nationalism* (London: Verso, 1983). Anderson proposes viewing the nation as "an imagined political community, imagined both as inherently limited and sovereign."

33 "Declaration of Lima," cited in *CIM Inter-American Commission of Women 1928–1973*, 10.

34 The declaration was drawn up and presented by the Mexican delegation to the Inter-American Commission of Women. Ward M. Morton, in his study, *Woman Suffrage in Mexico* (Gainesville: University of Florida Press, 1962), states that in anticipation of their victory in securing suffrage "the jubilant [Mexican] feminist organizations urged the delegation to the Eighth Pan American Conference in 1938 to take advantage of Mexico's progress toward women's rights by submitting a declaration on the subject" (37). The Mexican women's hopes were to founder as Congress buried the amendment that would have given them suffrage; it was not secured until 1953.

35 Doris Stevens Collection, Radcliffe College.

36 Ibid.

37 Charter of the United Nations.

38 Inter-American Conference for the Maintenance of Continental Peace and Security, Petropolis, Brazil, 1947.

39 The Rio Treaty served as the blueprint for NATO (North Atlantic Treaty Organization).

40 Papers of the Primer Congreso Interamericano de Mujeres, 1947, Collection of Alicia Moreau de Justo, Montevideo, Uruguay. I am grateful to Janet Greenberg for providing this document.

41 Ibid.

42 Ibid.

43 The reason the Guatemalan government particularly welcomed the women was in celebration of the overthrow of the Ubico dictatorship and establishment of civil liberties, including freedom of speech, under the administration of Juan José Arévalo.

15 Internationalizing married women's nationality (Ellen Carol DuBois)

1 Waldo Emerson Waltz, *The Nationality of Married Women*. Illinois Studies in Social Sciences (Urbana, IL: University of Illinois Press, 1937) vol. 22, no. 1, p. 13.

2 Waltz observed that this was an anomaly in Anglo-American law, which otherwise adhered to the rule of coverture for married women.

3 The United States did not make this change until 1907. See Nancy F. Cott, *Public Vows: A History of Marriage and the Nation* (Cambridge, MA: Harvard University Press, 2002).

4 Waltz, *Nationality*, p. 85.

5 Karen Knop and Christine Chinkin, "Remembering Chrystal Macmillan: Women's Equality and Nationality in International Law," *Michigan Journal of International Law*, (2001): 546.

6 "In international law, nationality secures rights for the individual by associating her with a state. Traditionally the subjects of international law are states; individuals are not subjects of international law. By associating the individual with the state, nationality makes one state's interference with the national of another a violation of the other state's sovereignty." Quoted in Knop and Chinkin, p. 537.

7 "Women Urge Parity with Male Citizens," *New York Times*, 19 February 1930, p. 9.

8 Arlette Gautier, "Legal Regulation of Marital Relations: An Historical and Comparative Approach," *Inernational Journal of Law, Policy, and the Family*, 19, 1 (April, 2005): 47–72.

9 James Brown Scott, *Observations on Nationality with Special Reference to the Hague Convention of April 12th 1930* (Oxford: Oxford University Press, 1931), p. 11.

10 E.M. Borchard, "The Citizenship of Native-Born American Women Who Married Foreigners Before March 2, 1907, and Acquired a Foreign Domicile." *The American Journal of International Law*, 29: 3 (July 1935): 396–422. After the Cable Act restored her citizenship, Bryan was able to run for Congress and was elected to the House for one term to represent Florida.

11 Note that American men who married women ineligible for naturalization by virtue of race did not lose their citizenship. This is documented in great detail in Waltz, *Nationality*.

12 They were however provided with naturalization procedures that were more expedited than those of other immigrants, while no such provisions were made in the reverse case, when the immigrant spouse was the man. I learned about the complexities of these changes through my own grandmother, born in Germany, who came to the United States in 1902 as a young child. She assumed that she would become a citizen when she married my American-born grandfather in 1923, but because of the passage of the Cable Law, when she went to vote in 1924, she was turned away as an alien. She was so humiliated that she did not try to exercise her rights again for over a decade, at which time she discovered that she actually did have American citizenship, by virtue of having come to the United States as the minor child of a woman who acquired citizenship by marriage to a naturalized immigrant in the years before the Cable Act.

13 The one exception was a few conservative Catholic women's groups, the opposition of which to legal reform seems to have been encouraged by the Vatican.

14 *League of Nations Conference for the Codification of International Law (1930)*, edited, with an introduction by Shabtai Rosenne, 4 vols. (Dobbs Ferry, NY: Oceana Publications, 1975), vol. 3, p. 319.

15 Diane Elizabeth Hill, "International Law for Women's Rights: The Equality Treaties Campaign of the National Women's Party and Reactions of the U.S. State Department and the National League of Women Voters (1928–1938)," Ph.D. thesis, University of California, Berkeley, 1999, p. 87.

16 "Memorandum of the First Codification Conference of the League of Nations," Chrystal Macmillan, *International Women's News*, 22, 4 (January 1928): 57.

17 Ibid. These two positions were not identical. The feminist principles of equality, personal autonomy, consent, and the disestablishment of marriage are not always compatible; what if a married woman chose to have her nationality changed to that of her husband? The tension between the IAWSEC's principles of autonomy and equality, and the insistence of the other feminist faction

on the sole principle of equality before the law may have played a role in the conflict between them on this and other matters, but that aspect will not be discussed in this article. Diane Hill touches on this in chapter two of her dissertation, op. cit. Also see Alice Paul to Jane Norman Smith, March 14, 1934, Smith Papers, Box 6.116, Schlesinger Library, Cambridge, MA. Paul renders Macmillan's position on nationality in terms of the IAWSEC's commitment to "protection."

18 Advertisement, *Het Vaderland*, 11 March 1930, p. 12.

19 "De Nationaliteit der Gehuwde Vrouw," *Het Vaderland*, 15 March 1930, evening edition, p. 2.

20 Sophosiba Breckinridge, *Marriage and the Civic Rights of Women* (Chicago: University of Chicago Press, 1931), p. 48. Borchard "The Hague Codification Conference," *The Nation*, 131, 3394 (23 July 1930): 94–95. Waltz, *Nationality,* p. 11.

21 "Hague Conference Adopts an Agenda," *New York Times,* 14 March 1930, p. 6; see Maria Vérone's account, "La Nationalité de la femme mariée (A la conférence de La Haye)," *L'Oeuvre,* 19 March 1930.

22 "De Codificatie Conferentie," *Het Vaderland,* 16 March 1930, p. 1

23 Ibid.

24 Only the United States and Germany sent women with full delegate status. (Although the United States was not a member of the League of Nations, it, along with the USSR, had been invited to send delegates, a lucky break for the female nationality activists as both countries had advanced laws on the subject.) However, the US woman delegate was Ruth Shipley, legendary "queen" of the Passport division, no friend of feminism. Emma Wold, a National Woman Party activist, was a technical adviser. The German delegation included Marie Elizabeth Luders, first German woman Ph.D. in political science, member of the Reichstag, and a champion of equal nationality laws for women. Not all accounts agree on the women's status. An article in *Equal Rights* (vol. 16, no. 11, 19 April 1930, p. 8) identifies Luders as a technical adviser and the second full delegate as Marcelle Renson of Belgium.

25 "The Hague: Dr. Wold's Account," *Equal Rights*, 16, 26 (2 August 1930): 204.

26 "International Vrouwenraad en Wereldbond voor Vrouwenkiesrecht," *Het Vaderland*, 14 March 1930, p. 1.

27 "Women Urge Parity with Male Citizens," *New York Times*, 19 February 1930, p. 9.

28 Doris Stevens to Viscountess Rhondda, 23 April 1929, Doris Stevens papers, Schlesinger Library.

29 Leila Rupp makes this point in arguing for Steven's youthful style even at middle age. "Is Feminism the Province of Old (or Middle-aged) Women?" *Journal of Women's History*, 12, 4 (2001): 164–173.

30 Leila Rupp, "Feminism and the Sexual Revolution in the Early Twentieth Century: The Case of Doris Stevens," *Feminist Studies*, 15, 2 (1989): 293.

31 Rosa Manus to Carrie Chapman Catt, Catt Papers, Library of Congress, 16 April 1930, reel 4.

32 US militants from the National Woman's Party formed this group after the International Women's Alliance for Suffrage and Equal Citizenship refused them membership at the 1926 Conference in Paris, at the insistence of their American rivals, the US League of Women Voters. For the formation of the IAWC in Havana in 1928, see Ellen DuBois, "A Momentary Transnational Sisterhood: Cuban/US Collaboration in the Formation of the Inter-American Commission on Women," in *An Intimate and Contested Relationship: The United States and Cuba*, ed. Alessandra Lorini (Florence: Firenze University Press, 2006). See also Francisca Miller's article in this volume and her book, *Latin American Women and the Search for Social Justice* (Hanover, NH: University of New England Press, 1991).

33 The IAWC's involvement on the nationality issue between its founding and The Hague Conference is documented in Muna Lee, "The Inter-American Commission on Women: A New International Venture," *Pan-American Magazine*, October 1929.

34 Doris Stevens to Clara Gonzales, 5 September 1929, from Doris Stevens Paper, Schlesinger Library. They were still expecting some collaboration with the IAWSEC.

35 "Doris Stevens returns from The Hague," Press Release, 19 May 1930, National Women's Party Papers, Library of Congress.

36 Stevens to Clara Gonzalez, 22 July 1936, Stevens Papers, Schlesinger Library.

37 Marta Vergara, *Memorias de una mujer irreverente* (Santiago, Chile: Zig-Zag, 1962), p. 88. In her dissertation, Hill concurs, following Cruchaga's gradual retreat from the bold nationality principles he had first championed.

38 Waltz, *Nationality*, p. 108. It seems reasonable to conclude that the Chilean proposal was meant only to put the principle on the table and to flush out a stronger position on the part of the conference, rather than with any expectation of passage.

39 A. Alvarez, "Impressions Left by the First Hague Conference for the Codification of International Law," *Transactions of the Grotius Society*, 16 (Problems of Peace and War, Papers Read before the Society in the Year 1930): 119–129.

40 "The American Dream," *Equal Rights*, 17:47 (26 December 1931): 371–373.

41 Doris Stevens to Alva Belmont, 17 May 1929, National Women's Party Papers. Through Scott's intervention, the Carnegie Endowment for Peace granted the IAWC $5000 for its work at The Hague.

42 Karen Rosemblatt, *Gendered Compromises: Political Cultures and the State in Chile, 1920–1950* (Chapel Hill, NC: University of North Carolina Press, 2000).

43 Vergara, *Memorias*, p. 86.

44 "Remarks on The Hague Conference by Fanny Bunand-Sevastos delivered before meeting of Maryland Branch of National Woman's Party, typescript, May 1930, Stevens Papers, Schlesinger Library, Fanny Bunand file.

45 Rosenne, *League of Nations Conference*, vol. 3, p. 1063.

46 Vergara, *Memorias*, p. 89.

47 Ibid., pp. 11, 45.

48 Marta Vergara, "One Week at the Hague, *Equal Rights*, 16, 25 (26 July 1930): 196.

49 Rosenne, *League of Nations Conference*, vol. 3, p. 1032.

50 "The feminist movement has made such progress in our country that last year we revised our law of nationality . . . so that [married women] now have practical freedom of choice." Rosenne, *League of Nations Conference*, vol. 3, p. 1027. US delegate Shipley spoke in favor of an amendment which would make the men's and women's positions equal rather than protect the woman's autonomy, and the primary concerns of which would have to do with the rights of the child.

51 *Het Vaderland*, 22 March 1930.

52 "The Hague: Dr. Wold's Account," *Equal Rights*, 16, 26 (2 August 1930): 204.

53 Simone Téry, "Doris Stevens of the Hague," *Equal Rights*, 16, 17 (22 March 1930): 131–133.

54 Vergara, "One Week at the Hague," p. 196.

55 Marta Vergara, "The Women at the Hague, "*Equal Rights*, 16, 7 (9 August 1930): 211.

56 *Ibid*. Editor's note.

57 "De Nationaliteit der Gehuwde Vrouw: De Evaringen en Verwacthingen der Ageerende Amerikaansche Dames," *Het Vaderland*, 8 April 1930, p. 2d. The subtitle translates as "the Experiences and Expectations of the Obstinate American Women." Thanks to Petry Kievet-Tyson, of the Dutch Institution for the Study of Arts and Sciences (NIAS) for this and other translations.

58 Ibid.

59 Vergara, "Women at the Hague."

60 The cartoon was mentioned by Bunand-Sevastos in her remarks before the Maryland Branch of NWP, op. cit. Thanks to Eline van der Ploeg, also of the NIAS, for superb detective work in locating this image.

61 Manus to Catt, 16 April 1930.

62 Vergara, "One Week at the Hague," p. 196.

63 Vergara, *Memorias*, p. 93.

64 Quoted in Grace Phelps, "Forty to One," reprinted from the *New York Tribune* in *Equal Rights,* 16:15 (17 May1930): 118.

65 *Het Vaderland*, 11 April 1930.

66 "Doris Stevens Returns from the Hague," IACW press release, 19 May 1930, National Woman's Party Papers, Library of Congress.

67 See "Forty to One," pp. 117–118.

68 Manus to Catt, 16 April 1930.

69 Vegara to Stevens, 10 October 1931, from Paris, thanking her for her help in securing her nomination. Stevens Papers, Schlesinger Library.

70 Phyllis Lovell, "Equal Rights in the Assembly," *Equal Rights*, 18, 41 (12 November 1932): 323.

71 Stevens to Vergara, 10 February 1931, Stevens Papers, Schlesinger Library.

72 This is an approach to the history, especially of international feminism – linking the personal and the political – most clearly developed in Mineke Bosch and Annette Kloosterman, eds. *Politics and Friendship: Letters from the International Woman Suffrage Alliance, 1902 – 1942* (Columbus, OH: Ohio State University, 1990).

73 Stevens to Vergara, 5 March 1940. Stevens Papers, Schlesinger Library. These photographs, part of the Doris Stevens papers, are available on the Visual Information Access site, Harvard University Libraries.

74 At various times: Dr. Rosa Welt Straus of Palestine; Miss May Oung of India; Mme Ana Godyevatz of Yugoslavia; Miss Margaret Whittemore of the United States; Mme Eugénie Meller of Hungary; Mlle Emilie Gourd of Switzerland; Mme van Der Schalk Schuster and Mme Bakker Nort both of Holland; Miss Alice Paul of the United States. And others.

75 In debates over women's equality and the fate of the Nationality Treaty during the 1930s at the League of Nations, several figures appear who would later play a role in women's rights at the UN, among them Bodil Begtrup of Denmark, destined to be the first chairwoman of the UN Committee on the Status of Women, and René Cassin, a French diplomat who would later work with Eleanor Roosevelt on the Universal Declaration of Human Rights.

76 Most notably, Minerva Bernardino of the Dominican Republic.

77 Vergara, "One Week at the Hague," p. 197.

78 Vergara, "The Women at the Hague," p. 211.

79 Rosemblatt, *Gendered Compromises*, p. 246. 1934 was the year that MEMCH, the socialist feminist organization, was formed, with Vergara in the leadership.

16 Inventing Commonwealth and Pan-Pacific feminisms (Angela Woollacott)

I am grateful to Mrinalini Sinha and the two reviewers for their thoughtful comments on the first version of this essay.

1 Leila J. Rupp, 'Constructing Internationalism: The Case of Transnational Women's Organizations, 1888–1945', *The American Historical Review*, 99 (1994), p. 1575.

2 Antoinette Burton, *Burdens of History: British Feminists, Indian Women, and Imperial Culture, 1865–1915* (University of North Carolina Press, Chapel Hill, 1994).

3 It is central to my argument here that I disagree with Leila Rupp's lumping the United States, Canada and Australia as the 'neo-Europes' together with Europe itself as a single global formation of women of European origin. Such a collapsing elides white-settler countries, emergent as nations but still in colonial relationships with European imperial powers, with the imperial powers and the US. In doing so, it obscures the colonial status of white women in these countries and their colonising of indigenous inhabitants, as well as their geopolitical locations, all of which were relevant to their positions within feminist internationalism. Leila J. Rupp, 'Challenging Imperialism in International Women's Organizations, 1888–1945', *NWSA Journal*, 8 (1996), p. 8.

4 Rupp, 'Challenging Imperialism', pp. 11 and 9.

5 'Australian and New Zealand Women Voters' Committee', *The Vote*, 22 July 1911, p. 164.

6 A. J. R. (ed.), *The Suffrage Annual and Women's Who's Who* (Stanley Paul & Co., London, 1913), p. 14.

7 'Woman Suffrage Union, British Dominions Overseas', *Jus Suffragii*, 8 (1 January 1914), p. 57.

8 *British Dominions Woman Suffrage Union: Report of First Conference and of First Year of Work*, pp. 3–6; 'British Dominions Woman Suffrage Union, Third Biennial Conference, 1918', *The Vote*, 7 June 1918, p. 277.

9 'Overseas Suffagists: Reception at Minerva Club', *The Vote*, 6 June 1924, p. 181.

10 *Jus Suffragii: The International Woman Suffrage News*, 18 (1924), p. 146; 'British Overseas Committee Pavilion', *The Vote*, 15 August 1924, p. 263.

11 'Phyllis', 'In the Looking Glass', *The British Australian and New Zealander*, 5 February 1925, p. 14.

12 'Bessie Rischbieth, O.B.E., an appreciation by M. Chave Collisson', *International Women's News*, 62 (1967) p. 46.

13 'British Dominions Women', *The Vote* 13 February 1925, p. 50; 'British Overseas Committee Conference', *Jus Suffragii*, 20 (1925), p. 86.

14 'British Commonwealth Women's Equality League', *Jus Suffragii*, 20 (1925), p. 133.

15 British Commonwealth League, *Report of Conference 'The Citizen Rights of Women within The British Empire' Caxton Hall July 9th & 10th, 1925*. The Fawcett Library at London Guildhall University holds a collection of all the British Commonwealth League conference reports.

16 British Commonwealth League, *Report of Conference*, pp. 32–3.

17 British Commonwealth League, *Report of Conference*, pp. 35–6.

18 Antoinette Burton, 'The Feminist Quest for Identity: British Imperial Suffragism and "Global Sisterhood" ', *Journal of Women's History*, 3 (1991), pp. 59–61.

19 British Dominions Woman Suffrage Union, *Report of First Conference and of First Year of Work*, pp. 2–3.

20 'British Dominions Woman Suffrage Union', *The Vote*, 24 May 1918, pp. 257–8.

21 'British Dominions Woman Suffrage Union Conference', *Jus Suffragii*, 12 (1918), p. 156.

22 *The Vote*, 6 June 1919, p. 214.

23 'Our Indian Meeting', *The Vote*, 16 July 1920, p. 123.

24 'The League of Nations and Women Overseas', *The Vote*, 26 September 1919, p. 342.

25 Fawcett Library, Vida Goldstein Papers, Box 67, 7/VDG 7, Manifold book – London, July–November 1919, pp. 59–60.

26 'Pan-Pacific Women's Conference Approaches', *Pan-Pacific Union Bulletin*, n.s. no. 102 (July 1928), p. 9.

27 Bessie M. Rischbieth, *March of Australian Women: A Record of Fifty Years' Struggle for Equal Citizenship* (Paterson Brokensha Pty Ltd, Perth, Australia, 1964), p. 123.

28 Rischbieth, *March of Australian Women*, p. 120.

29 *Women of the Pacific and Southeast Asia: A Record of the Proceedings of the Ninth Conference of the Pan-Pacific and Southeast Asia Women's Association* (The Australian Committee of the Pan-Pacific and Southeast Asia Women's Association, 1961), pp. 19–20.

30 *Women of the Pacific and Southeast Asia*, pp. 20–21.

31 *Women of the Pacific and Southeast Asia*, pp. 21–3.

32 For example, the 1929 BCL conference was supported by thirteen Australian societies, twelve British societies, two New Zealand societies, and one each from South Africa, India, Bermuda, Ceylon and Canada. British Commonwealth League, *Report of Conference Held June 5th and 6th, 1929*, pp. 6–7.

33 Raewyn Dalziel, 'Pan-Pacific and South-East Asia Women's Association 1931–', in *Women Together: A History of Women's Organisations in New Zealand*, ed. Anne Else (Daphne Brasell Associates Press, Wellington, 1993), pp. 88–90.

34 Doris M. Mitchell, *Sixty Years On: The Story of the Pan-Pacific South East Asia Women's Association 1928–1988: Australia's Part* (Pan-Pacific South East Asia Women's Association, Australia, 1977?), p. 4.

35 Kumari Jayawardena, *The White Woman's Other Burden: Western Women and South Asia During British Rule* (Routledge, New York & London, 1995), p. 265.

36 Bessie M. Rischbieth, 'Women's Influence in the Pacific: Where East and West Meet', *International Women's News*, 35 (1941), p. 65.

37 'List of Delegates According to Countries', *Pan-Pacific Union Bulletin*, n.s. no. 105 (October 1928), p. 13; *Australian Dictionary of Biography*, 9 (1983), p. 304.

38 'List of Delegates According to Countries', *Pan-Pacific Union Bulletin*, n.s. no. 105 (October 1928), pp. 13–14; and 'List of Delegates to the Pan-Pacific Women's Conference, Honolulu', *Pan-Pacific Union Bulletin*, n.s. no. 104 (September 1928), pp. 9–10.

39 Eleanor M. Hinder, 'Pan-Pacific Women's Conferences in Relation to World Conferences', *Pan-Pacific Union Bulletin*, n.s. no. 102 (July 1928), pp. 11–14.

40 *International Women's News*, 62 (1967), p. 46.

41 See, for example, Kate White, 'Bessie Rischbieth, Jessie Street and the end of first-wave feminism in Australia', in *Worth Her Salt: Women at work in Australia*, ed. Margaret Bevege, Margaret James and Carmel Shute (Hale & Iremonger, Sydney, 1982), pp. 319–29.

42 Karen M. Koral, 'Reflection of a Changing Empire: The British Empire Exhibition of 1924', unpublished MA thesis, Case Western Reserve University, 1994, p. 20.

43 Koral, 'Reflection of a Changing Empire', fig. 1, p. vi.

44 T. O. Lloyd, *The British Empire 1558–1983* (Oxford University Press, Oxford, 1984), p. 279.

45 Lloyd, *The British Empire*, p. 299.

46 Rischbieth, *March of Australian Women*, p. 121.

47 National Library of Australia, Bessie Rischbieth Papers, MS 2004/1/49.

48 British Commonwealth League, *Report of Conference Held June 30th and July 1st, 1927*, p. 7.

49 British Commonwealth League, *Report of Conference Held June 30th and July 1st, 1927*, pp. 9–10.

50 Chandra Talpade Mohanty, 'Under Western Eyes: Feminist Scholarship and Colonial Discourses', in *Third World Women and the Politics of Feminism*, ed. Mohanty, Ann Russo and Lourdes Torres (Indiana University Press, Bloomington and Indianapolis, 1991), p. 56.

51 British Commonwealth League, *Report of Conference Held June 30th and July 1st, 1927*, pp. 25–6, 42–3, 47.
52 'British Commonwealth League', *The Vote*, 4 November 1927, p. 350.
53 *Stri Dharma*, 13, (1930), pp. 83–5. I am grateful to Mrinalini Sinha for sharing this article with me. For a fuller analysis of the *Mother India* debate, see Mrinalini Sinha, 'Reading *Mother India*: Empire, Nation and the Female Voice', *Journal of Women's History*, 6 (1994), pp. 6–44, and her Introduction to *Katherine Mayo's Mother India*, ed. Mrinalini Sinha (Kali Press, New Delhi, 1998).
54 National Library of Australia, Bessie Rischbieth Papers, MS 2004/7/82, letter from Collisson to Rischbieth, 28 October 1927.
55 British Commonwealth League, *Report of Conference Held June 30th and July 1st, 1927*, p. 5.
56 British Commonwealth League, *Report of Conference Held June 30th and July 1st, 1927*, p. 19.
57 See for example British Commonwealth League, *Report of Conference Held June 30th and July 1st, 1927*, pp. 28–34; British Commonwealth League, *Report of Conference Held June 5th and 6th, 1929*, pp. 28–9; British Commonwealth League, *Report of Conference Held June 18th & 19th, 1930*, pp. 34–40; National Library of Australia, Bessie Rischbieth Papers, MS 2004/7/300 British Commonwealth League Annual Report, June 1931 to May 1932.
58 Fiona Paisley, 'White Women in the Field: Feminism, Cultural Relativism and Aboriginal Rights, 1920–1937', *Journal of Australian Studies*, 52 (1997), p. 114. See also Fiona Paisley, 'Citizens of their World: Australian Feminism and Indigenous Rights in the International Context, 1920s and 1930s', *Feminist Review*, 58 (1998), pp. 66–84.
59 Fiona Paisley, 'No Back Streets in the Bush: 1920s and 1930s Pro-Aboriginal White Women's Activism and the Trans-Australia Railway', *Australian Feminist Studies*, 12 (1997), esp. pp. 121–2. See also Fiona Paisley, 'Feminist Challenges to White Australia, 1990–1939', in *Sex, Power and Justice*, ed. D. Kirkby (Oxford University Press, Oxford, 1996), pp. 252–69.
60 National Library of Australia, Bessie Rischbieth Papers, MS 2004/7/98. Form letter from Chave Collisson written on BCL letterhead, 23 July 1929.
61 Catherine Martin's *The Incredible Journey* (Jonathan Cape, London, 1923) addressed the issue of Aboriginal children being taken from their mothers by telling the story of one such mother's heartbroken determination to get her child back. Katharine Susannah Prichard's *Coonardoo* (Jonathan Cape, London, 1929) represented both Aboriginal women's sexual exploitation by white men and, perhaps more controversially, the possibility of love between a white man and an Aboriginal woman.
62 Paisley, 'Feminist Challenges to White Australia', p. 268.
63 Constance Ternent Cooke spoke on Aboriginal women not only in the Commonwealth/imperial forum of the BCL, but also at the international forum of the Pan-Pacific Women's Conference in Honolulu in 1930; Mitchell, *Sixty Years On*, p. 4.
64 Paisley, 'Citizens of their World', esp. pp. 68–9.
65 Burton, 'The Feminist Quest for Identity', p. 49.
66 Minutes of the board meeting of the International Alliance of Women for Suffrage and Equal Citizenship in Brussels, 9–10 September 1936; Fawcett Library Archives, International Alliance of Women Papers, 2/IAW/10.2.
67 British Commonwealth League, *Report of Conference Held June 18th & 19th, 1930*.
68 Rischbieth, *March of Australian Women*, p. 121.
69 Rischbieth, *March of Australian Women*, p. 122.
70 Rischbieth, *March of Australian Women*, p. 122.
71 Ien Ang, 'I'm a Feminist But . . . "Other" Women and Postnational Feminism', in *Transitions: New Australian Feminisms*, ed. Barbara Caine and Rosemary Pringle (Allen & Unwin, St Leonards, NSW, 1995), pp. 60–61.
72 Bessie M. Rischbieth, 'The Geneva of the Future: An Australian Woman Looks Ahead', *The International Women's News*, 35 (1940–41), p. 42.
73 Marilyn Lake, 'Between Old Worlds and New: Feminist Citizenship, Nation and Race, the Destabilisation of Identity', in *Suffrage and Beyond: International Feminist Perspectives*, ed. Caroline Daley and Melanie Nolan (New York University Press, New York, 1994), pp. 290–91.

17 Feminism, social science, and the meanings of modernity (Ann Taylor Allen)

I would like to express my gratitude to the Stanford Institute for Research on Women and Gender and to the University of Louisville for providing the environment and the financial support for the preparation of this article. I also thank Karen Offen of the Stanford Institute and Marilyn Boxer of San Francisco State University for sharing the results of their research, and Karen Offen, Thomas R. Trautmann of the University of Michigan, and David Lindenfeld of Louisiana State University for reading and commenting on earlier versions of the article.

1 Robert Musil, *Der Mann ohne Eigenschaften*, 1930; quotation from the English translation, *The Man without Qualities*, Eithne Wilkins and Ernst Kaiser, trans. (New York, 1980), 3.

2 William R. Everdell, *The First Moderns: Profiles in the Origins of Twentieth-Century Thought* (Chicago, 1997), 10–11.

3 Fritz Stern, *The Politics of Cultural Despair: A Study in the Rise of the Germanic Ideology* (1961; rpt. edn., New York, 1965); Lawrence A. Scaff, *Fleeing the Iron Cage: Culture, Politics, and Modernity in the Thought of Max Weber* (Berkeley, Calif., 1989), 80; Eugen Weber, *France: Fin de Siècle* (Cambridge, Mass., 1986), 3. For other examples, see Arthur Mitzman, *Sociology and Estrangement: Three Sociologists of Imperial Germany* (New York, 1973); Mitzman, *The Iron Cage: An Historical Interpretation of Max Weber* (1970; rpt. edn., New Brunswick, N.J., 1985); Fritz Pappenheim, *The Alienation of Modern Man: An Interpretation Based on Marx and Tönnies* (1959; rpt. edn., New York, 1968); E. G. Jacoby, *Die moderne Gesellschaft im sozialwissenschaftlichen Denken von Ferdinand Tönnies: Eine biographische Einführung* (Stuttgart, 1971); *Degeneration: The Dark Side of Progress*, J. Edward Chamberlin and Sander L. Gilman, eds. (New York, 1985); Susan J. Navarette, *The Shape of Fear: Horror and the Fin de Siècle Culture of Decadence* (Lexington, Ky., 1998). Harry Liebersohn, *Fate and Utopia in German Sociology, 1870–1923* (Cambridge, Mass., 1988), dissents somewhat from this picture but emphasizes that the conventional view does emphasize "tragic pessimism" (2). H. Stuart Hughes, *Consciousness and Society: The Reorientation of European Social Thought, 1890–1930* (New York, 1958), stresses the problematic and pessimistic implications of research in the social sciences (329–35).

4 Terry Eagleton, "The Flight to the Real," in *Cultural Politics at the Fin de Siècle*, Sally Ledger and Scott McCracken, eds. (Cambridge, 1995), 13.

5 Carl E. Schorske, *Fin-de-siècle Vienna: Politics and Culture* (New York, 1980), 20.

6 Daniel J. Wilson, *Science, Community, and the Transformation of American Philosophy, 1860–1930* (Chicago, 1990), 121–49.

7 Modris Eksteins, *Rites of Spring: The Great War and the Birth of the Modern Age* (Boston, 1989), xiv.

8 *Fin-de-Siècle and Its Legacy*, Mikulas Teich and Roy Porter, eds. (Cambridge, 1990), 3.

9 Joan Kelly, "Did Women Have a Renaissance?" rpt. in *Women, History and Theory: The Essays of Joan Kelly* (Chicago, 1984), 19.

10 Dominick LaCapra, *Rethinking Intellectual History: Texts, Contexts, Language* (Ithaca, N.Y., 1983), 36–37.

11 Paraphrasing Karen Offen, I here define "feminist" as a person (male or female) who recognizes "the validity of women's own interpretation of their lived experiences and needs," protests against the institutionalized injustice perpetrated by men as a group against women as a group, and advocates the elimination of that injustice by challenging the various structures of authority or power that legitimate male prerogatives in a given society. Karen Offen, "Defining Feminism: A Comparative Historical Approach," *Signs* 14 (Autumn 1988): 152.

12 See, for example, George W. Stocking, Jr., *Victorian Anthropology* (New York, 1987), 186–238; Stocking, *After Tylor: British Social Anthropology, 1888–1951* (Madison, Wis., 1995), 3–160; Thomas R. Trautmann, *Lewis Henry Morgan and the Invention of Kinship* (Berkeley, Calif., 1987); Elizabeth Fee, "The Sexual Politics of Victorian Anthropology," in *Clio's Consciousness Raised: New Perspectives on the History of Women*, Mary S. Hartman and Lois W. Banner, eds. (New York, 1974), 86–102. Some excellent studies of American female intellectuals of this era, for example, Rosalind Rosenberg, *Beyond Separate Spheres: Intellectual Roots of Modern Feminism* (New Haven, Conn., 1982), and Desley Deacon, *Elsie Clews Parsons: Inventing Modern Life* (Chicago, 1997), have appeared, but their results have not been integrated into mainstream works of intellectual history. More works by feminist historians and theorists will be cited below.

13 Susan Moller Okin, *Women in Western Political Thought* (Princeton, N.J., 1979), 197–202; compare also Carole Pateman, "Genesis, Fathers, and the Political Liberty of Sons," in Pateman, *The Sexual Contract* (Stanford, Calif., 1988), 77–115; John Locke, *An Essay Concerning the True Original Extent and End of Civil Government*, 1690, rpt. in *The English Philosophers from*

Bacon to Mill, Edwin A. Burtt, ed. (New York, 1939), 434–35; Thomas Hobbes, *Leviathan*, 1651, rpt. in Burtt, *English Philosophers*, 193–94.

14 Joseph Campbell, "Introduction," in Johann Jakob Bachofen, *Myth, Religion, and Mother-Right: Selected Writings of J. J. Bachofen*, Ralph Manheim, trans. (Princeton, N.J., 1967), xxxiii.

15 E. A. Casaubon, *La femme est la famille* (Paris, 1834), 8; see also Claire Goldberg Moses, "The Evolution of Feminist Thought in France, 1829–1889" (PhD dissertation, George Washington University, 1978), 200–06; and Susan K. Grogan, *French Socialism and Sexual Difference: Women and the New Society, 1803–1844* (London, 1992).

16 Karen Offen, "The Beginnings of Scientific Women's History in France, 1830–1848," *Proceedings of the Eleventh Annual Meeting of the Western Society for French History, 3–5 November 1983*, John F. Sweets, ed. (Lawrence, Kans., 1984), 255–71.

17 Auguste Comte, "Social Statics; or Theory of the Spontaneous Order of Human Society," in *The Positive Philosophy of Auguste Comte*, Harriet Martineau, trans., 3 vols. (London, 1986), 2: 284; see also Terry R. Kandal, *The Woman Question in Classical Sociological Theory* (Miami, Fla., 1988), 7.

18 John Stuart Mill, *The Subjection of Women*, 1869, rpt. in *On Liberty; Representative Government; The Subjection of Women*, Millicent Garrett Fawcett, ed. (London, 1912), 432.

19 Henry Sumner Maine, *Ancient Law* (1861; rpt. edn., London, 1954), 100. See also Rosalind Coward, *Patriarchal Precedents: Sexuality and Social Relations* (London, 1983), 35–44; and Adam Kuper, "The Rise and Fall of Maine's Patriarchal Theory," in *The Victorian Achievement of Sir Henry Maine: A Centennial Reappraisal*, Alan Diamond, ed. (Cambridge, 1991), 99–110.

20 Mill, *Subjection of Women*, 430; compare Coward, *Patriarchal Precedents*, 31.

21 Johann Jakob Bachofen, "Lebens-Rückschau," 1854, rpt. in Bachofen, *Mutterrecht und Urreligion: Eine Auswahl*, Rudolf Marx, ed. (Stuttgart, 1954), 1–18; in English translation as "My Life in Retrospect," in Bachofen, *Myth, Religion, and Mother-Right*, 3–21. See also Karl Meuli's thorough biographical sketch, "Nachwort," *Johann Jakob Bachofens gesammelte Werke*, Meuli, ed., 10 vols. (Basel, 1943–), 3: 1012–79; and Lionel Gossman, *Orpheus Philologus: Bachofen versus Mommsen on the Study of Antiquity* (Philadelphia, 1983), 1–30.

22 On the chronological perspective of Bachofen and Maine, see Trautmann, *Lewis Henry Morgan*, 58–84.

23 For example, by Paula Webster, "Matriarchy: A Vision of Power," in Rayna R. Reiter, *Toward an Anthropology of Women* (New York, 1975), 143: "Bachofen's work has been appropriately criticized for its lack of empirical data and its substitution of mythology for history." Of course, very little such empirical data was available before 1861!

24 Johann Jakob Bachofen, "Mother-Right," excerpted and translated in *Myth, Religion, and Mother-Right*, 85; *Das Mutterrecht: eine Untersuchung über die Gynäcratie der alten Welt nach ihrer religiösen und rechtlichen Natur* (Stuttgart, 1861; rpt. of vols. 2 and 3 of *Bachofens gesammelte Werke*.

25 Bachofen, "Lebens-Rückschau," 11.

26 Bachofen, *Myth, Religion, and Mother-Right*, 79.

27 Bachofen, *Myth, Religion, and Mother-Right*, 80.

28 Bachofen, *Myth, Religion, and Mother-Right*, 100.

29 Bachofen, *Myth, Religion, and Mother-Right*, 109.

30 Joan Bamberger, "The Myth of Matriarchy," in *Woman, Culture, and Society*, Michelle Zimbalist Rosaldo and Louise Lamphere, eds. (Stanford, Calif., 1974), 265; compare also Coward, *Patriarchal Precedents*, 34.

31 LaCapra, *Rethinking Intellectual History*, 36–37.

32 On Enlightenment views of male supremacy, see Karen Offen, "Contextualizing the Theory and Practice of Feminism in Nineteenth-Century Europe," in *Becoming Visible: Women in European History*, 3rd edn., Renate Bridenthal, Claudia Koonz, and Merry Wiesner-Hanks, eds. (Boston, 1998), 327–55; compare Sherry Ortner, "Is Female to Male as Nature to Culture?" in Rosaldo and Lamphere, *Woman, Culture, and Society*, 67–88.

33 Bachofen, *Myth, Religion, and Mother-Right*, 118.

34 Trautmann, *Lewis Henry Morgan*, 58–83, 205–30; Thomas R. Trautmann, "The Revolution in Ethnological Time," *Man*, n.s., 27 (1992): 379–97.

35 Lewis Henry Morgan, *Ancient Society; or, Researches in the Lines of Human Progress, from Savagery through Barbarism to Civilization* (London, 1878), 59. See also Trautman, *Lewis Henry Morgan*. A survey of the various interpretations of Bachofen that, despite its very slight

attention to feminist interpretations, is still useful is *Das Mutterrecht von J. J. Bachofen in der Diskussion*, H.-J. Heinrichs, ed. (Frankfurt, 1987).

36 John Ferguson McLennan, *Primitive Marriage: An Inquiry into the Origin of the Form of Capture in Marriage Ceremonies*, Peter Riviere, ed. (1865; rpt. edn., Chicago, 1970).

37 Morgan, *Ancient Society*, 347; John Lubbock, *The Origin of Civilisation and the Primitive Condition of Man, Mental and Social Conditions of Savages* (London, 1870); compare Fee, "Sexual Politics," 94; and Trautmann, *Lewis Henry Morgan*, 179–204.

38 See Stocking, *After Tylor*, 3–34; and Uwe Wesel, *Der Mythos vom Matriarchat: Über Bachofens Mutterrecht und die Stellung der Frauen in frühen Gesellschaften* (Frankfurt, 1980).

39 Fee, "Sexual Politics," 100–03.

40 Karl Marx, *The Ethnological Notebooks of Karl Marx*, Lawrence Krader, trans. and ed. (Assen, 1972).

41 Friedrich Engels, *Der Ursprung der Familie, des Privateigentums, und des Staates*, 1884; quotation from the English translation, *The Origin of the Family, Private Property, and the State in the Light of the Researches of Lewis Henry Morgan* (New York, 1942), 50.

42 August Bebel, *Die Frau in der Vergangenheit, Gegenwart, und Zukunft* (Zurich, 1883); English translation, *Woman in the Past, Present and Future* (London, 1885); Paul Lafargue, *La question de la femme* (Paris, 1904).

43 Engels, *Origin of the Family*, 163; Bebel, *Woman in the Past, Present and Future*; compare Coward, *Patriarchal Precedents*, 146–71.

44 Herbert Spencer, *The Principles of Sociology*, 3 vols. (New York, 1901), 1: 654. Volume 1 was first published in 1876.

45 Lester Frank Ward, *Pure Sociology: A Treatise on the Origin and Spontaneous Development of Society* (New York, 1903), 314.

46 Ward, *Pure Sociology*, 297; Lester Frank Ward, "Our Better Halves," *The Forum* 6 (November 1888): 266–75. See also Clifford H. Scott, *Lester Frank Ward* (Boston, 1976).

47 Matilda Joslyn Gage, "Woman, Church, and State," in *History of Woman Suffrage*, Susan B. Anthony, Matilda Joslyn Gage, and Elizabeth Cady Stanton, eds., 3 vols. (Rochester, N.Y., 1881–82), 1: 753–99.

48 Elizabeth Cady Stanton, *Eighty Years and More*, 1898, intro. by Ellen Carol DuBois; afterword Ann D. Gordon (Boston, 1993), 430–31.

49 Elizabeth Cady Stanton, "The Matriarchate or Mother-Age," in *Transactions of the National Council of Women of the United States*, Rachel Foster Avery, ed. (Philadelphia, 1891), 223; see also the same text in *Free Thought Magazine* 19 (June 1901): 267–72; (July 1901): 320–25; Matilda Joslyn Gage, *Woman, Church, and State: A Historical Account of the Status of Woman through the Christian Ages: With Reminiscences of the Matriarchate* (1893; rpt. edn., New York, 1972), 225.

50 Gage, *Woman, Church, and State*, 16; Stanton, "Matriarchate," 221.

51 Gage, *Woman, Church, and State*, 43; see also Stanton, "Matriarchate," 226.

52 Stanton, "Matriarchate," 227; Gage, *Woman, Church, and State*; see also Karl Pearson, "Evidences of Mother-Right in the Customs of Medieval Witchcraft," in Pearson, *The Chances of Death and Other Studies in Evolution*, 2 vols. (London, 1897), 1–50.

53 Gage, *Woman, Church, and State*, 47; Stanton, "Matriarchate," 270.

54 Stanton, "Matriarchate," 218.

55 For a general discussion of Gage, Stanton, and matriarchal theories, see Donna A. Behnke, *Religious Issues in Nineteenth-Century Feminism* (Troy, N.Y., 1982), 159–65.

56 Among the most significant of these many works: Charles Letourneau, *La condition de la femme dans les diverses races et civilisations* (Paris, 1903); and Otis Tufton Mason, *Woman's Share in Primitive Culture* (1894; New York, 1899).

57 Stocking, *After Tylor*, 151–230.

58 Edward Westermarck, *The History of Human Marriage*, 3d edn. (London, 1903), 117.

59 James George Frazer, *The Golden Bough: Studies in the History of Oriental Religion*, 2 vols. (1914; rpt. edn., 1922), 2: 210–17.

60 C. Wright Mills, "Edward Alexander Westermarck and the Application of Ethnographic Methods to Marriage," in *An Introduction to the History of Sociology*, Harry Elmer Barnes, ed. (Chicago, 1965), 663, quoted in Deacon, *Elsie Clews Parsons*, 50.

61 Stocking, *After Tylor*, 230; Stocking, *Victorian Anthropology*, 326.

62 Ferdinand Tönnies, *Gemeinschaft und Gesellschaft: Grundbegriffe der reinen Soziologie* (1887; rpt. edn., Darmstadt, 1964), xxiv; quotation from the English translation of the preface in

Tönnies, *On Sociology: Pure, Applied and Empirical: Selected Writings*, Werner J. Cahnman and Rudolf Heberle, eds. (Chicago, 1971), 22.

63 Tönnies, *Gemeinschaft und Gesellschaft*, 148–51; Ferdinand Tönnies, "The Concept of Gemeinschaft," in Tönnies, *On Sociology*, 71.

64 Ferdinand Tönnies, "The Individual and the World in the Modern Age," in Tönnies, *On Sociology*, 288–317; see also David Lindenfeld, "Tönnies, the Mandarins and Modernism," *German Studies Review* 11 (February 1988): 60–77.

65 Compare Lindenfeld, "Tönnies, the Mandarins and Modernism," 66–77.

66 Ferdinand Tönnies, "Historicism, Rationalism, and the Industrial System," in Tönnies, *On Sociology*, 266–87.

67 Georg Simmel, "Weibliche Kultur," in Simmel, *Philosophische Kultur: Gesammelte Essais* (Leipzig, 1911); quotation from the English translation "Female Culture," in *George Simmel on Women, Sexuality, and Love*, Guy Oakes, trans. and ed. (New Haven, Conn., 1984), 67.

68 Simmel, "Female Culture," 101. On Simmel's view of women, see Kandal, *Woman Question*, 156–76.

69 Max Weber, "Die protestantische Ethik und der 'Geist' des Kapitalismus," *Archiv für Sozialwissenschaft* 20 (1905): 188; quotation from the English translation in *Max Weber: Selections in Translation*, W. G. Runciman, ed., Eric Matthews, trans. (Cambridge, 1978), 170.

70 Hughes, *Consciousness and Society*, 332.

71 Compare Fritz Ringer, *The Decline of the German Mandarins: The German Academic Community, 1890–1933* (Cambridge, Mass., 1969), 267–68.

72 Johann Jakob Bachofen, *Les droits de la mère dans l'antiquité: Préface de l'ouvrage de J-J Bachofen*, trans. and ed. by the Groupe Français d'Etudes Féministes (Paris, 1903), 14.

73 Jeanne Oddo-Deflou, intro., *Les droits de la mère*, 36–38. The translators acknowledged the work of Alexis Giraud-Teulon, *Etudes sur les societés anciennes: La mère chez certains peuples d'antiquité* (Paris, 1867), but criticized him for his skepticism about the existence of matriarchy as a universal stage of human evolution (*Les droits de la mère*, 13).

74 Oddo-Deflou, *Les droits de la mère*, 25; see also Cleyre Yvelin, ed., *Etude sur le féminisme dans l'antiquité* (Paris, 1908), 5–7.

75 Laurence Klejman and Florence Rochefort, *L'égalite en marche: Le féminisme sous la Troisième République* (Paris, 1989), 178–89.

76 Aline Valette, *Socialisme et sexualisme: Programme du Parti Socialiste Féminin* (Paris, 1893). On French socialist feminism, see Marilyn Boxer, "French Socialism, Feminism and the Family in the Third Republic," *Troisième République* (Spring–Fall 1977): 129–67. Boxer points out that Valette's theory of "sexualisme" was based on that of a male colleague, Dr. Paul Bonnier.

77 On Harrison's life and work, see the excellent biography of Sandra J. Peacock, *Jane Ellen Harrison: The Mask and the Self* (New Haven, Conn., 1988); see also Robert Ackerman, *The Myth and Ritual School: J. G. Frazer and the Cambridge Ritualists* (New York, 1991).

78 Friedrich Nietzsche, *Die Geburt der Tragödie aus dem Geiste der Musik* (Leipzig, 1872); English translation, *The Birth of Tragedy and The Genealogy of Morals*, Francis Golffing, trans. (New York, 1956).

79 Jane Ellen Harrison, *Prolegomena to the Study of Greek Religion* (Cambridge, 1903), 260. On the impact of Bachofen's thesis on classical scholarship, see Stella Gorgoudi, "Creating a Myth of Matriarchy," in Georges Duby and Michelle Perrot, eds., *A History of Women in the West*, 5 vols. (Cambridge, Mass., 1992), 1: 449–56.

80 Charlotte Perkins Gilman, *The Man-Made World; or, Our Androcentric Culture* (1911; rpt. edn., New York, 1970), i.

81 Mason, *Woman's Share in Primitive Culture*.

82 Gilman, *Man-Made World*, 183.

83 Gilman, *Man-Made World*, 36.

84 Charlotte Perkins Gilman, *Herland*, Ann J. Lane, intro. (New York, 1979).

85 Pearson, "Evidences of Mother-Right"; Mona Caird, *The Morality of Marriage and Other Essays* (London, 1897), 21–36; Ruth First and Ann Scott, *Olive Schreiner: A Biography* (London, 1980), 289.

86 Frances Swiney, *The Bar of Isis; or, The Law of the Mother* (London, 1909), 53, 43. See also Swiney, *The Awakening of Women; or, Woman's Part in Evolution*, 3d edn. (London, 1908).

87 George Robb, "Eugenics, Spirituality, and Sex Differentiation in Edwardian England: The Case of Frances Swiney," *Journal of Women's History* 10 (Autumn 1998): 108–09.

88 For example, "The Primal Power: Speech Delivered by Mrs. Perkins Gilman at the London Pavilion, Monday, May 19, 1913," *The Suffragette*, June 6, 1913; " 'The Real Devil': Lecture by Mrs. Perkins Gilman," *The Vote*, July 4, 1913; Frances Swiney, "Womanhood versus Motherhood," *The Malthusian*, November 15, 1909; see also articles by Swiney in *Westminster Review*, May 1901, October 1901, March 1905, April 1905.

89 On this movement in Britain, see Sheila Jeffreys, *The Spinster and Her Enemies: Feminism and Sexuality, 1880–1930* (London, 1985); and Lucy Bland, *Banishing the Beast: Sexuality and the Early Feminists* (New York, 1995).

90 Selma Sevenhuijsen, "Mothers as Citizens: Feminism, Evolutionary Theory and the Reform of Dutch Family Law, 1870–1910," in *Regulating Womanhood: Historical Essays on Marriage, Motherhood and Sexuality*, Carol Smart, ed. (London, 1992), 167–86.

91 Ann Taylor Allen, *Feminism and Motherhood in Germany, 1800–1914* (New Brunswick, N.J., 1991), 173–88; many more sources are given in the notes to this chapter.

92 Ellen Key, *The Renaissance of Motherhood*, Anna E. B. Fries, trans. (New York, 1914), 102–03, a collection of her essays in English.

93 Ellen Key, *Kvinnorörelsen* (Stockholm, 1909); quotation from the English translation, *The Woman Movement*, Mamah Bouton Borthwick, trans. (New York, 1912), 150.

94 Sevenhuijsen, "Mothers as Citizens," 172–74; and Selma Sevenhuijsen, *De Orde van het Vaderschap: Politieke Debatten over ongehuwd Moederschap, Afstamming en Huwelijk in Nederland, 1870–1900* (Amsterdam, 1987), 138–49; Allen, *Feminism and Motherhood*, 188–205.

95 Henriette Fürth, "Mutterschaft und Ehe," *Mutterschutz* 1 (1905): 28.

96 See, for example, Nancy F. Cott, *The Grounding of Modern Feminism* (New Haven, Conn., 1987), 40–41, on the attitudes of American feminists toward their European counterparts.

97 Marianne Weber, "Die historische Entwicklung des Eherechts," in *Frauenfragen und Frauengedanken* (Tübingen, 1919), 10–19. On Marianne Weber, see Guenther Roth, "Marianne Weber and Her Circle," new introduction to Marianne Weber, *Max Weber: A Biography* (New Brunswick, N.J., 1988), xv–lxi.

98 Marianne Weber, *Max Weber: Ein Lebensbild* (1926; rpt. edn., Heidelberg, 1950), 412; English translation, Marianne Weber, *Max Weber: A Biography*, Harry Zohn, ed. and trans. (New York, 1956), 373.

99 Marianne Weber, *Ehefrau und Mutter in der Rechtsentwicklung: Eine Einführung* (Tübingen, 1907), 24–77.

100 Max Weber, *Economy and Society: An Outline of Interpretive Sociology*, 1921, Ephraim Fischoff, *et al.*, trans., Guenther Roth and Claus Wittich, eds., 3 vols. (New York, 1968), 1: 370–72.

101 Marianne Weber, *Max Weber*, 380–90. Of course, the relationship of Max and Marianne and the ways in which it influenced Max's views on sexuality has been much discussed; see particularly Mitzman, *Iron Cage*, 277–98; Scaff, *Fleeing the Iron Cage*, 108–18; and Klaus Lichtblau, "The Protestant Ethic versus the 'New Ethic,' " in *Weber's Protestant Ethic: Origins, Evidence, Contexts*, Hartmut Lehmann and Guenther Roth, eds. (Cambridge, 1993), 179–94.

102 On Pelletier's education, see the excellent biography by Felicia Gordon, *The Integral Feminist: Madeleine Pelletier, 1874–1939* (Minneapolis, 1990), 24–74.

103 Madeleine Pelletier, *La femme en lutte pour ses droits* (Paris, 1908), 37.

104 Madeleine Pelletier, "Feminism, the Family and the Right to Abortion," Marilyn Boxer, trans., *French-American Review* 6 (Spring 1982): 3–24; Lily Braun, *Frauenarbeit und Hauswirtschaft* (Berlin, 1901); Henriette Fürth, *Die Hausfrau* (Munich, 1914); Charlotte Perkins Gilman, *Women and Economics* (Boston, 1898); Alice Melvin, "Abolition of Domestic Drudgery by Cooperative House-keeping," *The Freewoman* 1 (April 11, 1912): 410–12; H. G. Wells, *Socialism and the Family* (London, 1906).

105 Deacon, *Elsie Clews Parsons*, 113.

106 Elsie Clews Parsons, *The Family: An Ethnographical and Historical Outline with Descriptive Notes, Planned as a Text-Book for the Use of College Lecturers and of Directors of Home Reading Clubs* (New York, 1906), 297.

107 Parsons, *Family*, xi, 349.

108 *New York Herald*, November 18, 1906; *New York Evening Sun*, November 17, 1906; quoted in Deacon, *Elsie Clews Parsons*, 69.

109 On these relationships, see Martin Green, *The von Richthofen Sisters: The Triumphant and the Tragic Modes of Love; Else and Frieda von Richthofen, Otto Gross, Max Weber, and D. H. Lawrence in the Years 1870–1970* (New York, 1974).

110 Karlhans Kluncker, *Das geheime Deutschland: Über Stefan George und seinen Kreis* (Bonn, 1985), 97–107; see also Wolf Lepenies, *Between Literature and Science: The Rise of Sociology*, R. J. Hollingdale, trans. (Cambridge, 1988), 258–77.

111 Franziska Gräfin zu Reventlow, *Herrn Dames Aufzeichnungen, oder Begebenheiten aus einem merkwürdigen Stadtteil*, 1913, rpt. in Franziska Gräfin zu Reventlow, *Gesammelte Werke in einem Band*, Else Reventlow, ed. (Munich, 1925), 750–51.

112 Ludwig Klages, *Vom kosmogonischen Eros* (1922; rpt. edn., Bonn, 1963), 226; Carl G. Jung, "The Concept of the Collective Unconscious," in *The Archetypes and the Collective Unconscious*, 1936, rpt. in *The Collected Works of Carl G. Jung*, R. F. C. Hull, trans. (Princeton, N.J., 1970), 9: 87–110.

113 Reventlow, *Herrn Dames Aufzeichnungen*, 750–51.

114 Reventlow, *Herrn Dames Aufzeichnungen*, 759.

115 Kluncker, *Das geheime Deutschland*, 106.

116 Bram Dijkstra, *Idols of Perversity: Fantasies of Feminine Evil in Fin-de-Siècle Culture* (New York, 1986).

117 Compare Nancy A. Harrowitz and Barbara Hyams, *Jews and Gender: Responses to Otto Weininger* (Philadelphia, 1995).

118 H. G. Wells, *Ann Veronica* (1909, rpt. edn., London, 1993), 29.

119 Compare Frank J. Sulloway, *Freud, Biologist of the Mind: Beyond the Psychoanalytic Legend* (New York, 1979), 369–74.

120 On maternal archetypes, see Carl G. Jung, *Symbols of Transformation*, 1912, R. F. C. Hull, trans. (Princeton, N.J., 1956), 207–393; Richard Noll, *The Jung Cult: Origins of a Charismatic Movement* (Princeton, 1994), 169–76; Henri F. Ellenberger, *The Discovery of the Unconscious: The History and Evolution of Dynamic Psychiatry* (New York, 1970), 727–30; Erich Neumann, *The Great Mother: An Analysis of the Archetype* (Princeton, 1954), 28–29 and *passim*.

121 *The Freud-Jung Letters: The Correspondence between Sigmund Freud and C. G. Jung*, William McGuire, ed., Ralph Manheim and R. F. C. Hull, trans. (Princeton, N.J., 1974), 503 (Jung to Freud, May 8, 1912).

122 Noll, *Jung Cult*, 158–59.

123 McGuire, *Freud-Jung Letters*, 504 (Freud to Jung, May 14, 1912).

124 Stocking, *After Tylor*, 125–44.

125 J. J. Atkinson, *Primal Law* (London, 1903) (published in the same volume with Andrew Lang, *Social Origins*), 230–38.

126 Sigmund Freud, *Totem und Tabu: Einige Übereinstimmungen im Seelenleben der Wilden und Neurotiker* (Leipzig, 1913); rpt. of vol. 9 of Freud, *Gesammelte Werke chronologisch geordnet*, Anna Freud, ed., 17 vols. (London, 1947–55). Quotations are from the English translation, *Totem and Taboo: Resemblances between the Psychic Lives of Savages and Neurotics*, A. A. Brill, trans. (New York, 1918), 382.

127 Freud, *Totem and Taboo*, 192, 190.

128 For example, by Susan Kingsley Kent, *Making Peace: The Reconstruction of Gender in Interwar Britain* (Princeton, N.J., 1993), 126–30.

129 Ellenberger, *Discovery of the Unconscious*, 218–23; Noll, *Jung Cult*, 171.

130 Juliet Mitchell, *Psychoanalysis and Feminism: Freud, Reich, Laing, and Women* (New York, 1975), 16–29.

131 Freud, *Totem and Taboo*, 193.

132 Catherine Gascoigne Hartley, *The Truth about Woman* (New York, 1913); Hartley, *The Position of Woman in Primitive Society: A Study of the Matriarchy* (London, 1914).

133 For example, see "Evening Discussion Meetings, Mrs. Gallichan on 'Woman and Her Relationship to Man,'" *The Vote*, October 10, 1913. For biographical information on Hartley (1869–1929), who sometimes wrote under the name of Mrs. Walter Gallichan, see *Who Was Who, 1916–1928* (London, 1929), 471–72.

134 Hartley, *Position of Women in Primitive Society*, 266.

135 Stocking, *After Tylor*, 292.

136 Theresa Wobbe, "Mathilde Vaerting (1884–1977)," in *Frauen in den Kulturwissenschaften*, Barbara Hahn, ed. (Munich, 1994), 123–35, quotation p. 129.

137 Robert Briffault, *The Mothers: A Study of the Origins of Sentiment and Institutions*, 3 vols., 1927; abridged edn., Gordon Rattray Taylor, ed. (New York, 1959); Briffault and Bronislaw Malinowski, *Marriage Past and Present: A Debate between Robert Briffault and Bronislaw*

Malinowski, M. F. Ashley Montagu, ed. (Boston, 1956). The interchange published here dates from a radio broadcast of 1927.

138 Simone de Beauvoir, *Le deuxième sexe, I. Les faits et les mythes; II. L'expérience vécue* (Paris, 1949); Elizabeth Fisher, *Woman's Creation: Sexual Evolution and the Shaping of Society* (New York, 1979); Adrienne Rich, *Of Woman Born: Motherhood as Experience and Institution* (New York, 1976); Evelyn Reed, *Woman's Evolution: From Matriarchal Clan to Patriarchal Family* (New York, 1975); *Capitalist Patriarchy and the Case for Socialist Feminism*, Zillah R. Eisenstein, ed. (New York, 1979); Marilyn French, *Beyond Power: On Women, Men, and Morals* (New York, 1985).

139 Kathleen Gough, "The Origin of the Family," in Reiter, *Toward an Anthropology of Women*, 51–76; Coward, *Patriarchal Precedents*, 253–86; Fee, "Sexual Politics."

140 Parsons, *Family*, x.

141 Jane Ellen Harrison, *Homo Sum: Being a Letter to an Anti-Suffragist from an Anthropologist* (New York, 1912), 11.

142 Charles A. and Mary R. Beard, *The American Spirit: A Study of the Idea of Civilization in the United States* (New York, 1942), 397–419; Nancy F. Cott, *Putting Women on the Record: Mary Ritter Beard through Her Letters* (New Haven, Conn., 1991), 26–27. For some contemporary theories about the origin of the family, see (among many other examples) Gerda Lerner, *The Creation of Patriarchy* (New York, 1986); Margaret Ehrenberg, *Women in Prehistory* (Norman, Okla., 1989); Heide Göttner-Abendroth, *Das Matriarchat: Geschichte seiner Erforschung* (Stuttgart, 1995); Lawrence Osborne, "The Women Warriors," *Lingua Franca* 7 (December–January 1998): 50–58.

143 Eksteins, *Rites of Spring*, xiv; Richard L. Greaves, Robert Zaller, and Jennifer Tolbert Roberts, *Civilizations of the West: The Human Adventure* (New York, 1992), 813; John P. McKay, Bennett D. Hill, and John D. Buckler, *A History of Western Society: Since 1300*, 5th edn. (Boston, 1998), 927; Thomas F. X. Noble, *et al.*, *Western Civilization: The Continuing Experiment*, 2d edn. (Boston, 1998), 880; Eugen Weber, ed., *Movements, Currents, Trends: Aspects of European Thought in the Nineteenth and Twentieth Centuries* (Lexington, Mass., 1992), 203.

144 Hughes, *Consciousness and Society*, 15.

145 Cicely Hamilton, *A Pageant of Great Women* (London, 1910), 68. See also Lis Whitelaw, *The Life and Rebellious Times of Cicely Hamilton: Actress, Writer, Suffragist* (Columbus, Ohio, 1991), 86–88. Compare Liebersohn, *Fate and Utopia*, 194–96. Liebersohn stresses some of the utopian aspirations of this era and also finds the conventional emphasis on pessimism and alienation disproportionate. He does not, however, deal with the issue of gender relations.

18 Women's suffrage and revolution in the Russian Empire, 1905–1917 (Rochelle Goldberg Ruthchild)

I am indebted to Vicki Gabriner, Ellen Garvey, Rose Glickman, Esther Kingston-Mann, Maria Lähteenmäki, Tim Mixter, Deborah Pearlman, Elvira Wilbur, Elizabeth Wood, and the anonymous *Aspasia* reviewers for their comments on earlier drafts of this article. I am also very grateful for the meticulous editing of Maria Bucur, Francisca de Haan and Krassimira Daskalova and the encouragement of Karen Offen. Any errors are mine alone. This article has been lightly revised.

1 My definition of full women's suffrage is the unrestricted right to vote and the right to run for and hold elective office in a national entity. While individual western U.S. territories and states granted women universal suffrage, starting with the Wyoming (1869) and Utah (1870) Territories, U.S. women as a whole did not win suffrage until 1920. New Zealand women gained suffrage in 1893, but did not win rights to elective office until 1919. Women of all races won the right to vote and run for office in South Australia in 1894, and Victoria, New South Wales, and Tasmania soon after, but the federal constitution of 1902 denied suffrage to aboriginal women and men. Aborigines did not win federal suffrage in Australia until 1962. Finland remained part of the Russian Empire until 1917. *Suffrage and Beyond: International Feminist Perspectives*, eds. Caroline Daley and Melanie Nolan, New York: New York University Press, 1994, is particularly helpful on the suffrage movements in Australia and New Zealand. Daley and Nolan include Finland but not Russia in their 'Chronological List of Women's Suffrage

Dates', 349–352. Naomi Black, for example, is typical in arguing that 'equity feminism', or equal rights feminism 'has little impact on societies that do not have a tradition of individual rights and citizen action'. See Naomi Black, *Social Feminism*, Ithaca: Cornell University Press, 1989, 29. The 'nations most similar to England' quote is from Bonnie Anderson and Judith Zinsser, 'Asserting Women's Political and Legal Equality', in *A History of Their Own, Women in Europe from Pre-history to the Present*, rev. ed., 2 vols., New York: Oxford University Press, 2000, vol. 2, 367. The full quote is: 'In the first quarter of the twentieth century, women won the vote in nations most similar to England. In Scandinavia, feminists allied with liberals, socialists, and nationalists, and when those groups attained power, women won the franchise'. (367) The 'independent, Western' quote is from Francisco O. Ramirez, Suzanne Shanahan, and Yasemin Soysal, 'The Changing Logic of Political Citizenship: Cross-National Acquisition of Women's Suffrage Rights, 1890 to 1990', *American Sociological Review* vol. 62, no. 5 (October 1997): 735–745, 741. The 'minimal, class tension' quote is from Gisela Bock, *Women in European History*, trans. Allison Brown. Oxford: Blackwell, 2002, 145. John Markoff presents the periphery argument in his 'Margins, Centers, and Democracy: The Paradigmatic History of Women's Suffrage', *Signs* vol. 29, no. 1 (Autumn 2003): 85–116. Karen Offen, in *European Feminisms 1700–1950*, Stanford: Stanford University Press, 2000, makes the first serious attempt among women's historians to include Russia and Finland in a European narrative. On China's feminist movement, which won the right to vote in 1947, before the Chinese Revolution, see Louise Edwards, 'Woman's Suffrage in China: Challenging Scholarly Conventions', in *Pacific Historical Review* vol. 69, no. 4 (November 2000): 617–638, 618–619 (reprinted in this volume, Chapter 19).

2 For a thought-provoking contemporary analysis of the historical relationship between Russia and the West, see Esther Kingston-Mann, *In Search of the True West: Culture, Economics, and Problems of Russian Development*, Princeton: Princeton University Press, 1999.

3 'Chronological List', *Suffrage and Beyond*, 349–352. The timeline (743) in Ramirez et al., 'Changing Logic', gets the year right but the government wrong, attributing suffrage to the USSR, which was not formed until 1922. The Women's History Website maintained by Jone Johnson Lewis includes an 'International Woman Suffrage Timeline'. The 1917 entry for Russia states: 'When the Russian Czar is toppled, the Provisional Government grants universal suffrage with equality for women; later the new Soviet Russian constitution includes full suffrage to women'. See http://womenshistory.about.com/od/suffrage/a/intl_timeline.htm (accessed 24 February 2006) for the timeline. The Women in Politics World Chronology of Women's Suffrage has no 1917 listing for Russia, but instead lists 1918 as the year the Russian Federation granted women suffrage. See http://www.ipu.org/wmn-e/suffrage.htm (accessed 27 February 2006).

4 Books by Western historians about Russian women in the period covered by this article include, but are not limited to: Choi Chatterjee, *Celebrating Women: Gender, Festival Culture, and Bolshevik Ideology, 1910–1939*, Pittsburgh: University of Pittsburgh Press, 2002; Barbara Evans Clements, *Bolshevik Women*, Cambridge: Cambridge University Press, 1997; Barbara Alpern Engel, *Between the Fields and the City: Women, Work and Family in Russia, 1861–1914*, Cambridge: Cambridge University Press, 1994; Beate Fieseler, *Frauen auf dem Weg in die russische Sozial-demokratie, 1890–1917: Eine kollektive Biographie*, Stuttgart: Franz Steiner Verlag, 1995; Rose Glickman, *Russian Factory Women: Workplace and Society, 1880–1914*, Berkeley: University of California Press, 1984; Marcelline Hutton, *Russian and West European Women, 1860–1939: Dreams, Struggles, and Nightmares*, Lanham: Rowman and Littlefield, 2001; Laura Engelstein, *The Keys to Happiness: Sex and the Search for Modernity in Fin-de-Siecle Russia*, Ithaca: Cornell University Press, 1992; Jane McDermid and Anna Hillyar, *Midwives of the Revolution: Female Bolsheviks and Women Workers in 1917*, Athens: Ohio University Press, 1999; Anna Hillyar and Jane McDermid, *Revolutionary Women in Russia, 1870–1917*, Manchester: Manchester University Press, 2000; and Christine Ruane, *Gender, Class, and the Professionalization of Russian City Teachers, 1860–1914*, Pittsburgh: University of Pittsburgh Press, 1994. See note 5 for examples of the work of Russian historians of women.

5 The two major books and one dissertation in English about this topic date from the late 1970s and early 1980s and have received little attention from women's history scholars, with the notable exception of Karen Offen. The last Western monograph about the history of Russian feminism was published in 1984. Linda Edmondson has continued to publish and her critical analysis of Russian feminism has evolved from that presented in her *Feminism in Russia*, Stanford: Stanford University Press, 1984. One of her most recent articles is: 'Women's Rights,

Gender and Citizenship in Tsarist Russia, 1860–1920: the Question of Difference', in *Women's Rights and Human Rights*, eds. Patricia Grimshaw, Katie Holmes and Marilyn Lake, Hampshire: Palgrave, 2001, 153–167. Richard Stites in his *The Women's Liberation Movement in Russia, Feminism, Nihilism, and Bolshevism*, Princeton: Princeton University Press, 1978, rev. ed. 1991, puts feminism in the context of the range of women's activism in the pre-revolutionary period. Edmondson and Stites both downplay the significance of suffrage and judge the feminist movement ultimately to have failed. See also Rochelle Goldberg, 'The Russian Women's Movement: 1859–1917', unpublished Ph.D. thesis, University of Rochester, 1976. More recent Western surveys of Russian women's history uncritically repeat the claim made by socialists such as Aleksandra Kollontai that the feminists were out of touch with the masses, and downplay the diversity within the feminist movement. For example, Barbara Alpern Engel, in her *Women in Russia, 1700–2000*, Cambridge: Cambridge University Press, 2004, argues that: 'When, in the aftermath of the February Revolution, lower-class women grew more assertive, they rarely pursued women's political rights as such.' (135). Of the general histories of the Russian Revolution, Rex Wade devotes the most space to women's activism and the successful campaign for the vote, but he claims that the feminists were 'more closely tied to the Kadet Party' and links this to their 'generally middle- and upper-class social status'. See Rex A. Wade, *The Russian Revolution, 1917*, Cambridge: Cambridge University Press, 2000, 116. On women's suffrage as helping to legitimize parliamentary democracy but ultimately meaningless after the Bolshevik Revolution, see Richard Evans, *The Feminists*, New York: Barnes and Noble, 1977, rev. ed. 1979, 217–220. Post-Soviet Russian women's history scholars have aided enormously in showing the diversity of the feminist movement, publishing a number of articles and documents and bringing archival materials to light. See, for example, Svetlana Aivazova, *Russkie zhenshchiny v labirinte ravnopravii* (Russian women in the labyrinth of equal rights), Moscow: ZAO Redaktsionno-izdatel'skii kompleks Rusanova, 1998, 65; Irina I. Iukina, 'Formirovanie feministskoi ideologii v doreformennoi Rossii (Vtoraia polovina XIX-nachalo XX vekov)' (The forming of feminist ideology in pre-reform Russia [the second half of the nineteenth to the beginning of the twentieth century]) in *Zhenshchiny v istorii: vozmozhnost'byt' uvidennym* (Women in history: the possibility of being seen), ed. I.R. Chikalova, Minsk: Belorusskii gosudarstvennyi pedagogicheskii universitet, 2002, 229–240; Irina I. Iukina, 'Ol'ga Shapir—ideolog Rossiiskogo feminisma' (Olga Shapir—an ideologue of Russian feminism), in *'Ei ne dano prokladyvat' novye puti . . . '? Iz istorii zhenskogo dvizheniia v Rossii* ('Couldn't she blaze new trails . . . '? From the history of the women's movement in Russia), ed. O.R. Demidova, no. 2, St. Petersburg: 'Dorn', 1998, 116–127; Irina Iukina, *Istoriia zhenshchin Rossii: Zhenskoe dvizhenie i feminism (1850–e–1920–e gody: Materialy k bibliografii)* (The history of women in Russia: The women's movement and feminism (1850s–1920s: Materials for a bibliography), St. Petersburg: Aleteia, 2003; Irina I. Iukina and Iulia E. Guseva, *Zhenskii Peterburg. Opyt istoriko-kraevedcheskogo putevoditelia* (Women's Petersburg: An historical and regional guidebook), St. Petersburg: Aleteia, 2004; and O.A. Khasbulatova, *Opyt i traditsii zhenskogo dvizheniia v Rossii (1860–1917)* (The trials and traditions of the women's movement in Russia (1860–1917), Ivanovo: Ivanovo Gosudarstvennyi Universitet, 1994; and O.A. Khasbulatova and N.B. Gafisova, *Zhenskoe dvizhenie v Rossii (Vtoraia polovina XIX-nachalo XX veka)* (The women's movement in Russia [Second half of the nineteenth to the beginning of the twentieth-century]), Ivanovo: Izdatelstvo Ivanovo, 2003. See also V.I. Uspenskaia, 'Suffrazhizm v istorii feminizma i russkie feministki' (Suffragism in the history of feminism and Russian feminists), in *Zhenshchiny v sotsial'noi istorii Rossii* (Women in the social history of Russia), Tver': Universitet, 1997, 70–80. Uspenskaia does not refer to Edmondson or Grishina. On feminism and philanthropy, see Marina Liborakina, 'Women's Voluntarism and Philanthropy in Pre-revolutionary Russia: Building a Civil Society', *Voluntas* vol. 7, no. 4 (1996): 397–411. Natalia Pushkareva's generally impressive survey of Russian women's history, the first published in any language, does not mention Finnish women's suffrage but does note that Russian women 'received the right to vote in August 1917', before the U.S. or 'most European countries' (240). As is discussed later in this article, such a formulation gives little indication of the role of the feminists and their supporters in successfully demanding their rights. The formal decree on women's suffrage was part of the electoral law published by the Provisional Government on 20 July 1917. See Natalia Pushkareva, *Women in Russian History From the Tenth to the Twentieth Century*, ed. and trans. Eve Levin, Armonk: M.E. Sharpe, 1997, 208, 240.

6 For an excellent discussion and critique of Olympe de Gouges's feminist philosophy, see Joan Wallach Scott, "'A Woman Who Has Only Paradoxes to Offer'": Olympe de Gouges Claims Rights for Women', in *Rebel Daughters: Women and the French Revolution*, eds. Sara E. Melzer and Leslie W. Rabine, New York: Oxford University Press, 1992, 102–136. Olympe de Gouges, author of the *Declaration of the Rights of Woman*, was guillotined ostensibly for her opposition to Jacobin centralized rule in November 1793, but as much for her challenge to gender norms. The city prosecutor Chaumette condemned her as: 'that woman-man . . . This forgetfulness of the virtues of her sex led her to the scaffold'. (Scott, 'Woman Who Has Only Paradoxes to Offer', 115).

7 For an excellent discussion of the contradictory legacy of the French Revolution, see Scott, 'Woman Who Has Only Paradoxes to Offer', 102–103. For a different perspective, see Chapter 1 in this volume.

8 At this writing, only Saudi Arabia and the United Arab Emirates have not enacted women's suffrage. See http://www.iht.com/articles/2004/12/06/edeltahawy_ed3.php (accessed 24 February 2006).

9 The best summary of the 'first wave' of the U.S. women's movement remains Eleanor Flexner's *A Century of Struggle: The Women's Rights Movement in the United States*, Cambridge: Harvard University Press, 1959, 1975. Flexner's book has had multiple printings. Carrie Chapman Catt tallied up U.S. women's suffrage efforts as: '56 campaigns of referenda to male voters; 480 campaigns to urge Legislatures to submit suffrage amendments to voters; 47 campaigns to induce State constitutional conventions to write woman suffrage into State constitutions; 277 campaigns to persuade State party conventions to include woman suffrage planks; 30 campaigns to urge presidential party conventions to adopt woman suffrage . . . and 19 campaigns with 19 successive Congresses to get the federal amendment submitted and ratified'. Cited in Carole Pateman, 'Three Questions about Womanhood Suffrage', in *Suffrage and Beyond: International Feminist Perspectives*, 331–348, 332. Leading French revolutionary thinkers placed women beyond the bounds of citizenship. For Rousseau, women are 'subjects', not 'citizens'. See Siân Reynolds, *Women, State and Revolution: Essays on Power and Gender in Europe since 1789*, Brighton, Sussex: Wheatsheaf, 1986. Michelet and Proudhon were unabashedly misogynist. Proudhon asserted that: 'Woman is a diminutive of man in whom one organ is missing that would permit her to become adult'. See Bock, *Women in European History*, 92, for this quote and for a discussion of Michelet as well. The quote in the text is from Bock, 156.

10 See Markoff, 'Margins, Centers'. Although he highlights the Finnish suffrage victory and relates it to the upheaval in the Russian Empire (91–92, 105–106), Markoff does not include Russia proper and the rest of the Russian Empire in his survey. Edmondson, *Feminism*, 118–121, gives the most detailed discussion of the Finnish-Russian feminist connection. See also Stites, *Women's Liberation*, 198–199.

11 N. Mirovich, *Pobeda zhenskago dvizheniia v Finliandii* (The victory of the women's movement in Finland), Moscow, 1907, and in *Russkaia mysl'* no. 7, pt. 2 (1907): 118–136, 132–133. Future page number citations from Mirovich on Finland are from the *Russkaia mysl'* article. Edmondson, *Feminism*, 118–121, Stites, *Women's Liberation*, 198–199, Goldberg, 'Russian Women's Movement', 90–91, Aura Korppi-Tommola, 'Fighting Together for Freedom: Nationalism, Socialism, Feminism, and Women's Suffrage in Finland 1906', *Scandinavian Journal of History* vol. 15, no. 3 (1990): 181–191, 186–187; 'Woman Suffrage in Finland, 1906', http://www.pinn.net/~ sunshine/whm2003/finland.html (accessed 24 February 2006), 2, e-mail from Jason E. Lavery, 3 December 2003.

12 Korppi-Tommola, 'Fighting Together', 186–187; 'Woman Suffrage in Finland', 2–3. On Dr. Hultin, see Riitta Jallinoja, 'The Women's Liberation Movement in Finland: The social and political mobilization of women in Finland, 1880–1910', *Scandinavian Journal of History* vol. 5, no. 1 (1980): 37–49, 46. Jallinoja (44) translates the Union's name as the Feminist Union. Other sources translate it as the Women's Rights, or Women's Rights Movement Union. See *The Lady With the Bow: The Story of Finnish Women*, eds. Merja Manninen and Päivi Setälä, trans. by Michael Wynne-Ellis, Helsinki: Otava Publishing Company, 1990, 50, and Maria Lähteenmäki, 'The Foreign Contacts of the Finnish Working Women's Movement', *Scandinavian Journal of History* vol. 13, no. 1 (1988): 29–37, 31. On Mechelin as the father of the Finnish resistance, see Paul Miliukov, *Political Memoirs*, ed. Arther Mendel, trans. Carl Goldberg. Ann Arbor: University of Michigan Press, 1967, 211. On women and temperance

movements in the Russian Empire, see Patricia Herlihy, *The Alcoholic Empire*, Oxford: Oxford University Press, 2002.

13 Korppi-Tommola, 'Fighting Together', 187–188.

14 Irma Sulkunen, 'Suffrage and the Birth of the Civil State', *Lady With the Bow*, 52.

15 Ibid., 52–53.

16 Mirovich, *Pobeda*, 132–133.

17 Edmondson, *Feminism*, 117–121, has the best account of the Finnish suffrage struggle, including the Russian perspective. See also Goldberg, 'Russian Women's Movement', 91; Korppi-Tommola, 'Fighting Together', 188; Lähteenmäki, 'Foreign Contacts', 34; Stites, *Women's Liberation*, 198. For the Finnish name of the Women's Association, see Jallinoja, 'Women's Liberation Movement', 40.

18 Annie Furuhjelm, 'Report for the Finnish Women's Alliance', *International Woman Suffrage Alliance: Report of the Third Conference, Copenhagen, 7–11 August 1906*, London: Women's Printing Society, 1906, 75–79; Goldberg, 'Russian Women's Movement', 91; Jallinoja, 'Women's Liberation Movement', 47; Korppi-Tommola, 'Fighting Together', 188; *Lady With the Bow*, 46, 50–53.

19 On the Finnish struggle, see Mirovich, *Pobeda*, 118–136; Vera Figner, 'Zhenskoe dvizhenie v Finliandii' (The women's movement in Finland), *Pervyi zhenskii kalendar na 1908 g.* (First woman's calendar for 1908), ed. Praskov'ia Arian, St. Petersburg: n.p. 1908, pt. 5, 9–17; Furuhjelm, 'Report for the Finnish Women's Alliance', 75–79, Jallinoja 'Women's Liberation Movement', Korppi-Tommola, 'Fighting Together', 181–191, *Lady With the Bow*, 51, and Offen, *European Feminisms*, 215–216. The official history of the women's suffrage movement noted the Finnish achievement. See *The History of Woman Suffrage*, eds. Elizabeth Cady Stanton, Susan B. Anthony, Matilda Joslyn Gage and Ida Husted Harper, 6 vols., New York: National American Woman Suffrage Association, 1922, vol. 6, 771–773.

20 *Suffrage and Beyond*, 4–5, 349–352, Jallinoja, 'Women's Liberation Movement', 47–48; Edmondson, *Feminism*, 118–121.

21 See, for example, the excellent survey about Ukrainian women activists by Martha Bohachevsky-Chomiak, *Feminists Despite Themselves: Women in Ukrainian Community Life, 1884–1939*, Edmonton: Canadian Institute of Ukrainian Studies, University of Alberta, 1988.

22 Furujhelm's recollection about her meeting with Catt is in Jacqueline Van Voris, *Carrie Chapman Catt, A Public Life*, New York: Feminist Press, 1987, 62–63. The quote is on 63.

23 Edmondson, *Feminism*, 119. Catt, a founder of the IWSA, served as its President from 1904–1923. For an account of her life, see Van Voris, *Catt*.

24 The term *tolstyi zhurnal*, or thick journal, was applied in the late Imperial period to periodicals, usually with an oppositional bent, filled with literary, cultural, sociological, historical content, and popular with members of the intelligentsia. The journals were deliberately thick to discourage careful reading by the censors.

25 On Kollontai's childhood and her Finnish grandfather, see Aleksandra Kollontai, *Iz moei zhizni i raboty* (From my life and work), Moscow: Sovetskaia Rossiia, 1974, 17–21. A much more detailed account can be found in Aleksandra Kollontai, *Letopis' moei zhizni* (Chronicle of my life), ed. P.A. Popovkina, Moscow: Academia, 2004, 5–174. Eleven of Kollontai's first thirteen published articles, from 1898–1904, were about Finland. Kollontai's first book was *Zhizn' finlandskikh rabochikh* (The Life of Finnish Workers), St. Petersburg: Khudozhestvennoi pechati, 1903. Her third book, a collection of her early articles, was *Finliandiia i sotsializm: Sbornik statei* (Finland and Socialism: Collected essays), St. Petersburg: Malykh, 1906. On the reception of Kollontai's book on Finnish workers, see Beatrice Farnsworth, *Aleksandra Kollontai: Socialism, Feminism, and the Bolshevik Revolution*, Stanford: Stanford University Press, 1980, 22; and Barbara Evans Clements, *Bolshevik Feminist: the life of Aleksandra Kollontai*, Bloomington: Indiana University Press, 3–16. On Kollontai's pride in her Finnish blood, see Lähteenmäki, 'Foreign Contacts', 35.

26 Furuhjelm, 'Report', 75–79; Goldberg, 'Russian Women's Movement', 91; Edmondson, *Feminism*, 119. Lähteenmäki, 'Foreign Contacts', 35 mentions the Russian women at the Finnish conference. For the articles and pamphlets, see Mirovich, *Pobeda*, and Figner, *'Zhenskoe dvizhenie'*. For the Finnish-Russian feminists' letters of support, see *Gosudarstvennyi arkhiv Rossisskoi Federatsii* (State Archive of the Russian Federation, henceforth *GARF*), *'Soiuz ravnopravnosti zhenshchin'* (Women's Equal Rights Union), Fond 516, opis 1, delo 11, 5.

27 The law dated from 1864 and stipulated that the proxy could be any male who met the qualification himself, or a father, husband, son-in-law, or cousin. In 1890, the law was changed, eliminating some of the women's choices. The proxy had to be a relative, and the list of permissible relatives was extended to include grandsons and nephews. If a woman had no relatives, or had none she would trust with her proxy vote, she was out of luck. From S. Berednikov, 'Ob uchastie zhenshchin v zemskom samoupravlenii v Rossii' (About the participation of women in rural self-government in Russia), *Trudy pervogo Vserossiiskogo zhenskogo s"ezda v Peterburgie: 10–16 dekabriia 1908 goda* (Proceedings of the first all-Russian women's congress in St. Petersburg: 10–16 December 1908), Moscow: Tip. I.N. Kushnerova, 1909, 413–414.

28 Aleksandra Kollontai, *Sotsial'nyia osnovy zhenskago voprosa* (The Social bases of the woman question), St. Petersburg: Tip. 'Tovarishchestvo Zhudozh. Pechati', 1909, 21. For a fuller discussion of the entry of women and peasants into the political sphere, see Linda Edmondson, 'Women's rights, civil rights and the debate over citizenship in the 1905 Revolution', in *Women and Society in Russia and the Soviet Union*, ed. Linda Edmondson, Cambridge: Cambridge University Press, 1992, 77–100.

29 The 'ballast' quote is from Anna Kal'manovich, *Zhenskoe dvizhenie i ego zadachi* (The woman's movement and its tasks), St. Petersburg: Tip. Rabotnik, 1908, 1–2. On the failure to include women and accusations of 'untimeliness', see A. Tyrkova, 'Pervyi zhenskii s"ezd' (The first women's congress), in *Zarnitsy: Literaturno-politicheskii sbornik* (Lightning: Literary-political collection), no. 2 (1909): 172–209, 194; and Praskov'ia Arian, 'Zhenshchina i politika' (Woman and politics), *Pervyi zhenskii kalendar' na 1906 g.* (First woman's calendar for 1906), St. Petersburg: n.p. 1906, 386–399, 399. On the smirks and shrugs, see Liubov Gurevich's comments in *Ravnopravie zhenshchin: Tret'ii s"ezd soiuza ravnopravnosti zhenshchin: otchety i protokoly* (Women's equal rights: Third Congress of the Women's Equal Rights Union: Reports and protocols), St. Petersburg: Tip. Ia. Trei, 1906, 17.

30 In his voluminous writings, Miliukov barely mentions women's suffrage and never provides a serious description of the reasons for his initial opposition and his later change of heart. For a brief description of his public battle with his wife about suffrage, see Pavel N. Miliukov, *Vospominaniia* (Memoirs), 1859–1917, New York: Izd. Chekhova, 1955, 1, 308.

31 Ibid.

32 Ariadna Tyrkova, *Anna Pavlovna Filosofova i eia vremia* (Anna Pavlovna Filosofova and her time), Petrograd: M.O. Vol'f, 1915, 414.

33 Anna Shabanova, *Ocherk zhenskogo dvizheniia v Rossii* (An essay about the women's movement in Russia), St. Petersburg: Prosveschenie, 1912, 16. Witte's comments are in Tolstoi's diary of his term as Minister of Education, from 31 October 1905 to 24 April 1906. See *Vospominaniia Ministra Narodnogo Prosveshcheniia grafa I.I. Tolstogo 31 oktiabria 1905 g—24 aprelia 1906 g.* (The Memoirs of the Minister of Education Count I. I. Tolstoi from 31 October 1905–24 April 1906, Sostavitel' (Compiled by L.I. Tolstaia), Moscow: Greko-Latinskii Kabinet Iu. A. Shichalina, 1997, 74.

34 Shabanova, *Ocherk*, 16.

35 Ibid., 16; Praskov'ia Belenkaia Arian, 'Novyia techeniia v zhenskom dvizheniia v Rossii' (New trends in the women's movement in Russia), in *Pervyi zhenskii kalendar' na 1906 god* (First woman's calendar for 1906), St. Petersburg, n.p., 1906, 327–328; E.A. Chebysheva-Dmitrieva, 'O russkom zhenskom vzaimno-blagotvoritel'nom obshchestve v S-Peterburge' (About the Russian Women's Mutual Philanthropic Society in St. Petersburg), *Trudy pervogo Vserossiiskogo zhenskogo s"ezda*, 445–456.

36 Maria Pokrovskaia, 'Programmema zhenskoi progressivnoi partii' (The programme of the Women's Progressive Party), *Zhenskii vestnik* (Women's Herald), no. 1 (January 1906): 26–29. For two perspectives on Pokrovskaia, see: Rochelle Goldberg Ruthchild, 'Writing for Their Rights: Four Feminist Journalists: Mariia Chekhova, Liubov' Gurevich, Mariia Pokrovskaia, and Ariadna Tyrkova'; and Linda Edmondson, 'Mariia Pokrovskaia and *Zhenskii vestnik*: Feminist Separatism in Theory and Practice'. Both are in *An Improper Profession: Women, Gender, and Journalism in Late Imperial Russia*, eds. Barbara T. Norton and Jehanne M. Gheith, Durham and London: Duke University Press, 2001, 167–195; 196–221, respectively.

37 Maria Pokrovskaia, 'Osvoboditel'noe dvizhenie v Rossii' (The liberation movement in Russia), *Zhenskii vestnik*, no.12 (December 1905): 353–356, 354.

38 See for example, Pokrovskaia, *'Programmema'*, 26; 'Gosudarstvennaia Duma' (State Duma), *Zhenskii vestnik* (November 1905): 321–324; 'Novyi izbiratel'nyi zakon' (New electoral law), *Zhenskii vestnik* (July–August 1907): 161–162; *'Zhenshchiny ob'edinaites'* (Women unite), (January 1907): 1–7.

39 N. Mirovich, *Iz istorii zhenskogo dvizheniia v Rossii* (On the history of the women's movement in Russia). Moscow: Tip. I.D. Sytina, 1908, 4–11. A brief history, in English, of the Union, its platform and rules of organisation, can be found in the report from its delegation to the International Woman Suffrage Alliance Conference in Copenhagen. See *International Woman Suffrage Alliance: Report of Third Conference*. Copenhagen, 7–11 August 1906, 97–102.

40 Mirovich, *Iz istorii*, 4–11.

41 *GARF*, fond 516, *'Soiuz ravnopravnosti zhenshchin'* (Women's Equal Rights Union), opis 1, delo 3, 44–108.

42 For a flavour of Union meetings, see the report of the Union's Third Congress, *Ravnopravie zhenshchin: Tretii s"ezd soiuza ravnopravnosti zhenshchin* (Women's equal rights: Third Congress of the Women's Equal Rights Union).

43 Miliukov, *Vospominaniia* (Memoirs), 308.

44 Paul Miliukov, *God bor'by, Publitsisticheskaia khronika 1905–1906* (Year of struggle, Publicistic chronicle), St. Petersburg: Tip. Obschestvennaia pol'za, 1907, 401. For a more extensive overview of the woman question in the Duma, see Goldberg, 'Russian Women's Movement', 134–171, 283–312; Edmondson, *Feminism*, 135–142, 151–153; Stites, *Women's Liberation*, 206–210, 221–222, 283; and A.M. Karabanova, *'Zhenskii vopros v Gosudarstvennoi Dume v 1906–1917 godakh (Po materialam stenograficheskikh otchetov)'* (The woman question in the State Duma from 1906–1917 [On the basis of the materials in the stenographic reports]), *Zhenshchina v Rossiiskom obschestve* (Woman in Russian society), no. 1 (2002): 32–39.

45 *Otchet tsentral'nago komiteta konstitutsionno-demokraticheskoi partii (Partii Narodnoi Svobody) za dva goda s 18 oktiabria 1905 g. po oktiabr' 1907 g.* (Report of the central committee of the constitutional-democratic party [Party of People's Freedom] for the two years from 18 October 1905 to October 1907), St. Petersburg: Tipografiia tovarischestvo 'Obshchestvennaia pol'za', 1907, 54.

46 Ibid.

47 *Zhenskii vestnik* (March 1906): 93.

48 The address from the throne was in reality a short welcoming speech given by the Tsar at the Winter Palace to the Duma delegates on the day of their opening session. In the speech, he called the deputies the 'best people of the Russian land (*luchshikh liudei zemli russkoi*)'. The deputies often sarcastically alluded to this phrase. See V.A. Maklakov, *The First State Duma*, trans. Mary Belkin. Bloomington: Indiana University Press, 1964, 44–47.

49 Miliukov gives two different accounts of the drafting of the Duma's reply to the address from the throne. In *God bor'by*, a collection of articles and essays written at the time, he says that the thirty-three member commission drafted the address (404). In his memoirs, written in the late 1930s, he states that he and fellow Kadets Kokoshkin and Vinaver drafted the reply (Miliukov, *Vospominaniia*, vol.1, 372).

50 Miliukov, *Vospominaniia*, vol. 1, 373. Miliukov, Struve, and Nabokov, among the most influential Kadets, remained unenthusiastic, if not hostile, to pressing the issue of women's suffrage at that moment, claiming that the Duma address was about the present, not the future. The feminist Praskov'ia Arian called Miliukov and his allies 'little Robespierres, Dantons, and Mirabeaus', for their opposition to suffrage. See Stites, *Women's Liberation*, 214.

51 Terence Emmons, *The Formation of Political Parties and the First National Elections in Russia*, Cambridge: Harvard University Press, 1983, 356. The portrait of the Trudoviks has come largely from opponents or uneasy allies. The Mensheviks derided them as ineffective and in tow to the Kadets (*'na buksire za kadetami'*), Miliukov, *God bor'by*, 400. Miliukov considered the Trudovik leaders Aladin, Zhilkin, and Anikin, unimpressive, and regretted that the early co-operation between the two parties diminished. He blamed this on the growing influence of the 'Party intellectuals' (*'partiinie intelligenty'*). Miliukov, *Vospominaniia*, vol. 1, 367–368.

52 *Programmemy politicheskikh partii Rossii: konets XIX-nachalo XX vv.* (The programmes of the Russian political parties at the end of the nineteenth to the beginning of the twentieth centuries), ed. V.V. Shelokhaev, Moscow: ROSSPEN, 1995, 210.

53 *Gosudarstvennaia Duma: Stenograficheskie otchety. Pervyi sozyv* (State Duma: Stenographic reports, First convocation), 2 May 1906. t. 1. St. Petersburg: Gosudarstvennaia tipografiia, 1906, 84.

54 Ibid, 287.

55 *Konstitutionno-demokraticheskaia partiia. Zakonodatel'nye proekty i predpolozheniia partii narodnoi svobody 1905–1907* (Constitutional-democratic party. Legislative projects and proposals of the party of people's freedom 1905–07), St. Petersburg: 1907, 2–5.

56 Duma Stenographic reports, First session, 12 June 1906, 1213.

57 *Ravnopravie zhenshchin*, 51–52. Undaunted, the Union members printed up their report as a pamphlet, adding an introduction. I have not been able to find a copy of this pamphlet.

58 Ibid.

59 The main aim of the very complicated 3 June electoral law was to ensure the hegemony of the Russian male rural propertied class in the country's only legislative body. To preserve the 'Russian character' of the Duma, central Asia was completely disfranchised, and the number of Duma deputies allotted to other provinces was fixed by law in favour of the Russian population. The system of indirect voting through electoral colleges in each province, divided into four categories or *curiae* (landowners, city dwellers, peasants, and workers) was maintained and weighted more heavily by class. The other chief provisions were the following: 1. The number of cities allowed direct election of deputies was cut from twenty-six to seven (St. Petersburg, Moscow, Kiev, Odessa, Riga, Lodz, and Warsaw) and the representation weighted much more in favour of the wealthy urban bourgeoisie. 2. In the provincial electoral colleges, election of deputies was now done by all four *curiae* together. Though provision was made for minimal representation from all four groups, in fact, the majority of electors (landowners and wealthy urban bourgeoisie in all provinces) could pick the Duma deputies for all classes in their province. Duma deputies were selected only from those sitting in the curiae, with the exception of the five cities with direct elections. Sources: Emmons, *Formation*, 372–373; *'Gosudarstvennaia Duma'* (State Duma), *Entsklopedicheskii slovar' Granat* (Encyclopedic dictionary Granat'), seventh edition. Moscow, n.d., v. 16, 172–210, 204–208; 'Russia, Government and Administration', *Encyclopedia Britannica*, eleventh edition. Cambridge, England, 1911, v. 23, 873–875; Samuel Harper, *The New Electoral Law for the Russian Duma*. Chicago: University of Chicago Press, 1908, 2.

60 *'Ob izmenenii gorodskogo izbiratel'nogo zakona'* (On changes in the urban electoral law), *Prilozheniia k stenograficheskim otchetam Gos-oi Dumy* (Supplement to the stenographic reports of the State Duma), 5 vols., St. Petersburg: Gosudarstvennaia tipografiia, 1911, vol. 2, 2,434–2,448, 2,436.

61 'S novym godom' (Happy New Year), *Zhenskii vestnik* (January 1908): 1.

62 *Soiuz zhenshchin* (Women's Union), (December 1907): 2.

63 *Trudy pervogo Vserossiiskogo zhenskogo s"ezda*.

64 Anna M. Itkina, *Revoliutsioner, tribun, diplomat: stranitsy zhizni Aleksandry Mikhailovny Kollontai* (Revolutionary, orator, diplomat: pages from the life of Aleksandra Mikhailovna Kollontai), Moscow: Politizdat, 1970, 53–56. Kollontai, *Aleksandra, Iz moei zhizni i raboty*, 114.

65 *Trudy pervogo Vserossiiskogo zhenskogo s"ezda*, 495.

66 *Sten. otchety, Tretii sozyv, Sessiia V* (Duma stenographic reports, Third convocation, Fifth session), 15 February 1912, vol. 2, 2,163. For the full text of the proposal, see *Prilozheniia k stenograficheskim otchetam Gos-oi Dumy, Tretii sozyv, Sessiia V* (Supplement to the stenographic reports of the State Duma, Third convocation, Fifth session) St. Petersburg: Gosudarstvennaia tipografiia 1912, no. 336.

67 Ibid., no. 336.

68 S.V. Baumshtein, *'Zhenshchina-iurist'* (The woman lawyer), *Trudy pervogo Vserossiiskogo zhenskogo s"ezda*, 421–427, 426.

69 M.I. Pokrovskaia, 'Gosudarstvennyi Soviet i iuristki' (The State Council and women lawyers), *Zhenskii vestnik* (February 1913): 45; Shabanova, *Ocherk*, 30. Ivan G. Shcheglovitov, an 1881 graduate of the Imperial School of Jurisprudence, and an official in the Ministry of Justice from 1890, served as Minister of Justice from 1906–1915. After the Bolshevik Revolution he was arrested and executed. See Miliukov, *Political Memoirs*, 491; William G. Wagner, 'The Trojan Mare: Women's Rights and Civil Rights in Late Imperial Russia', in *Civil Rights in Imperial Russia*, eds. Olga Crisp and Linda Edmondson, Oxford: Oxford University Press, 1989, 65–84; and William G. Wagner, *Marriage, Property, and Law in Late Imperial Russia*, Oxford: Oxford University Press, 1994, 6–7. While documenting the differences among Tsarist officials on women's rights in 'The Trojan Mare', Wagner concludes: 'any substantial reform of women's legal position under an unchanged Tsarist regime appeared problematic' (84). The exceedingly

quick action by the government and the severity of the sentences for Sture and Shutliatikova in 1908 aroused public opinion and particularly incensed Bestuzhev students. See S.I. Strievskaia, 'Uchastie Bestuzhevok v revoliutsionnom dvizhenii' (The participation of Bestuzhev students in the revolutionary movement), in *Sankt-Peterburgskie vysshie zhenskie (Bestuzhevskie) kursy (1878–1918gg): Sbornik statei* (Saint Petersburg women's higher (Bestuzhev) courses (1878–1918): Collected essays), Leningrad, 1965, 30–73, 63.

70 Shabanova, *Ocherk*, 33; Vera Bil'shai, *Reshenie zhenskogo voprosa v SSSR* (The resolution of the woman question in the USSR), Moscow: Gos. izd. politicheskoi literatury, 1959, 78; Sofia Serditova, *Bol'sheviki v bor'be za zhenskie proletarskie massy, 1903 g.-fevral' 1917 g.* (The Bolsheviks in the struggle for the female proletarian masses), Moscow: Gos. izd. politicheskoi literatury, 1959, 78–79.

71 Shabanova, *Ocherk*, 31 Liechtenstein in 1984 became the last European state to grant women suffrage. See http://www.ipu.org/wmn-e/suffrage.html (accessed 26 February 2006)

72 'Samoderzhavie', 33; Bil'shai, *Reshenie*, 78; Serditova, *Bol'sheviki*, 78. On International Woman's Day in 1913, see Chatterjee, *Celebrating Women*, 21–29.

73 *Sten. otchety, Chetvertyi sozyv, Sessiia I* (Stenographic reports, Fourth convocation, First session, 13 March 1913, 3 vols. St. Petersburg: Gosudarstvennaia tipografiia, 1915, vol. 1, 2,176.

74 *Sten. otchety, Chetvertyi sozyv, Sessiia I* 13 March 1913, vol. 1, 2,174.

75 Ibid., 2177, Miliukov, *Vospominaniia*, 2 vols., vol. 2, 166.

76 On Miliukov's change on suffrage, see Stites, *Women's Liberation*, 222; Edmondson, *Feminism*, 152; Melissa Kirschke Stockdale, *Paul Miliukov and the quest for a liberal Russia, 1880–1918*, Ithaca: Cornell University Press, 1996, 198–200. For Miliukov's Duma remarks, see *Sten. otchety*, 13 March, 1913, 2,177.

77 Stites, *Women's Liberation*, 222; Miliukov, *Vospominaniia*, 2 vols., vol. 2, 166; Ariadna Tyrkova-Vil'iams, *To, chego bol'she ne budet: Vospominaniia izvestnoi pisatel'nitsy i obshchestvennoi deiatel'nitsy A.V. Tyrkovoi-Vil'iams (1869–1962), chast' vtoraia, Na putiakh k svobode* (That, which no longer can be: The memoirs of the prominent public figure A.V. Tyrkova-Williams (1869–1962), part two, On the path to freedom), ed. Diana Tevekelian, Moscow: Slovo, 1998, 459; Pokrovskaia, 'Podvinulis li my vpered' (Have we moved forward?) *Zhenskii vestnik* (April 1913): 97–98, 98.

78 Stites, *Women's Liberation*, 222; 'Gosudarstvennaia Duma i zhenshchina' (The State Duma and women), *Zhenskoe delo* (Woman's Cause), (1 April 1913): 1–4, 1.

79 'Gosudarstvennaia Duma i zhenshchina', 3–4; Mirovich, *Iz istorii*, 11–19; Liubov Gurevich, 'Otnoshenie k voprosu o zhenskom izbiratel'nym prave russkogo obshchestve, zemst i gorodov' (Regarding the question of women's suffrage in Russian society, rural councils, and cities), *Soiuz zhenshchin* (August–September 1907): 5–7; Miliukov, *Vospominaniia*, vol. 308–309; I.V. Gessen, *V dvukh vekakh, zhiznennyi otchet* (In two centuries, a life account), Berlin, 1937, 205; *Gosudarstvennaia Duma: Stenograficheskii otchety, 4 sozyv, Sessiia I* (State Duma: Stenographic record, Fourth convocation, First session), vol. 1 (13 March 1913): 2,174–2,179.

80 Repin and Gorkii are quoted in M.I. Pokrovskaia, 'Anketa' (Questionnaire), *Zhenskii vestnik* (July–August 1912): 151; on Tolstoi, see *Zhenskii vestnik* (July–August 1909):144. In a conversation with Natalia Nordman-Severova, Repin's wife, Tolstoi said: 'women should be equal before the law . . . . But in general, I consider women to be lower than men', *Zhenskoe delo*, (25 June 1910): 20. See also Goldberg, 'Russian Women's Movement', 280–283.

81 *Gosudarstvennaia Duma: Stenograficheskie otchety, Tretii sozyv, Sessiia IV* (State Duma: Stenographic reports, Third convocation, Fourth session), 17 February 1911, v. 2. St. Petersburg, 1911, 2,252–2,253.

82 M.I. Pokrovskaia, 'Shirokie krugi naseleniia ob izbiratel'nykh pravakh zhenshchin' (A wide range of the population on women's suffrage), *Zhenskii vestnik* (September 1912): 177–184.

83 On women's suffrage as an 'actual goal of the workers movement', and on the history and celebration of International Women's Day in Russia and the Soviet Union, see S. Liubimova, *50-letie mezhdunarodnogo zhenskogo dnia* (The fiftieth anniversary of International Women's Day), Moscow: Znanie, 1960, 6. See also Aleksandra Kollontai, *Mezhdunarodnyi den' rabotnits* (International Women Workers Day), Moscow: Gosizdat, 1920; Edmondson, *Feminism*, 153; Goldberg, 'Russian Women's Movement', 336–343, 352–354; Stites, *Women's Liberation*, 253; Chatterjee, *Celebrating Women*, 19; Philip S. Foner, *Women and the American Labor Movement*, New York: Free Press, 1979; Clara Zetkin, *Clara Zetkin, Selected Writings*, edited by Philip S. Foner. New York: International Publishers, 1984; Dale Ross, 'The Role of the

Women of Petrograd in War, Revolution and Counter-Revolution, 1914–1921', unpublished Ph.D. thesis, Rutgers University, 1973, 28. On the presence of the Finnish women, see Joyce Stevens, *A History of International Women's Day in Words and Images*, Marrickville, New South Wales: Southwood Press, 1985, 7. On International Women's Day in its first decade, see Temma Kaplan, 'On the Socialist Origins of International Women's Day', *Feminist Studies* 11, no. 1 (Spring 1985): 163–171.

84 Ralph Carter Elwood, *Inessa Armand: Revolutionary and Feminist*, Cambridge: Cambridge University Press, 1992, 105; Chatterjee, *Celebrating Women*, 168, note 38.

85 The fullest study in English of the celebration of International Women's Day in Russia is Chatterjee's *Celebrating Women*. On the 1913 celebration, see 21–29.

86 Serditova, *Bol'sheviki*, 88.

87 On the special issues, see Kollontai, *Iz moei*, 124; on *Pravda*, see A. Grigor'eva-Alekseeva, 'Vpervye v Rossii' (First in Russia), in *Zhenshchiny v revoliutsii* (Women in the revolution), ed. Aleksandra V.Artiukhina, Moscow: Gosudarstvennoe izdatel'stvo politicheskoi literatury, 1959, 93–111, 96. On the extent of the celebrations, see Ekaterina Bochkareva and Serafima Liubimova, *Svetlyi put': Kommunisticheskaia partiia sovetskogo soiuza—borets za svobodu, ravnopravie i schast'e zhenshchiny* (Bright path: The Communist Party of the Soviet Union—fighter for the freedom, equal rights and happiness of women), Moscow: Izdatel'stvo politicheskoi literatury, 1967, 43.

88 Chatterjee, *Celebrating Women*, 35 and note 81.

89 See Chatterjee, *Celebrating Women*, 34, for information on the feminist celebration of International Women's Day. See also Serditova, *Bol'sheviki*, 112; 122–123.

90 Bochkareva and Liubimova, *Svetlyi put'*, 43.

91 *Vsegda s vami: sbornik, posviashchennyi 50-letiiu zhurnala 'Rabotnitsa'* (Always with you: a collection, dedicated to the fiftieth anniversary of the journal 'Working woman'). ed. V. Vavilina, compiled by Aleksandra Artiukhina et al, Moscow: Pravda, 1964, 32–33.

92 Tsuyoshi Hasegawa, *The February Revolution: Petrograd, 1917*, Seattle: University of Washington Press, 1981, 78–79.

93 Food scarcity and high prices became a major issue. The price of bread had risen 600 percent over its pre-war level, eggs 500 percent, butter 900 percent, and staples such as soap had risen 221 percent. Ross, *Role of the Women of Petrograd*, 28.

94 The Tsarist police recognised the volatility of the women waiting for bread far more than did liberal and left activists. A quite prescient January 1917 police report reflected concern that: 'the mothers of families, exhausted from endless standing in line at the stores, tormented by the look of their half-starving and sick children are very likely closer now to revolution than Messrs. Miliukov, Rodichev and Company [the Kadets]'. Bil'shai, *Reshenie*, 96; Chatterjee, *Celebrating Women*, 44–45; Stites, *Women's Liberation*, 290, note 2.

95 On the leading role of radical male workers, see Diane P. Koenker and William G. Rosenberg, *Strikes and Revolution in Russia, 1917*, Princeton: Princeton University Press, 1989, where they argue, citing Leopold Haimson, that: 'the real force for change came from thousands of Vyborg metalworkers, . . . who effectively initiated the chain of events that would lead to the tsar's abdication eight days later' (96). On the role of social-democratic activists in February, see Michael Melancon, *The Socialist Revolutionaries and the Russian Anti-War Movement, 1914–1917*, Columbus: Ohio State University Press, 1990, 234. Richard Pipes, in his widely cited history of the Russian Revolution, argues that 'the February Revolution is often depicted as a worker revolt [but] it is important to emphasise that it was, first and foremost, a mutiny of peasant soldiers whom, to save money, the authorities had billeted in overcrowded facilities in the Empire's capital city'. Richard Pipes, *The Russian Revolution*, New York: Alfred A. Knopf, 1990, 278.

96 Chatterjee, *Celebrating Women*, 56.

97 E.N. Burdzhalov, *Vtoraia Russkaia Revoliutsiia: Vosstanie v Petrograd* (The Second Russian Revolution: The uprising in Petrograd), Moscow: Nauka, 1967, 119.

98 'Gibel' tsarskogo Petrograda: Fevral'skaia revoliutsiia glazami gradonachalnika A.P. Balk: Vospominaniia A.P. Balka iz arkhiva guverskogo institute voiny, revoliutsii i mira (Stenford, SShA), 1929 g.' (The downfall of Tsarist Petrograd: The February revolution through the eyes of Governor A.P. Balk: The memoirs of A.P. Balk from the archives of the Hoover Institute of War, Revolution, and Peace, Stanford, USA, 1929), *Russkoe proshloe* (Russian past), vol.1 (1991), 7–72, 26.

99   Recalling the February events in 1923, Kaiurov wrote: 'I myself had just the night before urged the women workers to show restraint and discipline, yet suddenly here was a strike. There seemed to be no purpose in it and no reason for it.' See V.N. Kaiurov, 'Shest' dnei fevral'skoi revoliutsii', *Proletarskaia revoliutsiia* vol.1, no. 13 (1923): 158, as cited in D.A. Longley, 'The *Mezhraionka* (Inter-district Committee), the Bolsheviks and International Women's Day: In Response to Michael Melançon', *Soviet Studies*, 41, no. 4 (October 1989): 625–645, 632.

100 Leon Trotsky, *Istoriia russkoi revoliutsii. tom I. Fevralskaia revoliutsii* (The history of the Russian Revolution, vol. 1, The February Revolution), 2 vols. Berlin: Izd. 'Granit', 1931, 126.

101 The leaflet is in Longley, '*Mezhraionka*', Appendix F, 'Pechatnyi listok Peterburgskogo Mezhduraionnogo Komiteta posviashchennyi Mezhdunarodnomu dniu rabotnits—23 fevralia 1917g.' (The printed leaflet of the Petersburg Inter-district dedicated to International Woman Workers Day—23 February 1917), 641–642. The Bolsheviks failed to produce a leaflet for International Women's Day because, according to activist Alexander Shliapnikov, their illegal press had not been repaired. Hasegawa (216) disputes Shliapnikov's claim, arguing that it was not lack of a printing press, but the Russian Bureau's priorities which determined the lack of a Bolshevik International Women's Day leaflet.

102 Longley, Appendix F, 641.

103 Ibid.

104 Bochkareva and Liubimova, *Svetlyi put'*, 52.

105 *Zhenskii vestnik* vol. 3 (March 1917): 1–3. The quote is on 1.

106 Burdzhalov, 206–207, 268–269; Hasegawa, 326, 379–380.

107 'Prava zhenshchin' (The rights of women), *Zhenskii vestnik* vol. 3 (March 1917): 41.

108 Tsentral'nyi istoricheskii arkhiv g. Moskvy (Central historical archive of the city of Moscow, henceforth TsGIA g. Moskvy), 'Maria Aleksandrovna Chekhova', fond 2251, opis 2, delo 248, 1–4.

109 'Prava zhenshchin', 40. Chekhova's description of the Kerensky episode and the telegram is in TsGIA g. Moskvy, fond 2251, opis 2, delo 247, pp. 1–4. The Kerensky quote is from *The Russian Provisional Government 1917*. Documents, selected and ed. by Robert Paul Browder and Alexander F. Kerensky. Stanford: Stanford University Press, 1961, 3 vols., 1, 173. The interview is cited in Ross, *Role of the Women of Petrograd*, 168–169.

110 See note 5, especially the quotes from Engel, Pushkareva, and Wade. McDermid and Hillyar make important contributions by making visible the role of women in the revolutionary movement and especially in the events of 1917. In *Midwives*, they acknowledge that women workers were concerned with 'justice', but emphasise the differences between the feminists and women workers (12, 174). See also Hillyar and McDermid, *Revolutionary Women in Russia*, 157, where they attribute the 'gulf between feminists and women workers' to the feminists' support for the war, as if the feminists and women workers were monolithic.

111 'Sobranie sluzhashchikh kreditnykh uchrezhdenii' (Meeting of credit union employees), *Pravda* 4 (9 March 1917): 3.

112 Anne Bobroff, 'The Bolsheviks and Working Women, 1905–1920', *Soviet Studies* 26, no. 4 (1974): 540–567, 558, 560. Anne Bobroff-Hajal, *Working Women in Russia under the Hunger Tsars: Political Activism and Daily Life*, Brooklyn, NY: Carlson Pub., 1994, 91.

113 *Rabochaia gazeta* (Workers gazette), 9 March 1917 for the meeting; *Pravda* (15 March 1917), for the Duma demonstration.

114 Robert Drumm, Bolshevik and Feminist Attempts to Organize Women, 1917', paper presented at the annual meeting of the New England Slavic Association, Storrs, CT, Apil 1976, 10.

115 *Pravda* (15 March 1917).

116 Clements, *Kollontai*, 111.

117 Olga Bobyleva, 'Privet russkoi rabotnitse' (Greetings to the Russian woman worker), *Pravda* (10 March 1917), 3–4, 3.

118 Ibid., 3–4.

119 Edwards, 'Women's Suffrage in China', 621.

120 Liubov Gurevich, *Pochemu nuzhno dat'zhenshchinam takiia zhe prava, kak muzhchinam* (Why is it necessary to give women the same rights as men), Petrograd: Izd. 'Znanie–Sila', 1917, 2. Most historians of the Russian revolutions of 1917, if they mention this demonstration or the women's suffrage victory at all, do so very briefly. For a more detailed eyewitness description of the march, see Olga Zakuta, *Kak v revoliutsionnoe vremia Vserossiiskaia Liga Ravnopraviia Zhenshchin dobylas' izbyratel'nykh prav dlia russkikh zhenshchin* (How during the Revolution

the All-Russian League for Women's Equal Rights gained suffrage for Russian women), Petrograd, 1917. Also available at www.vvsu.ru/grc/e-library/files/liga.doc (accessed 26 February 2006) Zakuta's description is additionally excerpted in Iukina, *Zhenskii Peterburg*, 260, 261.

121 *Jus Suffragii*, 1 November 1917, 26; *Rech'* (Speech), 21 March 1917; *Den'* (Day), 22 March 1917, 3; Edmondson, *Feminism*, 166; Stites, *Women's Liberation*, 292–293. The demonstration was peaceful; the closest it came to violence was when a 'Bolshevik agitator, probably Kollontai, just returned from exile, tried to address the women workers in the crowd, and was pushed off the steps of the Tauride Palace. She was furious that Figner sat in her car and did nothing to support Kollontai's right to free speech'. Stites, *Women's Liberation*, 293. To Stites, the demonstration 'had a disappointing, if not wholly unsuccessful outcome' (292).

122 The Soviet and Provisional Government leaders quick acceptance of the demonstrators' demands may be attributed to several factors, including their reluctance to forcibly disperse a crowd of women, the size of the crowd, their seeking to win support as progressive leaders, and the fact that they didn't have the forces necessary or willing to disperse the crowd. Those deputised by the city police to keep order during the march were members of women's organizations. See Zakuta, web version, 3.

123 *Rech'*, 22 March 1917, 4; A.V. Tyrkova, *Osvobozhdenie zhenshchiny* (Liberation of women), Petrograd: Tip. T-va P.F. 'El-Tip. N.Ia. Stoikovoi', 1917, 15; Ross, *Role of the Women of Petrograd*, 170; Gurevich, *Pochemu*, 3; Edmondson, *Feminism*, 165–166; Stites, *Women's Liberation*, 291–295; *Zhenskii vestnik* (April 1917): 49.

124 *Zakon o vyborakh v Uchreditel'nom Sobranie, offitsial'noe utverzhdennoe Vremennym Pravitel'stvom 20 iiuliia 1917 g.* (Election law for the Constituent Assembly, official confirmation of the Provisional Government 20 July 1917), Petrograd-Moscow, 1917, paragraphs 3–10. 'Statute on Elections to the Constituent Assembly', in Browder and Kerensky, *Provisional Government*, I, 455; *Uchreditel'noe Sobranie Rossiia 1918: Stengramma i drugie dokumenty* (The 1918 Russian Constituent Assembly: Stenographic record and other documents), ed. Tatiana E. Novitskaia, Moscow: Nedra, 1991; 'Ob utverzhdenii razdela i polozheniia o vyborakh v Uchreditel'noe sobranie. Postanovlenie Vremennogo pravitel'stva ot 20 iiuliia 1917 g.' (About the confirmation of issue and statute about elections to the Constituent Assembly. Decree of the Provisional Government of 20 July 1917), 13, 14; *Zhenskii vestnik* 5–6 (May-June 1917): 71–72; Ariadna Tyrkova-Williams, *From Liberty to Brest-Litovsk, The First Year of the Russian Revolution*, London, 1919, 197; Stites, *Women's Liberation*, 294; Edmondson, *Feminism*, 167. On Kuskova's role, see Barbara Norton, 'Laying the Foundation of Democracy in Russia: E.D. Kuskova's Contribution, February-October 1917', in *Women and Society*, 101–123.

125 L. G. Protasov, 'Zhenshchina v Vserossiiskoe Uchreditel'noe sobranie' (Women in the All-Russian Constituent Assembly), in *Ot muzhskikh i zhenskikh k gendernym issledovaniiam, Materialy mezhdunarodnoi nauchnoi konferentsii 20 apreliia 2001 goda* (From men's and women's to gender research, Materials for an international research conference 20 April 2001), ed. P.P. Shcherbinin, Tambov: Izd. Tambov Gosudarstvennyi Universitet, 2001, 51, for the quote.

126 On the voting percentages, see Ibid., 50.

127 J. Kevin Corder and Christina Wolbrecht, 'Incorporating Women Voters After Suffrage', unpublished paper, 22.

128 For more on Shishkina-Iavein's activism and her life after the Revolution (she survived the siege of Leningrad and died in that city after the Second World War, in 1947), see Natalia Bulanova, 'Zhenskoe politicheskoe liderstvo v Rossii: Pervyi opyt (Na primere syd'by P.N.Shishkinoi-Iavein)' (Women's political leadership in Russia: The first experience [The example of the fate of P.N. Shishkina-Iavein]), in *Variatsii na temu Gendera: Materialy III mezhvuzovskoi konferentsii molodykh issledovatelei 'Gendernye otnosheniia v sovremennom rossiiskom obshchestve* (Variations on the theme of Gender: Materials of the Third Inter-University conference of young researchers on the theme of 'Gender relations in contemporary Russian society), ed. T.A. Meleshko, M.V. Rabzhaeva, St. Petersburg: Aleteia, 2004, 70–74.

129 Stites, *Women's Liberation*, 301, for the list. Oliver Radkey, *Russia Goes to the Polls: The Election to the All-Russian Constituent Assembly, 1917*, Ithaca: Cornell University Press, 1989, 154, opp. 157, for the feminist vote totals. For the fullest account of women's participation in the Constituent Assembly elections, see Protasov, 'Zhenshchina', 46–54.

130 Protasov, 'Zhenshchina', 52–53, and Mark *Vishniak, Vserossiiskoe Uchreditel'noe Sobranie* (The All-Russian Constituent Assembly), Paris: Izd. Sovremennyiia Zapiski, 1932, 102. Many

of the women deputies died tragically. Spiridonova, Iakovleva, Slëtova, Perveeva, and Matveevskaia, perished in Stalinist camps or prisons. Bosh committed suicide. Breshkovskaia successfully emigrated to Czechoslovakia, dying there in 1934. Figner died in Moscow in 1942, having refused evacuation. Kollontai, conveniently sent out of the country in 1923 to Norway as the first Soviet woman ambassador (1923–1926, 1927–1930), served also as Ambassador to Mexico (1926–1927), and as Ambassador to Sweden (1930–1945). She died in Moscow in 1952, a year before Stalin died.

131 For a good description of the only day the Constituent Assembly met, see Vishniak, 98–116.

132 Gisela Bock argues that while women's suffrage did not result in dramatic changes, its long-term benefits for women are real. See *Women in European History*, 252. I am grateful to the editors for noting Bock's argument here.

133 See Gurevich, *Pochemu*; Edmondson, *Feminism*, 165–169, and Stites, *Women's Liberation*, 291–295. On the visit of the Pankhursts to Russia in this period, see Olga Shnyrova, 'Za svobodu! Za chest!' Suffrazhistskaia missiia v revoliutsionnuiu Rossiiu' ('For freedom! For respect!' The suffragist mission in revolutionary Russia), unpublished paper. On the significance of the Provisional Government legislation for Russia's women soldiers, see Melissa K. Stockdale, '"My Death for the Motherland is Happiness": Women, Patriotism, and Soldiering in Russia's Great War, 1914–1917', *American Historical Review* vol. 109, no. 1 (February 2004): 78–116, 111.

19 Women's suffrage in China (Louise Edwards)

1 Caroline Daley and Melanie Nolan, eds., *Suffrage and Beyond: International Feminist Perspectives* (Auckland, 1994), 351.

2 For example, Li Ziyun, an established scholar with a long record of research, claimed 1949 as "the year" that "Chinese women acquired the right to vote, something their sisters in the west had spent decades even centuries fighting for." Li Ziyun, "Women's Consciousness and Women's Writing," in Christina Kelley Gilmartin, *et al.*, eds., *Engendering China: Women, Culture, and the State* (Cambridge, Mass., 1994), 304–305.

3 Susan Blackburn has explored the problems for women's suffrage posed by a fragile national identity, nationalist struggles, and the colonial regime in Indonesia in her article, "Winning the Vote for Women in Indonesia," *Australian Feminist Studies*, 14 (1999), 207–218.

4 Carole Pateman, "Three Questions About Womanhood Suffrage," in Daley and Nolan, eds., *Suffrage and Beyond*, 346.

5 Ian Tyrrell, *Women's World, Women's Empire: The Woman's Christian Temperance Union in International Perspective, 1880–1930* (Chapel Hill, N.C., 1991).

6 See, for example, Ellen Carol DuBois, *Feminism and Suffrage: The Emergence of an Independent Women's Movement in America, 1848–1869* (Ithaca, N.Y., 1978); Patricia Grimshaw, *Women's Suffrage in New Zealand* (Auckland, 1987); Susan Kingsley Kent, *Sex and Suffrage in Britain, 1860–1914* (Princeton, N.J., 1987); Audrey Oldfield, *Woman Suffrage in Australia: A Gift or a Struggle?* (Melbourne, 1992).

7 To date, the women's suffrage movement in China is mentioned only briefly in broad studies of the transformation of Chinese women across the twentieth century. For example, Ono Kazuko, *Chinese Women in a Century of Revolution, 1850–1950* (Stanford, Calif., 1989), 86–89; Wang Zheng, *Women in the Chinese Enlightenment: Oral and Textual Histories* (Berkeley, 1999), 129, 183, 136; Lü Meiyi and Zheng Yongfu, *Zhongguo funü yundong, 1840–1921* [China's women's movement, 1840–1921] (Zhengzhou, 1991), 339–346.

8 Zhou Yaping, "Lun xinhai geming shiqi de funü canzheng yundong" [Discussing the women's suffrage movement of the 1911 Revolution Period], *Lishi dang'an* (Jing) [Historical Archives], 2 (1993), 118–123, 125.

9 Li Yu-ning, "Sun Yat-sen and Women's Transformation," *Chinese Studies in History* (Summer 1988), 62.

10 Luo Yanbin, "Zhongguo xin nüjie zazhi fakan ci" [On the publication of *China's New Women's World*] (1907), 15, in Tan Sheying, ed., *Zhongguo funü yundong shi* [A general history of the Chinese women's movement] (Nanjing, 1936). For more information in English on Luo Yanbin and other publishing enterprises by women during this period, see Charlotte Beahan, "Feminism and Nationalism in the Chinese Women's Press, 1902–1911," *Modern China*, 1 (1975), 379–416.

11 Ono, *Chinese Women in a Century of Revolution*, 86–89.

12 For a discussion of Jean-Jacques Rousseau, natural law, and women, see Christine Fauré, *Democracy Without Women: Feminism and the Rise of Liberal Individualism in France*, trans. by Claudia Gorbman and John Berks (Bloomington, Ind., 1991), 82–90. China's women's suffrage activists were unaware of the many problematic aspects of Rousseau's views on women identified by Fauré. Barbara Molony's article, "Women's Rights, Feminism, and Suffragism in Japan, 1870–1925," (Chapter 5 in this book) offers a useful comparison of the rhetoric of natural rights.

13 Lü and Zheng, *Zhongguo funü yundong*, 246. See Gayle Gullett, "Constructing the Woman Citizen and Struggling for the Vote in California, 1896–1911," and Corinne A. Pernet, "Chilean Feminists, the International Women's Movement, and Suffrage (1915 to 1950)," both in *Pacific Historical Review*, 69 (2000) (573–593 and 663–688, respectively) for comparisons with Californian and Chilean attitudes toward British suffragette tactics.

14 Xie Changfa, "Qingmo de liu Ri nüxuesheng ji qi huodong yu yingxiang" [The activities and influence of women students studying in Japan at the end of the Qing], *Jindai Zhongguo funü shi yanjiu* [Research on women in modern Chinese history], 4 (1996), 63–87. Interestingly, many Chilean suffragists had also studied abroad; see Pernet, "Chilean Feminists."

15 Qiu Jin, *Qiu Jin ji* [Collected works of Qiu Jin] (Shanghai, 1960, reprinted 1979); Bao Jialin, "Qiu Jin yu Qingmo funü yundong" [Qiu Jin and the late Qing women's movement], in Bao Jialin, ed., *Zhongguo funü shi lunji* [Collected essays on Chinese women's history] (Taipei, 1992), 346–382; Wang, *Women in the Chinese Enlightenment*, 42–43.

16 Xu Huiqi, "Tang Qunying yu 'Nüzi canzheng tongmenghui' " [Tang Qunying and the Women's Suffrage Alliance], *Guizhou shehui kexue* [Guizhou social sciences], 4 (1981), 30–37.

17 For a fuller discussion, see Li Chien-nung, *The Political History of China, 1840–1928* (Princeton, N.J., 1956).

18 Tan, *Zhongguo funü yundong tongshi*, 105–106, 97–104.

19 Wang, *Women in the Chinese Enlightenment*, 13. For discussion of women as icons of modernity within the male reform-minded intellectual's view, see Louise Edwards, "Policing the Modern Woman in Republican China," *Modern China*, 26 (April 2000), 115–147.

20 Jacqueline Nivard, "Women and the Women's Press: The Case of the *Ladies' Journal* (*Funü zazhi*), 1915–1931," *Republican China*, 10 (Nov. 1984), 37–56.

21 Christina Kelley Gilmartin, *Engendering the Chinese Revolution: Radical Women, Communist Politics and Mass Movements in the 1920s* (Berkeley, 1995), 81.

22 For more detail on Liu Wang Liming, see Wang, *Women in the Chinese Enlightenment*, 135–137; Lily Xiao Hong Lee, *et al.*, eds., *Biographical Dictionary of Chinese Women: The Twentieth Century 1912–2000* (Armonk, N.Y., 2003), 374–377.

23 For discussion of the status of widows in the Qing, see Paul Ropp, "The Seeds of Change: Reflections on the Condition of Women in the Early and Mid Ch'ing," *Signs: Journal of Women in Culture and Society*, 2 (1976), 5–23; Susan Mann, "Widows in the Kinship, Class and Community Structures of Qing Dynasty China," *Journal of Asian Studies*, 46 (1987), 37–55.

24 For an English translation, see Lawrence K. Rosinger, *China's Wartime Politics, 1937–1944* (Princeton, N.J., 1945), 70–85.

25 Louise Edwards, "From Gender Equality to Gender Difference: Feminist Campaigns for Quotas for Women in Politics 1936–1947," *Twentieth-Century China*, 24 (April 1999), 69–105.

26 Elisabeth Croll, *Changing Identities of Chinese Women: Rhetoric, Experience, and Self-Perception in Twentieth-Century China* (London, 1995).

27 Louise Edwards, "Women in the People's Republic of China: New Challenges to the CCP Grand Gender Narrative," in Edwards and M. Roces, eds., *Women in Asia: Tradition, Modernity and Globalisation* (Sydney, 2000), 59–84.

28 Wu Shuzhen, "Zhongguo funü canzheng yundong de lishi kaocha" [Observations on the history of the Chinese women's suffrage movement], *Zhongshan daxue xuebao: she ke ban* [Zhongshan university journal: social sciences edition], 2 (1990), 77–84, reprinted in *Funü zuzhi yu huodong* [Women's organizations and activities], 3 (1990), 32.

29 Phyllis Andors, *The Unfinished Liberation of Chinese Women, 1949–1980* (Bloomington, Ind., 1983), 20–21.

30 Wang, *Women in the Chinese Enlightenment*, 120.

31 Bernice J. Lee, "The Change in the Legal Status of Chinese Women in Civil Matters from Traditional Law to the Republican Civil Code" (Ph.D. dissertation, Sydney University, 1975).

32 Gilmartin, *Engendering the Chinese Revolution*; Ono, *Chinese Women in a Century of Revolution*; Wang, *Women in the Chinese Enlightenment*.

33 Christina Gilmartin, "Recent Developments in Research About Women in the PRC," *Republican China*, 10 (Nov. 1984), 57–66.

34 Richard Evans noted that the relationship of the European Marxists to the women's suffrage struggles around Europe were fraught with similar ambiguities about the value of parliamentarianism and the liberation of the masses from class oppression. Richard J. Evans, *Comrades and Sisters: Feminism, Socialism, and Pacifism in Europe, 1870–1945* (Sussex, Eng., 1987).

35 China's intellectuals have long been involved in the process of correctly "inheriting" the past to ensure its utility to the current CCP project of national reconstruction. See Kam Louie, *Inheriting Tradition: Interpretations of the Classical Philosophers in Communist China, 1949–1966* (Oxford, 1986).

36 Grimshaw, *Women's Suffrage in New Zealand*.

37 Oldfield, *Woman Suffrage in Australia*.

38 Ch'ien Tuan-sheng, *The Government and Politics of China, 1912–1949* (1950; Stanford, Calif., 1970), 325.

39 Xiang Jingyu, "Jinhou Zhongguo funü de guomin geming yundong" [The state of the Chinese women's national revolution movement], *Funü zazhi*, 10 (Jan. 1, 1924), reprinted in Zhonghua quanguo funü lianhehui funü yundong lishi yanjiu shi, eds., *Zhongguo funü yundong lishi ziliao, 1921–1927* [Materials on the history of the Chinese women's movement, 1921–1927] (Beijing, 1986), 109.

40 Xiang Jingyu, "Ping Wang Bihua de nüquan yundong tan" [Critique of Wang Bihua on the women's movement], *Funü zhoubao* [Women's weekly], 8 (Oct. 10, 1923), reprinted in Zhonghua quanguo funü lianhehui funü yundong lishi yanjiu shi, eds., *Zhongguo funü yundong lishi ziliao, 1921–1927*, 150–151.

41 Sheng Shusen, Tan Changchun, and Tao Zhisun, "Zhongguo nüquan yundong de xianqu, Tang Qunying," [The forerunner of the Chinese feminist movement, Tang Qunying], *Renwu* [Personages], 4 (1992), 82–90.

42 Song Qingling [1942], "Chinese Women's Fight for Freedom," trans. by Li Yu-ning, in Li Yu-ning, ed., *Chinese Women Through Chinese Eyes* (Armonk, N.Y., 1992), 91.

43 Roxanne Witke, "Women as Politicians in China of the 1920s," in Marilyn B. Young, ed., *Women in China: Studies in Social Change and Feminism* (Ann Arbor, Mich., 1973), 33.

44 Ono, *Chinese Women in a Century of Revolution*, 80.

45 Louise Edwards, "Chin Sung-ts'en's *A Tocsin for Women*: The Dexterous Merger of Radicalism and Conservatism in Feminism of the Early Twentieth Century," *Research on Women in Modern Chinese History* (June 1994), 117–140. The book itself was published by Datong shuju in Shanghai, 1903.

46 Her sister, Lin Zongxue, led one of China's women's armies during the anti-Qing movement, and her brother, Lin Baiyong, was prominent in the newspaper industry. Gao Kuixiang and Shen Jianguo, eds., *Zhonghua gujin nüjie pu* [Annals of ancient and modern women in China] (Beijing, 1991), 174.

47 Lin Zongsu, "Nüzi canzheng tongzhi hui xuanyan shu" [Manifesto of the women's suffrage comrades alliance], *Funü shibao* [Women's times], 5 (1912), 17–19.

48 See Zhang Binglin's formal written complaint to Sun: "I do not know whether women's political participation would be a good social custom or not, and, not daring myself to presume to have such knowledge, I think that the judgment of the appropriateness of such a measure should await public discussion. Yet, I have heard that Your Excellency gave approval in a few words to a certain woman's verbal request, even though the constitution has not yet been precisely enunciated. When unconsidered talk gets out of hand, once such statements are endorsed, things will become even more unruly." Zhang Binglin in Shanghai shehui kexueyuan, eds., *Xinhai geming zai Shanghai shiliao xuanji* [Selected historical materials on the 1911 revolution in Shanghai] (Shanghai, 1981), 777, trans. in Li, "Sun Yatsen and Women's Transformation," 63.

20 Rethinking the socialist construction and international career of the concept "bourgeois feminism" (Marilyn J. Boxer)

An earlier version of this essay was presented at the conference of the International Federation for Research in Women's History during the 20th International Congress of Historical Sciences in Sydney in July 2005. I owe special gratitude to my longtime colleagues Karen Offen and Jean Quataert, and to Gisela Bock and Geoff Eley, for invaluable close readings and suggestions; to the editors and anonymous readers of *The American Historical Review* for constructive criticism; and to Ann Taylor Allen, Naomi J. Andrews, Krassimira Daskalova, Carolyn Eichner, Joanne Ferraro, and Francisca de Haan for helpful comments.

1   For a portion of Zetkin's 1889 speech, translated by Susan G. Bell, see Susan Groag Bell and Karen M. Offen, eds., *Women, the Family, and Freedom: The Debate in Documents*, 2 vols. (Stanford, Calif., 1983), vol. 2: *1880–1950*, 87–91, quotations on 87, 90; also in Zetkin, *Clara Zetkin: Selected Writings*, ed. Philip S. Foner (New York, 1984), 45–50. For 1896, see Rosalie Schoenflies, Lina Morgenstern, Minna Cauer, Jeannette Schwerin, and Marie Raschke, eds., *Der Internationale Kongress für Frauenwerke und Frauenbestrebungen in Berlin, 19. bis 26. September 1896* (Berlin, 1897), 394–396, quotation on 394. At the latter conference, French feminist Eugénie Potonié-Pierre introduced the new word "feminism"; ibid., 40.

2   For a recent reference to Zetkin and her 1907 speech, see Kristen Ghodsee, "Feminism-by-Design: Emerging Capitalisms, Cultural Feminism, and Women's Nongovernmental Organizations in Post-socialist Eastern Europe," *Signs: Journal of Women in Culture and Society* 29, no. 3 (Spring 2004): 727–753, quotations on 732, 733. For other examples of the persistence of this idea, see Francisca de Haan, Krassimira Daskalova, and Anna Loufti, eds., *A Biographical Dictionary of Women's Movements and Feminisms in Central, Eastern, and South Eastern Europe, Nineteenth and Twentieth Centuries* (Budapest, 2006). German historian Gisela Bock finds the term "bourgeois feminism" to be "as ubiquitous today" as in Zetkin's day; personal communication, May 2006.

3   John R. Hall, "The Reworking of Class Analysis," in Hall, ed., *Reworking Class* (Ithaca, N.Y., 1997), 1–37. For new approaches to labor history particularly salient to understanding women and class, see Lenard R. Berlanstein, ed., *Rethinking Labor History: Essays on Discourse and Class Analysis* (Urbana, Ill., 1993), esp. William H. Sewell, Jr., "Toward a Post-Materialist Rhetoric for Labor History," 15–38. Kathleen Canning observes that gender analysis has "revitalized" the field of labor history; Canning, *Gender History in Practice: Historical Perspectives on Bodies, Class, and Citizenship* (Ithaca, N.Y., 2006), 124. On class and gender formation, see Leonore Davidoff and Catherine Hall, *Family Fortunes: Men and Women of the English Middle Class, 1780–1850* (Chicago, 1987); and Geoffrey Crossick and Heinz-Gerhard Haupt, *The Petite Bourgeoisie in Europe, 1780–1914: Enterprise, Family and Independence* (London, 1995), 97–98; also Ava Baron, "Gender and Labor History: Learning from the Past, Looking to the Future," in Baron, ed., *Work Engendered: Toward a New History of American Labor* (Ithaca, N.Y., 1991), 1–46. On "binary distinction," see Sonya O. Rose, "Class Formation and the Quintessential Worker," in Hall, *Reworking Class*, 133–166, esp. 139–144; and Rose, *Limited Livelihoods: Gender and Class in Nineteenth-Century England* (Berkeley, Calif., 1992), 193. On excluding women from the "public sphere," see the summary in Laura L. Frader and Sonya O. Rose, "Introduction: Gender and the Reconstruction of European Working-Class History," in Frader and Rose, eds., *Gender and Class in Modern Europe* (Ithaca, N.Y., 1996), 11–19.

4   For a pioneering analysis of the invention of "bourgeois feminism," see Françoise Picq, "'Bourgeois Feminism' in France: A Theory Developed by Socialist Women before World War I," trans. Irene Tilton, in Judith Friedlander, Blanche Wiesen Cook, Alice Kessler-Harris, and Carroll Smith-Rosenberg, eds., *Women in Culture and Politics: A Century of Change* (Bloomington, Ind., 1986), 330–343.

5   On the limitations of the European Left, and gender politics as its "greatest weakness," see Geoff Eley, *Forging Democracy: The History of the Left in Europe, 1850–2000* (Oxford, 2002), quotation on 112.

6   On "false women's emancipation," see F. A. Sorge, *Briefe und Auszüge aus Briefen von Joh. Phil. Becker, Jos. Dietzen, Friedrich Engels, Karl Marx an F. A. Sorge und Andere* (Stuttgart, 1921), 37; for "milliner," see Karl Marx, *Capital: A Critique of Political Economy*, vol. 1, trans. Samuel Moore and Edward Aveling (1867; repr., New York, 1902), 280–281; on "self-emancipation," see Marx, *Letters to Dr. Kugelmann* (New York, 1934), 82. Frederick Engels, *The Origin of the Family, Private Property and the State* (1884; repr., New York, 1942), 65–66; and Engels, *The Condition of the Working-Class in England in 1844*, trans. Florence Kelley Wischnewetsky (1845; repr., London, 1952), 181; on "asses," see Engels quoted by Hal Draper and Anne Lipow, "Marxist Women versus Bourgeois Feminism," *Socialist Register* 13 (1976): 179–226, quotation on 217.

7   August Bebel, *Woman under Socialism*, trans. from the German 33rd ed. by Daniel De Leon (New York, 1971), 5; originally published in 1883 as *Woman in the Past, Present, and Future*.

Feindliche is sometimes translated as "enemy"; see Draper and Lipow, "Marxist Women versus Bourgeois Feminism," 189. On the broader significance of translations and Bebel's pioneering use of "gender-neutral" terms, see Anne Lopes and Gary Roth, "A Note on Translation," in Lopes and Roth, *Men's Feminism: August Bebel and the German Socialist Movement* (Amherst, N.Y., 2000), 19–27. On Otto-Peters, see Lopes and Roth, *Men's Feminism*, 90. On Bebel's support of feminist legislative reform, see Bebel, *Woman under Socialism*, 112; also Richard J. Evans, *Comrades and Sisters: Feminism, Socialism, and Pacifism in Europe, 1870–1945* (Sussex, 1987), 28–29. For qualification of Bebel's feminism, see Richard Stites, *The Women's Liberation Movement in Russia: Feminism, Nihilism, and Bolshevism, 1860–1930* (Princeton, N.J., 1978), 234–236. For Bebel's 1878 speech on "more in common," see Lopes and Roth, *Men's Feminism*, 199.

8   Ute Frevert, *Women in German History: From Bourgeois Emancipation to Sexual Liberation* (New York, 1989), 141.

9   Clara Zetkin, *Zur Geschichte der proletarischen Frauenbewegung Deutschlands* (1928; repr., Berlin, 1958), 209. On Zetkin's formulation of socialist theory on women, see Werner Thönnessen, *The Emancipation of Women: The Rise and Decline of the Women's Movement in German Social Democracy, 1863–1933*, trans. Joris de Bres (1969; repr., Frankfurt-am-Main, 1973), 39–46. For Zetkin's reference to women as slaves, see Robert Stuart, "Whores and Angels: Women and the Family in the Discourse of French Marxism, 1882–1905," *European History Quarterly* 27, no. 3 (1997): 339–369, quotation on 343–344.

10 On "clean break," see Alfred G. Meyer, *The Feminism and Socialism of Lily Braun* (Bloomington, Ind., 1985), 52. For "extreme animosity," see Stites, *The Women's Liberation Movement*, 237. For "stupid dreams," see *Frauenrechtlerische Harmoniedüselei*, the title of Zetkin's response to a new feminist journal; *Die Gleichheit* 5, no. 1 (January 9, 1895): 6. See also the citation by Alfred G. Meyer in Lily Braun, *Selected Writings on Feminism and Socialism*, trans. and ed. Alfred G. Meyer (Bloomington, Ind., 1987), 43. Meyer translates Zetkin's title as "Women's Libbers' Stupid Dreams about Harmony." For "muddle-headed," see Jean H. Quataert, "Unequal Partners in an Uneasy Alliance: Women and the Working Class in Imperial Germany," in Marilyn J. Boxer and Jean H. Quataert, eds., *Socialist Women: European Socialist Feminism in the Nineteenth and Early Twentieth Centuries* (New York, 1978), 112–145, quotation on 116. For "untiring," see Quataert, "Feminist Tactics in German Social Democracy 1890–1914: A Dilemma," *IWK: Internationale Wissenschaftliche Korrespondenz zur Geschichte der deutschen Arbeiterbewegung* 13, no. 1 (March 1977): 48–65, quotation on 56 n. 41. For Pelletier, see Richard J. Evans, *The Feminists: Women's Emancipation Movements in Europe, America, and Australasia, 1840–1920* (London, 1977), 172. On "savage," see Richard J. Evans, "The Concept of Feminism: Notes for Practicing Historians," in Ruth-Ellen B. Joeres and Mary Jo Maynes, eds., *German Women in the Eighteenth and Nineteenth Centuries: A Social and Literary History* (Bloomington, Ind., 1986), 247–258, quotation on 248. Evans here emphasizes the "depth of the divisions" between the socialist women's movement and feminism (253). For "vicious," see n. 17 below. A recent biographer sees the Lutheranism of Zetkin's early years as partially responsible for her ideological rigidity; see Tânia Puschemat, *Clara Zetkin: Bürgerlichkeit und Marxismus: Eine Biographie* (Essen, 2003).

11 On bourgeois women's values, see Bonnie G. Smith, *Ladies of the Leisure Class: The Bourgeoises of Northern France in the Nineteenth Century* (Princeton, N.J., 1981). Smith opens her book with the question, "What is a bourgeois woman?"; ibid., 3. On "heroes," see Michelle Perrot, "1914: Great Feminist Expectations," in Helmut Gruber and Pamela Graves, eds., *Women and Socialism/Socialism and Women: Europe between the Two World Wars* (New York, 1998), 27. For "parasites," see Rosa Luxemburg, "Women's Suffrage and Class Struggle," in Luxemburg, *Selected Political Writings of Rosa Luxemburg*, ed. Dick Howard (New York, 1971), 216–222, quotation on 220.

12 Sarah Maza, *The Myth of the French Bourgeoisie: An Essay on the Social Imaginary, 1750–1850* (Cambridge, Mass., 2003). "'So bourgeois' [fashion hawker] Hugh mutters after her. 'So last year' "; observation at a New York City fashion show described in the *New York Times*, February 11, 2004, A26. On definitions of "bourgeois" in French dictionaries and popular usage, see Adeline Daumard, *Les Bourgeois et la bourgeoisie en France depuis 1815* ([Paris], 1987), 35–44.

13 Madeleine Pelletier once remarked, "What the socialists reprove isn't feminism. It's the feminists"; Pelletier, "Bourgeois Feminism and Socialist Feminism," *Le Socialiste*, May 5, 1907.

14 Shirley Gruner, "The Revolution of July 1830 and the Expression 'Bourgeoisie,' " *Historical Journal* 11, no. 3 (1968): 462–471, quotations on 469–471. Peter Gay, *The Bourgeois Experience: Victoria to Freud*, 5 vols., vol. 1: *Education of the Senses* (New York, 1984), 20; on writers and Flaubert as "bourgeoisophobus" see Gay, *Schnitzler's Century: The Making of Middle-Class Culture, 1815–1914* (London, 2001), 29. The other amorphous term with which "bourgeois" is sometimes linked, "middle class," carries less affect. Jürgen Kocka, who in his study of nineteenth-century German society uses the latter's adjectival form "interchangeably with 'bourgeois,' " points out that "the attractiveness of a concept rarely correlates with its precision . . . The middle class has never been a class, at least not in the Marxist sense"; Kocka, *Industrial Culture and Bourgeois Society: Business, Labor, and Bureaucracy in Modern Germany* (New York, 1999), 231–233.

15 Maza, *The Myth of the French Bourgeoisie*, 3, 5, 195.

16 Eleanor Hakim, speaking of her cohort of graduate students at the University of Wisconsin; Hakim, "The Tragedy of Hans Gerth," in Paul Buhle, ed., *History and the New Left: Madison, Wisconsin, 1950–1970* (Philadelphia, Pa., 1990), 252–263, quotation on 256.

17 Zetkin's adamant refusal to entertain collaboration with nonsocialist women and the rivalry for leadership are major themes of a study of feminism and German socialism that predates the resurgence of women's history. Its author sees Zetkin's "anti-feminism" as bordering on "fanaticism," and her presentations as "spirited, biting, and not infrequently vicious." See Jacqueline Strain, "Feminism and Political Radicalism in the German Social Democratic Movement, 1890–1914" (Ph.D. diss., University of California, Berkeley, 1964), 67, 81. For Zetkin's rivalry with Braun, see Jean H. Quataert, *Reluctant Feminists in German Social Democracy, 1885–1917* (Princeton, N.J., 1979), 107–133; on differences with Luise Zietz and others, see ibid., 164–165, 202–205.

18 Thus the split was less strong in Britain than in Germany. See Eley, *Forging Democracy*, 30–31; and Geoff Eley, "German Liberals, the Well-Ordered Public, and the Patriarchal Nation, 1860–1920," paper presented at the conference "Wilhelmine Germany and Edwardian Britain—Cultural Contacts and Transfers," University of Oxford, March 2006. I thank Professor Eley for sharing this paper with me.

19 For example, when a group of Swedish socialist women submitted a proposed resolution for the international socialist women's conference in 1910, chastising socialist men who deserted women whose children they had fathered, Zetkin appealed to them to withdraw it; Renée Frangeur, "Social Democrats and the Woman Question in Sweden: A History of Contradiction," in Gruber and Graves, *Women and Socialism/Socialism and Women*, 425–426.

20 On "mishmash commission," see Richard J. Evans, "Bourgeois Feminists and Women Socialists in Germany, 1894–1914: Lost Opportunity or Inevitable Conflict?" *Women's Studies International Quarterly* 3 (1980): 355–376, esp. 367–368.

21 For the controversy within German socialism over contraception, including strong statements against it by Clara Zetkin and Rosa Luxemburg, see R. P. Neuman, "Working Class Birth Control in Wilhelmine Germany," *Comparative Studies in Society and History* 20, no. 3 (1978): 408–428. On Zetkin's support for traditional gender roles, see Lopes and Roth, *Men's Feminism*, 200–201, and Karen Honeycutt, "Clara Zetkin: A Socialist Approach to the Problem of Woman's Oppression," *Feminist Studies* 3, no. 3/4 (Spring-Summer 1976): 131–144, esp. 135–136. For "haunted," see Quataert, *Reluctant Feminists*, 111.

22 Kollontai accompanied Zetkin on her 1909 visit to Britain; see Karen Hunt, *Equivocal Feminists: The Social Democratic Federation and the Woman Question, 1884–1911* (Cambridge, 1996), 68 n. 55. On Zetkin as Kollontai's mentor, see also Beatrice Farnsworth, *Aleksandra Kollontai: Socialism, Feminism, and the Bolshevik Revolution* (Stanford, Calif., 1980), 26. For Eleanor Marx, see Draper and Lipow, "Marxist Women versus Bourgeois Feminism," 225–226; emphasis in original. But Marx saw "no more in common between [feminist leader] Mrs. Fawcett and a laundress than we see between Rothschild and one of his employees"; ibid., 225.

23 Kollontai wrote *The Social Bases of the Woman Question* (1908) in preparation for the First All-Russian Women's Congress, and she held some fifty meetings with working women to coach them, before leading the group to the event "with clear instructions to disrupt it"; Farnsworth, *Aleksandra Kollontai*, 30–34, quotation on 33. For a detailed description of the 1908 congress, see Linda Harriet Edmondson, *Feminism in Russia, 1900–1917* (London, 1984), 86–93. For "antifeminist polemic," see Stites, *The Women's Liberation Movement*, 437; on harassment, see ibid., 252; on "class character," see Richard Stites, "Women and the Revolutionary Process in

Russia," in Renate Bridenthal, Susan Stuard, and Merry Wiesner-Hanks, eds., *Becoming Visible: Women in European History*, 3rd ed. (Boston, 1998), 424. Stites credits Kollontai with destroying the Russian Women's Union; Stites, *The Women's Liberation Movement*, 214. Kollontai wrote that "during the period of the first revolution . . . the bourgeois women's movement posed a serious threat to the unity of a working-class movement"; in Alexandra Kollontai, *Selected Writings*, ed. Alix Holt (New York, 1977), 50. Her comment on "unbridgeable gulf" is quoted in Stites, *The Women's Liberation Movement*, 228. For "scourge," see Beatrice Farnsworth, "Bolshevism, the Woman Question, and Aleksandra Kollontai," in Boxer and Quataert, *Socialist Women*, 186.

24 See Kollontai, *Selected Writings*.

25 For the full text of the appeal and repeat notices, see Marilyn J. Boxer, "Socialism Faces Feminism in France, 1879–1913" (Ph.D. diss., University of California, Riverside, 1975), 188, 191. "Confusionism" quoted in Boxer, "Socialism Faces Feminism," in Boxer and Quataert, *Socialist Women*, 92; on "letter," see Christine Bard, *Les Filles de Marianne: Histoire des féminismes, 1914–1940* (n.p., 1995), 90.

26 Charles Sowerwine, *Sisters or Citizens? Women and Socialism in France since 1876* (Cambridge, 1982), 134, 186; see also Sowerwine, *Les Femmes et le socialisme* (Paris, 1978). Paul Smith, *Feminism and the Third Republic: Women's Political and Civil Rights in France, 1918–1945* (Oxford, 1996), 80; Bard, *Les Filles de Marianne*, 345; Gruber, "French Women in the Crossfire of Class, Sex, Maternity, and Citizenship," in Gruber and Graves, *Women and Socialism/Socialism and Women*, 279–320, quotation on 283.

27 Henriëtte Roland Holst-Van der Schalk, *Een Woord aan de vrouwen der arbeidende klasse naar aanleiding der nat. tentoonstelling van vrouwen-arbeid* (Amsterdam, 1898), 19.

28 Maria Grever and Berteke Waaldijk, *Transforming the Public Sphere: The Dutch National Exhibition of Women's Labor in 1898*, trans. Mischa F. C. Hoyick and Robert E. Chesal (Durham, N.C., 2004), 48–49.

29 Patricia Hilden and Christine Bard offer some insight into the situation in the north of France and the southeast, respectively. Bard suggests that Saumoneau and the party line had some influence at Lyon; Bard, *Les Filles de Marianne*, 241. Regarding the major textile cities in the north, Hilden states, "In general, the national SFIO's campaign against bourgeois feminism found few echoes in the Nord federation"; Hilden, *Working Women and Socialist Politics in France, 1880–1914: A Regional Study* (Oxford, 1986), 256. Richard J. Evans, reporting on attitudes among Hamburg pub-goers toward women suffragists, cites some workingmen who, influenced by Zetkin's views, said, "the bourgeois feminists . . . are basically in favour of suppressing women workers"; in Evans, *Proletarians and Politics: Socialism, Protest and the Working Class in Germany before the First World War* (New York, 1990), 165.

30 For an illustrative case of the means through which the German party influenced others in the Second International, see Georges Haupt, *L'historien et le mouvement social* (Paris, 1980), 151–197.

31 See, e.g., the struggle of Anna Kuliscioff; Claire LaVigna, "The Marxist Ambivalence toward Women: Between Socialism and Feminism in the Italian Socialist Party," in Boxer and Quataert, *Socialist Women*, 146–181.

32 Ute Frevert, *Women in German History*, 146; I have altered the translation of *Frauenrechtlerinnen*, substituting the more common usage "women's righters" for "legalists." For a similar decision by Swedish Social Democrats in 1905, see Evans, *The Feminists*, 169.

33 Leila J. Rupp, *Worlds of Women: The Making of an International Women's Movement* (Princeton, N.J., 1997), 35. On suffrage as a divisive issue among internationalists, see ibid., 135–139.

34 On shifting views over collaboration, see also Evans, *The Feminists*, 170–177; on the United States., see Mari Jo Buhle, *Women and American Socialism, 1870–1920* (Urbana, Ill., 1981), 221–229. For Braun, see Meyer, *The Feminism and Socialism of Lily Braun*, 57–58; for Pelletier, see Sowerwine, *Sisters or Citizens?* 130; for the Austrian case, see Meyer, *The Feminism and Socialism of Lily Braun*, 53. Two French historians, Laurence Klejman and Florence Rochefort, assert that the real audience of the French socialist women leaders was male socialists; Klejman and Rochefort, *L'Egalité en marche: Le Féminisme sous la Troisième République* (Paris, 1989), 215.

35 On China, see Christina Gilmartin, "Gender, Politics, and Patriarchy in China: The Experiences of Early Women Communists, 1920–27," in Sonia Kruks, Rayna Rapp, and Marilyn B. Young,

eds., *Promissory Notes: Women in the Transition to Socialism* (New York, 1989), 101; on Vietnam, see Christine Pelzer White, "Vietnam: War, Socialism, and the Politics of Gender Relations," ibid., 177.

36 Mineke Bosch, "History and Historiography of First-Wave Feminism in the Netherlands, 1860–1922," in Sylvia Paletschek and Bianka Pietrow-Ennker, eds., *Women's Emancipation Movements in the Nineteenth Century: A European Perspective* (Stanford, Calif., 2004), 65.

37 Rupp, *Worlds of Women*, 47; see also Karen Offen, *European Feminisms, 1700–1950: A Political History* (Stanford, Calif., 2000), 386–387.

38 *The Woman Question: Selections from the Writings of Karl Marx, Frederick Engels, V.I. Lenin, Joseph Stalin* (New York, 1951), 89. Lenin's comment is also translated as "strong, ineradicable line against the bourgeois movement for the 'emancipation of women,' " in Lenin, *The Emancipation of Women: From the Writings of V. I. Lenin* (New York, 1966), 110. For early women's studies syllabi, see Sheila Tobias, ed., *Female Studies I* (Pittsburgh, Pa., 1970), and Florence Howe, ed., *Female Studies II* (Pittsburgh, Pa., 1970); for the first women's history course in the first women's studies program, taught by Roberta Salper, see Howe, *Female Studies II*, 89.

39 Judith Hole and Ellen Levine trace the influence of the left, old and new, through the beginnings of women's liberation in the United States in *Rebirth of Feminism* (New York, 1971), 114–122. Shulamith Firestone's *The Dialectic of Sex*, which blazed a meteoric path through the radical women's movement and appeared on many early women's studies course outlines, set out to perform the task left undone by the masters, to apply the dialectic method to the "sex class," women; Firestone, *The Dialectic of Sex: The Case for Feminist Revolution* (New York, 1970). See also the reflective essays in Rachel Blau Duplessis and Ann Snitow, eds., *The Feminist Memoir Project: Voices from Women's Liberation* (New York, 1998). For England, Sheila Rowbotham has provided a close analysis of the rebirth of feminism among women active in the New Left. See esp. Rowbotham, *Promise of a Dream: Remembering the Sixties* (London, 2001), and "Appreciating Our Beginnings," in Rowbotham, *Threads through Time: Writings in History and Autobiography* (London, 1999), 73–83. On "bourgeois character," see Kate Millett, *Sexual Politics* (Garden City, N.Y., 1970), 84; for "trap," see Robin Morgan, ed., *Sisterhood Is Powerful: An Anthology of Writings from the Women's Liberation Movement* (New York, 1970), xxii.

40 For Britain, see Barbara Caine, *English Feminism, 1780–1980* (Oxford, 1997), 256. For France, see Florence Rochefort, "Les féministes," in Jean-Jacques Becker and Gilles Candar, eds., *Histoire des gauches en France*, 2 vols., vol. 2: *XXe siècle: À l'épreuve de l'histoire* (Paris, 2004), 108. For aggressive ridicule, see Elaine Marks and Isabelle de Courtivron, eds., *New French Feminisms: An Anthology* (Amherst, Mass., 1980), x. On the new feminism in Italy as "genetically linked to the New Left," see Yasmine Ergas, "1968–79—Feminism and the Italian Party System: Women's Politics in a Decade of Turmoil," *Comparative Politics* 14, no. 3 (April 1982): 253–279, quotation on 256. For a survey that mentions socialist influence on second wave feminism in other European countries, including Greece, the Netherlands, and Spain, see Gisela Kaplan, *Contemporary Western European Feminism* (New York, 1992).

41 Betty Friedan, *The Feminine Mystique* (New York, 1963). For Friedan's political origins in the "old left," see Daniel Horowitz, *Betty Friedan and the Making of "The Feminine Mystique": The American Left, the Cold War, and Modern Feminism* (Amherst, Mass., 1998).

42 A 1968 strike by factory women helped spur organization by leftist women; see Rowbotham, *Threads through Time*, 80–81. Mitchell also noted, "The liberation of women remains a normative ideal, an adjunct to socialist theory, not structurally integrated into it . . . The family as it exists at present is, in fact, incompatible with the equality of the sexes"; Juliet Mitchell, "Women: The Longest Revolution," *New Left Review* 40 (November–December 1966): 11–37, quotations on 15, 36. On the need for new theory, see Mitchell, *Women's Estate* (New York, 1971), 90–91; for "liberal feminist," see ibid., 66. On the influence of Mitchell and Rowbotham, see, e.g., Anna Coote and Beatrix Campbell, *Sweet Freedom: The Struggle for Women's Liberation* (Oxford, 1982), 8–9.

43 Sheila Rowbotham, *Women, Resistance, and Revolution: A History of Women and Revolution in the Modern World* (1972; repr., New York, 1974), quotations on 35, 247. Rowbotham opens with protests by seventeenth-century aristocratic and bourgeois women, in a chapter she titles "Impudent Lasses."

44 On "bogey," see Sheila Rowbotham, "Introduction," in *The Daughters of Karl Marx: Family Correspondence, 1866–1898*, commentary and notes by Olga Meier, trans. and adapted by Faith

Evans (New York, 1979), xvii–xl, quotation on xxxv; on "caricatures" and "polarity," see Rowbotham, "The Women's Movement and Organizing for Socialism," in Rowbotham, Lynne Segal, and Hilary Wainwright, eds., *Beyond the Fragments: Feminism and the Making of Socialism* (London, 1979), 63–64 and 151 n. 19; on conventional stereotype, see Rowbotham, *Hidden from History: Rediscovering Women in History from the 17th Century to the Present* (1973; repr., New York, 1974), 79.

45 Rowbotham reflects on the links between radical history in Britain and the United States. as well as inspiration drawn from Western Marxist theorists whose work "illuminated aspects of women's oppression which were not part of conventional socialist ways of seeing." See Sheila Rowbotham, "New Entry Points from USA Women's Labour History," in Margaret Walsh, ed., *Working Out Gender: Perspectives from Labour History* (Aldershot, 1999), 9–28, quotation on 11.

46 Julia Swindells and Lisa Jardine, *What's Left? Women and Culture in the Labour Movement* (London, 1990), 12, 68; emphasis in original. They also state that for adding feminism to Marxist analysis, Mitchell "was promptly excommunicated by the *NLR* fraternity"; ibid., 70. "Cult of masculinity" is from Beatrix Campbell, *Wigan Pier Revisited: Poverty and Politics in the Eighties* (London, 1984), 98–99. Joan Wallach Scott also points to the difficulty of including women in the language of class; see "On Language, Gender, and Working-Class History," in Scott, *Gender and the Politics of History* (New York, 1988), 53–67, esp. 64–65.

47 Dorothy E. Smith, *Feminism and Marxism: A Place to Begin, a Way to Go* (Vancouver, 1977), 33; Sheila Rowbotham, *Woman's Consciousness, Man's World* (London, 1973), 38. Statements that both helped launch the new feminism and connected it to Marxism grew out of women's protests at meetings of SDS (Students for a Democratic Society), including widely distributed and much-anthologized essays by Roxanne Dunbar, "Female Liberation as the Basis for Socialist Revolution" (1968), and Margaret Benston, "The Political Economy of Women's Liberation" (1969). See also Lydia Sargent, ed., *Women and Revolution: A Discussion of the Unhappy Marriage of Marxism and Feminism* (Boston, 1981); Rowbotham, "Appreciating Our Beginnings," in Rowbotham, *Threads through Time*, 73–83; and Rowbotham, *Promise of a Dream*. A historian of the American left, James Weinstein, states, "Initially, the women's movement saw itself as entirely outside of, or even opposed to, the organized socialist movement, largely because socialist parties and groups had traditionally seen 'the woman question' as secondary to trade union or political electoral activity, but also because of the social conservatism of much of the socialist movement. Radical feminism grew up in opposition to the socialist movement in much the same way as black cultural nationalism emerged in reaction to the politics and social relations of the white left." Weinstein, *Ambiguous Legacy: The Left in American Politics* (New York, 1975), 165.

48 For a summary of socialist-feminist activism in the United States., see Red Apple Collective, "Socialist-Feminist Women's Unions: Past and Present," *Socialist Review* 38 (March–April 1978): 37–57.

49 The literature is huge. See, e.g., Annette Kuhn and AnnMarie Wolpe, eds., *Feminism and Materialism: Women and Modes of Production* (London, 1978); Batya Weinbaum, *The Curious Courtship of Women's Liberation and Socialism* (Boston, 1978); Zillah R. Eisenstein, ed., *Capitalist Patriarchy and the Case for Socialist Feminism* (New York, 1979); Michèle Barrett, *Women's Oppression Today: Problems in Marxist Feminist Analysis* (London, 1980); Cambridge Women's Studies Group, *Women in Society: Interdisciplinary Essays* (London, 1981); Sargent, *Women and Revolution*. On "polemicizing," see Mary-Alice Waters, *Feminism and the Marxist Movement* (New York, 1972), 35. On "dissatisfied," see Charnie Guettel, *Marxism and Feminism* (Toronto, 1974), 1. On "instruments," see Marlene Dixon, "Left-Wing Anti-Feminism: A Revisionist Disorder," *Synthesis: A Journal of Marxist-Leninist Debate* 1, no. 4 (Spring 1977): 31–43, quotation on 33. Socialist-feminists "disengaged from feminism," Beatrix Campbell later commented; Michèle Barrett, Beatrix Campbell, Anne Phillips, Angela Weir, and Elizabeth Wilson, "Feminism and Class Politics: A Round-Table Discussion," *Feminist Review* 23 (Summer 1986), 16.

50 Lise Vogel, *Marxism and the Oppression of Women: Toward a Unitary Theory* (New Brunswick, N.J., 1983), 108–109; Evans, *Proletarians and Politics*, 96.

51 At San Diego State University, where the first integrated program in women's studies was launched in 1970, the first chair offered the job was the Marxist Marlene Dixon, who declined but personally solicited another socialist feminist, Roberta Salper, who accepted. The initial curriculum included a course entitled "Status of Women under Various Economic Systems" that

highlighted communist societies. But after "three years of struggle," working "inside the beast" (their term for the university), the early San Diego State women's studies faculty asked themselves whether it was "a waste of our time . . . to be teaching and working with petty bourgeois students." The following year they decided it was, and, embattled with the administration over governance issues, they resigned en masse. For Dixon and Salper, see Roberta Salper, "Introduction," in Salper, ed., *Female Liberation: History and Current Politics* (New York, 1972), 22. On early San Diego State women's studies, see *Women's Studies Program: Three Years of Struggle* (San Diego, Calif., 1973), and Women's Studies Board, San Diego State College, *Women's Studies and Socialist Feminism* (San Diego, Calif., 1974); also Marilyn Jacoby Boxer, *When Women Ask the Questions: Creating Women's Studies in America* (Baltimore, Md., 1998), 164–166. On conflicts in women's studies, see also Ellen Messer-Davidow, *Disciplining Feminism: From Social Action to Academic Discourse* (Durham, N.C., 2002).

52 For course outlines, see Tobias, *Female Studies I*, and Howe, *Female Studies II*. Roxanne Dunbar's "Female Liberation as the Basis for Social Revolution," written early in 1969 as a response to an SDS resolution, was reprinted in Morgan, ed., *Sisterhood Is Powerful*, 477–492, which was a popular selection among academic feminists. Margaret Benston's "The Political Economy of Women's Liberation" (brochure, Boston, n.d.; reprinted from *Monthly Review*, September 1969) included writings from Lenin as an appendix.

53 Michèle Barrett and Anne Phillips, "Introduction," in Barrett and Phillips, eds., *Destabilizing Theory: Contemporary Feminist Debates* (Stanford, Calif., 1992), 2–3, emphases in original. On "Big Three," see Mary Maynard, "Beyond the 'Big Three': The Development of Feminist Theory in the 1990's," *Women's History Review* 4, no. 3 (1995): 259–281. As feminist theorist Donna J. Haraway points out, "Any . . . taxonomy is a re-inscription of history"; Haraway, *Simians, Cyborgs, and Women: The Reinvention of Nature* (New York, 1991), 159–160.

54 Zillah Eisenstein, "Developing a Theory of Capitalist Patriarchy and Socialist Feminism," in Eisenstein, *Capitalist Patriarchy and the Case for Socialist Feminism*, 5–40, quotation on 38 n. 27; The Combahee River Collective, "A Black Feminist Statement," in Gloria T. Hull, Patricia Bell Scott, and Barbara Smith, eds., *But Some of Us Are Brave* (Old Westbury, N.Y., 1982), 13–22, quotation on 20; Angela Y. Davis, "Foreword," in Foner, *Clara Zetkin*, 11.

55 For a sample "statement," see the following: "History—least of all labour history—is not an abstract intellectual pursuit. It is also a political statement, a personal choice about the past . . . It is to *Labour History*'s credit that it continues to provide a forum for 'activist' as well as academic, the young and innovative as well as the privileged and professional elite"; "Introduction," special issue, *Women, Work and the Labour Movement in Australia and Aotearoa/New Zealand*, ed. Raelene Frances and Bruce Scates, *Labour History* 61 (November 1991): x. For Woolf, see Virginia Woolf, *Three Guineas* (San Diego, 1938), 177 n. 13.

56 For one notable activist's memory of this concern, see the interview with Jane Fonda by Robin Morgan in *Ms.* 16, no. 1 (Winter 2006): 36.

57 Mme. Ghénia Avril de Sainte-Croix (writing as "Savioz"), "L'Indépendance économique de la femme," *L'Humanité*, January 17, 1907; she was co-founder of the National Council of French Women, author of *Le Féminisme* (Paris, 1907), and an international feminist activist. I thank Karen Offen for this reference; on Sainte-Croix, see Offen, "'La plus grande féministe de France': Mais qui est donc Madame Avril de Sainte-Croix?" *Archives du féminisme*, Bulletin no. 9 (December 2005): 46–54.

58 Among the exceptions are G. D. H. Cole, who includes a six-page chapter on "Socialism and the Rights of Women, 1914–1931" in Cole, *A History of Socialist Thought*, vol. 4, pt. 2: *Communism and Social Democracy, 1914–1931* (London, 1958), 839–845, and a chapter on Flora Tristan in vol. 1: *Socialist Thought: The Forerunners, 1789–1850* (London, 1953), 183–188; and George Lichtheim, who offers a brief discussion of Tristan as the "first socialist to have lived the connection between the emancipation of her sex and the ending of wage slavery," in Lichtheim, *The Origins of Socialism* (New York, 1969), 69.

59 The term is borrowed from Sonya Rose, "Class Formation." In Rose's view, "the 'quintessential worker problem' . . . has blinded historians from recognizing how both gender and race have been *constitutive* of class identities"; 139, emphasis in original. Although her focus is not on women, Carole Biewener's "Class and Socialist Politics in France," *Review of Radical Political Economics* 19, no. 2 (1987): 61–76, is useful for understanding how basic class concepts served to eclipse women's roles as workers.

60 Campbell, *Wigan Pier Revisited*, 97.

61 Michelle Perrot, "Twenty Years of Women's History in France: Preface to the English Edition," in Perrot, ed., *Writing Women's History*, trans. Felicia Pheasant (1984; repr., Oxford, 1992), viii–ix. See also the interview with Perrot about resistance to women's history by *gauchistes* in *Radical History Review* 37 (1987): 27–38.

62 Cf. Linda Harriet Edmondson's 1984 comment that most of the research on women in tsarist Russia had thus far focused on revolutionaries, with little attention given to the "bourgeois feminists," in Edmondson, *Feminism in Russia*, x.

63 Rowbotham, *Women, Resistance, and Revolution*.

64 Thönnessen, *The Emancipation of Women*, 10. Thönnessen sees the socialist turn to reformism, which he says favored "proletarian anti-feminism," as responsible for the demise of German socialism; ibid., 164–165.

65 Amy Hackett, "The German Women's Movement and Suffrage, 1890–1914: A Study of National Feminism," in Robert J. Bezucha, ed., *Modern European Social History* (Lexington, Mass., 1972), quotations on 355, 356.

66 For Ph.D. dissertations, see Karen Honeycutt, "Clara Zetkin: A Left-Wing Socialist and Feminist in Wilhelmian Germany" (Columbia University, 1975); Amy K. Hackett, "The Politics of Feminism in Wilhelmine Germany, 1890–1918" (Columbia University, 1976); and Boxer, "Socialism Faces Feminism in France, 1879–1913." Linda Edmondson lists eight dissertations on women in Russia between 1968 and 1981, all but one on women in radical movements; Edmondson, *Feminism in Russia*, 177.

67 Ann J. Lane, "Women in Society: A Critique of Frederick Engels," in Berenice A. Carroll, ed., *Liberating Women's History: Theoretical and Critical Essays* (Urbana, Ill., 1976), 4–25; and Amy Hackett, "Feminism and Liberalism in Wilhelmine Germany, 1890–1918," ibid., 127–136. It is worth noting that Lane, in her essay dating from 1972, criticizes the absence of women workers in E. P. Thompson's revisionist work. For criticism of Draper's and Lipow's stance on feminism, see Rowbotham, Segal, and Wainwright, *Beyond the Fragments*, 152 n. 27.

68 Draper and Lipow, "Marxist Women versus Bourgeois Feminism," 180, 189. Draper and Lipow trace the split back to a struggle for primacy within the German workers' movement between Lassalleans and Marxists; ibid., 182–183.

69 Richard J. Evans, "Bourgeois Feminists and Women Socialists in Germany, 1894–1914: Lost Opportunity or Inevitable Conflict?" *Women's Studies International Quarterly* 3 (1980): 355–376, quotation on 359. Evans titled chapter 2 of his *Comrades and Sisters* "The Impossible Alliance." Reasons for the vote included not unfounded fears of repression by police: in 1894, a women's "educational club" in Nuremberg was dissolved for sending a representative to a socialist meeting; see Quataert, "Feminist Tactics," 51.

70 See Sowerwine, *Sisters or Citizens?* 26–28; Sowerwine, "The Socialist Women's Movement from 1850 to 1940," in Renate Bridenthal, Claudia Koonz, and Susan Stuard, eds., *Becoming Visible: Women in European History*, 2nd ed. (Boston, 1987), 399–426, esp. 405–406; Boxer, "Socialism Faces Feminism in France, 1879–1913," 103–113. Claire Moses follows Sowerwine on this, in Moses, *French Feminism in the Nineteenth Century* (Albany, N.Y., 1984), 223–224. On factionalism among French feminists, see Wynona H. Wilkins, "The Paris International Feminist Congress of 1896 and Its French Antecedents," *North Dakota Quarterly* 43, no. 4 (Autumn 1975): 5–28. For "Auclert's biographer," see Steven C. Hause, *Hubertine Auclert: The French Suffragette* (New Haven, Conn., 1987), 67.

71 Robert Stuart, " 'Calm, with a Grave and Serious Temperament, Rather Male': French Marxism, Gender and Feminism, 1882–1905," *International Review of Social History* 41, pt. 1 (April 1996): 57–82, quotations on 76, 77.

72 Sowerwine, *Sisters or Citizens?* 75–77. For the *compte-rendu*, see *Congrès international de la condition & des droits des femmes tenu les 5, 6, 7 et 8 septembre 1900* (Paris, 1901), 73–79. The "bourgeois feminist" leader Maria Pognon reported that after the altercation, working women delegates to the conference stated their appreciation for her help over the previous year, and offered her their support. See Pognon, "Expliquons-nous," *La Petite République*, September 18, 1900, 1. Durand and Pognon both joined socialists to call for state support of mothers, unwed and married; Anne Cova, "French Feminism and Maternity: Theories and Politics, 1890–1918," in Pat Thane and Gisela Bock, eds., *Maternity and Gender Policies: Women and the Rise of the European Welfare States, 1880s–1950s* (London, 1991), 119–137, esp. 123–125. For a women's movement that viewed socialism as a "social poison," see Nancy R. Reagin, *A German Women's Movement: Class and Gender in Hanover, 1880–1933* (Chapel Hill, N.C., 1995), quotation on 73.

73 On Holland, see Grever and Waaldijk, *Transforming the Public Sphere*, 195–200. On Braun, see Meyer, *The Feminism and Socialism of Lily Braun*, quotations on 63, 64, and 142. Evans also follows Sowerwine on this; Evans, *Comrades and Sisters*, 40. Stites states that servants constituted a "blind spot" for feminists; Stites, *The Women's Liberation Movement*, 223. On Russia, see Rose Glickman, *Russian Factory Women: Workplace and Society, 1880–1914* (Berkeley, Calif., 1984), 243–244.

74 Boxer and Quataert, *Socialist Women*, 5–8. Exceptional work that did examine women's class status included Gerda Lerner, "The Lady and the Mill Girl: Changes in the Status of Women in the Age of Jackson," *Midcontinent American Studies Journal* 10, no. 1 (Spring 1969): 5–15, and two essays in Carroll, *Liberating Women's History*: Hilda Smith, "Feminism and the Methodology of Women's History," 368–384, and Sheila Ryan Johansson, "'Herstory's as History: A New Field or Another Fad?" 400–430.

75 Sowerwine writes, "Even in the countries where the socialist women's movement was weakest, it reached more women than the bourgeois feminists ever hoped to reach"; Sowerwine, "The Socialist Women's Movement," 421. If doubtful in other cases as well, this statement wholly ignores mass religious and patriotic women's movements that attracted large numbers in several countries; for the latter in Germany, see Frevert, *Women in German History*, 137. Picq writes that "socialist women abandoned working women"; Picq, "'Bourgeois Feminism' in France," 341. She refers to the infamous Couriau affair, in which French printers ejected a member for allowing his (union-qualified) wife to work in the trade, and only "bourgeois feminists" supported her protest.

76 Karen Offen, "Exploring the Sexual Politics of Republican Nationalism," in Robert Tombs, ed., *Nationhood and Nationalism in France: From Boulangism to the Great War, 1889–1918* (London, 1991), 195–205; Carolyn J. Eichner, *Surmounting the Barricades: Women in the Paris Commune* (Bloomington, Ind., 2004), 5, 9–10, 26, 61; Florence Rochefort, "The French Feminist Movement and Republicanism, 1868–1914," in Paletschek and Pietrow-Ennker, *Women's Emancipation Movements*, quotation on 78; Gisela Bock, *Women in European History*, trans. Allison Brown (Oxford, 2002), 119; Jean H. Quataert, *Staging Philanthropy: Patriotic Women and the National Imagination in Dynastic Germany, 1813–1916* (Ann Arbor, Mich., 2001), 82.

77 Claire Moses, "Debating the Present, Writing the Past: 'Feminism' in French History and Historiography," *Radical History Review* 52 (1979): 79–94, quotation on 84. In Moses's view, the grandmothers evoked "the National Woman's Party (suspect for its relationship to the Republican Party)," and the mothers, the members of the "National Organization for Women (suspect for its relationship to the Democratic Party)."

78 Sally Alexander, "Women, Class and Sexual Differences," *History Workshop Journal* 17 (Spring 1984): 125–149, quotation on 127.

79 Evans, *Comrades and Sisters*, 59. For women in the interwar French socialist party as "neither comrades nor sisters," see Gruber, "French Women in the Crossfire," 280.

80 Lopes and Roth, *Men's Feminism*, 45, 222.

81 See, e.g., Jeanne-Victoire [Jeanne Deroin], "Call to Women," *La Femme libre* 1, no. 1 (1832), in Bell and Offen, *Women, the Family, and Freedom*, vol. 1: *1750–1880*, 146–147; also Moses, *French Feminism in the Nineteenth Century*, 136–142; Eichner, *Surmounting the Barricades*, 2, 24, 69–95. Naomi J. Andrews demonstrates how "gender shaped socialism's definition of the good society" in the July Monarchy; Andrews, *Socialism's Muse: Gender in the Intellectual Landscape of French Romantic Socialism* (Lanham, Md., 2006), xvii.

82 On working-class women sympathetic to "bourgeois feminism" such as Jeanne Bouvier and Henriette Coulmy, see Bard, *Les Filles de Marianne*, esp. 184–186. On cross-class efforts, see, e.g., Frevert, *Women in German History*, 100–103. On opposition to Zetkin in the SPD, see Strain, "Feminism and Political Radicalism," 140–142, 208. On links between welfare work and the emergence of feminism, see Bock, *Women in European History*, 111–116.

83 On motherhood as an issue crossing "class" lines, see Ann Taylor Allen, *Feminism and Motherhood in Western Europe, 1890–1970: The Maternal Dilemma* (New York, 2005); for "parallel wars," see Ida Blom, "Modernity and the Norwegian Women's Movement from the 1880s to 1914: Changes and Continuities," in Paletschek and Pietrow-Ennker, *Women's Emancipation Movements*, 125–151, quotation on 138.

84 The term "litmus test" is used by Moses, "Debating the Present," 84, and by Sheila Rowbotham in *Women in Movement: Feminism and Social Action* (New York, 1992), 14. The wrong assumption appears in Ingrun Lafleur, "Five Socialist Women: Traditionalist Conflicts and

Socialist Visions in Austria, 1893–1934," in Boxer and Quataert, *Socialist Women*, 215–248, esp. 237. For the comparative study, see Ulla Wikander, Alice Kessler-Harris, and Jane Lewis, eds., *Protecting Women: Labor Legislation in Europe, the United States, and Australia, 1880–1920* (Urbana, Ill., 1995). In Scandinavia, opposition from trade union women who feared loss of work sometimes sufficed to quash proposals for restrictions; ibid., 215, 236–237, 247–248, 273–274. For a thoughtful comparative discussion of the controversy and its relation to citizenship and maternalism, see Bock, *Women in European History*, 158–173.

85 Class issues also arose in Latin America, for example, within the suffrage movement in Uruguay. Christine Ehrick suggests, however, that the familiar European/North American model does not really suit the Latin American context. See Ehrick, "*Madrinas* and Missionaries: Uruguay and the Pan-American Women's Movement," *Gender and History* 10, no. 3 (November 1998): 406–424.

86 See Ida Blom, "Prelude to Welfare States: Introduction," in Gruber and Graves, *Women and Socialism*, 415–420; Frangeur, "Socialist Democrats and the Woman Question in Sweden," and Hilda Rømer Christensen, "Socialist Feminists and Feminist Socialists in Denmark, 1920–1940," ibid., 478–503. These studies confirm Eley's point regarding the influence of relationships between liberal and socialist parties on degrees of collaboration among women's groups.

87 Martha Bohachevsky-Chomiak, *Feminists Despite Themselves: Women in Ukrainian Community Life, 1884–1939* (Edmonton, 1988), 80, and "Feminism in Ukrainian History," *Journal of Ukrainian Studies* 7, no. 1 (Spring 1982): 16–30, esp. 20. See also Bohachevsky-Chomiak, "Socialism and Feminism: The First Stages of Women's Organizations in the Eastern Part of the Austrian Empire," in Tora Yedlin, ed., *Women in Eastern Europe and the Soviet Union* (New York, 1980), 44–64.

88 Judith Szapor, "Sisters or Foes: The Shifting Front Lines of the Hungarian Women's Movements, 1896–1918," in Paletschek and Pietrow-Ennker, *Women's Emancipation Movements*, 189–205, quotations on 199; Andrea Petö, "Hungarian Women in Politics," in Joan W. Scott, Cora Kaplan, and Debra Keates, eds., *Transitions, Environments, Translations: Feminism in International Politics* (New York, 1997), 153–161, quotation on 159.

89 On the split into "broad" and "narrow" socialism, see Krassimira Daskalova, "Bulgarian Women in Movements, Laws, Discourses (1840s–1940s)," *Bulgarian Historical Review* 27, no. 1–2 (1999): 180–196, esp. 186–188; on stigma and stereotype, see Daskalova, "The Women's Movement in Bulgaria after Communism," in Scott, Kaplan, and Keates, *Transitions, Environments, Translations*, 162–175, quotations on 163 and 170.

90 Jill M. Bystydzienski, "The Feminist Movement in Poland: Why So Slow?" *Women's Studies International Forum* 24, no. 5 (2001): 501–511, quotation on 503.

91 Wang Zheng, *Women in the Chinese Enlightenment: Oral and Textual Histories* (Berkeley, Calif., 1999). The book is based on interviews with five members of the first generation of Chinese feminist activists. For transliterations and definitions of "feminism," see ibid., esp. 7–9, 133–134, 339–342; also Sasha Su-Ling Welland, "What Women Will Have Been: Reassessing Feminist Cultural Production in China—A Review Essay," *Signs: Journal of Women in Culture and Society* 31, no. 4 (Summer 2006): 949. Wang now refers to party work among women in Shanghai as "state feminism"; Wang, "'State Feminism'? Gender and Socialist State Formation in Maoist China," *Feminist Studies* 31, no. 3 (Fall 2005): 519–551.

92 Kumari Jayawardena, "Some Thoughts on the Left and the 'Woman Question' in South Asia," in Kruks, Rapp, and Young, *Promissory Notes*, 359–366, quotation on 363.

93 Kruks, Rapp, and Young, "Introduction," ibid., 7–12, quotation on 9.

94 On "capitulation," see Elizabeth Waters, "In the Shadow of the Comintern: The Communist Women's Movement, 1920–43," ibid., 29–56, quotation on 51; on "knuckled under," see Christina Gilmartin, "Gender, Politics, and Patriarchy in China: The Experiences of Early Women Communists, 1920–27," ibid., 82–105, quotation on 101; on individualism and traditional roles, see Christine Pelzer White, "Vietnam: War, Socialism, and the Politics of Gender Relations," ibid., 172–192, and Delia D. Aguilar, "Third World Revolution and First World Feminism: Toward a Dialogue," ibid., 338–344.

95 Kathleen Canning distinguishes usefully between class as an analytic concept and as "postulated identity or ideology"; Canning, "Gender and the Politics of Class Formation: Rethinking German Labor History," *AHR* 97, no. 3 (June 1992): 736–768, quotation on 767. Women, argues Diane P. Koenker, faced "exclusion from the male world of class"; see her "Men against Women on the Shop Floor in Early Soviet Russia: Gender and Class in the Socialist

Workplace," *AHR* 100, no. 5 (December 1995): 1438–1464, quotation on 1463. On masculine identity and class formation, see also Ava Baron, "On Looking at Men: Masculinity and the Making of a Gendered Working-Class History," in Ann-Louise Shapiro, ed., *Feminists Revision History* (New Brunswick, N.J., 1994), 146–171.

96 Florence Rochefort, "The French Feminist Movement and Republicanism, 1868–1914," in Paletschek and Pietrow-Ennker, *Women's Emancipation Movements*, 77–101, quotation on 86.

97 This was true especially of Bulgarian and Polish women; Francisca de Haan, Krassimira Daskalova, and Anna Loufti, "Introduction," in de Haan, Daskalova, and Loufti, *Biographical Dictionary of Women's Movements and Feminisms*, 9.

98 The journalist, Ida Heijermans, was the sister of a well-known socialist; Grever and Waaldijk, *Transforming the Public Sphere*, 202.

99 Nelly Roussel, *Quelques Lances rompues pour nos libertés* (Paris, 1910), 48.

100 Jeanne Bouvier, *Mes Mémoires: ou 59 années d'activité industrielle, sociale et intellectuelle d'une ouvrière, 1876–1935* (Paris, 1983), 243–244, also quoted in Bard, *Les Filles de Marianne*, 185; on teachers, ibid. On the role of intellectuals in the Second International, see Patricia van der Esch, *La Deuxième Internationale, 1889–1923* (Paris, 1957), 35–36. For weaknesses in the Marxist critique of the bourgeoisie, see Robert Stuart, *Marxism at Work: Ideology, Class and French Socialism during the Third Republic* (Cambridge, 1992). Stuart, on the other hand, credits the POF with identifying women clerks as "proletarian"; Stuart, "Gendered Labour in the Ideological Discourse of French Marxism: The Parti Ouvrier Français, 1882–1905," *Gender and History* 9, no. 1 (April 1997): 115.

101 Evans cites a prewar survey in Hamburg that found only 1,601 of 11,684 women members engaged in paid employment; Richard J. Evans, "Politics and the Family: Social Democracy and the Working-Class Family in Theory and Practice before 1914," in Richard J. Evans and W. R. Lee, eds., *The German Family: Essays on the Social History of the Family in Nineteenth- and Twentieth-Century Germany* (London, 1981), 266. Mary Nash cites an occupational survey of a 1926–1927 Spanish socialist women's group that found only 1 of 527 members working in an industrial occupation; Nash, "'Ideals of Redemption': Socialism and Women on the Left in Spain," in Gruber and Graves, *Women and Socialism*, 350–351. Of the approximately 1,000 members of the Bulgarian social democratic women's organization in 1922, 457 were housewives, 212 were "workers," 56 were "craftsmen," and about 75 were employed in clerical and professional occupations; Krassimira Daskalova, "Bulgarian Women's Movements (1850s–1940s)," in Edith Saurer, Margaareth Lanzinger, and Elisabeth Frysak, eds., *Women's Movements, Networks and Debates in Post-Communist Countries in the Nineteenth and Twentieth Centuries* (Weimar, 2006), 413–437. On wives, for France, see Claude Willard, *Les Guesdistes: Le mouvement socialiste en France, 1893–1905* (Paris, 1965), 362 n. 1; for Germany, see Evans, *Comrades and Sisters*, 61, and Quataert, *Reluctant Feminists*, 19; for the Netherlands, see Ulla Jansz, "Gender and Democratic Socialism in the Netherlands," in Gruber and Graves, *Women and Socialism*, 217; for Spain, see Nash, "Ideals of Redemption," 350; for Sweden, see Frangeur, "Social Democrats and the Woman Question," 428. For the British suffrage movement, see Olive Banks, *Becoming a Feminist: The Social Origins of "First Wave" Feminism* (Brighton, 1986), 11, 16; and Jiang Park, "The British Suffrage Activists of 1913: An Analysis," *Past and Present* 120 (August 1988): 147–162, esp. 157, 161. For the Netherlands, see Myriam Everard, "Het burgerlijk feminisme van de eerste golf: Annette Versluys-Poelman en haar kring," in Marjan Schwegman, Ulla Jansz, et al., eds., *Op het Strijdtoneel van de Politiek: Twaalfdejaarboek voor vrouwengeschiedinis* (Nijmegen, 1991), 106–137.

102 Sowerwine states that "the socialist women, if they were not so much of the working classes as they claimed, were nonetheless from class backgrounds very different from those of the feminists"; *Sisters or Citizens?* 186. Picq also challenges Sowerwine on this point; Picq, "'Bourgeois Feminism' in France," 330. Geoff Eley and Keith Nield point out that "socialist parties always contained a far richer sociology than a simple class-political argument would imply"; Eley and Nield, "Farewell to the Working Class?" *International Labor and Working-Class History* 57 (Spring 2000): 1–30, quotation on 20.

103 On identity politics, see Quataert, "Socialisms, Feminisms, and Agency: A Long View," *Journal of Modern History* 73 (September 2001): 603–616, quotation on 614.

104 On rejection of feminism in Central, Eastern, and Southeastern Europe after the fall of communism, see Tanya Renne, ed., *Ana's Land: Sisterhood in Eastern Europe* (Boulder, Colo., 1997), and Barbara Einhorn, "An Allergy to Feminism: Women's Movements Before and After 1989,"

chap. 6 in Einhorn, *Cinderella Goes to Market: Citizenship, Gender and Women's Movements in East Central Europe* (London, 1993). "Distaste for feminism is about the only thing in which there is great continuity between communism and capitalism," states Lynn Turgeon; Turgeon, "Afterword," in Valentine M. Moghadam, ed., *Democratic Reform and the Position of Women in Transitional Economies* (Oxford, 1993), 357.

105 Sylvia Paletschek and Bianka Pietrow-Ennker, "Women's Emancipation Movements in Europe in the Long Nineteenth Century: Conclusions," in Palestschek and Pietrow-Ennker, *Women's Emancipation Movements*, 301–333, quotation on 326. See also Virginia Sapiro, "A Woman's Struggle for a Language of Enlightenment and Virtue: Mary Wollstonecraft and Enlightenment 'Feminism,' " in Tjitske Akkerman and Siep Stuurman, eds., *Perspectives on Feminist Political Thought in European History from the Middle Ages to the Present* (London, 1998), 122–123; and Ulla Jansz, "Women or Workers? The 1889 Labor Law and the Debate on Protective Legislation in the Netherlands," in Wikander, Kessler-Harris, and Lewis, *Protecting Women*, 189.

106 Charles Sowerwine, "Socialist Women's Movement," in Bridenthal, Stuard, and Wiesner, *Becoming Visible*, 3rd ed., 383–384.

107 Offen, *European Feminisms*, 11. Olive Banks also sees the effects of socialism on feminism as "quite profound" and finds "the decline of 'first-wave' feminism" in Britain to have been "in part at least a consequence of its alliance with socialism"; Banks, *Becoming a Feminist*, 105, 160. Richard Evans blames divisions within the German women's movement for its failure to achieve a range of early-twentieth-century feminist goals, as well as for losing "the biggest battle of all—against the Nazis . . . almost without a shot being fired"; Evans, "Bourgeois Feminists and Women Socialists," 356.

108 Eley, *Forging Democracy*, 113. Eley points out that feminism "brings the principle of democracy to the center of the private sphere"; see Geoff Eley, "Nations, Publics, and Political Cultures: Placing Habermas in the Nineteenth Century," in Nicholas B. Dirks, Geoff Eley, and Sherry B. Ortner, eds., *Culture/Power/History: A Reader in Contemporary Social Theory* (Princeton, N.J., 1994), 318.

109 Cf. Robert Stuart's opinion that "[t]he vexed relationship between gender and class, between feminists and socialists, has shaped both the rise and fall of socialism's challenge to capital—the greatest ideological drama of our epoch"; Stuart, "Whores and Angels," 339.

110 Developing a different, women-oriented framework is one of the goals of an excellent recent study of socialism and feminism in England; see June Hannam and Karen Hunt, *Socialist Women: Britain, 1880s to 1920s* (London, 2002), esp. 202–206. For another recent study showing how complex, fluid, and situational the relationships were, see Annmarie Hughes, "Fragmented Feminists? The Influence of Class and Political Identity in Relations between the Glasgow and West of Scotland Suffrage Society and the Independent Labour Party in the West of Scotland, *c.* 1919–1932," *Women's History Review* 14, no. 1 (2005): 7–31.

INDEX

In this index, entries have been created using the indexer's judgement of significance and informative value – i.e. those elements which have substantive information content are included in the index while passing mentions with no significant information content are, with a very few exceptions, not indexed. To justify an index entry the material must be important enough in relation to the overall subject and context of the document, and contain information significant enough to warrant inclusion and be appropriate to the intended readership. This index does not include every single occurrence of any name, organization, publication, or term.